P9-BYE-665

America's Courts & the Criminal Justice System

Third Edition

America's Courts & the Criminal Justice System

Third Edition

David W. Neubauer
University of New Orleans

Brooks/Cole Publishing Company
Pacific Grove, California

Brooks/Cole Publishing Company
A Division of Wadsworth, Inc.

© 1988, 1984, 1979 by Wadsworth, Inc., Belmont, California, 94002. All rights reserved. No part of this book may be reproduced, stored in a retrieval system, or transcribed, in any form or by any means—electronic, mechanical, photocopying, recording, or otherwise—without the prior written permission of the publisher, Brooks/Cole Publishing Company, Pacific Grove, California 93950, a division of Wadsworth, Inc.

Printed in the United States of America
10   9   8   7   6   5   4   3   2   1

Library of Congress Cataloging-in-Publication Data

Neubauer, David W.
    America's courts and the criminal justice system.

    Includes bibliographies and index.
    1. Criminal courts—United States.   2. Criminal procedure—United States.   I. Title.
KF9619.N4   1988   345.73'01   87-27860
ISBN 0-534-09090-7   347.3051

Sponsoring Editor: *Claire Verduin*
Editorial Associate: *Linda Ruth Wright*
Production Editor: *Ellen Brownstein*
Manuscript Editor: *Catherine Cambron*
Permissions Editor: *Carline Haga*
Interior Design: *Cristina Simoni*
Cover Design: *Roy R. Neubaus*
Cover Photo: *Lee Hocker*
Art Coordinator: *Lisa Torri*
Interior Illustration: *Carl Brown*
Chapter Opening Illustrations: *Ron Grauer*
Typesetting: *Bookends Typesetting, Ashland, Oregon*
Cover Printing: *The Lehigh Press Company, Pennsauken, New Jersey*
Printing and Binding: *Maple-Vail Book Manufacturing Group, York, Pennsylvania*

PREFACE

This book is written for undergraduate courses that deal with America's criminal courts. That these courses (or parts of courses) are taught in departments as varied as criminal justice, political science, sociology, psychology, and social welfare highlights not only the pivotal role of the criminal courts within the criminal justice system but also their importance and impact upon society as a whole.

There has been only a limited range of teaching materials suitable for these classes. To be sure there are a number of case books, but these are written for law students and do not meet the needs of undergraduates. A few books are aimed at undergraduate students, but these often resemble their law school counterparts and are heavy with discussions of the history, structure, and philosophy of courts. Although these are important matters, the books project a rather sterile image of courthouse justice and omit what courts do in practice (and not in theory), how they do it, and, most importantly, why they do it.

This book is intended to fill the gap. Its focus is on the dynamics of the courthouse. The emphasis grows out of my own field research. Over the last two decades I have spent considerable time in state and federal courts in all parts of the nation. I have interviewed numerous judges, prosecutors, defense attorneys, probation officers, jailers, police officers, bail bondsmen, and occasionally defendants. I have also observed these officials in action and discussed with them their problems and their views of possible solutions. Throughout this book I have tried to convey to the reader this sense of being in the courthouse.

It is possible to stress the dynamics of courthouse justice because of the growing number of excellent studies of the criminal court process. Until the early 1970s there was little interest in the criminal courts. Courts, like police and corrections, were given an unhealthy out-of-sight, out-of-mind treatment. This is no longer the case. Social scientists, lawyers, and law professors now probe the workings of these important governmental bodies on a regular basis. This book will provide students with an overview of the current research.

Given the potential breadth of the material under discussion, I have had to focus on certain topics to the exclusion of others. First, this book focuses on the trial courts, not the appellate courts, although we will examine how the appellate courts affect the trial court process. Second, this book concentrates on the courts for adult offenders, not the juvenile courts. Because the structure, philosophy, and method of operation of the juvenile courts are quite different from those of courts dealing with adult offenders (typically seventeen years old or older, although the exact age varies from state to state), juvenile courts are best left to a separate discussion.

Writing this new edition has been both gratifying and stimulating. It is gratifying to learn that numerous professors, and I hope their students as well, have found the book useful. It is stimulating because it involves closely examining recent changes in both scholarship and public dialogue. This third edition represents more than an update. New features have been added. Highly controversial issues like the insanity defense (Chapter 4), the exclusionary rule (Chapter 12), the death penalty (Chapter 15), and racial discrimination in sentencing (Chapter 16) are given more expanded treatment. Appellate proceedings receive more expanded discussion in Chapter 14. Several chapters have been thoroughly revised. Chapter 9 now focuses more on the role in the judicial process of people who are not courthouse regulars, particularly victims. Chapter 10 has been recast to better highlight the case attrition that occurs in the early stages of the process from arrest through grand jury. Chapter 16 reflects major changes in sentencing laws that have taken place over the last few years. Finally, as a result of feedback from several users of the previous edition, the chapter on defense attorneys now directly follows the discussion of prosecutors. Throughout the updating, revising, and recasting of the third edition, however, the basic thrust and organization of the book have remained unaltered.

Acknowledgments

Writing the third edition has been made easier by the assistance and encouragement of people who deserve special recognition. As always, colleagues from a number of schools and institutions have offered valuable critiques. They include George Cole (University of Connecticut), Steve Flanders (Second Circuit Court of Appeals), Margaret Gilkison (Louisiana State University), Victory Flango (National Center for State Courts), John Gates (University of California at Davis), and Paul Wice (Drew University).

Thanks are also due to the reviewers of this edition: E. Stan Barnhill (University of Nevada at Reno), George F. Cole (University of Connecticut), Marc Gertz (Florida State University at Tallahassee), Ellen Hochstedler (University of Wisconsin at Milwaukee), Lou M. Holscher (Arizona State University at Tempe), N. Gary Holten (University of Central Florida), Jim Love (Lamar University, Beaumont, Texas), David M. Lukoff (University of Delaware at Newcastle) and Douglas Thomson (University of Illinois at Chicago).

Throughout the revising process Claire Verduin, criminal justice editor at Brooks/Cole, provided useful help and encouragement.

As in the previous editions, my wife and children deserve a special note of thanks for their love and support. I dedicate the book to my children in response to their bemusement at the idea that Daddy was busy writing a book.

David W. Neubauer

TO THE READER

Law and Structure

The starting point of this text is to provide readers with a working knowledge of the major structures and basic legal concepts that underlie the criminal courts. In deciding guilt or innocence and determining the appropriate punishment, the courts apply the criminal law through a complicated process termed *criminal procedure*. The structure of the courts, the nature of the criminal law they apply, and the procedures followed all have important consequences for how the courts dispense justice. But to understand the legal system one needs to know more than the legal rules. One also needs to understand the assumptions underlying these rules, the history of how they evolved, and the goals they seek to achieve. A discussion of the assumptions, history, and goals highlights why America's criminal justice process is not a unitary process but consists of a number of separate and sometimes competing units. It also points out conflicts over the goals the criminal courts are expected to achieve.

Although America's criminal court process is complicated, it is useful to focus on three essential issues. When presented with someone alleged to have violated the law—a defendant—the court process seeks to answer three questions. First, is the defendant guilty? That is, did the defendant violate the legal rules? If the defendant is found guilty, the court must then confront a second question: what penalty should be applied to the wrongdoer? The third question often precedes the first two: have the governmental officials—police and prosecutors, primarily—followed the rules for investigating crimes and convicting defendants? If the courts determine that the defendant's rights have been violated, they may either directly penalize the law enforcement officials (which is rarely done) or indirectly penalize them by letting the defendant escape punishment. Throughout this book we will be examining how the various stages of the criminal process are geared to provide answers to these three basic questions.

Dynamics of the Process

All too many books leave the false impression that an understanding of the formal law and major structures of the court is all that one needs to know about the criminal courts. This kind of analysis provides only a limited description of how the courts administer justice. The law is not self-executing. It is a dynamic process of applying abstract rules to concrete situations. Decisions about whether charges should be filed, the amount of bail to be required, and the sentence the convicted person will receive call for judges, prosecutors, and defense attorneys to make choices for which the formal law provides few precise guidelines. Thus the second objective of this book is to examine law in action—the dynamics of the criminal court process.

Invariably an examination of the law in action reveals a gap between how the law is supposed to operate and how it actually does operate. For example, the law in theory suggests that the guilt of defendants should be decided by a jury trial. Yet in practice, trials are rare. Most defendants plead guilty before any trial.

Problems

No treatment of the criminal courts would be complete without a discussion of the problems confronting the courts. Are the courts too slow? Are judges too soft in sentencing? Does the criminal court process discriminate against the poor? These are just a few of the questions about the operations of the criminal courts that this book will consider.

We can group the numerous problems under three general propositions. One goal of the courts is to protect society. To some, the courts are not properly fulfilling this role because they hamper efforts to fight crime. A second goal of the courts is to protect individual rights. To some, the courts have failed to provide fair and impartial justice by discriminating against the poor, the ignorant, and members of minority groups. Finally, many contend that the courts are so poorly managed that justice is delayed and innumerable inconveniences are experienced by witnesses, jurors, victims, and others.

Reform

Many organizations, groups, and individuals have probed the problems facing the criminal courts and proposed reforms. The fourth objective of this book is to discuss and analyze the reforms that have been suggested for what ails the courts.

Not all agree on the types of changes needed. Some argue that certain reforms will produce greater difficulties without solving the original problems. Therefore, this book will examine competing perspectives on the changes and reforms that are being proposed.

Organization of the Book

This book employs a spiral approach, beginning from a core of information and working outward to cover a wider range of relevant perspectives. I have begun with basic building blocks of knowledge and then proceeded to use these building blocks for a deeper analysis. Within each chapter, the initial emphasis is on the basics; the later material deals with more complicated issues.

The book is divided into five parts. After the introductory chapter, which examines the controversies surrounding the criminal courts, the three chapters of Part I give the reader an overview of the legal basis of the criminal courts:

criminal procedure, criminal law, and the organization of courts. Part II introduces the legal actors—judges, prosecutors, and defense attorneys—who on a day-to-day basis must make the decisions. The emphasis is on how the working relationships among these actors structure their exercise of discretion.

Part III follows the general stages cases pass through from arrest to the determination of guilt or innocence. Why cases are removed from the process and why cases are bargained out are prime concerns of this section.

Part IV focuses on the most important question in the criminal process: what sentence should be given to the guilty? Even though most of popular attention as well as legal analysis centers on the questions of legal guilt or innocence, the dynamics of the courthouse are geared to sentencing.

Part V identifies problems with the system and discusses several key aspects of reforming the criminal court process. Should the lower courts be abolished? Are the courts too slow? Should discretion be abolished?

Special Features

A number of special features will help make this introduction to the criminal court process more informative and enjoyable.

1. *Key Terms.* Any text should introduce the reader to the basic terminology of a particular field. This task is particularly important for a book on the criminal process because the law has a vocabulary all its own. To aid the reader key terms are highlighted throughout the text in **boldface.**

2. *Graphics.* Throughout the book, tables, figures, and charts focus on important material and present it in a lively way. Since readers are often interested in particular states, special effort has been made to provide important legal information for all fifty states.

3. *Boxed Quotations.* Scattered throughout the text are boxed quotations that express a perspective, provide historical background, or offer an interpretation. They are intended to round out the discussion in the text.

4. *Controversy.* How fairly, effectively, and efficiently the courts administer justice is a hotly debated topic. I have tried to capture varying viewpoints in sections labeled "Controversy." No attempt has been made to provide a pro and con position for every issue, but throughout the text as a whole I have tried to balance "liberal" and "conservative" viewpoints. I don't agree with all of the opinions expressed; neither should you. But understanding why people often disagree about matters such as plea bargaining, the death penalty, and so on is an important part of understanding how courts operate in mediating between conflicting points of view.

5. *Close-Up.* Usually at the end of each chapter, but in the middle of some, a "Close-Up" section gives an in-depth treatment of a topic. Many are designed to capture real-life experiences by looking at the people who make the decisions in the courthouse.

6. *Other Student Aids.* Each chapter ends with a conclusion, discussion questions, references, and suggestions for further reading. The book concludes with a detailed index.

CONTENTS

4 *What Is a Crime?* 63

PART II THE LEGAL ACTORS   89

5 *The Dynamics of Courthouse Justice* 91

6 *The Prosecutor* 109

CHAPTER 1

The Criminal Courts in Controversy

This is a book about America's criminal courts. It is about the history, values, traditions, and philosophy underlying the complex, sometimes contradictory, and often fragmented process by which defendants are found guilty—and sentenced to prison or placed on probation—or declared innocent. It is about the widespread controversy surrounding how the courts make these decisions and solutions proposed to correct the problems. It is about the defendants caught up in the process and what happens to the three-time losers, the scared young first offenders, and the business executives who are before the court to answer an indictment. But most of all, it is a book about the prosecutors, judges, defense attorneys, and juries who on a day-to-day basis must make the decisions about guilt or innocence, probation or prison, as well as the factors that guide selection among often hard choices. Throughout, attention is directed to the process by which the law is applied.

High crime rates and controversial Supreme Court decisions focus attention on the judicial branch of government. Local newspapers and television news broadcasts carry stories about crime and courts almost every day. Thus in a basic sense, the criminal courts need no introduction. We all know something about how they operate and some of the problems they face. The purpose of this introductory chapter is to build upon the public concern about the criminal courts by considering some basic topics. We will discuss why the courts are important, some of the problems they face, and the debate over their operations. Finally, we will suggest that courts are not mysterious separate entities but part of the larger social and governmental process.

The Pivotal Role of the Courts

criminal justice system

The term *criminal justice system* refers to the various agencies and institutions that are directly involved in the implementation of public policy concerning crime. The criminal justice system consists of three principal components: police, courts, and corrections. The courts play a pivotal role within this system because after a crime has been committed any formal action must be funneled through the courts. Only the courts can detain a person prior to trial. Only the courts can find a person guilty. Only the courts can sentence a person to prison. Alternatively, of course, the courts may release the suspect prior to trial, find him or her not guilty, or decide not to send the guilty to prison. The decisions that courts make (and how they make them) have important consequences for other components of the criminal justice system. The reverse is equally true: the operations of police and corrections have major impacts on the *criminal courts.*

criminal courts

A Fragmented Criminal Justice System

Although the three components of the criminal justice system are separate organizations, they are also tied together. Each component must interact with the other. This process is best visualized as three overlapping circles, one representing the police, another the courts, and the last corrections (see Figure 1-1). All three circles operate within a wider circle representing the general public.

Police, courts, and corrections of necessity work together. But the criminal justice system is neither uniform nor coordinated. The major components of the law enforcement and criminal justice system do not make up a smoothly functioning and internally consistent organization. Not only is each element fragmented and lacking coherence itself, but the separate elements often are not coordinated with each other, even though the operation of each has a direct bearing on the functioning of the others (Advisory Commission on Intergovernmental Relations). Moreover, the interrelationships between police, courts, and corrections are often marked by tension and conflict—and at times even hostility. Conflict results in part from competition for limited attention and funds from outside the system. But it also results from different perspectives on the common task of processing persons accused of breaking the law (National Advisory Commission on Criminal Justice Standards and Goals).

The competing perspectives of police, courts, and corrections (to say nothing of differing views within the court community itself) toward processing the

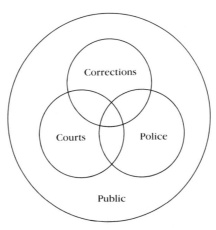

Figure 1-1 The overlapping circles of the criminal justice system.

accused have caused some to question whether America has a system of criminal justice or a nonsystem. Some argue that the process is so fragmented, splintered, divided, and decentralized that there is no overall coordination in the American justice process. Others disagree, arguing that it is still useful to view criminal justice as a system. They point out that the system has some overall purpose and an interrelationship among the various components; moreover, the term *system* does not necessarily mean that all actions must be rationally ordered. The criminal justice process is a living system composed of a number of parts characterized by competing goals. Tensions and conflicts among police, courts, and corrections therefore are not necessarily undesirable. Tensions arising from competing goals can provide important checks on other organizations. This friction is particularly evident in the criminal justice system, where the work of each component is evaluated by others: the police make arrests, yet the decision to charge is made by the prosecutor; the judge and jury rate the prosecutor's efforts. The very essence of the adversary process is conflict. Such contention ensures that multiple information sources will be considered.

Symbols of Justice

symbolic role

The importance of the courts cannot be measured solely in terms of their role within the criminal justice system (Hagan). The courts also play a meaningful *symbolic role.* The public looks to them as forums of fairness and impartiality. Public confidence in any democratic system of justice depends on public perception of the process as fair and just. Every citizen accused of a crime expects to have a day in court. At the same time, the public looks to the courts to punish wrongdoers. A conviction at trial is a public dramatization that those who violate society's rules will be punished. It also serves as a warning to potential wrongdoers. Americans believe that no one is above the law—no matter how high a position a person occupies, he or she may be convicted for criminal wrongdoing.

The Courts: A Consumer's Perspective

Given the pivotal role of the courts, many are concerned that these institutions have fallen far short of expectations. Some commonly voiced complaints concern excessive caseloads, lengthy delays, extensive backlogs, and inadequate financing. Judges, prosecutors, and defense attorneys have also been accused of being too ready to engage in plea bargaining and of imposing unduly lenient sentences. Appellate courts have been blamed for allowing obviously guilty defendants to go free.

A useful way to examine some of the problems and criticisms surrounding the courts is to view them through the eyes of their users. On a daily basis the courts require the presence of literally thousands of citizens to serve as jurors, to testify as witnesses, or to stand as defendants. These people, who use governmental services, have been labeled ***consumers of justice.*** Viewing the criminal court process through the eyes of these consumers—police officers, jurors, victims, witnesses, and defendants—highlights not only the importance of courts but also why many are so dissatisfied with their operations.

consumers of justice

In a democracy a government is expected to be responsive to the wishes and demands of its citizens. The satisfaction or dissatisfaction citizens find as consumers of court services play an important role in shaping their views and attitudes toward the government in general and the legal system in particular. Often, consumers are critical of court operations.

The Police

The police are the most regular users of the criminal courts. On a daily basis they must appear to request that charges be filed against those they have arrested, to testify at hearings, and to serve as witnesses during trial. To law enforcement personnel, the criminal courts represent a legal maze in which they have little control. Often they believe the process gives all the advantage to the guilty.

The police believe that bail turns the jail into a revolving door. Often those arrested are back on the streets within hours, some committing more crimes. It takes too long to get a case to trial. Evidence (heroin, for example) is thrown out of court on a technicality. Defendants are eventually allowed to plead guilty to a charge less serious than the one they allegedly committed. The sentences handed out are much too light. Thus, the police have come to believe that the courts frustrate their efforts to control crime.

Ordinary Citizens

Victims, witnesses, and jurors frequently come away from a brief encounter with the criminal courts with negative attitudes. Most of them are ordinary citizens, who consider their role a chance to serve their government. But to others their participation is an unwanted interruption of their daily lives. Often their appearance is postponed. When the case is finally heard, they still face long waits in crowded corridors deprived of simple amenities like a cup of coffee or a chair to sit on. During the trial (particularly if the charge is rape) the victims may feel they are on trial. It is no wonder that these consumers feel like unwelcome intruders in a system they find inefficient and mismanaged.

Defendants

Millions of Americans appear each year as defendants in a lower tribunal to answer charges as varied as driving too fast, creating a disturbance, or violating a city zoning ordinance. To many, their day in court consists of a long wait on a hard bench, a brief appearance before the judge, the pronouncement of a fine, and a quick calling of the next case. Such "cash register justice" often shatters the textbook image of justice.

The reactions of defendants accused of serious crimes reveal some contrasting images of the American criminal courts. Unlike their middle-class brethren, typical felony defendants hold no illusions about the courts. Educated not by the lofty premises of civics textbooks but instructed by their street peers, many view the courts as a game not much different from life on the streets. They see the behavior of the police, prosecutors, judges, and defense attorneys as essentially the same as the behavior of law violators: conning, manipulating, and lying (Casper). Indeed, in the minds of many defendants their major adversary is not the judge, police, or prosecutor, but their own defense attorney.

The General Public

Ultimately all citizens are consumers of the criminal courts. They perceive that they might need the protection of the courts, they view the courts in symbolic terms, and, of course, as taxpayers they pay the expenses of the courts. Public assessments about crime and the courts have remained remarkably constant over the last decade. A typical public opinion poll indicates the following:

- Eighty-three percent say that their best guess is that "the crime rate in this country is going up."
- Eighty percent think that "most crimes go unpunished these days."
- Eighty percent believe that courts "do not deal harshly enough with criminals."
- Sixty-eight percent think that "the police can't really do much about crime because the courts have put too many restrictions on the police."
- Fifty-five percent believe that "most judges have more sympathy for the criminals than for their victims" (Bureau of Justice Statistics).

Citizens express widespread dissatisfaction with the performance of the criminal courts. But it is important to point out that when asked more general questions American citizens are highly supportive of courts and judges (Fagan). Judges far more than legislators or public administrators retain the respect of the public.

- Seventy-five percent believe that judges are generally fair and honest in deciding each case.
- Ninety percent assume that if they were ever accused of a crime they would receive a fair trial (Curran and Spalding).

Debate over the Courts

A consensus has emerged that the criminal courts require change, but there is no agreement over what types of changes are in order. Even a brief review of the critical comments about the criminal courts discussed so far should indicate the varying and often conflicting views about what is wrong. Broadly, two differing diagnoses have been presented. One is that the courts have hindered effective law enforcement and therefore have produced inadequate protection of society. Conservatives see crime as the product of a breakdown of individual responsibility and self-control. They are concerned that criminals "beat the system" and "get off easy." In their view, the cure is to eliminate loopholes like the exclusionary rule, abolish the insanity defense, allow for preventive detention of dangerous offenders, and increase the certainty of punishment (Walker).

The alternative diagnosis stresses different causes. Liberals see crime not as a product of individual moral failure but as the result of social influences. They emphasize the need to reshape people through rehabilitation and to develop community-based sentencing alternatives, and they express skepticism about the extensive use of prison sentences. Moreover, they are concerned that the court system is fundamentally unfair to poor and minority defendants and thus support the decisions of the Warren Court expanding protections of criminal defendants (Jenkins). Liberals, however, are concerned about law-breaking. They see the need to protect the public from predatory criminals but at the same time believe that granting too much leeway to law enforcement officials will only result in the loss of freedom and civil liberties for all Americans.

The public dialogue on the issues facing the criminal courts is structured so that conservatives square off against liberals, hard-liners against those who are soft on crime. This sort of terminology, however, is not very helpful. Terms like ''soft on crime'' attract our attention to dialogue about the goals of the criminal courts, but they are not useful for systematic inquiry because they are too ambiguous and too emotional. More constructive in understanding the controversy over the criminal courts are the crime control and due process models developed by Herbert Packer. Although these models somewhat distort reality because they concentrate on extreme (polar) positions, they are quite useful because they examine in an unemotional way the competing values over the proper role of the criminal courts.

Crime Control Model

crime control model

The most important value in the ***crime control model*** is the repression of criminal conduct. Unless crime is controlled, the rights of the law-abiding citizens will not be protected, and the security of society will be diminished. To achieve this goal of repressing crime, the courts must process defendants efficiently. They should operate like an *assembly line*—rapidly removing defendants against whom there is inadequate evidence and quickly determining guilt according to evidence. The crime control model holds that informal fact-finding—initially by the police and later by the prosecutor—not only is the best way to determine if the defendant is in fact guilty but is also sufficiently foolproof to prevent the innocent from being falsely convicted. Accordingly, the crime control model stresses the necessity of speed and finality in the courts in order to achieve the priority of crime suppression.

Due Process Model

due process model

In contrast, the ***due process model*** emphasizes protecting the rights of the individual. Although adherents of the due process model do not downgrade the need for controlling crime, they believe that the sole pursuit of such a goal threatens individual rights and poses the threat of a tyrannical government. Thus, the key function of the courts is not the speed and finality projected in the crime control model but an insistence on a careful consideration of each case. The dominant image is one of the courts operating as an *obstacle course*. The due process model stresses the possibility of error in the informal fact-finding process and therefore insists on formal fact-finding to protect against mistakes made by the police and prosecutors. The proponent of the due process model believes the courts' priority should be to protect the rights of the individual. Any resulting decrease in the efficiency of the courts is the price paid in a democracy based on individual liberties.

Law and Politics

politics

The criminal courts do not stand in splendid isolation, removed from the rest of society; their activities are intimately intertwined with other social institutions, community norms, public opinion, and the actions (or inactions) of other members of the criminal justice system. Unfortunately the belief of many Americans that law and politics are (or at least should be) separate obscures the larger social context that affects the criminal courts. Judicial reformers, for instance, believe that the cure to court ills lies in removing *politics* from the process. In these contexts politics is a dirty word, standing for corruption, undue personal influence, dirty tricks, or partisan affairs. Such partial views of politics, however, cloud what is a vital process. The criminal courts are part of the "political process, by which authoritative decisions are made about who gets what in society" (Easton: 50).

CLOSE-UP

Reality versus Rhetoric: How Politicians Respond to the Crack Epidemic

It's an irresistible moment for politicians: an election year with a drug crisis. And the reaction has been all too predictable. . . . On Capitol Hill, Democrats vie with Republicans to see who can be more draconian. Around the nation, governors, mayors, and district attorneys pledge hard-line measures until their jurisdictions are crack-free. But amid the escalating rhetoric some skepticism is emerging. . . . While everyone wants swift and certain justice, no one is quite sure how to pay for it. What follows is a review of current antidrug proposals. Call it the Forthright Politician's Guide to Drug Enforcement.

More cops. Increasing the number of agents on the streets or on the borders will lead to more arrests and more recovered contraband. And if there's a local public nuisance—a schoolyard with a

drug trade, or a street corner occupied by junkies—aggressive cops can lawfully sweep those sectors clean, at least until they climb back into their cruisers. But, says Steven White, California's chief assistant attorney general for criminal cases, even the cops live in a zero-sum world. "Any time you push harder in one area, you have to pull back somewhere else," says White. In Miami, for example, federal prosecutors are praised for their drug efforts and criticized for giving other crimes less attention. A hard choice: more narcs or more robbery detectives?

More jail terms. More arrests will send more people to jail, at least temporarily. But the cells in state and local facilities are full. The Los Angeles County jail holds 20,000 inmates in a space allocated for 11,000. "As crowded as we are, we'll have

to find ways to deal with stricter enforcement," says Undersheriff Theodore Von Minden. Some ideas: early release; reopen old jails as Broward County, Fla., just did, or, as some drug agents hope, build some cheap, military-style barracks and call them prisons (not in their neighborhoods, of course). Some states like New York plan to erect more traditional prisons, but at $50,000 per cell that's not a revenue-neutral proposal.

Restricting plea bargains. In urban jurisdictions more than 90 percent of the cases end in guilty pleas. But in drug cases most appear to receive light sentences: in New York City last year, 55,000 narcotics arrests led to only 3,000 jail terms of more than 30 days. Tinkering with the system, though, can be tricky. In Los Angeles, District Attorney Ira Reiner wants to raise the

Applying this definition of politics to the activities of the criminal courts highlights some essential features of their operations. Certainly the decisions of the courts must be considered *authoritative;* only the courts have the legal power to detain suspects before trial or send those found guilty to prison. Because laws are unclear and resources limited, court officials must make important *decisions* about innocence or guilt, the nature of the charge, and the sentence. At times these decisions require choosing between competing values such as rights of the individual and protections for society. Finally, Easton's definition, by stressing *who gets what,* calls our attention to the importance of the authoritative decisions the courts make for defendants, victims of crimes, other components of the criminal justice system, and the general public.

Viewed from this perspective, criminal justice personnel engage in the same type of authoritative allocation of values as other governmental decision makers. The actions of legislators and mayors, for example, are generally viewed as political. The same holds true for the courts. At times these

---

cost of drug dealing, insisting on a six-month sentence rather than the current average of three days. Also, Reiner will ask for a suspended state prison term so that "the next time he's arrested on a drug charge, you file for a probation violation," and, after a brief hearing in front of a judge, the offender goes directly to jail. Using the probation gambit is sound, but here's the gamble: if dealers balk at the higher price for a guilty plea and demand a trial, can Reiner and the courts handle the load? Reiner says yes, but after the bluff-calling, the problem of adequate jail space remains.

Life sentences. New York's Gov. Mario Cuomo has suggested life imprisonment for crack dealers. In 1973 another ambitious New York governor, Nelson Rockefeller, promoted life terms for drug dealers. It didn't work that time; a study by the Association of the Bar of the City of New York found that juries balked at convicting dealers under the widely publicized law and that the deterrent effect passed quickly. Cuomo's proposal has political impact —it's hard for any opponent to sound harsher—but the practical import is slight. More important is Cuomo's idea to increase to three years the minimum sentence of all dealers; this will keep them off the streets a bit longer. But will the prospect of longer jail time scare dealers out of the business? Not if they don't believe they'll get caught.

Death penalty. Capital punishment is not available for drug pushers, and public officials ought to know that. U.S. Supreme Court precedent makes it nearly impossible to execute anyone but a killer. And should the court suddenly expand the list of death-eligible crimes, the procedural labyrinth surrounding capital punishment would still postpone the first execution into the next century.

"Obviously the criminal-justice system is not going to solve the drug problem," says New York's Cuomo. "But there's no question that given an episode like crack you have to do everything you can. Laws can have value in terms of attracting people's attention and help change attitudes." Yale Prof. David Musto teaches psychiatry and the history of medicine and has written about drug epidemics. He, too, recognizes the limits of law enforcement but sees some positive side effects in the new proposals. "These laws come out of the same anger and hatred that tend to lower demand for drugs," he says. He argues that tough laws get written when an epidemic has reached its final stage, one that he says can unfortunately last more than a decade.

Aric Press with Gerald Lubenow and Martin Kasindorf, "Reality versus Rhetoric: How Politicians Respond to the Crack Epidemic," *Newsweek,* September 8, 1986, p. 69.

political considerations are direct—for example, in the involvement of political parties in selecting members of the criminal justice community. At other times these political influences are indirect. For example, the officials who staff the courts—judges, prosecutors, and defense attorneys—are often lifelong members of their communities and therefore intimately acquainted with local values. Local community values are also transmitted to the criminal courts through decisions made by juries.

Conclusion

For decades the public was indifferent to the needs and problems of the criminal courts. Even many in the legal community seemed unconcerned with whether the criminal courts lived up to the lofty ideal of providing equal protection under the law. But in a few short years how America's criminal courts dispense justice has become a high-priority item. The courts, because of their pivotal position within the criminal justice system, became the focal point of much of this public concern. Particularly in the nation's largest cities, the rising crime rate is swelling the dockets of the criminal courts, thus taxing already inadequate facilities. Jails are overcrowded. Delay is a major problem. The quality of justice dispensed by the criminal courts is being questioned as well. Some say the courts coddle criminals; others believe the courts have failed to protect the rights of the accused. While some argue that legal technicalities needlessly free the guilty, others are alarmed that the courts dispense one type of justice to the rich and a different variety to the poor.

As citizens experience delay, inconveniences, frequent rescheduling of cases, and confusion when they appear as victims, witnesses, jurors, or defendants, they are increasingly voicing their dissatisfaction with the courts. For too long, they charge, the courts have been run as if they were a private club of judges and lawyers and not an important public body. This public dissatisfaction has forced courts to reexamine as well as alter many ways they do business. In turn, the criminal justice practitioners—the judges, prosecutors, and defense attorneys—have often been at the forefront in pointing out problems and deficiencies that require change.

For Discussion

1. Discuss with several friends any personal contacts they have had with the criminal justice system as victims, witnesses, jurors, or defendants. Were their experiences positive or negative? Why?
2. What are the most important problems facing the criminal courts? Why? What values do your choices of problem areas reflect?
3. How do the local papers cover the crime issue? For a week, count the number and type of crimes reported in the newspapers. How do these compare with official FBI crime statistics?
4. If you were a defendant in court, do you think you would be treated fairly and properly? Would your classmates feel the same way?

5. Do the local and state newspapers indicate any tensions among the principal criminal justice agencies (police, prosecutor, judge, defense attorney, corrections officials)?

6. Do you think that the criminal justice system in your community is fragmented? Are there any major gaps? For example, how easy is it to find information about a given case or defendant? Who benefits or suffers when the system is fragmented?

References

ADVISORY COMMISSION ON INTERGOVERNMENTAL RELATIONS. *State–Local Relations in the Criminal Justice System.* Washington, D.C.: Government Printing Office, 1977.

BUREAU OF JUSTICE STATISTICS, U.S. Department of Justice. *Sourcebook of Criminal Justice Statistics—1985.* Washington, D.C.: Government Printing Office, 1986.

CASPER, JONATHAN. *American Criminal Justice: The Defendant's Perspective.* Englewood Cliffs, N.J.: Prentice-Hall, 1972.

CURRAN, BARBARA, AND FRANCIS SPALDING. *The Legal Needs of the Public.* Chicago: American Bar Foundation, 1977.

EASTON, DAVID. *A Systems Analysis of Political Life.* New York: John Wiley, 1965.

FAGAN, RONALD. "Public Support for the Courts: An Examination of Alternative Explanations." *Journal of Criminal Justice* 9 (1981): 403–418.

HAGAN, JOHN. "The Symbolic Politics of Criminal Sanctions." In Stuart Nagel, Erika Fairchild, and Anthony Champagne, eds., *The Political Science of Criminal Justice.* Springfield, Ill.: Charles Thomas, 1983.

JENKINS, PHILIP. *Crime and Justice: Issues and Ideas.* Belmont, Calif.: Wadsworth, 1984.

NATIONAL ADVISORY COMMISSION ON CRIMINAL JUSTICE STANDARDS AND GOALS. *Report on Courts.* Washington, D.C.: Government Printing Office, 1973.

PACKER, HERBERT. *The Limits of the Criminal Sanction.* Palo Alto, Calif.: Stanford University Press, 1968.

WALKER, SAMUEL. *Sense and Nonsense About Crime.* Pacific Grove, Calif.: Brooks/Cole, 1985.

For Further Reading

BALBUS, ISAAC. *The Dialectics of Legal Repression.* New Brunswick, N.J.: Transaction Books, 1977.

CURRIE, ELLIOT. *Confronting Crime: An American Challenge.* New York: Pantheon, 1985.

PEPINSKY, HAROLD, AND PAUL JESILOW. *Myths that Cause Crime.* Cabin John, Md.: Seven Locks, 1984.

SCHEINGOLD, STUART. *The Politics of Law and Order.* New York: Longman, 1984.

SILBERMAN, CHARLES. *Criminal Violence, Criminal Justice.* New York: Random House, 1978.

WALKER, SAMUEL. *Sense and Nonsense About Crime.* Pacific Grove, Calif.: Brooks/Cole, 1985.

WILSON, JAMES Q. *Thinking About Crime.* Rev. ed. New York: Basic Books, 1983.

WILSON, JAMES Q., AND RICHARD HERNSTEIN. *Crime and Human Nature.* New York: Simon and Schuster, 1985.

PART I

THE
LEGAL
SYSTEM

Part I provides an introduction to basic legal concepts underlying the criminal courts.

Chapter 2 presents an overview of common law, the adversary system, and the twelve stages of the criminal court process. Its purpose is to tie together the various stages of a case that the remainder of the book analyzes individually.

Chapter 3 focuses on the organization of American courts. The consequences of the diversity of judicial bodies is the primary concern.

Chapter 4 centers on how the criminal law defines certain acts as illegal. An understanding of these definitions is an important first step in understanding discretion.

CHAPTER 2

How (and Why) Cases Move from Here to There

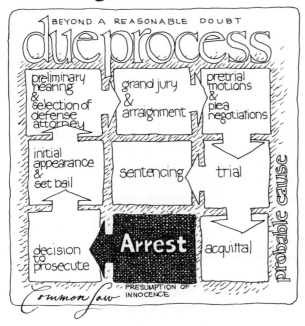

Most Americans possess an elementary knowledge about the criminal courts. They learned in high school civics courses that a person is presumed innocent until proven guilty. Press coverage of dramatic criminal cases has made them aware of the number of varying steps and procedures involved in a criminal prosecution. Television shows portray some of the difficulties that detectives, prosecutors, and defense attorneys face in fulfilling their responsibilities. But beyond these basics, the average American only dimly perceives how the courts actually dispense justice.

It is useful to begin with a broad overview of the nature and basis of the criminal law, the agencies charged with applying that law, and the steps in the criminal process. We can begin best by asking some basic questions. Why do we have law and courts? What functions and purposes does society assign to courts and law? What are the major agencies of the criminal courts? What tasks do they perform? What procedures are used in the criminal court process? Why are they used? Answering these questions will provide the reader with a core of knowledge that will dispel some (but certainly not all) the confusion and misunderstanding about criminal courts. Answering these questions will also explain how the numerous agencies and steps work together. Throughout this book, we will be dissecting each of the actors and steps individually; this broad overview will help show how all the pieces fit together.

However, a knowledge of the law, the agencies that apply the law, and the steps involved are only the beginning point in examining the operations of the criminal court process. Equally important is an examination of how these legal powers and legal procedures actually operate. A legal and structural analysis of the criminal courts omits the dynamics of the process. The interrelationship of judges, prosecutors, and defense attorneys has a major bearing on how the courts dispense justice. And each of these actors must make choices about how to dispense justice. These choices, far from being totally determined by the law, involve discretion. Therefore, this chapter will introduce some of the major concepts and analytical tools we need to analyze the dynamics of the criminal court process.

The Basis of Law

The basis of criminal law can be summarized in two words: human conflict. A controversy over how much money is owed, a quarrel between husband and wife, a collision at an intersection, a stolen television set are just a few examples of the great number of disputes that arise in and threaten to disrupt the normal activities of society. Business, transportation, and everyday activities depend on mechanisms for mediating inevitable human conflicts. Without such mechanisms, individual parties might seek private, nonpeaceful means of settlement. The proverbial feud between the Hatfields and the McCoys illustrates the disruptiveness of blood feuds, motivated by revenge—not only in the lives of individual parties directly involved but also in the larger society.

law

Law is a body of rules. These rules are found in a variety of sources: statutes, constitutions, court decisions, and administrative regulations. A key function of such rules is to prevent or at least minimize human conflict. By specifying the rules ahead of time, most people and organizations are able to conform their actions to the law. But if they do not, the law fulfills a second function: it provides a basis for resolving disputes.

Common Law

The American legal system traces its origins to England and is therefore referred to as Anglo-American law. Beginning in the twelfth century, judges traveled around England settling disputes by applying the norms and rules common to that area. Eventually these rules emerged into a national set of rules

common law

known as the *common law*. Common law is often referred to as judge-made law because initially the rules were determined by judges, not by legislative or executive bodies. Although today law is increasingly and primarily the product of statutes passed by legislative bodies or administrative regulations announced by executive agencies, judges still play a major role in determining the rules of society because they interpret and apply law. There are two principal divisions of common law: civil and criminal.

Civil Law

civil law

Most disputes that come to court involve private parties. Conflicts over owner-ship of property, failure to live up to the terms of a contract, or injuries suf-fered in an automobile accident are settled on the basis of the body of rules collectively known as *civil law.* A civil suit is brought by a private party to enforce a right or to seek payment for a wrong committed by another private party. These suits are brought because the courts possess powers that private parties do not: they can order a business to pay another business money owed

monetary damages

under a contract, grant a husband and wife a divorce, award *monetary damages* suffered for an injury received in an automobile accident, and so forth. The powers courts possess for settling disputes reveal an important dif-ference between law and other societal rules (such as norms or informal rules) for settling disputes: only law has the binding power of the state behind it. Thus civil cases are basically means by which private parties borrow govern-ment power for private ends.

plaintiff defendant

Most civil cases involve a request for monetary damages. The *plaintiff* (the person who starts a lawsuit) demands that the *defendant* (the person against whom a lawsuit is brought) pay money for the plaintiff's legal rights (an *injury*). For example, in a case involving an automobile accident, the in-jured party may request a sum of money to pay for hospital expenses, doc-tors' fees, lost wages, and general "pain and suffering." But in some instances, a suit for monetary damages cannot repair potential damages. If Farmer Jones's property is about to be flooded by a dam that Farmer Smith is building, Farmer Jones does not want to wait until his land is damaged to attempt to recover monetary damages; he wants to go on farming his land. Therefore, a second

---

Q U O T A T I O N

*C*ourts exist to settle arguments. Before there were courts, disputes had to be resolved by force. One tribe carried on a feud with another. Or, in medieval times, there was a formal combat between two armored knights. Around 750 years ago in England, courts began to take the place of combat. People had come to see that it would be better to have disputes settled without violence, and settled according to some logical rules. Judges were sent out from London, traveling a circuit on horseback, to decide arguments and maintain "the King's peace." And they slowly started to develop the rules that we call law.

Anthony Lewis, *Clarence Earl Gideon and the Supreme Court* (New York: Random House, 1972), p. 18.

equity
remedy
chancery
injunction

form of remedy, termed *equity,* developed in Anglo-American law. (Equity was originally a *remedy* requested from the king of England and therefore was termed *chancery.*) Equity requests an *injunction* (a court order) requiring the defendant either to perform a certain action or to stop a specified action. Thus Farmer Jones could seek a court order prohibiting Farmer Smith from building the dam. Equitable relief is more flexible and broad-based than requests for monetary damages. Jury trials are not available in equity cases.

Civil law is having an increasing impact on the criminal justice system. Civil suits alleging police brutality, charging discrimination in hiring, or arguing that prison facilities offer cruel and unusual punishment are just three examples. In turn, some requests for police or criminal court action are attempts to invoke criminal sanctions for essentially private disputes.

Criminal Law

criminal law

Although virtually all disputes are potentially disruptive to the overall functioning of society, some are viewed as so disruptive that they require special treatment; civil law remedies are not enough. There are several important differences between civil law and *criminal law.* One difference centers on who has been harmed. Civil suits are considered private matters whereas criminal violations involve public wrongs, which harm all of society. A second difference involves prosecution. Unlike the civil law, in which private parties file suit in court alleging an infringement of private rights, violations of public wrongs are prosecuted by the state. The type of penalties imposed on law violators is a third difference. In civil law the injured party receives compensation. Violators of the criminal law, however, are punished through the imposition of a prison sentence, a fine, a sentence of probation, or some similar action. The stress on punishment derives from the goal of criminal law to prevent and control crime. It is important to recognize that the criminal law is intended to supplement, not supplant, the civil law. Thus a person may be prosecuted criminally and the victim may also seek to recover civil damages for the same act.

Courts

courts

Courts and law go hand in hand; they provide a forum for resolving disputes through application of law. Obviously not all disputes in society are brought to the court. Some are privately resolved, sometimes in anticipation of what courts would do if they were brought to their attention. Certain types of conflicts—lovers' quarrels or disagreement over church doctrine, for instance—are not allowed to come to court. *Jurisdiction* is the legal term covering matters that courts are authorized to hear. Still other disputes are mediated by arbitration panels, insurance adjusters, marriage counselors, student grade appeal boards, and the like. While many of these alternative tribunals function somewhat like the courts, they are not courts.

jurisdiction

Four characteristics distinguish courts from other dispute-resolving institutions: courts (1) resolve disputes, (2) by *applying* them to the society's *legal* norms, and (3) do so *impartially* and (4) *independently* (Wheeler and Whitcomb: 5). Each of these is critical for understanding how courts adjudicate criminal cases.

The first characteristic of courts, that they resolve disputes, is a basic one. Courts formulate law on the basis of actual disagreements. Thus courts are passive. They do not seek out matters but wait for other parties to bring disputes to their attention. The second characteristic is that courts apply legal rules in solving disputes. That decisions are based upon law emphasizes rationality and reasoned explanation in the decision-making process. Thus the standards differ from those of marriage counselors, arbitrators, or student grade appeal committees, who may use a variety of standards in their work. The third characteristic, impartiality, means that each side will have an opportunity to present its case in court and that the court's decision will be fair, unbiased, and just. The fourth distinguishing characteristic of courts is independence. Courts are expected to resolve disputes free from outside pressures. This means no matter how much an accused criminal has outraged the public or governmental officials, a court is expected to judge the case dispassionately and on its individual merits.

America's courts, of which there are almost seventeen thousand, represent a bewildering array of names, types, functions, and geographical jurisdictions. Although we commonly speak of *the* American court system, the United States does not have a single uniform court structure. Rather it has fifty-one separate court systems, one in each of the fifty states, plus one for the national government. As a result, each state differs from its neighbor. (Chapter 3 will provide a detailed discussion of the organization and structure of America's courts.)

Rights of the Accused

In addition to preventing and controlling crime, the courts seek to protect the individual rights of each citizen. A key feature of a democracy is the insistence that the prevention and control of crime be accomplished within the framework of law. The criminal process embodies some of society's severest sanctions: detention before trial, confinement in prison after conviction, and, in certain limited situations, execution of the offender. Because the powers of the criminal courts are so great, there is concern that those powers not be abused or misapplied. Moreover, the Christian-Hebraic tradition places a high value on the worth of each individual citizen and therefore respects the individual liberty of each citizen.

Restrictions on the use and application of governmental power take the form of rights granted to the accused. One of the most fundamental protections is the right to be considered innocent until proven guilty. Another is the right to remain silent. Still another is the right to a trial by jury. These protections—found in the U.S. Constitution, the Bill of Rights, and the common law heritage—exist not to free the guilty but to protect the innocent. A criminal justice process based on the necessity of protecting individual liberties (of the innocent and guilty alike) obviously reduces the effectiveness of that process in fighting crime. The ideological foundations of Anglo-American criminal law have always recognized that freeing some of the guilty is the price willingly paid to ensure that too many innocent persons are not found guilty.

The American tradition of instituting limits on the use of governmental power flows from three basic concerns. The primary justification for providing constitutional safeguards for those caught in the net of the criminal process is to ensure that innocent persons are not harassed or wrongly convicted. The American legal system is premised on a distrust of human fact-finding. Because it fears human errors, the criminal court process provides multiple review points, believing that errors made at one step will be spotted during a later stage. The possibility of wrongly convicting an innocent person arises when honest mistakes are made by honorable people. But it also arises when dishonorable officials use the criminal justice process for less-than-honorable ends. Without built-in checks, the criminal justice process provides a quick and easy way for government leaders to dispose of their enemies. A common ploy in a totalitarian government is to charge persons with the ill-defined crime of being an "enemy of the state." The possibility of political misuse of the criminal justice process by tyrannical governments or tyrannical officials is a major concern in the Anglo-American heritage.

The third reason that democracies respect the rights of those accused or suspected of violating the criminal law is the need to maintain the respect and support of the community. Democratic governments derive their powers from the consent of the governed. Such support is undermined if power is applied arbitrarily. Law enforcement practices that are brutal, random, or overzealous are likely to produce fear and cynicism among the people, lawbreakers and law abiders alike. Such practices undermine the respect that law enforcement officials must have to enforce the law in a democracy. Even in a dictatorship efforts are often made to portray an image of a fair trial.

rule of law

A hallmark of American law, then, is that governmental officials must follow a regularized set of procedures in making decisions. The phrase ***rule of law*** stands for the idea that those who make decisions will do so by following the law. Although there is no precise definition of the rule of law, "its essential element is the reduction of arbitrariness by officials" (Skolnick: 8).

Q U O T A T I O N

*I*n a free society you have to take some risks. If you lock everybody up, or even if you lock up everybody you think might commit a crime, you'll be pretty safe, but you won't be free.

Senator Sam Ervin, quoted in Richard Harris, *Justice* (New York: Avon, 1969), p. 162.

In short, we expect our leaders to make decisions according to an agreed-upon set of legal procedures.

Due Process and the Bill of Rights

due process

The principal legal doctrine for limiting the arbitrariness by officials is **due process.** Due process of law is mentioned twice in the Constitution, once in the Fifth Amendment—"No person shall . . . be deprived of life, liberty or property without due process of law"—and in the Fourteenth Amendment—"No state shall deprive any person of life, liberty or property without due process of law." Like the concept of the rule of law, due process has a broad and somewhat elastic meaning with definitions varying in detail from situation to situation. The core of the idea of due process, however, is that a person should always have notice and a real chance to present his or her side in a legal dispute and that no law or government procedure should be arbitrary or unfair. The specific requirements of due process are regularly changed by the Supreme Court through interpretation of the Bill of Rights.

Bill of Rights Provisions Dealing with Criminal Procedure

Amendment IV.   The right of the people to be secure in their persons, houses, papers, and effects, against unreasonable searches and seizures, shall not be violated, and no warrants shall be issued, but upon probable cause, supported by oath or affirmation, and particularly describing the place to be searched, and the persons or things to be seized.

Amendment V.   No person shall be held to answer for a capital, or otherwise infamous crime, unless on a presentment or indictment of a Grand Jury, except in cases arising in the land or naval forces, or in the Militia, when in actual service in time of War or public danger; nor shall any person be subject for the same offence to be twice put in jeopardy of life or limb, nor shall be compelled in any criminal case to be a witness against himself, nor be deprived of life, liberty, or property, without due process of law; nor shall private property be taken for public use, without just compensation.

Amendment VI.   In all criminal prosecutions, the accused shall enjoy the right to a speedy and public trial, by an impartial jury of the state and district wherein the crime shall have been committed, which district shall have been previously ascertained by law, and to be informed of the nature and cause of the accusation; to be confronted with the witnesses against him; to have the compulsory process for obtaining witnesses in his favor, and to have the Assistance of Counsel for his defence.

Amendment VIII.   Excessive bail shall not be required nor excessive fines imposed, nor cruel and unusual punishment inflicted.

Bill of Rights.   The major obstacle to the ratification of the U.S. Constitution was the absence of specific protections for individual rights. Several of the most prominent leaders of the American Revolution opposed the adoption of the Constitution, fearing that the proposed national government posed as great a threat to the rights of the average American as had the king of England. Therefore shortly after the adoption of the Constitution, ten

Bill of Rights amendments, collectively known as the ***Bill of Rights,*** were adopted. Many of these protections—particularly the Fourth, Fifth, Sixth, and Eighth amendments—deal specifically with criminal procedure.

Originally the protections of the Bill of Rights restricted only the

incorporation national government. Through a legal doctrine known as ***incorporation,*** however, the Supreme Court determined that the due process clause of the Fourteenth Amendment made some provisions of the Bill of Rights applicable to the states as well. Not all protections of the Bill of Rights have been incorporated—only those viewed as essential to "the concept of ordered liberty." The major provisions of the Bill of Rights included the due process clause of the Fourteenth Amendment are protections against unreasonable searches and seizures (Fourth Amendment); protection against self-incrimination (Fifth); the right to counsel and trial by jury (Sixth); and the prohibition against cruel and unusual punishment (Eighth). Some have aptly called the Bill of Rights a constitutional code of criminal procedure.

State constitutions also contain bills of rights that are increasingly important in determining individual rights and liberties. As the U.S. Supreme Court has become more and more conservative, state supreme courts have treated state constitutions as an independent basis for establishing rights of privacy and due process.

Presumption of Innocence

One of the most fundamental protections recognized in the American criminal

presumption justice process is the right to be presumed innocent (termed ***presumption***

of innocence ***of innocence***). The state has the burden of proving defendants guilty of alleged crimes; defendants are not required to prove themselves innocent. This difference is fundamental. A moment's reflection makes clear how difficult it would be to prove that something did not happen or that a person did not do an alleged criminal act. Therefore a defendant is cloaked with the legal shield of innocence through the criminal justice process.

In meeting the obligation to prove the defendant guilty, the prosecution is

beyond a required to prove the defendant guilty ***beyond a reasonable doubt.*** This

reasonable legal yardstick measures the sufficiency of the evidence and means that the

doubt jury must be fully satisfied that the person is guilty. It does not mean the jury must be 100 percent convinced, but it comes close (Oran). The state's burden of proof beyond a reasonable doubt does not require that the state establish absolute certainty by eliminating all doubt whatsoever, only that it eliminate reasonable doubt. This criterion is more stringent than the burden of proof

preponder- in a civil case (involving two or more private parties) in which the yard-

ance of the stick is the ***preponderance of the evidence,*** meaning a slight majority of

evidence the evidence for one side or the other.

The Adversary System

adversary
system

A system of criminal justice is more than rules on paper (definitions of crime and rights granted to the accused, for example); it is also a plan for distributing power among judges, jurors, prosecutors, legislators, and so on. Thus, under Anglo-American law, only the legislature has the power to define crimes. In turn, the courts are entrusted with applying and interpreting that law in specific cases. The premise of the Anglo-American legal system is that the best way for courts to apply the law is through the *adversary system,* a battle between two differing parties. This system is viewed as the best way to determine guilt or innocence and at the same time protect the rights of the accused. Under the adversary system the burden is on the prosecutor to prove the defendant guilty beyond a reasonable doubt. The defense attorney is charged with arguing for the client's innocence and asserting legal protections. The judge serves as a neutral arbitrator who stands above the fight as a disinterested party to ensure that each side battles within the established rules. Finally, the decision is entrusted to the jury (although in some instances a judge alone may decide).

The adversary system builds three different types of safeguards into the criminal court process. First, it provides a forum for testing evidence. The reasoning is that when the two parties approach ''the facts from entirely different perspectives and objectives . . . [they] will uncover more of the truth than would investigators, however industrious and objective, seeking to compose a unified picture of what had occurred'' (American Bar Association: 3). Because American law views informal methods of fact-finding as subject to errors, it insists on a formal adversarial fact-finding process. Through cross-examination, each side has the opportunity to examine witnesses' truthfulness, to probe for possible biases, and to test what witnesses actually know, not what they think they know. The right to cross-examination is protected by the Sixth Amendment: ''In all criminal prosecutions, the accused shall enjoy the right . . . to be confronted with witnesses against him.''

The adversary system imposes a second type of safeguard by putting power in several different hands. Each actor is granted only limited powers and has limited powers to counteract the others. If the judge is biased or unfair, the jury has the ability to disregard the judge and reach a fair verdict. The opposite is also true. If the judge believes the jury has acted improperly, then the judge has the power to set aside the jury verdict and order a new trial. This diffusion of powers in the adversary system incorporates a series of checks and balances aimed at curbing political misuse of the criminal courts.

In diffusing power, the adversary system provides a third safeguard: it charges a specific actor—the defense attorney—with asserting the rights of the accused. Defense attorneys search out potential violations of the rights of the accused. They function as perpetual challengers in the criminal court process and, in theory at least, are ready at every juncture to challenge the government by insisting that the proper procedures be followed.

The Dispositional Process

An important first step in understanding how American courts dispense justice is to learn the basic legal concepts underlying the process. The common law heritage, the differing purposes of civil and criminal law, the structure of the courts, the reasons that protecting the rights of the accused is so valued, and the presumption of innocence within the adversary system are all basic to an understanding of the legal model of the criminal court process. But mastering these legal concepts is just the first step. They provide only an imperfect road map of the day-to-day realities of the courthouse.

The formal adversarial model is present only in a limited degree. Few cases ever go to trial. Most defendants either plead guilty or have their cases dismissed before trial. Instead of the conflict projected by the adversary model, judges, prosecutors, and defense attorneys cooperate on a number of matters. Whereas the main goal of the adversary model is to discover truth and decide guilt, a great deal of the court's attention is directed toward determining the appropriate penalty.

In short, there is a major gap between legal theory (law on the books) and how that law is applied on a daily basis (law in action). Although many persons find such a gap shocking, actually it is not; after all, no human institution ever lives up to the high ideals set out for it. If you spend five or ten minutes observing a stop sign on a well-traveled street, you will find that not all cars come to a complete stop, and some do not seem to slow down much at all. Yet at the same time, the stop sign (the law on the books in this example) clearly does affect the behavior of drivers (law in action). Realizing that law on the books is not the same as the law in action is only the second step in understanding how the courts dispense justice. The crucial task is to understand and explain why the law as practiced differs from the seeming intent of the formal rules. Toward this end a wide variety of studies of the criminal courts at the trial level have highlighted several important features about how the criminal courts operate. Assembly line justice, discretion, and the courtroom work group are concepts that describe how these institutions operate. These concepts also begin to suggest reasons for the deviations from the idealized version of the law.

Assembly Line Justice

A basic principle of the American legal system is that the courts will consider each case and each defendant individually. This expectation of individual attention is reinforced by fictionalized television prosecutors, judges, defense attorneys, and police officers who always have ample time to devote to a single case. To some, however, *assembly line justice* is a more realistic description of how the criminal courts operate. Particularly in the misdemeanor and traffic courts of large cities, dispositions are usually made with lightning speed. A person's day in court to answer a charge of speeding may consist of less than a minute before the judge.

assembly line justice

Assembly line justice is partially a reflection of the large number of cases that reach the court. Every year approximately two million felony cases and perhaps as many as ten million misdemeanor cases are begun. Although accurate and complete court statistics do not exist in the United States, these estimates provide some idea of the volume of cases requiring processing each year. Add to this the large number of ordinance violations (municipal code *violations*) and even larger numbers of traffic cases, and it becomes obvious that the criminal caseload of the courts is indeed staggering. Because of the large volume of cases, overworked officials often become more interested in moving the steady stream of cases than in individually weighing each case on the scales of justice. Particularly in large cities, there are tremendous pressures to move cases lest the backlog become worse and delays increase. Thus, unlike the trial model described by the law books, an administrative process geared to disposing of a large volume of cases is the dominant sort of law in action.

Discretion

discretion

Underlying the administrative nature of justice is ***discretion.*** Although the textbook image of justice portrays a mechanical process of merely applying rules of law to given cases, a closer examination shows that each of the actors possesses ample discretion: the prosecutor in charging and plea bargaining, the defense attorney in negotiating over a sentence, and the judge in imposing a sentence.

One reason actors in the criminal court community exercise discretion is that the law provides only minimal guidance for making decisions. The clearest example is sentencing. The criminal law specifies a potential range of penalties for each criminal offense: probation, prison, or a fine. The law, however, provides only the broadest standards for deciding where in the range of penalties a defendant's case should fall. Such discretionary decisions are required at virtually every step of the criminal court process. Judges, prosecutors, and defense attorneys also exercise discretion in an attempt to make the system fair. They seek individualized justice.

The Courtroom Work Group

courtroom work group

An important part of discretion in the criminal court process is the key role of the ***courtroom work group.*** Although we usually think of the criminal courts in terms of a conflict at trial, a more realistic appraisal is one of limited cooperation among the major participants. While defendants come and go, the judges, prosecutors, and defense attorneys work together daily. They are tied by more than a shared workplace, the courtroom; each is dependent on the others. For example, defense attorneys seldom have resources for investigating a case. They are dependent on the prosecutor for access to police reports and the like. Because prosecutors have more cases to try than time to try them, they are dependent on guilty pleas from the defense to secure convictions. Judges are dependent on prosecutor and defense negotiating pleas to prevent a backlog of cases from developing. Such cooperation is a two-way street. Those who work within the system can expect to receive some benefits. Defense attorneys who do not needlessly make additional work for the others are sometimes able to secure a lighter than normal sentence for their clients. On the other hand, those who challenge the system can expect sanctions. Defendants represented by uncooperative defense counsel sometimes receive longer prison terms than they would otherwise.

This courtroom work group is best described as a social organization. No individual actor works in social isolation; each can accomplish tasks only by interacting with the others. The network of cooperation underlying the courtroom community produces a commonly understood set of practices. Courts develop rules of thumb about how certain types of cases will be handled and what penalties will be applied.

The Criminal Court Process

The criminal court process is complicated. From the initial arrest to the final sentencing, a defendant's case passes through numerous stages. American law maintains that numerous—sometimes redundant—steps in the criminal process are the best way to ensure that individual rights are protected. Analytically, the criminal court trial process can be broken down into thirteen stages: arrest, the decision to prosecute, initial appearance, the setting of bail, holding a preliminary hearing, selecting a defense attorney, convening the grand jury, holding the arraignment, deciding pretrial motions, engaging in plea negotiations, conducting a trial, imposing sentence, and appeal.

These steps provide only a basic overview, however. Criminal procedure varies from state to state. The U.S. Supreme Court has ruled that certain steps are so vital—jury trial, for example—that they are required in all states, and for the federal government as well. Other procedures, however—most notably the grand jury—have been held by the Court to be less essential to the concept of "ordered liberty," and therefore states are not required to have them. To complicate matters even further, individual courts often adopt local rules that spell out additional details of criminal procedure. Procedural requirements also vary according to the severity of the offense.

The thirteen stages do not have to occur in a set order. For instance, a defendant may have an attorney even before arrest or may delay hiring one until almost the day of trial. Just as important, these separate steps are interrelated. The decision to charge, the outcome of the preliminary hearing, and the nature of the plea bargain all anticipate a jury verdict.

In outline form the steps of criminal procedure seem to suggest a streamlined process with defendants entering at the arrest stage and steadily moving through the various stages until conviction and eventually sentencing. This is not the case. The criminal process is filled with numerous detours. At each stage officials must decide either to advance the defendant's case to the next step, reroute it, or terminate it. Thus the thirteen stages are actually the forums for observing and analyzing the effects of discretion, assembly line justice, and the courtroom work group. Figure 2-1 provides a schematic representation of this funneling effect, showing that the criminal process acts as a series of screens. Much like a set of sieves that sorts rocks into various sizes, the steps of the criminal process sort defendants into various categories. The result is that many cases that enter the criminal court process are eliminated during early stages.

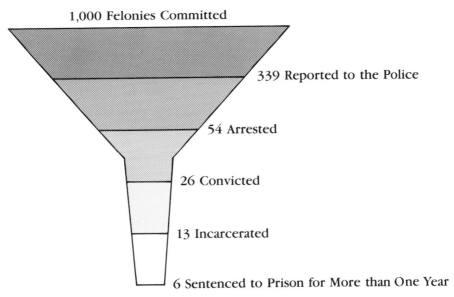

1,000 Felonies Committed

339 Reported to the Police

54 Arrested

26 Convicted

13 Incarcerated

6 Sentenced to Prison for More than One Year

Figure 2-1 Funneling effect of felony crimes
SOURCES: U.S. Department of Justice, Bureau of Justice
Statistics, *Report to the Nation on Crime and Justice*
(Washington, D.C.: Government Printing Office, 1983); Barbara
Boland with Ronald Sones, *The Prosecution of Felony Arrests,
1981* (Washington, D.C.: Government Printing Office, 1986).

Arrest.   The criminal process typically begins with a police decision to arrest
a suspect. In a small percentage of cases the police make arrests based on an
arrest warrant, a court document authorizing the police to take a person into custody. Most arrests, however, are made in the field without a warrant. Under common law, police officers have the power to take a person into
custody if they believe the person committed a felony (a major crime). But
if the crime is a misdemeanor (an offense less serious than a felony and usually
punishable by a fine or less than a year in jail), most states allow the police
to arrest only if the crime is committed in their presence.

    The police are able to arrest in only a small proportion of crimes. Nation-
wide, they make arrests in only 20 percent of serious crimes. As a result, only
a fraction of the nation's major crimes potentially reach the court.

Decision to prosecute.   After a suspect has been arrested and booked, the
police must seek legal authority to continue detaining the person. If the charge
is a minor one, the police may apply to a lower court judge for a complaint.
If the case is a serious one, however, the police are usually required to request
prosecution from the district attorney. The prosecutor acts as the key link between the police and the courts. This actor is the most important figure in
the criminal court process, controlling which defendants will be charged with

*arrest
warrant*

a crime, influencing bail setting, entering into plea bargains, and at times influencing the sentence as well. Prosecutors possess wide discretion in deciding whether criminal charges should be filed. During this initial evaluation a major consideration is the strength of the evidence. Factors other than the strength of the evidence may also play a role.

In almost every part of the country, the charging decision results in a significant number of arrested persons being released without the filing of criminal charges. Estimates place the number of cases never resulting in prosecution as high as 50 percent of those referred by the police to the prosecutor. Even when charges are accepted, the prosecutor may file a charge less serious than the police initially requested (for example, a misdemeanor rather than a felony).

Initial appearance.   An arrested person must be brought before a judge without unnecessary delay. In the United States the police are not allowed to detain a suspect for an indefinite period of time.

The initial appearance is the defendant's first encounter with the courts. At this time he or she is given a formal notice of the charges and the judge advises the defendant of the right to remain silent, the right to counsel, the right to bail, and the right to a preliminary hearing if applicable. In practice, judges make little effort to determine whether the defendant understands what is being explained. For felony defendants the initial appearance is a formality, because a defendant cannot enter a plea (guilty or innocent). For misdemeanor defendants, however, this step may be the only courtroom encounter. Roughly three out of four misdemeanor defendants plead guilty at the initial appearance and are sentenced immediately.

Bail.   Bond is usually set at the initial appearance. Because a defendant is considered innocent until proven guilty, American law allows virtually all defendants to remain at liberty before trial. Bail is a guarantee that the defendant will later appear for trial. Judges have wide latitude in setting the amount of bail.

bail

The most common form of ***bail*** is a cash bond. For felony defendants, bonds range from $1,000 to over $100,000. Because most defendants do not have that much cash on hand, they hire a bail bondsman who, in return for a 10 to 15 percent cash fee, will secure the defendant's pretrial release. An alternative to the cash bail system is release on recognizance. Defendants with strong ties to the community are viewed as unlikely to flee so they are released on their promise to return to court; no monetary bond is required. Defendants who cannot meet the bail bondsman's fees or qualify for release on recognizance must await trial in jail. On a typical day, American jails house about 115,000 adult defendants awaiting trial.

Preliminary hearing.   The preliminary hearing (termed a preliminary examination in some states) is designed to protect defendants against unwarranted prosecutions. It is the first time that a non-law-enforcement official (a judge)

probable cause

evaluates the strength of the evidence against the accused. At a preliminary hearing the prosecutor must show that there is ***probable cause*** to believe that the defendant committed the felony. Probable cause can be proved by showing that a crime has been committed and that it is likely that the defendant committed it. Evidence requirements, however, are less strict than during a trial. If the judicial officer determines that probable cause is present, the defendant is bound over to the grand jury. If not, the defendant is released and the charges dismissed.

The preliminary hearing is limited primarily to felony cases. Not all states require a preliminary hearing, and some limit its use to very serious crimes like murder for which the death penalty may be imposed. Where preliminary hearings are held, however, few cases are dismissed for lack of probable cause.

Defense attorneys. The Sixth Amendment specifies: "In all criminal prosecutions, the accused shall enjoy the right . . . to have the Assistance of Counsel for his defence." The U.S. Supreme Court has ruled that the right to counsel includes the obligation of the state to provide an attorney for those too poor to hire one of their own. The Court reasoned that the assistance of counsel constituted a vital protection because few nonlawyers are well versed enough in the law to conduct an adequate defense. The right to counsel applies not only to the trial itself but also to all other critical stages in the proceedings.

Most defendants—approximately 60 percent (and up to 80 percent in some large cities)—cannot afford to hire a lawyer. These indigent defendants are represented in one of two ways: assigned counsel or public defender. Under an assigned counsel system, a judge appoints a member of the local bar, sometimes without pay, to represent the defendant. But, increasingly, indigent defendants are represented by public defenders (paid government attorneys responsible for representing all indigent defendants). In small communities the public defender may be a part-time lawyer, but in larger communities, the staff consists of a dozen or more attorneys. Public defenders handle as many as 200 felony defendants per year, a caseload higher than the average prosecutor's.

Grand jury. Like the preliminary hearing, the grand jury is designed as a check on unwarranted prosecutions. The U.S. Constitution requires a grand jury in federal felonies, but the U.S. Supreme Court has held that a state is not required to have a grand jury. Only about half of the states use the grand jury. Grand juries usually consist of twenty-three members. If the majority of the grand jury believe that probable cause exists, a *true bill* is voted charging the defendant with a crime. A *no bill* (or no true bill) indicates that the grand jury found insufficient evidence to indict. No bills are very uncommon.

true bill
no bill

In practice the grand jury does not function as the independent check that legal theory would have it. By and large grand juries are dominated by the prosecutor. The prosecutor is the legal adviser to the grand jury and also determines which cases will be considered and which witnesses will be summoned. Thus, the grand jury indicts whom the prosecutors want indicted. Even no true bills are often the product of the prosecutor's assessment that the evidence against a particular defendant is weak. In rare cases, however, grand juries exhibit independence, and when they do so they wield great power.

CLOSE-UP

A Week Inside the Mills of Justice

"I don't want to die," 23-year-old Stanley Boyd pleads to the jurors about to decide whether he should be executed for fatally stabbing a friend. His mother is carried out of the courtroom wailing, "Oh Jesus, oh Jesus."

It is 10 p.m. in a dingy, otherwise deserted courthouse. Near midnight, the jury decides to spare Boyd, giving him a 50-year prison term with no parole.

The verdict is a dramatic moment during a week in St. Louis Circuit Court—five days that show vividly how justice is dispensed in America's urban courts. Events in a typical week confirm some widely held beliefs and disprove others.

For one thing, judges are swamped with work. The 28 men and three women on the bench here handle 50,000 matters each year, from vicious murders to doctors' errors to late rent checks. For another, civil cases take a long time to resolve—often two to four years to get to trial. The lag is typical of big cities, reports the National Center for State Courts. Some handle cases faster; others take five years or more.

Yet contrary to popular wisdom, trials are a rarity. Most criminal suspects plead guilty, and most money disputes are settled out of court, sometimes for large sums.

Monday: A Slow Beginning

Things get under way in civil court at 9:34 a.m. Monday, when Presiding Judge Gary Gaertner bounds into his courtroom. The big question in the minds of four dozen anxious lawyers gathered before him: Which of the 138 damage suits on the docket will get to trial? The only sure thing is Delores Brawley's malpractice suit against four physicians and a hospital, which tops the list. It's a 4-year-old case with a passel of lawyers and out-of-town witnesses. Delay would be a logistical nightmare.

For litigants here and in courtrooms around the nation—some who have waited years for justice—the process is a frustrating one that seems to drag on endlessly, only to come to a sudden end in high-pressure negotiations or a jury-deliberation room. To judges and lawyers steeped in the system, it takes on a rhythm and familiarity. New cases start at the bottom of the docket, slowly rising as older ones end. Lawsuits are like bottles of wine—they need time to mature, one lawyer observes.

Speedier Justice—for Suspects

Cases are moving a bit faster in criminal court, where a dozen judges must cope with an unending stream of violence and property offenses. Public concern nationwide in the 1970s about soaring crime—coupled with court limits on jail populations—prompted a crackdown on case backlogs. Here in St. Louis, more than 2,000 criminal charges used to clog the docket, resulting in delays of a year or more. Now, most of the 1,000 pending cases are disposed of within six months.

The key ingredient in the speedup is better planning. The small corps of prosecutors and defense lawyers, each handling dozens of cases, once gathered each week to juggle them in an often vain effort to see who could go to trial. Now, dangerous suspects are put at the top of the docket 10 days in advance to insure they will make it to trial.

Ready to go this week are 158 cases, including a long list of assaults, robberies and burglaries. Most result in guilty pleas. Still, many plead guilty only when confronted with an imminent trial. "They plead guilty when they see the whites of the jurors' eyes," remarks Circuit Atty. George Peach, in his ninth year as chief prosecutor here.

To avoid plea bargaining—reducing charges to induce a plea—Peach is giving tougher screening to cases brought by police, so they aren't pursued if evidence is weak. Result: Eighty-four percent admit guilt as charged. Public Defender Joseph Downey, whose staff aids 3 of 4 defendants in a city where most can't afford their own attorneys, says "sentence bargaining" is common. To encourage pleas, the prosecution offers in 1 of 4 cases to cut recommended terms—proposals almost always accepted by judges.

Midweek: Jury Call

Most citizens get their own glimpse of the justice system when they are summoned to the vast jury-assembly room. By Wednesday, nearly 500 persons have reported for a civic duty that pays all of $12 a day. Escaping service is difficult: No longer can one win automatic exemption just by being a teacher or more than 65 years old.

Jurors' first sight may be an unnerving one. To prevent violence, all visitors must pass through metal detectors. The rule has succeeded in keeping away those carrying firearms, although knives sometimes turn up; sheriff's deputies snicker about a woman angry at being searched who stalked off and returned nude.

After checking in, jurors lounge in rows of chairs, waiting for a call that could thrust them into a wide range of cases, from setting damages for a bus accident to determining a killer's fate. "You may be required to decide whether someone will die," defense lawyer Daniel Gralike tells jurors in a murder case.

Decision making isn't made any easier by poor working conditions that officials blame on a shoestring budget of 15 million dollars a year, $35 for each St. Louis resident. A state panel recently found the city's two old courthouses in "deplorable" shape. Observes Judge James Corcoran: "It's depressing. Windows haven't been washed in 10 years. Jurors have to sit for a week on uncomfortable wooden chairs." Many bathrooms are filthy or unusable, roofs leak and, says Judge Gaertner, "we work in firetraps."

Week's End: Plaintiffs Win, Criminals Lose

By Thursday, civil cases are beginning to produce damage verdicts and settlements, a few big but most small.

Robert Montgomery has accused a doctor and hospital of causing brain damage suffered by his 44-year-old wife Vera in a hysterectomy. After three days of trial, the case is settled for 3.2 million dollars. Why

the last-minute pact? "Until parties begin to see the evidence, they may not understand how successful or unsuccessful the case may be," says Judge James Gallagher.

In another case, Patricia Gray sued a friend and a quarry firm after she suffered head injuries when the friend crashed a vehicle into a 25-foot mining pit. Settlement: About $300,000, mostly covered by insurance.

A handful make it to a jury, but the verdicts are modest. Mary Kehres wins $7,200 against the city of St. Louis for whiplash and fractures suffered when she tripped on a protruding piece of sidewalk. Motorist James Porter gets $10,000—all he sought—over a collision with a bus, despite the bus driver's testimony that Porter was at fault.

A week isn't enough for some cases. Brawley's malpractice suit is declared a mistrial after eight days. It takes two full weeks for railroad worker Bill Welsh to win $500,000 for injuries suffered when a propane tank fell on his foot.

In addition to judging crimes and big damage cases, courts handle a host of everyday matters. During his lunch hour, Judge Robert Dowd, Jr., performs a wedding for a 68-year-old woman and a 72-year-old man. Dowd has just heard dozens of small claims. Rulings come within a day, but only after litigants get a chance to present their cases—most without attorneys. "I let people pour it all out," Dowd says. "I don't want them to say they came all the way downtown and weren't al-

lowed to tell the whole story." Typical case: A boy hits a playmate with a broom; his family wants reimbursement for the $180 emergency-room bill.

Criminal court is moving at a fast clip, too. Felonies used to be lumped together. Now, less serious crimes are sent to the "bulk division." Judge Evelyn Baker takes the bench at 2:30 p.m. Thursday to hear cases in assembly-line fashion. First up is Samuel Lanham, who admits stealing aluminum from a trailer-repair shop. Despite a prosecution call for six months in jail, he has no convictions on his record, and Baker orders six months' probation. It takes less than 20 minutes. So it goes until 7:45 p.m., when the last of 17 guilty pleas is accepted.

Friday is sentencing day. Before Judge Thomas O'Shea comes David Sanders, who robbed an armed courier of $100,000, possessed cocaine and resisted arrest. A prosecutor seeks a 60-year term; the defense—citing Sanders's clean record and cooperation with police—seeks probation. The judge's middle-ground ruling: 30 years.

Late Friday, prosecutor Henry Autrey heads into his partitioned office and drops into a chair under a sign saying, "Cubicle, sweet cubicle." He sighs, "It's been a tough week" and totals the results: Eight trials—4 convictions, 3 acquittals and a hung jury—and 90 guilty pleas. Law enforcement has scored a small victory over crime, but the battle begins anew next Monday.

Ted Gist, "In Court: A Week Inside the Mills of Justice," *U.S. News and World Report,* January 28, 1985, pp. 67–68. Copyright 1985 by U.S. News and World Report, Inc.

Arraignment.   Arraignment differs from the initial appearance, although the two terms are often used interchangeably. At the arraignment the defendant is given a copy of the formal charges (either the indictment or the bill of information), advised of his or her rights (usually more extensively than at the initial appearance), and called upon to enter a plea. This is the first time a felony defendant is called upon to enter a plea. The defendant can plead guilty (which is rare at this stage), not guilty (the usual plea), or *nolo contendere,* which means the defendant will not contest the charge but does not admit it.

motions

pleadings

Pretrial motions.   ***Motions*** are requests for the judge to make a legal ruling. During trial, lawyers will make various types of motions relating to the admissibility of evidence and the like. Similarly, before the trial certain kinds of legal questions require a determination. The process of making formal written motions along with written reasons are termed ***pleadings.*** A prosecutor may file a motion to require the defendant to produce documents or to give a handwriting sample, for example. Most motions, however, are filed by the defense. The most common ones are motions to suppress evidence (arguing that the police searched illegally) and motions to suppress a confession (contending that the confession was coerced, for example). Because many of these motions involve only questions of law, they can be decided at a hearing where the attorneys argue why the motion should—or should not—be granted.

Plea bargaining.   Most findings of guilt result not from a trial verdict but from a voluntary plea by the defendant. Roughly 80 to 90 percent of all convictions in felony cases (and an even higher percentage in misdemeanor and minor offense cases) result from a plea. Even when a case goes to trial, it is likely there were plea discussions.

Plea bargaining is pervasive but hardly uniform; indeed the numerous variations almost defy classification. It is important to bear in mind that plea bargaining is a general term that represents a variety of different practices and court traditions. Participation in plea bargaining varies. Some judges are active participants; others may refuse to take part. The nature of the final plea also varies. In some jurisdictions it is common for the defendant to plead to a less serious charge than the one initially charged (for example, the defendant might plead to simple robbery rather than armed robbery, the original charge). Or the defendant might plead to only some of the counts, and in return the government will dismiss other charges. In still another type, the defendant agrees to admit guilt in return for a specified sentence. And, finally, some pleas are entered without any promises whatsoever—the defendant pleads to all the charges as specified in the indictment or information.

Jury trials.   Along with the right to be presumed innocent until proven guilty, the right to a trial by jury is one of the most fundamental rights granted those accused of violating the criminal law.

A defendant can be tried either by a judge sitting alone (called a bench trial) or by a jury. A jury trial begins with the selection of twelve people (fewer in some cases). The prosecutor and the defense make opening statements, indicating what they think the evidence in the case will show. The prosecutor has the burden of proving the defendant guilty and is the first to call witnesses. Rules guide the type of evidence that may be introduced and how it may be interpreted. Witnesses are subject to cross-examination. When all evidence has been introduced, each side makes a closing argument to the jury, and the judge then instructs the jury about the law. The jurors retire to deliberate in secret. In most states jury verdicts must be unanimous, although a couple of states accept verdicts of ten out of twelve. While the details of the jury procedure vary from state to state, one factor is constant—the defendant's chances for an acquittal are not good.

sentencing   ***Sentencing.***   Most of the thirteen stages of the criminal process are concerned almost entirely with determining legal innocence or guilt. As important as the question of the defendant's guilt or innocence is, most of the time of the members of the courtroom work group is spent on deciding what sentence to impose on the guilty. Indeed, defendants are more concerned about the possible prison time they will have to serve than the question of guilt. Judges have wide discretion in imposing sentences. State or federal law specifies a potential penalty. Some states simply employ determinate sentencing, which means that the judge must sentence the defendant to a fixed number of years. Other states use indeterminate sentencing, which allows the judge to specify a sentencing range (say one to ten years). Alternatively, the judge may place the defendant on probation (the sentence is served in the community under supervision) for a fixed period or suspend the sentence (the jail or prison sentence is not served). In some states probation is specifically disallowed for certain categories of convictions, often armed robbery and first-degree murder. The law also may allow the judge to impose a fine, but this is rarely used in felony cases. The death penalty is allowed in many states. By and large the main decision is whether to place the defendant on probation or to impose a sentence for a certain period of time.

Clearly, the law offers a wide range of sentencing opinions. Furthermore, there is disagreement about the purpose of imposing sentence. At least four competing views on sentencing can be found in American society. Some say the sentence should be punishment, pure and simple. Others argue that sentences should be set to deter other wrongdoers. To others the purpose of sentencing should be to rehabilitate the defendant. Finally, some argue that defendants should be sentenced to protect society. Judges' sentencing decisions reflect these varying sentencing perspectives. Their rationales result in marked sentencing disparities.

Estimates indicate that a half of a million people are inmates in state and federal prisons. Although there is no accurate count on how many convicted defendants are on probation, the number is much higher. Indeed, the majority of defendants are placed on probation rather than incarcerated, but the ratio of probation to prison decisions varies from judge to judge and court to court.

Appeal.   Guilty defendants have the right to appeal their convictions to a higher court. In certain circumstances, most notably death penalty cases, an appeal is mandatory. In most cases, however, an appeal is discretionary. Defendants who plead guilty, for example, rarely appeal. Moreover, the doctrine of double jeopardy prevents a prosecutor from appealing a trial verdict of not guilty. Overall, the number of appeals is only a small proportion of guilty verdicts.

An appeal is based on claims that one or more errors of law were made during the criminal justice process. If the appellate court finds that error occurred during the trial, the conviction may be reversed and a new trial ordered. Defendants are not very successful on appeal.

Conclusion

The prosecution, conviction, and sentencing of a defendant is a complex, multifaceted, and somewhat fragmented process. It is through the criminal law that certain acts are defined as so threatening to the entire society that special sanctions are provided. Although the control and prevention of crime is a major goal of the law, this goal must be accomplished within the framework of the law. In particular, the law recognizes certain rights for all defendants. The courts are forums for deciding guilt or innocence and imposing sentence. But in turn the criminal courts are not a single entity. Under the adversary system, responsibilities are divided among judge, prosecutor, and defense attorney.

Because of its great commitment to fair treatment under the rule of law, the Anglo-American legal system specifies a number of steps in the criminal process. These steps are intentionally designed to be inefficient because inefficiency through multiple checkpoints is viewed as the best way to ensure that no errors are made. These multiple checkpoints function as screens, removing some defendants from the process, diverting others, and forwarding still more to the next stage. To speak of steps in the criminal process may be misleading because American justice involves numerous variations in the structure of these steps, the order in which they occur, and the way they operate in practice.

The structure of the courts, the nature of the law, and the steps in the criminal process provide only the beginning point, however, in understanding how the criminal courts dispense justice. These elements constitute the law on the books—the legal and structural components. But as we have argued, one must also understand the law in action. Although the formal model suggests the individual and separate treatment of all defendants, "assembly line justice" comes closer to describing the actual operations of the criminal courts. Similarly, a structural-legalistic discussion of the criminal courts stresses the conflict at trial, whereas studies have repeatedly shown limited cooperation because of pressures from the courtroom work group. Finally, whereas the civics book image projects a legal system that runs almost by itself, in practice discretion is involved in each of the major steps.

For Discussion

1. What are the most important differences between civil law and criminal law? What similarities do they share?
2. What are the major differences between the legal outlines of the criminal process (law on the books) and how the process actually operates (law in action)?
3. What are the most important protections given those accused of a crime? In a democracy could any of these protections be eliminated without sacrificing individual liberties?
4. How do decisions made during early stages of the criminal court process affect decisions made later? How might anticipation of the last steps of the criminal process—jury trial and sentencing—affect earlier stages?
5. What are some of the beneficial uses of discretion? What are some of the misuses of discretion? What are some ways that discretion could be used to inhibit the misuse of discretion? Would beneficial uses of discretion suffer?

References

AMERICAN BAR ASSOCIATION. *Standards Relating to the Prosecution Function and the Defense Function*. Chicago: American Bar Association, 1970.

NATIONAL CENTER FOR STATE COURTS, NATIONAL COURT STATISTICS PROJECT. *State Court Caseload Statistics: Annual Reports 1977 and 1978*. Washington, D.C.: Government Printing Office, 1980.

ORAN, DANIEL. *Law Dictionary for Nonlawyers*. 2d ed. St. Paul, Minn.: West, 1985.

PRESIDENT'S COMMISSION ON LAW ENFORCEMENT AND THE ADMINISTRATION OF JUSTICE. *Task Force Report: The Courts*. Washington, D.C.: Government Printing Office, 1967.

SKOLNICK, JEROME H. *Justice Without Trial—Law Enforcement in a Democratic Society*. New York: John Wiley, 1966.

WHEELER, RUSSELL, AND HOWARD WHITCOMB. *Judicial Administration: Text and Readings*. Englewood Cliffs, N.J.: Prentice-Hall, 1977.

For Further Reading

ABRAHAM, HENRY. *The Judicial Process*. 5th ed. New York: Oxford University Press, 1986.

BAUM, LAWRENCE. *American Courts: Process and Policy*. Boston: Houghton Mifflin, 1986.

CARP, ROBERT, AND RONALD STIDHAM. *The Federal Courts*. Washington, D.C.: Congressional Quarterly, 1985.

GLICK, HENRY. *Courts, Politics and Justice*. New York: McGraw-Hill, 1983.

ISRAEL, JEROLD, AND WAYNE LAFAVE. *Criminal Procedure: Constitutional Limitations*. St. Paul, Minn.: West Publishing, 1975.

JACOB, HERBERT. *Crime and Justice in Urban America*. Englewood Cliffs, N.J.: Prentice-Hall, 1980.

JACOB, HERBERT. *Justice in America: Courts, Lawyers and the Judicial Process*. 4th ed. Boston: Little, Brown, 1984.

JACOB, HERBERT. *Law and Politics in the United States*. Boston: Little, Brown, 1986.

KARLEN, DELMAR. *Anglo-American Criminal Justice*. New York: Oxford University Press, 1967.

MCLAUCHLAN, WILLIAM. *American Legal Process*. New York: John Wiley, 1977.

CHAPTER 3

Finding the Courthouse:
The Confusing Structure of American Courts

American courts present a bewildering variety of names, structures, functions, and types. Mayor's court, city court, justice of the peace, county court, superior court, district court, chancery court, and common pleas are just a few of more than two dozen names of courts found in America. If the varying names of the courts were the only problem, there would be no great difficulty—we could learn the names much as we learn classifications in biology. The drawback is that the names are seldom cues to either what the courts do or how they function. For example, if your case is in the supreme court, what level of court would you be in? If you thought the highest appellate court, you are probably right, unless you are in the state of New York. In New York the supreme court is the major trial court, and the highest appellate court is called the court of appeals. Not only do courts with similar names sometimes have different functions, the opposite is also true. Courts with different names may have roughly identical functions. Moreover, every state court system is somewhat different and, even within a state, the names, functions, and jurisdictions may vary and even overlap.

The purpose of this chapter is to provide some clarity in the sea of confusion over the structure and functions of American courts. We will begin with a discussion of the development of American courts and then move on to a consideration of some concepts basic to the structure and function of American courts. Next, using these basic concepts, we will examine the federal judicial system and then state court systems. Finally, we will examine the consequences of court organization for the operations of the criminal justice system.

How Courts Grew

Just as American law borrowed heavily from English common law, the organization of American courts reflects their English heritage. The ancient common law tradition was important in shaping current court systems. For example, Ohio and Pennsylvania call their major trial courts Courts of Common Pleas, a title taken directly from England. However, while certain traditions persist, court structures have also changed over time. Increases in population, the concentration of people in cities, and the shift from an agricultural to an industrial economy all necessitated changes in court organization. Such alterations, though, were far from automatic since basic political issues were often at stake. The clash of opposing economic interests, the debate over state versus national power, and outright partisanship are some political conflicts that account for the current structure of American courts.

Colonial Courts

During the colonial period, political power was concentrated in the hands of the governor, an appointee of the English king. Governors performed executive, legislative, and judicial functions. The courts in the early colonial period were rather simple institutions. The structure of these early American courts replicated English courts in form but not in substance. The complex, numerous, and highly specialized courts of the mother country were ill-suited to the needs of a small group of colonists trying to survive on the edge of the wilderness, so the colonists greatly simplified the English procedures.

The county courts stood at the heart of the American colonial government. Besides adjudicating cases they also performed important administrative functions (Friedman). Appeals from all courts were taken to the governor and the colonial council. As population increased and towns and villages became larger, new courts were created so that people would not have to travel long distances to have their cases heard. Through the years each colony modified its own court system according to variations in local demands, local customs, differing religious practices, and the nature of commercial trade. These early variations in legal rulings and court structures have persisted and contribute to the great variety of U.S. court systems today (Glick and Vines).

Early American Courts

After the American Revolution, a major dispute developed over whether there should be a federal court system separate from the state systems. When the U.S. Constitution was being drafted, the ***Anti-Federalists,*** who feared a strong national government and thought the new national government threatened both individual liberties and states' rights, wanted only a limited federal system. The Federalists, on the other hand, fearing the parochial prejudices of states, believed that lawsuits tried exclusively in state courts would put litigants (those involved in a suit) who were from out of state at a distinct disadvantage. Although the Federalists were successful in creating federal district courts (first in the Judiciary Act of 1789 and later in the Reorganization Act of 1801), the system adopted was a compromise that allayed some of the fears of the Anti-Federalists. These courts, empowered to enforce national law, were structured along state lines; they did not cut across state boundaries, and the selection process adopted ensured that judges would be residents of that state. Overall, the national courts were organized along local lines with each district court responsible for its own work under minimal supervision (Richardson and Vines).

Similar political disputes affected the state courts. After the Revolution the powers of the government were drastically reduced and taken over by the legislative bodies. But the structure of the state judiciaries remained largely unchanged. The former colonists, who viewed judicial action as coercive and arbitrary and distrusted lawyers and the common law, were not anxious to see the development of a large independent judiciary. Judicial decisions were scrutinized by state legislatures, which removed some judges from office or abolished specific courts in response to unpopular court decisions.

The distrust of the judiciary increased as courts declared legislative actions unconstitutional. Such actions were a major source of political conflict between legislatures and courts. The conflict often stemmed from opposing interests. Legislators were more responsive to policies that favored debtors (usually small farmers). Courts, on the other hand, reflected the views of creditors (merchants). In several instances state courts declared legislative acts favoring free money as unconstitutional. Out of this conflict over legislative and judicial power, though, the courts gradually emerged as an independent political institution.

Courts in a Modernizing Society

After the Civil War the structure of American courts changed in many important ways. Rapid industrialization produced fundamental changes in all aspects of American life, the law included. Increases in population, the growth of cities, and the rise of industrialization greatly expanded the volume of litigation. Moreover, the types of disputes coming to the courts changed as well. Not only did the growth of industry and commerce result in disputes over this new wealth, but the concentration of people in the cities (many of whom were immigrants), coupled with the pressures of industrial employment, meant the courts were faced with a new set of problems. The American courts, still reflecting the rural agrarian society of the early nineteenth century, were inadequate in the face of rising demands for services (Jacob).

Anti-Federalists

sporadic and unplanned growth

States and localities responded to the increased volume of litigation in a number of ways. City courts were created to deal with new types of cases in the urban areas; specialized courts were formed to handle specific classes of cases (small claims courts, juvenile courts, and family relations courts are examples); and more courts were added, often by specifying the court's jurisdiction in terms of a geographic boundary within the city. The result was *sporadic and unplanned growth.* Each court was a separate entity; each had a judge and a staff. Such an organizational structure meant there was no way to shift cases from an overloaded court to one with little to do. In addition, each court produced political patronage jobs for the city political machines. The development of courts in Chicago illustrates the confusion, complexity, and administrative problems that resulted from this sporadic and unplanned growth of American courts. In 1931 Chicago had 556 independent courts; the large majority were justice of the peace courts, which handled only minor offenses (Glick and Vines).

Other state and local courts included municipal, circuit, superior, county, probate, juvenile, and criminal courts. Sometimes other courts, such as the rackets court, were added to deal with special problems. The jurisdiction of these courts was not exclusive; that is, a case could be brought before a variety of courts depending on the legal and political advantages that each one offered. Factors such as court costs, the reputation of the judge, court delay, and the complexity of the court procedures were considered in determining which court to use. For example, a prosecuting attorney in a criminal case could choose a court likely to produce either a harsh or lenient judgment. Other attorneys sought to have their cases entered in courts with procedures so complex that they would entangle and confuse the opposition in legal technicalities. Partisan political considerations were also involved. The numerous justices of the peace competed for fees and therefore were often eager to trade favorable decisions for court business (Glick and Vines).

A Complex Court Structure

The sporadic and unplanned expansion of the American court system has resulted in an often confusing structure. In many states there are several courts in one county: several lower courts and one or perhaps two major trial courts. To add further confusion, some major trial courts have jurisdictions that overlap with those of lower courts. Moreover, there may be major variations in court jurisdiction from one county to the next within one state. An example is Maryland: "There are no less than 16 different types of courts, with little uniformity from one community to another. A lawyer venturing into another is likely to feel almost as bewildered as if he had gone into another state with an entirely different system of courts" (Institute of Judicial Administration: 11–12).

Basic Principles of American Courts

Although American courts may resemble a bramblebush of names, functions, and types, there are some basic principles underlying their organization. It is helpful to understand these basic principles of jurisdiction, the dual court system, and the differences between trial and appellate courts before embarking on a detailed discussion of any given court structure.

Jurisdiction

jurisdiction

Court structure is largely determined by the legal limitations on the types of cases a court may hear and decide. The persons over whom a court has power and the subject matter over which a court can make a legally binding decision are referred to as the court's *jurisdiction* (Oran). Constitutions, statutes, and court decisions define a court's jurisdiction. The authorization for the federal court system is found in Article III of the Constitution: "The judicial power of the United States shall be vested in one supreme court, and in such inferior courts as the congress may from time to time ordain and establish." This provision was deliberately left vague because the Founding Fathers were deeply divided over whether there should be a separate federal court system. Thus it was left to Congress to provide the working details of the federal court structure.

Similarly, state and municipal courts derive their power and authority from the respective state constitutions and state statutes. Typically, however, state constitutions are more detailed than the U.S. Constitution. In many states, for example, the names and geographical territories of the courts are individually

---

QUOTATION

*I*n short, despite experiments in diversity, colonial conditions shaped court organization in all, or almost all, colonies along similar lines in the 17th century. Court structures moved from the simple to the more complex, from the undifferentiated to the hierarchical. English models, English terms, and English customs were a more or less powerful influence everywhere. Executive, legislative, and judicial power were not clearly fenced off from each other. But as time went on, differentiation became more marked. Legislatures still heard appeals, but they conducted few or no trials.

The colonies had another trait in common. For all their geographic and political isolation, they owed some sort of allegiance to the crown. Their charters spoke explicitly of the duty to conform their laws to English laws. The distant king held at least some nominal authority, particularly in chartered colonies. Many colonies actively resisted English influence.

Lawrence Friedman, *A History of American Law,* 2d ed. (New York: Simon and Schuster, 1985), p. 46.

specified in the constitution. As a result, to create a new court to handle a rising caseload or to restructure the entire state court system requires a statewide constitutional amendment. As in the federal system, though, the legislative bodies flesh out the organizational skeleton provided in the state constitution by specifying the number of judgeships and the like. A court's jurisdiction can be classified according to three subcomponents: geographical jurisdiction, subject matter jurisdiction, and hierarchical jurisdiction.

Geographical jurisdiction.   Courts are authorized to hear and decide disputes arising within specified political boundaries (a city, a county, a group of counties). For example, a California court has no jurisdiction to try a person accused of committing a crime in Oregon. These geographical limitations on judicial powers present a number of problems for courts and law enforcement agencies. Sometimes it is difficult for a court to obtain personal jurisdiction over a defendant. If a defendant is being held in another part of the state, the court requests the cooperation of the other jurisdiction. But if that jurisdiction does not wish to relinquish control, either because the defendant has strong political ties or because it wishes to try the person first, heated exchanges can develop. Similarly, if a defendant has left the state, whether intending to avoid prosecution or not, the state may request extradition. Defendants in foreign countries present even more complex problems since the United States has no extradition treaty with some nations (Argentina, for example), and some nations will not extradite a person unless the alleged crime also violates their own law.

Subject matter jurisdiction.   Another key element of jurisdiction is subject matter. Trial courts of limited jurisdiction are restricted to hearing only a limited category of cases, typically misdemeanors and civil suits involving small sums of money. Trial courts of general jurisdiction are empowered to hear all other types of cases. In addition, certain types of cases are not allowed to be brought to court. The U.S. Supreme Court has ruled, for example, that courts have no jurisdiction to decide church disputes over doctrinal matters. Similarly, the U.S. Supreme Court will hear no cases involving political questions, although some ambiguity exists over what constitutes a political question.

Hierarchical jurisdiction.   The structure of courts also reflects differences in functions and responsibilities, referred to as original jurisdiction and appellate jurisdiction. ***Original jurisdiction*** means that a court has the authority to try a case and decide it. ***Appellate jurisdiction*** means that a court has the power to take cases on appeal already decided by a trial court. Trial courts are primarily courts of original jurisdiction, but they occasionally have limited appellate jurisdiction (for example, when a trial court hears appeals from lower trial courts like mayor's courts or a justice of the peace court). Appellate courts often have a very limited original jurisdiction. In disputes between states, the U.S. Supreme Court has original jurisdiction, and a number of state supreme courts have original jurisdiction in matters involving disbarment of attorneys.

original jurisdiction
appellate jurisdiction

Dual Court System

dual court system

America has a ***dual court system***: one national court structure and court structures in each of the fifty states. The end result is fifty-one separate court systems—one for the national government and fifty different ones in the states. The dual court system mirrors the federal system of government. In the federal system of government of the United States, powers are divided between the national government and the state governments, with each legally supreme in its own sphere. The two levels of government, however, share other powers, such as taxation and penalizing violators of their respective laws. Applying the federal principle to the courts, federal courts have exclusive power over violations of federal criminal law and state courts have the exclusive right to try those accused of breaking state laws. Figure 3-1 shows the ordering of cases in the dual court system. The division of responsibilities is not as clear-cut as it looks because the same judicial powers are shared by the state and federal courts. Civil suits between citizens of different states may be heard by either state or federal court. The possession of narcotics or the interstate transportation of a kidnap victim violates both state and federal laws, which means the accused could be tried twice. In addition, defendants convicted in state court may appeal to the U.S. Supreme Court, a federal court. Defendants convicted in state court may also seek a further review of their case in a U.S. District Court by filing a writ of *habeas corpus* (a claim that the person is being held illegally).

Trial and Appellate Courts

The principal difference between a trial and an appeal is that a trial focuses on facts whereas an appeal focuses on correctly interpreting the law. This distinction, of course, is not absolute. Fact-finding in the trial courts is guided by law. Likewise, appellate courts are sensitive to the facts of a case. Nonetheless, the major functional difference between these judicial bodies is the distinction between determining facts and interpreting the law.

trial court

Trial courts.   Virtually all cases, whether civil or criminal, begin in the ***trial court***. If the case is a criminal one, the trial court arraigns the defendant, sets bail, conducts a trial (or takes a guilty plea), and imposes sentence if the defendant is found guilty. If the case is a civil one, the trial court operates in much the same fashion, ensuring that each party is properly informed of the complaint, conducting pretrial procedures (such as settling disputes over exchange of information), conducting a trial or accepting an out-of-court settlement, and awarding damages. Because only trial courts hear disputes over facts, it is only in trial courts that witnesses appear. Trial courts are considered finders of fact, and the decision of a judge (or jury) about a factual dispute normally cannot be appealed (in Louisiana and Wisconsin, however, trial court findings of fact in civil cases are appealable). Although in theory every trial court decision may be appealed, most cases are settled without a trial; thus there is no appeal.

appellate court

Appeals courts.   The losing party in the trial court generally has the right to request an ***appellate court*** to review the case. In criminal cases, however, the constitutional protection against double jeopardy prevents the prosecutor from appealing if the judge or jury has returned a verdict of not guilty.

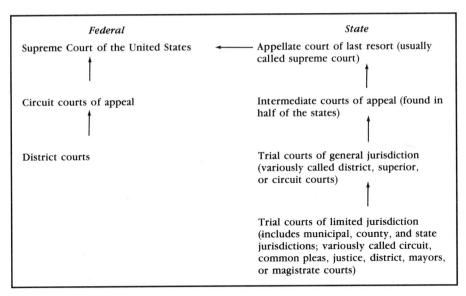

Figure 3-1   The dual court system of the United States and routes of appeal

The primary function of the appellate courts is to ensure that the trial courts correctly interpreted and applied the law. A second function is to devise new rules, reexamine old ones, and interpret unclear language of past court decisions or statutes (Wheeler and Whitcomb). Because their role is not the same, appellate courts operate very differently from trial courts. No witnesses are heard; no trials are conducted; and juries are never used.

appellant

brief
appellee

oral
argument

opinion of
the court

The appellate process begins when the ***appellant*** (the losing party in the lower court) files a notice of appeal. The appellant has several months to prepare a written ***brief*** explaining why the decision of the lower court was in error. The opposing party (the ***appellee***) also has the opportunity to prepare a brief setting forth arguments that the original decision was legally correct and should stand. The case is then set for ***oral argument,*** during which both sides are allotted a short time to present their arguments.

In deciding issues of law, appellate courts operate as collegial bodies—that is, decisions are made by a group of judges. There may be as few as three or as many as twenty-eight (as in the Ninth Circuit Court of Appeals). Appellate judges often provide written reasons justifying their decisions (trial court judges write opinions less often). If the case is an easy one, the ***opinion of the court*** may be very short, perhaps a sentence or two. But if the legal issues are important and/or complex, the court's opinion may run into dozens of pages. It is through such written opinions that appellate courts shape the law. Some legal issues are so close or involve such a number of conflicting legal problems that the judges do not always agree among themselves as to the correct answer. Those who disagree with the majority can write a dissenting opinion to explain their views and why they believe their fellow judges reached the wrong results.

If the appellate court finds that a legal error was committed (for example, illegally obtained evidence was admitted at trial) the court reverses and remands (sends back) the case to the trial court. This usually means that the defendant will be tried a second time. The chances of a criminal defendant winning on appeal are not very high, however.

Federal Courts

Only the federal courts operate over the entire territory of the United States. Federal courts are structured along state lines. Thus, although they enforce a uniform body of national criminal laws, local concerns influence the justice

---

QUOTATION

*A*n upper court can seldom do anything to correct a trial court's mistaken belief about the facts. Where, as happens in most cases, the testimony at the trial was oral, the upper court usually feels obliged to adopt the trial court's determination of the facts. Why? Because in such a case the trial court heard and saw the witnesses as they testified, but the upper court did not. The upper court has only a typewritten or printed record of the testimony. The trial court alone is in a position to interpret the demeanor-clues, this "language without words." An upper court, to use Judge Kennison's phrase, "has to operate in the partial vacuum of the printed record." A "stenographic transcript," wrote Judge Ulman, ". . . fails to reproduce tones of voice and hesitations of speech that often make a sentence mean the reverse of what the mere words signify. The best and most accurate record [of oral testimony] is like a dehydrated peach; it has neither the substance nor the flavor of the peach before it was dried." That is why, when testimony is taken in a trial court, an upper court, on appeal, in most instances accepts the facts as found by the trial court, when those findings can be supported by reasonable inferences from some witnesses' testimony, even if it is flatly contradicted in the testimony of other witnesses.

Jerome Frank, *Courts on Trial: Myth and Reality in American Justice* (New York: Princeton University Press, 1973), p. 23. (Copyright 1949 by Jerome Frank; copyright renewed © 1976 by Princeton University Press.) Reprinted by permission of Princeton University Press.

dispensed. As a result, there are important variations in the application of law, an indication that American courts are deeply rooted in a local heritage. The federal courts handle far fewer cases than do their state counterparts, although in general the cases they do hear tend to be more serious and complex. Because the federal courts are organized in a clear order of district courts, circuit courts of appeals, and the U.S. Supreme Court (see Figure 3-2), it is best to consider them before turning to the more varied structure of state courts.

District Courts

In the federal system, the district courts are trial courts of original jurisdiction. There is at least one U.S. District Court in each state; no district court crosses state lines (see Figure 3-2). Some states have more than one court. California, New York, and Texas, for instance, each have four. Altogether there are ninety-four district courts—eighty-nine within the fifty states, one in the District of Columbia, and four for the U.S. territories. The number of judges in each district ranges from two in sparsely populated Wyoming to twenty-seven in densely inhabited Manhattan (formally known as the Southern District of New York). Because district courts often encompass large geographical areas (for historical reasons, the western states tend to have only one court for each state), they hold court in various locations, termed *divisions*. While some districts hold court in only one division, others have as many as eight. In the

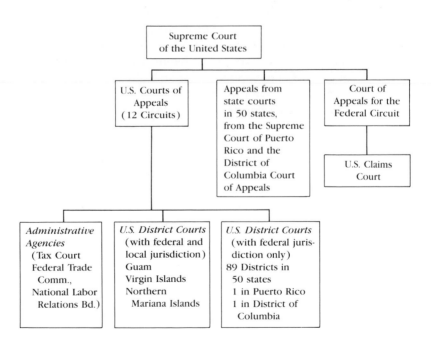

Figure 3-2   The U.S. court system. The lines show the routes of cases through appeals and Supreme Court grants of hearings. A few uncommon routes have been omitted.

TABLE 3-1   Workload of U.S. Courts, 1985

	Total cases filed	Minor criminal	Criminal	Civil
U.S. Supreme Court (9 judgeships)	5,006			
U.S. courts of appeal (156 judgeships)	33,360[a]		4,989	23,571
U.S. district courts (575 judgeships)	313,270		39,500	273,670
U.S. magistrates (253 full-time judgeships)[b]	363,687	90,757	120,143[c]	152,787

[a] Includes 3,179 appeals from administrative agencies.
[b] There are also 284 part-time U.S. magistrates.
[c] Initial proceedings in criminal cases.
SOURCE: Administrative Office of the United States Courts, *Annual Report of the Director, 1985* (Washington, D.C.: Government Printing Office, 1985).

U.S. territories, the district courts may also be responsible for local as well as federal matters.

The district courts are staffed by district court judges who are nominated by the president and confirmed by the Senate; they serve for life. District court judges possess full judicial powers, including conducting trials, accepting guilty pleas, and imposing sentences. In addition, there are 467 U.S. magistrates (only 280 of whom are full-time). Created by Congress in 1969 to replace the former position of U.S. commissioner (who had very limited powers), U.S. magistrates are empowered to hear petty and some minor offenses, as well as to conduct the preliminary stages of felony cases and numerous civil matters. U.S. magistrates are appointed for an eight-year term by the district court judges and do not have lifetime tenure.

The district courts have original jurisdiction over both civil and criminal cases; thus they are the trial courts for all violations of the federal criminal law other than those tried by U.S. magistrates. Federal criminal prosecutions have remained fairly constant through the past decades, averaging about forty thousand major cases per year. The volume of civil filings has been steadily increasing, however. As Table 3–1 shows, civil lawsuits consume more of the federal courts' time than criminal cases do. Although federal district courts handle far fewer cases than state trial courts, civil cases in federal court often raise more complex legal issues than those in state courts and the amount of money in controversy is also often quite a bit larger.

Courts of Appeals

Created in 1891 to relieve the U.S. Supreme Court of hearing the growing number of appeals, the circuit courts of appeals are the intermediate appellate courts of the federal system. Eleven of the circuits are identified by number and are organized regionally (see Figure 3-3). The twelfth circuit has jurisdiction over the District of Columbia. As in the district courts, the number of circuit court judges varies, depending somewhat on the population and volume of cases. The number of judges authorized for each circuit ranges from six

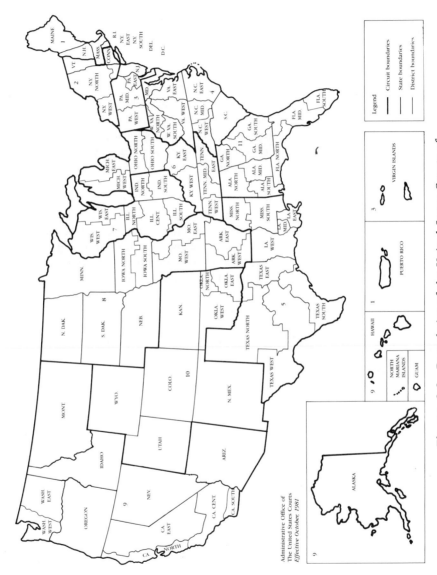

Figure 3-3 Boundaries of the United States Courts of Appeals and United States District Courts.

(the First Circuit) to twenty-eight (the Ninth Circuit). The chief judge (the most senior judge in terms of service, under seventy years of age) of each circuit has supervisory responsibilities for the circuit. Like district judges, circuit court of appeals judges are nominated by the president and confirmed by the Senate.

The circuit courts have jurisdiction to review the final decisions of the district court, as well as the power to act on certain legal issues that arise while a lawsuit is going on (called *interlocutory appeals*). In addition, the circuit courts hear appeals from a host of quasi-judicial tribunals like the National Labor Relations Board.

In fiscal year 1985, over thirty-three thousand appeals were filed in the circuit courts. As is true in the district courts, the volume of cases in the circuit courts has grown steadily since the early 1960s. During the past decade the number of cases being appealed doubled. The largest increase has been in civil appeals. Criminal appeals shot up dramatically from 1963 to 1973 but have leveled off since then. During the last decade, the number of criminal appeals has increased by less than 8 percent while the number of civil cases climbed by 122 percent.

The circuit courts normally utilize three-judge panels in deciding cases, which produces some differences in legal interpretation from panel to panel. In controversial cases, though, all the judges may sit together to decide the case. Such *en banc* hearings are rare, however; in 1985 only eighty-five were held in the entire nation. A decision by the circuit court exhausts the litigant's right to one appeal. A dissatisfied party may request the U.S. Supreme Court to hear the case, but such requests are rarely granted.

The U.S. Supreme Court

The highest court in the nation is the U.S. Supreme Court. It is composed of nine justices: eight associate justices and one chief justice (who is nominated specifically to that post by the president). Besides presiding over the Court's public sessions, the Chief Justice conducts the Court's conferences, assigns justices to write opinions (when the Chief Justice votes in the majority), and has supervisory power over the nation's courts. Like other judges appointed under Article III of the Constitution, justices of the Supreme Court are nominated by the president, require confirmation by the Senate, and serve for life.

writ of certiorari

The main way that cases proceed to the Supreme Court is through the ***writ of certiorari,*** an order to the lower court whose decision is being disputed to send up the records of the case so that the Supreme Court can determine whether the law has been correctly applied. The Court hears appeals from both circuit courts of appeals and state appellate courts of last resort. Although the U.S. Supreme Court is the only court in the nation to have authority over all fifty-one separate legal systems, this authority is actually a limited one.

rule of four

The Court does not have to hear a case unless it wants to. The discretionary power of the Court to determine which cases it will decide allows the Court to regulate its workload. In deciding whether to hear a case the Court employs the ***rule of four:*** four judges must vote to hear a case before it is placed on the docket. The Court hears only a small percentage of the requests for appeals. By law and custom a set of requirements evolved that must be met before a writ is granted. First, the litigant must have exhausted all other avenues of appeal. Second, the legal issue must involve a "substantial federal question" as defined by the particular Court. This means state supreme courts' interpretations of state law can be appealed to the U.S. Supreme Court only if there is an alleged violation of either federal law or the U.S. Constitution. For example, a suit contending that a state supreme court has misinterpreted the state's divorce law would not be heard because it involves only an interpretation of state law and does not raise a federal question. Therefore, the vast majority of state criminal cases are never reviewed by the U.S. Supreme Court.

Through its discretionary powers to hear appeals, the U.S. Supreme Court limits itself to deciding about two hundred cases a year. It has long been the tradition that the Court should not operate as the court of last resort, trying to see that justice is done in every case, but rather should marshal its time and energy to decide the most important policy questions of the day. The necessity for hearing only a small number of the potential cases coming to the Court is underscored by the rapid increase in case filings: 2,321 in 1963 to 5,006 in 1986, an increase of over 100 percent.

State Courts

State courts process the vast majority of cases. The courts in a single medium-sized state handle more cases than the entire federal system. The structure of state courts is less clear-cut than the three tiers of the federal system. Each state system is different. Although some states have adopted a unified court structure, in many there are still numerous local courts with overlapping jurisdictions. In examining the sometimes bewildering array of state courts, it is useful to divide state courts into four levels: trial courts of limited jurisdiction, trial courts of general jurisdiction, intermediate appellate courts, and courts of last resort.

Trial Courts of Limited Jurisdiction: Lower Courts

lower courts (inferior courts)

At the first level are trial courts of limited jurisdiction, sometimes referred to as *inferior courts* or more simply *lower courts.* The lower courts are by far the most numerous. They constitute 77 percent of the total number of judicial bodies. Variously called justices of the peace, city courts, county courts, magistrates, or municipal courts, the lower courts handle minor cases: traffic violations, ordinance violations, petty criminal cases, and civil disputes under a set amount (often $500 or less). Generally, lower courts are restricted to imposing a maximum fine of $1,000 and no more than a year in jail. In some states, though, they are authorized to levy fines as high as $5,000 and to sentence defendants to up to five years in prison. In addition, some of these courts are responsible for the preliminary stages of felony cases. Thus, trial courts of limited jurisdiction often hold arraignments, set bail, appoint counsel for indigents, and conduct preliminary examinations. Later the case is transferred to a trial court of general jurisdiction for trial (or plea) and sentencing.

TABLE 3-2   Estimated Case Filings in State Courts

Level of Court		Totals
Trial courts of limited and general jurisdiction[a]		80,580,851
Civil[b]	12,839,400	
Criminal[c]	10,511,116	
Juvenile	1,142,271	
Traffic[d]	57,287,920	
Intermediate appellate courts[e]		130,988
Courts of last resort[e]		59,968

[a] Data from Indiana, Mississippi, Nevada, and Ohio were not available.
[b] Tort, contract, small claims, domestic relations, and probate.
[c] Felonies, misdemeanors, ordinance violations (other than traffic), and miscellaneous criminal and preliminary hearings in courts of limited jurisdiction.
[d] Some states include parking violations as part of their traffic caseload, but others do not.
[e] Data from Indiana and Nevada were not available.
SOURCE: Bureau of Justice Statistics, *Case Filings in State Courts, 1983* (Washington, D.C.: U.S. Department of Justice, 1984).

trial de novo

The number of trial courts of limited (and sometimes special) jurisdiction varies from none in Idaho, Iowa, South Dakota, and Illinois (where their functions have been absorbed by the trial courts) to over a thousand in New York (1,507) and Texas (1,115).

The lower courts are not typically courts of record; no official verbatim transcript of the proceedings is made. Appeals from lower courts decisions are typically heard in a trial court of general jurisdiction, not in a state's appellate courts. Such an appeal is termed *trial de novo* because the case must be heard again in its entirety. There are an estimated fifteen to twenty thousand lower court judges, most of whom are not lawyers. Salaries of these justices of the peace, as they are often called, are usually quite low. Most lower courts are created by local governments—cities or counties—and therefore are not part of the state judiciary. Although the lower courts hear only minor cases, they are nonetheless quite important, for these are the courts where the vast majority of ordinary citizens have contact with their nation's judiciary (Table 3-2).

In trial courts of limited jurisdiction, proceedings are typically informal. Cases are processed on a mass basis. Trials are rare and most are disposed of quickly. Chapter 17 will discuss in greater detail the quality of justice dispensed by the nation's lowest and most neglected courts.

Trial Courts of General Jurisdiction: Major Trial Courts

major trial courts

The most common names for *major trial courts* are district, circuit, superior, supreme, or common pleas. Table 3-3 gives the exact names used in all states. The major trial courts have unlimited jurisdiction and therefore are the courts that dispose of serious criminal cases. Thus they hear all matters not specifically delegated to lower courts. In addition, they sometimes have shared jurisdiction (concurrent jurisdiction) with courts of limited jurisdiction; for example, they may also hear misdemeanor cases. The specific division of

TABLE 3-3 Major Trial Courts in Different States

Circuit court	Alabama, Arkansas,[a] Florida, Hawaii, Illinois, Indiana, Kentucky, Maryland, Michigan, Mississippi,[a] Missouri, Oregon, South Carolina, South Dakota, Tennessee,[a] Virginia, West Virginia, Wisconsin[b]
Court of common pleas	Ohio, Pennsylvania
District court	Colorado, Idaho, Iowa, Kansas, Louisiana, Minnesota, Montana, Nebraska, Nevada, New Mexico, North Dakota, Oklahoma, Texas, Utah, Wyoming
Superior court	Alaska, Arizona, California, Connecticut, Delaware,[a] District of Columbia, Georgia, Maine, New Hampshire, New Jersey,[b] North Carolina, Rhode Island, Vermont, Washington
Supreme court	New York[b]
Trial	Massachusetts

[a] Arkansas, Delaware, Mississippi, and Tennessee have separate chancery courts with equity jurisdiction.
[b] New Jersey, New York, and Wisconsin also have county courts.
SOURCES: Law Enforcement Assistance Administration (LEAA), *National Survey of Court Organization* (Washington, D.C.: Government Printing Office, 1973), p. 1; *National Survey of Court Organization 1975 Supplement to State Judicial Systems* (September 1975) and *National Survey of Court Organization 1977 Supplement to State Judicial Systems* (May 1977); The Council of State Governments, *The Book of the States, 1986–87* (Lexington, Ky.: LEAA, 1986).

jurisdiction between the inferior courts and general trial courts is specified by law, statutory or constitutional or both.

In most states these courts are divided into judicial districts or judicial circuits. The exact geographical boundaries of the trial courts of general jurisdiction depend somewhat on the volume of the cases but invariably follow existing political boundaries of counties. These districts or circuits in rural areas encompass several adjoining counties, and judges literally ride circuit, holding court in different counties on a fixed schedule. In larger counties where case volumes are larger, judges typically specialize. Such specialization may be either formal or informal. In New Orleans, for example, judges are formally specialized. The parish (county) has two district courts: civil district court and criminal district court. The judges are elected to one or the other court, and each court has separate support staff (sheriff, clerk of court, and so on). Chicago employs informal specialization. The chief judge of the circuit court of Cook County assigns judges to various divisions: criminal, family, juvenile, civil, and so on. Table 3-2 provides some basic workload data on the major trial courts.

Intermediate Courts of Appeals

At the beginning of this century, state court systems included only a single appellate body—the state supreme court. State courts, like their federal counterparts, faced a growth in appellate cases that threatened to overwhelm the state supreme court. State officials in thirty-six states responded by creating ***intermediate courts of appeals*** (Table 3-4). These courts must hear all properly filed appeals. Subsequent appeals are at the discretion of the higher court. Thus a decision by the state's intermediate appellate court is the final one for

intermediate courts of appeals

TABLE 3-4   Intermediate Courts of Appeals (Number of Judges)

Appeals court	Massachusetts (10)
Appellate court	Illinois (34), Connecticut (6)
Appellate division of superior court	New Jersey (28)
Appellate division of supreme court	New York (46)
Commonwealth court	Pennsylvania (9)
Court of appeals	Alaska (3), Arizona (18), Arkansas (6), California (73), Colorado (10), Georgia (9), Idaho (3), Indiana (12), Iowa (6), Kansas (7), Kentucky (14), Louisiana (48), Michigan (18), Minnesota (12), Missouri (32), New Mexico (7), North Carolina (12), Ohio (53), Oklahoma (12), Oregon (10), South Carolina (6), Tennessee (12), Texas (80), Virginia (10), Washington (16), Wisconsin (12)
Court of civil appeals	Alabama (3)
Court of criminal appeals	Alabama (5), Tennessee (9)
Court of special appeals	Maryland (13)
District court of appeals	Florida (45)
Intermediate court of appeals	Hawaii (3)
Superior court	Pennsylvania (15)

SOURCE: The Council of State Governments, *The Book of the States, 1986–87* (Lexington, Ky.: Council of State Governments, 1986).

most cases. Only a small fraction of the cases handled by trial courts ever reach the appellate courts.

The structure of the intermediate courts of appeals varies in several ways. Whereas some states have only a single court for the entire state, others provide separate courts for different regions. In most states these bodies hear both civil and criminal appeals. In the states of Alabama and Tennessee, however, there are separate courts of appeals for civil and criminal cases. Like their counterparts on the federal level, these courts typically employ rotating three-judge panels for deciding cases.

Supreme Court

state supreme court

The court of last resort is the ***state supreme court.*** In states without an intermediate court of appeal, the supreme court has no power to choose which cases will be placed on its docket. To complicate the picture further, both Texas and Oklahoma have two courts of last resort, the supreme court (civil) and the court of criminal appeals. The number of supreme court judges varies from a low of three in some states to as many as nine (see Table 3-5). Unlike the intermediate appellate courts, these courts do not use panels in making decisions. Rather, the entire court participates in deciding each case. The state supreme courts are the ultimate review board for matters involving interpretation of state law. The only avenue of appeal for a disgruntled litigant is the U.S. Supreme Court, but successful applications are few and must involve important questions of federal law.

Although state supreme courts vary greatly in the details of internal procedures used in deciding cases, most follow procedures roughly similar to those

TABLE 3-5 Courts of Last Resort in Different States (Number of Judges)

Supreme court	Alabama (9), Alaska (5), Arizona (5), Arkansas (7), California (7), Colorado (7), Connecticut (6), Delaware (5), Florida (7), Georgia (7), Hawaii (5), Idaho (5), Illinois (7), Indiana (5), Iowa (9), Kansas (7), Kentucky (7), Louisiana (7), Michigan (7), Minnesota (9), Mississippi (9), Missouri (7), Montana (7), Nebraska (7), Nevada (5), New Hampshire (5), New Jersey (7), New Mexico (5), North Carolina (7), North Dakota (5), Ohio (7), Oklahoma (9),[a] Oregon (7), Pennsylvania (7), Rhode Island (5), South Carolina (5), South Dakota (5), Tennessee (5), Texas (9),[a] Utah (5), Vermont (5), Virginia (7), Washington (9), Wisconsin (7), Wyoming (5)
Court of appeals	Maryland (7), New York (7)
Supreme judicial court	Maine (7), Massachusetts (7)
Court of criminal appeals	Oklahoma (3),[a] Texas (9)[a]
Supreme court of appeals	West Virginia (5)

[a]Two courts of last resort in these states.
SOURCES: U.S. Department of Justice, Bureau of Justice Statistics, *State Court Organization, 1980* (Washington, D.C.: Government Printing Office, 1982); The Council of State Governments, *The Book of the States, 1986–87* (Lexington, Ky.: Council of State Governments, 1986).

of the U.S. Supreme Court. State supreme courts, however, tend to have greater caseloads than the U.S. Supreme Court.

Court Unification

Since the turn of the century, the organization of American courts has been a central concern of court reformers. Groups such as the American Judicature Society and the American Bar Association believe that the multiplicity of courts is inefficient (because judges cannot be shifted to meet the growing volume of cases in other courts) and also inequitable (because the administration of justice is not uniform). Court reformers have placed a great emphasis on im-

unified court system

plementing a **unified court system.** The principal objective is to shift judicial administration from local control to centralized court management. The loose network of independent judges and courts bound together primarily by the appellate process would be replaced by a coherent organization with hierarchical lines of authority determining and enforcing policy. Greater authority would be concentrated in the state capital and less administrative independence would be granted local courts. Although court reformers differ about the exact details of a uniform court system, their efforts reflect five general principles (Berkson and Carbon).

Consolidated and Simplified Court Structure

Court reformers stress the need for a simple and uniform structure of courts for the entire state. The number of different types of trial courts would be reduced. In particular the myriad minor courts (which often have overlapping jurisdictions) would be consolidated in one county-level court. This would mean that variations between counties would be eliminated and replaced by a similar court structure throughout the state. Overall the court reformers envision a three-tier system: a state supreme court at the top; intermediate courts of appeal where the volume of cases makes it necessary; and a single trial court. (Chapter 17 discusses the movement to abolish locally controlled lower courts and to place them within the state judicial system.)

Centralized Administration

A second basic principle of the unified court system is centralized administration. The state supreme court working through court administrators would have the final authority and provide leadership for administering the state court system. The state court system would embody a genuine hierarchy of authority, with local court administrators required to follow the policy directives of the central office and held accountable by the state supreme court. Thus a centralized state office would supervise the work of judicial and nonjudicial personnel (clerks of court and so on).

Centralized Rulemaking

Reformers argue that the state supreme court should have the power to adopt uniform rules to be followed by all courts in the state. Examples of such rules would include criteria governing admission to the bar, procedures for disciplining errant attorneys, and time standards for disposing of cases. In addition judges could be temporarily assigned to other courts to alleviate backlogs and reduce delay. Centralized rulemaking would shift control from legislatures to judges and lawyers.

Centralized Judicial Budgeting

Centralized budgeting would give the state judicial administrator (who reports to the state supreme court) the authority to prepare a single budget for the entire state judiciary and send it directly to the legislature. The power of the governor to recommend a judicial budget would be eliminated. Likewise lower courts would be more dependent upon the supreme court for their monetary needs and less able to lobby local representatives directly. Thus decisions about allocating funds would be made at the state level, not at the local level as often occurs in many states.

Statewide Financing

Along with centralized judicial budgeting, reformers argue for the adoption of statewide financing of the judiciary. Although courts are mandated by state law, they are often financed in whole or in part by local governments. Given that courts are often not a high priority for local government, they end up with less than adequate local financing. State government, in contrast, has more money and therefore can better support necessary court services.

The Politics of Court Reorganization

The efforts of judicial reformers have achieved considerable success. Many states have substantially unified their court systems. In recent years, the states of Alabama, Arizona, Illinois, North Carolina, Kentucky, Oklahoma, Washington, Florida, Wisconsin, and Massachusetts have adopted new court structures. Significantly, however, only a very few states have adopted most or all of the principles suggested by court reformers. Several states, for example, have adopted a four-tier system (rather than the recommended three) by retaining magistrates or justices of the peace in separate courts. Along these same lines, a number of states have increased the responsibilities of centralized administration yet still allow significant supervisory power at the local level. Finally, the principle of statewide financing has not fared well. In many states county courts are still financed to a significant degree by the county (or an equivalent unit). Moreover, not all reform efforts have been successful. Some states (such as Tennessee) have considered and then rejected constitutional amendments to restructure their courts.

To understand why some reform proposals have been rejected while others have been significantly modified from the reformers' recommended principles, we need to examine the political dimensions of court reorganization. Battles over court organization are usually presented as dry technical issues involving case volume and efficiency. But such arguments really mask the underlying political dynamics.

Conflict over the structure, operations, and staffing of the courts has always been part of judicial politics. There are many groups that support court reform. Most prominent among these has been the lawyer elite. The American Bar Association is a long-time advocate of judicial reform. In 1913 elite members of the bar organized the American Judicature Society to conduct reform campaigns to improve the courts. Historically, middle-class reform organizations have also been involved. Organizations that grew out of the Progressive movement, like the League of Women Voters, endorse the ideals of court reform. More recently judicial reform has achieved wide official recognition and become the "government-approved" approach to judicial administration. The National Institute of Justice within the U.S. Justice Department and the private National Center for State Courts reflect a trend toward greater government involvement and leadership in the reform model of judicial administration (Glick).

Not everyone agrees with the goals or assumptions of court reform. Opposition stems from both philosophical and pragmatic considerations. Attempts to reorganize state court systems seldom generate much popular interest (Jacob). Thus the flow of public discussion favors those who support the status quo. The American Bar Association does not speak for all lawyers. General practice and trial lawyers are often in local courthouses and tend to think court reform would require unnecessary changes in their routines. Opposition to court reform also comes from judges and other court personnel who resist learning new procedures in new court organizations. While judges would not be eliminated by court unification, some would be required to take on new tasks, a change that they find uncomfortable. More specifically, nonlawyer judges oppose court reorganization because their jobs would be abolished under plans requiring all judges to be lawyers. This is why many court reform proposals include grandfather clauses allowing nonlawyer judges to remain in office. Court reform proposals can also become a political battleground between the Republican and Democratic parties (Glick). The party in power often perceives quite correctly that court reform will mean the loss of important patronage positions. On a broader scale, the Democratic party typically has its strongest support in urban areas, whereas the Republican party has greater dominance at the state level. The greater concentration of judicial power at the state level can produce a gain for the Republicans at the expense of the Democrats.

Any attempt to unify a state judicial system invariably brings opposition from local governments that wish to retain control of their local courts. Issues of local versus state authority also have important financial dimensions. As a result, most proposals to unify state court systems carry the provision that the state will pay all expenses of the local courts (thus relieving cities of millions of dollars in expense) but allow the local municipalities to retain revenues derived from court fines and court fees. Finally, many of the problems associated with the existing structure of courts are concentrated in the large cities. Rural politicians and rural lawyers, because they see no problems in their own area, are not sympathetic to major overhauls that would not benefit them but might mean a decreased control of local courts (Glick and Vines).

Despite these political obstacles, court reformers have made great strides in altering court structures. The changes adopted in a given state, however, reflect that state's political environment. Thus Alaska and Hawaii have highly unified courts that reflect the way in which territorial courts developed before statehood. Connecticut had state funding and appointed court clerks before its courts were highly consolidated because of the absence of county government in the state. North Carolina's courts are highly consolidated but elected county clerks remain powerful. And Maryland was able to unify its minor courts

QUOTATION

*H*istorians have generally viewed the creation of the courts of appeals as a response to increased federal litigation brought about by the "great increase in population" and the "general business revival which followed the civil war." The strain "imposed severe and increasing burdens on the overtaxed federal Supreme Court." We might assume from this explanation that the courts of appeals appeared on the American scene as a logical, painless, almost automatic response to postwar conditions. Such an assumption is erroneous. The creation of the courts of appeals was one of the most enduring struggles in American political history.

Richard Richardson, and Kenneth Vines, *The Politics of the Federal Courts* (Boston: Little, Brown, 1970).

into a statewide court of limited jurisdiction but was unable to overcome the resistance of the general jurisdiction trial courts, which remain locally funded and administered (Baar and Henderson).

Some have begun to question the assumptions and philosophy of the court reformers. These critics argue that the concept of a unified court system reflects a classical view of public administration, one that stresses a strong central administration rather than active participation by those most affected. Furthermore, the reformers hold a limited view of politics. In the words of Carl Baar, "The persistence of politics has been a failure not of court reformers but of those who have articulated reform arguments in the past." Some principles of a unified court system, it is believed, would not remove politics from the system but rather allow the governor much greater political control over the state's judiciary. Finally, the standard blueprint of court reorganization does not allow for a desirable diversity: instead, local diversity is considered illegitimate. For these reasons, a new generation of scholars, concerned about improving the quality of justice in American courts, now believes that the old principles of court reorganization hamper creative thinking about new directions for court reform (Gallas; Hudzik).

Consequences of Court Organization

How the courts are organized and administered has a profound effect on the way defendants are processed in the criminal courts as well as the type of justice that results.

Decentralization

Because there are fifty-one legal systems in America, there are significant differences in the law from one state to the next. On the civil side the grounds for divorce vary from rather rigid criteria in some states to rather minimal ones in others (of which Nevada is the most prominent example). On the criminal side differences in how crimes are defined are evident among the states.

Within each legal system there are also notable variations. The enforcement of the criminal law is almost entirely a local enterprise. Courts are structured on a local basis. The officials that staff the courts—judges, prosecutors, and defense attorneys—are often recruited from the community they now serve and thus reflect the sentiments of that community. Together these factors produce a system of justice with close ties to local communities. The direct result of the enforcement and application of the criminal law by local officials operating in courts reflecting the local community is that disparities exist between communities in matters like release on bail, delay in the courts, plea bargaining practices, and sentencing.

Local Control and Local Corruption

local control   *Local control* of justice has some obvious advantages. The courts are close to the people, and by and large the public respects the courts in America more than it does in Europe, where judges are viewed as faceless bureaucrats responding to the dictates of the national government, oblivious to local customs and needs. But local control has been the incubator for local corruption, local injustice, and, in some limited instances, local tyranny.

Every state invariably has a town or two where gambling and prostitution flourish because the city fathers agree to look the other way. Not surprisingly, they often receive monetary benefits from being so nearsighted. Recently, though, such activities have been decreasing due to the active interest of state police, state attorney generals, and/or federal prosecutors.

The locally administered criminal justice system has also been marked by pockets of injustice. At times the police and the courts have been the handmaidens of the local economic elite. In the South the police and the courts have hindered efforts to exercise civil rights by arresting or harassing those who sought to register to vote, eat at the whites-only lunch counter, or simply speak up to protest segregation.

The dual court system has provided a safety valve for checking the most flagrant abuses of local justice. The dual court system allows for alternative tribunals in some situations. Often, prosecution of local officials is conducted by federal officials.

Lack of Administrative Monitoring

A major peculiarity of America's judiciary is that within each state, the courts enjoy a great deal of independence. This is partly the result of the strong tradi-

---

CLOSE-UP

Why Federal Attorneys Are the Gang Busters Nowadays

Tomorrow in Federal Court in Brooklyn, a jury is to hear more disclosures about an alleged $30,000 payoff to former Taxi and Limousine Commissioner Jay L. Turoff and a million-dollar scheme to monopolize the city's taxi-meter business. On Wednesday, across the East River in Manhattan, Stanley M. Friedman, the former Bronx Democratic party leader, and three associates are scheduled to be sentenced in Federal Court for their roles in the corruption scandal at the city's Parking Violations Bureau. The two cases, both involving graft at high echelons of city govern-

ment, illustrate a growing tendency on the part of Federal authorities to snare major municipal corruption inquiries from the city's five district attorneys.

Successful corruption and organized-crime trials enhance a prosecutor's reputation. Thomas E. Dewey, in the late 1930's, moved from the District Attorney's office in Manhattan to the Governor's mansion and into two tries for the Presidency mainly because of his national reputation as a crime-busting district attorney. Thus, Federal attorneys and district attorneys have often clashed over jurisdictional rights for

cases destined to be heavily publicized.

Many experts, however, believe the upsurge in Federal corruption investigations is largely the result of aggressive United States attorneys' capitalizing on Federal laws and evidentiary rules that give them greater power to win indictments and convictions.

Trump cards held by Federal prosecutors over district attorneys include:

• Wider jurisdiction and bigger budgets to investigate matters that spill across county or state lines.
• The legal authority to obtain evidence from witnesses

tion of judicial independence in America: each judge rightly views himself or herself as supreme within his or her own court.

To be sure, local judges do not have total freedom in applying the law; appellate courts may review their decisions. But appellate court review is largely confined to the substance of the law and pronouncement of rules of procedure. Questions involving the substance of justice—the length of sentence, the amount of bail, and so on—are not reviewed by higher courts unless there has been gross abuse. Also, local prosecutors are essentially immune from supervision by state attorneys general. Local police are also outside of administrative review by the state police.

administrative monitoring

The lack of ***administrative monitoring*** is most directly seen in the absence of systematic and reliable data on the number of courts, the activities they perform, and the volume of cases they process. Beginning in 1922, the federal courts have operated under minimal administrative supervision. Data on case filings and closings are reported to the Administrative Office of the U.S. Courts, which publishes an annual report. Although most states have now created an administrative office for the state courts somewhat comparable to the Administrative Office of the U.S. Courts, these state bodies do not wield much power. Local courts do not necessarily report accurate data to the state administrator. Many lower courts, because they are run and administered by local governments, are not required to report data on case volume to the state

---

before a grand jury without granting total immunity from prosecution as local prosecutors must do.

• The ability to obtain indictments and convictions on conspiracy charges in Federal court with less proof than is required in the state system. Federal court rules, for example, permit a conviction on the uncorroborated testimony of a co-conspirator; state law requires independent confirmation.

• The use of the 1970 Racketeer Influenced and Corrupt Organizations Act, usually called RICO, which allows Federal prosecutors to seek a conviction on the basis of a "pattern" of activities constituting a criminal enterprise. The United States Attorney for the Southern District of the state, Rudolph W.

Giuliani, used the RICO law to convict Mr. Friedman last year on charges that he and his co-defendants converted the Parking Violations Bureau into a racketeering enterprise.

• A witness protection program that subsidizes Federal informants' efforts to start new lives elsewhere. State prosecutors lack a comparable program to encourage witnesses to cooperate.

• Smaller case loads and laws permitting the wholesale seizure of financial records.

In contrast, surging crime rates and congested criminal court calendars are compelling local district attorneys to give priority to clearing up

violent crimes. "Federal attorneys can control their calendars while a D.A. has to take every case brought to him by the police," said Jeremiah B. McKenna, chief counsel of the State Senate Crime Committee and a former assistant district attorney in Manhattan. "The D.A.'s have the primary responsibility to take care of street crime," said Edward A. McDonald, the head of the Justice Department's Organized Crime Strike Force in Brooklyn. "Our mandate is to investigate the more complex criminal activities that have a more pervasive impact on society."

Selwyn Raab, "Why Federal Attorneys Are the Gang-Busters Nowadays," *New York Times,* March 8, 1987, p. B-1. ©1987 by The New York Times Company. Reprinted by permission.

office. As a result, we cannot be sure how many courts there are in the United States or how many cases they process.

Choice of Courts

The multiplicity of local courts as well as the dual court system provides limited opportunities for the government to choose where to file charges. In many communities, when the police arrest for a minor criminal violation they have the choice of filing a state charge in a major trial court or a less serious local ordinance violation in a lower court. Often this choice is made on the basis of perceived advantages: which court will take up less of the officer's time (particularly if the officer is not paid for court appearances), the likely speed of the disposition, and the likely penalty the judge will hand out. Thus, in many cities police prefer to file the least serious charges because the local lower court will dispose of the case immediately and will probably hand out a heavier sentence than would a state court for the same offense. Similar choices occur in deciding between state or federal prosecution. Some criminal offenses involve a simultaneous violation of state and federal law. As a general rule federal officials will prosecute for major violations, leaving more minor prosecutions to state officials.

Conclusion

Because the courts are so diverse, finding the right courthouse confuses laymen and lawyers alike. Let a lawyer, now a U.S. magistrate, explain the problem:

> You stand on the courthouse steps trying to explain to your client that he's not going to get any money because his lawyer filed suit in the wrong court. The case involved a few hundred dollars. I filed suit in small claims court, but a few months later it turned out that all of the actions occurred in the next county. So I mailed the papers to the small claims court in the neighboring county. When we got there to try the case I found out that small claims court in the neighboring county has a different jurisdictional amount and I should have filed in county court. Only the statute of limitations had run out so I couldn't file there. Talk about your clients being mad. (Author's interview.)

The exact details of jurisdiction, names, and functions of courts vary greatly among states and often within a state as well. Such variations in court structure not only affect lawyers trying to decide where to file cases, but also have a wide-ranging impact on the entire criminal justice process. The local control of courts, the lack of administrative monitoring, the long history of local corruption, and the ability to choose a court for a criminal prosecution exert a long-term effect on the criminal court process.

Dissatisfaction with this system is legendary. But by and large, the judicial reformers have lacked the political power to make wholesale changes, mainly because there are so many built-in impediments to change. Nonetheless, court reformers have won a number of important victories. Although they have not been able to achieve widespread adoption of a three-tier system, every year at least one state makes significant advances.

For Discussion

1. Does your state have a unified system of lower courts? What are the names, functions, and jurisdictions of the lower courts in your state and city? What is the name of the major trial court(s) in your state? Is there an intermediate court of appeals? What is the name and jurisdiction of your state's court of last resort?

2. What U.S. district court governs your community? What circuit court of appeals governs your state?

3. Discuss with lawyers, judges, prosecutors, and police officers any informal rules for deciding in which court a minor criminal case will be filed.

4. Have there been any efforts to reorganize the courts in your state? How successful were these efforts? What factors aided these efforts? What factors tend to prevent court reorganization?

5. Given the difficulties of achieving court reorganization, would the time and effort of judicial reformers be better spent on other issues? Which ones?

6. What advantages would result from greater centralized administration of state courts? What disadvantages?

References

ADMINISTRATIVE OFFICE OF THE UNITED STATES COURTS. *Annual Report of the Director, 1985.* Washington, D.C.: Government Printing Office, 1986.

BAAR, CARL. "The Scope and Limits of Court Reform." *Justice System Journal* 5 (1980): 274–290.

BAAR, CARL, AND THOMAS HENDERSON. "Organizational Designs for State Court Systems." Paper presented at the annual meeting of the Law and Society Association, Madison, Wisconsin, 1980.

BERKSON, LARRY, AND SUSAN CARBON. *Court Unification: History, Politics, and Implementation.* Washington, D.C.: National Institute of Law Enforcement and Criminal Justice, 1978.

DAVIES, THOMAS. "Gresham's Law Revisited: Expedited Processing Techniques and the Allocation of Appellate Resources." *Justice System Journal* 6 (1981): 372–404.

FRIEDMAN, LAWRENCE. *A History of American Law.* 2d ed. New York: Simon and Schuster, 1985.

GALLAS, GEOFF. "Court Reform: Has It Been Built on an Adequate Foundation?" *Judicature* 63 (1979): 28.

GLICK, HENRY. *Courts, Politics, and Justice.* New York: McGraw-Hill, 1983.

GLICK, HENRY, AND KENNETH VINES. *State Court Systems.* Englewood Cliffs, N.J.: Prentice-Hall, 1973.

HUDZIK, JOHN. "Rethinking the Consequences of State Financing." *The Justice System Journal* 10 (1985): 135–158.

INSTITUTE OF JUDICIAL ADMINISTRATION. *Survey of the Judicial System of Maryland.* New York: Institute of Judicial Administration, 1967.

JACOB, HERBERT. *Justice in America,* 4th ed. Boston: Little, Brown, 1984.

LAW ENFORCEMENT ASSISTANCE ADMINISTRATION. *National Survey of Court Organization.* Washington, D.C.: Government Printing Office, 1973.

NEUBAUER, DAVID. "Winners and Losers Before the Louisiana Supreme Court: The Case of Criminal Appeals." Paper presented at the Annual Meeting of the Law and Society Association, 1985.

ORAN, DANIEL. *Law Dictionary for Nonlawyers.* 2d ed. St. Paul, Minn.: West Publishing, 1985.

RICHARDSON, RICHARD, AND KENNETH VINES. *The Politics of the Federal Courts.* Boston: Little, Brown, 1970.

WHEELER, RUSSELL, AND HOWARD WHITCOMB. *Judicial Administration: Text and Readings.* Englewood Cliffs, N.J.: Prentice-Hall, 1977.

For Further Reading

BERKSON, LARRY, AND SUSAN CARBON. *Court Unification: History, Politics, and Implementation.* Washington, D.C.: National Institute of Law Enforcement and Criminal Justice, 1978.

BRODER, JOSEPH, JOHN PORTER, AND WEBB SMOTHERS. ''The Hidden Consequences of Court Unification.'' *Judicature* 65 (1981): 10.

DUBOIS, PHILIP, ed. *The Analysis of Judicial Reform.* Lexington, Mass.: Lexington Books, 1982.

DUBOIS, PHILIP, ed. *The Politics of Judicial Reform.* Lexington, Mass.: Lexington Books, 1982.

FRIEDMAN, LAWRENCE. *A History of American Law.* 2d ed. New York: Simon and Schuster, 1985.

HENDERSON, THOMAS, AND CORNELIUS KERWIN. ''The Changing Character of Court Organization.'' *The Justice System Journal* 7 (1982): 449–469.

CHAPTER 4

What Is a Crime?

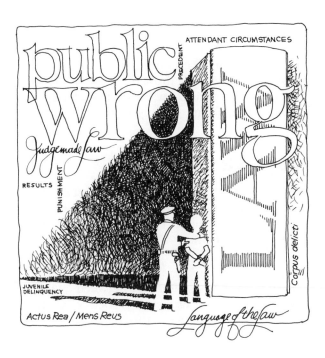

Mention the word *crime* to a cross section of people and you are likely to un-cover a variety of meanings. In popular usage crime often covers activities we don't like; thus we expect the law to punish the bad acts of others. But the word *crime* often implies not just bad acts but also immoral ones as well. Webster's dictionary, for example, defines crime as ''an offense against moral-ity,'' which makes it synonymous with *bad, evil,* or *sinful.* This linkage of crime with immorality suggests to some that the purpose of criminal law is to deter possible wrongdoers while at the same time educating the young or unwary. But most immediately, we associate *crime* with the muggings, rapes, and murders that fill the headlines of the morning newspaper or draw our at-tention on the nightly television news.

Popular views of crime, however, do not necessarily match up with its legal meanings. To be sure bad acts, immorality, deterrence, and education play a large role in how society comes to label some acts as violations of criminal law. But the legal definitions of crime are at the same time broader and narrower than popular usage. Crime in a legal sense, then, is not the same as activity we do not like or find immoral. Rather crime is what the legislature defines as acts prohibited by the criminal law.

This chapter focuses on the importance of legal definitions of crime for the operations of the criminal courts. The starting point is how crime is defined. We will examine the general principles underlying activities labeled criminal as well as the technical aspects of criminal definitions. Next, this chapter will explore the common law heritage that guides the development and application of these criminal definitions. Then we will look at the pattern of the American criminal law and attempts to revise it. Finally, we will discuss the consequences of the criminal law for the criminal courts. The criminal law constitutes the basic source of authority for the criminal courts. Before we can assess the type of justice produced by the courts, we need to know something about the law that is applied in reaching those results. Bear in mind that the United States has no uniform set of criminal laws. Instead, each jurisdiction enacts its own set of criminal prohibitions, leading to some important variations from state to state.

How Crimes Are Defined

Not all violations of the law are crimes. As Chapter 2 indicated, most disputes that come to court involve the civil law—that is, wrongs against individuals. Three criteria are involved when antisocial conduct is considered criminal: the wrong is public, punishable, and in violation of law.

Public Wrong

The involvement of a *public wrong* is the first difference between civil law and criminal law. A crime is considered a wrong against all of society, whereas a civil violation is considered a private matter between the parties directly involved. The concept of criminal law developed historically when the custom of considering wrongs private was replaced by the principle that the state is injured when one of its subjects is harmed.

Punishment

That a *punishment* must be provided is a second distinguishing feature of the criminal law. Punishment is viewed as necessary for protecting the public. It may be a fine, imprisonment, probation, suspended sentence, or death.

In setting penalties, the common law made a distinction between a felony and misdemeanor. But like so many other legal terms, the original rationale for the distinction has been lost. Although *felony* and **misdemeanor** are commonly used terms, there is no general agreement as to what they mean. In some states the distinction is made on the basis of where the guilty will be confined—felons in state prisons and misdemeanants in local jails. In other states, the distinction is based on the length of the sentence; generally a felony is punishable by imprisonment for over a year and misdemeanor by less than a year. In still other states, it is difficult to determine what criteria are used.

felony
misdemeanor

Because of this confusion the popular assumption that a felony is a more serious offense than a misdemeanor is not always accurate, although it is generally true.

Law

The third basic principle of the criminal law is that there can be no crime unless the activity has been made illegal. This is best expressed in the ancient Latin maxim, *nullum crimen, nulla poena, sine lege* (no crime, no punishment without law). Thus, before public wrongs can be considered criminal and before a punishment can be imposed for committing these public wrongs, both the public wrong and the punishment must be specifically stated in the *law*. The maxim of "no crime without law" expresses the fundamental concern of the common law that no innocent person should be subjected to the criminal process. The best way to ensure that an innocent person is not wrongly accused of violating the law is to require that criminal violations be known in advance so that law-abiding citizens can conform their behavior to the law. For this reason criminal statutes are interpreted strictly.

Elements of a Crime

corpus delicti The common law insists that criminal definitions be strictly interpreted. This fundamental requirement is expressed in the phrase **corpus delicti,** which means "body of the crime." The requirements for the body of the crime provide the technical (that is, legal) definitions of a crime. No behavior can be called criminal unless a guilty act was committed, with a guilty intent, and the guilty act and the guilty intent are related. In addition, a number of crimes are defined on the basis of attendant circumstances, specific results, or both. An understanding of the basic concepts embodied in statutory definitions of

Q U O T A T I O N

If two men had walked down Fifth Avenue a year ago—that would have been March, 1933—and one of them had a pint of whiskey in his pocket and the other had a hundred dollars in gold coin, the one with the whiskey would have been called a criminal and the one with the gold an honest citizen. If these two men, like Rip Van Winkle, slept for a year and again walked down Fifth Avenue, the man with the whiskey would be called an honest citizen and the one with the gold coin a criminal.

Samuel Insull, American financier, quoted in H. D. Schultz, *Panics and Crashes* (New Rochelle, N.Y.: Arlington House, 1972).

crime is essential for correctly interpreting specific definitions of crime. In turn, these basic concepts produce numerous categories of criminal activities (murder, voluntary manslaughter, and involuntary manslaughter, for example).

Guilty Act

guilty act (actus reus)

Before there can be a crime, there must be a ***guilty act (actus reus).*** Thus criminal liability occurs only after the voluntary doing of an act that results in criminal harm. The requirement of a guilty act reflects a fundamental principle of American law: no one should be punished solely for bad thoughts. There are different types of guilty acts, depending on the crime involved. For example, the guilty act in the crime of possession of an illegal drug is the possession. Differences in the nature of the guilty act account for many of the gradations of criminal offenses. To choose one obvious example, stealing property is considered separately from damaging property.

attempts

An important subdivision of the guilty act is a class of offenses labeled as ***attempts*** (for example, attempted burglary or attempted murder). The law does not want a person to avoid legal liability merely because someone or something prevented the commission of a crime. Typically, though, the penalties for attempt are less severe than if the act had succeeded. One result is that in some states, defendants often plead guilty to attempt to reduce the possible severity of the prison sentence.

Guilty Intent

guilty intent (mens rea)

Every common law crime consists of two elements, the guilty act itself and the accompanying mental state. The rationale is that criminal sanctions are not necessary for those who innocently cause harm. As Justice Holmes once pithily put it, "Even a dog distinguishes between being stumbled over and being kicked." The mental state required for a crime to have been committed is usually referred to as ***guilty intent*** or ***mens rea*** ("guilty mind"). Despite its importance in criminal law, guilty intent is difficult to define because it refers to a state of mind, a subjective condition. Some statutes, for example, specify the existence of specific intent; others require only general intent. Moreover, legislatively defined crimes have added new concepts of mental state to the traditional ones. Thus crimes differ in respect of the mental state the prosecution must prove existed in order to secure a criminal conviction. Larceny, for example, typically requires proof of a very great degree of intent; the prosecutor must prove that the defendant *intentionally* took property to which he *knew* he was not entitled, *intending* to deprive the rightful owner of possession *permanently.* Negligent homicide, on the other hand, is an example of a crime involving a lesser degree of intent; the prosecution need only show that the defendant *negligently* caused the death of another. Most crimes, though, require that the defendant knew he or she was doing something wrong. Also, the law assumes that people know the consequences of their acts. Thus a person cannot avoid legal liability by later saying "I didn't mean to do it."

Varying degrees of intent produce different categories of criminal offenses: the guilty act might be the same, but criminal liability varies. Homicide statutes illustrate this important variation. Murder requires proof that the defendant intended to kill or cause great bodily harm. In addition, most state statutes include deaths resulting from a felony (like armed robbery) under murder, even though the defendant did not specifically set out to kill the victim. Voluntary manslaughter involves death resulting from a sudden or intense passion. Involuntary manslaughter is involved if death occurred from an act performed recklessly. The following Illinois homicide statute illustrates these differences:

Article 9. Homicide

§9-1. Murder.   (a) A person who kills an individual without lawful justification commits murder if, in performing the acts which cause the death: (1) He either intends to kill or do great bodily harm to that individual or another, or knows that such acts will cause death to that individual or another; or (2) He knows that such acts create a strong probability of death or great bodily harm to that individual or another; or (3) He is attempting or committing a forcible felony other than voluntary manslaughter.

§9-2. Voluntary manslaughter.   (a) A person who kills an individual without lawful justification commits voluntary manslaughter if at the time of the killing he is acting under a sudden and intense passion resulting from serious provocation by: (1) The individual killed, or (2) Another whom the offender endeavors to kill, but he negligently or accidently causes the death of the individual killed. Serious provocation is conduct sufficient to excite an intense passion in a reasonable person. . . .

§9-3. Involuntary manslaughter and reckless homicide.   (a) A person who unintentionally kills an individual without lawful justification commits involuntary manslaughter if his acts whether lawful or unlawful which cause the death are such as are likely to cause death or great bodily harm to some individual, and he performs them recklessly, except in cases in which the cause of the death consists of the driving of a motor vehicle, in which case the person commits reckless homicide. . . . [Illinois Revised Statutes: Chapter 38, 1981.]

Note that if death occurred solely because of negligence, no criminal violation is involved. Here the civil law takes over; wrongful death is considered a private wrong.

One major consequence of the definition of different categories of homicide by criminal intent is varying penalties. Under Illinois law, a defendant convicted of murder may be sentenced to death or a minimum of fourteen years in prison. Conviction of voluntary manslaughter carries a maximum sentence of twenty years in prison, involuntary manslaughter ten years, and reckless homicide three years.

Fusion of Guilty Act and Guilty Intent

fusion of guilty act and guilty intent

The criminal law requires that the guilty act and the guilty mind occur together. Here is an example that illustrates this concept of *fusion of the guilty act and guilty intent.* Suppose a husband planned to kill his wife; he purchased some poison but never got around to putting the poison in her drink. The husband returns home late one night, an argument ensues, and he stabs her.

TABLE 4-1   Characteristics of the Most Common Serious Crimes

Crime	Definition	Facts
Homicide	Causing the death of another person without legal justification or excuse.	• Homicide is the least frequent violent crime. • 93% of the victims were slain in single-victim situations. • At least 55% of the murderers were relatives or acquaintances of the victim. • 24% of all murders occurred or were suspected to have occurred as the result of some felonious activity.
Rape	Unlawful sexual intercourse with a female, by force or without legal or factual consent.	• Most rapes involved a lone offender and a lone victim. • About 36% of the rapes were committed in the victim's home. • 58% of the rapes occurred at night, between 6 p.m. and 6 a.m.
Robbery	Unlawful taking or attempted taking of property that is in the immediate possession of another, by force or threat of force.	• Robbery is the violent crime that typically involves more than one offender (in about half of all cases). • Slightly less than half of all robberies involved the use of a weapon. • Less than 2% of the robberies reported to the police were bank robberies.
Assault	Unlawful intentional inflicting, or attempted inflicting, of injury upon the person of another. *Aggravated assault* is the unlawful intentional inflicting of serious bodily injury or unlawful threat or attempt to inflict bodily injury or death by means of a deadly or dangerous weapon with or without actual infliction of injury. *Simple assault* is the unlawful intentional inflicting of less than serious bodily injury without a deadly or dangerous weapon or an attempt or threat to inflict bodily injury without a deadly or dangerous weapon.	• Simple assault occurs more frequently than aggravated assault. • Assault is the most common type of violent crime.
Burglary	Unlawful entry of any fixed structure, vehicle, or vessel used for regular residence, industry, or business, with or without force, with the intent to commit a felony or larceny.	• 42% of all household burglaries occurred without *forced* entry. • In the burglary of more than 3 million American households, the offenders entered through an unlocked window or door or used a key (for example, a key "hidden" under a doormat). • About 34% of the no-force household burglaries were known to have occurred between 6 a.m. and 6 p.m.

TABLE 4-1   Characteristics of the Most Common Serious Crimes (*continued*)

Crime	Definition	Facts
		• Residential property was targeted in 67% of reported burglaries; nonresidential property accounted for the remaining 33%. • Three-quarters of the non-residential burglaries for which the time of occurrence was known took place at night.
Larceny (theft)	Unlawful taking or attempted taking of property other than a motor vehicle from the possession of another, by stealth, without force and without deceit, with intent to permanently deprive the owner of the property.	• Pocket picking and purse snatching most frequently occur inside nonresidential buildings or on street locations. • Unlike most other crimes, pocket picking and purse snatching affect the elderly as much as other age groups. • Most personal larcenies with contact occur during the daytime, but most household larcenies occur at night.
Motor vehicle theft	Unlawful taking or attempted taking of a self-propelled road vehicle owned by another, with the intent of depriving the owner of it permanently or temporarily.	• Motor vehicle theft is relatively well reported to the police because reporting is required for insurance claims and vehicles are more likely than other stolen property to be recovered. • About three-fifths of all motor vehicle thefts occurred at night.
Arson	Intentional damaging or destruction or attempted damaging or destruction by means of fire or explosion of the property without the consent of the owner, or of one's own property or that of another by fire or explosives with or without the intent to defraud.	• Single-family residences were the most frequent targets of arson. • More than 17% of all structures where arson occurred were not in use.

SOURCE: U.S. Department of Justice, Bureau of Justice Statistics, *Report to the Nation on Crime and Justice* (Washington, D.C.: Government Printing Office, 1983).

In this situation the intent to kill necessary for a murder conviction did not occur along with the death. Therefore the correct charge would be voluntary manslaughter.

Attendant Circumstances

attendant (accompanying) circumstances

Some crimes require the presence, or absence, of ***attendant (accompanying) circumstances.*** Most states differentiate between classes of theft on the basis of the amount stolen. In Illinois, for example, the law provides that theft of less than $300 is treated as a misdemeanor and over $300 as a felony. The amount stolen is the attendant circumstance.

Results

results

In a limited number of criminal offenses the **results** of the illegal act play a critical part in defining the crime. The difference between homicide and battery, for example, depends on whether the victim lived. A number of states distinguish between degrees of battery depending on how seriously the victim was injured. Note that the concept of result differs from that of intent. In all of the preceding examples, the defendant may have had the same intent. The only difference was how hearty the victim was or perhaps how skillful the defendant was in carrying out his or her intentions.

Legal Defenses

legal defenses

Under the law people who may have performed illegal acts may not be criminals because of a legally recognized justification for their actions or because legally they were not responsible for their actions. These **legal defenses** derive from how crime is defined. For example, guilty acts must be voluntary. A person who strikes another while having an epileptic seizure would not be guilty of assault because the act (hitting) was not voluntary. Similarly, the law recognizes the defense of duress when a person has been compelled to commit an illegal act because of threats or force. With this defense in essence the defendant is contending that he or she should be treated as a victim rather than a criminal. For example, if a bank robber threatens that unless you hand the teller a note demanding money a bomb will be detonated, you are acting under duress and cannot be found guilty.

The requirement of intent or a guilty mind produces several legal defenses to criminal offense. The law considers some types of persons incapable of forming criminal intent; therefore they cannot be legally held responsible for their actions. The prime examples are children. States vary, however, in how old children must be before they are presumed responsible for their actions. In most states, no child under seven can be held responsible for criminal actions. For children over seven, states differ in their definitions of *juvenile delinquency*. State juvenile delinquency laws are premised on the idea that those under a certain age have less responsibility for their actions than adults do.

juvenile delinquency

The Insanity Defense

The insanity defense is one of the most hotly debated topics in criminal law. It is rooted in a fundamental concept of Anglo-American law holding that before one can punish criminal behavior the individual must be blameworthy. Under the concept of mens rea, an insane person is not criminally responsible for his or her acts because he or she is incapable of having criminal intent. The question of what degree of insanity, mental illness, or mental disease makes a person blameless for otherwise criminal acts has been debated for years. This debate reflects marked philosophical divergences within American society concerning an individual's responsibility for his or her own acts. The lack of agreement is reflected in major differences between states concerning the extent to which a person's mental faculties must be impaired before he or she is considered insane. Table 4-2 lists the major criteria used in the United States.

TABLE 4-2 The Standards for Insanity Used by the States and the Circuits of the Federal Courts of Appeals

Insanity Standard	Jurisdiction
M'Naghten	Arizona, Florida, Iowa, Kansas, Louisiana, Minnesota, Mississippi, Nebraska, Nevada, New Jersey, North Carolina, Oklahoma, Pennsylvania, South Carolina, South Dakota, and Washington
M'Naghten *and* irresistible impulse	Colorado, Georgia, New Mexico, and Virginia
ALI	All federal circuits, Alabama, Alaska, Arkansas, California, Connecticut, Delaware, District of Columbia, Hawaii, Illinois, Indiana, Kentucky, Maine, Maryland, Massachusetts, Michigan, Missouri, Ohio, Oregon, Tennessee, Texas, Utah, Vermont, West Virginia, Wisconsin, and Wyoming
Product	New Hampshire
Other	New York, North Dakota, and Rhode Island
No standard	Idaho and Montana

SOURCE: Adapted from Ingo Keilitz and Junius P. Fulton, *The Insanity Defense and Its Alternatives: A Guide for Policymakers* (Williamsburg, Va.: National Center for State Courts, 1984), p. 15.

M'Naghten rule

The oldest test of insanity is the **M'Naghten rule,** which grew out of the murder of a private secretary to Sir Robert Peel in 1843 (Dow). The English law courts ruled that a person was insane when ''laboring under such a defect of reason, from disease of the mind, as not to know the nature and quality of the act he was doing, or if he did know it that he did not know he was doing what was wrong.'' More simply, the test focuses on knowing the difference between *right* and *wrong*. It is by far the most restrictive standard. Psychiatrists believe that the right and wrong test is difficult to apply and fails to take into account what we have learned about human behavior since the test was developed over a century ago. A number of American jurisdictions, however, currently utilize a modified version of the M'Naghten test (Keilitz and Fulton).

irresistible impulse

A few states supplement the M'Naghten rule with a slightly broader test, that of the **irresistible impulse.** The requirement is that the defendant was compelled by an irresistible impulse, even though he or she knew it was wrong, owing to a mental disease or defect that prevented the person from controlling his or her actions (Sigler).

substantial capacity

In recent years a number of states have followed the lead of the American Law Institute (ALI) and adopted a **substantial capacity** guideline. This test states that ''a person is not responsible for criminal conduct if at the time of such conduct and as a result of mental disease or defect he lacks substantial capacity either to appreciate the criminality of his conduct or to conform his conduct to the requirements of the law.'' The ALI standard has been characterized as a modernized combination of the M'Naghten test and the irresistible impulse test and is used by twenty-four states (Keilitz and Fulton).

Finally, two states—Idaho and Montana—have abolished the use of the insanity plea altogether (Dow). In Idaho, however, psychiatric evidence may be introduced on the issue of intent to commit a crime.

Typically a defendant who uses an insanity defense enters a dual plea of not guilty and not guilty by reason of insanity. Thus the burden of proof is on the

CONTROVERSY

A Needed Verdict: Guilty But Insane by Charles Nesson

To understand the true purpose of the insanity defense, one must first appreciate the broader aims of criminal law. The object of criminal trials is not simply to pass moral judgment on a defendant. Criminal process is an instrument of societal control. One of its most important objectives is to enhance the resolve of all good citizens to be law-abiding.

This is deterrence but not in the simplistic sense of pain versus gain. Law has a moralizing educational function. The idea is that punishment, as a concrete expression of society's disapproval of an act, helps to form and to strengthen the public's moral code and thereby affirm conscious and unconscious inhibitions against committing crime. As the French sociologist Emile Durkheim observed, there is an apparent paradox: "Punishment is above all designed to act upon upright people."

Back in the days of bedlams when psychiatric notions of insanity were extremely crude, criminal law could tolerate a defense for insane killers because they were obviously so different from the rest of us that it made no sense to judge them by human standards. There was no lesson to be learned

from punishing them any more than there would be from punishing a wild animal. The advance of psychiatry has now blurred the distinction between normal and crazy people.

John W. Hinckley, Jr. is not obviously insane. It took considerable expertise to convince attentive jurors of his insanity. A friend who attended the trial said to me, "If you had been there, you would understand how crazy this guy is." But to many of those who were not there and who, therefore, were not swept along by the testimony of the psychiatric experts, Mr. Hinckley seems like a kid who had a rough life and who lacked the moral fiber to deal with it.

This is not to deny that Mr. Hinckley is crazy but to recognize that there is a capacity for craziness in all of us. Lots of people have tough lives, many tougher than Mr. Hinckley's, and manage to cope. The Hinckley verdict let those people down. For anyone who experiences life as a struggle to act responsibly in the face of various temptations to let go, the

Hinckley verdict is demoralizing, an example of someone who let himself go and who has been exonerated because of it.

We need a new kind of verdict in criminal law—guilty but insane—"guilty" to express the objective truth that intentionally and unjustifiably killing someone is wrong, and that all people must resist temptations to murder, and "insane" to express the subjective truth about the defendant, arrived at with all the help that modern psychiatry can offer, that the defendant is sick and that his sickness contributed to his disposition to kill.

The consequence of the verdict "guilty but insane" should be the commitment of the defendant to the penal system under terms both legal and medical. Within the penal system, the defendant should receive medical treatment. But his ultimate release should be dependent on a judgment by appropriately constituted authority not only that he is no longer dangerous but also that he has served a sufficient term to affirm the rule of law.

Charles Nesson, "Guilty but Insane," New York Times, July 1, 1982, p. A19. ©1982 by The New York Times Company. Reprinted by permission. Charles Nesson, professor of law at Harvard Law School, teaches criminal law and evidence.

government, to show that the defendant committed the crime in question. The defense, however, bears the burden of proof as to insanity (see Chapter 14).

In recent years the insanity defense has sparked considerable controversy. The public perceives the insanity defense as a dodge used by tricky lawyers trying to gain sympathy for their guilty clients, who avoid punishment by pretending that they are insane. Heated outcries were heard when the jury acquitted would-be presidential assassin John Hinckley, Jr., as "not guilty by reason of insanity" (even though Hinckley was then confined to a mental institution). Public and professional displeasure has produced a rush to reform the insanity defense. For example, eight states (Alaska, Delaware, Georgia, Illinois, Indiana, Kentucky, Michigan, and New Mexico) have greatly altered the traditional insanity defense and made available the verdict "guilty but mentally ill" (Bureau of Justice Statistics). In states in which this verdict is available, it is an alternative to, but does not preclude, a verdict of "not guilty by reason of insanity" (Gardner). In these states, the person may be treated in a mental institution until recovery, and then transferred to a prison to serve the remainder of the sentence.

The often heated debate over the insanity defense is largely symbolic, however, because the insanity defense is rarely used in American courts. A recent study found that of the two million criminal cases in that year only 1,625 were found not guilty by reason of insanity (Steadman et al.) In his trial for the bizarre Tate-LaBianca murders, for example, defendant Charles Manson never raised insanity as a defense. Moreover, defense attorneys often use an insanity defense only as a last resort because numerous states make incarceration in a mental institution mandatory if the defendant is found not guilty by reason of insanity.

An Illustration of Elements of a Crime

corpus delicti

Corpus delicti (literally, "body of the crime") refers to the essential elements of the criminal act. All elements of a crime must be proved before the defendant can be convicted. For this reason, criminal statutes must be read closely because each clause constitutes a critical part of the offense. The common law definition of burglary is useful for demonstrating what we mean by the *elements of a crime.* It will also give us an opportunity to review our discussion thus far.

elements of a crime

At common law, the offense of burglary was defined as "breaking and entering the dwelling house of another, in the nighttime, with intent to commit a felony therein." Six elements are present: (1) "breaking" and (2) "entering," both of which involve guilty acts, (3) "dwelling house," (4) "of another," and (5) "in the nighttime." All are examples of attendant circumstances that must be present before the common law crime of burglary exists. The final element—(6) "with the intent to commit a felony therein"—involves mens rea. Note that results are not encompassed in common law burglary; there is no requirement that the person actually did take anything, only that he or she intended to commit a felony.

The common law definition seems to square with our image of the burglar: the stealthy nighttime prowler who breaks the back window and takes our color television set. But a closer examination reveals some peculiarities. Why was burglary limited to nighttime? Why was it restricted to a dwelling house? We normally think of a burglary of not only a house but also a car, business, trailer, and so on. In both instances the answer is that the common law judges, in formulating this definition, were responding to specific problems of earlier centuries. Obviously, in examining how crimes are defined, we need to examine the common law heritage from which these definitions were developed.

The Common Law Heritage

The American legal system is based on English common law. (Louisiana is the only exception; its civil legal system is based on the Napoleonic Code and the Continental legal heritage.) Common law originated sometime after the Norman conquest of England in 1066 and is derived from the practices of itinerant judges. Traveling from shire to shire (our word *sheriff* comes from this ancient English term), the judges settled disputes on the basis of the customs of the individual community; hence the name common law. Because the system of justice was locally based, the law varied from one community to another. Gradually the twin forces of an increasingly commercial economy and the drive of the English kings to consolidate their political control over the local noblemen produced a more uniform legal system for England. What is critically important is that in the development of the common law legal system, a distinctive way of doing business gradually emerged. There are three key characteristics of this common law heritage: the law was *judge-made* rather than legislatively enacted; the law was based on *precedent* (rulings in past cases guide decision making); and finally, it was *uncodified* (it could not be found in any one place).

Judge-Made Law

judge-made law

A key characteristic of the common law is that it is predominantly *judge-made law.* Initially the common law recognized a few basic rights. As English society, and later American society, became more complex, the judges adapted the old rights to new problems. Hence the law dealing with property, contracts, and torts (wrongs done to persons) developed from the English law courts. Even today the law in these areas is predominantly made by judges.

By the 1600s, the English judges had defined such felonies as murder, suicide, manslaughter, arson, robbery, larceny, rape, and mayhem. The common law defenses of insanity, infancy, self-defense, and coercion had also entered the law. These English criminal law concepts, often with some adaptations, were transplanted to America by the colonists. After the Revolution those common law crimes considered applicable to local conditions were retained. The process of the courts' creating and defining new crime continued in America during the nineteenth century. During this period offenses involving conspiracy and attempt were developed. Although today legislative bodies—not the courts—define crimes, statutory definitions often reflect common law heritage.

Precedent

precedent (stare decisis)

A second key characteristic of the common law is the doctrine of ***precedent,*** often referred to as ***stare decisis*** ("let the decision stand"). The doctrine of precedent requires a judge to decide a case by applying the rule of law found in previous cases provided the facts in the current case are similar to the facts in the previous cases. Figure 4-1 illustrates the citation system used in American law. Through following previous court decisions, the legal system promotes the twin goals of fairness and consistency.

The reliance of the common law on precedents reflects the law's approach to problem solving. Rather than issue a court opinion attempting to solve the entire range of a given legal problem, common law courts decide only as much of the case as they must to resolve the individual dispute. Broad rules and policy directives emerge only through the accumulation of court decisions over time. Unfortunately, many Americans make the mistake of translating common law heritage, particularly the doctrine of precedent, into a static view of the courts. Some critics of the Warren Court, for example, were fond of saying that it is no business of the courts to create new law, a position that conveniently ignores the entire history of Anglo-American law. Stated another way, common law courts have always been called on to shape the old law to new demands. The common law, though, is committed to stability by gradual change (hence the typical comment that the law and the courts are conservative institutions). One way courts achieve flexibility is in adapting old rights to new problems. For example, some prosecutors are attempting to adapt the old common law offense of nuisance and apply it to houses of prostitution and pornographic movie theaters. A second dimension of flexibility is the ability of courts to distinguish precedents. Recall that we said the doctrine of precedent involves previous cases with a similar set of facts. Courts sometimes simply state that the present set of facts differs from previous decisions and make another ruling. Finally, a court will occasionally (but very reluctantly) overturn a previous decision by stating that the previous court opinion was wrong.

Uncodified

uncodified

The third key characteristic of the common law is that it is ***uncodified;*** the law is not written in any one place. In deciding the legal meaning of a given crime (murder or burglary, for example), it is not sufficient to look just at the legislative act. One must also know how the courts have interpreted the statute. Further, in interpreting and applying the statute, one must be aware of possible legal defenses (insanity or age) that are not specifically mentioned in the law but exist nonetheless. To aid lawyers and others in determining the legal meaning of crimes, there are a variety of annotated works, books that contain the law plus commentary (history, explanations, and major court cases discussing the law). Although these books are helpful, they are intended only as guides. Annotated works are not official; they are not accepted by courts as definitive statements of the law.

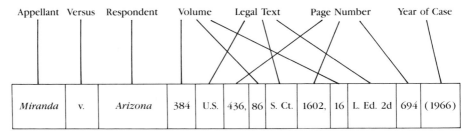

Students first confronted with legal citations are often bewildered by the array of numbers. But with a few basics in mind, these citations need not be confusing; they are very efficient aids in finding court decisions.

The full citation for *Miranda* is as follows: *Miranda* v. *Arizona* 384 U.S. 436, 86 S.Ct. 1602, 16 L.Ed.2d 694 (1966). The lead name in the case usually refers to the party who lost in the lower court and is seeking to overturn that decision. That party is called the *appellant*. The second name refers to the other party (or parties) who won at the lower level—in this instance the state of Arizona. The second party is called the *appellee* or, more simply, the *respondent*. Miranda is the appellant who is seeking to overturn his conviction. The state of Arizona is named as the respondent because criminal prosecutions are brought in the name of the state.

After the names of the parties come three sets of references. All decisions of the U.S. Supreme Court are reported in the *Supreme Court Reports,* which is published by the U.S. Government Printing Office. It is the official reporting system, and is abbreviated U.S. In addition, decisions of the Supreme Court are reported in two private reporting systems: the *Supreme Court Reporter,* which is abbreviated S.Ct., and in *Lawyers Supreme Court Reports, Lawyers Edition,* which is abbreviated L.Ed.2d.

The numbers preceding the abbreviation for the volume refer to the volume number. Thus *Miranda* can be found in volume number 384 of the United States *Supreme Court Reports.* The numbers after the abbreviation refer to the page number. Thus the *Miranda* decision in volume 384 begins on page 436, as well as volume 86 of the *Supreme Court Reporter* page 1602, and so on. Typically a library will carry only one of the reporting systems. Therefore the multiple references make it easy to locate the given case no matter to which of the three reporting systems one has access.

Decisions of other appellate courts at both the federal and state levels are reported in a similar manner in other volumes.

Figure 4-1   How to read legal citations

Common Law Criminal Definitions

Recall that earlier we provided the following common law definition of burglary: "breaking and entering the dwelling house of another in the nighttime with intent to commit a felony therein." Now that we have discussed the most salient characteristics of the common law heritage, we can consider some of the peculiarities of this definition of burglary. Even more important, we can also analyze the effects such a definition has on modern criminal law.

The common law definition of burglary was very limited. Key elements involved the attendant circumstances of nighttime and a dwelling house (which is different from a place of business or a car). Most of the common law definitions were defined very narrowly because conviction carried severe punishment—typically the death penalty. In this way, the courts sought to ease the severity of punishment by carefully restricting criminal definitions. But such constricted definitions of crime require reexamination as society changes. English judges were called upon to interpret the meaning of each of the six elements of the crime of burglary, and through the years the words took on different meanings.

Consider the meaning of *breaking*. Obviously, splintering a door with a hammer constitutes an act of breaking, but must breaking always involve physical force? Eventually the courts expanded the legal meaning of breaking beyond the seemingly common-sense requirement of physical force. Thus most courts ruled that pushing open a door already slightly ajar constituted breaking. The word *entering* presented similar problems. Again the law seems to envision a person walking into the house through the splintered door. But how much of the person must enter? The whole person or just an arm? The courts decided that even the slightest entry was sufficient. The courts eventually moved the legal definition further beyond our commonsensical notions by holding that the accused need not enter at all. Pushing a pole through a window also constituted entry, and if the accused employed an assistant (child, trained dog, or what have you) to do the actual entering, the accused was still deemed to have entered.

We could consider the other four elements of the common law crime of burglary, but by now the major points should be clear: the legal meanings of the words are not necessarily as clear as they first appear. New problems require rethinking old legal concepts. Sometimes these applications extend the meaning of the words far beyond what might have initially been envisioned. It is important to study the historical background because in many states laws on burglary (and most other crimes as well) are based on attempts to solve some of the problems raised by the common law definitions.

Although initially the common law courts defined criminal offenses, power to create and define criminal conduct gradually shifted from the courts to the legislature. Early in the nineteenth century legislators began to enact criminal statutes to cover gaps in court definitions of specific crimes rather than wait for the courts to cure the problem. By the beginning of the twentieth century, this shift was completed; most state legislators had enacted comprehensive criminal codes to replace the uncodified definitions produced by the courts. These statutory criminal offenses have been greatly influenced by the original common law definitions. Not only do the legislatively enacted criminal codes

---

Q U O T A T I O N

*I*t is revolting to have no better reason for a rule of law than that it was so laid down in the times of Henry IV. It is still more revolting if the grounds upon which it was laid down have vanished long since, and the rule simply persists from blind imitation of the past.

Justice Oliver Wendell Holmes, in an 1897 address reprinted in *Collected Legal Papers* (Boston: A. Harcourt, 1920), p. 187.

reflect the basic principles found in the common law definitions (mens rea, *actus reus,* and so on), but they often adopted the same words and phrases initially developed by the judges.

The Michigan burglary statute provides a convenient illustration of a legislatively enacted statute derived from judge-created criminal definitions:

750.110 Breaking and entering

Sec.110. Any person who shall break and enter with intent to commit any felony, or any larceny therein, any tent, hotel, office, store, shop, warehouse, barn, granary, factory or other building, structure, boat or ship, railroad car or any private apartment in any of such buildings or any unoccupied dwelling house, shall be guilty of a felony punishable by imprisonment in the state prison for not more than 10 years. Any person who breaks and enters any occupied dwelling house, with intent to commit any felony or larceny therein, shall be guilty of a felony punishable by imprisonment in the state prison for not more than 15 years. For the purpose of this section "any occupied dwelling house" includes one that does not require the physical presence of an occupant at the time of the breaking and entering but one which is habitually used as a place of abode.

A quick scanning of this definition of breaking and entering highlights many of the elements of burglary at the common law—breaking, entering, dwelling

QUOTATION

Does not the politicization of crime best explain the odd contours of criminal law controlling gambling, drug use, and sexual behavior? How else are we to understand the passage of these laws and the patterns of inclusion and exclusion? Horse racing is generally legal, but numbers gambling is considered criminal. Alcohol and Valium may be used legally, while the use of marijuana and cocaine is prohibited. It can hardly be argued that these distinctions reflect some natural moral order. Clearly, some segments are imposing their values on others—perhaps to demonstrate symbolically their superior status or perhaps to protect vested economic interests. Symbolic uses of the criminal law seem to have been paramount in the creation of Prohibition. Conversely, horse racing interests would be likely to suffer to the extent that other forms of gambling were legalized.

Stuart Scheingold, *The Politics of Law and Order* (New York: Longman, 1984), p. 22.

house, for example, have been retained. But there are some important differences. Note, for example, that nighttime is no longer included in the definition. Further, it is immediately obvious that the original common law definition—which took only a line and a half—has now been expanded into eleven lines. The added phrases are attempts to adapt the law to modern conditions and at the same time avoid some of the tortuous definitions the courts had been forced to provide.

That the Michigan law describes in great detail the meaning of an occupied dwelling clearly indicates that the legislature was trying to adapt the law to problems not present in medieval England. But even though the courts no longer create and define criminal conduct, they still play a role. It is still the responsibility of the appellate courts to clarify the meaning of legislative words. Similarly, as new problems appear, courts are often forced to interpret old law in the light of new situations.

The Crazy Quilt Pattern of Criminal Law

The common law heritage produces an important similarity in definitions of crime. In each state, criminal law reflects the same principles of how crimes are defined and interpreted. But there are important differences as well. As Chapter 3 indicated, the United States has fifty-one separate legal systems. Each has its own criminal code. Moreover, within each code important inconsistencies and sometimes contradictions appear. Consider the following. Under California law, breaking into the glove compartment of a car is punishable by a maximum sentence of fifteen years of imprisonment; stealing the entire car is punishable by a maximum of ten years. In Colorado, a defendant convicted of stealing a dog faces a maximum sentence of ten years; if the same defendant killed the dog, the maximum punishment is six months. These are just two examples cited by Marvin Frankel (a former U.S. district court judge particularly interested in sentencing disparities) of what he called the sometimes *crazy quilt pattern* of state criminal statutes. Not all criminal statutes are as obsolete or as inconsistent as these examples might suggest, but the above examples draw our attention to a major problem area—many states lack a consistent set of criminal definitions and penalties.

Changes in the criminal law occur in a piecemeal fashion. Legislators respond to practical problems in an ad hoc and pragmatic fashion. As specific deficiencies in the law become evident or new events arise, individual changes designed to cure isolated problems are voted into law.

Changes in the criminal law often reflect public concern about crime. Increases in crime invariably produce calls for the legislature to pass new laws. Thus a perceived crime wave—for example, a wave of armed robberies or rapes—stimulates elected officials to increase penalties. Prosecutors and attorney generals often use such public concern to lobby for harsher sentences. Likewise the emergence of new forms of deviance—computer crime and counterfeiting of records and tapes are the prime examples currently—often produce calls for new laws to cover existing loopholes.

As a result criminal laws seem to tumble out of our legislatures with great frequency and little reflection. Although there is some movement toward decriminalization of certain behavior, the general tendency is towards proliferation of criminal laws. In America more is often confused with better. (Sigler: 266.)

Another stimulus for legislative alteration of the criminal code is court decisions. Conflicting court interpretations often prompt legislative attempts to clarify conflicting court standards. Similarly, when a court declares a law unconstitutional, the legislature may pass a new law during the next session trying to remedy the deficiencies. After the U.S. Supreme Court's decision in *Gregg* v. *Georgia* (1976) upholding the Georgia death penalty law but striking down other state laws, a number of states drafted new laws attempting to reimpose capital punishment within the dictates of the Court's ruling. Court decisions invalidating laws, however, may draw no response; legislatures may not try to resurrect a law struck down by the courts (Wasby). Some laws struck down by the courts remain on the books, unrepealed though unenforced—a reminder that in a common law country the law is uncodified.

Whatever the source or cause of the piecemeal changes, the end product is a set of criminal laws with obsolete prohibitions and inconsistent penalties. Until recently, marijuana smoking was legally a more serious offense than using LSD (despite medical evidence clearly establishing LSD as a greater danger to health). The point is that no one set out to create such inconsistencies; they just happened. That changes in one section of the law may be inconsistent with another section of the law is not always immediately obvious. Recent legislative responses to armed robbery bring into focus the inconsistencies resulting from the historical accumulation of criminal prohibitions. As armed robberies increased, legislatures responded by increasing the penalty. Sometimes the unintentional result was that armed robbery was punished more severely than even murder. Contradictions such as this indicate a lack of agreement in American society about what behavior should be criminalized and what penalties are appropriate (Sigler). In practice, of course, judges and prosecutors treat murder as more serious than armed robbery.

One impediment to modernizing the criminal code is that the patchwork of criminal law is occasionally useful. After all, the criminal law really amounts to an arsenal of weapons that can be marshaled against those viewed as deviants (Arnold: 27). Sometimes ancient criminal prohibitions can be resurrected to prosecute notorious lawbreakers. This method has been aptly termed the "Al Capone theory of law making" (Newman). Al Capone, the notorious Chicago gangster leader, was never successfully prosecuted for his bootlegging, gambling, or prostitution activities. Instead he was convicted of income tax violation.

Consequences for the Criminal Court

The substantive criminal code constitutes the basic source of authority for law enforcement agencies. As a result, the nature of the criminal code has a profound effect on how law enforcement agencies function (but obviously does not account for all such activity). Sir Robert Peel, called "the father of the English police," recognized this early in the nineteenth century (Skolnick). Before introducing a new police system, he first reformed the criminal law. Prior to Peel's reforms, even minor offenses carried the death penalty. In the latter part of the twentieth century, the National Advisory Commission on Criminal Justice Standards and Goals also concluded that substantive criminal law revision "is a necessary concomitant to modernization of the criminal justice system" (Task Force on the Administration of Justice: 173). During the last twenty-five years, thirty-four states have codified their substantive criminal law or substantially revised their criminal codes. Nonetheless, internal contradictions in definitions of criminal violations often remain. The U.S. Congress, for example, has debated major reforms of the criminal code for almost two decades and has yet to pass a bill (Melone and Slagter). What constitutes a crime (as well as what does not) has major consequences for how the criminal courts dispense justice.

Law and Plea Bargaining

plea bargaining

The way crimes are defined has an important bearing on the entire administration of criminal justice. The next chapter will consider some of the specific ways that the criminal law produces discretion. At this point, though, we need to examine one specific aspect of discretion: ***plea bargaining.*** Variations in definitions of crimes, particularly the numerous differences in degrees of seriousness, make the criminal courts a likely arena for plea bargaining. The negotiation of pleas is bound to emerge when legislatively specified penalties are viewed by law appliers—judges, prosecutors, and defense attorneys—as not applicable to the defendants they see before them. Furthermore, the categories provide the vehicle for plea bargaining aimed at reducing the possible severity for a given offense. In at least one state, assault and battery involves five degrees (categories). Although the law must attempt to differentiate between, say, a punch thrown in anger and a deliberate gunshot wound that leaves its victim permanently paralyzed, too many different degrees of seriousness invite pleas to less serious offenses.

Another form of plea bargaining is count bargaining, in which the defendant pleads guilty to only some of the counts (charges) in the indictment, and the others are dismissed. Realistically, defendants often face the same penalty whether they plead to just one or all counts. Such bargaining is particularly common in federal district courts because the federal criminal law is ideally suited for multicount indictments. Multicount indictments facilitate count bargaining.

It should be obvious that the courts must apply the law as they find it. The corollary is that the courts often must rectify inconsistencies in that law. Disparities in possible sentences as provided in state statutes require judges, prosecutors, and defense attorneys to arrive at a workable penalty structure. Society would be outraged if serious crimes elicited the same punishment as minor ones, even if the law technically allowed both categories of offenses to be treated the same way.

Language of the Law

Americans pride themselves on living in a law-abiding nation. Our system takes seriously the notion that we are a society of laws, not of men. At the same time, though, Americans remain somewhat mystified by the law. Although in general the law is regarded with great respect, in particular applications of the law Americans are often less satisfied. The most common complaint is that the law is too technical. The image of the "Philadelphia lawyer" (a reference to slyness and trickery) symbolizes to many people a legal system in which the technicalities of the law stand in the way of proper conclusions. The public perceives that the criminal law is unduly technical. When a judge suppresses evidence (drugs, for example), the newspapers often report that the refusal to admit the drugs was based on a "technicality."

It is important to realize that the law must be technical; it must communicate precisely. In our everyday lives, we are able to communicate with our friends using ambiguous terms because the people we communicate with have similar reference points; they know what we mean. But we have all experienced situations in which disagreement with our friends, colleagues, spouses, or lovers—even our college professors—arose because of verbal misunderstandings. Only too late did we realize that we either did not say exactly what we meant or we used an ambiguous term; we meant one thing but they thought we meant another. The law seeks to avoid such ambiguities. Recall that the simple definition of burglary provided by the common law judges required amplification and clarification as situations changed. The meanings of *breaking, entering,* and *at night* required greater precision than we normally need in our ordinary conversations. Viewed from this vantage point, the law is technical because it must attempt to be unambiguous.

language of the law

Another reason that the **language of the law** mystifies laymen is not that the law is overly precise and technical but rather that it is not precise enough. We often turn to the law for answers to problems. In a number of situations the law is able to provide answers (for example, a competent lawyer is able to draft a will to meet the needs of the ordinary citizen). In developing areas of the law, however, the law is not settled. Not only does it lack precision when trying to grapple with emerging problems, at times statutes are drafted and court opinions written that contain ambiguities. The people who staff the legal system are only human. State legislators, pushed by the impending end of the session, pass hastily drafted legislation. The ambiguities appear only later. At other times legislators deliberately write ambiguous legislation in order to compromise and appear to give each side half a loaf. This deliberate use of ambiguous language is often done with the conscious intent to let the courts resolve the problem later. Thus, while laymen view the law as providing precision, legal professionals are likely to stress its ambiguity (Edelman).

Conclusion

There is a wide range of actions that we as individuals or as a society disapprove of, yet only some of these actions have been labeled criminal. Actions declared to constitute public wrongs (as distinct from personal wrongs) and

QUOTATION

*T*o a considerable degree, the legislature becomes an agency of harshness and the courts become agencies for protecting citizens from this harshness. The net effect between the legislature and the courthouse is a rather steady increase in statutory severity for certain crimes. Such legislative action follows an established pattern:

Step I.   Laws calling for severe punishments are passed by legislatures on the assumption that fear of great pain will terrorize the citizenry into conformity.

Step II.   Criminal justice personnel soften these severe penalties for most offenders (a) in the interests of justice, (b) in the interests of bureaucracy, and (c) in the interests of gaining acquiescence.

Step III.   The few defendants who then insist on a trial and are found guilty, or who in other ways refuse to cooperate, are punished more severely than those who acquiesce.

Step IV.   Legislatures, noting that most criminals by acquiescing avoid "the punishment prescribed by law," (a) increase the prescribed punishments and (b) try to limit the range of discretionary decision making used to soften the harsh penalties.

Step V.   The more severe punishments introduced in the preceding step are again softened for most offenders, as in Step II, with the result that the defendants not acquiescing are punished even more severely than they were at Step III.

Step VI.   The severity-softening-severity process is repeated. Several social trends suggest that it is legislators rather than court personnel who are out of step with the times.

From pages 95, 157, and 161 of *Justice by Consent: Plea Bargains in the American Courthouse,* by Arthur Rosett and Donald R. Cressey. Copyright © 1976 by J. B. Lippincott Company. By permission of Harper & Row Publishers, Inc.

labeled by a law, along with a penalty for violation, are legally criminal offenses. Although murder, robbery, and rape are defined as criminal in virtually every society, beyond these basics official definitions of criminal conduct vary. Gambling, for example, is illegal in most states but not in Nevada. What activity should be labeled criminal is the source of constant political discussion. Actions viewed as bad in the past may no longer be so considered. As society changes, so do public perceptions of public wrongs, and pressures develop to add more activities to the list of officially proscribed ones. Through all of this change, we must not lose sight of the essential fact that law is an integral part of society. Law is not imposed upon society; rather it reflects the sociology, economy, history, and politics of society. Law was created to help society, not the other way around.

For Discussion

1. How does the burglary statute of your state differ from the statutes reprinted in this chapter? Does your statute resemble the common law statute or the revised statute?

CLOSE-UP

Rape Laws in Midst of Revolution

American rape statutes, rooted in English common law, changed little for three centuries. But in the last decade, this corner of U.S. jurisprudence has been turned inside out, largely under pressure from women's groups.

Since the early 1970s, almost every state has made major changes in its rape laws.

The changes are of both form and substance, transforming the legal view of rape from a violent expression of sex to a sexual expression of violence. Yet rape law today remains an emotionally charged and legally troublesome issue in and out of court, not only for what it does but for what it doesn't do.

"The feeling is that now people are more likely to talk about it and report it," said Eunice Raigradski of the Na-

tional Center for Prevention and Control of Rape. "But rape is still greatly under-reported. And there are still problems in the legal process with convicting victims rather than rapists."

Many of the new rape laws do the following:

• Establish "degrees" of rape to reflect more accurately various types of sexual assault and set corresponding penalties.
• Rewrite the language so it is "neutered" and no longer limits rape to men's attacks on women.
• Wipe out requirements that women prove they resisted by "fighting back" physically.
• Remove requirements that women present corroborating evidence; cases can now

be decided solely on "her word against his."
• Allow for husbands to be charged with raping their wives.
• Impose tougher prison sentences.
• Include "shield" provisions blocking inquiries into a victim's past sexual experiences.

In a number of states, the laws no longer contain the word "rape." When "sexual assault" was substituted in Texas last year, for example, sponsors suggested victims might be more likely to report the crime if not faced with the stigma of the word "rape."

The new laws try to resolve the age-old legal question: What is rape?

Certainly it is rape when a stranger jumps out of a dark

2. State statutes typically give the date on which they were enacted. Compare these dates for a number of crimes and think about the following questions. Has your state criminal code been significantly rewritten in the last ten years? Are there any patterns of particular crimes (theft, for example) that periodically have been rewritten (perhaps to adjust for inflation)? Are any statutes out of date? Do you think the state statutes need to be rewritten?

3. State legislatures usually meet every other year (although some meet yearly). Look at the record of the last full legislative session to see what changes in the criminal code were proposed, by what groups, and which ones were enacted. Did any other proposed changes generate much public debate? Did any of these proposed changes appear to be merely symbolic efforts by legislators unlikely to change anything?

4. Each year the Federal Bureau of Investigation publishes the *Uniform Crime Reports,* available in most libraries. The most serious crimes are referred to as type I offenses and include murder and nonnegligent manslaughter, aggravated assault, forcible rape, robbery, burglary, larceny, and auto theft. Compare your state's definition of these offenses with

---

doorway and forces a woman to have intercourse at knifepoint. But is it rape when a husband physically forces his wife to have sex?

In 24 states, that husband can be charged with rape. In nine states he cannot be charged, and in 17 states he can be charged only under certain circumstances such as if the couple are living apart, have filed for legal separation or both.

The "neutering" of rape laws has given authorities more leeway to charge men with raping men, women with raping men and women with helping men rape other women. But that doesn't mean juries are willing to convict them.

In Hawaii earlier this year, a mistrial was declared after a jury failed to reach a verdict in a rape case against a woman accused of helping her boyfriend assault a tourist in a Waikiki hotel.

"We did not see how a woman could rape another woman," a juror said.

Rape, perhaps more than any other crime involving violence or the threat of violence, is subjective. It depends not so much on what happened, but what the participants were thinking. Unlike robbery, there is no missing money. Unlike murder, there is no dead body.

Rape involves a physical act that can be either an act of love or a violent felony. The legal problems come in deciding how the participants felt, how forcefully they expressed their feelings, how quickly they recognized the others' wishes and how they responded to those wishes.

Looking so closely into people's minds—and hearts—has never been a forte of a le-

gal system more geared toward judging people strictly according to their actions. Consequently, rape law remained relatively stagnant for decades.

For example, Idaho's 1983 rape law rewrote legislation from the 1890s. South Carolina's 1977 rape law changed a statute that had been basically unchanged since 1712. It wasn't until last year that Kansas wiped out the "fighting back" requirement; in Louisiana, penalties are still less stringent for rapists whose victims cannot prove they physically resisted.

The shield laws that now exist in most states are aimed at barring defense attorneys from putting the woman "on trial" by probing into her past sexual conduct.

Source: Timothy Harper, "Nation's Laws on Rape are in Midst of Revolution," Times-Picayune, April 29, 1984, p. 15. Copyright 1984 by Associated Press.

the definitions used in the *Uniform Crime Reports.* What serious crime under the *Uniform Crime Reports* fails to meet statutory requirements in your state?

You may also wish to talk to the official in the police department who regularly prepares their annual crime report about the problems of contrasting definitions of offenses such as burglary. Does the local police department keep two sets of figures? (They probably should.)

A discussion with a local prosecutor about these contrasting definitions might produce some interesting insights into problems of police departments enforcing the FBI definitions, not the state criminal code.

5. Divide the members of the class into teams. Assign each team to interview a key member of the criminal justice community—judge, prosecutor, defense attorney, police official, or beat cop—on problems they may see in the state's current criminal code. Do these officials perceive any major gaps in the criminal code—that is, acts that cannot now be punished but should be? Are there any major inconsistencies in the code? Do they think the state needs a comprehensive revision of the state penal code along the lines suggested by the National Advisory Commission? (If you go to school in a state that has revised its criminal code in the last few years, you can ask these people how the new code has worked out in practice.) Do not be surprised if the people interviewed do not agree. You may also consider interviewing some representatives in the community that are interested in the criminal law—the American Civil Liberties Union, the Catholic church, and good-government groups such as the League of Women Voters.

References

ARNOLD, THURMAN. "Law Enforcement." In *Criminal Justice: Law and Politics,* ed. George Cole. North Scituate, Mass.: Duxbury Press, 1972.

BUREAU OF JUSTICE STATISTICS, U.S. Department of Justice. *Report to the Nation on Crime and Justice.* Washington, D.C.: Government Printing Office, 1983.

DOW, PAUL. *Criminal Law.* Pacific Grove, Calif.: Brooks/Cole, 1985.

EDELMAN, MURRAY. *Symbolic Uses of Politics.* Chicago: University of Illinois Press, 1964.

GARDNER, THOMAS. *Criminal Law: Principles and Cases.* 3d ed. St. Paul, Minn.: West Publishing, 1985.

GARDNER, THOMAS, AND VICTOR MANIAN. *Criminal Law: Principles, Cases and Readings.* 4th ed. St. Paul, Minn.: West Publishing, 1980.

KEILITZ, INGO, AND JUNIUS FULTON. *The Insanity Defense and Its Alternatives: A Guide for Policymakers.* Williamsburg, Va.: National Center for State Courts, 1984.

MELONE, ALBERT, AND ROBERT SLAGTER. "Interest Group Politics and the Reform of the Federal Criminal Code." In *The Political Science of Criminal Justice,* ed. Stuart Nagel, Erika Fairchild, and Anthony Champagne. Springfield, Ill.: Charles Thomas, 1983.

NATIONAL ADVISORY COMMISSION ON CRIMINAL JUSTICE STANDARDS AND GOALS. *Courts.* Washington, D.C.: Government Printing Office, 1973.

NEWMAN, DONALD J. *Introduction to Criminal Justice.* Philadelphia: J. B. Lippincott, 1975.

QUINNEY, RICHARD. *Criminology: Analysis and Critique of Crime in America.* Boston: Little, Brown, 1975.

SIGLER, JAY. *Understanding Criminal Law.* Boston: Little, Brown, 1981.

STEADMAN, HENRY, JOHN MONAHAN, SHARON DAVIS, AND PAMELA ROBBINS. ''Mentally Disordered Offenders: National Survey of Patients and Facilities.'' *Law and Human Behavior* 6 (1982): 31–38.

SKOLNICK, JEROME H. *Justice Without Trial.* New York: John Wiley, 1966.

TASK FORCE ON THE ADMINISTRATION OF JUSTICE. *Task Force Reports: The Courts.* President's Commission on Law Enforcement and the Administration of Justice. Washington, D.C.: Government Printing Office, 1967.

WASBY, STEPHEN L. *The Impact of the United States Supreme Court.* Homewood, Ill.: Dorsey Press, 1970.

For Further Reading

ABRAHAM, HENRY. *The Judicial Process.* 4th ed. New York: Oxford University Press, 1980.

BERK, RICHARD, HAROLD BRACKMAN, AND SELMA LESSER. *A Measure of Justice: An Empirical Study of Changes in the California Penal Code, 1855–1976.* New York: Academic Press, 1977.

CAPLAN, LINCOLN. *The Insanity Defense and the Trial of John W. Hinckley, Jr.* Boston: D. R. Godine, 1984.

DOW, PAUL. *Criminal Law.* Pacific Grove, Calif.: Brooks/Cole, 1985.

FLETCHER, GEORGE. *Rethinking Criminal Law.* Boston: Little, Brown, 1978.

GUSFIELD, JOSEPH. *Symbolic Crusade: Status Politics and the American Temperance Movement.* Urbana: University of Illinois Press, 1963.

LAFAVE, WAYNE, AND AUSTIN SCOTT. *Criminal Law.* St. Paul, Minn.: West Publishing, 1972.

MORRIS, NORVAL, *Madness and the Criminal Law.* Chicago: University of Chicago Press, 1982.

SIGLER, JAY. *Understanding Criminal Law.* Boston: Little, Brown, 1981.

STATSKY, WILLIAM. *Legal Research Writing and Analysis: Some Starting Points.* St. Paul, Minn.: West Publishing, 1974.

PART II

THE LEGAL ACTORS

T he law is not self-executing. Prosecutors, judges, and defense attorneys must exercise discretion. The types of people recruited to these positions, the nature of the work they perform, and the pressures they must deal with are the concerns of the five chapters of Part II.

Chapter 5 analyzes the dynamics of courthouse justice with particular emphasis on how these separate actors work together as a group.

Chapter 6 discusses why the prosecutor is the most important member of the courtroom work group. The discretionary powers of the office structure virtually all of the decisions of the criminal courthouse.

The subject of Chapter 7 is the defense attorney. The nature of the attorney's clientele, the lack of great monetary rewards, and the effect of other members of the courtroom work group help explain why most defense attorneys act nothing like the famous television figure Perry Mason.

Chapter 8 considers the role of the judge. Of prime concern is how the judge shapes and in turn is shaped by the courtroom work group.

Chapter 9 examines the importance of witnesses, victims, and defendants in the decisions made by members of the courtroom work group.

CHAPTER 5

The Dynamics of Courthouse Justice

The popular picture of American criminal justice holds that a defendant's guilt or innocence is determined at trial after a hard-fought contest. The reality is strikingly different. Guilt is largely assumed: most defendants plead guilty after a series of mostly cooperative negotiations. Realizing that law on the books is not the same as law in action is only the beginning. Understanding and explaining *why* the law as practiced differs from the seeming intent of the formal rules is the crucial task.

This chapter examines the dynamics of courthouse justice by analyzing three major explanations for the great difference between the work of the courts and the textbook image of court combat and trials. The most commonly advanced reason is that there are too many cases. This explanation contains kernels of truth; however, it masks important considerations, not the least of which is that most criminal cases are routine. The second explanation focuses on discretion and begins to grapple with the day-to-day realities of courthouse

91

dynamics. The third centers on the courtroom work group and the complexities of interaction between courthouse regulars.

Assembly Line Justice and Excessive Caseloads

excessive caseloads

The most commonly advanced reason that criminal courts do not administer justice according to the textbook image is **excessive caseloads.** This orthodox explanation was put forth by the President's Commission on Law Enforcement and Administration of Justice:

> The crux of the problem is that there is a great disparity between the number of cases and the number of judges.
>
> It is not only judges who are in short supply. There are not enough prosecutors, defense counsel, and probation officers even in those courts where some of them are available. The deluge of cases is reflected in every aspect of the courts' work, from overcrowded corridors and courtrooms to the long calendars that do not allow more than cursory consideration of individual cases. (p. 31)

Strengths of the Explanation

The caseload explanation has the advantage of bringing out some important dimensions of these judicial bodies. No one disputes that the volume of cases is large. Particularly in large urban areas, there are pressures to move cases quickly. In direct and indirect ways, officials view one of their tasks as keeping the docket current; thus they seldom have much time to spend on any one case.

specialization

This explanation also focuses attention on **specialization.** In devising procedures for handling these large caseloads, court officials have usually opted for this important technique of mass society. Just as cars are built in a number of steps with each worker responsible for a small part of the overall product, workers in the criminal court specialize. This is most readily seen in the operations of big city public defenders. One assistant will conduct the initial interview with defendants, another will represent them at the initial appearance, another will argue pretrial motions, and yet another will conduct the plea negotiations, the trial, or both. Prosecutors' offices are similarly specialized, meaning that no single attorney follows a case from start to finish. The problem is that specific cases and defendants may not receive the individual attention they deserve.

group processing

The final strength of the case overload explanation is that it underscores the tendency for defendants accused of different and unrelated crimes to be processed in groups rather than individually. During initial appearances, defendants are often advised of their rights in one large group. This **group processing** at times even extends to the final plea. Defendants are also questioned in groups of various sizes about their desire to plead guilty. Moreover, court officials categorize defendants into easily identifiable classes on the basis of the nature of the crime and the background of the defendant. Thus, around courthouses, one often hears phrases like "he's just a harmless drunk" or "here's another peeping Tom." In turn, sentences are fixed on the basis of the defendant's membership in a given class rather than detailed individual attention.

Weakness of the Explanation

The excessive caseload explanation draws our attention to some important aspects of the criminal courts, but it also obscures as many aspects of the courts' process as it highlights. First of all, the stress is usually placed on the fact that these excessive caseloads are a modern problem; there are repeated references to the "rise" of plea bargaining, the "decline" of the trial, and the "twilight" of the adversary system. In fact, however, this position distorts history; for decades the courts have been characterized by too many cases. Even more important, plea bargaining predates any of the modern problems of the courts. Plea bargaining "began to appear during the early or mid-nineteenth century, and became institutionalized as a standard feature of American urban criminal courts in the last of the nineteenth century" (Haller: 273). To explain the excess of cases as a result of the growth of big cities and big city problems ignores the historical evidence.

The caseload explanation also detracts from an important point: most criminal cases are routine. They represent no disputed questions of law or fact. This observation has been documented in a study of litigation in two California counties from 1890 to 1970 (Friedman and Percival). The authors argued that dispute settlement is the function most clearly associated with the courts. Yet in most civil cases the courts were not called on to resolve any actual dispute; they merely provided a legal and formal authorization to a private

---

C O N T R O V E R S Y

Plea Bargaining Called Necessary Evil

Plea bargaining has been criticized for shortchanging society. Critics argue it is lenient. Prosecutors say it is justice. Almost everybody admits that at this time it is a necessary evil that society would be hard put to do without.

Prosecutors say that because of the volume of cases, there is no way every defendant could have a trial unless there were 50 criminal courts. There are six in Shelby County.

If defendants formed a union, went on strike against plea bargaining, and demanded a trial in every case, the system would collapse, one prosecutor said.

"We've got to have plea bargaining—it's a matter of necessity," said Criminal Court Judge William H. Williams. He had just finished disposing of about 60 cases in one week.

The average trial takes 2½ days, court records show. If Williams had been in trial, he would have disposed of 2 cases instead of 60.

The system, then, fosters few trials in comparison to the number of cases handled. . . .

But U.S. Supreme Court Chief Justice Warren Burger has called plea bargaining "an essential component of the administration of justice. Properly administered, it is to be encouraged."

John Triplett, *Commercial Appeal* (Memphis, Tenn.), January 27, 1975.

*routine
adminis-
tration*

settlement. The authors concluded that the courts engaged in ***routine administration***: "A matter is *routine* when a court has no disputed question of law or fact to decide. Routine administration means the processing or approving of undisputed matters" (p. 267). Civil cases are negotiated in a manner very similar to plea bargaining in criminal cases, for essentially the same reason. The courts are confronted with a steady stream of routine cases in which the only major question is the sentence to be imposed.

Excessive Caseloads Reconsidered

That caseloads are too heavy is part of the conventional wisdom surrounding the operations of criminal courts. Unfortunately, although often stated and restated, very little effort has been devoted to investigating this thesis.

Malcolm Feeley's study of two Connecticut courts is the first research to concentrate on the problem. Feeley compared two Connecticut courts, one with a heavy caseload, one with a light one. Although he expected that there would be major differences in how cases were processed and in the substance of justice handed out, the results indicated that the courts were remarkably similar. Neither court had many trials. In neither did the defense attorneys engage in pitched battle with the prosecution. Both courts set bail in roughly the same amounts and imposed roughly similar sentences. Each court spent the same amount of time per case, moving through its business "rapidly and mechanically." The only major difference was that the busier court was in session longer than the court with fewer cases.

Another study, this time of Chicago, concluded that "variations in caseloads did not affect the guilty plea decision, the sentence in guilty plea cases, or the decision to pursue a case to trial" (Nardulli). Practitioners in Miami, Detroit, the Bronx, and Pittsburgh believe that even an adequately funded criminal court system would dispose of relatively few cases by means of a trial (Church). The criminal court process cannot be understood solely on the basis of excessive caseloads because such an explanation omits too many important considerations.

Discretion

discretion

Discretion lies at the heart of the criminal justice process. Indeed, from the time a crime is committed until after sentence is imposed on the guilty, ***discretion*** is part of all the key decisions. Often the victim decides not to report the crime to the police. Even if the crime is known to the police, they may decide not to seek out the offender; or, if the offender is known, they may decide not to make an arrest. After arrest the prosecutor may decide not to prosecute. Once charges have been filed, a magistrate must make a decision about the amount of bail and whether there is sufficient probable cause to hold the defendant for the grand jury. In turn, grand juries have discretion over indictments, trial juries over conviction, and the judge over sentencing. Even after sentencing, prison officials exercise discretion in awarding "good time" (reducing the sentence for good behavior), and pardon and parole boards must decide whether to release on parole, grant a pardon, or both.

Clearly, discretion pervades the criminal justice process. Opinion is divided over whether such discretion is proper in a system premised on the equal application of the law. To some it can lead to tyranny and injustice. To others it is not only necessary but desirable, to prevent injustices. Many reform efforts are directed at reducing or at least structuring discretion.

Low Visibility

The existence and pervasiveness of discretion does not differentiate the courts from other organizations (for example, insurance executives must decide what types of claims are valid and establish procedures for processing them). What is distinctive about the criminal court process is not the existence of discretion but where that discretion is located.

In most organizations discretion increases as one moves up the administrative ladder; the lowest-ranking members perform routine tasks under fairly close supervision, which provides a relatively high degree of quality control. In the criminal justice system, however, discretion is exercised most frequently by the lowest members of the administrative hierarchy. Police officers, for example, have a great deal of discretion in deciding whether to arrest. Similarly, assistant district attorneys who decide whether prosecution is in order are typically the newest, least experienced members of the office.

low visibility Discretion in the criminal court process is of special concern because it is marked by *low visibility.* Since many of the key decisions are not directly observable, it is often difficult to determine what decisions are being made and on what basis they are made. In short, there is relatively little administrative monitoring, which can lead to inconsistencies. For example, one assistant district attorney might routinely refuse to prosecute for a given offense (say possession of small amounts of marijuana), while another will always file such charges. Such differences are also found in sentences judges impose. As a result of such policy inconsistencies, it is common for police officers to shop around for a prosecutor favorable to their view, or for a defense attorney to "judge shop" in hopes of getting a lenient sentence for the client.

The Basis of Discretion

Discretion flows from the substantive and procedural law. It is also the product of court officials' attempts to achieve the important goal of seeing that justice is done.

In part, discretion stems from the lack of a clear and coherent body of criminal law. This point is made by Wayne LaFave and Austin Scott in their widely used law school textbook, *Criminal Law.*

> It is important to note that in large measure such discretion is exercised because of the scope and state of the substantive criminal law. Because no legislature has succeeded in formulating a substantive criminal code which clearly encompasses all conduct intended to be made criminal and which clearly excludes all other conduct, the exercise of discretion in interpreting the legislative mandate is necessary. In part the problem is the result of poor draftsmanship and a failure to revise the criminal law to eliminate obsolete provisions. (pp. 18–19)

Because the criminal codes of the various states often contain contradictory prohibitions, judges, prosecutors, defense attorneys, and police officers must exercise discretion to rectify these problems. Moreover, the criminal law must be broad and general. Even carefully drafted statutes cannot anticipate every situation that might arise. For example, a law might be broadly written to ensure that some offenders that the legislature wishes to punish cannot escape through a loophole. But it is left to the criminal court community to remove those who fall under the law's broad mandate but whom the legislature meant to exclude (LaFave and Scott).

Similarly, in determining what penalties should be applied to a given criminal offense, legislators invariably set a penalty for the most heinous offender imaginable (Newman). Yet the vast majority of violators fall far short of being that bad. In context, events are less serious than the abstractions of the criminal law envision (Feeley). As a consequence courts must shape the penalties to the violators before them, not to the theoretical villains imagined when the penalty was enacted.

Some discretion, therefore, is the product of either ambiguous laws, laws that are broad and general, or laws that create so many prohibitions that priorities have to be assigned. In this sense the law provides too many guidelines. At other times discretion is the product of the failure of the law to provide any workable guidelines at all. On many important matters—most notably criteria for setting bail, standards for sentencing, and yardsticks for filing criminal charges—the appellate courts and legislative bodies are largely silent. In these areas local court officials have been left to develop their own guidelines.

Finally, discretion results from attempts by court officials to fulfill some very important but ill-defined goals of individualizing justice and seeing that justice is done. This is most graphically apparent during sentencing.

Legislative definitions of serious offenses are sometimes at odds with the court's definition of serious and threatening violations. For example, in attempting to combat the perceived increase in drug usage and crime related to drug usage, several states have increased the penalties upon conviction by specifying mandatory life imprisonment for a drug sale or mandating no parole. Criminal District Court Judge Jerome Winsberg of Orleans Parish (New Orleans) labels his state laws as having "no relationship to reality" (*Times-Picayune*). The drug sellers he sees in court are seldom the profiteering illegal businessmen envisioned by elected state legislators, but usually junkies making small sales to maintain their habit.

The Many Faces of Discretion

Although the pervasiveness of discretion is well accepted, no common meaning for the term exists. Political scientist George Cole provides a broad definition: "the authority to make decisions without reference to specific rules or facts, using instead one's own judgment" (Cole: 477). In context this seems to be the way the term is most often used, for it implies decisions made on the basis of an actor's personal values. But at other times discretion takes on an even more inclusive meaning. Sociologist Donald Newman, for example, writes that discretion is "the authority to choose among alternative actions or of not acting at all" (Newman: 479). This makes discretion synonymous with decision making. Some authors seem to adopt this definition when speaking of discretion, but such a view is not particularly helpful because it maintains that all decisions are discretionary. The danger is that discretion becomes merely a residual category for everything an author cannot otherwise explain. It is important, therefore, to recognize that there are three major subcomponents of discretion: legal judgments, policy priorities, and personal philosophies.

legal judgments

Legal judgments.   Many discretionary decisions in the criminal court process are made on the basis of ***legal judgments.*** A typical example would be a prosecutor who refuses to file a criminal charge (even though the police have made an arrest) because of her legal judgment that there is insufficient evidence to prove all the elements of the offense. Whether this would be considered discretion by everyone is not clear, but it is clear that decisions made by lawyers and nonlawyers alike about the law are a key element in decision making.

In turn, some legal judgments stem from a prediction about the likely outcome of a case at a later stage in the proceedings. Consider another example involving a prosecutor's decision not to charge a defendant. The prosecutor may believe that the defendant did violate the law but that no jury would convict. In a barroom brawl, there might be no legal question that the defendant struck the victim but the prosecutor may believe that a jury would decide that the victim had provoked the assault and therefore acquit.

Policy priorities.   Because criminal laws are so broad and general, there is a need for selective enforcement. We have all violated some law at some

---

QUOTATION

*E*ngraved in stone on the Department of Justice Building in Washington, on the Pennsylvania Avenue side where swarms of bureaucrats and others pass by, are these five words: "Where law ends tyranny begins" (William Pitt).

I think that in our system of government, where the law ends tyranny need not begin. Where law ends, discretion begins, and the exercise of discretion may mean either beneficence or tyranny, either justice or injustice, either reasonableness or arbitrariness.

Kenneth Culp Davis, *Discretionary Justice: A Preliminary Inquiry* (Urbana: University of Illinois Press, 1971), p. 3.

policy
priorities

time. Essentially the supply of criminal illegality is almost infinite. Yet the resources devoted to detecting wrongdoers and processing them through the courts (and later incarcerating them) are limited. Policy decisions must be made about priorities for enforcing the law. As a result, court officials employ a set of informal *policy priorities* in applying the law. Some prosecutors' offices, for example, have a house policy for prosecutions in minor theft or embezzlements. U.S. attorneys will not normally file embezzlement charges when the suspect is a young employee of a bank who stole small amounts and was fired when discovered. Similarly, prosecutors often have policies on possession of small amounts of marijuana. Overall, court officials devote more resources to prosecuting serious crimes like murder, rape, and armed robbery than more minor offenses.

personal
philosophies

Personal philosophies.   Some discretionary decisions obviously are a reflection of the decision makers' personal values and attitudes—their *personal philosophies.* Judges and prosecutors vary in what offenses they view as serious and deserving of a high priority. Burglaries are typically perceived as more threatening in small rural towns than they are in larger cities where burglary is a daily occurrence. Not only do judges, prosecutors, and others differ in their ranking of serious crimes, they also vary according to their views on the purpose of the criminal law. Those who believe that the courts can deter crime (through heavy sentences, for example) will behave differently from those who discount the general role the courts can play in deterrence.

Occasionally commentators charge that court officials decide what actions to take on a whim (Cole). No doubt in a small percentage of cases whim does affect the ultimate decision, but to argue that the decisions in the court system are systematically influenced by such whims is clearly mistaken (Neubauer).

The Courtroom Work Group

courtroom
work group

A defendant approaching the bench is surrounded by a dozen official and unofficial court personnel. In addition to the three legal actors embodied in the adversary model—judge, prosecutor, and defense attorney—those in attendance also include a host of support personnel without whom the court could not operate: a clerk, a court reporter, a bailiff, a police officer, a family court liaison official, a matron, and an interpreter. (A bail bondsman may also be in attendance.) This is the *courtroom work group*—the officials who on a day-to-day basis decide which cases will be carried forward, which defendant will be released on bail, what guilty pleas will be accepted and, finally and most important, what sentence will be imposed on the guilty.

courthouse
regulars

To even the most casual observer these *courthouse regulars* occupy a special status. They freely issue instructions (don't smoke, don't talk, don't read the newspaper) to the temporary visitors to the courthouse, though they smoke, talk, and read the newspaper themselves. The ordinary citizens—defendants, friends of defendants, victims, witnesses, and disinterested observers—sit on hard benches in the rear of the courtroom and may approach the bench through a gate dividing the courtroom only when specifically requested. The courthouse officials, on the other hand, enjoy easy access to the front part of the courtroom, freely passing the railing into the area near the judge's bench. The final indication of the special status of the courthouse regulars is the nature of their casual conversations. Courtrooms are subject to numerous and unpredictable periods of inactivity; during these times, the courthouse regulars engage in casual conversations demonstrating that they know each other well. Observers expecting to view an adversarial battle are struck by the cordiality of the opponents as they engage in casual conversations. Indeed, defense attorneys are much more likely to talk to their nominal adversary, the prosecutor, than to pass the time of day with their clients.

A number of studies have attempted to assess the activities of these officials (Blumberg; Neubauer; Eisenstein and Jacob). They have found a complex network of ongoing social relationships among judges, prosecutors, and defense attorneys who work together on a daily basis. The result is a level of cooperation not envisioned by the formal adversary model. Table 5-1 shows that in Philadelphia 83 percent of the district attorneys and public defenders cooperate always or often (Lichtenstein).

Not all studies, however, are agreed on the effects this cooperation has on the administration of justice. Some contend that the actors are so concerned with maintaining good relationships with the other courthouse regulars that they are not particularly interested in the justice meted out in individual cases. Nonetheless, these relationships are as important as they are complex. Given the complexity of this network we need some intellectual tools to guide our analysis. Toward this end James Eisenstein and Herbert Jacob have proposed *work groups* that the best way to analyze the network of ongoing relationships among the courthouse regulars is to view the courts as ***work groups.***

Work Group Formation

One of the major qualities differentiating modern societies from traditional ones is the existence in them of large formal organizations marked by numerous actors whose duties in pursuit of common interests are specialized and governed by specific rules of conduct. Certainly courts fall under this broad definition. But in certain ways the courts are also unique. The criminal courts are not a single organization but rather a collection of several separate institutions that gather in a common workplace, the courtroom. Whereas most large organizations—General Motors for example—consist of distinct divisions operating under a central leadership, the criminal courts consist of separate institutions without a hierarchical system of control. There is no central authority. A judge cannot reward a clerk, a prosecutor, or a public defender who performs well. The courts are not a central organization. Each of the courthouse regulars is a representative of a sponsoring institution, which in various ways monitors their activities, hires them, fires them, and rewards them. In turn, these sponsoring institutions have many clients with whom they interact and on whom they are dependent for support.

Interaction.   Every day the same group of courthouse regulars assembles in the same courtroom, sits or stands in the same places, and performs the

TABLE 5-1   Extent to which Assistant District Attorneys and Public Defenders Believe that They Cooperate with Each Other

Attorneys	Extent of cooperation				
	Always	*Often*	*Sometimes*	*Seldom*	*Never*
Assistant District Attorneys (n = 55)	33%	51%	14%	0%	2%
Public Defenders (n = 20)	30	50	20	0	0
Both ADAs and PDs (n = 75)	32	51	16	0	1

SOURCE: Michael Lichtenstein, "Public Defenders: Dimensions of Cooperation," *The Justice System Journal* 9 (1984): 105.

same tasks as the day before. The types of defendants and the types of crimes they are accused of committing remain constant too. Only the names of the victims, witnesses, and defendants are different. Thus, while defendants come and go, the judges, prosecutors, defense attorneys, clerks, bailiffs, and so on remain. These representatives from separate and independent sponsoring institutions are drawn together by a common task: each must do something about a given case.

None of these actors can perform his or her tasks independently; they must work together. These interactions are critical because none of the courthouse regulars can make decisions independently; each must consider the reactions of others. This is most readily seen in the work of the defense attorney. In representing the client, the defense attorney must consider the type of plea agreement the prosecutor may offer, the sentencing tendencies of the judge, the likelihood of a jury verdict of guilty, and the possibility that the probation officer will recommend probation. Prosecutors and judges fall into a similar pattern.

Through working together on a daily basis, a *limited* set of personal ties develops. Some researchers have suggested that these ties—developed through such activities as judges playing golf on the weekends with prosecutors or defense attorneys—are strong ones. Although in a few situations these ties are strong, they are hardly the major factor in courtroom dynamics. However, personal acquaintance does allow the participants to joke among themselves, particularly about difficult cases. More important, these personal interactions convey to each participant the pressures and problems faced by members of the other institutions.

Mutual interdependence.   Each member of the work group can achieve individual goals and accomplish separate tasks only through work group participation. The actors come to share common interests in disposing of cases. Hence cooperation—***mutual interdependence***—within the work group produces mutual benefits.

mutual inter-dependence

A judge who allows a backlog of cases to develop can expect to feel pressure from other judges or the chief judge to dispose of more cases. Assistant prosecutors are judged by their superiors not so much on how many cases they win but on how many they lose; the emphasis is on not losing by securing convictions. Defense attorneys face a more complicated set of incentives. Public defender organizations prefer to dispose of cases quickly because they have a limited number of attorneys to represent a large number of indigents. Private attorneys also need to move cases. Since most defendants are poor and can afford only a modest fee, private attorneys make their livelihoods by representing a large number of clients. The fee in each case is insufficient to allow the expenditure of much time on any given case, so there is a need for high turnover. In short all participants receive benefits from disposing of cases with minimal effort.

The Impact of Courtroom Work Groups

The key to understanding the criminal court process lies in understanding how the representatives of separate sponsoring institutions, each with its own needs and pressures, end up cooperating on a range of matters. Toward this end, the impact of courtroom work groups can be divided into five categories: shared decision making, shared norms, socialization, sticks and carrots, and goal modification (Clynch and Neubauer).

informal authority

Shared decision making.   In courtroom work groups, there are ***informal patterns of authority*** underlying the formal ones. Judges retain the legal authority to make the major decisions such as setting bail, adjudicating guilt (except if there is a jury trial), and imposing sentence, but they often rely on others. They may routinely follow the bail recommendations of the prosecutor, accept guilty plea agreements reached by defense and prosecution, or follow the recommendations of the probation officer. This does not mean that the judge is without power; these other actors in turn are sensitive to what the judge might do. Bail recommendations and sentence recommendations are the product of a two-way communication process. Prosecutors (and defense attorneys) know that in past situations a particular judge set bail in X amounts, so that is what they recommend in the current case.

These modifications of formal authority patterns are partially the result of control over information. Knowledge is power and whoever controls the knowledge has a great deal of power. Overall, prosecutors know the most about a case, defense attorneys less, and judges the least. As a result the nominal subordinates of judges can influence their decisions by selective information flow.

These informal patterns of authority result in a shared decision-making process that apportions power and responsibility. Judges, prosecutors, defense attorneys, bail officials, and others are aware that the decision they make can turn out to be wrong. A defendant who is released on bail may kill a police officer the next day. Since such dire results cannot be predicted ahead of time, the members of the courtroom work group share a sense that when one of their members looks bad, they all look bad. In our example, all the sponsoring institutions would face a great deal of public displeasure. Therefore it is highly functional for the members of the courtroom work group to diffuse power and responsibility. Decisions are made on a joint basis. If something later goes wrong, work group members have protected themselves: everyone thought it was a good idea at the time.

shared
norms

Shared norms.   The hallmark of work groups is regularity of behavior. This regularity is the product of ***shared norms*** about how each member should behave and what decisions are desirable. Courthouse workers can make their common work site a fractious and unpredictable place for carrying out assigned tasks, or, through cooperation, a predictable place to work. The greater the certainty, the less time and resources they need spend on each case. The shared norms that provide a structure and framework to what otherwise first appears to be an unstructured, almost chaotic process fall into three categories.

outsiders

The first shared norm involves shielding the work group from ***outsiders.*** The greatest uncertainty comes from outside forces that the members of the work group cannot control. For example, during a trial all participants are at the mercy of witnesses. Since witnesses' testimony at times produces surprises, the work group finds that witnesses' participation produces uncertainty. Similarly jurors are an unkown quantity. The courthouse regulars as much as possible seek to avoid such sources of uncertainty by making decisions among themselves on the basis of factors they can control. Plea bargaining provides the clearest example of such an effort.

A second set of shared norms centers on standards of personal and professional conduct. Attorneys are expected to stick by their word and never deliberately mislead. They are also expected to minimize surprises (Eisenstein and Jacob). Although in the television show Perry Mason often called in an unknown witness to win his case dramatically, members of the work group view such activities as a violation of social norms because surprise adds uncertainty to their work environment. Members who violate these rules of personal and professional conduct can expect sanctions from the other members of the work group.

normal
crime

The third set of shared norms relates to policy standards. As we noted, most of the matters before the courts are routine. And although each case is unique in that no two events are exactly similar, most cases fall in a limited number of categories. Just as a child learns to sort various four-legged animals into distinct categories of dog, cat, cow, and so on, the members of the work group develop concepts about types of crime and criminals. One study of public defenders has aptly labeled this phenomenon as the concept of the ***normal crime*** (Sudnow). The legal actors categorize crimes on the basis of the typical manner in which they are committed, the typical social characteristics of the defendants, the settings of the crimes, and the types of victims. Once a case has been placed into one of these categories, it is typically disposed of on the basis of a set pattern. In the community that Sudnow studied, child molesting cases were routinely reduced to loitering charges, drunkenness to disturbing the peace, and burglary to petty theft. The existence of such agreed-upon categorizations allows the members of the work group to dispose fairly rapidly of the large number of routine cases that require their attention. These policy norms are one solution to the problems facing the courtroom work group. They form a common orientation consisting of rules, understandings, and customs that accommodate the differing demands of the sponsoring institutions. A group sense of justice is the result.

Though the interests of the courthouse regulars are formally at odds, in operation they come to share common interests. The shared norms channel and limit conflict, but by no means eliminate it. Members of the work group still disagree, for example, over whether a defendant fits into the normal crime category or over whether a proposed sentence is too light. Their shared norms establish boundaries for what behavior is expected and which issues are debatable.

socialization

Socialization.   Court work groups have needs quite apart from the legal mandate of adjudicating cases; they must preserve the ongoing system. A problem common to all organizations is the need to break in new members, a process referred to as ***socialization.*** Through socialization by a variety of persons, newcomers are taught not only the formal requirements of the job (how motions are filed and so on) but also informal rules of behavior.

Newcomers learn not only from their peers but from other members of the social network. One veteran court aide put it this way:

> Most of the judges are pretty good—they rely on us. Sometimes you get a new judge who wants to do things his way. We have to break them in, train them. This court is very different. We have to break new judges in. It takes some of them some time to get adjusted to the way we do things. (Wiseman: 99)

sanctions

Sticks and carrots.   To be effective, social norms must be enforceable. Efficient routines are threatened not only by new members but also at times by current members of the work group. A variety of rewards (carrots) are available as benefits to those who follow the rules. In turn, some ***sanctions*** (sticks) may be applied to those who do not. By far the more effective is the carrot, because it operates indirectly and is less disruptive. The impositions of sanctions can result in counter-sanctions being applied, with the result that the network is disrupted even further.

In discussing sticks and carrots, let us again concentrate on the defense attorneys. Defense attorneys who do not unnecessarily disrupt routines are eligible for several types of rewards. First, they receive greater information from prosecutors, who more often have the resources to conduct an independent investigation. Prosecutors may show the police reports to cooperative defense attorneys or may be more willing to negotiate a slightly lesser-than-normal sentence. In return, defense attorneys are expected to avoid filing unnecessary motions, to be reasonably accommodating when the state needs more time to prepare, and to resist pushing too hard for sentence bargains.

As for sticks, a variety of sanctions are available for use against uncooperative defense attorneys. They may be allowed less access to case information, or the judge can keep them waiting. But mainly the clients of these attorneys are punished: they receive greater-than-normal penalties (Mileski). Ultimately, however, uncooperative members of the team are punished in some way. When asked what would happen if a prosecutor out of zeal or inexperience charged defendants with potential charges severe enough to discourage pleas of guilty, a judge replied as follows:

I would talk to him and try to teach him how I wanted him to conduct himself in my court. [And if that didn't work?] I often have occasion to see the district attorney—that is—on social occasions. If I am running the criminal department, he might ask me how things are going, and I'd suggest to him that the deputy he has in there isn't doing a very good job, and that I think he ought to be replaced. Usually, when I make such a judgment, the district attorney will go along with me. (Skolnick: 57)

***goal of
justice***

Goal modification. It is impossible to assess court work groups properly without considering the overall ***goal of justice*** that they are expected to achieve. A wide variety of studies have shown that organizations—General Motors, the police, the Social Security Administration, the courts, and so

CLOSE-UP

Chaos in the Courthouse

One of the first clues to the low status accorded the criminal courts (by both the general public as well as influential politicians), is their location. In at least half of the cities visited, the criminal courts were carefully tucked away from public view. The most common justification for these isolated and inconvenient locations was security. Since the pretrial detention facilities may be appended to the courthouse proper, it was necessary to place the entire structure out of the downtown business center. This was clearly the case in Chicago and New Orleans. . . .

Although criminal court buildings may have been constructed in a variety of architectural styles, they nevertheless all seem to possess the same imposing facade. Regardless of age, they present an image of stolidity and unyielding strength. Entrance is usually gained by climbing an excessive number of steps. For security reasons, there may be only one door open to the inner sanctum, funneling in all visitors through a crowded, narrow entranceway. . . .

Another side effect of these security precautions which can prove extremely discomforting to the inexperienced visitor is the practice of locking all courthouse lavatories. Use is restricted to permanent personnel who are issued personal keys. This decision was explained as being the result of hostile protests conducted in the late sixties and early seventies in which radical groups released their frustrations against the supposed inequities of our criminal justice system by blowing up courthouse lavatories. Other reasons for their limited use was their reputation as homosexual hangouts as well as ideal locales for muggings. The irony of the situation is that when they are open to the public, the facilities are so abused that sinks and toilets rarely work and towels and toilet paper are nonexistent.

The interior of the courthouse is usually distinguished by a massive lobby, with an impressively high, arched ceiling. In the center of the lobby is the omnipresent information booth which is invariably

unattended. A nearby bulletin board offers the only clue as to what cases are to be found in which courtrooms but the notices are usually outdated. In a distant corner is a small snack bar and a battery of telephones, a few of which are in service. . . .

Between nine to four o'clock each weekday, the cavernous lobby and most hallways are filled with animated conversations between lawyers, bail bondsmen, bailiffs, defendants, concerned family members, witnesses and a variety of other interested parties. For many bondsmen and private criminal lawyers these hallways are, in reality, their daytime offices. Although courthouses have attempted to reduce the cacophony in the hallways by providing for witness reception areas, lawyers' lounges, and other specialized and secluded hideaways, nearly everyone prefers to be near the action so as not to miss out on a business opportunity, or choice bit of gossip.

First-time visitors to the courthouse are frequently shocked by the amount of

forth—are greatly affected by the ultimate goals they are expected to fulfill. In some cases these overall goals are fairly precise: General Motors is expected to make a profit, a well-understood yardstick of achievement. But public bodies usually do not have such clear goals. Rather they have multiple often conflicting, and typically hard-to-measure ones. This is the case with the criminal courts. The public, the press, the defendants, the legal community, and the courthouse regulars all expect the courts to "do justice."

doing justice   This overall goal of ***doing justice*** produces a maze of difficulties for court officials. First, there is no agreement as to the meaning of justice. The courts are expected to do numerous things—respect individual liberties, protect the public, deter wrongdoers, punish the guilty, rehabilitate the transgressors.

---

badinage which transpires between the various members of the courtroom workgroup. . . .

Moving out of the hallways and into the courtroom, one notices a relative decrease in noise level, while the air quality improves appreciably. This is especially true in the spring and summer where most cities observe a policy of air-conditioning only the inside of the courtrooms, letting the hallways swelter without relief. The judge and bailiffs attempt to maintain an acceptable decibel level but disturbances are commonplace. It must be noted that the chaotic scenes depicted thus far pertain to only those courtrooms where pretrial proceedings are conducted such as initial arraignments, preliminary hearings, calendar, motions or arraignment. As one moves closer toward trial in a felony case, the courtroom scene becomes increasingly more tranquil. The end result is that the trial, which is a statistical rarity, is held in a quiet, sparsely-populated courtroom. The tedious and repetitive nature of most trials, in contrast to the public's misconception, serves to lull the most diligent observer into momentary lapses of daydreaming.

. . . The typical pretrial proceeding is conducted within a large courtroom. Entrance is gained through a double set of heavy doors. Once inside, the judge's elevated position becomes immediately apparent. Just below him is the court stenographer and the calendar clerk who attempts to control the scheduling of cases and keep the judge apprised of the relevant details of the case before him. Approximately 15 feet from the front of the bench are two tables reserved for the defense and prosecution, respectively. The prosecutor's table is piled high with manila folders representing those cases to be disposed of during the course of that day's business. This impressive pile of folders is invariably incomplete and results in last-minute scurrying by frantic assistant district attorneys trying to rectify the periodic lapses of the prosecutorial bureaucracy. If the other table is manned by a public defender, the mound of case folders nearly matches that of the prosecutor's. The private criminal lawyer maintains his own collection of case folders within the confines of his briefcase. Directly behind the defense and prosecution tables is a low railing or some other obstacle dividing the court officers (judges, lawyers, and clerks) from the general public who sit in several rows of benches. The first, and sometimes the second rows are reserved for police officers and lawyers who are waiting for their cases to be called. Sitting in the remaining rows are the defendants (those who have been free on bond or released on their own recognizance), family members, friends, and a variety of other observers. In the trial courts one finds large numbers of senior citizens who enjoy rooting for the prosecutor. They are often vocal in their thirst for severe sanctions against defendants whom they do not wish to have returned to their neighborhoods and continue to terrorize other elderly victims.

Indeed we often expect the courts to do all of these simultaneously, which is obviously impossible. Disagreement exists over which of these is the most important goal. Embedded in the overall goals of the court is a built-in conflict over what the end product should be. Just as important, there is no ready way to evaluate whether justice is actually being done. Courthouse statistics—the number of cases processed, the number of convictions, the number of trials—are substituted as measures of justice done. At the end of the month a supervisor need not ponder whether a subordinate achieved justice: he or she need only count how many cases were disposed of. The result is that the vague goals and complex needs of the organizations become hopelessly intermixed.

Variability in Court Work Groups

Virtually all criminal courts studied to date exemplify these patterns of how court work groups operate, but some important variations need to be considered.

- The stability of the work groups can vary (Church). Eisenstein and Jacob reported that work groups were much more stable in Chicago than in Baltimore, where rotation of key officials' jobs occurred more often and produced numerous disruptions of the ongoing network of relationships.
- Rules of behavior that guide the key actors vary from courtroom to courtroom. There is room for mavericks. Some defense attorneys march to a different drummer. They maintain hostile relations with prosecutors and exhibit many ''Perry Mason'' attributes of adversarial behavior. They do so at a price, however. They are seldom able to negotiate effectively for good deals. But at the same time, they tend to represent clients whom the court network is predisposed to treat harshly. In short, the normal range of sanctions and rewards does not apply to them.
- There are important variations in how judges control their courtrooms. Although the formal authority of the judge is shared with the informal network, judges respond in different ways. Some prefer to parcel out decisions to others and are therefore receptive to recommendations from prosecutors, probation officers, and perhaps even defense attorneys. Other judges play a much more dominant role. Most federal judges, for example, will not even allow the prosecutor or defense attorney to suggest a possible sentence.
- The content of the policy norms varies from community to community and from courtroom to courtroom. Property crimes are viewed as more threatening in rural areas than in urban ones; therefore the appropriate penalty for a defendant convicted of burglary in a rural area is more severe than for one convicted in a big city.

Conclusion

The actual operations of the criminal courts differ greatly from official expectations. Three concepts—excessive caseloads, discretion, and the courtroom work group—attempt to explain this gap between law in action and law on the books. Although courts are burdened with too many cases, excessive caseload volume is at best only a partial explanation for the behavior of the criminal courts. More important is the role discretion plays in the court system, shaping the dictates of formal law to the actual cases and defendants that come to the criminal courts. The courtroom work group concept emphasizes the interactions among the key actors in court. In the next three chapters, we will examine in greater depth how prosecutors, defense attorneys, and judges work within the courtroom work group, and why.

For Discussion

1. Throughout this book, we will discuss varying proposals for reducing the caseload of the courts. What problems might be helped by a reduction in caseload? What problems might remain largely the same? Why?

2. To many defendants, victims, and witnesses, a case in criminal court is a unique experience. Yet to the courthouse regulars most of these matters are quite routine. What effects might this situation have on the attitudes and expectations of the defendants, victims, witnesses, and others? On the courthouse regulars? Medical personnel adopt a professional, nonemotional response to sickness and accidents. Do the same factors apply to the courthouse regulars? What steps might be taken to alter this attitude of routine justice?

3. How does the courtroom work group affect the exercise of discretion?

4. Make a list of situations that you think are appropriate for discretion. Also list situations that are not appropriate for discretion or where discretion has been abused. What do your lists reveal about your own views of the goals of the criminal court process? Are your lists similar to or different from those of your classmates?

5. Observe a courtroom work group in your own community and talk to its members. How long have the same people worked together? Do they share common perceptions of normal crimes and appropriate penalties? What matters do they disagree over? What rewards and sanctions are used? Obtaining answers to these questions will not be easy. Why might the courthouse regulars be reluctant to discuss such matters?

6. In what ways might defendants receive a break depending on how well their defense attorneys cooperate with the courtroom work group? Some defendants receive a stiffer-than-normal penalty because the work group wishes to penalize the attorney. What might be done to correct this problem?

References

BLUMBERG, ABRAHAM S. *Criminal Justice.* New York: Quadrangle Books, 1970.

CHURCH, THOMAS. "Examining Local Legal Culture." *American Bar Foundation Research Journal 1985* (1985): 449–518.

CLYNCH, EDWARD, AND DAVID NEUBAUER. "Trial Courts as Organizations: A Critique and Synthesis." *Law and Policy Quarterly* 3 (January 1981): 69–94.

COLE, GEORGE F. "The Decision to Prosecute." *Law and Society Review* 4 (1970): 331.

EISENSTEIN, JAMES, AND HERBERT JACOB. *Felony Justice: An Organizational Analysis of Criminal Courts.* Boston: Little, Brown, 1977.

FEELEY, MALCOLM. *The Process Is the Punishment: Handling Cases in a Lower Criminal Court.* New York: Russell Sage Foundation, 1979.

FRIEDMAN, LAWRENCE, AND ROBERT PERCIVAL. "A Tale of Two Courts: Litigation in Alameda and San Benito Counties." *Law and Society Review* 10 (1976): 267.

HALLER, MARK. "Plea Bargaining: The Nineteenth-Century Context." *Law and Society Review* 13 (1979): 273.

LAFAVE, WAYNE, AND AUSTIN W. SCOTT, JR. *Criminal Law.* St. Paul, Minn.: West Publishing, 1972.

LICHTENSTEIN, MICHAEL. "Public Defenders: Dimensions of Cooperation." *Justice System Journal* 9 (1984): 102–110.

MILESKI, MAUREN. "Courtroom Encounters: An Observation Study of a Lower Criminal Court." *Law and Society Review* 5 (1971): 473.

NARDULLI, PETER. "The Caseload Controversy and the Study of Criminal Courts." *Journal of Criminal Law and Criminology* 70 (1979): 101.

NEUBAUER, DAVID W. *Criminal Justice in Middle America.* Morristown, N.J.: General Learning Press, 1974.

NEWMAN, DONALD. "Pleading Guilty for Considerations: A Study of Bargain Justice." *Journal of Criminal Law* 37 (1970): 665.

PRESIDENT'S COMMISSION ON LAW ENFORCEMENT AND ADMINISTRATION OF JUSTICE. *Task Force Report: The Courts.* Washington, D.C.: Government Printing Office, 1967.

SKOLNICK, JEROME H. *Justice Without Trial.* New York: John Wiley, 1966.

SUDNOW, DAVID. "Normal Crimes: Sociological Features of the Penal Code in a Public Defender Office." *Social Problems* 12 (1965): 254.

TIMES-PICAYUNE, February 26, 1976.

WISEMAN, JACQUELINE. *Stations of the Lost: The Treatment of Skid Row Alcoholics.* Englewood Cliffs, N.J.: Prentice-Hall, 1970.

For Further Reading

BURSTEIN, CAROLYN. "Criminal Case Processing from an Organizational Perspective: Current Research Trends." *Justice System Journal* 5 (1980): 258–273.

DAVIS, KENNETH C. *Discretionary Justice: A Preliminary Inquiry.* Urbana: University of Illinois Press, 1971.

EISENSTEIN, JAMES, AND HERBERT JACOB. *Felony Justice: An Organizational Analysis of Criminal Courts.* Boston: Little, Brown, 1977.

JACOB, HERBERT. "Courts as Organizations." In *Empirical Theories About Courts,* ed. Keith Boyum and Lynn Mather. New York: Longman, 1983, pp. 191–215.

LIPETZ, MARCIA. "Routines and Deviations: The Strength of the Courtroom Workgroup in a Misdemeanor Court." *International Journal of the Sociology of Law* 8 (1980): 47–60.

NARDULLI, PETER. *The Courtroom Elite: An Organizational Perspective on Criminal Justice.* Cambridge, Mass.: Ballinger, 1978.

NARDULLI, PETER, ROY FLEMMING, AND JAMES EISENSTEIN. "Unraveling the Complexities of Decision Making in Face-to-Face Groups: A Contextual Analysis of Plea-Bargained Sentences." *American Political Science Review* 78 (1984): 912–928.

NEUBAUER, DAVID W. *Criminal Justice in Middle America.* Morristown, N.J.: General Learning Press, 1974.

ROSETT, ARTHUR, AND DONALD P. CRESSEY. *Justice by Consent: Plea Bargaining in the American Courthouse.* Philadelphia: J. B. Lippincott, 1976.

CHAPTER 6

The Prosecutor

The prosecutor is the most powerful official in the criminal courts. From the time of arrest to the final disposition, how the prosecutor chooses to exercise discretion determines to a large extent which defendants are prosecuted, the type of bargains that will be struck, and the severity of the sentence.

These wide-ranging discretionary powers illustrate that the prosecutor occupies a central position in the criminal justice system. Whereas police, defense attorneys, judges, and probation officers specialize in a specific phase of the criminal justice process, the duties of the prosecutor bridge all these phases. This means that the prosecutor is the only official who must on a daily basis work with all the various actors of the criminal justice system. In turn, these various actors have conflicting views about how prosecutorial discretion should be used—the police push for harsher penalties, defense attorneys for giving their clients a break, and judges to clear the docket. As a result, the prosecutor stands center stage in an extremely complex and conflictive environment.

With the possible exception of big city mayors, prosecutors occupy uniquely powerful and highly visible positions.

This chapter examines a number of factors that affect how prosecutors exercise their wide-ranging discretionary powers. We will begin with a discussion of the decentralized organization of the prosecutor's office and then examine the key work requirements of the job. We will then turn our attention to the social forces that shape how these powers are actually applied. In particular we will look at the fact that most of the work of the office is carried out by young assistant attorneys, whose activities are greatly affected by their membership and acceptance in the courtroom work group. Finally, the chapter will focus on the conflicting goals that underlie the tasks of the American prosecutor.

Structure and Organization

prosecutor   The *prosecutor*, known as the district attorney in some jurisdictions and state's attorney in most others, is the chief law enforcement official of the community. The prosecutor works in the courthouse but is part of the executive branch of government. This independence from the judiciary is vital for the proper functioning of the adversary system, since prosecutors at times challenge judicial decisions.

Decentralization

decentralized   *Decentralized organization* is the key characteristic of the office of *organization*   prosecutor. In most states the district attorney has countywide responsibility, although some rural counties are grouped into prosecutorial districts (see Table 6-1). The actual division of responsibility follows local, state, and federal jurisdictional boundaries. In big cities, the prosecutor has a staff of more than a hundred full-time assistants. The largest office, that of the District Attorney for Los Angeles County, has over five hundred assistant prosecutors. The great majority of the nation's 2,700 prosecutor's offices, however, are small ones with no more than one or two assistants (U.S. Department of Justice). Frequently, rural prosecutors are part-time officials who also maintain a private law practice.

The activities of the prosecutor's office typically are not monitored by state *attorney*   officials. Although the *attorney general* is the state's chief law enforcement *general*   official, his or her authority over local criminal procedures is quite limited. In a handful of states the attorney general has no legal authority to intervene in or initiate local prosecutions. In other states this authority is limited to extreme conditions. Thus, the state attorney general exercises virtually no control or supervision over district attorneys. This lack of supervisory power, coupled with the decentralization of offices, means that local prosecutors enjoy almost total autonomy. Only the local voters have the power to evaluate the prosecutor's performance and vote the current officeholder out of office.

The decentralization of America's prosecutor authority results in divided responsibility. In a single city there are sometimes three separate prosecutors—city, county, and federal. Competition does occur between such separate

TABLE 6-1   Characteristics of Local Prosecutors

	Title	Area	Number of units	How selected	Term (years)
Alabama	District attorney	Judicial district	38	Elected	6
Alaska	(No local prosecutor)				
Arizona	County attorney	County	14	Elected	4
Arkansas	District prosecuting attorney	Judicial district	19	Elected	2
California	District attorney	County	58	Elected	4
Colorado	District attorney	Judicial district	22	Elected	4
Connecticut	State's attorney	Judicial district	9	Superior Court	4
Delaware	(No local prosecutor)				
Florida	State attorney	Judicial district	20	Elected	4
Georgia	District attorney	Judicial district	42	Elected	4
Hawaii	County or city prosecutor	County	7	Elected or appointed	4
Idaho	Prosecuting attorney	County	44	Elected	2
Illinois	State's attorney	County	102	Elected	4
Indiana	Prosecuting attorney	Judicial district	88	Elected	4
Iowa	County attorney	County	99	Elected	4
Kansas	County attorney	County	101	Elected	2
	District attorney	County	4	Elected	4
Kentucky	County attorney	County	120	Elected	4
	Commonwealth attorney	District	55	Elected	6
Louisiana	District attorney	Judicial district	40	Elected	6
Maine	District attorney	Judicial district	8	Elected	4
Maryland	State's attorney	County or city	24	Elected	4
Massachusetts	District attorney	Judicial district	10	Elected	4
Michigan	Prosecuting attorney	County	83	Elected	4
Minnesota	County attorney	County	87	Elected	4
Mississippi	District attorney	Judicial district	20	Elected	4
	County prosecuting attorney	County	63	Elected	4
Missouri	Prosecuting attorney	County	114	Elected	2
Montana	County attorney	County	56	Elected	4
Nebraska	County attorney	County	93	Elected	4
Nevada	District attorney	County	17	Elected	4
New Hampshire	County attorney	County	10	Elected	2
New Jersey	County prosecutor	County	21	Governor with consent of Senate	5
New Mexico	District attorney	Judicial district	13	Elected	4
New York	District attorney	County	62	Elected	4
North Carolina	District attorney	Judicial district	30	Elected	4
North Dakota	State's attorney	County	53	Elected	4
Ohio	Prosecuting attorney	County	88	Elected	4
Oklahoma	District attorney	District	27	Elected	2
Oregon	District attorney	County	36	Elected	4
Pennsylvania	District attorney	County	67	Elected	4
Rhode Island	(No local prosecutor)				
South Carolina	Circuit solicitor	Judicial district	16	Elected	4
South Dakota	State's attorney	County	64	Elected	4
Tennessee	District attorney general	Judicial district	17	Elected	8

(continued)

Table 6-1   Characteristics of Local Prosecutors (*continued*)

	Title	Area	Number of units	How selected	Term (years)
Texas	County attorney	County	191	Elected	4
	District attorney	District	70	Elected	4
Utah	County attorney	County	29	Elected	4
Vermont	State's attorney	County	14	Elected	4
Virginia	Commonwealth attorney	County or city	127	Elected	4
Washington	Prosecuting attorney	County	39	Elected	4
West Virginia	Prosecuting attorney	County	55	Elected	4
Wisconsin	District attorney	County	71	Elected	2
Wyoming	County and prosecuting attorney	County	23	Elected	4

U.S. Department of Justice, Law Enforcement Assistance Administration, National Criminal Justice Information and Statistics Service, *State and Local Prosecution and Civil Attorney Systems* (Washington, D.C.: Government Printing Office, 1978).

agencies over which office will prosecute which defendants. In addition, coordination on common problems is often lacking. Most major metropolitan areas encompass numerous counties and cities; gaps in jurisdiction allow sophisticated and organized criminal conspiracies to operate across several *special* boundaries. In response to such activities, some areas have created ***special*** ***prosecutor's*** ***prosecutor's offices*** to focus on organized crime in designated substantive *offices* areas.

Prosecutors as Public Officials

Most prosecutors are locally elected officials. The primary exceptions are U.S. attorneys, who are nominated by the president and confirmed by the Senate. In addition, in two eastern states (New Jersey and Connecticut) the local prosecutor is appointed and in three states (Alaska, Delaware, and Rhode Island), the state attorney general also serves as the local prosecutor (see Table 6-1).

The elected term is typically four years, although in some states it is only two. These elections indicate that the work of the American prosecutor is deeply set within the larger political process. For a lawyer interested in a political career, the prosecutor's office offers a launching pad. Numerous government officials—governors, judges, and legislators—began their careers as crusading prosecutors (Schlesinger). Not all prosecutors, though, plan to enter politics. Studies in Wisconsin and Kentucky, for example, indicated that more than half of the prosecutors had no further political ambitions. They viewed the office as useful for gaining visibility before establishing a private law practice (Jacob; Engstrom). Overall, most prosecutors are young. One survey indicated that about one half were serving their first term of office (Morgan and Alexander).

The tremendous power of the prosecutor's office means that political parties are very interested in controlling it. The county district attorney provides numerous opportunities for patronage. But even more fundamentally, political parties want one of their own supporters serving as district attorney to guarantee that their affairs will not be closely scrutinized and to act as a vehicle for harassing the opposition. This power is most aptly shown in Chicago. The Republican U.S. attorney, James Thompson (1971–1975) secured indictments and convictions against numerous Democratic officials and then used his record as U.S. attorney as the basis for winning the governorship of Illinois (1977–   ).

The Prosecutor at Work

The word *lawyer* usually evokes the image of someone arguing before a jury. Until the twentieth century, this was a good description. The most famous lawyers of the past—Daniel Webster and Clarence Darrow, for example—were skilled trial orators. But times have changed. The vast majority of American lawyers never try a case. The prosecutor's office, though, is one place where trials are still an important part of what lawyers do. The activities of American lawyers—and particularly the prosecutors—can be conveniently divided into five categories: fighting, negotiating, drafting, counseling, and administering (Mayer).

Fighting

fighting

A trial lawyer must be a ***fighter*** who likes to question witnesses, object to other lawyers' questions, and appeal to juries. A criminal case does not arrive in the prosecutor's office neatly packaged and awaiting the summoning of a jury. One of the most vital skills of an attorney is taking a disorganized case and preparing it for trial. Such case preparation and eventual trial involve numerous tactical decisions. Will this person make a good witness? How can we show the jury the strongest points of the case while minimizing the weaknesses? What type of defense is the opposition likely to mount, and how can it be countered? How can we introduce a vital piece of evidence on the borderline of admissibility? Obviously a working knowledge of the rules of

---

C O N T R O V E R S Y

Fuller Unseats Udolf as DA

Long after most election parties had ended and campaign supporters were in bed, district attorney opponents still were waiting for the results—that Andrew Fuller had defeated incumbent Bruce Udolf.

Fuller's supporters gathered at his house to man the phones, listen to radios and tally the results. When good news was announced, cheers began in the kitchen, and spread through the living room and downstairs into the den.

"I think we've run an issue-oriented campaign," Fuller said. "We've worked hard, traveled a lot of miles and talked to a lot of people. I feel like the large voter turnout was an indication that people of this area were interested in this race."

Meanwhile, Udolf has charged Fuller with running a "sleazy" campaign, demanding a public apology from him.

Suzanne Wood and Debbie McDonald, "Fuller Unseats Udolf as DA" *The Times* (Gainesville, Georgia), August 13, 1986, p.1.

evidence is the starting point. But perhaps equally important is insight into the psychological and sociological dynamics of juries, judges, defendants, and witnesses. What looks like an unbeatable case to a law professor may appear to be a case with major difficulties to a seasoned trial prosecutor.

Negotiating

negotiating

Only a handful of cases are ever tried; the rest are pled out or dismissed. One of the most important tasks of the prosecutor is to *negotiate* with the opposition. Reputation as a trial attorney is an important factor in negotiations. An advocate will exploit a weakness; poor trial attorneys therefore make poor negotiators as well. Like trial work, negotiating requires numerous tactical decisions. Does this type of case and type of defense attorney suggest that it is best to divulge the prosecutor's whole case in hopes of inducing a guilty plea? Or would it be better to play it close to the vest and tell the opposition nothing? During negotiations, attorneys must constantly reevaluate the weaknesses of their own case and the strengths of the opposition. For example, a victim's reluctance to testify may necessitate a lesser sentence than normal.

Drafting

drafting

briefs

Courts are paper bureaucracies. Like many other governmental bodies, no decisions can be made, no case advanced from one step to the next, without the proper paperwork. While the clerk of the court is primarily responsible for keeping these papers in order, the prosecutor is the one charged with *drafting*—preparing—these vital documents. Search warrants, for example, are often prepared by the prosecutor's office. When charges are filed, the prosecutor must specify the section of the criminal code that the defendant allegedly violated. The prosecutor must also prepare motions involving defense allegations that evidence was improperly seized or that a confession was coerced. Most of the prosecutor's legal research involves preparing such motions and *briefs* (the technical term for the form in which written arguments are presented to the court). At the close of the trial the prosecutor is involved in the preparation of the final charge to the jury. And after conviction, the prosecutor must prepare and argue before the appellate court. If documents are not properly prepared, either the case may be irretrievably lost or much extra effort may have to be expended later to remedy the initial mistake.

Counseling

counseling

A critical aspect of a lawyer's responsibility is advising and *counseling* clients. Just as patients judge doctors by their bedside manner, lawyers are often measured by their friendly, courteous, and understanding relationship with their clients. In the prosecutor's case, the counseling dimension is complicated because the prosecutor's client is the state. Nonetheless, prosecutors spend part of their time talking to victims, witnesses, and police officers. Before trial a lawyer must prepare witnesses by going over the questions to be asked, advising them how to testify, and telling them matters to be avoided. A poorly coached witness can easily cause an acquittal or a hung jury. Prosecutors counsel victims of crimes about why a plea bargain was entered into or why the charges were dropped. It is not unusual for a victim to want to prosecute to the fullest but for the lawyer to believe that no crime was committed. Prosecutors must also advise police about why a case is weak, what additional evidence is needed, and so on.

Administering

administer-
ing

Like the other members of the courtroom team, prosecutors handle a large volume of cases. A typical big city prosecutor, for example, has a yearly work-load of one hundred cases (Jacoby). A major concern of prosecutors is *administration*—keeping the cases moving. In doing so they carry out a number of important administrative responsibilities. In a number of jurisdictions, prosecutors are responsible for setting dates for trial; as the case approaches trial, they must make sure subpoenas are issued for all the witnesses they plan to call. Faced with numerous cases, district attorneys and their top aides must decide how to allocate resources. For example, should some attorneys be shifted from an existing section to make room for a new division in white-collar crime? In the largest offices, simply keeping the bureaucracy running—hiring new assistants, promoting deserving old assistants, preparing and fighting for the budget—consumes major amounts of time.

Assistant District Attorneys

On a day-to-day basis the work of the prosecutor's office is executed by the assistants. Recruiting, training, socializing, and supervising these assistant

---

QUOTATION

For the first week or two, I went to court with guys who had been here. Just sat there and watched. What struck me was the amount of things he [the prosecutor] has to do in the courtroom. The prosecutor runs the courtroom. Although the judge is theoretically in charge, we're standing there plea bargaining and calling the cases at the same time and chewing gum and telling the people to quiet down and setting bonds, and that's what amazed me. I never thought I would learn all the terms. What bothered me also was the paperwork. Not the Supreme Court decisions, not the *mens rea* or any of this other stuff, but the amount of junk that's in those files that you have to know. We never heard about this crap in law school.

Quoted in Milton Heumann, *Plea Bargaining* (Chicago: University of Chicago Press, 1978).

district attorneys have a major bearing on how prosecutorial power and discretion are exercised.

assistant district attorneys

Most ***assistant district attorneys*** (sometimes called deputy district attorneys) are hired directly after graduation from law school or after a short time in private practice. Typically, they have attended local law schools rather than the nation's most prestigious law schools, whose graduates prefer higher status, better paying jobs in civil practice. Traditionally, big city prosecutors hired assistants on the basis of party affiliation and the recommendations of ward leaders and elected officials. Increasingly, however, greater stress is being placed on merit selection, a trend exemplified by the Los Angeles prosecutor's office—the nation's largest and probably most professional—where hiring is on a civil service basis.

turnover

The ***turnover*** rate among assistant district attorneys is quite high. Most serve only an average of two to four years before entering private practice. Low salaries are one reason for the high turnover rate. Although starting salaries are generally competitive with those in private law offices, after a few years the salary levels are markedly less. The high rate of turnover is also a product of the nature of the office. Prosecutors' offices present numerous openings for braves, but only a few chiefs are needed. After two years on the job, the

---

CONTROVERSY

Stormy Prosecutor Roils Florida Political Waters

To his supporters, Robert W. Merkle is a folk hero, a combative Federal prosecutor who is undaunted by political pressure as he pursues corrupt officeholders and illegal drug traffickers, a colorful troubadour whose ballads and comical impressions have added a satirical edge to his battle with the legal and political establishments.

But to his critics, who include the state's Republican Governor, its two Democratic Senators, prominent lawyers and major newspapers, he is a reckless zealot who has abused the powers of his office and smeared the reputations of innocent people.

Mr. Merkle, a Republican who has been United States Attorney in Florida's Middle District since 1983, is at the center of a political contro-

versy that has reached the White House, where officials are considering whether to replace him to appease Gov. Bob Martinez, whose political allies include Jeb Bush, son of the Vice President. Mr. Merkle's term expired last April and since then he has served at the pleasure of the President.

The furor over the conduct of Mr. Merkle, a 42-year-old former football player at Notre Dame whose nickname is Mad Dog Merkle, crested earlier this month: Mr. Martinez, two days after his inauguration, found himself confronting Mr. Merkle in a Federal courtroom as a defense witness for Nelson Italiano, a prominent Tampa Democrat accused of mail fraud involving a cable television bribery scheme. Mr. Italiano was convicted.

Governor on Witness Stand

For almost five hours, the Governor, who was not charged with a crime, defended himself against the allegations of a government witness, Eddie Perdomo, who said he had given Mr. Martinez $8,000 in campaign contributions and cash gifts in 1979, when Mr. Martinez was a candidate for mayor of Tampa, as part of an attempt to buy favors for the cable television company.

While the Governor was testifying, his chief of staff, J. M. Stipanovich, said Mr. Martinez had called Mitch Daniels, the White House political director, to ask that President Reagan replace Mr. Merkle, a move that heightened the political drama surrounding the case. "There's nothing partisan about him,"

young assistants have learned about all they will learn—there are only a few ways to prosecute a burglary case and only a few possible defenses to counter. Young assistants looking for new challenges turn either to promotion to an elite, specialized unit within the office—armed robbery or murder, for example—where trials are more numerous and more demanding, or they turn to private practice. Finally, some assistants grow tired of the job. The criminal courthouse, with its constant, never-ending stream of society's losers, can become a depressing place to work. And constant trial work creates numerous physical and psychological pressures. Being a trial attorney is only for the young. Most assistants view their job as a brief way station toward a more lucrative and more varied private practice.

Learning the Job

Most assistant DAs have been admitted to the practice of law only recently and therefore are unfamiliar with the day-to-day realities of their profession. Although law schools provide an overview of major areas of the law—criminal law, tax, torts, and contracts, to name just a few—they give their students very little exposure to how law is actually practiced.

Mr. Stipanovich said in an interview. "This man believes he was commissioned by God to smite politicians."

Some critics contend that Mr. Merkle, whatever his legal skills, is tempermentally unsuited for his job, that he goes out of his way to personalize his battles with elected officials and lawyers. He can be as provocative outside the courtroom as inside, they say.

Mr. Merkle, the father of nine children, has won strong support from anti-abortion groups by denouncing the Supreme Court decision legalizing abortion as "judicial tyranny."

He often ends his speeches to local audiences by picking up his guitar and singing a song he composed, "My Heroes Have Always Been Lawyers," which some lawyers view as a slur on their profession.

"How can he not be popular with a lot of people?"

asked one lawyer here. "He goes out of his way to show his contempt for lawyers and politicians."

The St. Petersburg Times, a critic of Mr. Merkle, published two editorials this month calling for his dismissal, saying in one that Mr. Merkle "has built a record of prosecuting people without evidence to convict and smearing those he lacked evidence to indict."

The jury convicted Mr. Italiano of mail fraud, but apparently without giving much consideration to the allegations against Mr. Martinez. "We didn't really pay much attention to it," said Edward Heitger, the jury foreman.

At a news conference, Mr. Merkle defended his decision to present the Perdomo testimony against the Governor to

the jury, saying the Federal judge in the case had ruled that it was admissible to lay out the full scope of the bribery scheme. "If you accuse me of misconduct," he said, "then you are accusing the judge of misconduct."

His critics say the Martinez case is typical of the tactics Mr. Merkle has used to damage the reputations of other prominent citizens who were never charged with crimes. For example, they say, Mr. Merkle investigated E. J. Salcines, the Hillsborough County State Attorney, for three years, yet never brought charges against him. Mr. Salcines was defeated for re-election after news reports disclosed that he had invoked his Fifth Amendment rights against self-incrimination before a Federal grand jury.

Phil Gailey, "Stormy Prosecutor Roils Political Waters in Florida," *New York Times,* January 20, 1987, p. 7. ©1987 by The New York Times Company. Reprinted by permission.

training

For decades the position of assistant district attorney has provided young attorneys with the opportunity to serve an apprenticeship in legal practice primarily on the job. It was not unusual in the past for new employees—with no experience—to be sent into court their first day on the job. More recently large prosecutor offices have begun to provide new employees with a systematic introduction to the work to **train** them. New assistants are given a week of general orientation to the various divisions of the office, are allowed to watch various proceedings, and often observe veteran trial attorneys at work. Such formalized indoctrination is still relatively rare, however.

Young assistants quickly learn to ask questions of more experienced prosecutors, court clerks, and veteran police officers, who are willing to share their knowledge about courtroom procedures. Through this socialization process, new assistants learn the important unwritten rules about legal practice. The courthouse environment has developed shared conceptions of what types of violations should be punished and the appropriate penalties to be applied to such violations. Assistants learn that their performance (and chances for promotion) are measured by how promptly and efficiently they dispose of cases. They become sensitive to "hints"—for example, a judge complaining that prosecutors are bringing too many minor cases and a backlog is developing usually conveys the message to the new assistant that she is pressing too hard.

promotion

Promotions are also tied to reputations as a trial attorney. Assistants are invariably judged by the number of convictions they obtain. In the courthouse environment, though, not losing a case has a higher value than winning. Thus, young assistants learn that if the guilt of the defendant is doubtful or the offender is not dangerous, it is better to negotiate a plea rather than disrupt the courtroom routine by attempting to gain a jury conviction.

Promotions and Office Structure

As assistants gain experience and settle into the courthouse routine, they are promoted to more demanding and also more interesting tasks. Promotions are tied to office structure. In small prosecutors' offices, assistants are given a case at the time charges are filed to follow through arraignment, preliminary hearing, pretrial motions, trial, sentencing, and, if necessary, appeal. In these offices assistants are promoted by being given more serious cases. While such an assignment system reflects the lawyer–client relationship, it is administratively burdensome in large courthouses; assistants would spend much of their time moving from one courtroom to another and wasting time while waiting for their one or two cases to be called. Therefore most big city prosecutors assign personnel on a zone basis: screening, misdemeanor, arraignment, preliminary hearing, trial, and so on. Most commonly, prosecutors have specialized bureaus for major offenses (drug, homicide, armed robbery, and white-collar crime), which are staffed by most experienced trial attorneys. (Figure 6-1 provides a typical example.) These specialized units are the most prestigious mainly because trial work is plentiful and challenging. This means that on a regular basis one or two attorneys are regularly assigned to one courtroom with a given judge. The consequence is that through time prosecutors come to know the judge's views on sentencing and so on.

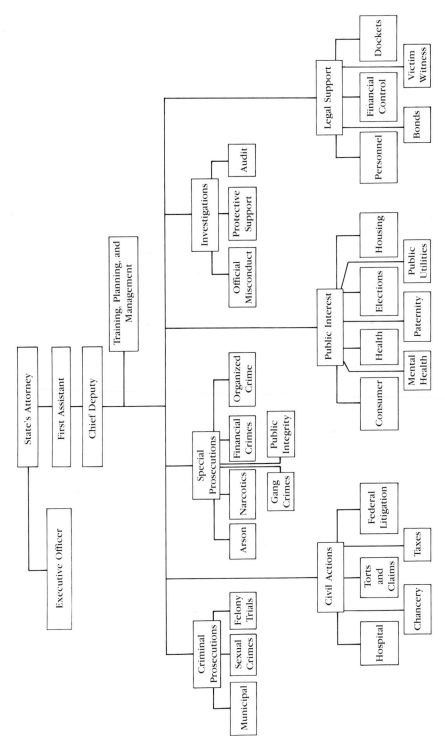

Figure 6-1 Office of the Cook County, Illinois, State's Attorney

Supervision

supervision Assistant district attorneys are ***supervised*** by a bureau chief, who is supposed to ensure that they follow policies of the office. Most prosecutors' offices have general policies, but these are often somewhat vague and in small offices are seldom even reduced to writing. They are simply part of what the young assistant learns informally.

For several reasons, however, assistant district attorneys enjoy fairly great freedom. Supervisors can exert only limited control over individual cases or individual assistants. They spend most of their time out of the office in the

CLOSE-UP

The Prosecutor: A Maze of Paper Work Without End

The defendant was dead, and to Michael J. Meagher, a 26-year-old assistant district attorney in Manhattan, this unexpected turn was less a cause for sentiment than for reassessing his caseload. It was the kind of thing that happened in his job, a job that lurched easily from boredom to bafflement.

Mr. Meagher learned of the death about 9 A.M. on June 15, a day when, as a junior prosecutor in an office of 320 lawyers, he was responsible for handling or helping to handle more than 100 misdemeanor cases in A.P. 1, one of the six "all purpose" parts of Criminal Court in Manhattan.

As usual, he had bicycled to work at 1 Hogan Place, in lower Manhattan, from his apartment near Gramercy Park. Mr. Meagher opened a steaming container of coffee and, amid the constant jangling of telephones, began poring over a two-foot-high stack of case files. In one, relating to an assault charge, he found a message saying the defendant had suddenly died.

"Well, that really helps me," Mr. Meagher mused aloud. But as with many matters in the congested Criminal Court, things were somewhat more complex. The dead man was scheduled to be a key witness for the prosecution in another case.

A Variety of Cases

Mr. Meagher hung the coat of his gray suit on the back of a chair, straightened his red paisley tie and hurried through the other files. There were cases of disorderly conduct, trespassing, petty larceny and drug possession, all marked for the day's calendar.

In nearly a year as a prosecutor—he was recruited by the District Attorney's office last spring, during his final semester at Cornell Law School—Mr. Meagher has had as many as 150 active cases of his own at one time. But in a criminal-justice system in which the vast majority of cases end in guilty pleas or dismissals, he has tried fewer than 10 cases and only three before a jury.

Mr. Meagher's appearances in A.P. 1 reflect only one of his duties as a $21,000-a-year assistant in Criminal Court.

At other times, he works in an arraignment part or in the complaint room; interviews police officers and witnesses and draws up charges; monitors lineups; orders laboratory reports on illegal substances; writes parole letters; works on his own cases, and, occasionally, drafts an appeal brief.

This day, June 15, was barely under way for him. With court scheduled to open at 9:30 A.M.—A.P. 1 is on the fourth floor of Criminal Court at 100 Centre Street, the same building that houses the District Attorney's office—Mr. Meagher badgered his colleagues for missing case notes, grabbed his jacket and bundle of files and dashed for the elevator.

Judge Leslie Snyder, who was appointed to the Criminal Court three months ago, presided—and mediated. Mr. Meagher, Russell Neufeld, a Legal Aid lawyer, and other lawyers plodded through the calendar for several hours, but much of what they had to say about this case or that was said off the record at bench conferences with the judge.

Some cases were dismissed for lack of witnesses or evidence. In a few, trial dates were set but will almost cer-

courtroom and therefore have difficulty being physically present to observe and possibly monitor the young DA's activities. Indeed, in crowded courthouses the trial assistants may have offices adjoining the judge's chambers and only rarely appear in the prosecutor's office at all. The effect of this lack of physical proximity is underscored by the types of decisions that must be made and how they are made. Each assistant has dozens of cases that require individual decisions on the basis of specific facts, unique witness problems, and so on. A supervisor has no way to monitor such situations except on the basis of what the assistant relates or writes in the file. Here as elsewhere,

---

tainly be delayed for lack of trial parts. Many pleas seemed dependent on a promise from Judge Snyder that the defendant would not be jailed. Mr. Meagher, juggling one bluejacketed misdemeanor file after another, was ordered to provide a number of defendants with "open file discovery," or access to the prosecution's records on the case. In many instances, the defendant did not appear, and Judge Snyder ordered the familiar P.R.W.O., parole revoked, warrant ordered.

"The joke in Criminal Court," Mr. Meagher remarked later, "is that trial is spelled P.R.W.O."

A grocery-store worker who had had a gun under disputed circumstances pleaded guilty to a reduced charge of criminal possession of a weapon. He stood before Judge Snyder with his hands behind his back, saying little. Sentencing was put off until August.

A man who had hit a police car while "coming from the wake of a very close friend" received a $250 fine and revocation of his license for drunken driving. A woman who was wanted for shoplifting and had apparently used dozens of aliases had her case postponed.

Perhaps the low point of

Mr. Meagher's morning came at 10:45, when Judge Snyder dismissed a drug case "for failure to prosecute." A laboratory report on the substance at issue, suspected to be cocaine, had been lost in the maze of paper work that accompanies any case through the system, and the judge said she would wait no longer for it.

At lunch, bought at a snack bar, Mr. Meagher washed down a yogurt with iced tea. He graduated from Marquette University in Milwaukee with a view to teaching American history in college. He earned a master's degree in history before opting for something with a prospect of "concrete problems that needed to be addressed."

"The most disappointing thing I've seen on the job is the way victims are treated by the system," he said. "If you've ever seen an innocent victim intimidated by a defendant or reduced to tears on a stand, well, it drives me insane. It's not hard to understand why a lot of people don't want to cooperate."

Mr. Meagher said he was also surprised by "how little

result we get from prosecuting chronic offenders."

"They keep coming back," he said. "You can affect some situations, but it's mostly at the margins."

At 2 P.M., Mr. Meagher was again wrapped in the mystery of A.P. 1.

In one case he brushed off a suggestion by Mr. Neufeld of Legal Aid that a recent crackdown on drunken drivers was the result of "political pressure" and needed to be tested constitutionally at trial. Why, Mr. Meagher asked, couldn't the defendant "count down from 10" when he was arrested? And "what about the two rum-and-Coke glasses on the front seat?"

Then he and Mr. Neufeld tangled over a case of a man charged with patronizing a prostitute.

"Is that being prosecuted these days?" Mr. Neufeld asked incredulously.

Mr. Meagher managed a smile. "It certainly is, unless there's a plea to the charge."

Judge Snyder looked at the combatants and adjourned the matter.

"Anyway," she sighed, "every case here gets decided on its own merits."

M. A. Farber, "The Prosecutor: A Maze of Paper Work Without End," *New York Times,* June 28, 1983, p. 13. © 1983 by The New York Times Company. Reprinted by permission.

information is power. Assistants can control their supervisors by selectively telling them what they think they should know (Neubauer).

Perhaps most important, assistant district attorneys are professionals licensed by society to exercise special and unique powers, most of which center on their ability to exercise judgment. Moreover, assistants view their brief tenure in office as an apprenticeship for learning the practice of law. Attempts by supervisors to control the work of the assistants invariably seriously erode the morale of the office, with assistants arguing that their professional status has been reduced to that of a clerk.

Attempts at Greater Supervision

The typical autonomy of the individual assistant district attorney has resulted in what Joan Jacoby has called the unit style. Each assistant makes his or her own decisions. A number of big city prosecutors have become concerned that this unit style allows too much unchecked discretion. In such cities as Detroit and New Orleans, prosecutors have imposed bureaucratic controls. Decisions on charging and plea bargaining are scrutinized by supervisors. A trial assistant, for example, is not allowed to offer a plea less than the original charge filed unless prior permission is granted. Moreover, these offices compile statistics on all aspects of the unit to allow supervisors to more effectively manage the work of the office and to spot any changes or potential problems. Head prosecutors believe that these management systems monitor prosecutorial discretion, minimize differences between individual assistants, and concentrate scarce crime-fighting resources (Jacoby).

Prosecutors and Courtroom Work Groups

Much of the prosecutor's time is spent working directly with other members of the courtroom work group. Even when interviewing witnesses, conducting legal research, or reviewing a file, the prosecutor is anticipating the reactions of judges and defendants. Thus the activities of prosecutors and assistant prosecutors can be understood only within the setting of the courtroom work group.

Generally the prosecutor is the most important member of the courtroom work group. How the prosecutor exercises the discretionary powers of the office sets the agenda for judges and defense attorneys—the types of cases prosecuted, the nature of plea agreements, and the sentences to be handed out. In addition, the prosecutor has more information about the case than anyone else: police reports, records of previous arrests and convictions, physical evidence, and laboratory tests.

A prosecutor's actions are in turn influenced by other members of the courtroom work group. Through the socialization process the assistant prosecutor's evaluation of a case is influenced by the courthouse environment. The pleas normally agreed to and the sentences typically imposed on the guilty reflect the shared norms of the courtroom.

Prosecutors who stray too far from accepted ways of doing things can expect sanctions. The judge may informally indicate that the state is pushing too hard for a harsh sentence. Or the judge may verbally chastise a district attorney in open court, thus threatening the attorney's status among peers. The defense attorney might not agree to a prosecutor's request for a continuance, might use delaying tactics to impair the state's efforts to schedule cases, or might even call for a jury trial, thus further disrupting the prosecutor's and the court's efforts to move the cases. (The prosecutor is not without countersanctions. These will be discussed in the following two chapters.)

The actions of the prosecutor, then, are constrained by other members of the courtroom work group. Within these constraints, effective assistant DAs are the ones who make tactical decisions that maximize their objectives. Prosecutors, for example, learn which defense attorneys have reputations for persuasiveness at trial. Attorneys with such reputations are more likely to obtain dismissals or reduced charges from the prosecutor. Assistants also learn which defense attorneys can be trusted and grant these people greater access to the prosecutor's information about the case. They are also more likely to be listened to when they present an argument that the case involves unusual circumstances. Prosecutors quickly learn the tendencies of the judge. No experienced prosecutor can afford to ignore how the judge wishes the courtroom to be run. On the other hand, the prosecutor can attempt to maneuver the case before a favorable judge and can also stress or withhold information to influence the judge's decision.

Contrasting Work Groups

The work of the prosecutor reflects two important considerations about America's criminal court process. First, prosecutors possess an immense amount of discretion. Second, they exercise this discretion in the context of other courtroom actors (the courtroom work group). In combination, these factors produce marked diversity. William McDonald cautions, therefore, that we must consider the domains of the prosecutor not as fixed by law and tradition but rather as blurred, shared, evolving, and open to negotiation. A study by Pamela Utz highlights this marked diversity. She examined two prosecutors' offices, in San Diego and Oakland, California. Despite the fact that both were operating within the same legal environment, Utz discovered contrasting operating styles.

The prosecutor in San Diego reflects an adversarial model. Assistant district attorneys presume that cases are serious, routinely overcharge, and set plea bargaining terms so high that many cases are forced to trial. Because there is a pronounced distrust of defense attorneys, plea bargaining involves a gamelike atmosphere. In general, the San Diego office is dedicated to the "full enforcement" of the law.

The operating style in Oakland, on the other hand, reflects a magisterial model. There are office policies about which types of cases involve serious violations of the law, and there are also strict standards in terms of charging. The office philosophy is that if the case is not "prison material," then there should be no trial. Plea bargaining proceeds on the basis that defense attorneys are fellow professionals. Overall, there appears to be more of a search for the truth in Oakland than in San Diego.

The contrasts in operating style between San Diego and Oakland reflect what James Eisenstein has labeled the competing perspectives of the law enforcement approach and the officer of the court approach. These competing perspectives are the subject of the next section.

Conflicting Goals

At first the goals of the prosecutor's office seem the model of simplicity: their job is to convict the guilty. But a closer examination shows that the goals are not as clear-cut as they first appear.

Prosecutors may define their main job in different ways. Some may serve primarily as trial counsel to the police department and thus reflect the views of the police. Others act as "house counsel" to the police; they give legal advice to the department on enforcement practices that will withstand challenge in court. Still others consider themselves mainly representatives of the court; they enforce rules designed to control police practices and act in other similar ways for the benefit of the accused. Finally, some prosecutors, as elected officials, try to reflect the opinion of the community in making their decisions (LaFave). The uncertainties about which of these tasks should come first create many of the dynamic issues facing American prosecutors.

On the one hand, prosecutors are law enforcement officials; this implies that their primary duty is to protect society. In the adversary system the prosecutor is expected to advocate the guilt of the defendant vigorously. But at the same time, the prosecutor is a lawyer and is therefore an *officer of the court*; that is, he or she has a duty to see that justice is done. Violations of the law must be prosecuted, but in a way that guarantees that the defendant's rights

officer of the court

Q U O T A T I O N

I get so damned pissed off and tired of these guys who come in and cry, "My guy's got a job" or "My guy's about to join the army," when he's got a rap sheet as long as your arm. His guy's a loser, and he's wailing on my desk about what a fine man he is. What really wins me is the guy who comes in and says, "O.K., what are we going to do with my criminal today? I know he has no redeeming social value. He's been a bad son of a bitch all his life, so just let me know your position. But frankly, you know, my feeling is that this is just not the case to nail him on. We all know if he does something serious, he's going." And before long the guy who approaches it this way has you wrapped around his little finger.

Quoted in Lief Carter, *The Limits of Order* (Lexington, Mass.: D. C. Heath, 1974), p. 87.

are respected and protected. In a 1935 Supreme Court decision, Justice Sutherland spelled out the limitations that the officer of the court obligation imposes on prosecutors: "He may prosecute with earnestness and vigor—indeed, he should do so. But while he may strike hard blows, he is not at liberty to strike foul ones. It is as much his duty to refrain from improper methods calculated to produce a wrongful conviction as it is to use every legitimate means to bring about a just one" (*Berger* v. *U.S.*, 295 U.S. 78, 1935).

The Supreme Court has held that because prosecutors are officers of the court, they have an obligation to provide the defense with information that may show innocence. Defense attorneys, though, are under no obligation to provide the prosecution with incriminating evidence. If prosecutors conceal or misrepresent evidence, such misbehavior can be sanctioned by a reversal of the conviction.

law enforcement approach

officer of the court approach

James Eisenstein has aptly labeled the two competing perspectives as the ***law enforcement approach*** and the ***officer of the court approach.*** Because of the varied environment in which prosecutors operate—pressures from judges, defense attorneys, police officers, and so on—it should not be surprising to discover that different prosecutors come to emphasize differing orientations. A survey of prosecutors in Kentucky found that almost half stated that they viewed their job in terms of being a law enforcement official, while the remainder came closer to the officer of the court orientation (Engstrom).

The differing orientations of American prosecutors appear to be related to varying goals. Prosecutors with a law enforcement orientation are more likely to stress punishing the guilty. And those with an officer of the court approach are more likely to define their major goal as securing convictions.

Police and Prosecutors

The police and prosecutor are commonly viewed as members of the same crime-fighting team. Newspapers often refer to police–prosecutor spokesmen, particularly when they are reporting on negative reactions to Supreme Court decisions. Television shows project the image of the prosecutor working with the police to fight crime. Such a linkage appears natural. Not only are police and prosecutor dedicated to the same overall goal—imposing sanctions on criminal behavior—but they also work together on a day-to-day basis. Each is dependent on the other. The prosecutor must rely on the police to provide the evidence necessary for a conviction. Similarly, the police are not satisfied merely with arresting an offender; they also want sanctions applied and therefore look to the prosecutor to ensure that the guilty are convicted and sentenced.

Embedded in this relationship, however, are potentials for conflict. Police spokesmen, for example, are often publicly critical of the local district attorney for dismissing too many cases or bargaining too many out. In turn, prosecutors are often privately critical of the police for conducting inadequate investigations. In *Helter Skelter*, Vincent Bugliosi describes how he was able to secure a conviction against Charles Manson for the bloody ritualistic murders of several Hollywood celebrities, including the movie actress Sharon Tate. One of the minor themes of the book is how the prosecutor's office had to overcome slip-shod investigation by the Los Angeles Police Department. Studies in California, Wisconsin, and Illinois have shown varying degrees of tension between the prosecutor's office and the police departments (Carter; Milner; Neubauer).

The Prosecutor as Police Legal Adviser

Prosecutors depend on the police for their raw materials: arrests and investigations. How the police conduct investigations and the legality of the searches they make affect how the prosecutor processes cases and the likelihood of obtaining a conviction. If the police do not prepare complete and accurate reports—if, for instance, they fail to provide full names and addresses of victims and witnesses, leave out details of how the crime was committed, or neglect to include vital laboratory reports—the prosecutor may be forced to

---

QUOTATION

*T*he prosecutor should be aware of the importance of the function of his office for other agencies of the criminal justice system and for the public at large. He should maintain relationships that encourage interchange of views and information and that maximize coordination of the various agencies of the criminal justice system.

The prosecutor should maintain regular liaison with the police department in order to provide legal advice to the police, to identify mutual problems and to develop solutions to those problems. He should participate in police training programs and keep the police informed about current developments in law enforcement, such as significant court decisions. He should develop and maintain a liaison with the police legal adviser in those areas relating to police-prosecutor relationships.

The prosecutor should develop for the use of the police a basic police report form that includes all relevant information about the offense and the offender necessary for charging, plea negotiations, and trial. The completed form should be routinely forwarded to the prosecutor's office after the offender has been processed by the police. Police officers should be informed by the prosecutor of the disposition of any case with which they were involved and the reason for the disposition.

National Advisory Commission on Criminal Justice Standards and Goals, *Courts* (Washington, D.C.: Government Printing Office, 1973), p. 247.

drop charges. District attorneys also depend on police officers to testify before grand juries, during pretrial hearings, and at trials. If police officers forget court appearances or are not subpoenaed, cases may be delayed or lost altogether. The police often believe that an arrest closes the case, but the prosecutors believe they need additional information to win in court.

Inadequate police reports present a classic illustration of non-coordination within the criminal justice system. Most police officers have only a limited knowledge of the criminal law and the evidence required to sustain a conviction in court. Prosecutors, however, have done little to bridge the gap. Few try to provide legal counsel to the police (President's Commission). By and large, the contacts between police and prosecutor are routine and formalized: the police file reports, which the prosecutors process. Over time, individual police officers, usually detectives, often develop a working relationship with specific prosecutors. Rarely, however, do the top officials of the organizations confer on mutual problems. For example, when the Prairie City (Illinois) prosecutor's office was faced with a question of how to handle domestic disturbances, it made a policy decision that the police would be responsible for determining whether criminal charges should be filed. Although this policy had a major impact on the police, the police chief and his staff were not contacted. Moreover, most prosecutor's offices do not require that the assistants spend time at the police station or on patrol seeing the process through the eyes of the policemen. When assistants do spend time riding with the police, it is usually without encouragement from their superiors.

Police View the Prosecutor

Police voice a number of complaints about prosecutors. One is that prosecutors review cases superficially and do not prosecute when they should. The police also generally dislike plea bargaining practices, believing that DAs allow too many defendants to escape with light penalties. They are also frustrated by the absence of legal advice for police and complain that prosecutors display condescending attitudes toward them.

Varying Perspectives on the Law

Tensions between police and prosecutors are partially the result of inadequate communication between the two separate organizations. But conflict between the two is also the product of varying perspectives on the law. Police and prosecutors see the law in very different terms.

Police and prosecutors usually come from different social backgrounds (Skolnick; McNamara; Reiss and Bordua; Niederhoffer). Most policemen are recruited from the working class; prosecutors are likely to have middle-class backgrounds. These differences in social background are magnified by differences in education. Most police seldom have worked beyond a high school diploma, but all prosecutors are college graduates with a professional degree. The police and prosecutors also approach their law enforcement jobs from decidedly different vantage points. For police officers, particularly detectives, their job is a permanent career; for prosecutors, law enforcement is a way station on the road to private legal practice.

These differences in social background, education, and career commitments produce markedly different perspectives on the law. An in-depth study of police reactions to the law showed the police are hostile to the formal law, especially to the procedural restrictions on their activities. For example, police officers view themselves as experts in criminal investigation, but the courts refuse to recognize such expertise, a refusal the police regard as unjustified (Skolnick). Thus, standards conflict about what the police should do. One set of standards is based on norms of the police organization and another set is based on the law. As Reiss and Bordua comment, the courts often find fault with an officer's conduct that may have been "well within the reasonable limits of departmental policy or regulation" (Reiss and Bordua). Police often view the procedural restrictions of the law as unreasonable. Prosecutors, however, view the law from a different perspective. To be sure, prosecutors may be critical of some restrictions on the police. Nevertheless prosecutors have been trained in the law and the law's dedication to protecting individual rights. They are more likely to understand the reasons for such restrictions and are not as critical of procedural restrictions on the police.

Two types of prosecutorial decisions illustrate these differing perspectives. During the charging decision, the police and prosecutor often have divergent expectations. The police think that a valid arrest should be followed by prosecution. To the district attorney, however, a reasonable and valid arrest might not produce sufficient evidence for conviction. The same differences arise during the drafting of search warrants. Typically the police come to the district attorney's office, state their problem, and ask how to search (or perform similar tasks) in conformity with the law. They want answers. But the prosecutors are unable to provide the certainty that the police desire. Where the police see simple problems, the prosecutors see complex issues and respond, "It's six of this and half a dozen of the other."

Reformers often assume that increased contact between the prosecutor and police will lead to a higher level of legal sophistication on the part of the latter. What they fail to realize is that fundamentally different views of the law are involved. Indeed, increased contacts may only produce increased friction. I spent six months observing the activities of a prosecutor's office in central Illinois and witnessed several police–prosecutor meetings that led to abrasive interactions, not educational dialogue. Both sides became more annoyed without attempting to understand the other's position (Neubauer).

The Work Environment

The work environments of the police and the prosecutor produce different perspectives, too. The primary task of police officers is to locate and arrest suspects; prosecutors are primarily interested in convicting. For the police the most relevant area is the scene of the crime; for the prosecutor the arena is the courtroom. Prosecutors spend most of their time in court or talking with defense attorneys and judges outside of court. In short, they find themselves in the middle. The police view the prosecutor as their spokesman in court; however, the prosecutor must work with the judges and defense attorneys and is subject to their pressures. One major pressure is the need to dispose of cases.

Prosecutors have many more cases than they can try. As a result, most cases are disposed of by bargaining with the defendant and reaching a compromise. Not surprisingly, the police may view such compromises as selling them out.

> Police get conditioned to the idea that we are the only people with our finger in the criminal dike in this country. They feel that everyone else "lets him go." Police differ from the D.A. The D.A. is satisfied with the conviction, finding him guilty. But police want him punished. They become outraged when the result of their work is ignored. "What if they let him off, I get him tomorrow: those bastards kiss him on the cheek and let 'em go," is their attitude of how the D.A. and the judge handle their cases. (Reiss and Bordua: 37)

It is apparent that the police and prosecutor want different results from the ultimate court process. The police want vindication: a conviction for the crime charged is positive reinforcement that the police officer is doing his or her job. Prosecutors, however, pursue goals other than convictions.

Conclusion

The prosecutor is the most important official in the criminal courts system. By law and custom, prosecutors possess wide-ranging discretionary powers. The exercise of this discretion makes for the dynamics of the courthouse. In effect, all others involved in the criminal courts—judges, defense attorneys, probation officers, juries, witnesses, and so on—must react to the decisions made by the prosecutor. But as we have seen, the law imposes few formal restrictions on the use of these discretionary powers. Not only are prosecutors' offices decentralized, they are also headed by locally elected officials. Moreover, the young assistants who make most of the key decisions are generally attorneys fresh out of law school with little background in how the law is actually administered. Most will serve only a short time before entering the private practice of law.

This does not mean that prosecutorial discretion is uncontrolled; rather it is influenced by other members of the courtroom work group. Through the socialization process and the occasional application of sanctions, young prosecutors are educated in the norms of the courtroom work groups.

For Discussion

1. How important do you think local autonomy is in the operations of the prosecutor? What benefits and drawbacks would act to control prosecutors at the state level?

2. Given that prosecutors are generally elected officials, what effect does this have? Is it desirable to have the chief law enforcement official responsive to public opinion?

3. Interview a prosecutor. Of the five major tasks—fighting, negotiating, counseling, drafting, and administering—what are the most important? Why? Which tasks take the most time?

4. What kinds of controls should be placed on an assistant prosecutor's discretion?

5. Discuss the ways prosecutorial discretion is influenced by courtroom work groups. If possible, discuss with a prosecutor his or her relationships with judges and defense attorneys.

6. Check local newspapers to see how much is written about the local prosecutor. What do these news items indicate about the goals of the local prosecutor?

7. If you were a prosecutor, would you stress the law enforcement or the officer of the court approach? Why?

References

BUGLIOSI, VINCENT, WITH CURT GENTRY. *Helter Skelter.* New York: Bantam Books, 1974.

CARTER, LIEF H. *The Limits of Order.* Lexington, Mass: D. C. Heath, 1974.

EISENSTEIN, JAMES. "The Federal Prosecutor and His Environment." Paper delivered at the annual meeting of the American Political Science Association, Washington, D.C., September 2–7, 1968.

ENGSTROM, RICHARD. "Political Ambitions and the Prosecutorial Office." *Journal of Politics* 33 (1971): 190.

JACOB, HERBERT. "Judicial Insulation—Elections, Direct Participation, and Public Attention to the Courts in Wisconsin." *Wisconsin Law Review* (Summer 1966): 812.

JACOBY, JOAN. *The American Prosecutor: A Search for Identity.* Lexington, Mass.: D. C. Heath, 1980.

LAFAVE, WAYNE. *Arrest: The Decision to Take a Suspect into Custody.* Boston: Little, Brown, 1965.

MCDONALD, WILLIAM. "The Prosecutor's Domain," in *The Prosecutor,* ed. William McDonald. Beverly Hills, Calif: Sage Publications, 1979.

MCNAMARA, JOHN. "Uncertainties in Police Work," in *The Police: Six Sociological Essays,* ed. David Bordua, pp. 163–252. New York: John Wiley, 1967.

MAYER, MARTIN. *The Lawyers.* New York: Dell Publishing, 1968.

MILNER, NEAL. *The Court and Local Law Enforcement.* Beverly Hills, Calif: Sage Publications, 1971.

MORGAN, ROBERT, AND C. E. ALEXANDER. "A Survey of Local Prosecutors." *State Government* 47 (1972): 42.

NEUBAUER, DAVID. *Criminal Justice in Middle America.* Morristown, N.J.: General Learning Press, 1974.

NIEDERHOFFER, ARTHUR. *Behind the Shield.* Garden City, N.Y.: Doubleday, 1969.

THE PRESIDENT'S COMMISSION ON LAW ENFORCEMENT AND ADMINISTRATION OF JUSTICE. *Task Force Report: The Police.* Washington, D.C.: Government Printing Office, 1967.

REISS, ALBERT J., AND DAVID BORDUA. "Environment and Organization: A Perspective on the Police." In *The Police: Six Sociological Essays,* ed. David Bordua. New York: John Wiley, 1967.

SCHLESINGER, JOSEPH. *Ambition and Politics: Political Careers in the United States.* Chicago: Rand McNally, 1966.

SKOLNICK, JEROME. *Justice Without Trial.* New York: John Wiley, 1967.

U.S. DEPARTMENT OF JUSTICE. Law Enforcement Assistance Administration. *State and Local Prosecution and Civil Attorney Systems.* Washington, D.C.: Government Printing Office, 1978.

UTZ, PAMELA. "Two Models of Prosecutorial Professionalism." In *The Prosecutor,* ed. William McDonald. Beverly Hills, Calif.: Sage Publications, 1979.

For Further Reading

CARTER, LIEF H. *The Limits of Order.* Lexington, Mass.: D. C. Heath, 1974.

DEWEY, THOMAS. *Twenty Against the Underworld.* Garden City, N.Y.: Doubleday, 1974.

EISENSTEIN, JAMES. *Counsel for the United States: U.S. Attorneys in the Political and Legal System.* Baltimore: Johns Hopkins University Press, 1978.

FEELEY, MALCOLM, AND MARK LAZERSON. "Police–Prosecutor Relationships: An Interorganizational Perspective." In *Empirical Theories About Courts,* ed. Keith Boyum and Lynn Mather. New York: Longman, 1983, pp. 216–243.

JACOBY, JOAN. *The American Prosecutor: A Search for Identity.* Lexington, Mass.: D. C. Heath, 1980.

LEZAK, SIDNEY, AND MAUREEN LEONARD. "The Prosecutor's Discretion: Out of the Closet, Not Out of Control." In *Discretion, Justice, and Democracy,* ed. Carl Pinkele and William Louthan. Ames: Iowa State University Press, 1985.

MCDONALD, WILLIAM, ed. *The Prosecutor.* Beverly Hills, Calif.: Sage Publications, 1979.

MILLER, FRANK. *Prosecution: The Decision to Charge a Suspect with a Crime.* Boston: Little, Brown, 1969.

NEUBAUER, DAVID. *Criminal Justice in Middle America.* Morristown, N.J.: General Learning Press, 1974.

NISSMAN, DAVID, AND ED HAGEN. *The Prosecution Function.* Lexington, Mass.: Lexington Books, 1982.

WEIMER, DAVID. *Improving Prosecution? The Inducement and Implementation of Innovations for Prosecution Management.* Westport, Conn.: Greenwood Press, 1980.

CHAPTER 7

Defense Attorneys

In America, the phrase *defense attorney* makes most people think of Perry Mason. As rerun on late-night television, the fictionalized character of Perry Mason embodies our image of the defense attorney fighting to free his falsely accused client. He always succeeded. The public often contrasts this favorable image with a less complimentary one of real attorneys. Concerned about rising crime rates, many Americans also view the defense attorney as a conniver who uses legal technicalities to free the guilty. In the eyes of other members of the legal profession, the defense attorney is a virtual outcast who knows little law and who may engage in unethical behavior. To a client, the one whose future is literally in the lawyer's hands, the defense attorney is often perceived as just another member of the courthouse gang who does not fight hard enough.

This chapter assesses these conflicting images against the daily realities of the small proportion of the legal profession that represents defendants accused of violating the criminal law. The picture is a complicated one. Some defense attorneys suffer from all the shortcomings mentioned by their critics. Others do not. But all face day-to-day problems and challenges not usually encountered by the bulk of American lawyers who represent higher status clients. The key topics of this chapter are the factors influencing the type of legal assistance available to those who appear in criminal courts: the legal right to counsel, the tasks defense attorneys must perform, the relationship they have with courtroom work groups, the nature of the criminal bar, the relationship between lawyer and client, and, finally, differing systems for providing legal assistance to the poor.

The Right to Counsel

right to counsel

Like most other provisions of the U.S. Constitution, the Sixth Amendment has a different meaning today than it did when first inserted into the Constitution. Under the ancient common law, defendants could be tried without a lawyer, even if they wanted to hire their own. The Sixth Amendment was meant to correct this situation by providing the *right to counsel*. But until the early 1960s, this provision did not extend to many felony defendants too poor to hire their own lawyer. A significant minority had to face the legal maze of the courts by themselves. Often this meant that the quality of justice a defendant received depended on the quantity of money she or he possessed.

Gideon v. Wainwright

In *Gideon v. Wainwright* (372 U.S. 335, 1963), the Supreme Court reversed earlier interpretations of the Sixth Amendment. In *Gideon* the Court held that indigent (poor) defendants charged with a felony were entitled to the services of a lawyer paid by the government. Justice Hugo Black's opinion for the Court is worth quoting at length because it aptly summarizes the importance of counsel in the adversary system.

> In our adversary system of criminal justice, any person hailed into court, who is too poor to hire a lawyer, cannot be assured a fair trial unless counsel is provided for him. This seems to us to be an obvious truth . . . there are few defendants charged with crime, few indeed, who fail to hire the best lawyers they can get to prepare and present their defenses.
>
> That government hires lawyers to prosecute and defendants who have the money hire lawyers to defend are the strongest indications of the widespread belief that lawyers in criminal courts are necessities, not luxuries.

Argersinger v. Hamlin

But as so often happens, answering one question raises several new ones. Thus in the wake of *Gideon,* the Court wrestled with the question of extending the right to counsel to include not only felony defendants but also those accused of minor violations (misdemeanor or ordinance violations) as well. In *Argersinger v. Hamlin* (407 U.S. 25, 1972), the Court ruled that "absent a knowing and intelligent waiver, no person may be imprisoned for any offense, whether classified as petty, misdemeanor, or felony, unless he was represented by counsel." This decision requires trial judges to decide before sentencing if a jail sentence is likely; if it is not, there is no need to appoint counsel. Few of the nation's lower courts, however, have taken steps to implement the Court's *Argersinger* decision (Krantz et al.).

The *Gideon* decision spawned another important question: where in the criminal process does the right to counsel begin (and end)? Some argued that the right to legal representation is applicable only after a defendant is officially charged with a crime and brought into court, but the Supreme Court adopted a more expansive view. Note that the Sixth Amendment protects the right to counsel in "all criminal prosecutions," not just the criminal trial. Thus, a defendant is entitled to legal representation at "critical stages" of prosecutions; that is, at every stage "where substantial rights of the accused may be affected" that require the "guiding hand of counsel" (*Mempa* v. *Rhay,* 389 U.S. 128, 1967). These critical stages include arraignment and the preliminary hearing, but not the initial appearance.

Some extensions of *Gideon* proved more controversial than the initial decision itself. In *Miranda* and companion cases, the right to counsel was extended to the police station to include police interrogations and police lineups. Not only did the Warren Court steadily extend the right to counsel at trial and prior to trial, they also applied the right to post-trial proceedings. Working on the assumption that a person's right to one appeal can be effective only if counsel is available, the Court held that indigents have the right to court-appointed counsel for the appeal as well as free transcripts of the trial. To quote the Court, "There can be no equal justice where the kind of trial a man gets depends on the money he has" (*Griffin* v. *Illinois,* 351 U.S. 12, 1956).

Defense Attorneys at Work

advocate

To a large extent, the adversary system depends on defense attorneys. Lawyers are expected to be ***advocates*** for their client's case, arguing for legal innocence. As one defense counsel phrased it, "If the attorney does not appear to be taking the side of the defendant, then no one will" (Neubauer: 73). The adversary system also charges defense attorneys with ensuring that defendants' constitutional rights are respected. Thus, irrespective of guilt or innocence, the defense attorney is a ***challenger*** who must seek out possible violations of these rights. Attorneys must also be ***counselors*** and advise their clients. Finally, defense attorneys must fulfill these responsibilities within the framework established by legal ethics. The zealous advocacy of a client's case is not the same thing as winning at all costs. As a member of the legal profession, a lawyer's advocacy of a client's case is limited by professional obligations. Attorneys are officers of the court and must follow court rules. They cannot deliberately mislead the court by providing false information. Nor can they knowingly allow the use of perjured testimony.

challenger
counselor

We can best dissect the multiple (and sometimes conflicting) responsibilities of defense attorneys by examining their work in fighting, negotiating, drafting, counseling, and administering.

Fighting

The objectives of defense attorneys are diametrically opposed to those of the prosecutor. Whereas the state seeks to prove the defendant guilty, defense attorneys seek to disprove the criminal charges. Under the adversary system, *fighting* they are charged with zealously advocating their clients' cases to ensure that the defendants receive justice. The defense attorney as *fighter* is most visible during trial. Through cross-examination, for example, defense attorneys search for weaknesses in the state's case. In most trials attorneys seek to convince the jury that the defendant is not guilty beyond a reasonable doubt by presenting a case of their own. Throughout the trial the defense attorney manages the case and must make important tactical and strategic decisions. (Chapter 14 will discuss some of the factors guiding such decisions.)

Negotiating

The defense attorney's role as advocate is not confined soley to trial. The lawyer's dual role as advocate and counselor produces conflicting yardsticks for assessing the work performed. How do we define winning? For Perry Mason, winning meant an acquittal. And most defendants define winning in this way. A study of over two thousand writs of habeas corpus filed by Florida prisoners demonstrated that defendants believed it was their lawyer's job to ''get them off'' no matter how guilty they were (Kerper). Such expectations are unrealistic. As the ABA Standards on the Administration of Justice spell out, lawyers who define success as gaining an acquittal are doomed to disappointment (Nelson). An experienced Los Angeles public defender explains: ''What is our job as a criminal lawyer in most instances? Number one is . . . no kidding, we know the man's done it, or we feel he's done it, he may deny it, but the question is: *Can they prove it?* The next thing is: *Can we mitigate it?* Of course you can always find something good to say about the guy—to mitigate it. Those are the two things that are important, and that's what you do'' (Mather: 278). Thus many defense attorneys define winning in terms of securing probation, avoiding a felony conviction by accepting a plea to a misdemeanor, or avoiding a long prison sentence. Such alternative goals to gaining an outright acquittal focus on sentencing, whereas the prescribed role of advocate centers on contesting guilt or innocence.

negotiating One attorney put it this way: ''Given the situation, what is the best that can be done for my client'' (Neubauer: 74). Often the best that can be done for the client is to *negotiate* the best possible deal.

Drafting

drafting Under the adversary system, defense attorneys are also charged with protecting the defendant's constitutional rights. The defense attorney is thus a challenger whose role is to keep the adversary system honest. Defense attorneys are catalysts who question whether the police or prosecutor have acted properly. Most of these activities occur when the attorneys file motions they have *drafted* to suppress confessions or evidence because the police acted improperly. Or defense attorneys may file a motion for a change of venue because of prejudicial pretrial publicity. In many instances, defense attorneys file pretrial motions in an effort to gain a tactical advantage over the prosecutor.

Counseling

counseling One of the most important tasks of defense attorneys is *counseling*. As advocates, defense attorneys are expected to champion their client's cases. But

as counselors, they must advise their clients about the possible legal consequences involved. Thus lawyers must fully and dispassionately evaluate the
strengths and the weaknesses of the prosecutor's case, assess the probable success of various legal defenses, and—most important—weigh the likelihood of
a jury conviction or acquittal. In appraising the risks and outlining the options,
lawyers interpret the law to their clients, who are often unversed in what the
law considers important, what the law demands, and what the law views as
irrelevant. (Later in this chapter we will examine why the counseling role is
a difficult one for the defense attorney.)

Administering

Like prosecutors, defense attorneys represent numerous clients at the same
time. Typically, though, the caseload of defense attorneys is heavier than that
of prosecutors. Moreover these cases are all at different stages of the criminal
court process. Defense attorneys must keep numerous balls in the air trying
to meet various scheduled court appearances: initial appearances, bail hearings, arraignments, pretrial motions, plea bargaining sessions, trial settings, and
sentencing hearings. On a typical day defense attorneys must appear in several
different courts and thus spend part of their day waiting for everyone else to
assemble. Besides scheduling personal court appearances, defense attorneys
administering are also responsible for other *administrative* duties: making sure that
necessary witnesses are subpoenaed to be in court, filing motions on time, and
so on.

The fact that a lawyer represents numerous defendants typically means that
there is often insufficient time to investigate each case thoroughly. Like judges
and prosecutors, defense attorneys must be able to process many cases. Consider the assessment by a public defender of a former colleague: "She wasn't
a good PD [public defender] in the sense that she couldn't handle cases on
a volume basis. She wanted to act like a private lawyer and the Office couldn't
afford to give her that much time. She was eased out of the office" (Platt and
Pollock: 254).

Defense Attorneys and Courtroom Work Groups

How defense attorneys perform their multiple tasks as fighters, negotiators,
counselors, drafters, and administrators is directly tied to their relationship
with other members of the courtroom work group.

Although the names and faces of defendants change daily, the defense attorneys who represent them are a regular fixture of the criminal court. Typically
assistant public defenders are permanently assigned to a single courtroom and
work every day with the same judge, the same prosecutor(s), the same court
reporter, and the same clerk of court. Similarly, private defense attorneys—
although they practice before several judges—are a permanent fixture in the
criminal courts, for in any city only a handful of lawyers dominate the representation of fee-paying criminal defendants. This daily interaction of the criminal
bar with the court community shapes the type and quality of legal represen-

tation received by those accused of violating the law. Whereas the adversary system stresses the combative role of the defense attorney, the day-to-day activities of the courtroom work group stress cooperation.

Rewards and Sanctions

rewards

Defense attorneys who maintain a cooperative stance toward judges, prosecutors, and clerks can expect to reap some **rewards**. Defense attorneys have limited (and in some instances nonexistent) investigative resources. Prosecutors can provide cooperative defense attorneys with information about the cases by letting them examine the police reports, revealing the names of witnesses, and so on. Private defense attorneys may need the court's cooperation in collecting fees from the defendant. Thus judges will grant continuances to cooperative defense attorneys who need more time and leverage to obtain their fee.

sanctions

The court community can also apply **sanctions** to defense attorneys who violate the norms. For example, the clerk can refuse to provide beneficial scheduling of cases or the judge can drag out a trial by continuously interrupting it for other business. These actions indirectly reduce a lawyer's income-generating ability. Other sanctions are more direct. A judge can criticize a lawyer in front of his or her client (thus scaring away potential clients in the courtroom) or can refuse to appoint certain attorneys to represent indigents, a significant source of income for some lawyers (Nardulli). A final category of sanctions involves the prosecutor's adopting a tougher stance during bargaining by not reducing charges or by recommending a longer-than-normal prison sentence.

CONTROVERSY

How Can You Represent the Guilty?

The duty of the defense counsel is to represent the client zealously within the bounds of the law. . . . The general public views these duties of the defense counsel with understandable suspicion and probably contempt. The public often asks a defense counsel how it feels to represent a person they know to be guilty when that person is acquitted of the charge. By doing so the questioner mistakenly believes that the attorney *alone* "engineered" the outcome, thereby ignoring the fact that the decision was by a jury of 12 citizens . . . or

a judge who simply decided that the prosecutor did not have enough evidence to prove the charge beyond a reasonable doubt. In order to get this point across to the public they should be asked how they would feel as an attorney representing a client whom they believe was innocent which client was found guilty. It really comes down to a person giving their opinion from the position that they occupy at the time they are posing the question.

In 1770 Captain Thomas Preston and the British soldiers under his command were prosecuted for the killings in the Boston Massacre. An attorney successfully defended all but two of the soldiers and was called a traitor to the cause. In time the devotion of the attorney to the cause of representing the unpopular was vindicated. The attorney was John Adams who was to become the second President of the United States.

J. Radley Herold, "The Duty of the Defense Counsel," *Westchester Bar Journal* 12 (1985): 217. Reprinted by permission.

Sanctions against defense attorneys are not often invoked, but when they are, they can have far-reaching effects. Every court community can point to an attorney who was sanctioned, with the result that the attorney either no longer practices criminal law in the area or has mended his or her ways.

Variations in Cooperation

Defense attorneys are the least powerful members of the courtroom work group. Because of the numerous sanctions that can be applied to defense attorneys, they are forced into a reactive posture. Moreover, the lack of a central organization against the unified prosecutor's office further decreases their ability to exert a systematic influence on how criminal cases are processed.

Members of the defense bar respond to pressures of the courtroom work groups in various ways. Prosecutors assess defense attorneys in terms of "reasonableness," that is, ability to "discern a generous offer of settlement and to be willing to encourage his client to accept such an offer" (Skolnick: 58). Based on Skolnick's criterion, attorneys fell into three categories. One category consisted of defense attorneys who handled few criminal cases. One might suppose that the prosecutor preferred dealing with such inexperienced attorneys, but they did not. Because these attorneys did not know the ropes, they were too unpredictable and often caused administrative problems. In another category were attorneys who had active criminal practices and maintained a hostile relationship with the prosecutor's office. Known as "gamblers," these attorneys exemplified the aggressive, fighting advocate, but because they either won big or lost big, they also served to show the other attorneys the disadvantage of this posture. The final category of attorneys consisted of both public defenders and private attorneys who represented the large number of defendants. These attorneys worked within the system.

An Assessment

Given the defense attorneys' regular interaction with the criminal court community, do defendants receive the type of legal representation they should or do the defense attorneys' ties to the courthouse conflict with the adversary ideal? Some studies argue that the defense attorneys' ties to the court community mean that the defendants' best interests are not represented (Sudnow; Blumberg). Others, however, have concluded that defendants' best interests are not eroded when their attorneys adopt a cooperative posture (Skolnick; Neubauer).

A sociologist studied a public defender's office and concluded that the public defender and prosecutor had adopted a common orientation to cases. He found that public defenders were more interested that a given case fit under one of several categories of offenses than in determining whether the event met the proper penal code provisions. As a result, the public defenders seldom geared their work to securing acquittals for their clients. They took it for granted that those before the courts were guilty and were to be treated accordingly (Sudnow). Thus, from the beginning, the presumption of guilt permeated the public defenders' assessment of cases.

A study of a large New York court likened the practice of law to a confidence game in which both sides—defendant and attorney—must have larceny at heart (Blumberg, 1967b). The lawyer regulars of metropolitan court sought to preserve their relations with the court at all costs. The judges and prosecutors depended on the defense attorneys to suggest that defendants plead guilty. The author placed great stress on the fact that it is the defense attorney who first suggested a guilty plea to the defendant—a suggestion that a number of defendants initially respond to in a negative way because they expect their attorney to be their champion.

Still another study concluded that the defendant's best interests are not eroded by the defense attorney's ties to the courtroom community; in fact the clients do better as a result of a cooperative posture. Working within the system will benefit the client because the prosecutor will be more amenable to disclosing information helpful to the defense, the bargains struck will be more favorable, and the defendant will not be penalized for the hostility of the defense attorney. Furthermore, attorneys identified as agitators may harm their clients' causes because prosecutors and judges will hand out longer sentences (Skolnick: 61). Similarly, it appears that attorneys who maintain friendly relationships with the court community are better able to act as counselors to defendants because they are better able to predict what the reactions of the court community will be to individual cases (Neubauer).

We need to place this discussion of the interaction of the defense attorney with the criminal court community in perspective lest we leave the impression that the adversary ideal has no meaning whatsoever. The legal system, civil and criminal, is based on controversy. Norms of cooperation work to channel such controversy into constructive avenues. All too often advocacy is falsely equated with antagonism. Although defense attorneys exchange pleasantries with judges and prosecutors, their personal contacts with these officials outside the courtroom are much more limited than some studies suggest (Mather).

Another qualification to bear in mind is that cooperative attorneys do not bargain out every case. They also take cases to trial. If the defense attorney thinks the prosecutor is driving too hard a bargain or that the state cannot prove its case to the jury, a trial will be recommended. Furthermore there is no evidence that during a trial cooperative attorneys do not argue the case to the best of their abilities.

The Criminal Bar

solo practitioners Law offices of **solo practitioners** are a permanent feature of urban architecture. They can be found huddled around the stone edifice of the criminal courts and interspersed between the neon lights garishly proclaiming "Harry's 24-Hour Bail Bonds." In Detroit they are called the Clinton Street Bar and in Washington, D.C., the "Fifth Streeters"—titles that are not meant to be complimentary. These lawyers spend little time in their offices; they are most often at the courthouse socializing with other members of the courtroom work group. Often dressed in bright colors, they can be observed soliciting new clients in the corridors in violation of the legal profession's canons of ethics. Their proximity to the criminal courts and the bail bondsmen and the sparseness of the law books in their offices are good indicators that the law practiced from these offices bears little resemblance to our Perry Mason notions about defense attorneys. A number of factors account for the low economic and professional status of the criminal bar.

CLOSE-UP

The Defense Lawyer: A Daily Ritual of Deals and Delays

Robynn Abrams spends much of her time waiting.

Nine months after joining the Legal Aid Society and beginning her work in Criminal Court in Manhattan, Miss Abrams, who is 30 years old, has seen only two of her cases get as far as a hearing, and neither has gone to trial. The rest have been dismissed or plea-bargained or, most often, simply adjourned.

"It's frustrating, because sometimes you don't feel like a lawyer, but like a traffic cop," she said. "It's embarrassing to be part of a system where you have to tell your client for the umpteenth time, 'Your case isn't going today.'"

For Miss Abrams, born in the Bronx, raised in Plainview, L.I., working for Legal Aid is the fulfillment of a dream, nurtured during her college days at the State University's college in Plattsburgh, when she taught English to inmates at the Clinton Correctional Facility, then at the John Jay College of Criminal Justice and Cardozo Law School, as well as in brief stints in the City Police Department and the Brooklyn District Attorney's office.

On June 15, she arrived at the Legal Aid offices at 80 Lafayette Street at 9:30 A.M. From the outset, she waited; only one elevator was working, and a line had formed. Her desk was strewn with what she called "other peoples' lives"—manila file folders, one for each case she was to handle that day.

In one, a 21-year-old man was charged with assaulting a woman last August after a performance of "Harlem Renaissance," a musical revue at a midtown theater. The case had been adjourned 11 times before.

In the world of Criminal Court, where most courtroom appearances seem like station breaks, trials are epic events calling for special preparation. Miss Abrams had reviewed the case for three hours the night before and had prepared questions for jury selection.

There were other items on the agenda. A 19-year-old was charged with possessing stolen property—his friend's moped had a stolen license plate. The prosecution has offered him a "violation"—harsher than a parking ticket, softer than a misdemeanor—an offer Miss Abrams declined to accept.

Another man, charged with stealing eight pairs of socks from Macy's and now being held on Rikers Island in $1,000 bail, was to return to court; last time the case was adjourned because the clerk's office could not find his court papers.

At around 10 o'clock, Miss Abrams took the five-minute walk over to Criminal Court and glided past the aphorisms carved into the stone of the entryway. "Why should there not be a patient confidence in the ultimate justice of the people?" one of them reads.

Her goals are less lofty. "I don't think people come here anymore thinking, 'I'm going to change the system,'" she said. "It's more like fighting the system, making sure the people I come into contact with don't get stepped on."

In the world of Criminal Court, lawyering is a matter of circulating and bargaining and striking quick deals—and that is a task for which Miss Abrams, lithe and chatty, seemed well equipped.

Outside All-Purpose Part 9, the frenetic routine began. Within the first hour and a half, Miss Abrams, seeming more like a floor trader on the New York Stock Exchange than an advocate, greeted one defendant; checked the hold-

Stratification of the Bar

stratification of the bar

A diverse array of lawyers appears in criminal court, reflecting the *stratification of the bar.* The availability of lawyers and the type of law they practice has been influenced by two major forces: urbanization and specialization. Although the law has always been an urban profession, the small-town lawyers who handled a wide variety of cases were once more typical than they are

---

ing pen to see if another had arrived from Rikers Island; asked if any trial parts were available; greeted Judge Jay Gold with a "hiya, judge," and met with John McCusker and Michelle Lehr, the prosecutors handling two of her cases.

Even before the day began, Miss Abrams's schedule had been thrown into disarray. Miss Lehr had called the previous afternoon; she was not ready to try the case of a Manhattan man charged with assaulting his former lover and threatening her over the phone, so it had to be adjourned, for the eighth time.

Then Mr. McCusker, who the day before had said he was ready to try the theater assault, told Miss Abrams that the police officer expected to testify was not available. Another adjournment.

It was time for the daily ritual of rescheduling, acted out on this day in huddles at the edge of the Complaint Room. One case was set for July 7, but the other proved more difficult. Mr. McCusker will be away the first two weeks of July, a co-defendant will be in Puerto Rico after that, and his attorney, Joel E. Abramson, will be away all of August. They agreed on September.

Although it is Legal Aid that is generally accused of obstruction, Miss Abrams said later, in many instances it is the prosecution that seeks postponement.

At 12:07, a breakthrough: Mr. McCusker offered Miss Abrams an "A.C.D." in the moped case. The case will be adjourned and, six months hence, dismissed if the defendant does not get into any other trouble.

Agreeing to a plea bargain is one thing; hammering it through it is another. For 45 minutes, Miss Abrams waited, watched and whispered with Casey Donovan, another Legal Aid lawyer, as a Russian immigrant charged with drunken driving testified in his own defense. Lunchtime was from 1 to 2, and when court reopened at 2:25, the moped case was finally called. Twenty-six seconds later, it was settled.

Like most defendants, this one heard little and understood less of what was going on in the huddle at the bench. Miss Abrams came back to explain. "All you have to do is keep cool for six months," she told him. "This is better than a trial. This way they can't go after your friend."

He smiled wanly, walked out of Criminal Court and out of Robynn Abrams's life. He didn't thank her.

"I don't expect gratitude from my clients," she said. "It sounds corny, but it's almost my pleasure to represent them. Also, many of them feel wronged by their being in court. So why should they feel grateful to me?"

Evenings, at her Greenwich Village apartment, Miss Abrams will do "mindless" things—lift weights, watch TV, play with her cats—all in a largely futile attempt to keep her mind off work. "I have dreams about my clients," she said. "The other night, I dreamt one of them was horribly killed at Rikers. Or I'll think, 'Oh, God, should I have pled that person? Will I get that offer again?'"

There are, indeed, times when she wonders why she subjects herself to it all.

"I walk into the courtroom, and I find it very depressing looking around," she said. "Everyone sitting there is treated very badly, and nobody's ever really being helped."

But Miss Abrams said the frustrations magnify the accomplishments, the lives that are turned around. "Sometimes I think I've helped someone start a new life," she said. "If there comes a day when I feel I'm not being caring enough, I'll leave."

David Margolick, "The Defense Lawyer: A Daily Ritual of Deals and Delays," *New York Times,* June 28, 1983, p. 13. © 1983 by The New York Times Company. Reprinted by permission.

today. As wealth and population became increasingly concentrated in large cities, so too did lawyers. The growing complexity of society has meant that lawyers can no longer be generalists; they must concentrate on mastering a few areas of the law. Most lawyers specialize (drafting wills, contracts, and so on). Increasingly the practice of criminal law is also highly specialized. The increase in appellate court decisions involving criminal law and criminal procedure requires a large investment of a lawyer's time and energy to keep abreast of changes in the law. But most lawyers never handle criminal cases, largely because other areas of the law are much more lucrative. Studies of private attorneys in such differing cities as Denver, Washington, D.C., and Prairie City, Illinois, reached the same conclusion: the bulk of non-indigent defendants are represented by a handful of attorneys (Taylor et al.; LEAA; Neubauer).

Legal practice in the urban bar can be divided into three parts. First there is an inner circle, which handles the work of banks, utilities, and large corporations. The law firms of the inner circle are quite large (up to three hundred partners in New York, Chicago, and Los Angeles). These lawyers are recruited from the nation's most prestigious law schools, earn large salaries, and almost never appear in criminal court. Another circle includes lawyers representing interests opposed to those of the inner circle—the injured party in personal injury cases, small- to medium-sized businesses, and so on. Most practicing attorneys fall into this category. They earn a comfortable living. They also rarely handle criminal cases. The major exception is that in most communities there is at least one attorney known for being a good trial advocate. This person will occasionally represent criminal clients who can afford a substantial fee.

The bulk of the attorneys who appear in criminal court are drawn from the third or outer circle. They are often referred to as solo practitioners because they practice alone or share an office with another attorney. In sharp contrast to the elitist backgrounds of the big corporation attorneys, solo practitioners have often worked their way up from working-class backgrounds. Many are members of a racial or ethnic minority and in past years were often immigrants' children. They typically graduated from the least prestigious law schools (often night programs at city colleges).

Solo practitioners are the least prestigious members of the legal profession. They are viewed by other lawyers as having little legal ability. Economically, they barely eke out an existence. In essence this outer ring handles all the legal business that other lawyers find either too messy or too financially unrewarding. Divorces, small personal injury cases, and criminal cases make up the bulk of their cases.

The stratification of the legal profession affects the criminal courts in two major ways. First, a few attorneys handle most of the criminal cases. For this group of courtroom regulars, criminal cases constitute a dominant part of their economic livelihood. Second, because few lawyers practice criminal law, bar associations have little interest in the work of criminal courts. Most of the time of the bar associations is spent considering matters of the better paying and more socially acceptable business and middle-class clients. Short of a major scandal that forces the attention of the organized bar, the criminal courts are given an out-of-sight, out-of-mind treatment.

Not all private defense attorneys, however, fall into the pattern of being essentially unethical, poorly trained wholesalers. This pattern appears to predominate in America's older central cities. Newer cities tend to have a different type of defense bar, attorneys who are younger, more skilled, and more committed to providing quality representation (Stover). The old-time solo practitioner appears to be a vanishing breed. A study of private defense bars in nine U.S. cities reported that as the older attorneys of this type die or retire, they are not being replaced (Wice, 1978). Part of the reason is economic pressure. Public defenders are now available to provide legal services. Younger attorneys are more professionally and ethically committed to providing higher quality legal services to criminal indigents. They prefer working for public defenders' offices than eking out an economic existence as a solo practitioner.

Environment of Practice

It is no accident that in many large cities, there is a distinct criminal bar. Low status, low fees, and the difficulty in securing clients are three factors that shape the availability of lawyers to represent those accused of violating the law. These factors are also a reflection of the problems associated with trying to dispense justice in America's courthouses.

Low status. Most lawyers view criminal cases as unsavory. Criminal clients are not noted for being honest with their attorneys. Representing criminal defendants also produces few chances for victory; most defendants either plead guilty or are found guilty by a judge or jury. Moreover, many lawyers who represent middle-class clients do not want accused drug peddlers brushing shoulders in the waiting room with their regular clients. And despite the legal assumption of innocence until guilt is proved, once defendants are arrested the public assumes they are guilty. As a result, the general public perceives attorneys as freeing known robbers and rapists to return to the streets. Law professor Murray Schwartz succinctly notes: "Realistically, the lawyer who defends notoriously unpopular clients runs a risk of identification in the public mind (and not infrequently in the mind of his own profession) with his client" (Kaplan: 259).

Securing cases. To earn a living, lawyers first need clients. Securing clients often presents greater problems for lawyers who handle criminal cases than for those who practice strictly civil law. Unlike the attorneys in large or even medium-sized law firms who represent regular clients over long periods of time, defense attorneys seldom have such regular clientele. Accordingly, a part of their time is spent *securing cases.*

securing cases

The criminal lawyer's most important commodity in securing clients is his or her reputation. This reputation often develops on the basis of the lawyer's handling of a specific case. A lawyer's reputation is important in several ways. First, defendants want a specific attorney to represent them, not a firm of lawyers. Such preferences may result from recommendations from satisfied past clients. Second, attorneys who do not practice criminal law often refer clients to a specific lawyer who does. Third, a repeat offender may seek out the previous attorney, if he or she felt the lawyer had provided good representation in the past. Finally, judges may formally or informally assign a case to a lawyer (Wice, 1978).

In securing clients, defense attorneys often rely on policemen, bail bondsmen, and court clerks to give their names to defendants who need counsel. In return, the attorney compensates the referee. Such practices, of course, may violate legal ethics. To secure cases, solo practitioners are known as "joiners" because they spread their name by belonging to as many groups as possible. The need to secure cases is also a reason solo practitioners are often active in local politics. Not only do their names become familiar, but their hopes for a future appointment, perhaps as a judge, are also thus improved.

CLOSE-UP

Setting the Fee

How does the lawyer determine the amount of the fee? One San Francisco lawyer speaking at Nate Cohn's criminal law seminar answered this question with the vague answer of "what is reasonable," and when pressed as to what he considered a reasonable fee, he only half jokingly replied, "It is as much as you can get. . . ."

Most of the lawyers interviewed did not exhibit such a blatant disregard for their clients' welfare and were very thoughtful about how to set a proper and just fee. Most complained that this was by far the lousiest aspect of their job and felt very uncomfortable during any financial deliberations.

The most critical factor shaping the legal representation of defendants is economics. From these fees lawyers must pay for an office, perhaps a secretary, their out-of-pocket expenses, and, of course, themselves. Because of the small fees involved in any single case, private attorneys must handle a large number of

cases and thus cannot afford to devote much time to any single case. In purely economic terms, it is more profitable to bargain the case out (a few minutes in the prosecutor's office) than to engage in a lengthy trial because the fee is set on the basis of representation of the case rather than on a per-hour basis.

For private attorneys, collecting fees is an important but difficult task. A defendant found guilty is not likely to want to pay for losing and might not be able to pay. Even in the unlikely event the client is acquitted, collecting fees is just as difficult, for the lawyer no longer has any leverage. Defendants quickly become forgetful of, if not ungrateful for, the services performed by counsel. As a result, attorneys demand their fees in advance and sometimes work out a time payment plan with the payments coinciding with

scheduled court appearances. A commonly retold story involves defense attorneys requesting a continuance because "Mr. Green" has not yet arrived. This code for the lack of payment of the fee is typically honored by court officials (Mayer: 160). Other techniques for obtaining a fee from clients may involve solicitation of the defendant's family to pressure them to contribute. At other times, attorneys will take whatever the defendant has in his or her pocket. Judge Charles Halleck of the superior court in Washington, D.C., observed, "Sometimes the attorney asks a jailed defendant 'You got $15 or $25? Here let me hold it for you.'" Later that becomes part of the fee (Downie: 176). Despite all these efforts, however, the majority of fees go partially unpaid.

Reprinted from Paul Wice, *Criminal Lawyers: An Endangered Species,* p. 111. © 1978 by Paul Wice. Reprinted by permission of Sage Publications, Inc.

fees

Fees.   Obtaining clients is only half the problem facing private attorneys who represent criminal clients. The second half is collecting the *fee.* There has been a myth that criminal lawyers receive fabulous salaries. Although a few have become quite wealthy, most earn a modest middle-class living (Wice, 1978).

The three most important considerations in setting the fee are the seriousness of the offense, the amount of time it will take the lawyer to deal with the case, and the client's ability to pay. It is hazardous to estimate specific fees, but one study provides the following ranges: $500–$1,000 for misdemeanor (drunk driving included); $1,000–$2,500 for a nontrial felony; and $2,000+ for a felony trial (Wice, 1978). Well-known criminal lawyers may charge their well-heeled clients considerably more, however.

Providing Indigents with Attorneys

Most defendants cannot afford to hire a lawyer. A survey conducted by the National Legal Aid and Defender Association (Benner et al.: 83) estimated that nationwide 65 percent of felony defendants were legally indigent (too poor to pay a private attorney). The indigency rate approaches 75 percent in urban courthouses (Wice, 1985). Obviously the Supreme Court's decision in *Gideon* that the state must provide attorneys for the poor applies to a substantial number of criminal defendants.

The stage of the criminal proceedings when counsel is provided varies from jurisdiction to jurisdiction. In some areas the court appoints an attorney to represent the indigent as early as the initial appearance. In other areas, however, appointment may be delayed until later in the case (see Table 7-1), a practice that can undermine the effectiveness of court-appointed counsel.

indigency standards

Who qualifies for court-appointed counsel also varies. Some judges apply stringent ***indigency standards*** before appointing counsel. For example, in a number of counties, defendants are disqualified from receiving court-appointed lawyers if a monetary bond has been posted, even though that might exhaust all their money. In other areas, however, eligibility standards are less stringent. In big-city courts, judges rarely inquire into the financial capabilities of defendants to determine whether they satisfy the court's definition of indigency. Most judges seem to feel that if a defendant is willing to settle for a public defender, then he or she is not likely to possess the funds necessary to hire a private attorney (Wice, 1985).

How best to provide legal representation for the poor has been a vital issue of long standing for the courts and the legal profession. In the United States, there are two primary methods: the assigned counsel system (attorneys are appointed by the judge on a case-by-case basis) and the public defender system (a salaried public official represents all indigent defendants). Each system has its supporters and critics. The debate over the advantages and disadvantages of the assigned counsel versus the public defender highlight some important issues involving the quality of legal representation provided the poor.

Assigned Counsel

assigned counsel

The ***assigned counsel*** system is used in almost two thirds of the counties in the United States. However, assigned counsel serve only about one third

TABLE 7-1 Speed of Assigning Counsel for Indigent Defendants

Entry into case		Percentage of counties
Within	1 day	33
	2 days	25
	3 days	19
Within	1 week	11
	3 weeks	9
After	3 weeks	3

SOURCE: Robert Spangenberg, Beverly Lee, Michael Battaglia, Patricia Smith, and A. David Davis, *National Criminal Defense Systems Study: Final Report* (Washington, D.C.: Bureau of Justice Statistics, U.S. Department of Justice, 1986).

of the nation's population. The assigned counsel system reflects the traditional way that professions like the law have responded to charity cases: lawyers represent indigent defendants on a case-by-case basis. Appointments are made by the judge from a list which may consist of all practicing attorneys in the jurisdiction or only those who have volunteered to defend indigents.

Critics contend that the result of the system is that the least qualified lawyers are appointed to defend indigents. In most counties the only attorneys who volunteer are either young attorneys who desire courtroom experience or those who seek numerous appointments to make a living. Even where appointments are rotated among all members of the practicing bar (as in New Jersey or Houston), there is no guarantee that the lawyer selected is qualified to handle the increasing complexity of the criminal law; the appointee may be a skilled real estate or a good probate attorney, but these skills are not readily transferable to the dynamics of a criminal trial. This overall pattern that assigned counsel are recent law school graduates or old "has-beens," to quote a Seattle judge, is confirmed by a study of lawyers in Oregon showing that court-appointed attorneys were younger, less experienced, and rated by other members of the bar as less competent than retained counsel (Moore).

The availability of lawyers willing to serve as assigned counsel is directly related to financial compensation. In some jurisdictions attorneys are expected to represent indigents as part of their professional responsibility without being paid (pro bono). In most areas, though, assigned counsel are paid, but the fees are typically below those charged in private practice. The financial problems facing some states and localities has also meant that some fees due lawyers have not been paid (Wice, 1985). Assigned counsel systems seldom provide funds to hire investigators or secure services of expert witnesses, further weakening the ability to provide a thorough defense. Even where court-appointed attorneys are paid, compensation is minimal, adding another obstacle to qualified attorneys who might serve (Silverstein). Inadequate compensation pressures attorneys to dispose of such cases quickly in order to devote time to fee-paying clients. An Oregon district attorney made the following observation: "Counsel for indigents very often display an attitude of 'let's get it over with.' The same lawyer, whom I know to be a veritable tiger for a paying client, is in many cases a pussy cat when representing the indigent client. Such are the economic facts of life" (Moore: 283).

To its backers, a major benefit of the assigned counsel system is that it disperses the responsibility for defending the poor among the practicing lawyers. To many the overall lack of organization and coordination makes the assigned counsel system unsuited for modern criminal courts, particularly in large or medium-sized jurisdictions. According to the President's Commission on Law Enforcement, a central administration program is necessary for an assigned criminal system to function properly. A prime benefit of central administration is that it can provide for investigative staff and secure the services of expert witnesses. The lack of overall supervision and coordination also means that the quality of appointed attorneys is not monitored. Only a small percentage of assigned counsel systems employ formal procedures for removing attorneys from assigned counsel lists.

Public Defender

public defender

The ***public defender*** is a twentieth-century response to the problem of providing legal representation for the indigent. Under the defender system a salaried lawyer (working full-time or part-time for the jurisdiction) represents criminal indigents in the jurisdiction. Los Angeles was the first city to create a public defender office in 1914. In subsequent decades the program spread slowly; by 1965, the National Legal Aid and Defender Association—the national organization that promotes better legal representation for civil as well as criminal indigents—reported programs in only 117 counties. Since 1965 public defender programs have spread rapidly because of Supreme Court decisions (*Gideon* and later *Argersinger*) as well as increased concern for more adequate representation of indigents.

Today the public defender system is used in one third of all U.S. counties. It predominates in most big cities and has also been adopted in a number of medium-sized jurisdictions. Fourteen states have established statewide, state-funded programs (Spangenberg et al.). In addition several states provide for a state appellate defender who handles all indigent appeals.

Proponents of the public defender system cite several arguments in favor of its adoption. One is that a lawyer paid to represent indigents on a continuous basis will devote more attention to cases than a court-appointed attorney who is not compensated at all or only minimally. And many members of the practicing bar like the idea that they no longer have to take time away from fee-paying cases to meet their professional obligations.

A second advantage often claimed for the public defender system is that it provides more experienced, competent counsel. Because public defenders concentrate on criminal cases, they can keep abreast of changes in the law, and the day-to-day courtroom work keeps their trial skills sharp. By contrast, assigned counsel often are neither knowledgeable in criminal law nor specialists in trial work. The public defender is also likely to be more knowledgeable about informal norms and is therefore in a better position to counsel defendants and negotiate the best possible deal.

Finally, a defender system "assures continuity and consistency in the defense of the poor" (Silverstein: 47). Issues that transcend individual cases—criteria for pretrial release, police practices, and so forth—are more likely to be considered by a permanent, ongoing organization than under appointment systems.

But critics contend that public defenders—as paid employees of the state—will not provide a vigorous defense because they are tied too closely to the courtroom work group. Edward Bennett Williams, a nationally known defense attorney, has even suggested that the prosecutor and public defender are like two professional wrestlers; they fight each other in a different town every night, making sure that they do not hurt each other. In a similar vein, David Sudnow, a sociologist, writes:

> He [the public defender] will not cause any serious trouble for the routine motion of the court conviction process. Laws will not be challenged, cases will not be tried to test the constitutionality of procedures and statutes, judges will not be personally degraded, police will be free from scrutiny to decide the legitimacy of their operations, and the community will not be condemned for its segregative practices against Negroes. The PD's defense is completely proper, in accord with correct legal procedure, and specifically amoral in its import, manner of delivery, and perceived implications for the propriety of the prosecution enterprise. (p. 273)

A number of studies have compared the adequacy of representation provided by assigned counsel to that of public defender's offices. The dominant conclusion is that there is not much difference (Taylor et al.; Wice, 1985). Problems often identified with public defenders are in reality not all that unique. Rather they reflect difficulties associated with lawyers—whether paid or court-appointed—who maintain close ties with other members of the courtroom work group.

Lawyers and Clients

The adversary system is premised on a good working relationship between lawyer and client. The American legal system surrounds the lawyer–client relationship with special protections. In order to be an effective advocate and counselor, the lawyer must know all the facts of a case. Thus any information communicated by the client is treated as *privileged communication;* it cannot be disclosed without the client's consent. (There are certain exceptions, however. For example, if a client tells her lawyer that a crime is about to be committed, the lawyer as an officer of the court is required to bring such knowledge to the attention of the proper authorities.) Based on this trust and a full exchange of information, the attorney assumes the difficult task of advocating a client's case. In civil litigation the relationship between lawyer and client is often (but not always) characterized by such trust and full disclosure. In criminal cases, however, the relationship may be marked by distrust and hostility.

privileged communication

Lawyers View Their Clients

A study in Oakland, California, revealed that getting along with clients was one of the most difficult tasks of public defenders. Many eventually left the office because of the difficulty of dealing with their clients, who were often sullen, distrustful, ungrateful, and dishonest in dealing with them (Platt and Pollock). At times defendants tell their attorneys implausible stories, invent alibis, and/or withhold key information. The defendant's lack of candor greatly complicates the job of the attorney in representing the defendant. The following example illustrates: "A legal secretary, indicted for forgery and embezzlement, told her public defender that she had no prior record. But during the sentencing hearing it emerged that she had several previous East Coast convictions for similar offenses. Knowledge of these previous convictions would have greatly altered the public defender's approach to the case" (Mather: 282).

The lack of trust in the lawyer–client relationship may be determined by the necessity of the lawyer to prepare the client for a less than total victory. To return to the counselor role, the defense attorney must at some point inform the defendant that given the crime, the prior record, facts of the case, and so forth, it is likely that the person will be imprisoned. Since defendants involved in the criminal process typically live a day-to-day existence postponing bad news, such statements are not to their liking. Preparing the client for less than total victory obviously clashes with traditional notions that the attorney should always win.

Q U O T A T I O N

It may often be a lawyer's duty to emphasize in harsh terms the force of the prosecution's evidence: "What about this fact? Is it going to go away? How the hell would you vote if you were a juror in your case?" It may sometimes be a lawyer's duty to say bluntly, "I cannot possibly beat this case. You are going to spend a long time in jail, and the only question is how long." It may even be a lawyer's duty to use the kind of language illustrated by a recent Massachusetts case: "The jury will fry your ass." "You're going to die if you take the stand." "You will burn if you do not change your plea." "The jury wants your blood."

Albert Alschuler, "The Defense Attorney's Role in Plea Bargaining." Reprinted by permission of The Yale Law Journal Company and Fred B. Rothman & Company from *The Yale Law Journal,* Vol. 84, p. 1307.

Ultimately it is the defendant's choice whether to accept the attorney's advice to plead guilty or to go to trial. The importance of the defendant making the final decision is underscored by a Los Angeles public defender: "You know, the DAs can holler all they want about what fools we are sometimes to turn down their deals. But you gotta remember that we've got our clients to answer to. We're not free agents in this thing like the DAs are" (Mather: 281).

Lawyers differ in their ability to influence their clients. Private attorneys find their advice accepted more readily than court-appointed lawyers do, a difference partially accounted for by the type of commitments the defendant has made. Whereas the indigent defendant has no choice in receiving the services of a public defender or assigned counsel, defendants with private attorneys have a choice because they have selected their counsel themselves.

Defendants View Their Lawyers

Often defendants view their lawyers, whether public or private, with suspicion if not bitterness. This is particularly the case with court-appointed attorneys, whom many defendants consider the same as any other government-paid attorney. Some defendants think public defenders will not work hard on their case because they are paid whether they win or not. To others, the defense attorney has ambitions to become a judge or prosecutor and therefore does not want to antagonize the court system by fighting too hard. Overall, then, many defendants view the public defender as no different from the prosecutor. In prison, "PD" stands not for "public defender" but for "prison deliverer." In what has become an almost classic statement, a Connecticut prisoner responded to Jonathan Casper's question as to whether he had a lawyer when he went to court with the barbed comment, "No, I had a public defender."

A partial explanation for a breakdown of trust between the client and public defender involves the absence of one-to-one contact. Most public defender offices are organized on a functional basis. Attorneys are assigned to various courtrooms and/or responsibilities—arraignment court, preliminary hearing, trial sections, and so on. Each defendant sees several public defenders, all of whom are supposed to be working for him or her. This segmented approach to representation for indigents—which a number of progressive public defender programs are trying to counter—decreases the likelihood that a bond of trust will develop between attorney and client.

This form of representation also increases the probability that some defendants will be overlooked and no attorney will work on their cases or talk to them. One can certainly understand the frustration of this thirty-three-year-old accused murderer with no previous record:

"I figured that with he being my defense attorney, that as soon as that grand jury was over—because he's not allowed in the hearing—that he would call me and then want to find out what went on. After that grand jury I never saw him for two months." "You stayed in jail?" "Yeah." (Casper: 8)

Nor do such experiences appear to be atypical. The same interviewer reported that the bulk of public defenders spent only five to ten minutes with the defendants, usually hurried conversations in the bullpen (room where jailed prisoners are temporarily held awaiting court appearance) or corridors (Casper).

Quite clearly not all of defendants' criticisms of their lawyers are valid. But valid or not, defendants' lack of trust and confidence in their lawyers is a major force in shaping the dynamics of courthouse justice. Defendants try to con their lawyers and the lawyers respond by exhibiting disbelief when defendants state unrealistic expectations or invent implausible alibis.

Conclusion

Perhaps nowhere else is there a greater contrast between the images and realities of the criminal court process than in the activities of the defense attorney. Unlike Perry Mason who always successfully defended innocent clients, most defense attorneys plea bargain out the steady stream of factually guilty defendants. Defense attorneys in representing clients must serve as advocate, counselor, and challenger, all within the canons of legal ethics. These conflicting duties account for some, but certainly not all, of the criticism surrounding them. Mainly because of economic forces, only a handful of lawyers represent criminal defendants, and for decades these lawyers have been the less qualified members of the bar. Today, however, most defendants are represented by court-appointed attorneys. Opinion is divided over which is the better method for providing court-appointed counsel.

For Discussion

1. Does your community use assigned counsel or public defenders? Interview a judge, prosecutor, and/or defense attorney to get their views on which system is best and why. Which system do you think is best?
2. Examine local newspapers. Are references to defense attorneys favorable or unfavorable?
3. Interview a public defender and/or a private defense attorney. What are the major problems they face in representing clients?
4. If you need to hire a lawyer for a criminal case, what type of lawyer is available? How would you go about finding a good defense attorney?
5. Why do many defense attorneys maintain a cooperative stance with prosecutors? In what ways does such cooperation enable the defense attorney to represent the client better? In what ways does such cooperation jeopardize the rights of the defendant?
6. You are the defense attorney. Your client denies guilt. What are your responsibilities? If the defendant admits guilt, would these responsibilities be similar or different? Why?
7. Discuss with a prosecutor his or her relationship with defense attorneys. How does the DA evaluate the effectiveness of defense attorneys as advocates for their clients?

References

ATTORNEY GENERAL'S COMMITTEE ON POVERTY AND THE ADMINISTRATION OF FEDERAL CRIMINAL JUSTICE. *Report.* Washington, D.C.: Government Printing Office, 1963.

BLUMBERG, ABRAHAM. *Criminal Justice.* Chicago: Quadrangle Books, 1967a.

——."The Practice of Law as a Confidence Game." *Law and Society Review* 1 (June 1967b): 15–39.

CASPER, JONATHAN. *American Criminal Justice: The Defendant's Perspective.* Englewood Cliffs, N.J.: Prentice-Hall, 1972.

DOWNIE, LEONARD, JR. *Justice Denied: The Case for Reform of the Courts.* New York: Praeger, 1971.

KAPLAN, JOHN. *Criminal Justice: Introductory Cases and Materials.* Mineola, N.Y.: Foundation Press, 1973.

KERPER, HAZEL B. *Introduction to the Criminal Justice System.* St. Paul, Minn.: West Publishing, 1972.

KRANTZ, SHELDON, CHARLES SMITH, DAVID ROSSMAN, PAUL FROYD, AND JANIS HOFFMAN. *Right to Counsel in Criminal Cases: The Mandate of Argersinger v. Hamlin.* Cambridge, Mass.: Ballinger, 1976.

LAW ENFORCEMENT ASSISTANCE ADMINISTRATION (LEAA). *The D.C. Public Defender Service.* Vol. 1: *Policies and Procedures.* Washington, D.C.: Government Printing Office, 1974.

MATHER, LYNN. "The Outsider in the Courtroom: An Alternative Role for the Defense." In *The Potential for Reform of Criminal Justice,* ed. Herbert Jacob. Beverly Hills, Calif.: Sage Publications, 1974.

MAYER, MARTIN. *The Lawyers.* New York: Dell, 1968.

MOORE, MICHAEL. "The Right to Counsel for Indigents in Oregon." *Oregon Law Review* 44 (1965): 255–300.

NARDULLI, PETER. *The Courtroom Elite: An Organizational Perspective on Criminal Justice.* Cambridge, Mass.: Ballinger, 1978.

NELSON, DOROTHY W. *Cases and Materials on Judicial Administration and the Administration of Justice.* St. Paul, Minn.: West Publishing, 1974.

NEUBAUER, DAVID. *Criminal Justice in Middle America.* Morristown, N.J.: General Learning Press, 1974.

PLATT, ANTHONY, AND RANDI POLLOCK. "Channeling Lawyers: The Careers of Public Defenders." In *The Potential for Reform of Criminal Justice,* ed. Herbert Jacob. Beverly Hills, Calif.: Sage Publications, 1974.

THE PRESIDENT'S COMMISSION ON LAW ENFORCEMENT AND ADMINISTRATION OF JUSTICE. *Task Force Report: The Courts.* Washington, D.C.: Government Printing Office, 1967.

SILVERSTEIN, LEE. *Defense of the Poor.* Chicago: American Bar Foundation, 1965.

SKOLNICK, JEROME. "Social Control in the Adversary System." *The Journal of Conflict Resolution* 11 (March 1967): 52–70.

SPANGENBERG, ROBERT, BEVERLY LEE, MICHAEL BATTAGLIA, PATRICIA SMITH, AND A. DAVID DAVIS. *National Criminal Defense Systems Study: Final Report.* Washington, D.C.: Bureau of Justice Statistics, U.S. Department of Justice, 1986.

STOVER, ROBERT V. "The Indigent's Right to Counsel: How Much Does It Help?" Paper presented at the annual meeting of the Midwest Political Science Association, Chicago, Illinois, May 3–5, 1973.

SUDNOW, DAVID. "Normal Crimes: Sociological Features of the Penal Code in a Public Defender Office." *Social Problems* 12 (1965): 209–215.

TAYLOR, JEAN, THOMAS STANLEY, BARBARA DEFLORIO, AND LYNE SEEKAMP. "An Analysis of Defense Counsel in the Processing of Felony Defendants in Denver, Colorado." *Denver Law Journal* 50 (1973): 9–44.

WICE, PAUL. *Criminal Lawyers: An Endangered Species.* Beverly Hills, Calif.: Sage Publications, 1978.

——. *Chaos in the Courthouse: The Inner Workings of the Urban Criminal Courts.* New York: Praeger, 1985.

For Further Reading

BLUMBERG, ABRAHAM. *Criminal Justice.* Chicago: Quadrangle Books, 1967.

HOULDEN, PAULINE, AND STEVEN BALKIN. "Costs and Quality of Indigent Defense: Ad Hoc vs. Coordinated Assignments of the Private Bar Within a Mixed System." *The Justice System Journal* 10 (1985): 159.

LAW ENFORCEMENT ASSISTANCE ADMINISTRATION (LEAA). *The D.C. Public Defender Service: An Exemplary Project.* Washington, D.C.: Government Printing Office, 1974.

MCDONALD, WILLIAM, ed. *The Defense Counsel.* Beverly Hills, Calif.: Sage Publications, 1983.

SKOLNICK, JEROME. "Social Control in the Adversary System." *Journal of Conflict Resolution* 11 (March 1967): 52–70.

WICE, PAUL. *Criminal Lawyers: An Endangered Species.* Beverly Hills, Calif.: Sage Publications, 1978.

CHAPTER **8**

Judges

The judge is the symbol of justice for most Americans. Of all the actors in the criminal justice process, the public holds the judge most responsible for ensuring that the system operates fairly and impartially. Thus we commonly equate the quality of justice with the quality of the judge. The judge and the symbol of justice is reinforced by the mystique surrounding the position—the flowing black robes, the gavel, and the honorific "all rise" when the judge enters the courtroom.

As important as these symbols are, though, they sometimes raise obstacles to understanding what judges actually do and how they influence the criminal justice process. The symbols of the bench coupled with its vast array of legal powers often cause us to overestimate the actual powers of the judge and ignore the importance of the other actors in the courtroom work group. At the same time, the mystique of the office often results in an underestimation of the role of the judge. Judges are not merely impartial black-robed umpires who hand down decisions according to clear and unwavering rules. "This view of the judge as an invisible interpreter of the law, as a part of the courtroom with no more individual personality than a witness chair or a jury box, is a fiction that judges themselves have done much to perpetuate" (Jackson: vii).

The purpose of this chapter is to untangle the conflicting notions about what judges do and how they do it. We will begin by examining the powers and responsibilities of the judge and how various pressures (the large number of cases, for example) have eroded the ideal image of a judge's power. Next we will consider the judge as a member of the courtroom community. A judge's actions are shaped and influenced by actions of prosecutors, other judges, and defense attorneys, among others. Yet at the same time, the type of justice handed out varies from one judge to another. A persistent concern is whether judges are as qualified as they should be. Therefore, we will examine three suggestions for improving the quality of the judiciary: merit selection, increased training, and mechanisms for removing unfit judges.

Judges at Work

The formal powers of judges extend throughout the criminal court process. From arrest to final disposition, the accused face judges whenever decisions affecting their futures are made. Judges set bail and revoke it; they determine whether there is sufficient probable cause to hold defendants; they rule on pretrial motions to exclude evidence; they accept pleas of guilty; if there is a trial, they preside; and after conviction they set punishment. Throughout the process judges are expected to discharge these powers and responsibilities judiciously and without the appearance of impropriety.

Although we tend to think of judges primarily in terms of presiding at trials, their work is much more varied. Much of their work day is spent conducting hearings, accepting guilty pleas, imposing sentence, or working in their office (called **chambers**). In carrying out the responsibilities of the office, judges mainly react to the work of prosecutors and defense attorneys.

More than five thousand judges in courts of general jurisdiction were asked about their typical work day (Ryan et al.). Table 8-1 summarizes the variety of tasks judges engage in, using the same categories employed in Chapter 6: fighting, negotiating, drafting, counseling, and administering.

Fighting

Serving as an umpire during trial is a primary task of judges. Indeed, seven out of ten judges with a criminal assignment report that on a typical day they preside over a trial (Ryan et al.). While presiding at trial judges are expected to be neutral and not intervene to the undue advantage of either side. Because no legal code can furnish clear, unambiguous rules for every case, judges must use discretion in determining how the law applies to the particular facts of the case. They are the final arbiter of the law for the legal questions that may arise during trials: what questions may be asked potential jurors, what evidence is admissible, what instructions of law should be given the jury. Incorrect

TABLE 8-1   Trial Judges' Common Work Day

Tasks	Percent of judges engaging in task daily
Fighting	
Reading case files	70%
Civil or criminal calendar	52
Presiding at non-jury trial	45
Presiding at jury trial	44
Waiting time	42
Negotiating	
Case-related discussions with attorneys	48
Socializing with attorneys and others	39
Settlement discussions	32
Plea negotiation discussions	19
Drafting	
Keeping up with the law	68
Preparing/writing decisions, judgments, orders	56
Counseling	
Attending bar association meetings	0
Talking to civic groups	0
Teaching	0
Administering	
General administrative work	71

SOURCE: Adapted with permission of The Free Press, a Division of Macmillan, Inc. from *American Trial Judges* by John Paul Ryan, Allan Ashman, Bruce D. Sales, Sandra Sane-Dubow. Copyright © 1980 by The American Judicature Society.

rulings on matters like these may result in an appellate court ruling that judicial error was committed and a new trial is required.

Negotiating

negotiating Most criminal convictions result not from a finding of guilt but from the defendant's plea of guilty. As Table 8-1 documents, negotiating activities form a common part of the judge's work day. Judges vary greatly in the extent to which they participate in such plea bargaining negotiations. Some are active participants; along with prosecutors and defense attorneys, they discuss the evidence in the case, the type of charge the defendant will plead, and the sentence to be imposed. Others, however, refuse to participate. In these cases, the defense and prosecution take into consideration the judge's past practices.

Drafting

drafting Only on rare occasions do trial judges draft legal opinions setting forth reasons for their decisions. But they do rule on numerous legal motions drafted by the prosecutor or defense. They are required by law to sign search warrants. They must rule on defense motions to exclude evidence because of improper police conduct or to change the site of the trial because of prejudicial pretrial publicity. Most of these matters are fairly routine and receive only brief examination by the judge. Thus contrary to popular perceptions, trial judges in criminal cases seldom decide complex legal issues. The Ryan study (see Table 8-1) indicates, however, that drafting documents and keeping up with the law are tasks judges commonly engage in.

Counseling

counseling

Although prosecutors and defense attorneys must deal with clients, trial judges have no direct counseling role. Indeed, canons of judicial ethics generally prohibit judges from dealing directly with victims, witnesses, defendants, or police officers. Occasionally, however, judges will offer advice to police officers on how to draft a warrant properly. Similarly, some judges try to ensure that jurors and witnesses are treated fairly and courteously. Table 8-1 indicates, however, that counseling activities are not part of the trial judge's common work day.

Administering

docket

Judges must also be administrators. Judges try to keep their ***dockets*** (the calendar of cases scheduled to be heard) current. One major management task is the scheduling of cases. Dates for hearing pretrial motions and dates for trial

---

Q U O T A T I O N

*T*his is the dilemma of a judge and of many officials in the legal system. Following the rule of law may result in hardship and essential unfairness. Ignoring the law is a violation of one's oath of office, an illegal act, and a destruction of the system. Some choose to ignore the law in the interests of "justice." Others mechanically follow precedent. Neither course is satisfactory. The judge who frees a defendant knows that in most instances the state cannot appeal. Unless there is an election in the offing and the prosecutor chooses to use this case as a political issue, there will be no repercussions. But it is his duty, as it is that of the accused, to obey the law. If the judge is not restrained by the law, who will be? On the other hand, it is unrealistic to say, "Let the defendant appeal." In the long period between the trial judge's ruling and that of the higher court, if it hears the appeal, a human being will be in jail. One does not easily deprive a person of his liberty without very compelling reasons. Almost every day, the guardians of the law are torn between these conflicting pulls.

Judge Lois Forer, *The Death of the Law* (New York: David McKay, 1975), pp. 85–86. © 1975 by Lois G. Forer.

*administer-
ing*

must be established. How generously judges grant an attorney's requests for continuances (additional time) greatly affects how speedily or slowly cases are disposed of. Another major management problem is keeping track of the cases and all the papers involved in a specific case. Lost cases or lost paper can have serious consequences. Assisting judges in these administrative tasks are bailiffs, clerks, and/or law clerks. In large courts the administrative tasks are so time-consuming that one or more judges are designated *chief judges* and devote almost full time to administering the court. In a growing number of courts, particularly in large ones, court administrators may also be present.

chief judge

Benefits of the Job

In discharging their duties, judges enjoy some distinct benefits of office. Traditionally they have been surrounded with a high level of prestige and respect. Lawyers address the judge as ''your honor,'' and all rise when the judge enters or leaves the courtroom. For many lawyers, a judgeship is the capstone to a successful career. Judges also enjoy other trappings of office. Federal judges enjoy life terms, as do judges in a handful of states. More commonly, terms of office range from six to ten years, considerably longer than those of other public office holders—a reflection of the independence of the American judiciary.

Judicial salaries are not the highest incomes of the legal profession, but they are higher than the average of other criminal justice personnel. Salaries of general jurisdiction trial judges range from $47,000 to $82,000. The average salary is $61,000. For some lawyers, a judicial salary represents an increase over that received in private practice and it is certainly more secure. For others, however, a judgeship represents a significant decrease in earning power. For almost a decade, Congress refused to raise the $40,000 pay of federal judges (since increased to $89,500), which led to the resignation of a number of young competent judges as well as difficulties in attracting good lawyers to fill the resulting vacancies.

Many judgeships carry with them considerable patronage powers. Court posts of bailiff, clerks, commissioners, reporters, probation officers, and secretaries must be filled. Since many of these positions are usually not covered by civil service, judges can award such positions to friends, relatives, campaign workers, and party leaders. In some cities judicial staff positions are a significant reservoir for party patronage.

Frustrations of the Job

The pressures of today's criminal justice system mean that the ideals surrounding the judge are not always borne out by the reality. Trial court judges in the nation's largest cities face sometimes staggering caseloads. Instead of having time to reflect on challenging legal questions or to consider the proper sentence for a convicted felon, trial judges must move cases, acting more like administrators in a bureaucracy than judicial sages. As a New York judge put it:

> It is clear that the ''grand tradition'' judge, the aloof, brooding, charismatic figure in the Old Testament tradition, is hardly a real figure. The reality is the

working judge who must be politician, administrator, bureaucrat, and lawyer in order to cope with a crushing calendar of cases. A Metropolitan Court judge might well ask, "Did John Marshall or Oliver Wendell Holmes ever have to clear a calendar like mine?" (Blumberg: 120)

Moreover, the judge's actions are limited by the system—lawyers are late, court documents get lost, jails are crowded. Added to these general constraints is the overall low prestige of criminal court judges, who occupy the lowest rung within the judicial system. Like the other actors in the criminal justice system, the judge becomes tainted by close association with defendants who are perceived as societal outcasts.

Thus the frustrations of the criminal trial court judge are many. Some judges prefer the relative peace of civil court where dockets are less crowded, courtrooms quieter, legal issues more intriguing, and witnesses more honest than the criminal court atmosphere of too many cases, too much noise, too many routine (and often dull) cases, and too many fabricated stories. Other judges, however, like the camaraderie of the criminal court.

Judges Within the Courtroom Work Group

The public believes judges are the principal decision makers in courts. Often they are not. Instead they defer to the judgments of other members of the courtroom work group—prosecutors, witnesses, defense attorneys, psychiatrists, clerks, jail wardens, sheriff's deputies—who may have a greater knowledge about particular cases. Thus judges often accept bail recommendations offered by prosecutors, plea agreements struck by defense and prosecution, and sentences recommended by the probation officer. In short, while judges still retain the formal legal powers of their office, they often informally share these powers with other members of the courtroom work group.

Sanctions can be applied against judges who deviate from the consensus of the courtroom work group. Defense attorneys and prosecutors can foul up judges' scheduling of cases by requesting continuances, being unprepared, or failing to have witnesses present when required. Particularly in big-city courts, judges who fall too far behind on disposing of the docket feel pressures from other judges, especially the chief judge. Judges who fall behind may be transferred to less desirable duties.

Differences Among Judges

By no means are judges totally controlled by the courtroom work group. As the most prestigious members of the group, they can bring numerous pressures to bear on prosecutors, defense attorneys, probation officers, and others. A verbal rebuke to a defense attorney in open court, a comment to the head prosecutor that the assistant is not performing satisfactorily, or a suggestion to the attorneys that they should get together on a specific case are examples of judicial actions that can go a long way toward shaping how the courtroom work group disposes of cases.

The amount of actual influence a judge exerts on the other members of the courtroom work group depends on several factors. Judges themselves are one factor. Some judges are active leaders of the courtroom work group. One study found that of a group of Colorado judges, some ran a "tight ship" (Beaney). They pressured attorneys to be in court on time, for example. These judges fully participated in courthouse dynamics. On the other hand, some judges ran a "loose ship," allowing, for example, the attorneys to have as many

CLOSE-UP

The Judge: Racing Through a 118-Case Day

They were all part of a fast parade in Judge Irving Lang's courtroom. People who spoke Spanish or Rumanian or Chinese. Defendants who didn't know who or where their attorneys were. Lawyers with more cases than they could handle, seeking long adjournments.

"A couple of weeks?" asked one.

"Think in terms of days, not weeks, counselor," Judge Lang advised.

Judge Lang takes pride in his ability to race through a calendar of 100 cases or more—disposing of a good percentage through dismissals or plea bargains—and be finished before 5 o'clock, the official close of the court day.

That satisfaction was not to be allowed him on June 15, much to the chagrin of his court officers in All-Purpose Part 5 in Manhattan. All day the officers had reminded him that they wanted to get away early for a 6 o'clock softball game in Queens.

But 118 cases stood between them and the ball game: cases in which records would be incomplete, lawyers or clients or witnesses would be missing, lawyers would be poorly prepared, pleas would be negotiated, motions would

be made, objections would be raised and Judge Lang would have just a few minutes to devote to each.

He would finish at exactly 5 o'clock.

At 10:05, he took the bench—robeless, as is his style—a full half-hour after defendants, their families and their attorneys had begun filing in.

The defendants stood behind a table placed several feet from the judge. They waited—nervously if this was their first arrest, at ease if they were old hands—as their attorneys tried to strike deals with judge and prosecutor during off-the-record chats at the bench.

The tone of these conversations depended on whether the young lawyers—prosecutors from District Attorney Robert M. Morgenthau's office and, in most cases, defense lawyers from the Legal Aid Society—were prepared to bargain from what Judge Lang thought were reasonable positions.

Frequently, he chided a lawyer for trying to hold out for too much. At times, he advised against a guilty plea, criticized a defense lawyer for knowing next to nothing about a client or criticized the

assistant district attorney for a lack of information about a case.

From Prosecutor to Judge

For Judge Lang, who is 54 years old and has served on the bench since 1969, his own experience is the key to his approach. For 10 years, he was an assistant district attorney under Frank S. Hogan in Manhattan, eventually rising to chief of the Narcotics Bureau. After that, he served three years as a member and counsel to the state's Narcotics Addiction Control Commission.

Judge Lang earns $57,299 a year. Court officers, who oversee the security, the paper work and the ceaseless parade of people who come before the judge, earn in the neighborhood of $30,000.

By contrast, the defendants, for the most part, live on the fringes of society. The judge and prosecutors look at the compendium of their past arrests and convictions—known as rap sheets—see that they live in certain neighborhoods, check out their manner of dress and speech, view how they walk and quickly size them up as career thief, career prostitute, career burglar, career criminal. This gulf between their world and that of

continuances as they requested. Such judges have in essence abdicated responsibility to prosecutors, defense attorneys, and others.

A second factor affecting the role of the judge within the courtroom work group is the stability of the work group. In this case stability refers to the length of time a judge works with the same set of basic actors. Greater familiarity

Judge Lang and his crew of officers must be bridged in the three or four minutes they will have before him.

"You can tell a lot from a cold piece of paper," the judge said, flipping through the record of past arrests and convictions of a defendant whose name had just been called.

"Burglar's tools, burglar's tools, grand larceny"—he ticked off the cases as he went through the several sheets that made up the man's criminal history.

"He's a car thief," he explained.

But even with the emphasis on speed, Judge Lang said, justice is not sacrificed.

"The fact that we do things in a short period of time does not mean that you have not assessed a number of factors," he said. "While they're calling a case, I'm looking at the complaint, the criminal record, the R.O.R. sheet. So, by the time the defendant's actually in front of the bench, I know what the charges are and the weaknesses or gaps in the facts. When you have a high volume, if you don't act with a certain degree of quickness, you get backed up in a traffic jam.

"There's no reason that an incident that took five minutes should take five days to recount."

Several times he dismissed cases because of dissatisfaction with the prosecutor. Once he

told Jonathan D. Siegel, the assistant district attorney on duty in AP-5, "I'm not here to act as a clerk for the D.A.'s office by adjourning cases that don't move with celerity."

At 10:29 and on his seventh case, Judge Lang took the first of 15 guilty pleas and passed sentence. A woman, a clerk in a novelty shop in the Times Square area, had been arrested for selling lethal weapons. She pleaded guilty to a reduced charge of disorderly conduct, and because this was her first arrest, Judge Lang questioned her about whether her decision to forgo a trial was voluntary. He barked out questions in rapid-fire succession as she nodded nonstop.

Finally he said: "$50 or 5 days. Watch what you sell."

By lunch break at 1:10, Judge Lang had handled 59 cases. He returned to court at 2:45.

The afternoon brought its own frustrations, often involving defendants for whom warrants had been issued when they failed to appear. When they strolled in after lunch, warrants had to be vacated and court papers retrieved.

Warnings From the Judge
"There's a general perception that you can come when you want to, and that as long as you show up voluntarily, the

judge is not going to do anything," he said.

To each of a half-dozen people he saw in succession, Judge Lang issued the same warning: If they were not present at 9:30 on their next court date, he would throw them in jail.

At 3:30, a court officer told Judge Lang: "We've got to really move. Go into high gear."

"Yeah, we've got to move," Judge Lang agreed.

A case that had been pending for six months was adjourned, this time because no lawyer had come. "We haven't got the facilities to handle every loitering and hypodermic needle charge like that," the judge said. "We just eventually give them a conditional discharge or something."

A conditional discharge—which sets a defendant free with at most a lecture after he has pleaded guilty, usually to a reduced charge—means nothing to most defendants, Judge Lang said. But if the defendant is a repeat offender, he added, at some point the conditional discharges will come back to haunt him.

"Finally, one day someone will look at the record and say enough is enough," Judge Lang said. "At that point, he will get a jail sentence."

E.R. Shipp, "The Judge: Racing Through a 118-Case Day," *New York Times,* June 28, 1983, p. 13. © 1983 by The New York Times Company. Reprinted by permission.

among work group members means smoother negotiations, more common use of informal arrangements (rather than formalities), and a better knowledge about sentences a certain judge is likely to mete out (Eisenstein and Jacob).

Yet a third factor is the size of the court—that is, the number of judges on the court. In small courts judges rarely specialize; rather each one handles all stages of a case. Sixty percent of American judges serve on courts with nine or fewer judges. In large courts, with twenty-six or more judges, the work environment is strikingly different. Judges are assigned to specific stages of cases. As a result, ***judge shopping*** is a common practice in some big-city criminal courts. By the strategic use of motions for continuances and motions for a change of venue (a request for another judge), defense attorneys attempt to maneuver their clients before the judge they perceive as most favorable. Such judge shopping is the most direct evidence of variations between judges. Although organizational pressures work to provide a certain degree of consistency among judges, any examination of a multi-judge court immediately shows that judges differ in terms of sentences handed out, how they run their courtroom, and the number of cases pending. A mastery of these judicial differences is often as necessary for the practicing attorney as knowledge about the law and rules of procedure.

judge
shopping

Quality and Qualifications of Judges

In large measure the quality of justice depends on the quality of the judges who dispense it. As the noted American jurist Benjamin Cardozo once put it: "In the long run, there is no guarantee of justice except the personality of the judge" (Cardozo: 149). Unfortunately there is no agreed-upon set of criteria about what personality good judges should have—to say nothing about their legal talent and insight into human affairs.

"Scratch the average person's idea of what a judge should be and it's basically Solomon," says Yale law professor Geoffrey Hazard (Jackson: 7). We expect judges to be honest, patient, wise, tolerant, compassionate, strong, decisive, articulate, courageous—a list of virtues similar to those in Boy Scout handbooks (Jackson).

The difficulties of establishing the qualities of a good judge, to say nothing of determining what constitutes a poor judge, are summarized by the President's Commission: "Although it is possible to identify such factors as professional imcompetence, laziness, or intemperance which should disqualify a lawyer from becoming a judge, it is much more difficult to choose confidently the potentially superior judge from among a number of aspirants who appear generally qualified" (p. 66).

Gauging the correct type of judicial personality is particularly perplexing because of the wide array of both formal and informal tasks judges must perform. Moreover, a number of these tasks—keeping the docket moving comes to mind—are not directly related to legal wisdom or other seemingly obvious qualifications. Thus, while there is a strong reform movement to recruit better quality men and women to the bench (which often means more learned), many of those who become judges have more modest credentials that are probably better suited to the actual functions that trial judges perform (Jacob, 1973).

Despite the lack of clarity in what attributes a good judge should possess, one central conclusion stands out. Some judges do not fulfill the high minimal standards. They are senile, prejudiced, vindictive, tyrannical, lazy, and sometimes corrupt.

Although many factors have a bearing on the quality of judicial personnel—salary, length of term, prestige, independence, and personal satisfaction with the job—the factor considered most important by legal reformers is judicial selection. The training of judges and removal of poor judges are additional methods prominently mentioned for upgrading the quality of judges.

Varying Roads to a Judgeship

A variety of methods are used to select judges: partisan elections, nonpartisan elections, executive appointment, legislative election, or merit selection (usually referred to as the Missouri Bar Plan). Moreover in some states, different procedures are used for varying levels of the judiciary. Table 8-2 shows that there is a definite regional pattern in what states use which methods. Partisan elections are concentrated in the South, nonpartisan elections in the West and upper Midwest, legislative elections and executive appointments in the East, and merit selection west of the Mississippi River.

Formal selection methods are not always a guide to how judges are actually selected, however. When a judicial vacancy occurs, interim selection methods are needed. Gubernatorial appointment and merit selection predominate in filling temporary vacancies. In the populous state of California, for example, 88 percent of the trial judges initially were appointed by the governor to fill a temporary vacancy. Indeed, a recent study estimated that half of all trial judges initially received their position through some form of interim selection (Ryan et al.). It is the combination, therefore, of formal selection and initial selection methods that accounts for how trial judges first arrive on the bench.

Executive Appointments

In the early years of the republic, judges were selected by executive appointment or election by the legislature. Today, however, these methods of judicial selection are used in only a handful of jurisdictions. Three states use election by the legislature and a few others still employ gubernatorial appointment. All federal judges are selected by executive appointment. A number of studies have examined the political dynamics involved in the selection of federal judges (Grossman).

The U.S. Constitution specifies that the president has the power to nominate judges with the advice and consent of two thirds of the Senate. Based on this constitutional authorization, both the president and Senate have a voice in the selection process. When a judgeship becomes vacant, the deputy attorney general of the U.S. Department of Justice (the executive official authorized by

TABLE 8-2   Initial (and Interim) Selection Methods of Trial Judges in the States

Partisan election		Nonpartisan election		Gubernatorial appointment	
Alabama	(G or M)	California	(G)	Connecticut	(G)
Arkansas	(G)	Florida	(M)	Delaware	(G-M)
Georgia	(G-M)	Idaho	(M)	Maine	(G)
Illinois	(SC)	Kentucky	(M)	Massachusetts	(G-M)
Louisiana	(SC)	Michigan	(G)	New Hampshire	(G)
Mississippi	(G)	Minnesota	(G)	New Jersey	(G)
New Mexico	(G)	Montana	(M)	Rhode Island	(G)
New York	(G-M)	Nevada	(M)		
North Carolina	(G-M)	North Dakota	(M)		
Pennsylvania	(G-M)	Ohio	(G)		
Tennessee	(G)	Oklahoma	(G-M)		
Texas	(G)	Oregon	(G)		
West Virginia	(G)	South Dakota	(G-M)		
		Washington	(G)		
		Wisconsin	(G)		

Merit		Legislative selection		Hybrids	
Alaska	(M)	South Carolina	(G or LS)	Partisan or merit, depending on locale:	
Colorado	(M)	Virginia	(G)	Indiana	(G)
D.C.	(M)			Kansas	(G)
Hawaii	(M)			Missouri	(G or M)
Iowa	(M)			Nonpartisan or merit, depending on locale:	
Maryland	(M)			Arizona	(G)
Nebraska	(M)				
Utah	(M)				
Vermont	(M)				
Wyoming	(M)				

Note: Codes for interim appointments: G = gubernatorial appointment; M = merit appointment; G-M = gubernatorial appointment, but merit system currently in effect by executive order; G or M = gubernatorial appointment or merit depending upon locale; SC = state supreme court appointment; LS = legislative selection.
SOURCES: Adapted with permission of The Free Press, a Division of Macmillan, Inc. from *American Trial Judges* by John Paul Ryan, Allan Ashman, Bruce D. Sales, Sandra Sane-Dubow. Copyright © 1980 by The American Judicature Society. New information from Council of State Governments, *The Book of the States: 1986–87 Edition.* Lexington, Ky.: Council of State Governments, 1986.

the president to handle judicial nominees) searches for qualified lawyers by consulting party leaders of the state where the vacancy occurred, campaign supporters, U.S. senators, and prominent members of the bar. This initial and private screening has been known to take a year or longer when there are conflicts within the president's party over who should be selected.

After the president has submitted his nomination for the vacant judicial post, the process shifts to the Senate. Most nominations are routine. After a hearing by the Senate Judiciary Committee, the full Senate usually confirms. But if the nomination is controversial, the committee hearings and Senate vote become the focus of great political activity. When President Johnson nominated his friend Justice Abraham Fortas to be chief justice of the Supreme Court, the Judiciary Committee delayed its formal vote; eventually the president withdrew the nomination and Justice Fortas resigned from the Court due to charges of impropriety. Similarly, President Nixon's nomination of justices on two separate occasions were defeated in the Senate after bitter and divisive debates. Senators also influence federal judicial selections through the informal power of senatorial courtesy. Senators expect to be consulted before the president nominates a person for a judicial vacancy from their state if the president belongs to the same party as the senator. A senator who is not consulted may declare the nominee personally unacceptable, and senators from other states—finding strength in numbers—will follow their colleagues' preferences and not approve the presidential nominations. Through this process, senators can make specific recommendations as to who they think is qualified (former campaign managers come to mind) or exercise a direct veto over persons they find unacceptable (political enemies, for example). Procedural changes in the Senate Judiciary Committee, however, have recently lessened the influence of senatorial courtesy (Slotnick).

American Bar Association

Although the ***American Bar Association*** (ABA), the national lawyers' association, enjoys no formal role in the screening of nominees for the federal bench, it plays an increasingly influential role through its Standing Committee on Federal Judiciary (Slotnick). The committee investigates potential nominees by consulting with members of the legal profession and law professors. It then ranks the candidates as "unqualified," "qualified," "well qualified," or "exceptionally well qualified." Although the president—not the American Bar Association—has the sole power to nominate, most presidents do not wish to name someone who will later be declared unqualified. Therefore the deputy attorney general usually seeks ABA's recommendations prior to nomination, which often eliminates some potential nominees. This process produces federal judges with two defining attributes: judges who belong to the president's party and who have often been active in politics.

State appointive systems resemble the presidential system for selecting federal judges, except at the state level there is no equivalent of senatorial courtesy. Like federal appointees, governors tend to nominate those who have been active in their campaigns. At times governors have been known to make appointments to strengthen their position within a geographical area or with a specific group of voters (Crow).

In recent years some governors informally have allowed bar associations to examine the qualifications of potential nominees. State bar associations are gaining an increasing role much like the ABA influence on federal judicial appointees. But unlike in the federal process, governors have greater independence to ignore bar association advice.

Election of Judges

election

More than half the states select judges through popular *election,* either partisan or nonpartisan. The concept of an elected judiciary emerged during the Jacksonian era as part of a larger movement aimed at democratizing the political process. It was spearheaded by reformers who believed that an elitist judiciary did not square with the ideology of a government controlled by the people (Dubois). According to this philosophy, there should be no special qualifications for public office; the voters should decide who was most qualified. A number of states adopted judicial elections using partisan ballots. One result was that party bosses used judicial posts as patronage to reward the party faithful.

At the turn of the century, a counter-trend began. Spurred by widespread corruption in city governments resulting from dominance of political parties, the Progressive movement sought to weaken the influence of the parties. One major technique was the nonpartisan ballot: officials would run for office not on the basis of party affiliation but on personal qualifications. Nevertheless, even where nonpartisan elections are employed, partisan influences are often present. A fair estimate is that in half of the states using nonpartisan judicial ballots, the political parties play some role (Jacob, 1978). For example, both Minnesota and Michigan use nonpartisan ballots, but judicial candidates are endorsed or nominated by parties, receive party support during campaigns, and are readily identified with party labels (Glick and Vines).

CONTROVERSY

Reagan Judicial Nominations

Perhaps an unprecedented number of controversial lower court nominations were considered by the 99th Congress. Several of them resulted in roll-call votes on the floor of the Senate. Certainly it is hard to recall when so much national attention was given by the media to lower court judgeships. In part, this was a result of the participation of interest groups such as People for the American Way, which mounted a major campaign against two Reagan administration nominees, Jefferson B. Sessions, III, to a federal district judgeship in Alabama, and Daniel A. Manion to the U.S. Court of Appeals for the Seventh Circuit.

Sessions, serving as U.S. Attorney for the southern district of Alabama since 1981, was actively backed by Alabama Republican Senator Jeremiah Denton. Sessions received a split rating from the

ABA, with a substantial majority voting *Qualified* and a minority voting *Not Qualified*. Although that in itself would not seriously undermine a nomination during the 99th Congress, the opposition of Alabama blacks to the nomination did. In 1985, Sessions prosecuted on voting fraud charges three black civil rights leaders, but the trial ended in acquittals. Alabama blacks saw Sessions as insensitive if not hostile to the rights of blacks. The investigator for the Democrats on the Senate Judiciary Committee uncovered evidence of Sessions' insensitivity that produced unfavorable publicity for Sessions, the Reagan administration, and Senator Denton. Sessions was called back for further hearings. In his defense, he argued that the damaging remarks attributed to him were said in jest or taken out of context. He

denied being racially prejudiced. The administration claimed that opposition to Sessions was political and was essentially grounded in Sessions' conservative views. The Senate Judiciary Committee, at the urging of Senator Biden, finally voted 10 to 8 against the nomination, with Alabama's other senator, Democrat Howell Heflin, voting with the majority. With the Sessions nomination effectively killed, the nomination was formally withdrawn on July 31, 1986. In November, Denton was narrowly defeated for reelection. His defeat was widely attributed to the heavy black vote against him.

The fate of the Manion nomination was ultimately different, but only after a bitter national debate in which the President himself vigorously defended the nomination and campaigned for senatorial

Campaigns for American judgeships are generally low-key, low-visibility affairs marked by the absence of controversy. Voter turnout is low. Judges are seldom voted out of office. Studies in various states indicate that less than 5 percent of the judges were ever defeated for reelection (Jacob, 1978). The electoral sway of the incumbent judge is so powerful (indeed the title *judge* is typically listed on the ballot) that sitting judges are seldom even opposed for reelection. Although many judges are never opposed for reelection and fewer still are turned out of office, the possibilities still exist. The most recent such case was that of Chief Justice Rose Bird of the California Supreme Court. She was strongly opposed by conservatives, particularly for her opposition to the death penalty, and in November 1986 was defeated in a retention election. Two other justices were also defeated—Cruz Reynoso and Joseph Grodin (Wold and Culver). Elected judges do spend part of their time maintaining contact with the local voters. Maintaining visibility and close ties to lawyers is perhaps the best insurance a judge can buy against having to wage a potentially costly campaign for reelection.

votes—unprecedented for a president on behalf of a lower court nomination. The supporters of Manion argued that Manion was attacked because of his conservative views and because of his previous activities with his late father, Clarence Manion (dean of the law school at the University of Notre Dame), a founder of the extremist John Birch Society. Although not a member of the Birch Society himself, Manion, according to his supporters, was being smeared in a manner that smacked of McCarthyism at its worst, guilt by association. Manion's opponents, on the other hand, argued that he lacked a record of distinction and achievement that was expected of appointees to the courts of appeals. They questioned his ability to be an unbiased judge. Furthermore, they doubted his legal competence on the basis of briefs that Manion had submitted to the Judiciary Committee as representative of his legal ability. Manion, like Sessions, received a split vote from the ABA with a substantial majority voting *Qualified* and a minority *Not Qualified*. The Senate Judiciary Committee was evenly split (9-9) on the nomination but voted to send it to the Senate floor without recommendation.

Lobbying by the administration was fierce, and one Republican senator, Slade Gorton of Washington, who had indicated his intention to vote against Manion, switched sides and suggested that he did so after the administration agreed to nominate Gorton's moderate Democrat candidate for a federal district judgeship in Washington. Other stories emerged of Republican senators extracting from Justice officials sympathetic treatment for their preferred candidates for district judgeships. On June 26, 1986, the Senate voted on the Manion nomination. The vote was 47-47, with Vice President Bush ready to break the tie by voting for Manion. But in a parliamentary maneuver, Senate Minority Leader Robert Byrd switched his vote from a vote against confirmation to a vote for confirmation. This made the confirmation vote 48 to 46, but gave Byrd the opportunity to immediately move for reconsideration of the vote.

Technically, Manion was confirmed, but there was doubt because the Senate had on its table the vote to reconsider. Finally, after weeks of political jockeying and continued nationwide media coverage, the Senate voted on July 23 to defeat the motion to reconsider by a vote of 49 to 50. The administration won, but at the cost of a bruising battle. Gorton was hurt politically in his home state of Washington, where he had been favored to win reelection, and in November he was narrowly defeated.

Sheldon Goldman, "Controversial Nominations," *Judicature* 70 (1987): 336. Reprinted by permission.

Merit Selection

"Remove the courts from politics" has been the longstanding cry of judicial reformers who point to three adverse effects of the popular election of judges. First, popular election has failed to encourage the ablest lawyers to seek judicial posts and works to discourage qualified persons from considering running because they wish to avoid the ordeal of an election. Second, popular election may suggest the appearance of impropriety because it provides an incentive for judges to decide cases in a popular manner. Thus, "an elective system does little to dissuade minority groups from believing that an elected judge must pander to the popular viewpoint in order to remain in judicial office" (National Advisory Commission: 146). Third, the elective system is a contest in which the electorate is least likely to be informed about the merits of the candidates. Implicit in these and other arguments of judicial reformers is the identification of poor judges with political hacks subservient to the party that initially slated them for a judgeship.

Missouri Bar Plan

To cure these ills, legal reformers advocate merit selection, also known as the **Missouri Bar Plan** because that state was the first to adopt it in 1940. Merit selection has won increasing acceptance. A number of states now utilize the plan to select all the judges in the state or just for appellate court selection (see Table 8-2). In addition, a number of other states have actively considered adopting merit selection. The growing importance of merit selection is demonstrated by the fact that all states which have altered judicial selection techniques in recent years have adopted some form of the Missouri Bar Plan. Even in states that have not formally adopted merit selection, governors often use "voluntary merit plans" to fill temporary vacancies (Dubois).

Merit selection is actually a hybrid system incorporating elements from other judicial selection methods: gubernatorial appointment, popular election, citizen involvement, and—most important—a formalized role for the legal profession. In its present form, merit selection calls for the establishment of a judicial nominating commission composed of lawyers and lay persons who suggest a list of qualified nominees (usually three) to the governor. The state's chief executive makes the final selection but is limited to choosing from those nominated by the commission. After a short period of service on the bench (typically one year) the new judge stands uncontested before the voters. The sole question is "should Judge X be retained in office?" If the incumbent judge wins a majority of affirmative votes, he or she earns a full term of office. Each subsequent term is secured through another uncontested "retention ballot." Most judges are returned to the bench by a healthy margin, often receiving over 80 percent of the vote. Only a handful of judges have been removed from office (Baum). Over a twenty-year period only twenty-two trial court judges were defeated in 1,864 retention elections. Nine of these defeats occurred in Illinois, which requires a judge to receive a minimum of 60 percent of the popular vote to remain on the bench (Hall and Aspin).

Although backers of the Missouri Bar Plan contend that it will significantly improve the type of judges selected and remove the courts from politics, studies of the merit selection system in operation have reached different conclusions.

Although the politics of judicial selection has been altered, it has not been removed; in fact, removing politics does not seem possible. What the reformers presumably mean is the removal of "partisan" politics. In operation, the Missouri Bar Plan has reduced the influence of political parties while at the same time greatly increasing the power of the legal profession (Watson and Downing). Merit selection procedures were also used by President Carter for affirmative action purposes. During his term of office a higher proportion of women and racial minorities were appointed to the federal bench than were appointed by other presidents.

Which System Is Best?

The debate over the best method for selecting state judges has raged for decades. Partisan and nonpartisan elections, employed in a majority of states, are supported by those who believe elections are the most appropriate method for guaranteeing the popular accountability of state judicial policy makers. Critics, on the other hand, assert that elections are fundamentally inconsistent with the principle of judicial independence, which is vital for neutral and impartial judicial decision making. Less philosophically, these competing perspectives find expression in tension between the legal profession and political parties over influencing judicial selections. The different methods of judicial selection heighten or diminish the influence of the bar or the influence of political parties.

In evaluating which selection system is "best," a key criterion is whether one system produces better judges than another. That is, do the judges in one system differ from those in others? Certainly it is part of judicial folklore that they do. Conversations with appointed judges indicate that some believe they would never have attained their position if they had to run for election. On the other hand, discussions with elected judges show that many believe that they would never have been selected under an appointment system. The only attribute these judges share in common is that they appear to fellow judges, members of the bar, and outside observers to be good judges. Several studies have systematically analyzed the folklore of the judges and supporters of one system over another and concluded that different selection systems are associated with different backgrounds of judges.

Where legislators appoint judges, it is quite clear that former legislators are more likely to be selected than in other systems. Similarly, elected systems elevate to the bench a higher proportion of persons who have held local political office. By contrast, where the governor appoints, the system benefits those who have held state office (such as legislators). We can perhaps best evaluate these differences by asking what systems appear to favor candidates with local political office, which typically means the elected local district attorney. Under the Missouri Bar Plan and elective systems, former DAs are more often selected as judges. Where the executive or legislature makes the selection, though, fewer DAs become judges.

Varying backgrounds of judges are related to differing selection systems, but by and large the differences are rather small. When judges' prior political experience, local ties, party affiliation, and quality of legal education have been analyzed, the systems of judicial selection do not appear to be very different. Pulling together the findings of many diverse studies, Nagel concluded that elected and appointed systems do not differ "as much in their results or in the behavior of voters and appointers as the debate in literature would have us believe" (Nagel: 36). Canon reached a similar conclusion in studying state supreme court judges: "Institutional mechanisms surrounding recruitment do not have the impact on personal characteristics which advocates of competing selection systems often imply they have" (Canon: 588).

Similarities in Judges' Backgrounds

Although the United States uses a wide variety of methods for selecting judges, it is important to note that overall judges share some important similarities, similarities that may be of even greater importance than the differences (Table 8-3). In general, judges are males from the upper middle class, and their backgrounds reflect the attributes of that class: they are more often white and Protestant and they are better educated than the average American.

Another similarity is that most judges were born in the community in which they serve. Trial court judges are usually appointed from particular districts. This local selection results in elevating persons who were born in that area and often attended local or state colleges before going on to a law school within the state. (The only major exception is in New England, where the schools have a strong regional orientation.) These patterns are revealed in a study of Louisiana judges. Over 90 percent of Louisiana judges were born in the state, 75 percent attended college within the state, and most of the rest attended a southern school (Vines).

Finally, judges are seldom newcomers to political life. As Table 8-3 shows, almost three out of four state supreme court judges surveyed held a prior non-judicial political office. Trial court judges also have held prior office, with the model category being district attorney or state legislator. Eighty percent of federal judges had prior governmental experience. Before becoming judges, they had some familiarity with the range of public issues that governments as well as courts must address. These factors mean that few political mavericks survive the series of screens that precede becoming a judge. The process tends to eliminate those who hold views and exhibit behavior widely different from those of the mainstream of local community sentiment.

How selection systems recruit judges with attitudes reflecting those of the local community is shown in a study of Pittsburgh and Minneapolis. These two cities were chosen because of major differences in their political systems and their methods of judicial selection. In Pittsburgh judicial selections reflect a highly politicized environment dominated by the Democratic machine. Lawyers wanting to be judges patiently "wait in line" because of the party's need to maintain ethnic and religious balance on the judicial ticket (Levin). As a result, almost all Pittsburgh judges held government positions prior to coming to the bench and some still remain active in party affairs. Because of the dominance of partisan politics in the city, it is widely accepted that courts should be staffed with party workers. Bar associations play only a very limited role

TABLE 8-3   Characteristics of State Supreme Court Judges and Federal Appeals Court Judges

	State supreme court judges 1980–81 N = 300	Federal appeals court judges (Carter appointees)* N = 56
Race and sex		
Female	3.1%	19.6%
Black	0.6	16.1
Religious affiliation		
Protestant	60.2	60.7
Catholic	23.9	23.2
Jewish	11.6	16.1
Other	4.2	NDA
Government career experience		
Prosecutor	21.5	32.1
Previous judicial	62.9	53.6
Type of undergraduate school		
State	55.2	30.4
Private	34.0	50.0
Prestigious	10.8	19.6
Type of law school		
State	66.0	39.3
Private	12.6	19.6
Prestigious	16.2	41.1
Proprietary	5.2	0.0
Type of law practice		
Solo	26.1	1.8
2–4 partners	54.0	3.6
Larger firm	19.9	26.9
Average age upon reaching court	53.0	51.9

SOURCES: Henry Glick and Craig Emmert, "Stability and Change: Characteristics of State Supreme Court Judges," *Judicature* 70 (1986): 107, 109; Sheldon Goldman, "Reorganizing the Judiciary: The First Term Appointments," *Judicature* 68 (1985): 313, 324–325. Reprinted by permission.

in judicial selection, and there is little support for efforts to reform the judiciary.

The political culture of Minneapolis is strikingly different. It is a "good government or reformed city" with a weak political machine. Political parties have only a limited role in judicial selection; instead the bar association is quite influential. Before a judicial election the Minneapolis Bar Association polls its members, and the winner in the lawyers' poll almost always wins in the general election. If a vacancy occurs, the governor appoints judges according to the preferences of the bar association. As a result of this selection process, Minneapolis judges are seldom drawn from party activists; they tend to be lawyers in large, business-oriented law firms.

The vastly different political cultures and judicial selection processes in Pittsburgh and Minneapolis produce judges with contrasting judicial philosophies. Minneapolis judges are more oriented to the needs of "society" than toward the defendant. Typically they are more concerned with universal legal requirements and adopt a formalistic approach; that is, they see the purpose of sentencing in terms of punishment and deterrence and make few efforts to individualize justice.

Pittsburgh judges, on the other hand, stress common sense and practical day-to-day experiences in making decisions. In place of abstract and universal legal principles, they attempt to reach "just" solutions. Courtrooms are run informally. In short, Pittsburgh judges place a high premium on individualizing justice and little on deterrence or punishment.

These opposing judicial philosophies produce contrasting sentences. Pittsburgh judges are more lenient than those in Minneapolis. A higher percentage of defendants are placed on probation, and when a prison sentence is imposed, it is shorter. Overall, black defendants are treated more favorably in Pittsburgh than in Minneapolis (Levin).

Learning to Be a Judge

Unlike most other countries, the United States does not rely on a group of career judges who undergo special training beyond a law degree. Our various methods of judicial selection all essentially recruit judicial amateurs to the bench who have no practical experience or systematic exposure to the judicial world. Many new judges find that being a judge varies greatly from what they had expected. Robert Carp and Russell Wheeler studied the experiences of newly appointed federal judges. In an appropriately titled article, "Sink or Swim: The Socialization of a Federal District Judge," they found that new federal judges experience three general kinds of problems. First is mastering new areas of substantive and procedural law. In sharp contrast to private lawyers who specialize in a few areas of the law, judges must be generalists; they must rule on a diverse range of legal matters, some of which they were exposed to in law school but some of which are entirely new. Many federal judges (but fewer state judges) therefore come to the bench with no background in criminal law and pro-

CLOSE-UP

Women in the Judiciary

Until this century, the number of women judges in America was so small that one could literally count them all on one hand. The first woman on the bench in this country, Esther Morris (who, incidentally, was not a lawyer), was appointed to serve as a justice of the peace in the Territory of Wyoming in 1870. At the end of the nineteenth century, no other state had selected any women judges, nor had any women been appointed to serve in the federal judiciary.

The twentieth century began witnessing changes, though not very quickly. By 1950, women had achieved at least token representation on the bench. It was not until 1979, however, that every state could report that its bench had included at least one woman judge. [As of 1982, there were 549 female judges serving on state courts. As part of his affirmative action program, President Carter appointed forty women to the federal bench.]

Susan Carbon, "Women in the Judiciary." *Judicature,* 65 (1984): 285.

cedure. It is still possible for a judge who the day before had made his living drafting corporate indentures to be called upon to rule on the validity of a search or to charge a jury on the law of entrapment.

A second set of problems facing new judges is administrative in nature. Supervising the court staff, efficiently and wisely using their time, and managing the hundreds of cases on the court's docket are types of problems many judges have never previously faced.

Finally, new judges experience psychological discomfort in adjusting to their new job. The bench can be a lonely place. Another difficult psychological problem is sentencing. Most judges find sentencing the hardest part of being a judge. A federal judge in Louisiana summarized this difficulty: ''You see so many pathetic people and you're never sure of what is a right or a fair sentence'' (Carp and Wheeler: 373). Some judges have difficulty in abandoning the adversary role that marked their legal careers. One judge indicated ''the major problem along these lines is that a judge has got to look at both sides of the case whereas an attorney need only look at one'' (Carp and Wheeler: 373).

Mastering new areas of the law, administering the court, and psychologically adjusting to the new role are all challenges that confront new judges. But judges are assisted by a variety of other people in learning how to deal with the problems facing them. Fellow trial judges are the first and foremost training agents. Through formal meetings, but mainly through more informal exchanges, judges discuss common problems and possible techniques. Lawyers who appear in court are another source that judges can mine to learn what the law says in an area new to them. Local court staff—clerks, bailiffs, secretaries, probation officers, and law clerks—often provide new judges with advice on administrative or procedural matters. But in the end judges must rely on themselves. Through reading in the law library and seeking out knowledgeable persons, judges engage in self-education.

Q U O T A T I O N

*A*fter you become a federal judge some people tend to avoid you. For instance, you lose all your lawyer friends and generally you have to begin to make new friends. I guess the lawyers are afraid that they will some day have a case before you and it would be awkward for them if they were on too close terms with you. I guess other people think a judge is sort of aloof and they don't feel so much at ease with you as they did before.

Quoted in Robert Carp and Russell Wheeler, ''Sink or Swim: The Socialization of a Federal District Judge,'' *Journal of Public Law* 21 (1972): 372–373. Reprinted by permission of the *Emory Law Journal* of the Emory University School of Law.

Judicial Education

A major development in the last few years has been judicial training schools and seminars to ease the adjustment problems of new judges. Such programs are by no means limited to new judges. Even veterans of the bench may benefit from a systematic exposure to administrative techniques for keeping the docket current or from seminars on rapidly changing areas of the law.

judicial education   *Judicial education* in America caught on during the 1960s. Until then the idea that judges should go back to school was not widely accepted, mainly because it might appear to downgrade the judiciary, which was supposed to know the law. Under the prodding of the American Bar Association and Supreme Court Justice Tom Clark, judicial education programs were developed. In 1956 the Institute for Judicial Administration initiated seminars for state appeals court judges. The National Judicial College conducts one- to four-week summer courses for trial judges. The Federal Judicial Center conducts seminars for newly appointed federal judges as well as continuing education seminars for veteran judges. Other such national programs have sprung up. At the state level, however, institutionalization of training programs for new judges or yearly educational conferences for all judges has been slower.

Judging the Judges

Although judicial selection techniques attempt to recruit Solomon-like figures to the bench and although judicial education programs can fill in a new judge's deficiencies and keep sitting judges abreast of changes in the law, the troublesome problem still remains: what should be done with unfit judges? At issue is how to devise a system for removing unfit judges while at the same time guaranteeing an independent judiciary.

The need for such protections is illustrated by attempts of the ultraconservative John Birch Society to impeach Chief Justice Warren in the 1960s. The Impeach Earl Warren campaign charged the Supreme Court with making "unconstitutional . . . pro-Communist racial integration policies." These critics of Earl Warren were attempting to remove him not because of a lack of ability as a judge but because they disagreed with the Court's decisions on racial integration, freedom of religion, and criminal procedure. Protections against unpopular court rulings constitute the hallmark of an independent judiciary. Yet judicial independence is not an end in itself. As University of Chicago law professor Philip Kurland has put it, "the provisions for securing the independence of the judiciary were not created for the benefit of the judges, but for the benefit of the judged" (quoted in Byrd: 267).

Proper judicial conduct is indispensable to the confidence of the people in their judiciary, a confidence that itself is indispensable to the rule of law (Greenberg). In recent years such public confidence has been eroded by scandals surrounding the courts. Two judges of the Illinois Supreme Court were forced to resign in 1969. In California, New Mexico, New York, Florida, and Oklahoma—to name just a few other states—judicial conduct has been called into question, resulting in investigations, indictments, and resignations of some judges.

The fundamental problem is that judges—whether elected or appointed— exercise more power with less accountability than any other officials in our society. Moreover, formal methods for removing unfit judges—recall elections and impeachment—are generally so cumbersome that they have seldom been used.

judicial conduct commission

A more workable method for dealing with unfit judges is the ***judicial conduct commission.*** In 1960, California became the first state to adopt a modern, permanent, and practical machinery for disciplining its judges. In response to the mounting public clamor for accountability on the part of governmental officials, every state has followed California's pioneering lead. More than thirty states have implemented judicial disciplinary mechanisms that replicate the California model (Brooks). The remaining states have adopted a variety of permanent institutionalized mechanisms for enforcing judicial discipline, most but not all of which have borrowed some elements from the California model (Tesitor).

Under the California model, a commission on judicial qualifications or conduct is created as an arm of the state's highest court. The members of the commission typically consist of judges, lawyers, and prominent laymen. They investigate allegations of judicial misconduct and, when appropriate, hear testimony. If the commission finds in favor of the judge, the investigation is closed and the matter is permanently concluded. Alternatively, the commission may recommend a sanction of private admonishment, public censure, retirement, or removal.

The state supreme court retains the final power to discipline errant judges. Although commissions are armed with the potent weapon of a public recommendation, they prefer to act more informally. If the information suggests judicial misconduct, the commission conducts a confidential conference and discusses the matter with the judge, who has an opportunity to rebut the charges. The commission may try to correct the matter. Most importantly, though, it usually seeks to force the voluntary retirement of the judge. The informal pressures and the threat of bringing public proceedings are apparently enough to force the judge in question off the bench. The complaints and investigations remain confidential unless the commission finds it necessary to seek a reprimand or removal before the state supreme court. This confidentiality is essential lest a judge's reputation be tarnished by a crank complaint. Many complaints are issued against judges by disgruntled litigants whose charge is no more serious than that the judge did not rule in their favor.

In 1980, Congress passed the first major change since 1939 in the self-governance mechanism of the federal judiciary. The Judicial Councils Reform and Judicial Conduct and Disability Act laid out a precise and exacting mechanism for administering and acting on complaints against federal judges. Complaints are initially heard by the judicial councils (the administrative arm of each U.S. Circuit Court). Most result in either a finding of no misconduct or the imposition of non-public sanctions. However, if there is substantial evidence of serious misconduct, the judicial council sends a written report to the Judicial Conference, the policy-making arm of the federal judiciary. The Judicial Conference can recommend that the House consider impeachment procedures.

Article II of the Constitution provides for the removal of the president, vice-president, or civil officers of the United States—including federal judges—for crimes of "treason, bribery, or other high crimes and misdemeanors." The *impeachment* House must first vote articles of ***impeachment*** specifying the specific charges. Impeachment is not a conviction, but rather allegations of wrongdoing roughly equivalent to a grand jury indictment. The trial on the articles of impeachment is conducted before the Senate. Conviction requires a two-thirds vote of the senators present and carries with it removal from office and disqualification to hold any future office.

An unprecedented series of allegations of misconduct against three different federal judges since 1981 highlight the interlocking relationships between criminal prosecutions, impeachment, and the new statutory scheme. Former Chief Judge Harry Claiborne of the District of Nevada was the first federal judge in over fifty years to face formal impeachment charges. He was convicted by a federal jury of income tax evasion. In 1986, while serving a two-year sentence in federal prison, the Senate found Claiborne guilty on three of four impeachment articles by the required two-thirds vote and removed him from the bench. In another case, Chief Judge Walter Nixon of the Southern District of Mississippi was convicted on criminal charges with the appeal pending. No misconduct proceedings have been filed against him, but the history of the Claiborne matter suggests that an impeachment proceeding is probable if the charges are sustained on appeal and he does not resign. Finally, U.S. District Judge Alcee Hastings was indicted for soliciting a $150,000 bribe from two convicted racketeers. He was acquitted of the charge by a jury but the codefendant was convicted. The Eleventh Circuit, in a 381-page report, concluded that Hastings was guilty and had fabricated his defense and that he should be removed from office. The Judicial Conference has recommended that the House consider impeachment proceedings against Judge Hastings. Meanwhile the judge continues to hear cases.

Conclusion

The workaday world of the trial judge bears little resemblance to the high expectations we have about the role of the judge. The trial judge is expected to dispose of a large caseload but is often frustrated by the lack of preparation of the attorneys, missing defendants, misplaced files, little time to reflect, and, probably most important, insufficient control over many vital aspects of the case. For these and other reasons, judges depend on other members of the courtroom work group. Some depend heavily on the prosecutors and defense attorneys and probation officers, feeling content to let them make the difficult decisions. Others, however, are much more active participants and are truly leaders of the courtroom work group.

To a large extent the public's impression of justice is shaped by the trial judge's demeanor and the dignity the judge imparts to the proceedings. Given the very high ideals society holds for judges, however, not all measure up. To a certain extent, this is because we expect too much of judges, as if we think merely placing a black robe on a lawyer will eradicate all the shortcomings the person already had. Ultimately, the quality of judges ranges from some who are highly competent and extremely dedicated, to many who are average, to a few who fall below minimal standards.

For Discussion

1. What are the most important tasks that a judge performs? How do these tasks differ from popular images citizens hold about judges? Why?
2. What system of judicial selection do you think is best? What dangers do you perceive in letting bar associations select judges? What dangers do you perceive in letting the voting public choose?
3. Discuss with a judge his or her first year on the bench. Did the judge consider herself or himself prepared? What unexpected problems did he or she encounter?
4. Examine local news coverage of judges. What issues do the media bring up? Do you think these stories show the full range of tasks and difficulties that judges must deal with?
5. Are judges and lawyers too protective of judges who do not live up to our expectations? What procedures would you recommend for removing unfit judges?

References

BAUM, LAWRENCE. "The Electoral Fates of Incumbent Judges in the Ohio Court of Common Pleas." *Judicature* 66 (1983): 420.

BEANEY, WILLIAM. "Relationships, Role Conceptions, and Discretion among the District Court Judges of Colorado." Paper presented to the annual meeting of the American Political Science Association, Washington, D.C., 1970.

BLUMBERG, ABRAHAM. *Criminal Justice.* Chicago: Quadrangle Books, 1967.

BROOKS, DANIEL. "Penalizing Judges Who Appeal Disciplinary Sanctions: The Unconstitutionality of 'Upping the Ante.'" *Judicature* 69 (1985): 95.

BYRD, HARRY. "Has Life Tenure Outlived Its Time?" *Judicature* 59 (1976): 266.

CANON, BRADLEY. "The Impact of Formal Selection Processes on the Characteristics of Judges—Reconsidered." *Law & Society Review* 6 (May 1972): 579–594.

CARBON, SUSAN, AND LARRY BERKSON. *Judicial Retention Elections in the United States.* Chicago: American Judicature Society, 1980.

CARDOZO, BENJAMIN. *The Nature of the Judicial Process.* New Haven, Conn.: Yale University Press, 1921.

CARP, ROBERT, AND RUSSELL WHEELER. "Sink or Swim: The Socialization of a Federal District Judge." *Journal of Public Law* 21 (1972): 359–394.

CROW, JOHN. "Subterranean Politics: A Judge Is Chosen." *Journal of Public Law* 12 (1963): 275–289.

DUBOIS, PHILIP. *From Ballot to Bench: Judicial Elections and the Quest for Accountability.* Austin: University of Texas Press, 1980.

DUCAT, CRAIG, AND VICTOR FLANGO. "In Search of Qualified Judges: An Inquiry into the Relevance of Judicial Selection Research." DeKalb, Ill.: Center for Developmental Studies, Northern Illinois University, 1975.

EISENSTEIN, JAMES, AND HERBERT JACOB. *Felony Justice: An Organizational Analysis of Criminal Courts.* Boston: Little, Brown, 1977.

GLICK, HENRY ROBERT, AND KENNETH N. VINES. *State Court Systems.* Englewood Cliffs, N.J.: Prentice-Hall, 1973.

GREENBERG, FRANK. "The Task of Judging the Judges." *Judicature* 59 (1976): 458–467.

GROSSMAN, JOEL. *Lawyers and Judges: The ABA and the Politics of Judicial Selection.* New York: John Wiley, 1965.

HALL, WILLIAM, AND LARRY ASPIN. "What Twenty Years of Judicial Retention Elections Have Told Us." *Judicature* 70 (1987): 340.

JACKSON, DONALD DALE. *Judges.* New York: Atheneum, 1974.

JACOB, HERBERT. *Urban Justice: Law and Order in American Cities.* Englewood Cliffs, N.J.: Prentice-Hall, 1973.

——. *Justice in America: Courts, Lawyers, and the Judicial Process,* 3d ed. Boston: Little, Brown, 1978.

LEVIN, MARTIN A. "Urban Politics and Policy Outcomes: The Criminal Courts." In *Criminal Justice: Law and Politics,* 2d ed., ed. George F. Cole. North Scituate, Mass.: Duxbury Press, 1976.

NAGEL, STUART. *Comparing Elected and Appointed Judicial Systems.* Beverly Hills, Calif.: Sage Publications, 1973.

NATIONAL ADVISORY COMMISSION ON CRIMINAL JUSTICE STANDARDS AND GOALS. *Courts.* Washington, D.C.: Government Printing Office, 1973.

PRESIDENT'S COMMISSION ON LAW ENFORCEMENT AND ADMINISTRATION OF JUSTICE. *Task Force Report: The Courts.* Washington, D.C.: Government Printing Office, 1967.

RYAN, JOHN PAUL, ALLAN ASHMAN, BRUCE SALES, AND SANDRA SANE-DUBOW. *American Trial Judges.* New York: The Free Press, 1980.

SLOTNICK, ELLIOT. "The Changing Role of the Senate Judiciary Committee." *Judicature* 62 (1979): 502–510.

——. "The ABA Standing Committee on Federal Judiciary: A Contemporary Assessment." *Judicature* 66 (1983): 385.

TESITOR, IRENE. *Judicial Conduct Organizations.* Chicago: American Judicature Society, 1978.

VINES, KENNETH. "The Selection of Judges in Louisiana." *Tulane Studies in Political Science* 8 (1962): 99–119.

WATSON, RICHARD, AND RONDAL DOWNING. *The Politics of the Bench and Bar: Judicial Selection under the Missouri Nonpartisan Court Plan.* New York: John Wiley, 1969.

WOLD, JOHN, AND JOHN CULVER. "The Defeat of the California Justices: The Campaign, the Electorate, and the Issue of Judicial Accountability." *Judicature* 70 (1987): 348.

For Further Reading

CRAMER, JAMES, ed. *Courts and Judges.* Beverly Hills, Calif.: Sage Publications, 1981.

DUBOIS, PHILIP. *From Ballot to Bench: Judicial Elections and the Quest for Accountability.* Austin: University of Texas Press, 1980.

GROSSMAN, JOEL. *Lawyers and Judges: The ABA and the Politics of Judicial Selection.* New York: John Wiley, 1965.

JACKSON, DONALD DALE. *Judges.* New York: Atheneum, 1974.

WATSON, RICHARD, AND RONDAL DOWNING. *The Politics of the Bench and Bar: Judicial Selection under the Missouri Nonpartisan Court Plan.* New York: John Wiley, 1969.

CHAPTER 9

Defendants, Victims, and Witnesses

When we think about the criminal courts, our minds immediately focus on the members of the courtroom work group: prosecutors, defense attorneys, and judges. We are less likely to think about the other participants: victims, witnesses, or even defendants. Yet these other actors are also important.

clientele

The activities of organizations are shaped by their ***clientele,*** or the persons they deal with. Clientele shape the processing and handling of demands for services, the tasks to be performed, and public assessments of the organization. Conflicts often arise between the organization and those it must deal with. The courts are no exception. The clientele of criminal courts affect the court process in several important ways.

First, defendants and victims greatly influence workload. Courts are passive institutions. They do not seek out cases to decide; rather they are dependent on others to bring matters to their attention. How many cases are filed, as well as the kinds of cases brought to court, are determined by the decisions of others—police, victims, and of course those who violate the law in the first place. Thus the courtroom work group has very little control over its workload. Second, victims, witnesses, and defendants are the consumers of the court process. As Chapter 1 indicated, democratic governments are expected to be responsive to the wishes and demands of their citizens. As we shall see, victims and witnesses often complain about how the courts handle their cases.

Victims, witnesses, and defendants are both subjects and objects of the criminal justice process. Their importance for how the courtroom work group administers justice on a day-to-day basis is the subject of this chapter.

The Defendant

defendant

The ***defendant*** is supposed to stand at the center of the criminal court drama. Yet the typical felony defendant is largely powerless to control his fate—more object to be acted on than the key to what happens. Those accused of violating the criminal law are a diverse lot. Although crimes of violence dominate the headlines, most defendants are not dangerous; they are charged with property or drug offenses. A small group of career criminals are responsible for a disproportionate share of some offenses (Moore), but for other defendants the particular case represents the only time that they will be in court. Although many defendants are economically impoverished, accusations against high-ranking government officials, big businessmen, and prominent local citizens demonstrate that defendants come from all social strata. This diversity aside, the vast majority of violators conform to a definite profile. Compared to the average citizen, felony defendants are significantly younger, overwhelmingly male, disproportionately members of racial minorities, more likely to come from broken homes, less educated, more likely to be unemployed, and less likely to be married (Gertz). Violent offenders are much more likely to have experienced abuse and violence in their families (Bureau of Justice Statistics). By the time the court sorting process has ended, those sentenced to prison consist of an even higher proportion of poor, young, illiterate, black males (Table 9-1). Thus the typical felony defendant is one of society's losers, possessing few of the skills needed to successfully compete in an increasingly technological society.

Because most defendants are poor and uneducated, they are ill-equipped to deal with the technical abstractions of the criminal court process. Many are incapable of understanding even the simplest instructions about the right to bail or the presumption of innocence. Many are too inarticulate to aid their attorney in preparing a defense. Many hold unfavorable attitudes toward the law and the criminal justice system and thus regard the judge and all other court personnel, including their defense attorneys, with hostility and distrust.

> As a result, the huge majority of defendants . . . submit to the painful consequences of conviction but do not know for certain whether they committed any of the crimes of which they are accused. Such defendants are so unschooled in law that they form no firm opinion about their technical innocence or guilt. Neither do they actually agree or disagree that it is just to punish them. They do not know enough about themselves to tell the lawyers what to do. (Rosett and Cressey: 146)

TABLE 9-1 Profile of Prison Inmates

Age (median)	27 years
Sex (male)	96%
Race:	
White	49.6%
Black	47.8%
Other	2.5%
Education (mean years)	11.2 years
Prior incarceration record	64%
Current offense:	
Violent	58%
Property	31%
Drugs	7%
Pre-arrest employment status:	
Full-time	60%
Part-time	10%
Not employed	30%
Pre-arrest annual income:	
Less than $3,000	19%
$3,000–$9,000	30%
$10,000 +	25%

SOURCE: Bureau of Justice Statistics, "Prisons and Prisoners" (Washington, D.C.: U.S. Department of Justice, 1982).

Criminal courts are a depressing place to work. Judges, prosecutors, and defense attorneys seldom come away from their day's activities with a sense of accomplishment, for many of the criminal cases involve social problems like drug addiction, marital problems, lack of education, and mental illness, over which the court personnel have no control. Many cases stem from disputes between people who knew one another. An in-depth study of felony case dispositions in New York City by the Vera Institute (a nonprofit group devoted to criminal justice reform) summed it up this way:

> The incidents that give rise to arrest are frequently not the kind that the court system is able to deal with satisfactorily. At the root of much of the crime brought to court is anger—simple or complicated anger between two or more people who know each other. Expressions of anger result in the commission of technical felonies, yet defense attorneys, judges and prosecutors recognize that in many cases conviction and prison sentences are inappropriate responses. High rates of dismissal or charge reduction appear to be a reflection of the system's effort to carry out the *intent* of the law—as judges and other participants perceive it—though not necessarily the letter of the law. (xv)

Court personnel have little empathy with or understanding of the types of defendants whose fates they must decide. Members of the courtroom work group are essentially middle class. Little in their backgrounds or training has equipped them to deal with violations of the law committed by the poor.

Victims and Witnesses

victims
witnesses

Victims and *witnesses* are the forgotten people in the criminal justice system. Fictional and nonfictional treatments of the court process direct attention to the criminal as victim rather than to the victim as victim (Elias). Thus, although there is an enormous literature on offenders, much less is known about victims. In the view of many, the courts, along with the rest of the criminal justice community, have ignored the interests of victims and witnesses.

Courts Through the Eyes of Victims and Witnesses

Crime victims once played a prominent role in the criminal process. Before the American Revolution, victims were the central figures in the criminal justice drama. Criminals' fates were closely tied to their victims' wishes (Karmen). But when crime became viewed as an offense against the state (see Chapter 4) the victim was assigned a subordinate role (Elias). ''Now victims are merely bit players, upstaged by the government's prosecutors, and their testimony is presented as just another piece of evidence in the state's case against the accused'' (Karmen: 3).

Several studies have documented the hardships victims and witnesses face while participating in the criminal court process (Knudten et al.; Ash;

CLOSE-UP

The Typical Defendant?

One of the troublesome aspects of visiting a criminal courthouse is that it soon becomes apparent that it is impossible to detect the appearance of a typical defendant. As the various defendants appear before the judge, they are indistinguishable from most other city inhabitants from the same community. It is true that the court's clientele is disproportionately young and poor, but beyond these broad clues, there are no physical indicators distinguishing the victims from the defendants.

Aside from being young and poor, the typical defendant appearing before a felony court is likely to have prior experience with the criminal law. It is continually amazing to me how defendants so young have compiled so exhaustive a record of anti-social behavior in so short a period of time. With so many diversion programs designed to help the first offender, and the caseload pressures facing the

courts, only first-time offenders accused of a very serious crime are likely to reach the felony courtroom. The average felon can be best categorized as falling into one of three groups: (1) violent sociopaths who present a serious threat to society, (2) recidivists who cannot seem to fit into society, but do not present a threat in terms of physical violence, and (3) the isolated case of an individual acting out of a unique set of circumstances which has triggered his criminal behavior.

The first group seems in need of psychological aid in order to curb sociopathic tendencies, while the latter group needs career counseling and other forms of vocational and educational rehabilitation. The second group does seem to have the potential for being capable of rehabilitation, but this category also contains a

high percentage of professional criminals who believe that arrest and incarceration are simply occupational hazards. These include professional safecrackers, burglars, and receivers of stolen property. They have selected criminal activity because of its perceived lucrative returns and are not generally very good candidates for rehabilitation.

The third category is a highly diverse group. It contains a large number of middle class, white-collar criminals who occasionally fall within the jurisdiction of the urban courts but are much more likely to be found in the federal district court. These defendants are commonly involved in major drug cases or complex economic crimes such as fraud, bribery, or extortion.

From *Chaos in the Courthouse: The Inner Workings of Urban Criminal Courts* by Paul B. Wice. Copyright © 1985 by Praeger Publishers. Reprinted by permission of Praeger Publishers.

Cannavale and Falcon; Davis; Connick and Davis). Some represent minor inconveniences, like getting to the courthouse and finding a parking place. Other hardships are more major.

- Repeated court appearances, some of which were continued with no reason given.
- Long waits in uncomfortable surroundings.
- Inadequate notification of court dates.
- Loss of income from taking a day off from work.
- Fear of retaliation by the defendant.

The victim as witness.   Victims and witnesses also face major problems while testifying in court. Because few people are accustomed to testifying, lawyers must coach their witnesses ahead of time to answer only the question asked, to speak forcibly (but not belligerently), and not to become rattled by cross-examination. Even after such preparation, though, many witnesses are uncomfortable during cross-examination as the defense attorney attempts to tie their story into knots and discredit them.

Most of what we know about the ordeal of testifying in court comes from studies of rape victims (Resick). A study by Holmstrom and Burgess, both of whom counsel rape victims in Boston City Hospital, found that the victim, rather than the defendant, is put on trial. Holmstrom and Burgess followed the cases of fourteen women who testified in court during a rape trial. Often the trauma is significant: the victim must publicly repeat in specific detail how the rape occurred. Moreover, the legal definition of rape, in Massachusetts as well as other states, adds to the humiliation. Rape is sexual penetration against the woman's will; the defense often seeks to blame the victim by suggesting that she consented, did not resist, was provocatively dressed, and so on. It can take little to discredit the victim. Since the Holmstrom and Burgess study, a number of states have passed legislation limiting inquiry into a rape victim's past sexual conduct.

Support for the system.   Somewhat surprisingly, despite the problems and frustrations experienced, victims and witnesses still express overall support for the court process (Hagan). In Milwaukee those surveyed indicated that they were satisfied or very satisfied with the handling of their case by the police (81 percent), district attorney (75 percent), and judge (66 percent). Less than 15 percent said they were dissatisfied (Knudten et al.). Favorable judgments were independent of whether a victim was satisfied with the eventual outcome of the case (Stookey and Oman).

Victims Through the Eyes of the Court

The criminal courts confront a double-bind with regard to victims. On the one hand, victims are valued for the cases they bring to the system. Their misfortunes become the raw material of the court process. On the other hand, individual victims represent a potential source of irrationality in the process. The personal and often emotional involvement of victims in the crime experience can generate particularized demands for case outcomes that have little to do with the public interest. Prosecutors, for example, may perceive that the victim's demands for public justice actually mask a desire for private vengeance (Hagan).

Lack of cooperation.   A number of victims and witnesses are reluctant to become involved in the criminal justice process. Half of all major crimes are never reported to the police; even when they are, not all victims wish to prosecute. They may fear reprisal by the suspect, or they may prefer not to go through the ordeal of the court process. Some specific witness-related problems include giving the police incorrect addresses, refusing to sign a complaint, failing to show up in court, and offering testimony that is confused, garbled, or contradicted by other facts. Witness-related problems result in a significant number of cases in which the prosecutor refuses to file charges or the case is later dismissed. In Indianapolis, for example, 40 percent of cases dropped from the process before trial were attributed to witness problems. Comparable figures for other cities are Golden, Colorado (20 percent), New Orleans (40 percent), and Los Angeles (70 percent) (Boland et al.).

Not all uncooperative behavior can be blamed on victims and witnesses, however. The court process can be equally at fault. In Washington, D.C., a study focused on what it called "noncooperative" witnesses reported that 41 percent were never told they should contact the prosecutor, 62 percent were never notified of court appearances, and 43 percent stated that the police, prosecutor, and judge all failed to explain the witnesses' rights and duties (Cannavale and Falcon). Apart from this failure to communicate, the report also concluded that "prosecutors misinterpreted the witnesses' intentions and therefore regarded them as uncooperative, when indeed such a decision was premature at best and incorrect at worst" (Meyer: 1). Moreover, the longer the case is delayed, the more likely it is that witnesses will not appear when summoned.

Victim characteristics.   How a case is handled is determined by the identity of the victim as well as the offender. In Toronto, many victims who successfully pursued their cases through the criminal justice system were not individuals but organizations, particularly commercial organizations (Hagan). Prosecutors allocate their limited resources to the cases that they believe constitute the most "trouble." Not surprisingly, such judgments correlate with the desire for high conviction rates. Prosecutors assume that judges and juries will find the claims of certain kinds of victims credible and acceptable, and not those of others (Stanko). The troubles of older, white, male, employed victims are considered more worthy of public processing (Myers and Hagan), whereas victims of violent crime tend to be young, nonwhite males, divorced or never married, low-income, and unemployed (Bureau of Justice Statistics; Elias). Cases involving a prior relationship between the victim and defendant are often viewed by court officials as private disputes rather than offenses against the entire community. In domestic disturbance cases, for example, many women call the police in order to stop the violence but later refuse to sign a complaint, thus effectively ending the case.

The following case illustrates how prosecutors' perceptions of victims affects decision making.

> An auxiliary police officer watched a woman approach a man as he emerged from a liquor store. It was dark. The officer thought he saw a knife flash in her hand, and the man seemed to hand her some money. She fled, and the officer went to the aid of the victim, taking him to the hospital for treatment.
>
> The officer saw the woman on the street a few days later and arrested her for first degree robbery on the victim's sworn complaint. It was presumably a "high quality" arrest—identification of the perpetrator by an eye-witness, not from mugshots or a lineup, but in a crowd. Yet, shortly thereafter, this apparently airtight case was dismissed on the prosecutor's motion.
>
> What the victim had not explained to the police was that the defendant, an alcoholic, had been his girlfriend for the past five years; that they had been drinking together the night of the incident; that she had taken some money from him and got angry when he took it back; that she had flown into a fury when he then gave her only a dollar outside the liquor store; and that she had slashed at him with a pen knife in anger and run off. He had been sufficiently annoyed to have her charged with robbery, but, as the judge who dismissed the case said, "He wasn't really injured. Before it got into court they had kissed and made up." In fact, the victim actually approached the defense attorney before the hearing and asked him to prevail upon the judge and the Assistant District Attorney (ADA) to dismiss the charges against his girlfriend. (Vera Institute of Justice: xii)

This case is one of many cited by the Vera Institute to support its finding that in half of all felony arrests, the victim had a prior relationship with the defendant. Prior relationships were frequent in cases of homicide and assault, where they were expected, but they were also frequent in cases of robbery, where they were not. Criminal court officials, therefore, regard these crimes as not very serious.

Aiding Victims and Witnesses

For decades reformers have urged that victims and witnesses be accorded better treatment. In 1931, the National Commission on Law Observance and Enforcement concluded that effective administration of public justice requires willing witnesses, but testifying in court imposed unreasonable burdens on citizens. Similarly, in 1938 the American Bar Association found that witness fees were deplorably low, courthouse accommodations were inadequate and uncomfortable, and witnesses were frequently summoned to court numerous times only to have the case continued. But it was not until the 1960s that consistent attention was devoted to the problems faced by victims and witnesses in the court and ways to improve the situation (Karmen). The President's Commission on Law Enforcement and Administration of Justice highlighted a "growing concern that the average citizen identifies himself less and less with the criminal process and its officials."

In the last decade, concern for victims and witnesses of crime has risen to a crescendo. Government at the federal, state, and local level has begun to focus on the problem through legislation, funding, and research. In 1982 Congress passed the Victim and Witness Protection Act, which requires the U.S. attorney general to develop and implement guidelines that effectively promote the observance of victim and witness rights. The resulting memorandum, issued on July 12, 1983, expands victim and witness assistance even beyond what was called for in the act (Goldstein). Similarly, in 1983 the President's Task Force on Victims of Crime stressed the need for achieving a balance between the needs and rights of the victim and those of the defendant. More than thirty states have passed victim rights initiatives. Growing interest in aiding victims and witnesses is reflected in three programs in particular.

Victim/Witness Assistance Programs

Victim/witness assistance programs encourage cooperation in the conviction of criminals by reducing the inconvenience citizens face when appearing in court. Typical activities include providing comfortable and secure waiting areas, aiding in collecting witness fees, assisting with the prompt return of stolen property that has been recovered, and encouraging officials to take strong action if victim/witnesses are threatened by defendants. These programs—many of them based in or working closely with prosecutors' offices—also provide victim/witnesses with a clearer understanding of the court process by distributing brochures, explaining court procedures, and notifying witnesses of upcoming court dates (Davis). The Law Enforcement Assistance Administration funded more than ninety victim/witness projects. The Victims of Crime

CONTROVERSY

Recognizing the Rights of Crime Victims

Statistics gloss over one of the most troublesome consequences of crime in America today. For every crime counted, there are innocent victims: those directly assaulted, those whose homes and businesses are entered and rifled, as well as the families, neighbors, and loved ones who share in the victims' pain and loss or who must cope with their own losses as survivors. That law-and-order process designed to apprehend those who break the law, to enforce our penal code against those who would evade it, and to lead the victimized through the judiciary's procedural maze falls down on the job with that final assignment. These individuals—the victims of robberies or assaults, the families who are victimized by a loved one's murder, the businessperson whose enterprise has been victimized by vandals or employees—become ciphers in a game the sole purpose of which is closing the case. Emotional trauma, social stigma, tangible losses or physical injury go unattended to by police, prosecutors, and all strata of criminal justice officials. An ability to separate a victim's personal well-being from his or her victimization appears to be a job criteria for criminal justice officials. The old TV star, Sergeant Joe Friday of "Dragnet," played the role adeptly with his automatic line, "Just the facts, ma'am."

Senator John Heinz (R.–Penn.), "Recognizing the Rights of Crime Victims," *USA Today, 113,* 1984: 80.

Act and the Justice Assistance Act, both passed by Congress in 1984, provide increased funding for victim services (Finn).

victim/witness assistance programs

Victim/witness assistance programs are based on two assumptions. First, the cooperation of victim/witnesses is essential to prosecutors if they are to win convictions. Second, many victim/witnesses fail to cooperate with court officials because the cost of involvement is too high in terms of lost time, inconvenience, exposure to retaliation, discomfort, and psychological stress (Davis).

Evaluations of victim/witness assistance programs have yielded mixed results. A study of Prince George's County, Maryland, found that a victim's willingness to cooperate in the future was positively associated with considerate treatment by criminal justice personnel (Norton). Records kept by a program in Peoria, Illinois, likewise indicated that victim/witnesses receiving help were more likely to appear when summoned than those who had not been aided (National Institute of Justice). But no such impact was found in Brooklyn; those helped by the program appeared at the same rate as those who were not aided. Moreover, there was no change in the rate of case dismissals. Although the project's services were highly rated by users, they did not affect the users' opinions of the court system (Davis).

Victim Compensation Programs

The criminal justice system in the United States is offender-oriented, focusing on the apprehension, prosecution, and punishment of wrongdoers. While emphasizing the rehabilitation of offenders, the system has done little to help victims recover from the financial and emotional problems that they suffer. Civil lawsuits (see Chapter 2) are of little relevance because most criminal defendants have no money to pay monetary damages for personal injuries or damage to property. An increasingly used technique is restitution, whereby the court orders the defendant to pay the victim for the losses suffered (see Chapter 15).

When restitution by the offender is an inadequate or impractical method for financial reimbursement, compensation by a third party is the only alternative. An insurance company is an example of such a third party; but many victims, because they are poor, do not have insurance covering medical expenses or property losses. The government is another sort of third party.

victim compensation programs

Victim compensation programs rest on the premise that the government should counterbalance losses suffered by victims of criminal acts.

The first compensation program in the United States began in California in 1965. Since then thirty-nine states have enacted legislation providing compensation for at least some classes of crime victims. All programs establish eligibility requirements for claimants. Typically, some types of victims—for instance, relatives and accomplices of the offender—are ineligible for awards. Most programs provide for recovery of medical expenses and some lost earnings; none reimburses the victim for lost or damaged property. The maximum amount paid in damages is typically $10,000 to $15,000. Payments are made from state-administered funds. Many laws create boards or commissions to determine claims, although in some states claims are decided by the courts or existing workers' compensation agencies (Anderson and Woodard).

Victim compensation programs appear to provide clear benefits to victims of crime. But the actual results of such programs require careful scrutiny. Preliminary evaluations of compensation programs have yielded findings disappointing for administrators (Karmen). Compensation programs are intended to improve the attitudes of victims toward the criminal justice system, but this improvement does not occur (Doerner). Indeed cumbersome administrative procedures lead to added frustrations and increased alienation. Strict eligibility requirements mean that as many as two-thirds of claimants never receive any money (Elias).

Victim's Bill of Rights

victim's bill of rights

Nowhere is awakened concern about victims of crime more readily apparent than in proposals for a *victim's bill of rights.* Apart from the title they share, however, these proposals differ markedly, reflecting different philosophies.

The President's Task Force on Victims of Crime submitted sixty-eight separate recommendations aimed at achieving a balance between the needs and rights of the victim and those of the defendant (Table 9-2). Also in 1982, California voters approved Proposition 8 by a two-to-one margin. Known as the "Victim's Bill of Rights," it added twelve controversial provisions to the state constitution and the criminal code. These versions reflect the rallying cry of the law-and-order movement, which has it that the courts protect the rights of defendants rather than the rights of victims. Premised on the notion that defendants escape too easily from the court process, these proposals stress largely substantive changes in the law, such as abolishing the exclusionary rule, limiting bail, restricting plea bargaining, and imposing stiffer sentences.

Other proposed victim's bill of rights are less ideological, emphasizing improving court procedures to better the lot of victims and witnesses. One example is the fifteen-point proposal of the International Society of Victimology. More recently the National Conference of the Judiciary on the Rights of Victims of Crime adopted a Statement of Recommended Judicial Practices, suggesting (1) fair treatment of victims and witnesses through better information about court procedures, (2) victim participation and input through all stages of judicial proceedings, and (3) better protection of victims and witnesses from harassment, threats, intimidation, and harm.

The Politics of Aiding Victims

After a long period of neglect, aiding victims has become good politics. Everyone agrees that victims and witnesses should be treated better during the court process. But political rhetoric should not be allowed to obscure some important issues.

Although enthusiasm for helping victims is clearly growing, the willingness to pay for the necessary services is declining. A number of innovative and imaginative programs like rape crisis centers and shelters for battered women have sought to provide needed services for victims of crime. Yet the federal government has greatly reduced or totally eliminated funding for these efforts. At the same time, fiscal problems and tax reduction efforts mean that state

TABLE 9-2 Recommendations for Federal and State Action, President's Task Force on Victims of Crime

1. Legislation should be proposed and enacted to ensure that addresses of victims and witnesses are not made public or available to the defense, absent a clear need as determined by the court.
2. Legislation should be proposed and enacted to ensure that designated victim counseling is legally privileged and not subject to defense discovery or subpoena.
3. Legislation should be proposed and enacted to ensure that hearsay is admissible and sufficient in preliminary hearings, so that victims need not testify in person.
4. Legislation should be proposed and enacted to amend the bail laws to accomplish the following:
   a. Allow courts to deny bail to persons found by clear and convincing evidence to present a danger to the community.
   b. Give the prosecution the right to expedited appeal of adverse bail determinations, analogous to the right presently held by the defendant.
   c. Codify existing case law defining the authority of the court to detain defendants as to whom no conditions of release are adequate to ensure appearance at trial;
   d. Reverse, in the case of serious crimes, any standard that presumptively favors release of convicted persons awaiting sentence or appealing their convictions;
   e. Require defendants to refrain from criminal activity as a mandatory condition of release; and
   f. Provide penalties for failing to appear while released on bond or personal recognizance that are more closely proportionate to the penalties for the offense with which the defendant was originally charged.
5. Legislation should be proposed and enacted to abolish the exclusionary rule as it applies to Fourth Amendment issues.
6. Legislation should be proposed and enacted to open parole release hearings to the public.
7. Legislation should be proposed and enacted to abolish parole and limit judicial discretion in sentencing.
8. Legislation should be proposed and enacted to require that school officials report violent offenses against students or teachers, or the possession of weapons or narcotics on school grounds. The knowing failure to make such a report to the police, or deterring others from doing so, should be designated a misdemeanor.
9. Legislation should be proposed and enacted to make available to businesses and organizations the sexual assault, child molestation, and pornography arrest records of prospective and present employees whose work will bring them in regular contact with children.
10. Legislation should be proposed and enacted to accomplish the following:
   a. Require victim impact statements at sentencing;
   b. Provide for the protection of victims and witnesses from intimidation;
   c. Require restitution in all cases, unless the court provides specific reasons for failing to require it;
   d. Develop and implement guidelines for the fair treatment of crime victims and witnesses; and
   e. Prohibit a criminal from making any profit from the sale of the story of his crime. Any proceeds should be used to provide full restitution to his victims, pay the expenses of his prosecution, and finally, assist the crime victim compensation fund.
11. Legislation should be proposed and enacted to establish or expand employee assistance programs for victims of crime employed by government.
12. Legislation should be proposed and enacted to ensure that sexual assault victims are not required to assume the cost of physical examinations and materials used to obtain evidence.

SOURCE: President's Task Force on Victims of Crime, *Final Report* (Washington, D.C.: U.S. Government Printing Office), 1982, pp. 17–18.

and local governments are also unable to provide such funding. Overall, legislators and other government officials find voting for victim-oriented legislation politically advantageous; but when it comes to voting money for another ''welfare program,'' they are much more hesitant.

Moreover, it is unclear how much aid victims and witnesses receive from these programs. Once enacted, programs do not always work as intended. Elias concluded that victim compensation laws were exercises in symbolic politics. Few claimants ever received compensation; the laws provided "political placebos" with few concrete, tangible benefits for victims. Similarly, victim/witness assistance programs appear to be important first steps in providing better services to citizens who find themselves thrust into the criminal court process. But not all agree that the benefits of these programs actually aid the victim. Sociologist William McDonald charges that "some projects that are billed as 'assisting victims' are more accurately described as assisting the criminal justice system and extending government control over victims. Whether the victims so controlled would regard the project as 'assisting' them is problematic" (p. 35). Some victims do not wish to become involved.

In 1975, the National Organization for Victim Assistance was founded. It is difficult to organize crime victims politically, however, because they share little aside from their misfortune. However, other social movements have discovered that their goals coincide with those of particular groups of victims. The most important contributors to the cause of victims are the women's movement, law-and-order advocates, civil rights and civil liberties groups, and child welfare advocates (Karmen). The active interest of these strange political bedfellows suggests that beneath the rhetoric about aiding victims of crimes, there are important disagreements over goals and priorities.

Differing versions of the victim's bill of rights provide a case in point. Although everyone agrees that victims and witnesses should be treated better, the important question is "at whose expense?" Some versions emphasize protecting the rights of victims by denying privileges and benefits to suspects, defendants, and prisoners. This type of the victim's bill of rights is the most recent example of the conflict between the due process model and the crime control model highlighted in Chapter 1. Other versions emphasize improving the welfare of victims at the expense of the privileges and options enjoyed by members of the courtroom work group (Karmen). Law professor Norval Morris, for one, believes that victims should have the opportunity to be

C O N T R O V E R S Y

The Rhetoric About Victim's Rights Is Demagoguery

Crime inflicts terrible pain and suffering on its victims. Without question, the best thing that can be done for victims and potential victims is to reduce the astronomical level of predatory crime in America. Unfortunately, the proposals advanced on behalf of the rights of victims will not accomplish that. Most of the rhetoric about victim's rights is demagoguery: playing upon the very real feelings of pain, fear, and outrage to advance dubious proposals. The so-called "victim's bill of rights" will do nothing for victims and nothing to reduce crime. If anything, these proposals will trample on established constitutional rights, which do in fact protect victims.

Samuel Walker, "What Have Civil Liberties Ever Done for Crime Victims? Plenty!" *ACJS Today* (October 1982): 4–5; American Civil Liberties Union, *The Rights of Crime Victims* (New York: Bantam Books).

present during plea bargaining but not to have veto power. Similarly, Rosett and Cressey argue that additional efforts must be made to bring the criminal courts back to the people by breaking down barriers between courts and citizens. Members of the courtroom work group understandably resist limitations on their powers and responsibilities. Finally, straight victim compensation programs aid victims at the expense of a third group: taxpayers.

Conclusion

Victims and witnesses provide the raw material for the court process. The complaints they bring, the credibility of their stories, and their willingness to participate directly affect the courtroom work group's activities. Victims and witnesses are valued because they provide the raw material for the court process, but members of the courtroom work group do not respond uncritically to the demands for their services. They find some stories more believable than others, and some claims more worthy than others.

The clientele shapes the criminal court process in a less obvious way. Most defendants are young, illiterate, impoverished, and disproportionately members of minority groups. Many victims share similar traits. They are also poor, unversed in the way of the courts, and disproportionately members of minority groups. The net result is that the criminal courts are poor people's institutions. They share many characteristics of other institutions like welfare offices and charity hospitals that deal almost exclusively with the poor. Unlike the middle class, the poor are accustomed to accepting the conditions they find themselves in. They do not protest long waits before government officials can see them, nor do they demand that the building they wait in offer amenities. In cities with separate civil and criminal courts, the former are typically newer and cleaner. Such contrasts emphasize the differing clientele of civil and criminal courts, and also highlight major differences in how victims and witnesses are treated.

For Discussion

1. Interview several people who have been witnesses in criminal court. What problems do they mention? Did they find their experience satisfying or frustrating?
2. What programs would you recommend for improving court treatment of victims and witnesses?
3. While you are in court, observe the facial expressions and body motions of the defendants. What might they indicate? For a representative day in court, prepare a tally of the age, race, sex, poverty level, and so on of both witnesses and defendants. How does this profile compare to Table 9-1?
4. How do the characteristics of defendants in criminal courts shape the process? Why do judges, prosecutors, defense attorneys, and probation officers often believe that because of the nature of the court's clientele, cases are really less serious than they legally appear to be?

References

AMERICAN BAR ASSOCIATION. "Recommendations of the Committee on Improvements in the Administration of Justice of the Section of Judicial Administration (As approved by the Assembly and House of Delegates, July 27, 1938)." Chicago, 1938.

ANDERSON, JOHN, AND PAUL WOODARD. "Victim and Witness Assistance: New State Laws and the System's Response." *Judicature* 68 (1985): 221.

ASH, MICHAEL. "On Witnesses: A Radical Critique of Criminal Court Proceedings." *Notre Dame Lawyer* 48 (1972): 386.

BOLAND, BARBARA, ELIZABETH BRADY, HERBERT TYSON, AND JOHN BASSLER. *The Prosecution of Felony Arrests.* Washington, D.C.: Institute for Law and Social Research, 1982.

BUREAU OF JUSTICE STATISTICS. *Report to the Nation on Crime and Justice: The Data.* Washington, D.C.: U.S. Department of Justice, 1983.

CANNAVALE, F., AND W. FALCON. *Witness Cooperation.* Lexington, Mass.: D. C. Heath, 1976.

CONNICK, ELIZABETH, AND ROBERT DAVIS. "Examining the Problems of Witness Intimidation." *Judicature* 66 (1983): 438.

DAVIS, ROBERT. "Victim/Witness Noncooperation: A Second Look at a Persistent Phenomenon." *Journal of Criminal Justice* 11 (1983): 287.

DOERNER, WILLIAM. "Impact of Crime Compensation on Victim's Attitudes Toward the Criminal Justice System." *Victimology* 5 (1980): 61.

ELIAS, ROBERT. *Victims of the System: Crime Victims and Compensation in American Politics and Criminal Justice.* New Brunswick, N.J.: Transaction Books, 1983.

FINN, PETER. "Collaboration Between the Judiciary and Victim-Witness Assistance Programs." *Judicature* 69 (1986): 192.

GERTZ, MARC. "Comparative Justice: A Study of Five Connecticut Courts." Paper presented at the annual meeting of the New England Political Science Association, Durham, New Hampshire, April 9–11, 1976.

GOLDSTEIN, ABRAHAM. "The Victim and Prosecutorial Discretion: The Federal Victim and Witness Protection Act of 1982." *Law and Contemporary Problems* 47 (1984): 225.

HAGAN, JOHN. *Victims Before the Law: The Organizational Domination of Criminal Law.* Toronto: Butterworths, 1983.

HOLMSTROM, LYNDA, AND ANN BURGESS. "Rape: The Victim Goes on Trial." In *Victimology: A New Focus,* ed. Israel Drapkin and Emilio Viano, pp. 31–48. Lexington, Mass.: D. C. Heath, 1975.

KARMEN, ANDREW. *Crime Victims: An Introduction to Victimology.* Pacific Grove, Calif.: Brooks/Cole, 1984.

KNUDTEN, RICHARD, ANTHONY MEADER, MARY KNUDTEN, AND WILLIAM DOERNER. "The Victim in the Administration of Criminal Justice: Problems and Perceptions." In *Criminal Justice and the Victim,* ed. William McDonald, pp. 115–146. Beverly Hills, Calif.: Sage Publications, 1976.

MCDONALD, WILLIAM F., ed. *Criminal Justice and the Victim.* Beverly Hills, Calif: Sage Publications, 1976.

MEYER, EUGENE. "Witnesses' Feelings Misread." *Washington Post,* December 14, 1975.

MOORE, MARK, SUSAN ESTRICH, DANIEL MCGILLIS, AND WILLIAM SPELMAN. *Dangerous Offenders: The Elusive Target of Justice.* Cambridge, Mass.: Harvard University Press, 1984.

MORRIS, NORVAL. *The Future of Imprisonment.* Chicago: University of Chicago Press, 1974.

MYERS, MARTHA, AND JOHN HAGAN. "Private and Public Trouble: Prosecutors and the Allocation of Court Resources." *Social Problems* 26 (1979): 439.

NATIONAL ADVISORY COMMISSION ON CRIMINAL JUSTICE STANDARDS AND GOALS. *Courts.* Washington, D.C.: Government Printing Office, 1973,

NATIONAL COMMISSION ON LAW OBSERVANCE AND ENFORCEMENT. *Report on the Cost of Crime,* no. 12. Washington, D.C.: Government Printing Office, 1931.

NATIONAL INSTITUTE OF JUSTICE. *Exemplary Projects: Focus for 1982—Projects to Combat Violent Crime.* Washington, D.C.: U.S. Department of Justice, 1982.

NORTON, LEE. "Witness Involvement in the Criminal Justice System and Intention to Cooperate in Future Prosecutions." *Journal of Criminal Justice* 11 (1983): 143.

PRESIDENT'S COMMISSION ON LAW ENFORCEMENT AND CRIMINAL JUSTICE. *Task Force Report: The Courts.* Washington, D.C.: Government Printing Office, 1967.

PRESIDENT'S TASK FORCE ON VICTIMS OF CRIME. *Final Report.* Washington, D.C.: Government Printing Office, 1982.

RESICK, PATRICIA. "The Trauma of Rape and the Criminal Justice System." *Justice System Journal* 9 (1984): 52.

ROSETT, ARTHUR, AND DONALD CRESSEY. *Justice by Consent.* Philadelphia: J. B. Lippincott, 1976.

STANKO, ELIZABETH. "The Impact of Victim Assessment on Prosecutors' Screening Decisions: The Case of the New York County District Attorney's Office." *Law and Society Review* 16 (1981–1982): 225.

STOOKEY, JOHN, AND COLLEEN OMAN. "The Victim's Perspective on American Criminal Justice." Paper presented at the annual meeting of the Midwest Political Science Association, Chicago, Illinois, April 29–May 1, 1976.

VERA INSTITUTE OF JUSTICE. *Felony Arrests: Their Prosecution and Disposition in New York City's Courts.* New York: Vera Institute of Justice, 1977.

WALKER, SAMUEL. *Sense and Nonsense About Crime: A Policy Guide.* Pacific Grove, Calif.: Brooks/Cole, 1985.

For Further Reading

ANDERSON, JOHN, AND PAUL WOODARD. "Victim and Witness Assistance: New State Laws and the System's Response." *Judicature* 68 (1985): 221.

CANNAVALLE, F. J. *Witness Cooperation with a Handbook of Witness Management.* Lexington, Mass.: D. C. Heath, 1975.

FINN, PETER. "Collaboration Between the Judiciary and Victim-Witness Assistance Programs." *Judicature* 69 (1986): 192.

GRAHAM, MICHAEL. *Witness Intimidation: The Law's Response.* Westport, Conn.: Quorum Books, 1985.

HAGAN, JOHN. *Victims Before the Law: The Organizational Domination of Criminal Law.* Toronto: Butterworths, 1983.

HOLMSTROM, LYNDA, AND ANA BURGESS. *The Victim of Rape: Institutional Reactions.* New York: John Wiley, 1978.

MCDONALD, WILLIAM, ed. *Criminal Justice and the Victim.* Beverly Hills, Calif.: Sage Publications, 1976.

MOORE, MARK, SUSAN ESTRICH, DANIEL MCGILLIS, AND WILLIAM SPELMAN. *Dangerous Offenders: The Elusive Target of Justice.* Cambridge, Mass.: Harvard University Press, 1984.

RAFTER, NICOLE, AND ELIZABETH STANKO. *Judge, Lawyer, Victim, Thief: Women, Gender Roles and Criminal Justice.* Boston: Northeastern University Press, 1982.

PART III

IS THE DEFENDANT GUILTY?

T he five chapters of Part III follow the steps of criminal prosecution from arrest to the determination of guilt or innocence. The central concerns are why many cases are eliminated from the process early and why most cases end not with a trial but a plea of guilty.

Chapter 10 looks at case screening. Well before trial, many cases are eliminated by actions of prosecutors, grand juries, and/or preliminary hearings.

Chapter 11 focuses on the American bail system.

Chapter 12 considers the preparation of cases for trial. The primary topics are discovery and the suppression of evidence.

Plea bargaining is a much publicized but little understood part of the criminal court process. Why cases are pled out and whether plea bargaining is fair are the central topics in Chapter 13.

Chapter 14 examines the trial process: Selection of a jury, presentation of evidence, and the eventual jury verdict. Even though only a handful of cases go to trial, jury verdicts nonetheless have a major impact on how the courts exercise discretion.

CHAPTER 10

After the Arrest:
Case Attrition

Cases do not automatically move through the criminal justice process. At numerous stages in the proceedings, prosecutors, judges, police officers, and victims have the option of advancing a case to the next step, seeking an alternative disposition, or dropping the case altogether. These screening decisions result in significant case attrition.

This chapter discusses the early stages of a criminal case, focusing on when and why case attrition occurs. We will begin at the beginning, with arrests, and proceed through prosecutorial screening, the preliminary hearing, and the grand jury. The decisions made at these early points set the tone, tenor, quality, and quantity of cases moving through the criminal court process (Jacoby). Clearly the volume of cases is directly tied to screening decisions. It is common in many areas for roughly half of the defendants to have their charges dismissed during these early stages. Moreover, later stages in the proceedings, like plea bargaining, reflect how cases were initially screened. It is a long-standing practice in many courts, for instance, for prosecutors to overcharge a defendant by filing accusations more serious than the evidence indicates in order to provide themselves leverage for later offering the defendant the opportunity to plead to a less serious charge.

The charging process also has important consequences for defendants. Once a suspect is formally charged with a crime, the full power of the criminal court process comes into effect. Unless bond is posted, the accused must await trial in jail. He or she may have to raise money to hire a lawyer. The person's reputation may be damaged. Thus, the criminal court process imposes significant penalties even on defendants who are later acquitted or have their cases dismissed.

Arrests

Beginning in 1964, the United States experienced a dramatic increase in crime. For almost two decades crimes known to the police increased much faster than population. In 1980, however, this trend leveled off. By 1985 rates of property offenses had dropped significantly and rates of violent crimes had decreased slightly (Bureau of Justice Statistics, 1986). The public, though, still perceives that crime is on the increase. Relatively few crimes ever result in criminal court action.

arrest   Most criminal cases begin with an arrest. Every year the police ***arrest*** almost eleven million persons for non-traffic offenses—mostly minor ones like simple assault, public drunkenness, petty theft, possession of small amounts of marijuana, and so on. Of these arrests, however, 2.3 million are for the serious crimes of homicide, rape, arson, aggravated assault, robbery, burglary, auto theft, and larceny over fifty dollars. These eight crimes, considered in the FBI's

type I offenses   *Uniform Crime Report* as ***type I offenses*** and generally referred to as ***index***
index crimes   ***crimes,*** are the ones that produce headlines about rising crime rates. Note, though, that some other serious crimes (possession of drugs, for one) are not included. Also, many types of crimes committed primarily by the upper class—fraud and stock manipulations, for instance—are also excluded even though their economic costs are as great as the costs of crimes committed by the poor. Contrary to public perceptions, most felony arrests are for nonviolent offenses involving burglary and larceny. Only one out of five arrests for type I offenses involve homicide, rape, robbery, or aggravated assault.

Although the volume of arrests for serious crimes is heavy, they represent only a fraction of the crimes committed. The *Uniform Crime Reports* are based only on crimes known to the police. Only 36 percent of the personal and household offenses measured in the National Crime Survey's yearly sample of households were reported to the police—a rate of reporting that remained basically unchanged throughout the 1980s (Bureau of Justice Statistics, 1986). Moreover, of the crimes brought to the attention of the police, only about 19

police   percent result in an arrest. ***Police clearance*** by arrest varies greatly by the
clearance   type of crime involved: 43 percent of violent crimes result in arrest compared to only 17 percent of property offenses (Bureau of Justice Statistics, 1983). Even after arrest, the police may determine that the crime report is unfounded or that there is insufficient evidence to hold the suspect.

The vast majority of crimes never reach the courts. Nonetheless, the workload of the criminal courts is heavy. The very visible increase in crime during the 1960s and 1970s swelled court dockets as well. Other factors also add to the workload of the courts. One is the shift in the types of cases being prosecuted. In an effort to fight the alarming increase in drug usage, law enforcement officials have increasingly sought to prosecute major drug dealers rather than street-level pushers, who are easier to apprehend and prosecute. Similarly, public pressures have resulted in more prosecution of major white-collar crimes. These types of cases are more complex than run-of-the-mill prosecutions for possession of small amounts of illicit drugs or felony theft. In addition, during the 1960s and 1970s, appellate courts, led by the U.S. Supreme Court, imposed additional procedural requirements (*Miranda* warnings, for example). Taken together, these factors have increased the workload of the criminal courts because they require that more time be devoted to case preparation.

Police Screening

police screening

Most police departments forward those arrested to the prosecutor without conducting a review of the strength of the case. In general the police prefer to leave assessments of legal matters to prosecutors. "In deciding to invoke the criminal process the police are guided by the strong belief that analysis of the evidence both in regard to its admissibility and its weight are matters that should be decided by higher authority" (McIntyre, 1968: 469). This lack of *police screening* is particularly important because it means that in some communities the police department effectively controls the decision to prosecute.

Police procedures have a lot to do with whether or not arrests result in convictions. Police officers, in responding to calls from victims and witnesses, are not always fully aware of the critical importance to the success of the case in court of recovering physical evidence. A review of 14,865 arrests in the District of Columbia indicated that when the arresting officer recovers tangible evidence, a conviction is more likely. When the police manage to bring more cooperative witnesses to the prosecutor, the probability of conviction likewise increases. When the police are able to make an arrest soon after the offense, tangible evidence is more often recovered and conviction is again more likely (Forst et al.).

Police officers vary in providing the prosecutor with sufficient evidence for a conviction. Studies old and new have called for improvement in the investigative and evidence-gathering functions of the police. One report noted that prosecutors complained that police tend to be sloppy in their investigations, often missing important evidence and improperly seizing, marking, or storing the items they do gather (Battelle Law and Justice Study Center). A seven-city study found that 12 percent of the officers produced half of all convictions, whereas 22 percent produced no arrests resulting in conviction. This difference in performance sprang not from personal characteristics of the officers or experience. Rather the most important factor was the successful officers' "persistence in finding and interviewing witnesses and in supporting witnesses through the trial, as well as being particularly conscious of the gathering and maintenance of evidence'' (Forst et al.).

Police departments also vary in the quality of arrests referred to the district attorney. Where prosecutors deal with numerous police departments one often finds that some departments have a better record of forwarding the evidence necessary for a successful conviction. In Salt Lake City, for example, prosecutors accept 85 percent of the felony arrests made by the sheriff's office, compared to 67 percent of those made by the police department. The same pattern appears in Los Angeles: 86 percent acceptance for the sheriff arrests compared with 60 percent for police arrests (Brosi). Prosecutors perceive that some police agencies conduct more thorough investigations than others (Neubauer, 1974b).

Filing of Charges

*charging
document
corpus delicti*

The criminal court process begins with the filing of a formal, written accusation alleging that a specified person or persons committed a specific offense or offenses. The ***charging document*** includes a brief description of the date and location of the offense. All the essential elements (***corpus delicti***) of the crime must be specified. Applicable state and federal law governs technical wording, procedures for making minor amendments, and so on. These formal, written accusations satisfy the Sixth Amendment provision that a defendant be given information upon which to prepare a defense.

complaint

information

*arrest
warrant*

There are four types of charging documents: the complaint, information, arrest warrant, and indictment (which will be discussed later). Which one is used depends on the severity of the offense, the applicable state or federal law, and local customs. ***Complaints*** must be supported by oath or affirmation of either the victim or the arresting officer. They are most commonly used in prosecuting misdemeanor offenses or city ordinance violations. An ***information*** is virtually identical in form to the complaint except that it is signed by the prosecutor. A bill of information is required in felony prosecutions in most non–grand jury states. In grand jury states, they are used for initiating felony charges pending grand jury action. ***Arrest warrants*** are issued by a judicial officer—typically a lower court judge or magistrate. On rare occasions, the warrant is issued prior to arrest. For most street crimes, however, the police arrest the suspect and then apply for an arrest warrant. In such instances, some states require that the prosecutor approve the request in writing before an arrest warrant can be issued (McIntyre, 1967).

Prosecutorial Control of the Charging Decision

The prosecutor controls the doors to the courthouse. He or she can decide whether charges should be filed and what the proper charge should be. Although the law demands prosecution for "all known criminal conduct," the courts have traditionally granted prosecutors wide discretion in deciding whether to file charges. For example, there are no legislative or judicial standards governing which cases merit prosecution and which should be declined. Moreover, if a prosecutor refuses to file charges no review of this decision is possible; courts have consistently refused to order a prosecutor to proceed with a case.

prosecutorial domination of the charging process

The prosecutor has the legal authority to ***dominate the charging process.*** Some choose to share this authority with the police. An American Bar Foundation study concluded that some prosecutors defer to the police (Miller). In these communities the police file criminal charges with minimal supervision by the prosecutor. In essence, these prosecutors have transferred their decision-making power to the police (Mellon et al.). In others, the prosecutor retains the formal authority to file charges, but the police influence the prosecutor's decision. Studies of Oakland (Skolnick), of Seattle (Cole), and of assistant U.S. attorneys (Eisenstein) indicate that the police and prosecutor jointly discuss cases before charges are filed. The influence of the police in such an interchange is revealed by Skolnick's finding that police pressure resulted in suspects being charged on the basis of weak evidence or being initially overcharged.

In communities where prosecutors choose to control the filing of criminal charges, a substantial percentage (a third to a half) of persons arrested are released without the filing of criminal charges. I analyzed all non-traffic arrests for a month in a medium-sized Illinois community and found that a third of police arrests resulted in no criminal charges being filed (Neubauer, 1974a). Another study likewise concluded that in court systems with strong prosecutorial screening, up to half of all felony arrests do not result in criminal charges (Boland et al.).

One of the major recommendations of the National Advisory Commission on Criminal Justice Standards and Goals was that prosecutors should exercise the dominant role in the charging decision. The primary justification is efficiency. Removing weak cases and cases that do not warrant prosecution eliminates the need for judges and other court personnel to devote time to them. Moreover, civilian witnesses and police officers are not required to appear, which translates into additional savings on witnesses and police overtime and allows civilians and police alike to use their time in more productive ways (Rossman and Hoffman).

Arguments in favor of prosecutorial control of the charging decision that are anchored in a view that such actions will increase "efficiency" neglect something vital:

> Those who have studied the pretrial screening process have failed to see it as part of either the prosecutorial system or the criminal justice system. The result is, in part, a failure to see pretrial screening as part of a continuum rather than as an isolated act and as a means to an end, the disposition of a case, rather than as a goal in itself. Screening cannot be separated from the larger system of which it is part if it is to be evaluated. It is an implicit part of that system, and must be treated as such. (Jacoby: 12)

Disregarding the relationship between police and prosecutor is a major cause of the failure to see prosecutorial screening as tied to the entire criminal justice process. Prosecutorial control of the charging decision is resisted by the police. Every arrest rejected by the prosecutor is an implicit criticism of the arresting officer. When District Attorney Harry Connick established a tough screening policy in New Orleans, the case rejection rate went up to 46 percent. The police responded publicly, refusing to believe that they were "wrong" in half the arrests they made (*Times-Picayune*). Moreover, in some jurisdictions the police rely on the initial charging policies of the prosecutor to protect them from civil lawsuits for false arrest. Accommodating prosecutors may file charges they would otherwise reject just to convince the defendant that the arrest was lawful, or they may require the defendant to sign a release waiving any claim of false arrest. Tough prosecutorial screening policies disrupt such arrangements. In addition, the police may rely on overcharging as a means of developing snitches: they may promise to drop charges if the arrestee agrees to cooperate. Prosecutorial dominance of the charging decision obviously alters such practices (McDonald). As a result, some prosecutors choose to maintain

CLOSE-UP

Shackled Prisoners Find Night Court No Place for Laughs

The five men stumbled into the courtroom a little past 11 p.m., chained and tired, wearing iron shackles and somber stares.

All of them were arrested only a few hours ago.

Morris allegedly used a gun to rob a store, MacArthur is accused of stealing money from a gas station, Ricky allegedly hit a policewoman, Alvin is booked with beating up his son, and 17-year-old Marshall, the youngest of the group, is booked with rape.

They sat down silently, looking as if they couldn't believe they were actually here. So much has happened since the sun went down. So much has changed.

Three armed deputies with bowling-pin forearms stood in corners of the room, watching and yawning. Five bondsmen with greased hair and wearing a lot of jewelry took notes. A sign stuck to a post in the middle of the near-empty room warned spectators: "Do Not Talk To The Inmates. If So, You Will Be TOLD To Leave."

But no one was there to read it. No family, no relatives, no friends tonight at Magistrate Court. There were only five people on the agenda.

Only five? This won't take long, the court crew said, this is just another night. In they come, out they go.

"Magistrate Court is the first contact the criminal has with the criminal justice system," Judge Anthony Russo says as he flips through the pages of Car and Parts magazine. A "M*A*S*H" rerun is on television.

"These people are bewildered," Russo says, "their life has just turned around."

Magistrate Court operates from a small room in a corner of the Orleans Parish Criminal Courts Building at Tulane and Broad avenues. The building's huge corridors are empty this late at night. When a heel hits the floor, the sound bounces off the walls.

Court will begin in a few minutes. This is nothing like that television show, "Night Court," Russo says. That hap-

pens in Municipal Court, and it's not at night anymore. Magistrate Court is not funny.

Everyone arrested in New Orleans after 6 p.m. and before 10:30 p.m. comes here. Everyone. They are led in chained, the judge reviews their case, and sets bond. Anyone arrested after 10:30 p.m. must wait until morning for a bond hearing.

Families come often, sitting in shock, hoping the bond is low enough to pay. If it's not, this might be their last look at a loved one for a while.

Russo has done this about three nights a week for 12 years, so there's no reason to get excited tonight. He leans back in his chair and smiles a lot when he talks.

"There's no such thing as a light season," he says. "You know what we tell people? We give them this speech, 'Crime is a seven-day-a-week, 365-day-a-year business. We work holidays and weekends, to protect you, the law-abiding citizens.'"

He pauses and smiles.

good working relationships with their police departments and to demonstrate that they are part of the law enforcement team "by granting police a major voice in the charging decision" (Neubauer, 1974a).

Preliminary Hearing

preliminary hearing **preliminary examination**

The **preliminary hearing** (or **preliminary examination,** as it is called in some states) represents the first time that a case is reviewed by someone other than a law enforcement official. An arrested person is entitled to a timely hearing before a neutral judge to determine whether probable cause exists to detain the defendant prior to trial (*Gerstein* v. *Pugh,* 420 U.S. 103, 1975). Typically held before a lower court judge, the preliminary hearing is

---

"Man, it just never stops. And summer is the biggest season, because of the hot weather. People are out."

Especially at night.

Meeting the Attorney
Peeling paint fills the white walls of the courtroom. Venetian blinds are crooked and dirty. The neon sign from Irma's Bail Bonds on Broad sneaks through the blinds from the darkness.

The five men sit side-by-side on a scuffed wooden bench. They listen to Bruce Netterville, the public defender, who warns them not to say anything tonight in court.

"I'm the first person they see that's really on their side," Netterville says later. "These people have no self-esteem. What future do they have? They are overwhelmingly black and overwhelmingly poor."

The five men here tonight look overwhelmingly dazed. Ricky plays with the strings on his cutoff jeans. Morris slouches, his eyes half-shut. MacArthur just stares. Alvin rubs his goatee. Marshall sits upright, like he's preparing to salute.

Each of the men has been

here before. Morris has seven prior felony arrests. Mac-Arthur has 16.

Marshall, No. H1878186, is last. He has been arrested on the most serious crime: aggravated rape.

"How old are you, sir?" asks Russo.

"Seventeen, sir," Marshall replies.

"What do you do?" asks Russo.

"I'm a student, sir," Marshall replies.

"Can you afford an attorney?"

"No sir."

The prosecutor reads Marshall's record: "Your honor, he has 13 pending felony charges, five for burglary, five for illegal possession of stolen goods, three for theft charges. No prior convictions."

"Bond is set at $250,000," Russo says. Marshall sits down without expression.

The five chained men then stand up and start to walk back to Central Lockup. A deputy approaches Ricky.

"I'm going to ask you one question," he says in a tough

whisper. "Man, did you really hit a policewoman?"

Ricky just stares. The deputy sneers.

Five Is a Slow Night
This really was a slow night, Maraldo says a few minutes after the five men leave. On some nights, she says, 30 arrested people come in here, all hooked together with that big chain.

"We didn't even have any family members tonight," Maraldo says. "We usually have a lot."

"Nope, this was a pretty hardcore group," Russo says.

Russo must work until 6 a.m., waiting to sign arrest warrants. Maraldo has a lot of paperwork to finish.

"We never have had any trouble," Russo says. "You know why? Did you notice that when I spoke to them out there, I said, 'sir'? You know, that works. That's probably one of the first times in their lives they've been treated with respect."

Rene Sanchez, "Shackled Prisoners Find Night Court No Place for Laughs," *Times-Picayune,* August 25, 1986, p. 1. Reprinted by permission from the Times-Picayune Publishing Corp.

designed "to prevent hasty, malicious, improvident, and oppressive prosecutions, to protect the person charged from open and public accusations of crime, to avoid both for the defendant and the public the expense of a public trial, to save the defendant from the humiliation and anxiety involved in public prosecution, and to discover whether or not there are substantial grounds upon which a prosecution may be based" (*Thies* v. *State,* 178 Wis. 98, 1922). Beyond its legal rationale of protecting an innocent defendant from being held on baseless charges, the preliminary hearing often serves an important informal function as well. It gives the defense attorney an overview of the evidence against the client and provides the opportunity for discovery (see Chapter 12).

bind over

In non-grand jury states, the preliminary hearing is the sole procedure for determining whether sufficient evidence exists to justify holding the defendant. In grand jury states, the preliminary hearing **binds over** the accused for possible indictment. As a result, a magistrate's ruling that there is insufficient evidence does not necessarily end the case. The prosecutor can take the case directly to the grand jury (Gilboy).

probable cause

hearsay evidence

During a preliminary hearing the state does not have to prove the defendant guilty beyond a reasonable doubt, as would be required during a trial. Rather, all that is necessary is that the prosecutor establish **probable cause** that a crime has been committed and that the defendant committed the crime. Typically **hearsay evidence** (secondhand evidence) is admissible. Generally the defense does not have the right to cross-examine witnesses, although some states and some judges permit attorneys to ask witnesses questions. The situation in Chicago illustrates the diversity of practices. During most preliminary hearings, evidentiary rules are not strictly enforced. But in murder cases the judge permits hearsay testimony only for minor matters, such as the chain of possession of physical evidence (the murder weapon, for example). For critical matters like the identification of the assailant, the judge insists on occurrence witnesses' testimony (Gilboy).

Waiving the Preliminary Hearing

For a variety of reasons, many defendants and/or their attorneys choose to waive the preliminary hearing. An American Bar Foundation study found that in 28 percent of the cases in Detroit and 34 percent in Wichita, Kansas, the preliminary hearing was waived (Miller). This pattern holds in other communities as well. A limited number of waivers are the result of an unrepresented defendant not realizing that a preliminary hearing may be useful. Normally, however, waiving the preliminary hearing requires a positive step. Thus, if the defendant is confused, the judge will typically conduct the preliminary hearing. Waivers of hearings may also be the product of defense counsel perceptions that the holding of a preliminary hearing might work to the defendant's disadvantage. For example, in a rape case, the defense attorney may prefer to reduce potential prejudicial pretrial publicity and at the same time hope that if the defense waits long enough, the victim's testimony will change. Such a waiver involves a tactical decision that the information to be gained from holding a preliminary does not outweigh the potential damage to the defendant's case. At other times, though, waivers result from defense attorneys adopting a cooperative stance toward judge and prosecutor and not forcing them to waste time. Many Detroit defense attorneys waive the preliminary hearing for this reason (Eisenstein and Jacob: 221).

The Preliminary Hearing in Practice

Although the legal purpose of the preliminary hearing is simple, the actual conduct of these hearings is quite complex. In some jurisdictions they resemble minitrials and last an hour or more. More typically, though, they last less than a minute. In some jurisdictions they are an important stage in the proceedings because cases are screened; in others they are a perfunctory step in which probable cause is found to exist in virtually every case. To complicate matters further, preliminary hearings are rare in some courts. Given this widespread variability, it is virtually impossible to make any blanket statement about the importance and significance of the preliminary hearing. Various studies, however, do reveal four major patterns.

Preliminary hearings seldom held.   In some jurisdictions preliminary hearings are almost never held. The prime example is the federal courts. The majority of federal criminal cases begin not with an arrest but with a grand jury indictment, meaning that there is no need for a preliminary hearing. But even when there is a street arrest, it is common practice in federal courts to seek a grand jury indictment before the ten-day period required for conducting the preliminary hearing. As a consequence, probable cause hearings are held in a very small percentage of cases in the federal courts. Similar practices are found at the state level.

Short and routine preliminary hearings.   Probably the most common practice is for preliminary hearings to be short and routine. A typical case involves a police detective testifying from a police report he did not write to the effect that a Mrs. Jones had reported a crime was committed. Then a minimal amount of information would be given as to why the police arrested Mr. Smith. The total time consumed is generally no more than a minute or two.

Such short and routine preliminary hearings seldom result in a finding that probable cause does not exist. My own study of Prairie City, Illinois, for example, documented that only 2 percent of the defendants had their cases terminated at the preliminary hearing (1974b: 132–134). Often defense attorneys view such judicial proceedings as useless and are inclined to waive them.

Preliminary hearing as a minitrial.   For decades Los Angeles has used the preliminary hearing in a unique fashion: it is actually a minitrial where the prosecution calls all of its principal witnesses and the defense is allowed to call witnesses and cross-examine the state's witnesses. (Not insignificantly, Los Angeles was the setting for the books and television series on Perry Mason.) But despite the time-consuming process of conducting a full-fledged minitrial, the rate of no probable cause findings is small. Only about 10 percent of cases are dismissed or reduced to a misdemeanor at this stage (Greenwood et al.). This low rate results from extensive prosecutorial screening before the preliminary hearing. Although few cases are screened out of the system, the preliminary hearing in Los Angeles has a major impact on the court process, since a transcript of the proceedings is made. Many cases are disposed of not by a guilty plea or a trial but by the opposing parties submitting the transcript to a judge (termed *submission on the transcript*). After reading the transcript the judge typically finds the defendant guilty after a brief bench trial (Mather).

submission on the transcript

Preliminary hearing as a screening device.   Although in most areas the preliminary hearing is largely ceremonial, resulting in few cases being screened out of the criminal process, in a few courts it is quite significant. In Chicago and Brooklyn, for example, the preliminary hearing is a major stage of the proceedings. Because the prosecutor has not previously reviewed the case, it is left to the judge to separate the strong cases from the weak ones. As a result the preliminary hearing is a major stage in Chicago, where 80 percent of the cases are disposed of by dismissal or reduction to a less serious misdemeanor. Similarly, in Brooklyn 65 percent of felony cases receive a final disposition during the preliminary hearing (McIntyre and Lippman).

McIntyre explored what he called the "judicial dominance of charging process." His research provides a good insight into the Chicago process as well as a useful overview of some of the major factors shaping the screening process. After a routine felony arrest, the Chicago police alone decide whether to file a complaint. They seldom drop a case. Thus the state's attorney neither reviews a case prior to filing nor has any contact with it until the preliminary hearing. It is therefore the judge's responsibility to screen cases. As a result only 20 percent of the approximately sixteen thousand preliminary hearing cases yearly in Chicago are bound over to the grand jury. Of the remainder, a large number are dismissed either because there was insufficient evidence, the victim did not appear (thus indicating a reluctance to prosecute), or the court determined that key evidence (often illicit narcotics) had to be suppressed because it was obtained by means of illegal search and seizure. In addition, a number of felony cases were reduced to misdemeanor charges either because the evidence was not sufficient to sustain a felony or because the judge believed the defendant was not a threat to society. In short, the screening and charging decisions that in most communities are made by the prosecutor or the police and prosecutor together are in Chicago dominated by the judiciary. This practice is a longstanding one dating at least to the 1920s and has survived numerous changes in court personnel and legal procedure.

McIntyre argues that the system is unique to Chicago because of important political reasons, mainly that the Chicago judges "are less susceptible to criticisms for showing leniency" than the police or prosecutor are. The preliminary hearing allows the police to build an impressive record of "crime clearance rates" unhampered by a lack of prosecution. At the same time, these procedures allow the prosecutor to point to a high conviction rate (after the preliminary hearing) without the necessity of making the type of decision that could be viewed as unduly lenient.

Grand Juries

grand jury
indictment

A **grand jury** differs from a trial jury. Whereas the grand jury determines probable cause and returns an accusation (an **indictment**), the trial jury determines guilt or innocence. Similar institutions existed in ancient Greece, Rome, Scandinavia, and Normandy. It emerged in English law in 1176 during a political struggle among King Henry II, the church, and noblemen. At first criminal accusations originated with members of the grand jury themselves, but gradually this body came to consider accusations from outsiders as well. The jurors heard witnesses and, if convinced there were grounds for trial, returned an indictment. Grand juries also considered accusations brought before them by prosecutors, returning a **true bill** (an indictment) if they found the accusation true and a **no true bill** if they found it false. Historically, therefore, the grand jury has two functions: to serve as an investigatory body and to act as a buffer between the state and its citizens to prevent the government from using the criminal process against its enemies.

true bill
no true bill

After the American Revolution, the grand jury was incorporated into the Fifth Amendment to the Constitution, which provides that "no person shall be held to answer for a capital, or otherwise infamous crime, unless on a presentment or indictment of a grand jury." The archaic phrase "otherwise infamous crime" has been interpreted to mean felonies. This provision, however, applies only to federal prosecutions. In *Hurtado* v. *California* (1884), the Supreme Court held that states had the option of using either an indictment or information. In nineteen states the grand jury is the exclusive means of initiating prosecution for all felonies. In a few, it is required only for capital offenses. In the remainder, the grand jury is an optional investigative body (see Table 10-1).

The size of grand juries varies greatly from as few as six jurors (Indiana) to sixteen or seventeen to as many as twenty-three. Grand jurors are normally randomly selected in a manner similar to the selection of trial jurors. In a handful of states, however, judges, county boards, jury commissioners, or sheriffs are allowed to exercise discretion.

The Grand Jury in Operation

Grand juries are empaneled (formally created) for a set period of time (typically three months). During this time they meet periodically to consider the cases brought to them by the prosecutor and to conduct other investigations. If a grand jury is conducting a major and complex investigation, its time may be extended by the court.

The work of the grand jury is shaped by a number of legal dimensions that differ greatly from the legal protections found elsewhere in the criminal court process. One of these is secrecy. Since the grand jury may find insufficient evidence to indict, it works in secret (the rest of the process is required to be public) to shield those merely under investigation. Another unique aspect is that indictments are returned by a plurality vote (unanimity is required in most trial juries). In most states one half to two thirds of the votes are

TABLE 10-1   Grand Jury Requirements

Grand jury indictment required	Grand jury indictment optional	Grand jury lacks authority to indict
All crimes	Arizona	Pennsylvania
New Jersey	Arkansas	
South Carolina	California	
Tennessee	Colorado	
Virginia	Idaho	
	Illinois	
All felonies	Indiana	
Alabama	Iowa	
Alaska	Kansas	
Delaware	Maryland	
District of Columbia	Michigan	
Georgia	Missouri	
Hawaii	Montana	
Kentucky	Nebraska	
Maine	Nevada	
Mississippi	New Mexico	
New Hampshire	North Dakota	
New York	Oklahoma	
North Carolina	Oregon	
Ohio	South Dakota	
Texas	Utah	
West Virginia	Vermont	
	Washington	
Capital crimes only	Wisconsin	
Connecticut	Wyoming	
Florida		
Louisiana		
Massachusetts		
Minnesota		
Rhode Island		

SOURCE: Deborah Emerson, *Grand Jury Reform: A Review of Key Issues* (Washington, D.C.: U.S. Department of Justice, National Institute of Justice, 1983).

sufficient to hand up an indictment. By contrast, trial jurors can convict only if the jurors are unanimous or, in a very few states, near unanimous. Finally, witnesses before the grand jury have no right to representation by an attorney. Although defendants may have a lawyer at all vital stages of a criminal prosecution, none is allowed at this stage. Nor do suspects have the right to go before the grand jury to protest their innocence or even to present their version of the facts.

The work of the grand jury is shaped by its unique relationship with the prosecutor. In the vast majority of states, grand juries are considered part of the judicial branch of government. In theory at least, the prosecutor functions only as a legal adviser to the grand jury. But in practice, the prosecutor dominates. Grand jurors hear only the witnesses summoned by the prosecutor. And as laymen, they are heavily influenced by the legal advice of the prosecutor.

The net result is that grand juries often function as rubber stamp for the prosecutor. A study of the Harris County (Houston), Texas, grand jury found that the average time spent per case was only five minutes; in 80 percent of the cases there was no discussion by members of the grand jury; rarely did members voice a dissent; and finally, the grand jury approved virtually all of the prosecutor's recommendations (Carp). Similarly, in one recent year federal grand juries returned over seventeen thousand indictments, but only sixty-eight no true bills. In Chicago, grand juries indicted 100 percent of the murder cases presented (Gilboy). In short, grand juries indict whomever the prosecutor wants indicted.

Nor are no true bills necessarily an indication that grand juries fulfill a significant screening function. A prosecutor who believes a case is weak subtly conveys this feeling. One assistant prosecutor I interviewed says that grand jurors "get the feeling when we're not pressing a case real hard" (Neubauer, 1974b: 134). In turn, the secrecy of the grand jury proceedings may lead prosecutors to use it as a "safety valve." That is, if a case involves a prominent citizen, has received extensive publicity, or both, the prosecutor may hesitate to dismiss the case even though a conviction appears unlikely.

Abolish or Reform the Grand Jury?

The grand jury system has been the object of various criticisms. Whereas in theory the grand jury serves as a watchdog on the prosecutor, some portray the grand jury as "the prosecutor's darling," a "puppet," or a "rubber stamp." To William Campbell, U.S. District Court judge for the Northern District of Illinois, "the grand jury is the total captive of the prosecutor who, if he is candid, will concede that he can indict anybody at any time, for almost anything, before any grand jury." This lack of independence leads critics to characterize the screening function of grand juries as meaningless, costly, and time-consuming, and grand juries themselves as peopled by untrained laymen. These concerns have prompted a call for the **abolition of the grand jury.** Early in this century, judicial reformers succeeded in abolishing grand juries in some states. More recently the National Advisory Commission has urged abolition largely as a way to streamline the court process and avoid unnecessary case delay. Abolition efforts are rarely successful, however, because they require a constitutional amendment.

abolition of the grand jury

Other critics go farther, arguing that grand jury proceedings trample due process rights. Some contend that grand juries have been misused to serve partisan political ends, harassing and punishing those who criticize the government. The cases most often cited include prominent opponents of the Vietnam War and more recently members of the Puerto Rican Independence Movement (Deutsch). Thus concern has been voiced that the grand jury "has become an instrument of the very prosecutorial misconduct it was supposed to buffer the citizen against" (Pizzigati). These critics seek to **reform grand jury proceedings** by developing procedures to guarantee the rights of witnesses and targets of grand jury investigations (Emerson). One principal suggestion is that a witness be granted the right to have an attorney present during questioning; witnesses called before a federal grand jury are not allowed to have an attorney present, although some states do grant this right. Two major concerns about the power of grand juries focus on immunity and contempt.

reform grand jury proceedings

immunity

transactional immunity

Immunity.   A common complaint about grand juries involves *immunity.* The Fifth Amendment protects a person against self-incrimination. In 1893 Congress passed a statute that permitted the granting of *transactional immunity.* In exchange for a witness's testimony, the prosecutor agrees not to prosecute the witness for any crimes admitted—a practice often referred to as "turning state's evidence."

use immunity

The Organized Crime Control Act of 1970 added a new and more limited form of immunity. Under *use immunity,* the government may not use a witness's grand jury testimony to prosecute that person. However, if the state acquires evidence of a crime independently of that testimony, the witness may be prosecuted. The Supreme Court has held that use immunity does not violate the Fifth Amendment's prohibition against self-incrimination (*Kastigar* v. *United States,* 406 U.S. 441, 1972). Use immunity provides witnesses less protection than transactional immunity. A witness may not refuse the government's offer of immunity; failure to testify may result in contempt of court charges and a jail term.

contempt power

Contempt power.   Grand juries possess *contempt power* so that they can compel witnesses to provide testimony needed for a criminal investigation. Critics contend that some prosecutors call political dissidents to testify to find out information unrelated to criminal activity. The contempt power can also be used for punishment. A prosecutor may call a witness knowing that she or he will refuse to testify and then have the witness jailed. A witness who refuses to testify can be confined for an indefinite period of time until they "purge" themselves of contempt by providing the requested information. In this way a person can be imprisoned without a trial. This has happened mainly to newspaper reporters. In *Branzburg* v. *Hayes* (408 U.S. 665, 1972), the Supreme Court ruled that journalists must testify before a grand jury. As a result, some journalists have gone to jail rather than reveal their confidential sources, because they believe that to do so would erode the freedom of the press protected by the First Amendment.

Funneling Effect

It is important to reemphasize that the criminal court process is not streamlined. After an arrest, cases do not automatically move from prosecutorial screening to preliminary hearing to the grand jury and then to the trial court. Rather, discretion is exercised at each stage of the process, with the result that some cases are dropped, others forwarded to the next step, and still others diverted elsewhere. Figure 10-1 shows the funneling effect for felony cases. The largest drop-off occurs when victims of crime do not report the offense to the police. Of crimes reported to the police, only a relative handful lead to an arrest.

case attrition

prosecutorial screening

A detailed picture of *case attrition* during the court process emerges in a study of thirty-seven urban prosecutors summarized in the tree diagram of Figure 10-2. For every one hundred arrests, twenty-nine are rejected, diverted, or referred to other jurisdictions during *prosecutorial screening.* Of those

1,000 felonies committed
  339 reported to the police
    54 arrested
    26 convicted
    13 incarcerated
      6 sentenced to prison for more than one year

Figure 10-1 Funneling effect of felony crimes
SOURCES: U.S. Department of Justice, Bureau of Justice Statistics, *Report to the Nation on Crime and Justice* (Washington, D.C.: Government Printing Office, 1983); Barbara Boland with Ronald Stones, *The Prosecution of Felony Arrests, 1981* (Washington, D.C.: U.S. Department of Justice, Bureau of Justice Statistics, 1986).

nolle prosequi

that survive the initial hurdle, twenty-two are later dismissed by the prosecutor through a ***nolle prosequi*** (or *nolle* for short). Overall, half of all arrests do not survive to the trial stage. The high attrition rate of felony cases early in the process contrasts sharply with the small percentage of acquittals during the trial phase. Once cases reach the felony court, relatively few are dismissed. Most end in either a plea or a trial (Boland and Stones). The early

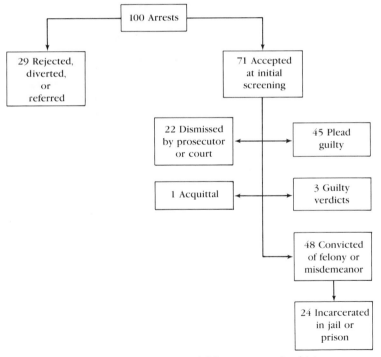

Figure 10-2 Case attrition of felony arrests in thirty-seven urban prosecutors' offices SOURCE: Barbara Boland with Ronald Stones, *The Prosecution of Felony Arrests, 1981* (Washington, D.C.: U.S. Department of Justice, Bureau of Justice Statistics, 1986).

decisions of the prosecutor are thus much more important in terminating cases than the later activities of judges and juries.

In most courts, there is a 50 percent case attrition rate. However, there are important variations between courts in the stage at which cases are dropped. Table 10-2 shows an inverse relationship between early prosecutorial screening and later case dismissals. In New Orleans, for example, many cases are eliminated during prosecutorial screening, with only a handful dismissed at later stages. Conversely, in Manhattan few cases are initially declined by prosecutors, leading to a high rate of case dismissals later in the process.

Variations in the stage in which most case attrition occurs reflect differences in state law, the structure of state courts, and local traditions. Consider prosecutorial screening. In states with two levels of trial courts and dual prosecutors, felony court prosecutors have discretion over the charging decisions made by local prosecutors in the lower courts. Similarly, some states allow police officers to use arrest warrants for filing charges without prosecutorial review (Jacoby). Thus, a critical stage for case screening and case attrition in one court may be of little importance in another jurisdiction. In Los Angeles and Detroit, for example, prosecutors make the important screening decisions, meaning that the preliminary hearing is relatively unimportant. By contrast, in Chicago, Brooklyn, and Houston, where prosecutors tend to defer to the police during the charging phase, significant case attrition occurs at the preliminary hearing (McIntyre and Lippman).

Why Attrition Occurs

Case attrition is the product of a complex set of factors; among them are the relationships between the major actors in the criminal justice system, patterns of informal authority within the courtroom work group, the backlog of cases on the court's docket, and community standards defining serious criminal activity. Several recent studies have examined the norms of courthouse justice and indicate that sufficiency of the evidence, case priorities, and substantive assessments are the most important reasons for case attrition. These categories parallel the threefold categorization of discretion developed in Chapter 5: legal judgments, policy priorities, and personal standards of justice. Like other attempts to understand discretion, these categories are not mutually exclusive—some screening decisions are based on more than one criterion.

Sufficiency of the Evidence

Is there sufficient evidence to prove the elements of the offense? This is the most important question that prosecutors and court officials must answer in deciding whether to file charges or whether to dismiss the case if charges have already been filed. Studies in Seattle (Cole), Prairie City, Illinois (Neubauer, 1974b), Chicago (Gilboy), Jacksonville, Florida, and San Diego (Feeney, Dill, and Weir) report that sufficiency of the evidence is an important consideration during prosecutorial screening. One assistant district attorney phrased it this way: "When I examine the police report I have to feel that I could go to trial with the case tomorrow. All the elements of prosecution must be

TABLE 10-2 Fraction of Total Attrition that Occurs at Screening and after Court Charges Are Filed

Jurisdiction	Percent of total attrition occurring:	
	At screening	After filing
New Orleans	90%	10%
Denver	79	21
Los Angeles	76	24
Lansing	75	25
Minneapolis	74	26
San Diego	68	32
Greeley	65	35
Miami	64	36
Dallas*	61	39
Salt Lake City	51	49
Golden	45	55
Washington, D.C.	31	69
Tallahassee	16	84
Manhattan	9	91

*Attrition after filing and after indictment are the same because there is no case processing in the lower court.
SOURCE: Barbara Boland with Ronald Stones, *The Prosecution of Felony Arrests, 1981* (Washington, D.C.: U.S. Department of Justice, Bureau of Justice Statistics, 1986).

present before I file charges (Neubauer, 1974a: 118). Similarly, when 855 prosecutors in fifteen urban jurisdictions were asked whether they would accept or decline prosecution for thirty standard cases, the legal-evidentiary strength of the case emerged as the most important factor (Jacoby et al.).

A large percentage of arrests are rejected during prosecutorial screening because of insufficient evidence. Looking at Table 10-3, we find that of cases in which prosecution was declined, insufficient evidence was the major reason, with the percentage ranging from 61 percent in Manhattan to 30 percent in Washington, D.C. Witness problems (discussed in Chapter 9) constitute another type of evidence problem, and they are another important reason for declining prosecution. Insufficient evidence and witness problems are also typically cited as reasons cases are dismissed after charges are filed (Boland with Stones).

probable cause

prosecutable case

Focusing on the strength of the state's case introduces an important change in evaluative standards; from an initial concern with *probable cause,* the emphasis shifts to whether it is a *prosecutable case.* At the preliminary hearing the judge determines whether there is probable cause—that a crime has been committed and there are grounds to believe that the suspect probably committed it. From the prosecutor's perspective, however, probable cause is too gross a yardstick; even though it is present, a case may still be legally weak. Thus, a prosecutable case is not one merely satisfying probable cause, a standard required of police in making an arrest and used by the judge

TABLE 10-3 Reasons Felony Arrests Are Declined for Prosecution

Jurisdiction	Number of declined cases*	Percent of declinations due to:							
		Insufficient evidence	Witness problems	Due process problems	Interest of justice	Plea on another case	Referral to diversion	Referral for other prosecution	Other
Golden	41	59%	27%	2%	5%	2%	2%	2%	0%
Greeley	235	52	7	0	38	0	1	2	0
Manhattan	995	61	23	5	4	0	–	3	4
New Orleans	4,114	38	30	12	8	0	7	4	–
Salt Lake City	973	58	12	1	8	1	2	19	–
San Diego	4,940	54	15	6	9	1	0	9	7
Washington, D.C.	1,535	30	24	–	13	0	–	3	29

Note: Declined cases include diversions and cases referred for other prosecution.
–Insufficient data to calculate.
*Excludes cases for which reasons are unknown.
SOURCE: Barbara Boland with Ronald Stones, *The Prosecution of Felony Arrests, 1981* (Washington, D.C.: U.S. Department of Justice, Bureau of Justice Statistics, 1986), p. 17.

in the administration of the preliminary hearing. Rather, it is a case that meets the standards of proof necessary to convict. Skolnick distinguishes between factual and legal guilt. Prosecutors who emphasize factual guilt focus on whether the suspect committed the crime. In contrast, those who decide on the basis of legal guilt look at what can be proved about the suspect's activities.

Case Priorities

case priorities

Case attrition also results from general prosecutorial policies about *case priorities.* Just as police departments have informal norms governing arrests (they will not arrest for gambling among friends in private homes, for example), criminal courts have similar yardsticks. For example, a number of U.S. attorneys will not prosecute bank tellers who embezzle small amounts of money (generally under $100 to $300), get caught, and lose their jobs. The stigmatization of being caught and losing the job is viewed as punishment enough. Similarly, numerous local and state prosecutors have virtually decriminalized possession of small amounts of marijuana by refusing to file charges. The study of the Los Angeles County district attorney's office found that informal office policies controlled the charging decision. The office was reluctant to prosecute interfamily assaults, neighborhood squabbles, and noncommercial gambling ("Prosecutorial Discretion"). Prosecutors devote greater resources to more serious offenses (Gilboy; Jacoby et al.).

Substantive Assessments

substantive assessments

The judicial process is expected to individualize justice. *Substantive assessments* of justice—attitudes of members of the courtroom work group about what actions should not be punished—constitute the third category of criteria guiding screening. In Chapter 5, we argued that this constitutes the third subcomponent of discretion. When McIntyre studied screening in Chicago, he found that many cases are dropped or reduced for reasons other than failure to establish guilt (1968). And even if the evidence was strong, a defendant might not be prosecuted if his conduct and background indicated that he was not a genuine threat to society (1968). In Detroit, among other places, a different phrase is used—prosecution would serve no useful purpose—but the thought is the same (McIntyre, 1967). In Table 10-3, these reasons for rejection are included under the category of "interest of justice."

An important dimension of personal standards of justice involves a subjective decision on the part of the prosecutor that the case is not as serious as the legal charge suggests. In most courthouses, officials refer to some cases as "cheap" or "garbage" cases. Rosett and Cressey provide the following example. An old man stumbled drunkenly into a liquor store waving a cap pistol and demanding a bottle of whiskey. Even though all the elements of the offense of armed robbery were clearly present, the judge, complaining witness, and prosecutor did not take the case seriously. It was viewed as a "cheap" robbery. Decisions not to file charges in cheap cases reflected the effort of court officials to produce substantive justice.

Written Guidelines

Prosecutorial screening is not random. Decisions to decline prosecution or to dismiss cases that have already been filed are made after weighing the sufficiency of the evidence, considering general policies, and finally applying in a limited way personal standards of justice. These shared norms of the courtroom work group (see Chapter 5) are not uniformly applied, however. Assistant prosecutors in the same office evaluate similar cases differently. There are also significant differences between prosecutor's offices. A survey of United States attorneys found wide variations in prosecution policies regarding narcotics violations, bank fraud, theft from interstate shipment, illegal aliens, forgery of Treasury checks, and thirty other offenses. Where one district may prosecute, another may decide that a similar case is not serious enough or does not involve a large enough loss of money to merit prosecution (Pear).

These inconsistencies reflect the absence of legislative or appellate standards governing prosecutorial screening. Greater attention is being devoted to the

QUOTATION

Whenever we are reminded of our high crime rate by some new atrocity, our thoughts instinctively turn to the law and its enforcement agencies in the expectation that they can do something to curb the outrage. The truth is that law enforcement, important and essential as it is, cannot by itself significantly reduce crime. . . .

The system offers few opportunities for radical change. Dismissal rates probably can be tightened by more circumspect collection of evidence by the police, by lightening the burden on the complaining witness, and by diminishing his dominant position in the prosecution process. . . . Dismissal rates could be cut by some ten percentage points. . . .

But whether these improvements of the enforcement system would have a significant impact on our high level of crime is a very different question. Since it is unlikely that the police can substantially increase the number of arrests for index crimes, it is unlikely that the attrition of the law enforcement process [in New York City] would noticeably change. One thousand committed crimes would be followed by, say, forty-six convictions instead of the present thirty-six.

Hans Zeisel, *The Limits of Law Enforcement* (Chicago, University of Chicago Press, 1982), pp. 15, 51–52. Reprinted by permission.

*written
guidelines*

problem, however, through the development of ***written guidelines*** (Comptroller General). The United States Department of Justice has adopted a policy statement, entitled *Principles of Federal Prosecution,* designed to foster more uniform practices (see Table 10-4). Similarly, the vast majority of U.S. attorneys and a growing number of urban prosecutors have formulated written criteria for their offices. These written standards are intended to guide internal decisions, not to create any legally enforceable rights. Their actual impact is unclear. One salutary effect is that in the process of writing guidelines, prosecutor's offices are forced to confront existing inconsistencies. The final guidelines, though, tend to be general and thus allow for some differences in application.

The Criminal Justice Wedding Cake

The tyranny of criminal justice statistics is that they treat all cases in the same way. A homicide counts the same as a $75 theft, which under state law is petty larceny but is reported in the *Uniform Crime Reports* (adopted in the thirties) as a major felony. Merely counting the number of criminal events gets in the way of understanding how and why court officials treat murder cases differently from petty thefts.

To understand case attrition, Samuel Walker suggests that it is useful to view criminal justice as a wedding cake (Figure 10-3). The wedding cake model is based on the observation that criminal justice officials handle different kinds of cases very differently. Within each layer there is a high degree of consistency; the greatest disparities are found between cases in different layers. An examination of these layers illuminates Frank Zimring's comment on the paradox of American criminal justice: "The problem is not that our system is too lenient, or too severe; sadly, it is both."

Celebrated Cases

The top layer of the wedding cake consists of a few very celebrated cases. These are the cases that dominate the news. Trials of Jean Harris, John Hinckley, Count von Bulow, and Firestine are prominent examples. Equally newsworthy are those accused of bizarre crimes like mass murders. Likewise each year local communities have a few celebrated cases either because a local notable has been charged with a serious crime or because the crime itself was particularly heinous.

*celebrated
cases*

Celebrated cases are exceptional because they *are* so celebrated. From the moment the case begins, criminal justice officials treat them as exceptional, making sure that every last detail of the judicial process is followed. The cases are also extraordinary because they involve the rarest of criminal court events, the full jury trial. All the controversial matters are aired in public, to the fascination of the viewing and reading public. Like morality plays of old and soap operas of today, public attention is focused on the battle between good and evil, although who is playing which role is not always obvious.

Because of the publicity surrounding them, celebrated cases have a tremendous impact on public perceptions of criminal justice. On one level, these cases reinforce civic book notions that defendants will receive their day in court,

Table 10-4 United States Department of Justice Principles of Federal Prosecution

Initiating and declining prosecution

1. If the attorney for the government has probable cause to believe that a person has committed a federal offense within his jurisdiction, he should consider whether to:
   (a) request or conduct further investigation;
   (b) commence or recommend prosecution;
   (c) decline prosecution and refer the matter for prosecutorial consideration in another jurisdiction;
   (d) decline prosecution and initiate or recommend pretrial diversion or other non-criminal disposition; or
   (e) decline prosecution without taking other action.
2. The attorney for the government should commence or recommend federal prosecution if he believes that the person's conduct constitutes a federal offense and that the admissible evidence will probably be sufficient to obtain and sustain a conviction, unless, in his judgment, prosecution should be declined because:
   (a) no substantial federal interest would be served by prosecution;
   (b) the person is subject to effective prosecution in another jurisdiction; or
   (c) there exists an adequate non-criminal alternative to prosecution.
3. In determining whether prosecution should be declined because no substantial federal interest would be served by prosecution, the attorney for the government should weigh all relevant considerations, including:
   (a) federal law enforcement priorities;
   (b) the nature and seriousness of the offense;
   (c) the deterrent effect of prosecution;
   (d) the person's culpability in connection with the offense;
   (e) the person's history with respect to criminal activity;
   (f) the person's willingness to cooperate in the investigation or prosecution of others; and
   (g) the probable sentence or other consequences if the person is convicted.
4. In determining whether prosecution should be declined because the person is subject to effective prosecution in another jurisdiction, the attorney for the government should weigh all relevant considerations, including:
   (a) the strength of the other jurisdiction's interest in prosecution;
   (b) the other jurisdiction's ability and willingness to prosecute effectively; and
   (c) the probable sentence or other consequences if the person is convicted in the other jurisdiction.

SOURCE: *Principles of Federal Prosecution* (Washington, D.C.: U.S. Department of Justice, 1980).

complete with a Perry Mason–type defense counsel and an attentive jury. But on another level, celebrated cases highlight the public's worst fears—the rich often get off scot free because they can afford an expensive attorney. All too many seem to beat the rap. People assume that the court process ordinarily functions this way; clearly it does not. Celebrated cases are atypical. They do not reflect how the courts operate on a day-to-day basis.

Serious Felonies

The second layer of the wedding cake consists of serious felonies. The third includes lesser felonies. The courtroom work group distinguishes between the second and third levels on the basis of three principal criteria: the seriousness of the crime, the criminal record of the suspect, and the relationship between the victim and the offender. Court actors focus on "how much the case is worth." Serious cases end up on the second layer; the "not-so serious" ones on the third.

There is, of course, no automatic formula for sorting cases into serious and not-so-serious felonies; the primary key is a commonsense judgment about the

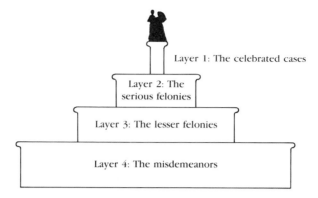

Figure 10-3 The criminal justice wedding cake
SOURCE: Samuel Walker, *Sense and Nonsense about Crime: A Policy Guide* (Pacific Grove, CA: Brooks/Cole, 1985).

facts of the case. Serious crimes most often include crimes of violence like murder, robbery, and rape. But this is not always the case. A suspect's long criminal record might transform an ordinary felony into a serious one, at least in the eyes of the prosecuting attorney. Conversely, what first appears to be a serious offense might be downgraded because the victim and the offender knew one another. Thus what starts out as an armed robbery might later be viewed as essentially a private disagreement over money owed, with the criminal act a means of seeking redress outside accepted channels.

Analysis of the true seriousness of a case is part of the everyday language of the courthouse actors. Serious cases are routinely referred to as "heavy" cases or "real" crimes. The less serious ones as "garbage," "bullshit," or simply not real crimes. The practical consequences are that second-layer felonies are treated as serious indeed, with considerable attention devoted to their processing. Third-layer crimes, on the other hand, receive less attention and are treated in a routine and lenient manner.

The Lower Depths

The bottom layer is a world unto itself. It consists of a staggering volume of misdemeanor cases, which far outstrip the number of felony cases. About half are "public order" offenses like disorderly conduct, public drunkenness, disturbing the peace, and so on. Only about a third involve crimes against property or persons, many of which are petty thefts or physical disagreements between "friends" or acquaintances. Rarely do these defendants have any social standing. In the eyes of the courtroom work group, few of these cases are worth much at all. Relatively little time is devoted to their processing. They are typically handled by a different court from the felony cases and processed in a strikingly different manner. Dispositions are arrived at in a routine manner. Defendants are arraigned en masse. Guilt is rarely contested. Even more rarely are the punishments harsh. For these reasons, the lower courts will be treated separately in Chapter 17.

Conclusion

Case attrition is the dominant reality of American criminal justice. In statistical profile, the process resembles a funnel—wide at the top, narrow at the end. Fewer than half of all crimes are ever reported to the police. Only one in five of the crimes known to the police results in an arrest. Thus most crimes never reach the courts. Of the small subset of criminal events referred to court officials, half are dropped following prosecutorial screening, preliminary hearings, or grand jury deliberations. Prosecutors and judges decline to prosecute or later dismiss charges that have been filed because the case lacks sufficient evidence, falls too low on the priority list, or is viewed as a "cheap" case. The wedding cake model highlights this sorting process. Considerable resources are devoted to serious felonies. Lesser felonies receive less attention; they are more likely to be filtered out of the system.

The decisions made during the early stages of the criminal court process set the context for how cases are disposed of later during plea bargaining or trial. After a case survives the initial hurdles, the courtroom work group operates on the assumption that the defendant is guilty. This produces an anomaly: the closer a case approaches to trial, the greater the likelihood the defendant will be found guilty. Once a case reaches the felony courts, the vast majority of defendants are found guilty. Thus the important decisions about innocence or guilt are made early in the process by judges and prosecutors, not, as the adversary system projects, late in the process by lay jurors.

For Discussion

1. In the most recent volume of the FBI's *Uniform Crime Reports,* look up your local community. How many crimes were reported? How many arrests? Is your community similar to or different from the national average? What proportion of arrests involve crimes of violence?

2. Interview a local police official about police standards for arrest and procedures for booking a suspect. Do they make any efforts to screen cases before forwarding the case to the prosecutor? Also inquire about their perceptions of prosecutorial charging standards. Are these too stringent?

3. If you were a prosecutor, what standards would you employ in deciding which cases to file? What types of cases do you think should not be prosecuted? Prosecuted more vigorously? Why?

4. Interview the prosecutor(s) in your community who handle the charging decision. What procedures and criteria do they use? How do they evaluate the quality and thoroughness of police investigations? Ask for specific examples. Also interview a trial prosecutor. Ask if they have too many minor cases.

5. Observe a preliminary hearing. How long does it take? What witnesses were called? Does the preliminary hearing function as a major stage in the criminal process?

6. Does your state use a grand jury? If so, for what cases? Since grand jury proceedings are secret, you cannot observe them in operation. You can,

however, interview a prosecutor and ask what cases are sent to the grand jury and why, what procedures are followed, and whether grand juries ever refuse to indict and why.

7. Do you think the grand jury should be abolished? Do you think it currently fulfills its historical purpose of protecting citizens from governmental persecution?

8. Where does screening occur in your community?

References

BAKER, NEWMAN. "The Prosecutor—Initiation of Prosecution." *Journal of Criminal Law, Criminology and Police Science* 23 (January–February 1933): 770–796.

BALCH, ROBERT. "Deferred Prosecution: The Juvenilization of the Criminal Justice System." *Federal Probation* (June 1974).

BATTELLE LAW AND JUSTICE STUDY CENTER. *Forcible Rape: A National Survey of Responses by Prosecutors*. Washington, D.C.: Government Printing Office, 1977.

BOLAND, BARBARA, ELIZABETH BRADY, HERBERT TYSON, AND JOHN BASSLER. *The Prosecution of Felony Arrests*. Washington, D.C.: Institute for Law and Social Research, 1982.

BOLAND, BARBARA, WITH RONALD STONES. *The Prosecution of Felony Arrests, 1981*. Washington, D.C.: U.S. Department of Justice, Bureau of Justice Statistics, 1986.

BROSI, KATHLEEN. *A Cross-City Comparison of Felony Case Processing*. Washington, D.C.: Institute for Law and Social Research, 1979.

BUREAU OF JUSTICE STATISTICS. *Report to the Nation on Crime and Justice: The Data*. Washington, D.C.: U.S. Department of Justice, 1983.

———. "Criminal Victimization, 1985." Washington, D.C.: U.S. Department of Justice, 1986.

CAMPBELL, WILLIAM. "Eliminate the Grand Jury." *Journal of Criminal Law and Criminology* 64 (1973): 174.

CARP, ROBERT. "The Behavior of Grand Juries: Acquiescence or Justice?" *Social Science Quarterly* (March 1975): 853–870.

COLE, GEORGE. "The Decision to Prosecute." *Law and Society Review* 4 (February 1970): 313–343.

COMPTROLLER GENERAL OF THE UNITED STATES. *Greater Oversight and Uniformity Needed in U.S. Attorneys' Prosecutive Policies*. Washington, D.C.: General Accounting Office, 1982.

DEUTSCH, MICHAEL. "The Improper Use of the Federal Grand Jury: An Instrument for the Internment of Political Activists." *Journal of Criminal Law and Criminology* 75 (1984): 1159.

EISENSTEIN, JAMES. "The Federal Prosecutor and His Environment." Paper presented at the annual meeting of the American Political Science Association, Washington, D.C., 1968.

———, and Herbert Jacob. *Felony Justice: An Organizational Analysis of Criminal Courts*. Boston: Little, Brown, 1977.

EMERSON, DEBORAH. *Grand Jury Reform—A Review of Key Issues*. Washington, D.C.: U.S. Department of Justice, National Institute of Justice, 1983.

FEDERAL BUREAU OF INVESTIGATION (FBI). *Uniform Crime Reports—1981*. Washington, D.C.: Government Printing Office, 1982.

FEENEY, FLOYD, FORREST DILL, AND ADRIANNE WEIR. *Arrests Without Conviction: How Often They Occur and Why*. Washington, D.C.: U.S. Department of Justice, National Institute of Justice, 1983.

FINN, PETER, AND ALAN HOFFMAN. *Prosecution of Economic Crimes*. Washington, D.C.: LEAA, National Institute of Law Enforcement and Criminal Justice, 1976.

FORST, BRIAN, FRANK LEAHY, JEAN SHIRHALL, HERBERT TYSON, AND JOHN BARTOLOMEO. *Arrest Convictability as a Measure of Police Performance*. Washington, D.C.: U.S. Department of Justice, National Institute of Justice, 1981.

FORST, BRIAN, J. LUCIANOVIC, AND S. COX. *What Happens After Arrest? A Court Perspective of Police Operations in the District of Columbia.* Washington, D.C.: Law Enforcement Assistance Administration, 1977.

GILBOY, JANET. "Prosecutors' Discretionary Use of the Grand Jury to Initiate or to Reinitiate Prosecution." *American Bar Foundation Research Journal* 1984 (1984): 176.

GOLDMAN, SHELDON, AND THOMAS JAHNIGE. *The Federal Courts as a Political System.* New York: Harper & Row, 1971.

GREENWOOD, PETER, SORREL WILDHORN, EUGENE POGGIO, MICHAEL STRUMWASSER, AND PETER DELEON. *Prosecution of Adult Felony Defendants in Los Angeles County: A Policy Perspective.* Lexington, Mass.: D. C. Heath, 1976.

JACOBY, JOAN. *The Prosecutor's Charging Decision: A Policy Perspective.* Washington, D.C.: Government Printing Office, 1977.

JACOBY, JOAN, LEONARD MELLON, EDWARD RATLEDGE, AND STANLEY TURNER. *Prosecutorial Decisionmaking: A National Study.* Washington, D.C.: U.S. Department of Justice, National Institute of Justice, 1982.

MATHER, LYNN M. "Some Determinants of the Method of Case Disposition: Decisionmaking by Public Defenders in Los Angeles." *Law and Society Review* 8 (1974): 187.

MCDONALD, WILLIAM F., ed. *Criminal Justice and the Victim.* Beverly Hills, Calif.: Sage Publications, 1976.

MCINTYRE, DONALD. "A Study of Judicial Dominance of the Charging Decision." *Journal of Criminal Law, Criminology and Police Science* 59 (1968): 463–490.

——, ed. *Law Enforcement in the Metropolis.* Chicago: American Bar Foundation, 1967.

——, AND DAVID LIPPMAN. "Prosecutors and Disposition of Felony Cases." *American Bar Association Journal* 56 (1970): 1156.

MELLON, LEONARD, JOAN JACOBY, AND MARION BREWER. "The Prosecutor Constrained by His Environment: A New Look at Discretionary Justice in the United States." *Journal of Criminal Law and Criminology* 72 (1981): 52.

MILLER, FRANK. *Prosecution: The Decision to Charge a Suspect with a Crime.* Boston: Little, Brown, 1969.

NATIONAL ADVISORY COMMISSION ON CRIMINAL JUSTICE STANDARDS AND GOALS. *Report on Courts.* Washington, D.C.: Government Printing Office, 1973.

NEUBAUER, DAVID. "After the Arrest: The Charging Decision in Prairie City." *Law and Society Review* 8 (Spring 1974a): 495–517.

——. *Criminal Justice in Middle America.* Morristown, N.J.: General Learning Press, 1974b.

PEAR, ROBERT. "Disparity Reported in U.S. Prosecutions." *New York Times,* January 7, 1980, p. 1.

PIZZIGATI, SAM. Personal interview, March 18, 1977.

"Prosecutorial Discretion in the Initiation of Criminal Complaints." *Southern California Law Review* 42 (1969): 519–545.

ROBINSON, TIMOTHY. "Two Prosecutors Eye Rules to Curb Grand Jury Power." *Washington Post,* June 3, 1975.

ROSSMAN, DAVID, AND JAN HOFFMAN. *Intake Screening: A Proposal for Massachusetts District Attorneys.* Boston: Center for Criminal Justice, Boston University, 1975.

SKOLNICK, JEROME. *Justice Without Trial.* New York: John Wiley, 1966.

TIMES-PICAYUNE, May 5, 1973.

VORENBERG, ELIZABETH, AND JAMES VORENBERG. "Early Diversion from the Criminal Justice System: Practice in Search of a Theory." In *Prisoners in America,* ed. Lloyd E. Oblin, Englewood Cliffs, N.J.: Prentice-Hall, 1973.

ZIMRING, FRANKLIN, SHEILA O'MALLEY, AND JOEL EIGEN. "Punishing Homicide in Philadelphia: Perspectives on the Death Penalty." *University of Chicago Law Review* 43 (1976): 252.

For Further Reading

ALPERT, GEOFFREY, AND THOMAS PETERSEN. "The Grand Jury Report: A Magic Lantern or an Agent of Social Control?" *Justice Quarterly* 2 (1985): 23.

CLARK, LEROY. *The Grand Jury: The Use and Abuse of Political Power.* New York: Quadrangle Books, 1972.

EMERSON, DEBORAH, AND NANCY AMES. *The Role of the Grand Jury and the Preliminary Hearing in Pretrial Screening.* Washington, D.C.: U.S. Department of Justice, National Institute of Justice, 1984.

FRANKEL, MARVIN, AND GARY NAFTALIS. *The Grand Jury: An Institution on Trial.* New York: Hill & Wang, 1977.

GREENWOOD, PETER, SORREL WILDHORN, EUGENE POGGIO, MICHAEL STRUMWASSER, AND PETER DELEON. *Prosecution of Adult Felony Defendants in Los Angeles County: A Policy Perspective.* Lexington, Mass.: D. C. Heath, 1976.

MILLER, FRANK. *Prosecution: The Decision to Charge a Suspect with a Crime.* Boston: Little, Brown, 1969.

NEUBAUER, DAVID. *Criminal Justice in Middle America.* Morristown, N.J.: General Learning Press, 1974.

ZEISEL, HANS. *The Limits of Law Enforcement.* Chicago: University of Chicago Press, 1983.

CHAPTER 11

Freedom for Sale

Bail represents a defendant's first major encounter with the courts. For the price of the bondsman's fee the accused can purchase freedom and return to home, family, the streets, or whatever. Bail also represents the arresting officer's first major encounter with the courts, but for the police it means that the defendant may have the opportunity to commit more crimes while awaiting trial. These competing perspectives fuel the often-heated debate over how effectively America's system of monetary bail operates.

This chapter examines how America's system of pretrial release works, the factors that shape its operation, and the consequences of these decisions. Some of the key areas discussed include whether bail discriminates against the poor, whether it unfairly exposes the general public to risks of being victimized, whether defendants released on bail later appear for trial, and suggested alternatives.

The Monetary Bail System

bail

Bail is a guarantee. In return for being released from jail, the accused promises to return to court as needed. This promise is guaranteed by posting money or property with the court. If the defendant appears in court when requested, the security is returned. If she or he fails to appear, however, the security can be forfeited.

The practice of allowing defendants to be released from jail pending trial originated in thirteenth-century English common law, largely as a convenience to local sheriffs. The colonists brought the concept of bail with them across the Atlantic, where it eventually became embedded in the Eighth Amendment, which provides that "excessive bail shall not be required." The United States Supreme Court has never decided whether the excessive bail clause estab-

right to bail

lishes a **right to bail.** Federal law and the constitutions in most states create the right to bail. There are limitations, however. Defendants accused of a capital offense have no right to bail, because no security is viewed as large enough to deter an accused from fleeing to save his life. Courts have also historically refused to allow bail if there is a risk of flight or if the defendant, upon release, might obstruct justice (Berg).

Bail Procedures

bail procedures

Shortly after arrest, a defendant is brought before a judge who sets the conditions of release. **Bail procedures** vary according to the seriousness of the crime and the city involved. Those arrested for minor misdemeanors can be released fairly quickly by posting bail at the police station. In most com-

bail schedule emergency bail schedule

munities the lower court judges have adopted a fixed **bail schedule** (also known as an **emergency bail schedule**), which specifies an exact amount for each offense. Table 11-1 provides some additional details on bail setting in a few of the nation's largest cities.

Bail procedures for felony or serious misdemeanor cases are considerably more complex. The arrestee must appear before the central court for the setting of bail. As a result, those accused of serious crimes remain in police custody a number of hours (and sometimes over the weekend) before they have the opportunity to make bail. Some police departments attempt to circumvent judicial rules requiring a bail hearing "without unnecessary delay" in order to question suspects (Wice).

Forms of Bail

cash

Once bail has been set, a defendant can gain pretrial release in four basic ways. First, the accused may post the full amount of the bond in **cash** with the court. All of this money will be returned when all court appearances are satisfied. Because it requires a large amount of cash, this form of bail is seldom used. The typical bail amount for a minor felony is $1,000, for example, and most persons—particularly felony defendants—cannot easily and quickly raise

property bond

that much money. The second method for securing pretrial release is a **property bond**. Most states allow a defendant (or friends and relatives) to

TABLE 11-1 The Initial Bail-Setting Stage

City	Who sets the bail		Where it is done		How it is done	
	Misdemeanor	Felony	Misdemeanor	Felony	Misdemeanor	Felony
Washington	Desk sergeant	Judge	Stationhouse	Court of general session	Schedule	Discretion
San Francisco	Clerk of criminal court	Judge	Hall of justice	Hall of justice	Schedule	Discretion
Los Angeles	Police captain	Judge	Stationhouse	Regional Courthouse	Schedule	Discretion
Oakland	Police captain	Judge	Stationhouse	Courthouse	Schedule	Discretion
Detroit	Desk sergeant or arresting magistrate	Arresting magistrate	Police station	Hall of justice	Schedule	Discretion
Chicago	Desk sergeant	Judge of bond court	Police station	Bond court or electronically	Schedule	Discretion
St. Louis	Desk sergeant	Judge	Police station	Police station or courthouse	Schedule	Flexible schedule
Baltimore	Desk sergeant	Judge	Police station	Police court	Schedule	Schedule
Indianapolis	Turnkey	Turnkey	City jail	City jail	Schedule	Schedule
Atlanta	Police	Police	Police headquarters	Police headquarters	Discretion schedule	Discretion schedule
Philadelphia	Desk sergeant	Magistrate and district attorney	Stationhouse	Police headquarters	Schedule	Schedule

NOTE: Wice personally visited the eleven cities and, in addition, contacted a total of seventy-two by mailed questionnaires. This is the only study to date of bail practices and procedures in the United States.

SOURCE: Reprinted by permission of the publisher from *Freedom for Sale* by Paul B. Wice (Lexington, Mass.: D. C. Heath and Company), p. 26.

personal recognizance

use a piece of property as collateral. If the defendant fails to appear in court, the property is forfeited. Property bonds are also rarely used because courts generally require that the equity in the property must be double the amount of the bond. Thus a $1,000 bond requires equity of at least $2,000. A third alternative for making bail is ***personal recognizance.*** Judges are allowed to release defendants from jail without monetary bail if they believe the person is not likely to flee. Personal bonds are used most often for defendants accused of minor crimes and for prominent members of the community.

bail bondsman

Because most of those arrested lack ready cash, do not own property, or lack social clout to qualify, the first three options for making bail are only abstractions. The majority of those released prior to trial use the fourth method: they hire a ***bail bondsman,*** a middleman, to post bail. Bondsmen post the amount required and charge a fee for their services, typically 10 percent of the amount of the bond. Thus a bondsman normally would collect $100 for writing a $1,000 bond. None of that money is refundable.

America's system of monetary bail means that those who are rich enough or have rich friends can buy their freedom and await trial on the streets. But the poor await trial in jail. Thus what began in medieval England as a humane innovation has evolved into a regressive practice. On any given day, there are approximately 235,000 adults held in jail (not prison), nearly 116,000 of whom have not been convicted of any crime (Bureau of Justice Statistics, 1986). Average daily population figures, though, greatly underestimate the high volume of transactions that occur. In a typical year there are more than 8 million admissions and 7.9 million releases (Bureau of Justice Statistics, 1984). Thus a very large number of defendants are released on bail after spending several days in jail while friends or relatives try to obtain the necessary funds to meet the bondsman's fee.

Conflicting Theories of Bail

Administration of bail has been greatly influenced by a longstanding division over the purposes of bail. The basic question is whether society should release a defendant who is probably guilty before trial. Pretrial release, for example, is very limited in the Continental legal system. American law, however, deeply suspicious of the possibility of a misuse of official power, refuses to allow officials to detain anyone merely accused of a crime, except under very limited circumstances. And this is the source of the conflict.

Ensuring appearance at trial. In theory the only purpose of bail is to ensure that the defendant appears in court for trial. Under this theory, a judge is supposed to fix bail in an amount calculated to guarantee the accused's availability for court hearing. This view of bail flows from the adversarial premise that a person is innocent until proven guilty and therefore should not suffer any hardships—such as a stay in jail—while awaiting trial.

Protecting society. The assumption that bail should be set solely to assure the defendant's appearance in court, however, does not do away with the central issues raised by practices in the Continental legal system—what to do with potentially dangerous defendants or those who might commit additional crimes while awaiting trial. A study in eight urban jurisdictions, for example, concluded that about 15 percent of those released were rearrested while on pretrial conditional release (Toborg). Informally, judges can deliberately set bail so high that defendants perceived to be dangerous will be unable to post bail and therefore await trial in jail. A survey of seventy-two major U.S. cities found that over half of those questioned stated that they set bail in this manner (Wice). More recently preventive detention has been formally authorized in some jurisdictions.

In practice, America's bail system represents a compromise between the legally recognized purpose of setting bail to assure reappearance for trial and the belief that some defendants should be allowed out of jail until their trial. Throughout this chapter we will see how these competing views affect the daily realities of bail setting and how these unresolved conflicting purposes lead various officials to manipulate the process.

The Context of Bail Setting

Deciding whom to release prior to trial and whom to detain pending trial poses critical problems for American courts. At the heart of the problem are efforts to balance the conflicting theories of bail: the right to bail as guaranteed by the Constitution and the need to protect society. As Roy Fleming argues, one can imagine two improbable extremes. On the one hand, the courts could release all defendants prior to trial. On the other, they could hold every suspect. But neither of these extremes is possible. Freeing all those accused of

---

$Q \quad U \quad O \quad T \quad A \quad T \quad I \quad O \quad N$

*P*unishment before trial, then, shares the same features as sentencing following conviction. Defendants lose their liberty, spend time in jail, and incur financial penalties. What distinguishes them, of course, is the finding of guilt through legal process that forges the link between crime and punishment. At the time bail conditions are imposed or reconsidered, this link is missing. As a matter of public policy and legal principle, therefore, if the presumption of innocence is to have substantive meaning, the scope and cost of pretrial sanctioning should be minimized for the maximum number of defendants.

From *Punishment Before Trial: An Organizational Perspective of Felony Bail Processes* by Roy B. Flemming. Copyright © 1982 by Longman, Inc. All rights reserved.

murder, robbery, and rape is politically unfeasible, no matter what the chances are of the accused later appearing in court. Similarly, jailing all is not possible because prisons are simply not large enough. Nevertheless, court officials must make decisions every day that fashion a balance between these competing demands (Flemming).

Legal protections like the right to bail are meaningful only in the context of the policies that execute those protections. Only rarely do judges directly decide that a defendant should remain in jail pending trial. Rather, this important decision is made indirectly, when the amount of bail is fixed. The higher the bail, the less likely the accused will be able to secure pretrial release. A study in New York City found that half the defendants for whom a bail was set could not make that amount of money and therefore remained in jail pending trial (Zeisel). As the amount of bail increases, fewer defendants are able to secure pretrial release.

Trial court judges have a great deal of discretion in fixing bail. Statutory law, for example, provides few specifics of how much money should be required. Appellate courts have spent even less time deciding what criteria should be used. While the Eighth Amendment protects against excessive bail, appellate courts will reduce a trial judge's bail amount only in the rare event that flagrant abuse can be proved. In practice, trial court judges have virtually unlimited legal discretion in determining the amount of bail.

The political and institutional factors that shape pretrial release policy in a court involve the context of bail setting because they determine the range of choices available to court officials. Uncertainty, risk, and jail resources are primary factors influencing bail setting.

Uncertainty

Uncertainty is a major problem facing court officials in making bail decisions. The defendant appears in court for bail setting a few short hours after arrest. Because the time span is short, only a limited amount of information is available. In all likelihood the defendants are total strangers to the court officials. Moreover, the details of the alleged crime—the who, what, when, where, and especially the why—are troublingly vague. Thus, when setting bail judges do not have information on the strength of the evidence against the accused (Nagel). Compounding the information void is the lack of adequate facts about the defendant's past criminal history. In some courts police "rap sheets" (lists of prior arrests) are available, but in others they are not. Moreover, rap sheets typically contain only information on prior arrests and not on how the case was eventually disposed of (dismissal, plea, or prison, for example). Defendants may, of course, volunteer information on their background, prior experience with the court, and so on, but understandably court officials may view this information as unreliable.

Faced with limited information, some of which may prove to be either incomplete or inaccurate, court officials must make a number of decisions. Is this specific defendant likely to appear in court? Is he or she dangerous to the community? What kind of bail is most appropriate? In the context of the crime and the defendant, what is "reasonable" or "nonexcessive" bail? The scarcity of knowledge means that defendants may be classified incorrectly as good or bad candidates for release and the wrong bail decisions made.

Risk

The uncertainty court officials face during bail setting is aggravated by the risks involved. Potentially any defendant released on bail may commit another crime. This is how one judge expressed this risk factor:

> If you let [the defendant] out on personal recognizance, with the understanding that he would reappear again for trial, and then the victim was badly injured, or killed, you have the problem of the newspapers coming [out] in a very critical vein. You have to have some security for the particular judge. (Suffet, 323)

Police groups, newspapers, district attorneys and the general public may criticize a judge severely for granting pretrial release to defendants. In New York City, for example, a judge was nicknamed ''Turn 'Em Loose Bruce'' by the Patrolman's Benevolent Association. The judge was later reassigned to civil court after a series of public controversies about his setting low bail for defendants accused of violent crimes.

It is important to recognize that in bail setting judges and other court officials may make two types of mistakes. Type 1 errors involve releasing a defendant who later commits another crime or fails to appear in court. Type 2 involves detaining a suspect who should have been released. These two types of errors are inversely related; that is, the more type 2 errors, the fewer type 1. Type 2 errors, however, are hidden. They appear only if a major tragedy occurs—a suicide in jail for example. Type 1 errors, on the other hand, form the stuff of which newspaper headlines are made. In short, judges face public criticism mainly for type 1 errors. Thus, in assessing the risk factors, court officials tend to err on the conservative side, preferring to make type 2 rather than type 1 errors.

Jail Conditions

The context of bail setting involves not only uncertainty and risk, but also available resources. In this situation the jail is the principal limiting factor. In most big cities jails regularly hold more than their capacity. As a result, court officials are forced to make uncomfortable decisions: they may believe that the defendant should be held in jail awaiting trial, but realize that arrestees who have committed more serious offenses have already filled the jail. Several studies have found that as jails become overcrowded, or threaten to exceed their capacity, bail-setting practices become more lenient (Roth and Wice; Flemming).

The Process of Bail Setting

bail tariffs

The principal way that court officials respond to the context of bail setting (uncertainty, risk, and limited jail capacity) is through the application of bail tariffs. **Bail tariffs** are rules of thumb, general guidelines concerning the proper bail amount. Judges do not ponder each case as a totally isolated event; rather, based on past experience the bail tariff provides cues and guidelines for evaluating specific cases. It "involves a search by officials to establish whether or not they should follow custom" (Flemming: 29). In some communities bail tariffs are written guidelines; in others they exist informally but have a major impact nonetheless. Two factors are particularly important in shaping bail tariffs: the seriousness of the crime and the prior criminal record of the defendant.

Seriousness of the Crime

seriousness of the crime

By far the most important consideration in setting bail is the **seriousness of the crime.** The amount of bail almost always is related to this criterion. For example, a study of bail practices in seventy-two cities reported that 86 percent of the judges believed that the seriousness of the charge was the most important pretrial release criterion in their city. The assumption underlying this belief is that the more serious the crime, the greater the urge to forfeit bail and therefore the greater the financial costs should be for such flight (Wice). An analysis of almost 5,600 cases in one borough of New York City offers further evidence of this point. The severity of the charge was inversely related to bail release (Nagel). The same pattern emerges in Philadelphia (Figure 11-1). It is a common practice for judges to use a bail schedule, which they determine themselves. For each offense a normal amount of bail is specified, with the judge or magistrate responsible for setting bail having the discretion to require more or less.

Prior Criminal Record

prior criminal record

A second criterion used in setting the amount of bond is the defendant's **prior criminal record.** Typically defendants with prior criminal records have bond set higher than normal for the offense charged. Eighty-five percent of the judges in one survey reported using the defendant's prior criminal record and found it important (Wice). Similarly, in New York City defendants with prior criminal records were more likely to await trial in jail (Nagel).

Situational Justice

situational justice

The use of bail tariffs allows the courts to set bail rather rapidly for most defendants. After a consideration of the charge and the prior record, the judge typically announced the bail amount or may agree to grant a recognizance bond. This does not mean that all bail settings are automatic. Judges often seek to produce **situational justice,** in which they weigh the individual facets of the case and the defendant. Judges also employ hunches. In the face of so little knowledge, judges may construct honesty tests like the following.

> "Have you ever been arrested anywhere in the world since the day you were born to this day?" The defendant replied that he was arrested two or three years ago. "What for?" "I forget," the defendant answers.
> "Weren't you arrested this year. In April? Weren't you in the Wayne County Jail for a day or so? On the 26th?" The judge asks the questions without giving the defendant a chance to reply.

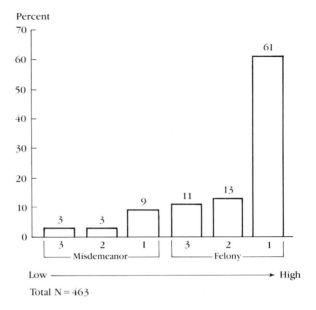

Figure 11-1 Seriousness of charges of detained defendants in Philadelphia prisons on November 13, 1980: felony–misdemeanor gradings SOURCE: John Goldkamp, "Questioning the Practice of Pretrial Detention: Some Empirical Evidence from Philadelphia," *Journal of Criminal Law and Criminology* 74 (1983): 1568.

After pausing a moment, the judge informed the defendant he had a "pretty bad memory" and added, "Have to have a bondsman for people with bad memories." He set surety bail at $1,000.

The defendant then spoke up and told the judge that he hadn't thought it was very important to remember the charge in the earlier case. The judge smiles. "You didn't think it was very important? Well, bond isn't either." (Flemming: 57)

Bail Setting and the Courtroom Work Group

In the majority of cases, bail setting involves a unilateral decision-making process—the judge reviews the case and sets a bond amount (Flemming). There are two important ways, however, for members of the courtroom work group to influence this decision. One is direct: the actors seek to provide information and thus influence the decision.

The police can influence a judge's bail decision in their selection of charges. They can deliberately overcharge—for example, arrest for a felony rather than a more appropriate misdemeanor—in order to increase the amount of bail or to punish defendants (Wice). In Des Moines, Iowa, for example, the police arrested men for drunk driving even when they knew they lacked evidence to obtain a conviction: "The boys figured the defendant would at least be rapped for the bond [defendants pay a bail bondsman $25 to write a $300 bond] and also spend a night in jail" is how one police captain justified such practice (James: 114). Such police practices can often be traced to the view that bail allows defendants to "beat the system." Frustrated and angered by what they see as undue leniency, the police seek to manipulate the court process for their own ends (Wice).

Next to the judge, the prosecutor is the most important actor in setting bail. The prosecutor is often present during the initial appearance when bail is set,

---

C O N T R O V E R S Y

More Details in Bond Hearings Needed

Before bonds are set in criminal cases, judges in Houston, Atlanta and Memphis know more about a defendant and his alleged crime than New Orleans judges.

"I don't have enough information for anything," said magistrate Judge Gerard Hansen, who sets most of the bonds in Criminal District Court. "And the more information I have, the better judge I can be."

Recently, what judges know about defendants when setting and reducing bonds came under scrutiny after a man with four felony convictions had his bond reduced when a check of the local computer showed none of his previous convictions or arrests.

When a defendant appears before a magistrate, prosecutors usually have only a police arrest register that gives personal information such as age and address and the bare minimum on the alleged crime, such as location, time and date and a one- or two-sentence description of the act, Hansen said. The information on the computer arrest register is taken from field reports submitted by police officers.

Hansen said information such as the quantity of drugs seized and the condition of victims make it easier for him to determine the bond. But this information is rarely included on the arrest registers, he said.

Hansen also gets a copy of a defendant's New Orleans Police Department rap sheet, which covers arrests in a six-parish area as far back as 1973. In most cases, earlier arrests are available, said Capt. Wayne Levet, who runs the department's record room.

Regular Criminal District Court judges may also set or reduce bonds. The judges said they check rap sheets and arrest registers, but wish they could get a defendant's FBI rap sheet, which is a nationwide list of his crimes. Although it takes more than a month to get such records, they could be available for repeat offenders. Levet said when the sheets come in from Washington, copies are given to the Police Department and district attorney's office.

"I think it would be appropriate if the system is to work properly if the district attorney would produce whatever records he has," said Judge Miriam Waltzer. "It's not only very frustrating, but very scary. You think you have a first-offender, but find the person has been through the system many, many times. I cannot know something that is not given to me."

District Attorney Harry Connick said it isn't his office's responsibility to provide judges with information, but the office does it as a courtesy to the courts.

"We have no legal standing to speak officially about a person's criminal history," Connick said. Besides, he said, the district attorney's office doesn't keep all the FBI rap sheets; that's the Police Department's job.

With only sketchy details available, New Orleans judges are asked to decide what price a person accused of a crime will pay for his freedom.

Alex Martin, "Judges Need More Details in Bond Hearings," *Times-Picayune,* February 20, 1987, p. B-1. Reprinted by permission from the Times—Picayune Publishing Corp.

and through time the judges come to know and respect the prosecutor's assessments. An excellent study of bail setting in the New York criminal court explores the interaction among judges, prosecutor, and defense attorney (Suffet). The author observed 1,473 bail settings. In 49 percent the judge made the decision without discussing the matter with the attorneys. Thirty-eight percent of the time the judge set bail in the amount suggested by either the prosecutor or defense. One point of interest, therefore, is that in a large proportion of cases the judge, prosecutor, and defense attorney apparently agreed on how much bond should be required. Such lack of disagreement is the result of widely accepted standards.

Of equal interest are the cases in which there was disagreement. When the participants disagreed, the prosecutor was more influential than the defense attorney. One reason is that prosecutors have more prestige; they are more likely to make the initial suggestion. Moreover, when prosecutors thought the judge's initial bail suggestion was too low, they were successful 80 percent of the time in getting the amount increased. When the situation was reversed, however, the defense attorney was less successful. The author concluded that the prosecutor's ability to influence bail setting derived from the fact that the judge and prosecutor held similar views about the proper amount of bail, and these views were reciprocally supportive (Suffet).

Besides these direct attempts of members of the courtroom work group to influence bail setting, important indirect factors are at work as well. Note that in Suffet's study agreement was relatively high about proper amounts of bail. This shared point of view has an important consequence: it diffuses responsibility. In releasing defendants on bail, there is no way to avoid making mistakes. If a number of people thought release for a particular defendant was acceptable, it is much more difficult later to single out the judge for blame if a crime is committed.

Geographic Differences

Pretrial release policies and practices vary widely in America's criminal courts. Table 11-2 illustrates these important variations for two cities: Detroit and Baltimore. In use of release on recognizance (ROR), for example, Detroit grants ROR for almost half the cases compared with only 12 percent in Baltimore. Other studies have documented similar disparities in other cities as well (Thomas, 1970). Likewise, the amount of cash bail required varies between courts. The typical cash bail in Baltimore is more than double the amount required in the Motor City. An earlier study found the same disparities (Silverstein). Finally and most important, the actual rate of pretrial release of felony defendants exhibits marked differences. To cite the sharpest contrast, Thomas reports that in Kansas City 63 percent of the defendants await trial in jail compared with only 13 percent in Minneapolis.

The National Jail Census (U.S. Department of Justice) found that half of the jailed inmates were in just six states: California, New York, Texas, Florida, Pennsylvania, and Georgia. Since these states include only one fourth of the nation's population and some of the most populous states with high crime rates

TABLE 11-2 Bail-Setting Policies for Felony Defendants in Detroit and Baltimore

| | Percent of defendants | |
Bail decisions	Detroit	Baltimore
Recognizance release	48.8	11.8
Cash bails	48.2	75.3
Remands (no bail allowed)	3.0	12.9
Total	100.0	100.0
Median cash bail	$2,000	$4,650
Number	1536	1676

SOURCE: From *Punishment Before Trial: An Organizational Perspective of Felony Bail Processes* by Roy B. Flemming. Copyright © 1982 by Longman, Inc. All rights reserved.

(such as Illinois, Ohio, and Michigan) are not included while some smaller ones are, the only conclusion is that defendants' chances of pretrial release are heavily dependent on the community where they are arrested.

These differences in the scope and cost of pretrial punishment are not the result of differences in crime severity. When studies include controls for the seriousness of the crime, they have found that variations in ROR use, cash bail amounts, and overall pretrial release rates persist. Rather these variations reflect important differences in the political dynamics surrounding pretrial release policies and procedures. The influence of different members of the courtroom work group varies. In one court the prosecutor may play a dominant role, usually urging high bail amounts. In another the prosecutor may play no role at all; the judge sets bail quite independently.

The Flemming study uncovers another important dimension of these political dynamics. His analysis explains the markedly different bail policies found in Table 11-2. Both cities faced a jail crisis—overcrowding, riots, unsanitary conditions, and so forth. In Detroit, however, the federal court imposed a maximum capacity on the jail population. This court order forced the judges of Detroit Recorder's Court to alter their bail policies and practices. In Baltimore, on the other hand, the federal court ordered some improvements in the local jail but did not impose a cap on the jail population. The state courts, therefore, were not under the same pressure as their counterparts in Detroit to make changes.

The disparities between the two cities, though, run deeper than a federal court order. In Detroit, pro-defendant groups are politically active. Their activities forced the judges to respond. By contrast, in Baltimore the dominant political culture is conservative. Pro-defendant groups in particular and black political activity in general are not very influential. Moreover, in Baltimore bail is determined not by judges but by commissioners. These low status court officials are more vulnerable to negative sanctions. Thus within the context of bail setting—uncertainty, risk, and limited jail resources—the political environment of Detroit supported bail reform, whereas the dynamics of Baltimore supported more punitive policies.

Bail Bondsmen

Clustered around urban courthouses are the bright neon lights of the bail bondsmen. Boldly proclaiming "Bail Bonds, 24-Hour Service" they are a constant reminder that freedom is available—for a price. Bail bondsmen are as important to America's monetary bail system as they are controversial. Reformers believe that the bondsman is a cardinal flaw in the system, a parasite who preys on human misery. For decades, reformers have been bringing to light the sometimes flagrant abuses of the bondsmen, contending that they are a constant source of corruption and collusion in the criminal courts. For these reasons abolition of the bail bondsmen is a key objective of many reformers. In a handful of states the bondsmen have, in effect, been driven out of business by bail reform.

What little is known about bail bondsmen has been strongly biased by the reform-oriented literature. Grand jury investigations, legislative studies, journalistic exposés, and perhaps most important, the reports of two national commissions have portrayed bondsmen as fixers of cases and corrupters of the system. In short, bail bondsmen have been viewed as essential links in the chain of official corruption. Forrest Dill, however, spent several months studying bail bondsmen in two California cities. He concluded that past studies leave the simplistic and incorrect impression that the bondsman is an isolated sore. Commenting on the linkage of bondsmen to official corruption, Dill argues that "such findings contain an element of truth, of course, but it is hardly surprising that bail bondsmen in corrupt jurisdictions participate in corrupting practices" (p. 643). He persuasively argues that to understand the role of bondsmen in the criminal justice system, one must examine two aspects of their existence: the business setting and the court setting.

The Business Setting

Bondsmen are small businessmen. But the business they are in is a unique one. By allowing commercial middlemen to post bond, the state has created a business operation within the criminal courts. The bondsman is a private government subcontractor. In essence, the key decisions on pretrial release have been transferred from public officials to a private party who represents neither the interests of the courts nor the interests of the defendant.

surety bond

Bail bondsmen make money by providing a specialized form of insurance. For a nonrefundable fee, they post a ***surety bond*** with the court. If the defendant does not appear for trial, the bondsman is responsible for the full amount of the bond. For assuming this risk, the bondsman is permitted to charge a fee, usually 10 percent.

Bail bondsmen almost never directly post a cash surety with the court. Instead they purchase a surety bond from a major insurance company, which charges 30 percent of the bondsman's fee. Thus if the total amount of the bail is $1,000, the bondsman receives $100 from the client and keeps $70 of it. The profit margin in each case is seldom large, so bondsmen need to find enough clients willing to purchase their services while simultaneously accepting only those who present a minimal risk of fleeing.

Securing clients. Competition among local bondsmen to gain "good" clients is stiff. Since the only legitimate business techniques bondsmen may use are quite limited and engaged in by all—advertising and a reputation for prompt, courteous, twenty-four-hour service—bondsmen must rely on other techniques, sometimes legal and sometimes not, to ensure a steady supply of clients.

There are four major sources of clients. In descending order of importance, first are family and friends. After the defendant is taken into custody and is allowed to make one or two telephone calls, the family or friend often seeks out a bondsman. A second way the clients come to the bondsman is more direct. Defendants with prior court experience know how to contact bondsmen who have provided good service in the past. Defense attorneys are a third source of referrals. Lawyers may legitimately refer a client to a bondsman, but at times bondsmen and lawyers exchange favors. For example, bondsmen can help lawyers by providing knowledge about the defendant's financial situation, by referring clients to a specific lawyer (which is illegal), or by giving kickbacks (which are also illegal). In turn, defense attorneys may reciprocate with information, or fees for referrals (also illegal). Police officers, court clerks, or bailiffs are the fourth source of clients. Again it may be a subtle suggestion—"I hear Al's Bail Bonding Service is good"—or it may be more direct—pointing to a particular bondsman's number in the phone book and pushing a quarter in the defendant's hand. Sometimes such referrals stem from an attempt to be helpful, but more often there is an expectation that the person making the referral will be compensated in some way.

Reducing risks. Once bondsmen have made contact with a particular defendant, they must decide whether they are willing to take the person as a client. In general, bondsmen consider the following types of defendants bad risks: first offenders (because they are likely to panic); recidivists whose new crime is more serious than previous ones; and violent defendants (they may harm the bondsman). In assessing which defendants are financially reliable, bondsmen use the very criteria ignored by the court: employment history, family situation, and roots in the community. If a defendant is marginal, bondsmen may require the posting of collateral in addition to the fee. Bail bondsmen may also revoke the bond of any client they fear might be contemplating flight (but they are under no obligation to rebate the fee).

Contrary to popular belief, bondsmen do not accept just anyone as a client. They prefer to write bonds when the bail is low because their risks are also low. Thus many bondsmen make a living by posting collateral for numerous defendants accused of minor crimes and an occasional large bond when repayment is assured.

Bond jumping. After a bondsman has decided to accept a defendant as a client, a key factor determining whether there will be a ***bond forfeiture*** is the degree of supervision the bondsman exercises over the client. Although some bondsmen work long and hard to maintain contact with their clients, most are quite lax (Wice). Once a defendant skips, however, bondsmen attempt to find the person.

***bond
forfeiture***

jump bond

Bail bondsmen have extraordinary legal powers over bailed defendants who *jump bond* and flee. When the bondsman makes bail, the clients are required to sign a contract waiving the right to extradition and allowing the bondsman to retrieve them from wherever they have fled. These powers exceed any possessed by law enforcement officials. For example, a bondsman can retrieve a fugitive who has crossed state lines much more easily than the police can. Law enforcement officials must follow formal extradition procedures that do not apply to the bondsman because his apprehension of the defendant is viewed as a private right stemming from the bond contract. The bondsman need not even secure a warrant. Some law enforcement officials contend that the bondsman renders an important service to the state by retrieving bond jumpers (National Conference on Bail and Criminal Justice). However, chasing bond jumpers is often too expensive since the bondsman must hire a "trace skipper" to locate the person and then pay for the travel expenses. As a result, bondsmen often find it unprofitable to chase defendants. Abuses of these powers over bond jumpers—including murder and kidnapping—have long been noted.

Bail Bondsmen and the Courtroom Work Group

Experienced bail bondsmen are on a first-name basis with court personnel—bailiffs, clerks, prosecutors, and so on—who represent a vital part of their business. Bondsmen are often financial contributors to judges' reelection campaigns. Each of these officials can help (or hinder). As one bondsman noted: "The court clerk is probably one of the most important people I have to deal with. He moves cases, he can get information to the judge, and he has control over various calendar matters. When he's not willing to help you out, he can make life very difficult. He knows he's important, and he acts like it" (Dill: 658). The relationships between bail bondsmen and the courts are reciprocal.

Bondsmen aid the courts.   One way that bondsmen help the courts is by managing the population of arrested persons. This insight is as obvious as it is basic. Without an organization like the bail bondsmen, the courts would be faced with an intolerably large jail population or would be forced to make major alterations in their own procedures. For decades the bail bondsmen have been the course of least resistance. At the same time, bondsmen may also cooperate in preventing some defendants from being released. When court officials desire that a particular defendant not be released, the bondsmen often cooperate by refusing to post surety.

Bondsmen also help the courts by directing defendants through the bureaucratic maze of the court system. Defendants come to the court with varying backgrounds and differing expectations and thus have the potential for disrupting the smooth operations of the court system. Bondsmen know the local routines and help educate their clients to accept these routines. They urge unrepresented clients to hire a lawyer if the case is a major one. They may ease the defendant's anxiety. And in some cases, they encourage defendants to plead guilty.

Shortly after lunch on another afternoon, a young man who had been charged with littering and possessing open containers of beer in his car stopped by to see Al [a bondsman] about his case. He was apprehensive about the outcome because the girl who had been arrested with him had already "copped out as charged." He asked: "What will happen if I change my earlier plea to guilty?"

Al answered: "It won't make any difference. They got the girl and all they want are guilty pleas. The judge will fine you $25, and that will be the end of it."

Al was correct. Later that afternoon the client returned and jubilantly told Al, "It's all over. I got out for $29." (Dill: 655–656)

Like defense attorneys and probation officers, therefore, bail bondsmen are "agent mediators." They help defendants adapt to and accept their newly acquired role of defendant.

The court aids the bondsmen.   The major financial risk facing bondsmen is that clients will jump bond and ***fail to appear*** in court, and the entire amount of the bond will have to be made good. Yet in many cities, forfeited bonds regularly go uncollected. During one year, 318 bonds were forfeited in St. Louis, but 304 were set aside by the court (Wice). To encourage bondsmen to seek out and find those who have fled, states allow a grace period before bonds can be forfeited (ranging from a short two weeks in Detroit to a rather lengthy 180 days in California). But the key reason that many bonds go uncollected is the discretionary power of judges to exonerate bondsmen from outstanding bonds. In many cities, bondsmen will not have to pay a bond forfeiture if they can convince the judge that they made every effort to find the missing client (Wice). But these considerations cannot explain all of the uncollected bonds. One newspaper estimated that $2 million in bond forfeitures went uncollected in Dallas. In New Orleans the figure was almost $1 million. Such large amounts of uncollected bond forfeitures often result from judges deliberately not trying to collect. Given the reciprocal relationships between the bondsmen and the court, and the help the bondsmen offer the courts, the major way the courts can help the bondsmen is by not trying to collect bond forfeitures

*failure
to appear*

Effects of Bail

Pretrial detention affects not only those detained but has an important impact on the criminal court process as well. Despite the fact that detained defendants are presumed innocent until proven guilty, they suffer the same disadvantages as those incarcerated after conviction. Economically they may lose jobs. Socially they are stigmatized by the jail label. Psychologically they are subjected to stress, anxiety, and isolation. Physically they are held in a violence-prone atmosphere. The President's Commission on Law Enforcement and Criminal Justice chose the following examples to dramatize the human toll that pretrial detention may exact.

—A man was jailed on a serious charge brought last Christmas Eve. He could not afford bail and spent 101 days in jail until a hearing. Then the complainant admitted the charge was false.

—A man could not raise $300 bail. He spent 54 days in jail waiting trial for a traffic offense, for which he could have been sentenced to no more than five days.

—A man spent two months in jail before being acquitted. In that period he lost his job, and his car, and his family was split up. He did not find another job for four months. (p. 30)

But the effects of pretrial detention are not limited to those detained. The decision on bail—made within the first hours of contact with the court—reverberates through all subsequent stages of the court proceedings. In a variety of ways detained defendants are at a disadvantage during pretrial, plea bargaining, trial, and sentencing.

Jail Conditions

jail conditions

Jail conditions are often poor. Many big city jails and some county ones are chronically overcrowded. Many regularly hold twice their intended capacity; four inmates may be housed in a six-by-nine-foot cell, confined to their cells, or in a narrow adjoining corridor (Goldfarb). Idleness is the norm. Rehabilitative services are notably lacking. Prisoners are let out of their cells only for meals or an occasional but short period of recreation. Food may be of low quality and nutritionally poor. Medical care may be lacking. Physically jails are often ugly, ancient, almost medieval structures. Jail is a brutal environment. The threat of attack—including homosexual rape—is always present. And because jails are so overcrowded, it is often impossible to separate young defendants from old, novices from career criminals, the especially vulnerable from the likely aggressors.

It is into this undesirable atmosphere that all who cannot pay the bondsman's fee are thrust. One author has likened the American jail to the twentieth-century poorhouse (Goldfarb). The inmates are disproportionately poor and disproportionately members of minority groups. Perhaps because jails hold society's outcasts, relatively little is known about them. Until the National Jail Census, there were no statistics on how many jails there were in the country; the census found 4,037 adult jails. Interestingly, the number of jails has declined in recent years to 3,338 (Bureau of Justice Statistics, 1984). By all accounts the conditions in jails (which hold those awaiting trial) are significantly worse than in prison. Indeed, because pretrial detainees have not been convicted they have fewer rights and privileges than those in the same jail who have been convicted. They are not eligible to participate in rehabilitation programs, for example.

Overcrowded conditions and dilapidated physical structures have drawn attention to local jails since at least the mid-1960s. Local officials have been inactive in correcting these conditions (Price, Weber, and Perlman). Increasingly in recent years prisoners have filed suits in federal court contending that the conditions in the county jails violate the Eighth Amendment prohibition against "cruel and unusual punishment" (Culbertson and Schneider). As a result, federal court supervision of local jails is extensive. Of the 621 largest jails in the nation, almost half (46 percent) are under court order, and 134 are being required to reduce jail populations. An additional 150 are under orders to improve the conditions of confinement by reducing crowding in living units, furnishing adequate recreational facilities, improving medical services, providing an adequate diet, or revising jail practices (Bureau of Justice Statistics, 1986).

Legal Consequences

Pretrial detention has a great impact on the legal processing of defendants. Detained defendants exist in a state of limbo. While sitting and waiting, their primary concern is what is going to happen with their case. But jail isolates them from any control over their fate. At times it is difficult for them to communicate with their attorneys. Months may pass between contacts with their lawyer. And because they are detained, defendants cannot help their lawyer in preparing a defense. Most defense attorneys, for example, lack the resources of an investigator to search out witnesses favorable to the defendant.

Pretrial detention places great pressure on defendants. They are anxious and uncertain over their case, and this anxiety and uncertainty significantly affect tactical decisions. In some instances, delay may be to the defendant's advantage. Even so, waiting is much easier out of jail. Moreover, the time spent

"dead time" awaiting trial may be *"dead time,"* time not counted in the final sentence. Thus pressures build on defendants to get the process over with. Some prefer to plead guilty and be done with it. At least after sentencing, defendants know how much time they will have to serve, when they will be eligible for parole, and that the time served will be in the state prison.

A predominant concern of bail research centers on the discriminatory impact of bail practices. Simply put, do defendants in jail have higher rates of conviction and prison sentence? Table 11-3 presents data from the Manhattan

---

Q U O T A T I O N

*V*iewed from the perspective of maintaining the plea-bargaining system, pretrial detention and demoralizing conditions in jails are highly functional. They discourage the defendant from bargaining too hard; they place a high price upon filing motions or demanding a trial; they encourage him to rat out his friends in order to end his own ordeal. This is not to argue that those in authority consciously plan rotten jails; clearly most are concerned about jail conditions. But it is to suggest that such conditions are functional, do serve the needs of the production ethic that dominates our criminal justice system.

Jonathan Casper, *American Criminal Justice: The Defendant's Perspective,* ©1972, p. 67. Reprinted by permission of Prentice-Hall, Inc., Englewood Cliffs, New Jersey.

TABLE 11-3   Case Dispositions, by Jail Status and Charge

Charge	At liberty before trial		Detained before trial	
	Percent convicted	*Total cases*	*Percent convicted*	*Total cases*
Assault	23	126	59	128
Grand larceny	43	96	72	156
Robbery	51	35	58	100
Dangerous weapons	43	23	57	21
Narcotics	52	33	38	42
Sex crimes	10	49	14	28
Others	30	47	78	23

SOURCE: Ares, Rankin, and Sturz, "The Manhattan Bail Project: An Interim Report on the Use of Pre-Trial Parole," *N.Y.U. Law Review* 38 (1963): 67, 84.

bail project, the first systematic investigation of the effects of bail on the criminal court process. Conducted by the Vera Institute of Justice in 1963, the data clearly show that detained defendants are more likely to be convicted. Almost three out of five persons charged with assault and detained before trial were convicted; but only one of five (23 percent) of those charged with the same offense but not detained were convicted. Another study of preventive detention found that defendants' chances of being convicted increased by at least 20 percent when they were detained before trial (Ervin).

The effects of pretrial detention continue after conviction and sentencing. Detained defendants have a greater likelihood of being sentenced to prison and for longer terms than those who posted bond. Often pretrial detention has stripped defendants of attributes that might contribute to a lighter sentence. If they had a job, they have lost it, and their family lives have been disrupted, therefore making them poorer probation risks. Those who have been detained present a very different physical appearance in court. Dressed in jail garb, with a pallid complexion caused by confinement, detained defendants are less able to project a favorable image. Finally, the special status of detained defendants is underscored by the fact that they are brought to court in handcuffs by sheriff deputies who maintain a watchful vigilance, another cue that society has already labeled these people as dangerous.

These findings, that jailed defendants are more likely to be convicted and also more likely to be sentenced to prison, have been disputed by more recent research. After analyzing over eight thousand criminal cases from 1975 in Philadelphia, John Goldkamp found that jailed defendants did not differ from their bailed counterparts in terms of findings of guilt. At all the significant stages—dismissal, diversion, and trial—jailed defendants were as likely as bailed ones to receive a favorable disposition. When it came to sentencing, however, jailed defendants were more likely to be sentenced to prison, but interestingly the length of the sentence was not related to bail status (Goldkamp, 1980). Similarly, the three-city study of Chicago, Baltimore, and Detroit revealed that there was no uniform impact of bail status on either findings of guilt or sentencing (although in some cities in some situations there was an impact) (Eisenstein and Jacob). The emerging literature in the field is not easily summarized.

Perhaps the best response is provided by Goldkamp. Does bail status negatively affect the defendant's case? His verdict is "it depends."

Failure to Appear

bench warrant (capias)

Not all defendants on pretrial appear in court when required. Skipping bail entails several consequences. First, bail is forfeited. Second, a warrant is issued for the suspect's arrest. This warrant is termed a **bench warrant** or a **capias** and commands the sheriff or police to take a person into custody. The person must be delivered to the judge issuing the warrant and cannot make bail. Finally, failure to appear often subjects the defendant to a separate criminal charge of bond jumping.

Nationally the nonappearance rate varies from 3 to 7 percent (Table 11-4). But as with so many other areas of the criminal system, reliable figures are extremely hard to come by. Typically a failure to appear involves several court agencies—judges, clerks, police, and prosecutor—whose activities are not well coordinated. In addition, many courts do not keep such records, or if they do, they usually keep them in a careless and unreliable manner. Moreover data on failure to appear can easily be manipulated either to show the success of pretrial release or to discredit it. Note in Table 11-4 that Detroit seems to have an extremely high forfeiture rate. During the time the statistics were gathered, the court was under pressure to keep pretrial release to a minimum and used two forms of statistical manipulation to make it seem as if release did not work. First, a strict definition was used. A defendant who was even a minute late was counted as skipping. (Most of the nonappearing defendants actually showed up within two days.) Second, when a defendant fled, the Detroit court counted each missed court appearance as a separate count. Discounting these statistical manipulations, the failure-to-appear rate in Detroit came close to the national average.

Defendants who fail to appear do not always intend to do so. Failure-to-appear rates are closely tied to practices within the court itself. A number of defendants do not show up because they were not given clear notice of the next appearance date. The noise of the courtroom or language barriers often mean that defendants are confused about when to appear next. Similarly, most courts still keep records by hand. Simple clerical errors as to the defendant's correct name or current address often mean that notices are never delivered. Perhaps above all, many courts are simply unwilling to try to communicate with defendants while they are on pretrial release. The lack of proper administrative procedures continues after defendants have failed to appear. In many communities, the sheriff or police are lax in serving bench warrants.

Another way that courts themselves contribute to nonappearances is by lengthy delay in disposing of the case. As the time from arrest to trial increases, the rate of nonappearances rises even faster. Crimes committed while out on bail are also tied to delay in court disposition. A study in Charlotte, North Carolina, for example, estimated that every additional two-week delay increased by 5 percent the chances a defendant either would not appear or would commit another crime (Clarke et al.).

TABLE 11-4 Forfeiture Rates

	Rate	Source of statistics and clarification
Chicago	8.7%	Clerk of circuit court of Cook County (1969)
Philadelphia	4.0%	Estimate by court administrator (1970)
Indianapolis	5.4%	Survey by Indianapolis Bail Project (1969) surety bonds
Detroit	24.0%	Recorders court annual report (1969): 8% for surety bonds, 40% for personal bonds
Baltimore	5.0%	Estimate by public officials and bondsmen
Atlanta	7.0%	Exact figure from district attorney's office
St. Louis	5.0%	Exact figure from clerk of circuit court, criminal division
Washington	3.7%	Exact figure from the report of the D.C. judicial court, Report on the Operation of Bail (1969)

SOURCE: Reprinted by permission of the publisher, from *Freedom for Sale* by Paul B. Wice (Lexington, Mass.: Lexington Books, D. C. Heath and Company. Copyright 1974, D. C. Heath and Company), p. 67.

A basic question in evaluating the effectiveness of bail is how well judges (in their bail-setting decisions) are able to predict the likelihood of a defendant's appearance. The study in Charlotte provides some tentative answers. The authors found that numerous variables thought to be important were not: age, race, sex, income, and seriousness of the crime *were not* related to nonappearance. Thus the factor most used by the courts in setting bail—severity of the crime—is, at least in this one community, not related to the final outcome (Clarke et al.). More recent research underscores this point. Separate studies in Washington, D.C. (Roth and Wice) and New York City (Zeisel) concluded that the most dangerous defendants jumped bail the least. By contrast those accused of more minor offenses had higher rates of failure to appear. The Charlotte study found that the only other major factor related to failure to appear was the criminal history of the defendant. At least this one factor used in setting bail has some relationship to the intended results.

Toward Bail Reform

For decades, the monetary bail system has been the subject of extensive debate. The fairness and effectiveness of pretrial detention has been questioned from several perspectives. The bail reform movement of the 1960s and 1970s was largely concerned with correcting inequities. Requiring suspects to buy their freedom was viewed as unfairly discriminating against the poor. To make bail fairer, reformers advocated using citations in lieu of arrest, a 10 percent bail deposit system, and bail reform projects. These programs offer new ways to accomplish the historical goal of bail—to guarantee appearance for trial. During the 1980s concern shifted to the linkage between bail and crime. Allowing dangerous defendants to post bail was viewed as unnecessarily exposing the public to the risk of further victimization. To better protect the public, these critics urged the adoption of preventive detention. Detaining some suspects without bail is designed to adapt constitutional provisions to the current realities of high crime rates.

These competing viewpoints are reflected in two major pieces of federal legislation. The Bail Reform Act of 1966 created a presumption favoring pretrial release. Unless the judge is convinced that pretrial release "will not reasonably assure the appearance of the person as required," the defendant is to be released. The 1984 Bail Reform Act made wholesale revisions in the earlier law. Its emphasis on protecting the safety of the community represents a major shift in philosophy. In setting bail, a federal judge may now consider danger to the community and may deny bail altogether when the accused is found to be a "grave danger to others." Whereas release of the defendant was the primary intent of the earlier law, ***detention*** plays a prominent role in the new one.

detention

Citation in Lieu of Arrest

Every year the police arrest almost eleven million people, most of them for minor offenses. But even though the violations are minor, they are often treated the same as felonies; the person is arrested, booked at the police station, and must pay a bondsman to secure release.

*citation in
lieu of arrest*

An alternative to requiring those arrested for minor offenses to post bond is a ***citation in lieu of arrest.*** A citation works much like an ordinary traffic ticket. Suspects are given a summons directing them to appear in court at a given time and place. These are commonly used for a specified list of misdemeanors.

Citation programs have proven quite successful. In California, for example, defendants given a citation in lieu of arrest failed to appear only 4.5 percent of the time (Kalmanoff). Yet only a handful of cities have adopted such programs. One of the reasons is that programs like these are strongly opposed by bail bondsmen, who have sufficient political muscle to block enactment of the necessary legislation. Just as important, adoption of a citation-in-lieu-of-arrest program requires the coordinated efforts of several independent agencies—local police departments, lower court judges, clerks of court, and so on—each of which dislikes any change in its routine. Moreover, bail reform has no built-in political constituency because it is viewed by the public as helping criminals. Programs like these are a low-priority item. And even when formally adopted, citation programs may prove ineffective. Police officers are naturally suspicious and therefore reluctant to issue citations. Without strong backing from police administrators, citation in lieu of arrest can remain empty legislation.

Ten Percent Bail Deposit

Bail bondsmen charge a nonrefundable 10 percent fee for posting bond. Given that bondsmen seem to perform few services for their fee and have often been sources of corruption, bail reformers have attempted to legislate an economic end run around the bondsmen. In a handful of states (Illinois, Pennsylvania, and Kentucky) as well as the U.S. courts, defendants may gain pretrial release by posting 10 percent of the bond amount with the court. At this point there is no difference between what the bondsman charges and what the court requires. But when the defendant makes all scheduled court appearances, the court will refund 90 percent of the amount posted with the court. (It uses the extra 10 percent to cover the costs of administering the program.) Defendants who fail to appear, however, are still liable for the full face amount of the bond.

10 percent
bail deposit

The **10 percent bail deposit** program directly threatens the bail bond industry. Indeed, in Illinois, the first state to adopt this program, bondsmen have virtually disappeared. In other states, however, bondsmen have been successful in defeating such programs in the legislature.

Bail Reform Projects

Bail reformers have been critical of traditional methods of bail setting because the bail amount is fixed not on the basis of whether the defendant will likely appear in court but on the basis of the crime charged. Moreover, the court makes no attempt to determine which defendants are good risks. **Bail reform projects** seek to remedy these deficiencies by investigating the background of arrested persons and then recommending **release on recognizance** (release without bail) for those who are reliable.

bail reform
projects
release on
recognizances
(ROR)

First developed and tested by the Vera Institute of Justice in New York City, the program works as follows. A program worker (either a paid staff member or a volunteer law student) interviews the defendant shortly after arrest about family, job, prior criminal record, and length of time in the community. Persons deemed good risks are recommended for release on recognizance. Not all defendants are eligible for the program, however. Those arrested for serious charges like murder, armed robbery, or sale of drugs are excluded in most communities. After a person has been released on recognizance, the bail reform project makes follow-up contacts to ensure that the defendant knows when the court appearance is scheduled and will show up.

The guiding assumption of the Vera Project is that defendants with ties to the community are not likely to flee. And by providing information about these ties (which normally is not available when bail is set), the program provides a more workable way for making sure that the wrong persons are not detained prior to trial. Research has confirmed the operating assumption. Where bail reform projects have been tried, the rate of nonappearance for those released on recognizance has been lower than for those released through bail bondsmen (Wice). Supporters also argue that bail reform projects save money. Because more defendants are being released, costs for holding these persons in jail are significantly reduced.

There are often major gaps between an idea in theory and its actual implementation; this is true of bail reform projects. Although a number of cities have implemented bail reform programs, there are often important differences in the administration of these programs.

Bail reform projects must operate in a very restricted political atmosphere. Programs aimed at helping those accused of crime face an uphill battle. Moreover, there are often conflicts among judges, court administrators, prosecutors, defense attorneys, and the police about who will control and administer the programs. In several cities Wice visited such disputes have seriously weakened the effectiveness of the programs.

In an effort to head off possible negative public relations, bail reform projects have maintained a conservative stance by selecting only the most reliable persons for pretrial release. As a result, bail reform projects, like all too many other criminal justice reforms, end up concentrating government resources on those least in need. The initial concern was with truly poor defendants, many from the inner cities and members of minorities; but in practice bail reform has been least able to help this group. A study of the pretrial release program in Charlotte found that most of the defendants released by the program would have been released on recognizance anyway or would have been able to hire a bondsman. Thus the pretrial release program made only a slight dent in the percentage of defendants released prior to trial (Clarke et al.). A study in an unnamed eastern city concluded:

> Thus, to the degree that recognizance standards emphasize employment history, length of residence, and social ties (which is the case in Metro City and other cities), they tend to screen out precisely those defendants who are most likely to have difficulty making financial bail in the first place. (Flemming et al.: 969)

The net result is that bail reform programs seem to release those who would have posted cash bail anyway; the overall pretrial release rate is more dependent on jail capacity than on the reform efforts (Mahoney).

Preventive Detention

preventive detention

Adherents of the crime control model assume that current bail practices do not successfully restrain dangerous defendants. They point to defendants who commit crimes while out of jail on pretrial release. The suggested alternative is *preventive detention,* which allows judges to hold suspects without bail if they are accused of committing a dangerous or violent crime and locking them up is deemed necessary for community safety. More than half the states have adopted some form of preventive detention either by constitutional amendment or by legislative enactment.

The best-known example of preventive detention is the Comprehensive Crime Control Act of 1984. A judge may order defendants who have previously been released on bail detained for up to ten days. The most controversial provisions authorized preventive detention for defendants accused of serious crimes. After a detention hearing, the defendant may be held in jail without bail for up to ninety days pending trial if the judge finds "clear and convincing evidence" that there is a risk of flight, obstruction of justice will occur, or that the suspect is dangerous. The law also creates a presumption against pretrial release for major drug dealers. The Supreme Court has upheld the 1984 Bail Reform Act, ruling that Congress enacted preventive detention not as a punishment for dangerous individuals but as a potential solution to the pressing social problem of crimes committed by persons on bail (*U.S.* v. *Salerno,* 55 LW 4663).

Although the 1984 Act expands the court's power to detain individuals prior to trial, the pretrial release of most defendants is still expected (Berg). It is too early to determine whether preventive detention orders will be sought in substantial numbers. Some have suggested that prosecutors may avoid the law's elaborate procedural requirements by employing the usual practice of requesting high bond amounts (Cohen). This was certainly the case in Washington, D.C., whose law served as the basis for the 1984 federal law. Prosecutors rarely requested detention hearings and less than two out of every thousand felony defendants were detained (Thomas).

Civil libertarians view preventive detention laws as a threat to constitutional values. More specifically, critics view predictions of dangerousness as very unreliable. A variety of studies indicate that the criteria used in setting bail are poor predictors of the likelihood that the defendant will later appear in court as scheduled or will commit further crimes while out on bail (Goldkamp, 1983). Given these problems, civil libertarians advocate reducing trial court delay (Chapter 18) as a better approach to reducing crimes committed while defendants are out on bail.

CLOSE-UP

Bail? Sorry, the Prosecutor Thinks You Might Be Dangerous

When federal drug agents arrested Marlen Ramallo on June 3 on charges of importing cocaine, the 33-year-old Alexandria, Va., mother of two got a surprise: She was jailed and denied bond.

Despite her lack of a criminal record and her ties to the Northern Virginia community, Ramallo was held under a controversial 22-month-old law that allows federal prosecutors to keep suspects in custody if they are considered "dangerous to the community" or likely to flee before trial.

Under the old law, Ramallo, a native of Bolivia who prosecutors say they feared would flee because of her associations with reputed drug dealers, probably would have been released on bond. Ramallo, who is married to an American, pleaded guilty to a drug conspiracy charge after six weeks in jail. Later she was sentenced to 18 months in prison, with credit for the time she had served.

Enacted as part of a tough-

ening of federal criminal laws in general and drug trafficking statutes in particular, the 1984 Bail Reform Act has resulted in the pretrial detention of an estimated 7,000 people, prompting Justice Department officials to hail the law as a "remarkable success."

"We have many instances to show where we have been able to detain people who were really dangerous whom we could not detain under old law," says Deputy Assistant Attorney General James I. K. Knapp. Almost half of those detained were accused of narcotics offenses, he says.

Civil libertarians and defense lawyers are more critical of the law. While some lawyers say the changes make it less likely that only poor suspects who cannot afford the high bonds in drug cases will be jailed, others question the law's effectiveness, fairness and constitutionality.

"Now, for the first time in

200 years, the government can keep a person in jail without bond in a noncapital case," says John K. Zwerling, an Alexandria defense attorney.

"We see it as a strong violation of one of the fundamental foundations of our legal system—that a defendant is presumed innocent until found guilty at trial," says Judy Goldberg, an American Civil Liberties Union legislative analyst.

Supporters and critics agree that federal judges and magistrates have accepted the bail changes more rapidly than expected, granting more than 80 percent of prosecutors' requests for preventive detention. They have granted them far more frequently than judges in jurisdictions that have had preventive detention statutes for several years, such as the District of Columbia, according to bail expert John P. Bellassai.

Caryle Murphy, *The Washington Post National Weekly Edition,* September 15, 1986, p. 31. Reprinted by permission.

Conclusion

Bail serves several purposes in the American court system, some legally sanctioned, others definitely extralegal. Bail is used to guarantee a defendant's appearance at trial, to protect society by holding those perceived to be dangerous, to punish those accused (but not yet convicted) of violating the law, and to lubricate the system by softening defendants up to enter a plea of guilty. These varying purposes are partially the result of the tension between conflicting principles. Although the law recognizes that the only legal purpose of bail is to guarantee a suspect's future appearance at trial, in practice court officials perceive a need to protect society. Out of these conflicting principles arise compromises. Bail setting is also influenced by the conditions under which it must be executed. Shortly after arrest, based on at best sketchy information, a decision must be made.

Few are happy with how the system actually operates. Some defendants are held in jail who clearly should not be. Others are released who threaten society. Until recently such problems attracted little attention. The course of least resistance was to delegate the responsibility to private businessmen—bail bondsmen. Now a great deal of rethinking is focused on improving the system.

For Discussion

1. Under the Constitution, what is the purpose of bail? What additional purposes does bail fulfill in practice? Why?
2. Do you think that for certain defendants, bail should not be allowed? What kinds of cases?
3. You are the judge. In setting bail, how may the nature of the crime, the characteristics of the defendant, the conditions in the local jail, and local community pressures influence your decision?
4. Examine the local newspapers. Have there been reports of defendants committing crimes while out on bail? Have there been reports on poor conditions in the local jail? How might these reports affect bail setting?
5. Attend a court session where bail is set. Does the prosecutor make bail recommendations? The defense attorney? Does the judge appear to be influenced by these recommendations? What information is available in setting bail?
6. Using court records and other sources if necessary, determine the amount of bond set in various types of cases. Also try to determine what forms of bail predominate—recognizance, bondsmen, and so on. Try to estimate the percentage of defendants who are released on bail.
7. Interview a judge, prosecutor, defense attorney, and bail bondsman. Determine bail-setting criteria in your community. Also ask about problems these officials perceive in the bail process.
8. Check your telephone directory. How many bondsmen are listed?

References

BERG, KENNETH. "The Bail Reform Act of 1984." *Emory Law Journal* 34 (1985): 687.

BUREAU OF JUSTICE STATISTICS. *The 1983 Jail Census.* Washington, D.C.: U.S. Department of Justice, 1984.

——. *Jail Inmates 1984.* Washington, D.C.: U.S. Department of Justice, 1986.

CLARKE, STEVENS, JEAN FREEMAN, AND GARY KOCH. *The Effectiveness of Bail Systems: An Analysis of Failure to Appear in Court and Rearrest While on Bail.* Chapel Hill: Institute of Government, University of North Carolina, 1976.

COHEN, FRED. "Special Feature: An Introduction to the New Federal Crime Control Act." *Criminal Law Bulletin* 21 (1985): 330.

CULBERTSON, ROBERT, AND ELIZABETH SCHNEIDER. "National Survey of County Jails." In *Preliminary Report.* Washington, D.C.: National Sheriffs Association, 1982.

DILL, FORREST. "Discretion, Exchange and Social Control: Bail Bondsmen in Criminal Courts." *Law and Society Review* 9 (Summer 1975): 639–674.

EISENSTEIN, JAMES, AND HERBERT JACOB. *Felony Justice: An Organizational Analysis of Criminal Courts.* Boston: Little, Brown, 1977.

ERVIN, S. J. *Preventive Detention.* Chicago: Urban Research Corp., 1971.

FLEMMING, ROY. *Punishment Before Trial: An Organizational Perspective on Felony Bail Process.* New York: Longman, 1982.

——, C. KOHFELD, AND THOMAS UHLMAN. "The Limits of Bail Reform: A Quasi-Experimental Analysis." *Law and Society Review* 14 (Summer 1980): 947–976.

GOLDFARB, RONALD. *Ransom: A Critique of the American Bail System.* New York: Harper & Row, 1965.

GOLDKAMP, JOHN. "The Effects of Detention of Judicial Decisions: A Closer Look." *Justice System Journal* 5 (1980): 234–257.

——. "Questioning the Practice of Pretrial Detention: Some Empirical Evidence from Philadelphia." *The Journal of Criminal Law and Criminology* 74 (1983): 1556.

JAMES, HOWARD. *Crisis in the Courts.* New York: David McKay, 1971.

KALMANOFF, ALAN. *Criminal Justice: Enforcement and Administration.* Boston: Little, Brown, 1976.

MAHONEY, BARRY. "Evaluating Pretrial Release Program." Paper presented at the annual meeting of the American Political Science Association, Chicago, Illinois, 1976.

NAGEL, ILENE. "The Legal/Extra-Legal Controversy: Judicial Decisions in Pretrial Release." *Law and Society Review* 17 (1983): 481.

NATIONAL CONFERENCE ON BAIL AND CRIMINAL JUSTICE. *Proceedings and Interim Report.* Washington, D.C.: Government Printing Office, 1965.

POWERS, RICHARD. "Detention Under the Federal Bail Reform Act of 1984." *Criminal Law Bulletin* 21 (1985): 413.

PRESIDENT'S COMMISSION ON LAW ENFORCEMENT AND ADMINISTRATION OF JUSTICE. *Task Force Report: The Courts.* Washington, D.C.: Government Printing Office, 1967.

PRICE, ALBERT, CHARLES WEBER, AND ELLIS PERLMAN. "Judicial Discretion and Jail Overcrowding." *Justice System Journal* 8 (1983): 222.

ROTH, JEFFREY, AND PAUL WICE. *Pretrial Release and Misconduct in the District of Columbia.* Washington, D.C.: Institute for Law and Social Research, 1980.

SILVERSTEIN, LEE. "Bail in the State Courts—A Field Study and Report." *Minnesota Law Review* 50 (1966): 621.

SUFFET, FREDERICK. "Bail Setting: A Study of Courtroom Interaction." *Crime and Delinquency* 12 (October 1966): 318.

THOMAS, WAYNE. *The Current State of Bail Reform: Bail Projects.* Davis, Calif.: Center on the Administration of Justice, 1970.

——. *Bail Reform in America.* Berkeley: University of California Press, 1976.

TOBORG, MARY. *Pretrial Release: A National Evaluation of Practices and Outcomes.* Washington, D.C.: National Institute of Justice, 1982.

U.S. DEPARTMENT OF JUSTICE, BUREAU OF JUSTICE STATISTICS. *Profile of Jail Inmates: Sociodemographic Findings from the 1978 Survey of Inmates of Local Jails.* Washington, D.C.: Government Printing Office, 1980.

U.S. DEPARTMENT OF JUSTICE, LAW ENFORCEMENT ASSISTANCE ADMINISTRATION 1980. *Jail Census.* Washington, D.C.: Government Printing Office, 1981.

WICE, PAUL. *Freedom for Sale.* Lexington, Mass.: D. C. Heath, Lexington Books, 1974.

ZEISEL, HANS. "Bail Revisited." *American Bar Foundation Research Journal* (1976): 769.

For Further Reading

ERVIN, S. J. *Preventive Detention.* Chicago: Urban Research Corp., 1971.

FLEMMING, ROY. *Punishment Before Trial: An Organizational Perspective on Felony Bail Process.* New York: Longman, 1982.

FREED, DANIEL, AND PATRICIA WALD. *Bail in the United States.* Washington, D.C.: National Conference on Bail and Criminal Justice, 1964.

GOLDFARB, RONALD. *Ransom: A Critique of the American Bail System.* New York: Harper & Row, 1965.

GOLDKAMP, JOHN. *Two Classes of Accused: A Study of Bail and Detention in American Justice.* Cambridge, Mass.: Ballinger, 1979.

SHAUGHNESSY, EDWARD. *Bail and Preventive Detention in New York.* Washington, D.C.: University Press of America, 1982.

TOBORG, MARY. "Bail Bondsmen and Criminal Courts." *Justice System Journal* 8 (1983): 141.

WICE, PAUL. *Freedom for Sale.* Lexington, Mass.: D. C. Heath, Lexington Books, 1974.

CHAPTER **12**

Preparing for Trial

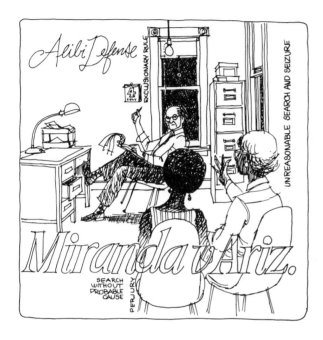

"You have the right to remain silent. You have the right to a lawyer. If you cannot afford a lawyer, one will be provided for you. Anything you say can be used against you." This police ritual can be witnessed almost every night on prime-time television. Invariably the information is delivered in a perfunctory manner, the detective reading from the ***Miranda card*** in a monotone. These *Miranda* warnings are the most controversial part of the Supreme Court's revolution in criminal justice. Responding to criticisms that police procedures were unfair and that the police were not adhering to the procedural requirements of the law, the Supreme Court imposed additional restrictions on police investigative techniques, such as searches, interrogations, and line-ups. In turn the Court's decisions produced extensive national controversy. Based on *Miranda* and similar cases, trial judges sometimes rule that otherwise valid evidence cannot be admitted at trial.

Miranda card

This chapter examines some of the diverse activities that may occur between arraignment and the final disposition (either a guilty plea or a trial). We will begin with the gathering of evidence, termed *discovery*. Next we will discuss how and why some evidence is excluded from trial.

Discovery

discovery

The informal and formal exchange of information between prosecution and defense is referred to as **discovery.** Results of laboratory analysis, medical examinations, fingerprint results, ballistics tests, written statements of witnesses, defendants' confessions, lists of potential witnesses, police reports, and so on are some prominent examples of information that prosecutors often gather and defense attorneys want to know prior to trial. This knowledge can help each party strengthen its own case as well as plan responses to the opposition's litigation strategy. Discovery seeks to assure that the adversary system does not give one side an unfair advantage over another. Does the notion of a fair trial require the prosecutor to disclose such information to the defense? What of the defense attorney? Should there be an obligation for the defense to disclose aspects of its case, or would this erode the basic protection that a defendant is innocent until proven guilty? These questions echo current debate over the extent of pretrial discovery.

The guiding assumption of the adversary system is that truth will emerge after a struggle at trial. In an influential article, though, Supreme Court Justice William Brennan questioned whether criminal trials were a sporting event or a quest for the truth. Historically civil trials were largely sporting events, with decisions heavily dependent upon the technical skills of the lawyers. In an effort to eliminate the worst aspects of such contests, the Federal Rules of Civil Procedure were adopted for U.S. courts in 1938, and most states have since followed the federal example. These rules reflect the philosophy that prior to trial, every party in a civil action is entitled to the disclosure of all relevant information in the possession of any person, unless that information is privileged (Wright). These discovery rules are intended to "make a trial less a game of blind man's bluff and more a fair contest with the basic issues and facts disclosed to the fullest practicable manner" (*U.S.* v. *Procter and Gamble Co.,* 356 U.S. 677, 683, 1958).

Justice Brennan believes that the liberal discovery rules of civil procedure should apply to criminal cases as well; he based his argument on the fact that defense attorneys seldom have the investigative resources the state does. Most defense attorneys have difficulty preparing criminal cases. Typically defendants are unable to aid the attorney either because they are too inarticulate and/or because they are held in jail prior to trial, preventing them from searching for witnesses. Thus defense attorneys may go to trial not knowing what evidence they must defend their clients against. This position would make it mandatory for prosecutors to inform the defense of virtually all evidence in their possession.

Only a handful of states, however, have adopted Justice Brennan's position. In most states mandatory prosecutorial disclosure is much more limited. This counter-theory was expressed by the New Jersey Supreme Court in *State* v. *Tune* (13 N.J. 203, 1953): "Liberal procedures for discovery in preparation for trial are essential to any modern judicial system in which the search for truth in the aid of justice is paramount and in which concealment and surprise are not to be tolerated. However, such liberal fact-finding procedures are not to be used to defeat the ends of justice.'' The court went on to cite examples in which prosecutorial disclosure might result in the defendant's taking undue advantage. For example, the defendant, knowing of the state's case, might procure perjured testimony or might harass and intimidate witnesses who are likely to testify (Saltzburg).

These competing philosophies have resulted in considerable variation among jurisdictions over the type of information that is discoverable. Some jurisdictions allow only limited discovery. The trial court has the discretion to order the prosecutor to disclose the defendant's confession and/or other physical documents, but that is all. Other jurisdictions take a middle ground. Discovery of confessions and physical evidence is a matter of right, but discovery of the other items (witnesses' statements, for example) is more difficult. Finally, a few states have adopted Justice Brennan's position of liberal discovery. There is a presumption strongly in favor of prosecutorial disclosure with only certain narrow exceptions (Kamisar, et al.).

Prosecutorial Disclosure

A few jurisdictions have an office policy prohibiting assistant prosecutors from disclosing any information not required by law. More typically, however, assistant DAs voluntarily disclose to defense attorneys certain aspects of the state's case. Such informal discovery operates within the norms of cooperation of courtroom work groups. Defense attorneys who maintain good relationships with prosecutors and are viewed as trustworthy (that is, they will not use information for nefarious purposes) receive selected information about the case. Conversely defense attorneys who maintain hostile relationships with the prosecutor and/or represent clients who are viewed as troublemakers (the two frequently go together) find the prosecutors holding the cards as tightly to the vest as the law allows.

informal prosecutorial disclosure

Informal prosecutorial disclosure does not stem from a basic sympathy for the defendant. Rather it flows from a long-held courthouse theory that an advance glimpse at the prosecutor's case often encourages a guilty plea.

According to prosecutors, defendants often tell their lawyers only part of what happened. Therefore the defense attorney who learns what evidence the prosecutor possesses can use it to show the defendant that contesting the matter may be hopeless. The following case involving a liquor store burglary is a good illustration. The client told his attorney that the police had stopped him several blocks from the alleged break-in and that he had nothing to do with it. The prosecutor relayed a different version. According to the police reports, the squad car was on routine patrol checking stores. When the squad car pulled into the parking lot, its headlights illuminated someone inside the store. The officers went to the back of the store and observed a suspect leaving the store and entering a car. They chased the car, stopped it several blocks away, discovered the car "loaded with goodies," and arrested the defendant. After such disclosures, the prosecutors contend that the lawyer goes back to his client and says, "You lied to me, you bastard. Tell me the truth or I'll pull out of the case" (Neubauer: 200). Prosecutors, however, are not prone to revealing weaknesses in their case—only the strengths.

Mandatory Disclosure

mandatory disclosure

Growing discontent with the discovery system has prompted American courts to expand **mandatory disclosure** by the prosecutor cautiously. In *Brady* v. *Maryland* (373 U.S. 83, 1963) the Supreme Court held that due process of law is violated when prosecutors hide evidence in their possession that might be favorable to the defense. Similarly, in *Jencks* v. *U.S.* (353 U.S. 651, 1957) the Court ruled that prior inconsistent statements of a witness must be made available to the defense. Read together, these decisions stand for the proposition that as officers of the court, prosecutors can no more suppress evidence than they can knowingly use perjured testimony. These decisions, however, were technically limited to trial; the prosecution must disclose such information to the defense after the witness has testified at trial so it can be used for cross-examination. Some courts, however, have broadened the ruling to require disclosure prior to trial.

Defense and Disclosure

As noted earlier, defense attorneys often encounter major stumbling blocks in obtaining information that can be valuable for constructing a defense at trial. In addition to relying on informal prosecutorial disclosure, resourceful defense attorneys may employ a variety of proceedings not directly designed for discovery purposes. Filing a pretrial motion to suppress evidence may disclose facts related to the defense because key government witnesses will testify. And the preliminary hearing, intended to test the sufficiency of the evidence for holding the defendant, affords an opportunity for the defense to hear at least part of the story of some critical witnesses (Uviller).

alibi defense

Defense attorneys understandably press for broader discovery laws. A major issue in broadening discovery involves the extent to which the defense should also be required to disclose relevant materials in their files. A few states, for example, require that the defense file a notice of **alibi defense** (the crime was committed while the defendant was somewhere else), complete with a list of witnesses to be called to support the alibi. Such notice prior to trial allows the prosecutor to investigate the backgrounds of these witnesses and thus be prepared to undermine the defendant's contention that he or she was somewhere else when the crime was committed. Some proposals go even further. Under rule 16 of the Federal Rules of Criminal Procedure, the defense can require the prosecutor to divulge certain types of information only by agreeing to reciprocal discovery by the prosecutor.

Exclusionary Rules

The decade of the 1960s witnessed the first attempt by the Supreme Court to exercise strong policy control over the administration of criminal justice. The nation's highest court began to apply to the state courts some of the more specific requirements of the Bill of Rights. Earlier opinions enunciating vague standards of "due process" were replaced by decisions specifying precise rules. The Bill of Rights was transformed from a collection of general constitutional principles to a code of criminal procedure. General constitutional requirements were transformed to specific policy standards. These sweeping changes in constitutional interpretation have been appropriately called by Fred Graham the ***due process revolution.***

due process
revolution

Unfortunately for the Supreme Court, its attempt to nationalize, rationalize, and constitutionalize the criminal justice system came at a time of rising crime, riots, political violence, and assassinations. To the public there appeared to be a connection between the new trends of "judicial permissiveness" and the breakdown of law and order. The justices were accused of "coddling criminals" and "handcuffing the police." The most controversial decisions dealt with police gathering of evidence. Otherwise valid and trustworthy evidence was excluded from trial. Dollree Mapp's pornography conviction was reversed because the police had illegally searched her house. Ernesto Miranda's rape conviction was overturned because the police had not advised him of his constitutional right to remain silent before he confessed. (During the retrial, however, Miranda was convicted.)

CLOSE-UP

The Realities of Discovery

Whether a court system utilizes open or closed discovery is of crucial importance to the defense attorney. It can greatly affect the lawyer's relationship with his client. In an open system, the lawyer can go straight to the prosecutor's files and obtain an official set of the facts of the case, which usually amount to the essentials of the state's case against the defendant. By learning the facts of the prosecutor's case, the defense attorney need not face the difficult task of trying to force his client to voluntarily disclose this information. Nearly all lawyers interviewed felt that clients' veracity is questionable and in need of thorough verification. This forces the attorney to devote extra hours, frequently wasted, verifying a client's version of the facts, which also puts a strain on their relationship—especially when the attorney is forced to confront the defendant with his prevarications.

A lack of adequate discovery may also impede an early or at least an intelligent plea negotiation, which may eventually result in a jury trial and severe sentence or a premature settlement of the case without an aggressive defense. In the cities which tended toward closed discovery, there was often a failure to plea bargain, and a large number went to trial, frequently without a jury. Philadelphia is probably the best example of a city whose district attorney has taken a hard stance toward giving information to the defense attorney, and where, as a result, an extremely large percentage of cases go to trial—albeit nonjury trials, which are frequently described as "slow pleas." At the other extreme, Los Angeles and Denver with very open discovery policies, probably try only one-third of the percentage of cases tried in Philadelphia. They are also able to initiate their plea bargaining at an earlier time and are therefore blessed with significantly smaller backlog than is found in most cities with closed discovery.

exclusionary
rule

The ***exclusionary rule*** prohibits the prosecutor from using illegally obtained evidence during a trial. It is the Supreme Court's sole technique for enforcing several vital protections of the Bill of Rights. Its adoption has been justified on three grounds. The first is a normative argument: a court of law should not participate in or condone illegal conduct. The second reflects an empirical assessment: excluding evidence will deter law enforcement officials from illegal behavior. The final justification is based on experience: alternative remedies, like civil suits for damages against police officers for misconduct, are unworkable.

The exclusionary rule is commonly associated with the search and seizure of physical evidence, but in fact there are three distinct exclusionary rules. One applies to the identification of suspects. In *U.S.* v. *Wade* (388 U.S. 218, 1967) the high court held that police line-ups constitute a critical stage of the prosecutorial process, and defendants therefore have the right to be assisted by counsel. In later decisions, identifications of suspects were excluded from trial because the line-up was improperly conducted. The other exclusionary rules relate to confessions and searches.

Confessions

Miranda
"free and
voluntary"
confessions
physical
coercion

In ***Miranda,*** the Court added to earlier decisions on confessions. The traditional rule was that only confessions that were ***"free and voluntary"*** would be admitted at trial. Confessions obtained by ***physical coercion*** (beatings or torture, for example) were not allowed into evidence because they were not trustworthy; someone in fear of a beating is likely to say what his or her antagonists want to hear. In the 1930s the Court rejected confessions based on physical coercion, and subsequently such practices largely ceased. The Court then was confronted with the slightly different issue of confessions obtained as a result of lengthy interrogations, psychological ploys,

---

QUOTATION

*T*he exclusionary rule rests on the absurd proposition that a law enforcement error, no matter how technical, can be used to justify throwing an entire case out of court, no matter how guilty the defendant or how heinous the crime.

The plain consequence of treating the wrongs equally is a grievous miscarriage of justice: the criminal goes free; the officer receives no effective reprimand; and the only ones who really suffer are the people of the community.

President Ronald Reagan, speech in New Orleans
quoted in the *New York Times,* September 29, 1981.

psychological
coercion

and the like. The Court reasoned that confessions based on **psycho-logical coercion** should be rejected just as if they were based on physical coercion because such statements were not likely to be free and voluntary. But it is not easy to define what constitutes psychological coercion, and in over twenty cases the Court sought to spell out what factors the trial court should use in making this determination. The Court's standards, however, were far from precise.

Miranda
warnings

In an attempt at greater precision, the Court adopted specific procedures for police interrogations. In what are widely known as **Miranda warnings,** the police are required to tell a suspect:

- You have a right to remain silent.
- Anything you say may be used against you.
- You have the right to have a lawyer present.
- You have the right to court-appointed counsel if you are indigent.

In addition, the Court shifted the burden of proof from the defense, which previously had to prove that a confession was not "free and voluntary," to the police and prosecutor, who now must prove that they have advised the defendant of his or her constitutional rights (*Miranda* v. *Arizona,* 384 U.S. 436, 1966). Figure 12-1 provides an example of the form police departments use to comply with the decision.

The composition of the Supreme Court changed significantly with the four Nixon appointments, and so did a number of decisions interpreting the scope of the *Miranda* warnings. For example, in *Harris* v. *New York* (401 U.S. 222, 1971) the Court held that a prosecutor may use a confession obtained without constitutional warnings to prove that a defendant who testifies is lying. Similarly, in *New York* v. *Quarles* (104 S. Ct. 2626, 1984) then Justice (now Chief Justice) Rehnquist found that overriding considerations of public safety justified the police officer's failure to provide *Miranda* warnings before asking questions about the location of a weapon apparently abandoned just before arrest. Thus, the more conservative Burger court somewhat limited the *Miranda* requirements by carving out exceptions.

Searches

In *Mapp,* the U.S. Supreme Court ruled that the Fourth Amendment imposes the exclusionary rule on state court proceedings. The Fourth Amendment provides: "The right of the people to be secure in their persons, houses, papers and effects against unreasonable search and seizure, shall not be violated."

unreasonable
search and
seizure
search with-
out probable
cause

But what constitutes an **unreasonable search and seizure**?

Historically, the gathering of physical evidence was governed by the common law rule that "if the constable blunders, the crook should not go free." This meant that if the police conducted an illegal search (**search without probable cause**), the evidence obtained still could be used. Evidence was admitted in court if it was reliable, trustworthy, and relevant. How the police obtained the evidence was considered a separate issue. Thus there were no effective controls on search and seizure; law enforcement officials who searched illegally faced no sanctions.

Metropolitan Police Department Warning as to Your Rights

You are under arrest. Before we ask you any questions, you must understand what your rights are.

You have the right to remain silent. You are not required to say anything to us at any time or to answer any questions. Anything you say can be used against you in court.

You have the right to talk to a lawyer for advice before we question you and to have him with you during questioning.

If you cannot afford a lawyer and want one, a lawyer will be provided for you.

If you want to answer questions now without a lawyer present you will still have the right to stop answering at any time. You also have the right to stop answering at any time until you talk to a lawyer.

Waiver

1. Have you read or had read to you the warning as to your rights?

   _____

2. Do you understand these rights? _____

3. Do you wish to answer any questions? _____

4. Are you willing to answer questions without having an attorney present? _____

5. Signature of defendant on line below.

   _____

6. Time _____ Date _____

7. Signature of officer _____

8. Signature of witness _____

Figure 12-1 This is a typical form required for all interrogations. Similar forms are used throughout the United States. SOURCE: U.S. Department of Justice, Law Enforcement Assistance Administration, *The D.C. Public Defender Service, Vol. II: Training Materials* (Washington, D.C.: Government Printing Office, 1975), p. 58.

Early in the twentieth century the Supreme Court modified the common law tradition by adopting the exclusionary rule, holding that the Fourth Amendment barred the use of evidence secured through an illegal search and seizure (*Weeks* v. *U.S.*, 232 U.S. 383, 1914). But this ruling was applied very narrowly. Only federal law enforcement officials were covered; state law enforcement officials were exempt. After World War II, the Court extended the privacy component of *Weeks* to the states. But the divided Court refused to impose the exclusionary rule (*Wolf* v. *Colorado,* 338 U.S. 25, 1949). Although some states—for instance, California—did adopt it, many took no effective action to curb illegal searches. Twelve years later *Wolf* was overturned by a bare 5 to 4 vote. In a bellwether decision, the exclusionary rule was extended to the states (*Mapp* v. *Ohio,* 367 U.S. 643, 1961). Evidence obtained during an illegal search and seizure would no longer be admitted.

Almost three decades later, the exclusionary rule requirements remain highly controversial. The nature of the debate has changed, however. Initially, critics called for its abolition (Oaks; Wilkey); now, they just suggest modifications. This shift in thinking is reflected in the Reagan administration's Attorney General Task Force on Violent Crime. Although composed largely of long-standing critics of the exclusionary rule, the final report called only for its modification, not its abolition. The American Law Institute has proposed a "substantial violation" test. Chief Justice Burger has urged an "egregious violation standard" (*Brewer* v. *Williams,* 430 U.S. 422, 1977). More recently, some have proposed an exception for "good faith" or "reasonable mistakes" by the police. To the critics, modifications along these lines would reduce the number of arrests lost because of illegal searches. The sanction would be more proportional to the seriousness of the violation of the Fourth Amendment (Jensen and Hart). A few state and federal courts have adopted one variant or another of the good faith exception to the exclusionary rule (Burkoff). The Supreme Court, however, has recognized an "honest mistake" or good faith exception to the exclusionary rule only in extremely narrow and limited circumstances (*U.S.* v. *Leon,* 468 U.S. 897, 1984; *Illinois* v. *Krull,* 55 LW 4291, 1987).

Critics and supporters of the exclusionary rule agree on one central point: the grounds for a lawful search are complex and highly technical. For example, if an officer seizes illegal contraband, like cocaine, pursuant to a search warrant, the evidence may later be suppressed if the judge finds that the warrant was improperly drafted. Moreover, appellate courts continuously rule on what constitutes an unreasonable search and seizure. Broadly speaking, searches fall into two categories: searches based on a warrant and warrantless searches.

Search Warrants

*search
warrant*

A ***search warrant*** is a written document signed by a judge or magistrate authorizing a law enforcement officer to conduct a search. The Fourth Amendment specifies that "no Warrants shall issue, but upon probable cause, supported by Oath or affirmation, and particularly describing the place to be searched and the persons or things to be seized." A recent study by the National Center for State Courts provides considerable insight into how search warrants are obtained in seven cities (Van Duizend, Sutton, and Carter).

Once a police officer decides that a search warrant is necessary, the officer usually goes back to the station house to prepare the application, affidavit, and warrant. Three alternative procedures are used. In a few jurisdictions search warrant applications are prepared by a deputy prosecutor on the basis of information provided by the officer. In other localities the prosecutor systematically reviews all search warrant applications before they are presented to the magistrate. Finally, in rural areas a significant number of warrants are obtained by telephone.

Once preliminary approval has been obtained from the prosecutor or the officer's supervisor, the applicant goes to the courthouse, or if court is not in session, to the home of a judge. The review by the magistrate or judge seldom takes long. It usually consists of a hushed conversation at the bench or a presentation in chambers after the judge has called a brief recess. Outright rejection is rare. "Most of the police officer interviewees could not remember having a search warrant application turned down." Of eighty-four warrant proceedings observed, only seven resulted in denial of the application (8 percent).

The next step is the execution of the warrant. The officer serves the warrant, conducts the search, and seizes evidence. Officers mainly search private residences and impounded vehicles for drugs or stolen goods. Statutory law generally requires that the officer file a "return" in court indicating what items were seized, if any.

The authors concluded "It is a sizable overstatement . . . to say that the warrant review process routinely operates as it was intended. For example, it was clear in many cases that the review process was largely perfunctory, and apparent that some judges regarded themselves more as allies of law enforcement than as independent reviewers of evidence" (Van Duizend, Sutton, and Carter).

Warrantless Searches

Obtaining a search warrant is still a relatively rare phenomenon although more frequent than in pre-*Mapp* days. For a host of reasons, police officers and even some judges view the process of securing a search warrant as burdensome and time-consuming. It is not surprising, therefore that many law enforcement officers regard the search warrant as the option of last resort. In their eyes, there are many easier ways to get the evidence or otherwise make a case against the accused.

warrantless search *consent search* The vast majority of searches are conducted without warrant. One common form of *warrantless search* is a *consent search.* The person must freely and voluntarily consent to be searched; but listening to law enforcement officers leads to the conclusion that consent is the easiest thing in the world to obtain. As one Mountain City detective explained, you just make an offer that cannot be refused.

> [You] tell the guy, "Let me come in and take a look at your house." And he says, "No, I don't want to." And then you tell him, "Then I'm going to leave Sam here, and he's going to live with you until we come back [with a search warrant]. Now we can do it either way." And very rarely do the people say, "Go get your search warrant then." (Van Duizend, Sutton, and Carter)

incident to a lawful arrest *plain view* The police may also lawfully search without a warrant if the search is *incident to a lawful arrest* or if the evidence is in *plain view.* The precise meaning of probable cause remains elusive, however. The grounds for a warrantless search vary depending on what is being searched; it is easier to search a car than a person's house.

The Exclusionary Rule and the Courtroom Work Group

The police must often make immediate decisions about searching or interrogating a suspect. They don't have time to consult a lawyer about the complex and constantly evolving law governing search and seizure or confessions. Yet these on-the-spot decisions made on the street may later be challenged in court as violations of suspects' constitutional rights. Thus even though the exclusionary rule is directed at the police, its actual enforcement occurs in the courts, particularly the trial courts.

Pretrial Motions

pretrial motions

A defense attorney who believes that his or her client was subjected to an illegal search, provided a confession because of improper police activity, or was identified in a defective police line-up can file a motion to suppress the evidence. Most states require that objections be made prior to trial. But several states continue to treat suppression of evidence as subject to the "usual principle that the admissibility of evidence is determined when it is tendered [presented] and not in advance of trial" (Kamisar et al.: 729). There are also important variations in when such *pretrial motions* must be filed. In some jurisdictions, they may be filed at any time prior to trial, which means that the defense attorneys can wait until the day of trial to raise an objection with the result that the trial is usually delayed. Other jurisdictions specify that the trial judge can require that pretrial motions be filed in advance of trial to prevent the defense from dragging out the proceedings.

A hearing is held on the motion, and the defense attorney has the burden of proving that the search was illegal or that the confession was coerced. The

CONTROVERSY

Unconstitutional Conduct

A court which admits [illegally seized evidence] . . . manifests a willingness to tolerate the unconstitutional conduct which produced it. How can the police and the citizenry be expected to "believe that the government truly meant to forbid the conduct in the first place."

A court which admits the evidence in a case involving a "run of the mill" Fourth Amendment violation demonstrates an insufficient commitment to the guarantee against unreasonable search and seizure. It demonstrates "the contrast between morality professed by society and immorality practiced on its behalf." It signifies the government officials need not always "be subjected to the same rules of conduct that are commands to the citizens."

Yale Kamisar, "Is the Exclusionary Rule an 'Illogical' or 'Unnatural' Interpretation of the Fourth Amendment?" *Judicature* 78 (1978): 83–84.

only exception involves an allegation that the *Miranda* warnings were not given, in which case the state has the burden of proof. The judge's ruling in the pretrial hearing is binding on the later trial.

Pretrial hearings on a motion to suppress evidence are best characterized as "swearing matches." As one defense attorney phrased it, "The real question in Supreme Court cases is what's going on at the police station" (Neubauer: 167). Seldom is there unbiased, independent evidence of what happened. The only witnesses are the participants—police and defendant—and not surprisingly they give different versions of what happened. As James Vorenberg, who was executive director of the President's Commission on Law Enforcement and Administration, notes, *Miranda* "just moves the battleground from the voluntariness of the confession back to the voluntariness of the waiver . . . the police have done pretty well with these swearing contests over the years" (quoted in Cipes: 55).

In cases in which the defense questions the legality of the search or a confession, the dominant issue involves the facts of the case. The dispute over the facts structures and apportions the roles that the police, defense attorneys, judges, and prosecutors play. Defense attorneys are forced into a catalytic role since they must search out the issues. Judges, by virtue of their power as fact finders at hearings, become the supreme umpires that legal theory indicated they should be. Prosecutors are forced into a passive role. Although pretrial motions place the prosecutor in a defensive posture, they are not at a major disadvantage because the police typically are able to provide information indicating compliance.

Defense Attorney as Prime Mover

Defense attorneys, charged with protecting the constitutional rights of the defendant, are the prime movers in suppression matters. Unless they object, it is assumed that law enforcement officials behaved properly.

For the defense a number of benefits flow from filing pretrial motions to suppress. If the motion is granted, the case will be won because the prosecutor will dismiss the case for lack of evidence. Even if the motion is denied, the defense may be able to discover information that may later prove valuable at trial. Moreover, filing a pretrial motion keeps options open. The defense may later decide to plea bargain the case, for example.

Despite the advantages, defense attorneys face major barriers in raising objections. According to many defense attorneys, the police follow proper procedures most of the time. The task of the lawyer is to separate the out-of-the-ordinary situation from the more numerous ones in which the police have not violated Supreme Court rulings. It is not an easy task. As one lawyer commented: "Illegal searches are hard to get at. . . . The defendant doesn't know if the police had probable cause. Sometimes the police get an anonymous phone call that a burglary is in progress. . . . Or the police get a tip that guns are in a car. Well, the prosecutor doesn't tell you that. You have to root around to find out if probable cause existed. You have to ask, 'How did the police get to it in the first place?' A search without probable cause is hard to find out about" (Neubauer: 173).

Possible violations of *Mapp* or *Miranda* do not come into the lawyer's office prepackaged, just awaiting a court hearing. On the contrary the lawyer must frame the issue and determine whether enough facts exist to support her contention. Often the attorney is unaided by her client. As the lawyer just quoted went on to say, "For the defendant the case starts when he's arrested. Search and seizure and probable cause, however, start before that."

Not only is it difficult for a defense attorney to develop evidence to support a motion to suppress, it also requires a thorough knowledge of changing appellate court decisions on these matters. As with most other areas in a complex society, only a specialist possesses the necessary knowledge and skill to effectively handle a given problem. The impact of the Supreme Court decisions is tied to the existence of lawyers who keep up on the changes in the law. A study of four Wisconsin cities found that lawyers varied in their knowledge and use of *Miranda* (Milner). In some cities, such as Green Bay, lawyers had only limited knowledge of the Court's decision. In several communities, however, there was at least one lawyer who was particularly knowledgeable about the decision, and it was only in those towns that challenges were raised in court (Milner: 111–113).

Defense attorneys' activities in filing pretrial motions are also influenced by the informal norms of the courtroom work group. Pretrial motions require extra work not only for the defense attorney but for the judge and prosecutor as well. Moreover, they often contribute to delay. Defense attorneys who file too many frivolous motions or use them to harass the judge and/or prosecutor can be sanctioned in a variety of ways. One prosecutor told me about a defense attorney who had filed numerous motions in a case, apparently just to make the DA work harder; after winning the motion unexpectedly he gloated over the victory. The DA replied simply that he may have won the battle but not the war. In a subsequent case the defense attorney's client received a harsher than normal sentence; the defense attorney is now much more selective in filing pretrial motions. In a similar manner, judges can make uncooperative defense attorneys wait for their cases to be called or refuse to appoint them for indigent defendants.

The courtroom work group has another side, however. For cooperative defense attorneys, it can provide informal avenues of protest. A defense attorney I interviewed believed that one police officer consistently violated procedural rules. But rather than challenge him through formal means, the attorney chose a different route.

> Very few officers use improper means to get a statement. I know because I hear about it when it does occur. But one particular officer I have heard complaints about from all types of defendants—all races, creeds, crimes, situations, etc. In all of these cases invalid promises are being made to defendants. Invalid promises to get him probation, to keep the case out of the paper, or that no charges will be filed. Of course the officer later denies making any promises. By way of contrast, I have never heard a complaint about some officers.
>
> I have recently informed the court and the state's attorney about this particular officer. If he is not stopped, then I will make a vendetta out of this. I

will take case after case until there is enough evidence that they will have to believe that this officer is not telling the truth.

We had the same situation with the sheriff's department. I went to the boss and laid it on the line and it was stopped.

This may sound horrible, but it is the most effective means to stop this sort of thing. Motions to suppress in court don't get anywhere so it is better to try and get to the source. (Neubauer: 178)

There was every indication that his informal approach proved effective.

The Defensive Posture of the Prosecutor

A pretrial motion to suppress evidence represents only liabilities for prosecutors. At a minimum, they must do extra work. At a maximum, they may lose the case entirely. Even if they win the suppression motion, they may have to expend extra effort defending that decision on appeal, where they may again lose.

Despite these drawbacks, however, prosecutors maintain the upper hand. For once they need only defend, because in reality the defense attorney bears the burden of proof. Since the police control the information involved, prosecutors are generally in a favorable position to argue against excluding evidence. For example, in most instances the police are able to obtain the defendant's signature on the *Miranda* warning form, which indicates compliance with *Miranda*. Similarly, in a search and seizure case the officers know enough law to know how to testify in order to avoid suppression of evidence. Finally, if the DA finds a case with potential problems, it can be dropped.

Trial Judges as Decision Makers

The decision to suppress evidence rests with the trial judge. After hearing the witness and viewing the physical evidence (if any), the judge makes a legal ruling based on appellate court decisions. Thus trial court judges are key policy makers in applying and implementing Supreme Court decisions concerning confessions and search and seizure.

A pretrial motion is essentially a clash over the facts. Returning to the example of the pretrial motion concerning the armed robbery that may have been faked, recall that the judge accepted the police version of the facts and upheld the confession. Such findings are seldom reviewed by appellate courts. On appeal, upper courts examine whether the law was correctly applied by the trial judge. They will rarely scrutinize the facts to which the law was applied. Such deference toward trial judges is based on their proximity to the event. Only trial judges have the opportunity to observe directly how witnesses testify—their responsiveness to questions, their attempts at concealment. Such nuances are not reflected in the trial court transcript. A prosecutor pointed to an additional reason why appellate courts do not scrutinize the trial judge's finding of fact.

If a defense attorney appeals on an unsuccessful pretrial motion, the appellate court would have to find that the trial judge abused his discretion. When an appeals court reverses in one of these cases they are saying that another judge abused his discretion. They are understandably reluctant to do so. Normally appellate courts accept the trial judge finding of fact because he is closer to the action. (Neubauer: 175)

The trial court judge possesses virtually unfettered discretion in making findings of fact. This discretionary power can be used to buttress the judge's opinion on how a matter should be decided. As one attorney put it, "A judge who knows what he is doing can keep making findings of fact so that no appellate court can ever rule he didn't apply the law properly" (Neubauer: 175). Thus a judge out of sympathy with Supreme Court decisions, by making findings of facts, can distinguish the given case from the decision that in theory should govern.

How judges view the truthfulness of police officers' testimony is an important consideration. A study of eight newly appointed judges to the city of Detroit's Recorders Court highlights variations in how judges assess the truthfulness of police testimony (Luskin: 35–36). The author analyzed charges of carrying a concealed weapon (CCW) on one's person without a permit to do so and carrying a pistol in a motor vehicle without a permit. CCWs are police-initiated and usually occur in the course of writing a ticket for a traffic violation when the police officer sees the weapon "on view." Since the police officers cannot search a car or person in the course of issuing a ticket, they must have seen the weapon or a portion of it without a search. Whether this is what happened—the defense often claims it is not—the arresting officer

CLOSE-UP

Confession in Nichole Killing Stands, Judge Rules

A state judge refused Thursday to throw out the confession of a LaPlace man charged with the rape and slaying of an 8-year-old Terrytown girl last summer. District Judge G. Walton Caire ruled that John Francis Wille, 22, gave the confession freely and without coercion. At a pretrial hearing Thursday in Edgard, Caire also refused to throw out Wille's indictments and denied a defense motion to reject his identification in a photographic line-up.

Wille is scheduled to stand trial on Oct. 6 on first-degree murder and aggravated rape charges in the slaying of Nichole Lopatta, who was kidnapped from in front of her home June 2, 1985. Her body was found four days later off a desolate stretch of highway north of LaPlace. He also is charged with second-degree murder in the mutilation death of Billy A. Phillips, 25, of Tickfaw, La. whose body was found near Nichole's the same day.

Defense attorneys George Oubre and Robert Becnel had asked that Wille's confession be suppressed because he was pressured into confessing. Wille's attorneys tried to establish that the only reason Wille confessed was because

threats were made against his sister and his girlfriend.

But Caire said testimony during a July 7 hearing showed that Wille's rights were not violated. Wille was read his rights and was aware of what he was doing when he confessed, and authorities did not threaten or use force against him, Caire said. Caire also said that officers did not discriminate against Wille when they used a photographic line-up to identify him as the man who entered a Popeye's restaurant in Kenner shortly after the slayings.

Barri Marsh, "Confession in Nichole Killing Stands, Judge Rules," *Times-Picayune/States-Item,* August 1, 1986. Reprinted by permission from the Times-Picayune Publishing Corp.

will testify that the gun "slid out from under the seat when the car stopped" or "the gun butt was protruding from under some papers on the car seat."

Four judges believed that the police officers frequently lied or at least colored their stories. For a period, one judge kept a list of police officers he thought often gave less than truthful testimony. If these judges found the police officer's story was "too incredible" about the weapons search, they would dismiss the case without a suppression motion. What is particularly interesting is that this group of four judges included one strong advocate of gun control, two former prosecutors, and one former defense attorney. Hence their attitudes reflect their experience on the bench more than their personal ideas formed prior to donning the black robe. Three other judges, however, held different views. One rated the police as lying only infrequently about the circumstances of arrests and searches. (The views of the eighth judge could not be determined.)

Costs of the Exclusionary Rule

A key question in the ongoing debate over the exclusionary rule centers on its costs. In a widely cited dissent, then Chief Justice Burger summed up the critics' position as follows: "Some clear demonstration of the benefits and effectiveness of the exclusionary rule is required to justify it in view of the high price it exacts from society—the release of countless guilty criminals" (*Bivens* v. *Six Unknown Federal Narcotics Agents,* 403 U.S. 388, 1971).

Assessing how many convictions are lost because of the exclusionary rule is difficult for reasons discussed in Chapter 10; case attrition occurs at numerous stages of the proceedings and for various reasons. Several recent studies shed considerable light on the topic.

Exclusionary rules can lead to the freeing of apparently guilty defendants during prosecutorial screening. Prosecutors may refuse to file charges because of a search and seizure problem, a tainted confession, or a defective police line-up; but this occurs very infrequently. The Government Accounting Office examined case rejections by U.S. attorneys and found that only 0.4 percent of the time was search and seizure cited as the primary reason. Similarly, a study of seven communities reports that an average of 2.0 percent of the rejections were for *Mapp* or *Miranda* reasons (Boland et al.). The most controversial study analyzed 86,033 felony cases rejected for prosecution in California. The National Institute of Justice report found 4,130 (4.8 percent) rejected for search and seizure reasons. The NIJ conclusion that these figures indicate a "major impact of the exclusionary rule" has been challenged as misleading and exaggerated (Davies). Indeed, compared to lack of evidence and witness problems, *Mapp* and *Miranda* are minor sources of case attrition.

After charges are filed, case attrition can also occur when judges grant pretrial motions to suppress. A nine-county study concluded, however, that relatively few pretrial motions to suppress evidence are filed (Nardulli). In less than 8 percent of the cases did the defense file one or more motions to exclude evidence. Once filed, pretrial motions are rarely successful. Challenges to identifications or confessions were granted only 5 percent of the time. Challenges to gathering physical evidence were somewhat more likely to be granted by the judge but the rate was still a low 17 percent. Interestingly, not all defendants who successfully suppressed evidence escaped conviction; some were convicted anyway.

Piecing together the various stages of the criminal court process leads to the conclusion that the exclusionary rule has a truly marginal effect on the criminal court system (Nardulli). Examining case attrition data from California, Davies calculated that only 0.8 percent (eight out of a thousand) arrests were rejected because of *Mapp* and *Miranda.* As for cases filed, Nardulli calculated for his nine communities that 0.57 percent (6 out of a thousand) convictions were lost due to exclusionary rules. Moreover, of the lost convictions only 20 percent were for serious crimes. Weapons and drug cases are the most likely to involve questions of police conduct.

Conclusion

This chapter has examined several important aspects of what occurs while cases are being prepared for trial. One is discovery, the formal or informal exchange of information. What information is subject to discovery varies greatly. Typically, though, defense attorneys who are cooperative members of the courtroom work group receive more information than others. Another important aspect of preparing for trial centers on suppression of evidence. Confessions and physical evidence that have been illegally obtained cannot be used at trial. If the defense believes this has occurred, it files a pretrial motion to suppress the evidence. Prosecutors are usually in a favorable position to show that the evidence was obtained legally.

When an accused pleads not guilty at arraignment, a date for trial is set and bail continued. Typically by this time the defendant is represented by counsel. The plea entered at arraignment may be made with the intention of going to trial or to gain a tactical advantage. The defendant may plan to plead guilty later but may be delaying in order to await assignment of the case to a different judge. The not-guilty plea also allows time for the defense to learn more about the case.

Preparation for trial may be very brief: the day of trial the defense and prosecution may quickly scan their individual files. Or it may be extensive: in a big murder trial, for example, both sides devote considerable time to interviewing witnesses, examining physical evidence, and arguing legal motions.

For Discussion

1. What type of discovery law does your state have? Do you think that the defense should have the right to discover the entire case of the state? Do you think there should be a reciprocal requirement for the defense?
2. Discuss with a defense attorney and prosecutor how they prepare for trial. Also ask about their views of the state's discovery law and informal discovery practices.

3. By examining court files and talking to court officials, try to determine how many motions to suppress are filed and how many are granted.

4. Observe a pretrial hearing to suppress evidence. To what extent does the judge's decision depend on what version of the facts he or she accepts?

5. Examine the local newspapers to see how often the press reports that evidence is suppressed. What types of reactions do these stories report—favorable or unfavorable?

References

AMERICAN LAW INSTITUTE. *A Model Code of Pre-Arraignment Procedure: Proposed Official Draft Complete Text and Commentary.* Philadelphia: American Law Institute, 1975.

ATTORNEY GENERAL'S TASK FORCE ON VIOLENT CRIME. *Final Report.* Washington, D.C.: U.S. Department of Justice, 1981.

BOLAND, BARBARA, ELIZABETH BRADY, HERBERT TYSON, AND JOHN BASSLER. *The Prosecution of Felony Arrests.* Washington, D.C.: Institute for Law and Social Research, 1982.

BRENNAN, JUSTICE WILLIAM. "The Criminal Prosecution: Sporting Event or Quest for Truth?" *Washington University Law Quarterly* (1963): 279–294.

BROSI, KATHLEEN. *A Cross-City Comparison of Felony Case Processing.* Washington, D.C.: Institute for Law and Social Research, 1979.

BURKOFF, JOHN. "Exclusionary Rules." In *Encyclopedia of Crime and Justice,* ed. Sanford Kadish. New York: Free Press, 1983.

CIPES, ROBERT. "Crime, Confessions and the Court." *Atlantic Monthly,* (September 1966), 55.

COMPTROLLER GENERAL OF THE UNITED STATES. *Impact of the Exclusionary Rule on Federal Criminal Prosecutions.* Washington, D.C.: General Accounting Office, 1979.

DAVIES, THOMAS. "A Hard Look at What We Know (and Still Need to Learn) About the 'Costs' of the Exclusionary Rule: The NIJ Study and Other Studies of 'Lost Arrests.'" *American Bar Foundation Research Journal* 1983 (1983): 611.

GRAHAM, FRED. *The Self-Inflicted Wound.* New York: Macmillan, 1970.

JENSEN, D. LOWELL, AND ROSEMARY HART. "The Good Faith Restatement of the Exclusionary Rule." *Journal of Criminal Law and Criminology* 73 (1982): 916.

KAMISAR, YALE, WAYNE LAFAVE, AND JEROLD ISRAEL. *Modern Criminal Procedure,* 4th ed. St. Paul, Minn.: West Publishing, 1974.

LUSKIN, MARY LEE. "Determinants of Change in Judges' Decisions to Bind Over Defendants for Trial." Paper presented at meeting of American Political Science Association, September 2–5, 1976.

MATHER, LYNN. "The Outsider in the Courtroom: An Alternative Role for the Defense." In *The Potential for Reform of Criminal Justice,* ed. Herbert Jacob. Beverly Hills, Calif.: Sage Publications, 1974.

MILNER, NEAL. *The Court and Local Law Enforcement.* Beverly Hills, Calif.: Sage Publications, 1971.

NARDULLI, PETER. "The Societal Cost of the Exclusionary Rule: An Empirical Assessment." *American Bar Foundation Research Journal* 1983 (1983): 585.

NEUBAUER, DAVID. *Criminal Justice in Middle America.* Morristown, N.J.: General Learning Press, 1974.

OAKS, DALLIN. "Studying the Exclusionary Rule in Search and Seizure." *University of Chicago Law Review* 37 (1970): 665–753.

SALTZBURG, STEPHEN. "Discovery." In *Encyclopedia of Crime and Justice,* ed. Sanford Kadish. New York: Free Press, 1983.

UVILLER, H. RICHARD. *The Process of Criminal Justice: Adjudication.* St. Paul, Minn.: West Publishing, 1975.

VAN DUIZEND, RICHARD, L. PAUL SUTTON, AND CHARLOTTE CARTER. *The Search Warrant Process.* Williamsburg, Va.: The National Center for State Courts, 1984.

VERA INSTITUTE OF JUSTICE. *Felony Arrests: Their Prosecution and Disposition in New York City's Courts.* New York: Longman, 1981.

WASBY, STEPHEN. *The Impact of the United States Supreme Court: Some Perspectives.* Homewood, Ill.: Dorsey Press, 1970.

WILKEY, MALCOLM. "The Exclusionary Rule: Why Suppress Valid Evidence?" *Judicature* 62 (1978): 214–232.

WRIGHT, CHARLES. *Handbook of the Law of Federal Courts,* 2d ed. St. Paul, Minn.: West Publishing, 1970.

For Further Reading

BAKER, LIVA. *Miranda: Crime, Law and Politics.* New York: Antheneum, 1983.

CANON, BRADLEY. "The Exclusionary Rule: Have Critics Proven That It Doesn't Deter Police?" *Judicature* 62 (1979): 398–403.

KAMISAR, YALE. "Is the Exclusionary Rule an 'Illogical' or 'Unnatural' Interpretation of the Fourth Amendment?" *Judicature* 62 (1978): 66–84.

MILNER, NEAL. *The Court and Local Law Enforcement.* Beverly Hills, Calif.: Sage Publications, 1971.

NISSMAN, D. E., HAGEN, AND P. BROOKS. *Law of Confessions.* Rochester, New York: Lawyers Co-operative Publishing, 1985.

SCHLESINGER, STEVEN. *Exclusionary Injustice: The Problem of Illegally Obtained Evidence.* New York: Marcel Dekker, 1977.

"The Exclusionary Rule: Have Proponents Proven That it is a Deterrent to Police?" *Judicature* 62 (1979): 404–409.

WASBY, STEPHEN. *The Impact of the United States Supreme Court: Some Perspectives.* Homewood, Ill.: Dorsey Press, 1970.

WILKEY, MALCOLM. "The Exclusionary Rule: Why Suppress Valid Evidence?" *Judicature* 62 (1978): 214–232.

CHAPTER 13

Negotiated Justice and the Plea of Guilty

In the United States, criminal justice is popularly equated with trials. Yet, only a handful of defendants are ever tried. Most plead guilty. The vast majority of convictions result not from a guilty verdict following a contested trial but rather from a voluntary plea by the accused.

Plea bargaining is very controversial. To some, it erodes the cornerstones of the adversary system: the presumption of innocence and the right to trial. To others, it allows the guilty to escape with a light penalty. To still others, it is a modern-day necessity if the courts are to dispose of their large caseloads. All agree, however, that it is the most important stage of the criminal court process.

What is plea bargaining? What forms does it take? Why would prosecutors accept a plea of guilty to a lesser charge when there is the possibility of convicting the defendant on a more serious charge? Why would defendants waive their right to be presumed innocent at trial and instead plead guilty to charges as serious as armed robbery or second-degree murder? Are the judge's routine questions of a defendant entering a guilty plea really important? Is plea bargaining a fair and equitable procedure? Why is it that in a system of justice premised on trials, the vast majority of cases are never tried? These are some of the questions this chapter seeks to answer.

The Many Faces of Plea Bargaining

Guilty pleas are the bread and butter of the American criminal courts. They outnumber trials by more than five to one at the federal level and by about ten to one at the state and local level (Bureau of Justice Statistics). The data in Table 13-1 demonstrate the pervasiveness of guilty pleas. Most guilty pleas are the result of plea bargaining. The prosecutor, defense attorney, defendant, and sometimes the judge reach an accommodation on the disposition of the case. We can best define ***plea bargaining*** as the process through which a defendant pleads guilty to a criminal charge with the expectation of receiving some consideration from the state.

plea bargaining

Plea bargaining is hardly new. There is considerable evidence that it became a common practice sometime after the civil war (Alschuler, 1979; Friedman). Some even trace its roots earlier into medieval English history (Sanborn). What is new is the amount of attention plea negotiations have recently received. During the early decades of this century it was only sporadically discussed. Although the crime surveys of the 1920s reported the dominance of plea bargaining (Illinois Association; Moley), most courts persistently denied its existence. It was not until the 1960s that plea bargaining emerged as a controversial national issue.

One indication of this controversy are the words used to describe negotiated settlements in criminal cases. Currently, the two most popular names are ***plea bargaining*** and ***plea negotiation.*** These terms, often used interchangeably, evoke negative images suggesting that the courts are ''bargaining with criminals'' (Sanborn). Other, even more pejorative phrases, like ''copping a plea'' or ''striking a deal,'' are sometimes used. Moreover, there is no agreement among court officials about what is meant by *plea bargaining.* Some prosecutors refuse to admit that they engage in bargaining; they simply call it something else (Miller et al.).

plea negotiation

This debate over names also indicates that plea bargaining is a very general term encompassing a wide range of practices. The data in Table 13-1 show that there are extensive differences among jurisdictions in the ratio of pleas to trials. In some courthouses, trials are rare indeed. In others, trials are more common. Any discussion of negotiated justice, therefore, must start with the recognition that there are important variations both in the types of plea agreements negotiated and the process by which such agreements are reached.

Types of Plea Agreements

explicit bargaining
implicit bargaining

There are important differences in the types of plea agreements that result from negotiations. Some plea agreements are ***explicit***: the defendant pleads guilty with a specific understanding. Others are ***implicit***: the defendant pleads guilty in general anticipation of receiving a lenient sentence. Typically plea agreements take one of three forms.

TABLE 13-1 Number of Pleas per Trial, Caseloads, and Crime Rates (Based on All Felony Arrests) for Selected Jurisdictions

Jurisdiction	Pleas per trial	Pleas and trials	Index crime rate	Population
Geneva, Illinois	37	680	6,400	278,000
Manhattan, New York	24	17,033	13,800	1,428,000
Cobb County, Georgia	22	1,456	8,800	298,000
Littleton, Colorado	19	699	8,400	330,000
Golden, Colorado	18	1,129	5,200	374,000
Rhode Island	15	3,250	9,100	947,000
Colorado Springs, Colorado	12	809	8,200	317,000
St. Louis, Missouri	10	2,533	14,300	453,000
Salt Lake, Utah	9	1,338	11,700	619,000
Lansing, Michigan	8	1,057	6,300	272,000
Tallahassee, Florida	7	684	12,000	202,000
Washington, D.C.	5	4,024	10,000	638,000
New Orleans, Louisiana[a]	4	3,103	9,600	557,000
Portland, Oregon[a]	4	2,986	11,200	563,000
Jurisdiction median	11	1,400	9,400	414,000

[a] Approximately half the trials in New Orleans and Portland are bench trials (heard by a judge only without a jury). When bench trials are excluded, both jurisdictions still have a plea-to-trial ratio below the 14-jurisdiction median.
SOURCE: Bureau of Justice Statistics, "The Prevalence of Guilty Pleas," in *Bureau of Justice Statistics Special Report* (Washington, D.C.: U.S. Department of Justice, 1984).

charge bargaining

Charge bargaining. One inducement a prosecutor can offer in return for a plea of guilty is a reduction of charges (***charge bargaining***). A defendant may be allowed to plead guilty to robbery rather than the original charge of armed robbery, for example. Or a defendant enters a plea to misdemeanor theft rather than the initial accusation of felony theft. The principal effect of a plea to a less serious charge is to reduce the potential sentence. Some offenses carry a very stiff maximum sentence. A plea to a lesser charge therefore greatly reduces the possible prison term the defendant will have to serve. Bargains for reduced charges are most commonly found in jurisdictions where the state's criminal code is rigid and/or where prosecutors routinely overcharge to begin with. Thus some charge reductions reflect the probability that the prosecutor would not be able to prove the original charge in a trial.

count bargaining

Count bargaining. Another common type of plea agreement is called ***count bargaining.*** In return for a defendant's plea of guilty to one (or more) criminal charges, the prosecutor dismisses all other pending charges. For instance, a defendant accused of three burglaries would plead guilty to only one burglary charge, with the two remaining accusations being dismissed. Count bargaining is typically used in situations in which the defendant engages in what is in essence a single criminal act, but the law specifies several separate and often technical criminal violations. For example, in a forgery case the defendant may be charged not only with forgery but also with uttering (circulating) a forged document, as well as obtaining property by false pretenses (Alschuler, 1968).

Like charge reduction agreements, a count bargain reduces the potential sentence but in a very different manner. A defendant charged with many counts theoretically could receive a maximum sentence of something like 135 years, a figure arrived at by multiplying the number of charges by the maximum jail term for each charge and assuming that the judge will sentence the defendant to serve the sentences consecutively (one after another). Such figures are totally unrealistic, because consecutive sentences are very rare. In practice, the defendant will often receive the same penalty no matter how few (or how many) charges are involved.

Sentence bargaining.   The third common form of plea agreement is called

sentence bargaining

plea on the nose

sentence bargaining. A plea of guilty is entered in exchange for a promise of leniency in sentencing. There may be a promise that the defendant will be placed on probation or that the prison term will be no more than a given figure, say five years. Typically, in a sentence bargain the defendant pleads to the original charge (often termed a ***plea on the nose***), although in some

---

Q U O T A T I O N

Discussions of plea bargaining often conjure up images of a Middle Eastern bazaar, in which each transaction appears as a new and distinct encounter, unencumbered by precedent or past association. Every interchange involves higgling and haggling anew, in an effort to obtain the best possible deal. The reality of American lower courts is different. They are more akin to modern supermarkets, in which prices for various commodities have been clearly established and labeled in advance. Arriving at an exchange in this context is not an explicit bargaining process—"You do this for me and I'll do that for you"—designed to reach a mutually acceptable agreement. To the extent that there is any negotiation at all, it usually focuses on the nature of the case, and the establishment of relevant "facts"—facts that flow from various interpretations of what is and is not said in the police report, rap sheet, and the like. . . . The term plea bargaining has come to refer to almost any type of negotiation, even one in which the defense successfully convinced the prosecutor to drop all charges, which is clearly not a *plea* bargain in the conventional sense of the term.

Malcolm Feeley, "Pleading Guilty in Lower Courts," *Law and Society Review* 13 (1979): 462.

areas sentence bargaining operates in conjunction with either count bargaining or charge reduction bargaining.

Invariably, in sentence bargaining the defendant receives less than the maximum penalty. To some this is an indication that defendants get off too easily. Realistically, though, only defendants with long criminal records who have committed particularly heinous crimes will receive the maximum. In practice, *normal* courts impose sentence on the basis of ***normal penalties*** for specific crimes *penalties* involving typical types of defendants. Thus in sentence bargaining the sentence agreed to is the one typically imposed in similar cases.

The Bargaining Process

The process by which a plea agreement is reached varies greatly from court to court and often from judge to judge in a given jurisdiction. Some judges are major participants in the bargaining process. They will, for example, agree ahead of time that if the defendant enters a plea of guilty, a specific sentence will be imposed (sentence bargaining). Other judges refuse to participate in bargaining at all. In their courtrooms, prosecutors dominate the bargaining process.

How negotiations are conducted varies. At times negotiations are rather casual:

> The elevator doors opened into a smoky, crowded corridor at the Hall of Justice. Stepping out, a deputy public defender encounters a deputy district attorney.
>
> "Hey," said the defender hurriedly, "How about Alvarado? We plead and you recommend 45 days."
>
> "No way," replied the D.A.'s man. "Gotta have at least 90."
>
> "Oh," said the defender, moving on down the corridor, "We'll think about 60." (Hager)

Contrast this example with the institutionalization of plea bargaining in Detroit's Recorders Court, where for every four judges there is only one assistant prosecutor authorized to negotiate guilty pleas. After the state has made an offer, the defense attorney must sign a form indicating the nature of the plea bargain offered. To complicate matters still further, a handful of courts (Baltimore, Pittsburgh, and Los Angeles are prime examples) employ a pro-*slow plea* cedure termed a ***slow plea*** (part plea, part trial). A slow plea involves a short (usually fifteen-minute) bench trial in which the defense does not contest the issue of guilt but rather presents favorable evidence about the defendant in hopes that the judge will impose a light sentence (Levin; Mather, 1974; Eisenstein and Jacob).

The Context of Plea Bargaining

These varying practices illustrate that the process of negotiated justice does not operate in isolation from the other stages of the criminal court process. What has gone before—the setting of bail, the return of a grand jury indictment, and the prosecutor's evaluation of the strengths of a case are prime examples—is intimately intertwined with how courts dispose of cases on a plea. The opposite is equally true. Throughout the history of a case, decisions on bail, indictment, or screening have been premised on the knowledge that the vast majority of defendants end up pleading guilty. The place to begin in analyzing the diversity of negotiated justice is with the context of plea bargaining.

The common explanation for plea bargaining is that the courts have too many cases. Plea bargaining is usually portrayed as a regrettable but necessary expedient for disposing of cases. Chapter 5 argued that although this explanation contains some truth, it obscures too many important facets of what the courts do and why they do it. Certainly the press of cases and lack of adequate resources shape the criminal court process, plea bargaining included. Certainly because prosecutors need to move cases, they agree to a more lenient plea than they might prefer.

But the excess caseload hypothesis cannot explain why plea bargaining is as prevalent in courts with heavy caseloads as it is in courts with relatively few cases (Eisenstein and Jacob). Variations in plea bargaining rates among the fourteen cities reported on in Table 13-1 bear this out. Among the high plea jurisdictions (those with a high ratio of pleas to trials) are four suburban counties (Geneva, Illinois; Cobb County, Georgia; Golden and Littleton, Colorado) with generally low crime rates and average or below average caseloads. With the exception of Manhattan, there does not appear to be a strong association between the size of the caseload and the plea bargaining rate. The vast differences in the ratio of pleas to trials across jurisdictions reflect primarily differences in prosecution and police, not crime rates or court resources (Boland and Forst).

A similar conclusion emerges in a study of Miami, Pittsburgh, Detroit, and the Bronx. Members of the courtroom work group were presented with twelve hypothetical cases and asked, "Assuming that prosecution, defense, and the court have adequate resources to deal with their caseloads in a fair and expeditious manner, how do you believe this case should be resolved?" (Church, 1985: 474). The responses indicate that relatively few of the cases would be disposed of by a trial. Furthermore, there was little support for the notion that practitioners consider negotiated guilty pleas a necessary but illegitimate response to inadequate court system resources.

The principal weakness of the excessive caseload hypothesis is that it assumes a purely mechanical process, ignoring the underlying dynamics. It seems to suggest that if there were only more judges, prosecutors, defense attorneys, and courtrooms, there would be many more trials, and the penalties imposed on the guilty would also increase. Such a view ignores the context of plea bargaining. Plea bargaining is a response to some fundamental issues, the first of which centers on the question of guilt.

Presumption of Factual Guilt

It is important to recall from Chapter 10 that the bulk of legally innocent defendants are removed from the criminal court process during the screening process through the preliminary hearing, grand jury, and/or the prosecutor's charging decision. By the time a case reaches the trial stage, the courtroom work group presumes that the defendant is probably guilty. Survival through the prior processing means that prosecutors, defense attorneys, and judges alike perceive that trial defendants are in serious trouble (Eisenstein and Jacob).

dead bang
case
slam dunk

The following case illustrates what some court officials term a ***dead bang case,*** or a ***slam dunk,*** a case with very strong evidence against the defendant and with no credible explanation by the defendant for innocence (Mather, 1974: 198).

> A neighbor saw a young black man entering the rear door of the house. The police were called and arrested the defendant, Ronald Phillips (not his actual name but the case is a real one nonetheless) within a block of the house in possession of a color TV set. According to Phillips the TV came from his ''Aunt's'' house. (Winsberg)

One Illinois state's attorney summarized the strong evidence of guilt in cases like this one: ''The pervasiveness of the facts should indicate to any competent attorney that the element of prosecution is present and a successful prosecution is forthcoming'' (Neubauer: 200).

No two cases are ever the same, of course. Many discussions of plea bargains leave the false impression that the attorneys haggle only over the sentence. This is not true. Courtroom work groups spend a lot of time discussing and analyzing how the crime was committed, the nature of the victims and witnesses, and the background of the defendant. In most cases, however, there is little likelihood that the defendant will be acquitted outright, only that he or she might be convicted of a less serious offense. The question of what charge the facts will support is an important part of plea bargaining.

Costs and Risks of Trial

The possibility of trial greatly influences negotiations. Trials are a costly and time-consuming means for establishing guilt. Consider our earlier example. To try Ronald Phillip's case would probably take two days and require the presence of the judge, bailiff, clerk, defense attorney, prosecutor, and court reporter. During this period, none could devote much time to the numerous other cases requiring disposition. Moreover each would be forced to spend time preparing for this trial. A trial would also require the presence of numerous non-court personnel: police officers, witnesses, victims, the defendant, and twelve jurors. For each of these persons, a trial represents an intrusion into their daily lives.

Based on these considerations, all members of the courtroom work group have a common interest in disposing of cases and avoiding unnecessary trials. Their reasons diverge: judges and prosecutors want high disposition rates in order to prevent case backlogs and to present a public impression that the process is running smoothly. Public defenders prefer quick dispositions because they lack enough people to handle the caseload. Because most clients of private defense attorneys can afford only a modest fee, these attorneys are dependent on high case turnover to earn enough money. All members of the courtroom work group, then, have more cases to try than time (or resources) to try them (Eisenstein and Jacob).

To a large extent, then, a trial is a mutual penalty that all parties seek to avoid through plea bargaining. To be sure, not all trials are avoided. But through plea bargaining scarce trial resources can be applied to the cases that need to be tried.

What to Do with the Guilty

The adversary proceedings of trial are designed to resolve conflict over guilt or innocence. In practice, however, it is not the issue of legal guilt that is disputed but what sentence to impose. Decisions on sentencing do not involve the simple, alternative, "yes or no" issue of guilt presented at trial. Rather they incorporate difficult judgment issues about the type of the crime and the nature of the defendant. Moreover, because of the standards of evidence, the information relevant to sentencing is not easily introduced at trial (Mather). Unlike a trial, plea bargaining does focus on what to do with an offender—particularly how much leniency is appropriate. The case of Ronald Phillips illustrates these factors. Whether the stolen color television came from Phillip's aunt's house is not relevant to the issue of legal guilt. It may, however, be highly important when it comes to sentencing. For if the victim was really his aunt, this might

---

Q U O T A T I O N

Prosecutors and state's attorneys learn that their roles primarily entail the processing of factually guilty defendants. Contrary to their expectations that problems of establishing factual guilt would be central to their job, they find that in most cases the evidence in the file is sufficient to conclude (and prove) that the defendant is factually guilty. . . . Of the cases that remain after the initial screening, the prosecutor believes the majority of defendants to be factually guilty.

Furthermore, he finds that defense attorneys only infrequently contest the prosector's own conclusion that the defendant is guilty. In their initial approach to the prosecutor they may raise the possibility that the defendant is factually innocent, but in most subsequent discussions their advances focus on disposition and not on the problem of factual guilt. Thus, from the prosecutor's own reading of the file (after screening) and from the comments of his "adversary," he learns that he begins with the upper hand; more often than not, the factual guilt of the defendant is not really disputable.

Milton Heumann, *Plea Bargaining* (Chicago: University of Chicago Press, 1978), p. 100.

suggest that the crime was not one of economic motive but stemmed from a family dispute. (In this case, however, it turned out the victim was not truly Phillip's aunt.)

Criminal statutes are broad and encompassing. The courtroom work group is called upon to apply these broad prohibitions to very specific and variable cases. They are concerned with adjusting the penalties to the specifics of the crime and the defendant. In the interest of fairness, they seek to individualize justice. Consider a case with two codefendants of unequal culpability—for example, an armed robbery involving an experienced robber who employed a youthful accomplice as a driver. Technically both are equally guilty, but in the interest of fairness and justice, the prosecutor may legitimately decide to make a concession to the young accomplice but none to the prime mover. How members of the courtroom work group individualize justice is greatly shaped by the criminal code under which they work.

The Criminal Code

The dynamics and goals of plea bargaining reflect the legal definitions of crimes and the penalty structure provided for them. The close relationship between plea bargaining practices and the state's sentencing structure is illustrated by Donald Newman's study of plea bargaining in three states: Wisconsin, Michigan, and Kansas. Newman uses the following common type of burglary to illustrate the point.

> A defendant was arrested by a policeman in the act of stealing electrical appliances from a warehouse at 3:00 A.M. He had gained entry to the building by forcing a rear door with a crowbar. (Newman: 55)

In Wisconsin, the defendant would probably be charged with burglary and plead on the nose to that offense. In Michigan, by contrast, the defendant would likely be charged with breaking and entering in the nighttime and later would plead to the reduced charge of breaking and entering in the daytime. In Kansas, on the other hand, the initial charge would be first-degree burglary with a later plea to the lesser offense of third-degree burglary. These differences in customary ways of dealing with cases are largely the result of differences in sentencing structure in the states. In Wisconsin sentencing laws are very flexible, leaving great discretion to the judge. As a result guilty pleas involve little explicit bargaining. In Michigan and Kansas, legislative statutes have fixed sentencing to allow for little judicial discretion in sentencing. As a result, these states are marked by a widespread use of explicit bargaining, especially charge reduction bargaining (Newman). Often members of the courtroom work group enter into plea agreements because they perceive the penalties to be inappropriately harsh.

Sentencing provisions in many states are very severe because those who draft the laws have in mind the worst offenders: professional, hardened, and violent criminals. But courtroom work groups rarely encounter such stereotyped bad guys. Most defendants are less threatening and less dangerous than the formal law envisions. Where legislative definitions of serious offenses are at odds with the courts' definition of serious and threatening violations, plea bargaining provides the flexibility to make adjustments.

Bargaining and Courtroom Work Groups

Plea bargaining is a contest involving the prosecutor, defendant, defense counsel, and, at times, the judge. Each party has its own objectives. Each attempts to structure the situation to its own advantage by employing tactics to improve its bargaining position. Each views success in reaching its objectives from its own perspective. Within these conflicting objectives accommodations are possible because each side can achieve its objectives only by making concessions on other matters. Plea bargaining is typical of "most bargaining situations which ultimately involve some range of possible outcomes within

CLOSE-UP

The Name of the Game Is Plea Bargaining

The public defender stuck a patent-leather loafer on the lowest rung of the holding cell and wedged an elbow in between the gray steel bars. "Cedric," he said quietly, "Cedric, listen to me, please."

Cedric looked back at him without an emotion crossing the flat, black expanse of his face.

"Cedric, how are we going to explain the coats in the back of the car?" the defender asked. "Somebody's going to want to know how they got there."

The pale sunlight came into the cell in neat squares through the wire mesh windows. On the floor behind Cedric, bundled heaps of men tried to escape into unconsciousness. Every now and then one would mumble in his half-sleep or lash out with a savage elbow to protect his floorspace.

"Uh, look," Cedric said, the barest of smiles on his lips. "We just say somebody threw them there, you know, was running by and threw them in."

Kent Brody, the defender, took his foot off the cross-bar and looked directly at Cedric. They were both young, each almost with a baby face, but more than just jail bars separated them.

"Cedric, there comes a time to face facts," Brody said. "The facts of the case are against you. We both know it. They offered a better deal than I thought. They offered flat time on the armed robbery and that would cover the arson and the probation violation. I assumed they'd give a spread, but they are offering you flat time, Cedric."

Cedric was not impressed. He gripped the bars, but casually, his slim body leaning gently against the steel, he said nothing.

"OK," said Brody, "Four years is a long time, but armed robbery carries a minimum of four to life, Cedric. You don't want it. OK. But if you get convicted, it won't be the minimum."

There was a pause and Cedric spoke softly. "Fight it," he said.

"Sure," Brody said. "Fine.

OK now, so what's our defense? How'd the stuff get in the car, Cedric?"

Cedric Malthia may not know much about the law, but he knows what he likes. And he doesn't like the idea of going to prison for four years in exchange for saying he held up a clothing store at gunpoint. No, for a four-year sentence he was not going to say it.

Now if Brody had gotten him the deal he asked for, it might have been different. If that gun had been made to magically disappear and he had been offered two on a simple robbery, now that he might go along with. He might save the state the trouble of proving him guilty for that. He might take the plea bargain if they would agree to two. . . .

But Cedric was not cooperating. Not yet, anyway. For while the system may be in a hurry, Cedric had nothing but time.

Excerpted from a *Chicago Sun-Times* article by Roger Simon. © With permission of the Chicago Sun-Times, Inc., 1987.

which each party would rather make a concession than fail to reach agreement at all'' (Schelling: 70). Bargaining is also possible because each of the legal actors understands the context of plea bargaining: the presumption of guilt, the costs and uncertainties of trial, the concern with arriving at an appropriate sentence, and the nature of the criminal code. All these factors influence bargaining positions.

Prosecutors

To the prosecutor, a plea bargain represents the certainty of conviction without the risks of trial. Recall that prosecutors emphasize convictions. Because they value the deterrent objectives of law enforcement, they prefer that those guilty of a crime be convicted of some charge rather than escape with no conviction at all. Not incidentally, a conviction by a plea also allows prosecutors to project to the public the image of criminals being convicted.

The certainty and finality of a defendant's pleading guilty contrasts sharply with the potential risks at trial. During trial a number of unexpected things can occur, most of them to the detriment of the prosecutor. The victim may refuse to cooperate. Witnesses' testimony may differ significantly from earlier statements made in investigative reports. A witness may make an unfavorable impression on the jury. Moreover, there is always the possibility that a mistrial (in which the judge ends the trial without a verdict because of a major defect in the proceedings) will be declared, and even after a jury verdict of guilty the appellate courts may reverse, meaning that the whole process must be repeated.

Plea bargains can also benefit prosecutors. Police reward informants with promises of reduced charges or leniency, promises they expect prosecutors to honor. Through plea bargaining the prosecutor can accommodate such requests. Similarly prosecutors use plea bargains to reward cooperative defendants. A typical example is a crime involving a major figure and a secondary one. In exchange for providing evidence against the major figure, the secondary one may be allowed to enter a plea to a less serious charge, greatly increasing the likelihood that the major figure will be convicted.

In seeking a conviction through a guilty plea, the prosecutor is in a unique position to control the negotiating process. To begin with, the prosecutor proceeds from a position of strength: in most cases the state has sufficient evidence for conviction. A survey of chief prosecutors in various states showed that the strength of the state's case was the most important motivation (85 percent) in this bargaining decision (Vetri). If, however, the case is weak, the prosecutor can avoid the embarrassment of losing a case at trial by either dismissing it all together or offering such a good deal that the defendant cannot refuse.

To improve their bargaining position, it is common practice for some prosecutors to overcharge deliberately.

"Sure, it's a lever," says one San Francisco prosecutor, referring to his office's practice of charging every non-automobile homicide as murder. With unusual candor he adds, "And we charge theft, burglary, and the possession of burglar's tools, because we know that if we charged only burglary there would be a trial." (Alschuler, 1968: 90)

This is not a universal practice, however. The chief assistant prosecutor of Minneapolis described attempts to reduce charges as follows.

> It's the attitude of my boss, and it was the attitude of his predecessor, that we stick with the charge on the "information" unless some new evidence comes up. When we move to reduce a charge our boss asks us if the evidence was good when the "information" was issued. Then he wants to know what we have learned since to justify a reduction. . . . We also don't reduce charges as much as the East because we're not yet in that position of tremendous caseload pressure. (Levin: 70–71)

Prosecutors, of course, control several of the forms of plea bargaining, including the ability to offer a charge reduction or a count bargain. In general, they can threaten to throw the book at a defendant who does not plead. Or they may refuse to bargain at all. If the crime is a serious one and the defendant is viewed as very dangerous, the prosecutor may force the defendant either to plead on the nose with no sentencing concessions or run the additional risk of trial.

Defendant

But if a plea gives the prosecutor a much sought-after conviction, why do defendants plead guilty? To understand plea bargaining it is important to recognize that it is often in the defendant's best interest to give up the right to be presumed innocent at a trial. The primary benefit of a plea is the possibility of a lenient sentence.

Around the courthouse, it is a common perception that defendants who refuse to plead guilty receive harsher sentences. Sometimes the penalty for going to trial works indirectly. For example, a judge may impose a higher sentence because the defendant compounded the crime by lying on the witness stand or getting some friends to perjure themselves. Or during a trial the full details of the crime will emerge—often to the detriment of the defendant. On a plea, though, the judge will be shielded from such details. Finally, a prosecutor may agree not to invoke the state career criminal provisions that impose higher penalties for those with a prior felony conviction.

Pleading guilty may also benefit defendants in ways not directly tied to sentencing. For poor defendants unable to post bail, a guilty plea can mean an immediate release either on probation or for time served or a transfer to better prison facilities and the beginning of serving the sentence. A plea can also mean the opportunity to avoid a conviction for a crime with an undesirable label—for instance, *rapist*—by pleading to an offense with a less pejorative title, and to avoid the possibly embarrassing publicity of a trial.

Ultimately defendants must decide whether to go along with the plea bargain or take their chances at trial. Few defendants are in a position to make a reasoned choice between the advantages of a plea and the disadvantages of a trial; most are poor, inarticulate, and have little formal education. For these defendants the experience in the courts is like their life on the streets: one goes along. Often softened up by the experience in jail awaiting trial, many defendants find that entering a plea is the best way to go along and avoid the possibility of even harsher penalties.

Defense Counsel

If the prosecutor enters negotiations from a position of strength, the opposite is true of defense attorneys, who have few bargaining chips. They may, however, attempt to gain some tactical advantages through several maneuvers. For one, they can seek to drag out the case in hopes that witnesses and victims lose interest or otherwise become unavailable. For another, they may file pretrial motions either to suppress the confession or evidence that was seized. Finally they can threaten to go to trial. But if the chances of winning are not high—and they rarely are—they must also consider the strong possibility that after a trial conviction, the defendant may be penalized with a higher prison sentence.

Because the defense starts from a position of weakness, it is generally up to the defense attorney to initiate plea discussions. These discussions may occur at any time in the case—shortly after arrest, at the arraignment on the indictment, or, most likely, shortly before the trial date. The lawyers' main resource is their knowledge of the courtroom work group—the types of pleas the prosecutor usually enters, the type of sentence the judge normally imposes in cases like this, and so on.

Defense attorneys act as classic negotiators, trying to get the best deal possible for their clients while at the same time explaining to the clients the realistic alternatives. As we noted in Chapter 7, there can be conflict between these two roles. A defense attorney, for example, may negotiate what she considers the best deal given the circumstances only to have her client refuse to go along.

In this relationship there is an understandable concern that a few defense attorneys manipulate clients. For example, defense attorneys might tell a client that the prosecutor is pushing a hard deal in this case and is insisting on a seven-year jail term. The defendant says he will not do more than four. Yet the defense attorney and prosecutor have not yet talked. When later they do, the prosecutor suggests a five-year sentence, the defense attorney says his client wants probation but he might agree. When the defendant is informed that the state will go with five, the impression is left that the defense attorney is really a great bargainer (Winsberg). The judge who provided this example concluded by saying that if he has any indication that the defense attorney is manipulating his client in such a fashion, he will monitor the attorney closely.

Judges

Several factors limit a judge's ability to control, supervise, or participate in plea bargaining. Given the division of powers in the adversary system, judges are reluctant to intrude on prosecutorial discretion. Prosecutors control many of the key bargaining mechanisms—specifically the charges filed and the charges to allow the defendant to plead to. Thus, when a prosecutor, defense attorney, and defendant have agreed either to a count bargaining or a charge reduction bargaining, the judge has no legal authority to refuse to accept the plea.

Even more fundamentally, however, the judge knows relatively little about each case. Only the prosecutor, defendant, and defense attorney know the evidence for and against the defendant. Without a knowledge of why the parties agreed to a plea bargain, it is obviously difficult for a judge to reject a plea agreement. In short, the judge is dependent on the prosecutor and, to a lesser extent, the defense attorney.

Within these restraints, though, judges have a limited ability to shape the plea bargaining process. The extent to which they are involved in the process varies greatly. A survey of state trial court judges revealed four basic patterns. Some judges are actively involved in plea negotiations. They make recommendations about the disposition of cases. Seven percent of the judges surveyed fell into this category. A second set of judges is indirectly involved. They review the recommendations made by defense and prosecutor. Twenty percent of the judges reported such participation. Next, a small percentage of judges (4 percent) attend plea discussions but do not participate. By far the largest category involves judges who do not attend plea negotiating sessions; rather, their role is limited to ratifying agreements reached by others. Fully 69 percent of the judges fell into this category (Ryan and Alfini). Even judges who only ratify plea negotiations can have an important impact on the process. Regular members of the courtroom work group know the sentence the judge is likely to impose. Therefore they negotiate case dispositions incorporating these sentencing expectations. On rare occasions judges may reject a plea agreement. Such rejections serve to set a baseline for future negotiations.

The extent to which a judge is actively involved in the plea bargaining negotiations is influenced by a number of factors. One is the judge's perceptions of his or her negotiating skills. Judges who view themselves as having good negotiating skills are more likely to be active participants. Judges in large cities are also more likely to be active participants. More stable courtroom work groups tend to encourage judicial involvement. In addition, a judge's expectation that a trial will be lengthy encourages his or her active participation. Acting to discourage judicial involvement are state rules and state court decisions. Some states have adopted clear statements prohibiting judges from participating in plea negotiations. In these states, naturally, judicial participation is rare (Ryan and Alfini). It appears that judicial participation is shaped by forces involving the judge's individual talents as well as the type of court over which he or she presides.

Dynamics of Bargaining

Negotiations are a group activity typically conducted in busy, noisy, public courtrooms. As one enters these courtrooms, the initial impression is of constant talking and endless movement. While the judge is hearing a pretrial motion in one case, a prosecutor and defense attorney are engaged in an animated conversation about a charge reduction in another. Meanwhile, in more hushed tones, a public defender is briefing his client about why a continuance will be requested, and nearby a mother is talking to her son who is being held in jail. These numerous conversations occur while other participants are constantly moving in and out. Police officers leave after testifying in a motion to suppress, bail bondsmen arrive to check on their clients, clerks bring in new files and lawyers search for the prosecutor assigned to their case. Occasionally the noise becomes so loud that the judge or bailiff demands silence—a request that usually produces only a temporary reduction in the decibel level.

On the surface, courtrooms appear disorganized. In fact, there is an underlying order to the many and diverse activities that occur (Maynard). Interaction norms control the face-to-face encounters of the participants. Decision-making norms govern the substance of the negotiations.

Interaction Norms

Courtrooms are the site of numerous simultaneous conversations. Despite the seeming chaos, who talks to whom, when, and where is governed by a certain kind of order.

audience section

Physically, the courtroom is divided into three distinct regions. The first is the **audience section** where defendants, friends, family, and witnesses are allowed. A railing divides this public section from the **lawyers' region.**

lawyers' region

Here activity tends to occur around one or more tables reserved for the lawyers. The jury box is considered part of the lawyer's turf because prosecuting and defense attorneys may use it to conduct their negotiations and conferences. The third area is the **judge's region,** with a raised bench, and

judge's region

a witness stand (which is unused during pretrial and settlement). In front of the bench and to the side are desks for clerks, court recorders, and often a probation officer (Maynard).

judicial encounters

In this physical setting, there is a decided social order to who talks to whom and when. Participants accord the highest ranking to **judicial encounters.** The judge's activities dominate all other courtroom interactions. Thus, when the judge calls a case the other participants involved in that matter are immediately expected to drop all other business and proceed to the

negotiational encounters

front of the court. Next in order of social importance are **negotiational encounters** that take place between the lawyers. The two parties do not sit down and discuss all of their cases one by one; rather negotiations occur in fits and starts. For example, a discussion about a plea in exchange for time served may be interrupted when the judge calls another case and resumed later

lawyer–client encounters

when both lawyers are free. The lowest social ranking is given to **lawyer–client encounters.** These conversations occur largely at the behest of the lawyer. Clients are expected to be ready when their lawyers inquire about the facts of the case or want to relay information about ongoing plea negotiations. A conversation initiated by a client is not viewed as obligatory; that is, the lawyer can end it at any time, something that would not happen in a lawyer–lawyer interchange. Prosecutors will not interrupt a lawyer's conversation with a client although the judge will (Maynard).

Decision-Making Norms

Through working together on a daily basis, the members of the courtroom work group come to understand the problems and demands of the others. They develop shared conceptions of how certain types of cases and defendants should be treated. Everyone except the outsider or the novice knows these customs of the courthouse.

Plea bargaining is a complex process that exhibits important variations between jurisdictions. Nonetheless, a variety of studies in different courts point to important similarities in shared norms. The most important is the seriousness of the offense. The more serious the crime charged, the harder the prosecutor bargains (Mather, 1979; Nardulli et al.). The next most important is the defendant's criminal record. Those with prior convictions receive fewer concessions during bargaining (Alschuler, 1979; Nardulli; Springer). Another key consideration is the strength of the prosecutor's case. The stronger the evidence against the defendant, the fewer concessions offered (Adams).

These shared norms structure plea negotiations. In each courtroom work group there is a well-understood set of allowable reductions. Based on the manner in which the crime is committed and the background of the defendant, nighttime burglary will be reduced to daytime burglary, drunkenness to disturbing the peace, and so on. Writing about a misdemeanor court, Malcolm Feeley offers an economic analogy of shared norms.

> It is the salesman's stock-in-trade to represent a "going rate" as if it were a special sale price offered only once. The gap between theoretical exposure and the standard rate allows defense attorneys and prosecutors to function much the same way, making the defendant think he is getting a special "deal" when in fact he is getting the standard rate. Together prosecutors and defense attorneys operate like discount stores, pointing to a never-used high list price and then marketing the product as a supposedly "special" sale price, thereby appearing to provide substantial savings to those who act quickly. (p.191)

Contrary to many popular fears, defendants are not allowed to plead to just any charge. If a defendant has been charged with armed robbery, the defense attorney knows that the credibility of her bargaining position will be destroyed if she suggests a plea to disturbing the peace. Such a plea would be out of line with how things are normally done. Courtroom work groups have similar shared norms about sentencing.

On the basis of these shared norms, all parties know what is open for bargaining and what is not. The following example is a good one.

> On a three count forgery case, the defense attorney asks the D.A., "Can I have one count?" The D.A. says, "Yes, which one?" The defense attorney says "Count 2." And that's it. No bargain has been made. No promise made that counts 1 and 3 will be dismissed in exchange for the plea to count 2. *It's simply that everyone knows what the standard practice is.* (Mather, 1974: 199)

These shared norms provide a baseline around which specific cases are disposed of. Around this baseline sentence, there will be upward or downward adjustments depending on the circumstances of the individual case.

Why Cases Go to Trial

Although most cases are disposed of by a guilty plea, an important percentage (10 to 20 percent) of defendants are tried. Cases go to trial when the parties cannot settle a case through negotiation. Thus in large measure the factors that shape plea bargaining—the strength of the prosecutor's case and the severity of the penalty—are the same ones that enter into the decision to go to trial.

Defense attorneys recommend a trial when the risks of trial are low and the possible gains are high.

reasonable doubt

This broad calculation leads to two very different types of trial cases. In one, the possible gains for the defendant are high because there is a chance of an acquittal. There may be **reasonable doubt** that the defendant committed any crime, or two sets of witnesses may tell conflicting versions of what happened (Neubauer). A second category of cases going to trial involves situations in which the prison sentence will be high. Even though a judge or jury is not likely to return a not guilty verdict, the defendant may still decide that the slim possibility of an acquittal is worth the risk of the trial penalty.

Not all trial cases, however, are the result of such rational calculations. Some defendants want a trial no matter what. Judges, prosecutors, and defense attorneys label as irrational defendants who refuse to recognize the realities of the criminal justice system and insist on a trial even when the state has a strong case (Neubauer).

The net effect of these plea versus trial considerations is that some types of cases are more likely to go to trial than others. Table 13-2 presents data from a study in a large metropolitan court, Los Angeles. Property offenses (burglary, theft, forgery) are unlikely to go to trial because the state is apt to have a strong case (usually buttressed by the presence of indisputable physical evidence) and the prison sentence will not be long. Serious crimes like murder, rape, and robbery are much more likely to be tried. In these crimes of violence, there may be reasonable doubt because the victim may have provoked the attack. Moreover, a convicted defendant is likely to serve a long prison term and therefore more disposed to take the chances on an outright acquittal.

There are widespread variations in the decision to go to trial. Southern states have an average of seventy trials per hundred thousand people compared to the national average of thirty-four (Kalven and Zeisel). In some rural areas, trials occur only once a decade, but in other rural places, trials are more common.

Jury Trial Penalty

jury trial penalty

Although most defendants plead guilty, a significant minority of cases do go to trial. As previously indicated, it is a common assumption in courthouses around the nation that defendants who do not enter a plea of guilty can expect to receive harsher sentences. Typically called the *jury trial penalty,* the notion reflects the philosophy, "He takes some of my time, I take some of his." Here *time* refers to the hours spent hearing evidence presented to a jury (Uhlman and Walker). This is how one judge expressed his philosophy:

> If someone has a trial and it's apparent that there is some question of a good defense . . . then the sentence is probably no harsher than it would have been if he'd entered a plea. It's a delight to have a good trial, handled by a good attorney. He knows what he is doing and comes up with sharp things during the trial. . . . But I think there are times when you see a completely frivolous trial which . . . is a waste of everyone's time. Take the guy who is caught with his hand in the till, and there's no question but that he's guilty. And the case is still

TABLE 13-2   Rank Ordering of Trial Disposition of Felony Defendants in Los Angeles Superior Court, 1970

Offense	Total defendants	Percentage of defendants disposed of by full court or jury
Homicide	398	36.1%
Kidnapping	189	28.0
Rape, forcible	391	27.1
Other sex offenses	769	22.9
Robbery	1,875	22.2
Assault	1,640	21.5
Opiates	1,250	16.8
Hit and run	109	13.7
Theft, except auto	2,092	11.1
Deadly weapons	377	10.6
Burglary	4,670	10.4
Manslaughter, vehicular	69	10.1
Theft, auto	1,582	9.4
Drunk driving	371	8.6
Marijuana	5,529	8.2
Dangerous drugs	6,851	8.2
Other drug violation	194	7.2
Forgery and checks	2,107	6.2
Bookmaking	701	5.0
Escape	146	2.7
Other	261	16.8
Total	31,571	11.6%

SOURCE: Bureau of Criminal Statistics, State of California, n.d. Cited in Lynn Mather, "Some Determinants of the Method of Case Disposition: Decision-Making by Public Defenders in Los Angeles," *Law and Society Review* 8 (Winter 1974): 248.

tried, and his hands are still in the till, and he hasn't been able to get them out, and you wonder why he's wasted everyone's time. . . . (Heumann: 142)

Several studies provide empirical documentation for these courthouse perceptions. One study of a major eastern city concluded that "the cost of a jury trial for convicted defendants in Metro City is high: sentences are substantially more severe than for other defendants" (Uhlman and Walker: 337). The same conclusions emerged in a study of three California counties (Brereton and Casper). Such findings, however, have not gone unchallenged. Research conducted on some other courts was unable to document the existence of a jury trial penalty. In their three-city study, Eisenstein and Jacob concluded that "the effect of dispositional mode was insignificant in accounting for the variance in sentence length" (p. 270). Their conclusion was supported by a study in Washington, D.C. (Rhodes). Read together, these various studies suggest that it is very difficult to make conclusions about nationwide practices, because of the tremendous discrepancies among jurisdictions. Moreover, it appears that the jury trial penalty may be applied more selectively than earlier research indicated.

Despite the uncertainty over the extent of the jury trial penalty, the U.S. Supreme Court has clearly sanctioned the practice. A Kentucky defendant accused of forging an $88.30 check was offered a five-year prison sentence if he entered a plea of guilty. But the prosecutor indicated that if the defendant rejected the offer, the state would seek to impose life imprisonment because of the defendant's previous two felony convictions. Such enhanced sentences for habitual criminals were allowed at that time by Kentucky law. The defendant rejected the plea, went to trial, was convicted, and was eventually sentenced to life imprisonment. In *Bordenkircher* v. *Hayes* (434 U.S. 357, 1978), the high court held, "The course of conduct engaged in by the prosecutor in this case, which no more than openly presented the defendant with the unpleasant alternative of forgoing trial or facing charges on which he was plainly subject to prosecution" did not violate constitutional protections. In dissent, however, Justice Powell noted that the offer of five years in prison "hardly could be characterized as a generous offer." He was clearly troubled that "persons convicted of rape and murder often are not punished so severely" as this check forger.

Copping a Plea

"Your honor, my client wishes at this time to withdraw his previous plea of not guilty and wishes at this time to enter a plea of guilty." In phrases very similar to this one, defense attorneys indicate that the case is about to end; the defendant is ready to plead. A plea of guilty is more than an admission of conduct; it is a conviction that also involves a defendant's waiver of the most vital rights of the court process: presumption of innocence, jury trial, and confrontation of witnesses (*Boykin* v. *Alabama,* 395 U.S. 238, 1969).

For defendants in a crowded urban court, the entry of the plea may be nothing more than a hurried, confused period of standing before a judge and mumbling the expected words. For others, it represents a careful proceeding. Until fairly recently, the taking of a guilty plea operated in an informal manner and was largely dependent on what local court officials believed should be done. Because the courts and the legal process as a whole were reluctant to recognize the existence of plea bargaining, little statutory or case law guided the process. Under the leadership of Chief Justice Warren Burger, however, the U.S. Supreme Court has sought to set standards for the plea bargaining process.

Questioning the Defendant

nolo contendere

In limited circumstances a defendant will enter a plea of **nolo contendere**—Latin for "I will not contest it." While a plea of nolo contendere has the same results in criminal proceedings as a plea of guilty, it cannot be used in a civil proceeding as a defendant's admission of guilt. Thus, this plea is usually entered when civil proceedings and liabilities may result. Most defendants, however, plead guilty to one or more charges listed in the charging document. Before a defendant's plea of guilty can be accepted, the judge must question the defendant. This was not always the case. Judges merely accepted the attorney's statement that the defendant wanted to plead guilty. But in *Boykin* v. *Alabama* in 1969, the Supreme Court ruled: "It was error, for the trial judge to accept petitioner's guilty plea without an affirmative showing that it was intelligent and voluntary."

In questioning the defendant, the judge inquires whether the defendant understands the nature of the charge, the possible penalty upon conviction, whether any threats were made, if the defendant is satisfied with the services of defense counsel, and whether the defendant realizes that a plea waives right ***Boykin form*** to a jury trial. A typical ***Boykin form*** is shown in Figure 13-1. In theory, such questioning serves to ensure that the guilty plea reflects the defendant's own choice, is made with a general understanding of the charges and consequences of conviction, and was not improperly influenced by prosecution, law enforcement officials, or the defendant's own attorney. Such questioning also provides an official court record designed to prevent defendants from later contending they were forced to plead guilty.

Some courts go a step further by also requiring that a brief summary of the case be entered in the record. Either a law enforcement officer or the prosecutor states that if a trial were held, the evidence would show the defendant is guilty and then proceeds to summarize the evidence sufficient to prove each of the elements of the offense. The defendant then has the opportunity to offer any corrections or additions.

Accepting a Plea

Judges have discretion in deciding whether to accept the defendant's plea of guilty. Some judges refuse to do so unless the defendant fully admits guilt. If the defendant wishes to plead guilty but refuses to admit any wrongdoing, the judge may reject the plea and order the case to be tried. Other judges insist on a less stringent admission of wrongdoing. This issue arose in a case where the defendant was indicted for first-degree murder, a capital offense. The defendant protested his innocence but entered a plea anyway, saying: "I pleaded guilty on second-degree murder because they said there is too much evidence, but I ain't shot no man. . . . I just pleaded guilty because they said if I didn't they would gas me for it. . . . I'm not guilty but I pleaded guilty." The Court held that given the defendant's desire to avoid the death penalty and the existence of substantial evidence of guilt, the plea of guilty was valid (*Alford* v. *North Carolina*, 400 U.S. 25, 1971).

Placing the Plea Agreement on the Record

Until the mid-1960s, plea negotiations were still officially denied. As a result, the taking of a plea was often a sham. The defendant was expected to lie and deny that a deal had been made. This is how one defendant described the experience.

> Did your lawyer tell you how to answer them beforehand? No, but you know how to answer them. He [the judge] asked me, you know, like had you ever been—you haven't been offered any kind of deal or nothing. He didn't put in that word, but it was meant the same thing. You have to say "No." If anybody's in the courtroom, you gotta make a little show for them. (Casper: 84)

CRIMINAL DISTRICT COURT
PARISH OF ORLEANS
STATE OF LOUISIANA
SECTION "C"

JUDGE JEROME M. WINSBERG

STATE OF LOUISIANA   CASE NO. _____
    VERSUS
                                        VIO. _____
_____

WAIVER OF CONSTITUTIONAL RIGHTS
PLEA OF GUILTY

I, _____, before my Plea of Guilty to the crime of _____, have been informed and understand the charge to which I'm pleading guilty. _____

I understand that I have a right to trial by Judge or Jury, and if convicted, a right to appeal. And by entering a plea of guilty in this case, I am waiving my rights to trial and appeal. _____

The acts constituting the offense to which I am pleading guilty have been explained to me as well as the fact that for this crime I could possibly receive a sentence of _____.

I understand that by pleading guilty that I am waiving my rights to confront and cross examine the witnesses who accuse me of the crime charged, and to compulsory process of the Court to require witnesses to appear and testify for me. _____

I am entering a plea of guilty to this crime because I am, in fact, guilty of this crime. _____

I have not been forced, threatened or intimidated into making this plea. _____

I am fully satisfied with the handling of my case by my attorney and the way in which he has represented me. _____

I further understand that I am waiving my right against self-incrimination, that at my trial I would not have to testify, and if I did not testify, neither the Judge nor the Jury could hold that against me. I also give up the right not to say anything against myself, or against my interest, such as I am doing by pleading guilty. _____

I understand that if I elected to have a trial, I have a right to have competent counsel to represent me at trial. And if I was unable to pay for counsel, the Court would appoint competent counsel to represent me, but by entering the plea of guilty, I am waiving these rights. _____

If a plea bargain agreement has been made, I understand that no other promises which may have been made to me other than as set out hereinabove in this plea bargain are enforceable or binding. _____

The Judge has addressed me personally as to all of these matters and he has given me the opportunity to make any statement I desire. _____

_____	_____
DATE	DEFENDANT
_____	_____
JUDGE	ATTORNEY FOR THE DEFENDANT

Figure 13-1 Institutionalizing plea bargaining—
a sample *Boykin* form

To prevent the possibility of covering up plea bargaining, some courts now require that a plea agreement be placed on the record. This public disclosure allows defendants and attorneys to correct any misunderstandings.

To ensure fairness in negotiations between defense and prosecution, the law now provides defendants with a limited right to withdraw a guilty plea. In the case of *Santobello* v. *New York* (404 U.S. 257, 1971), the prosecutor agreed to permit the defendant to plead to a less serious offense and to make no recommendations as to sentencing. Months later at the sentencing hearing, however, a new prosecutor, apparently ignorant of his colleague's commitment, recommended the maximum sentence, which the judge imposed. The defendant was not allowed to withdraw the plea. Chief Justice Burger's opinion ordered that the defendant be allowed to withdraw the plea, arguing, "When a plea rests in any significant degree on a promise or agreement of the prosecutor, so that it can be said to be a part of the inducement or consideration, such promise must be fulfilled."

But Is This Justice?

Plea bargaining is a hotly debated topic that people either strongly favor or strongly oppose. What is particularly interesting is that opposition comes from persons with contrasting ideological positions. Civil libertarians as well as law and order spokesmen see it as a danger, but often for different reasons. But not all opposition to plea bargaining can be categorized along a continuum from individual rights to societal protection. Many legal professionals are also concerned that plea bargaining reduces the courthouse to a place where guilt or innocence, prison or probation are negotiated just as one might haggle over the price of copper jugs at a Turkish bazaar (Rubin). They see it as justice on the cheap and therefore inherently destructive of the concept that the rule of law exists to protect society. What unites these otherwise contrasting perspectives is the concern that plea bargaining works to make the jobs of the judge, prosecutor, and defense attorney much easier but sacrifices the legitimate interests of the police, victim, witnesses, defendant, and the public in general.

An evaluation of the type of justice resulting from plea bargaining must recognize the overriding fact stressed earlier in this chapter: plea bargaining encompasses a wide variety of very different practices. The debate over the merits and demerits of bargaining reflects contrasting perceptions of realities. For instance, defenders of plea bargaining tend to see guilty pleas occurring when the state has a very strong case, while opponents tend to see it occurring most frequently where the evidence is weak. Proponents see plea bargaining as a reflection of an experienced defense counsel's perception of the likely result of trial. Opponents, on the other hand, are more inclined to see a bargained agreement as the product of tactical considerations and inherent biases in the system (Nardulli).

Does Plea Bargaining Sacrifice the Rights of the Defendant?

Supporters of the values of the due process model are concerned that plea bargaining undercuts the protections afforded individuals. This view is aptly expressed by the leading academic critic of plea bargaining, law professor Albert Alschuler:

> [T]he plea bargaining system is an inherently irrational method of administering justice. . . . [It] subjects defense attorneys to serious temptations to disregard their clients' interests. . . . Today's guilty-plea system leads even able, conscientious, and highly motivated attorneys to make decisions that are not really in their clients' interests. (1975: 1180)

A prime concern of due process adherents is that a criminal court process geared to produce guilty pleas negates the fundamental protection of the adversary system—a public trial where the defendant is presumed innocent—for plea bargaining discourages trials by imposing a penalty on those who lose at trial. They therefore advocate abolishing bargaining in favor of a vast increase in the number of trials. Such a position, however, ignores the reality of criminal courts: in most cases there is no substantial disagreement over the facts. Moreover, civil libertarian critics look to the jury as the proper forum for sifting guilt from innocence. Yet experienced trial attorneys often have grave doubts about such an approach. In the words of a Los Angeles public defender:

> If you've got an exceptional case—one which is weak and there's a good chance that the defendant may be innocent—then you don't want to take it before a jury because you never know what they'll do. And besides you don't want to try it because it's such a bad case. So you chamberize with the judge. (Mather: 202)

Some are concerned that plea bargaining works to shield police misconduct from scrutiny. Questions about police adherence to constitutional protections against illegal search and seizure, for example, are compromised away in the bargaining process.

A final concern is that in a criminal court process geared to guilty pleas, an innocent defendant might be forced to enter a plea of guilty. Consider the statement of a minor Louisiana politician who contended he was forced into pleading guilty to charges of vote fraud despite his innocence: "I was faced with six felonies and 41 years. . . . I didn't have the time or money to clear my name" (Degruy and Simon: 1). It is difficult to evaluate such a statement, for any protestations of innocence after entering a plea of guilty are obviously self-serving. Given that courts are human institutions, it is unlikely that an innocent defendant has never been pressured to plead, but there is no evidence that this is a systemic problem. Questions of doubtful validity are screened throughout the court process. And, the vast majority of defense attorneys will not let their clients enter a plea unless they are convinced that there is enough evidence for a guilty verdict. Even when the guilty enter a plea, due process advocates suspect that the defendant receives few advantages.

Do the Guilty Benefit?

If holders of due process values are uneasy that plea bargaining jeopardizes the rights of the individual, the backers of the crime control model express the opposite concern. They believe plea bargaining allows defendants to avoid

C O N T R O V E R S Y

Wall Street Executive Pleads Guilty

NEW YORK—A leading Wall Street investment banker, turned in by stock speculator Ivan Boesky, tearfully admitted insider trading charges Friday and said he had agreed to surrender about $9 million to the government.

Martin A. Siegel, 38, pleaded guilty to conspiracy and tax evasion in U.S. District Court as part of the widening insider trading investigation that has shaken the securities industry the past year.

Siegel is the confidential informant whose knowledge led prosecutors to charge three other top-level Wall Street executives on Thursday with insider trading, U.S. Attorney Rudolph Giuliani said.

In a separate civil matter, a complaint by the Securities and Exchange Commission charged that Boesky paid Siegel $700,000 for secret information that helped Boesky's companies make $33 million trading stock.

Three times, in late 1982, 1983 and 1984, Boesky couriers met Siegel in a "conspicuous public location" in midtown Manhattan, exchanged passwords with him and handed him a briefcase stuffed with cash, the SEC complaint said.

Siegel, without admitting or denying the allegation, agreed to relinquish $4.3 million in cash, and securities worth more than $4.7 million, for a total of about $9 million, said Gary Lynch, the SEC's enforcement chief. He also is barred from the securities industry for life.

Though Siegel's only alleged profit was the $700,000, "We wanted him to disgorge more than he had put in his pocket," Lynch said. He said the SEC demanded the $9 million to settle the matter, arriving at the sum by figuring Siegel's alleged responsibility for Boesky's profit.

In the biggest insider trading case thus far, Boesky in November agreed to pay a record $100 million in penalties and to plead guilty to an unspecified criminal charge. He also is barred from the securities industry for life.

Boesky has been cooperating with prosecutors, and he led them to Siegel, who in turn agreed to cooperate, Giuliani said.

Associated Press, "Wall Street Executive Pleads Guilty," *New Orleans Times-Picayune*, February 14, 1987, p. 1.

a guilty label for crimes they actually committed, results in lenient sentences, and in general gives criminal wrongdoers the impression that the courts and the law are easily manipulated.

The police in particular much prefer a conviction on the crime charged rather than a plea to a lesser one. In the words of one detective in downstate Illinois: "When we arrest them, they should be found guilty on that charge, not some lesser charge. I don't believe in reduced charges; they should be made to answer" (Neubauer: 61). Law enforcement officials often equate plea bargaining with excessive leniency.

It is not a difficult task to single out individual cases in which these law enforcement criticisms of plea bargaining have merit. But the argument obscures too much. In particular, it confuses cause with effect. A bargained agreement on reduced charges, for example, may be the product of initial overcharging and/or of evidence problems that surface later. Moreover, such criticisms suggest that in plea bargaining anything goes—the prosecutor and judge will make any deal to dispose of a case. Yet each court employs a more or less consistent approach to what charge or count reductions are customary, plus a set of sentencing rules of thumb. Many of the law enforcement criticisms of plea bargaining may be reduced to an overall displeasure with the leniency of the courts. Whether sentences are too harsh or too lenient should be a separate issue from the vehicle for reaching these sentencing dispositions—plea bargaining.

Abolishing/Reforming Plea Bargaining

In recent years, some court systems have attempted to either abolish or reform plea bargaining. Such efforts conform to one of the most controversial recommendations of the National Advisory Commission on Criminal Justice Standards and Goals:

> As soon as possible. . . negotiations between prosecutors and defendants—either personally or through their attorneys—concerning concessions to be made in return for guilty pleas should be prohibited. In the event that the prosecution makes a recommendation as to sentence, it should not be affected by the willingness of the defendant to plead guilty to some or all of the offenses with which he is charged. A plea of guilty should not be considered by the court in determining the sentence to be imposed. (p. 46)

This recommendation was prompted primarily by the commission's view that plea bargaining produces undue leniency.

The main weakness of the commission's recommendation to abolish plea bargaining is that it refuses to recognize the context of plea bargaining. Rosett and Cressey forcefully make this point:

> These proposals ignore the underlying conflicts to which negotiation is a response. They assume that justice can be administered without confronting these differences. They seek an idealized criminal law that is clear and precise, and that does not have to accommodate messy disagreements and accidents. Such proposed cures are futile. (p. 95)

Many efforts to abolish plea bargaining are really surface changes, unresponsive to the dynamics of the courthouse.

Faced with mounting public criticism and professional concern, prosecutors and judges in a number of American communities have tried to alter traditional plea bargaining practices. The state of Alaska and the cities of New Orleans and El Paso are commonly identified with efforts to abolish plea bargaining altogether. Other communities, such as Detroit and Denver, have sought to reform the process by regularizing it.

Drawing conclusions from these efforts, however, is somewhat difficult. The reason traces back to the original theme of this chapter—plea bargaining practices are quite varied. In some instances attempts of a given jurisdiction to abolish plea bargaining often mean that they simply abolished one form of plea bargaining, typically sentence bargaining, but continued other practices. Moreover, the changes instituted in a given court may represent a major departure from past practice in that jurisdiction but might be commonplace elsewhere. Claims that plea bargaining has been abolished or that major reforms have been instituted require critical analysis. As a result of a growing number of studies of such efforts, we can point to some important areas of interest.

In analyzing the impact of changes in plea bargaining practices, a basic question is whether the changes were indeed implemented. Written policy changes do not always alter the behavior of the court actors. Efforts in Denver to adopt mandatory pretrial conferences, for example, met with resistance from defense attorneys and others. As a result the programs did not have their intended impact and were later dropped (Nimmer and Krauthaus). A similar finding was reported by Lief Carter, who studied a county in northern California where the grand jury had publicly criticized plea bargaining for bestowing undue leniency. In response, the prosecutor tried to eliminate plea bargaining. The defense attorneys, however, began to take more cases to trial. After the

---

C O N T R O V E R S Y

Should the Government Agree to Plea Bargain?

In determining whether it would be appropriate to enter into a plea agreement, the attorney for the government should weigh all relevant considerations, including:

(a) the defendant's willingness to cooperate in the investigation or prosecution of others;
(b) the defendant's history with respect to criminal activity;
(c) the nature and seriousness of the offense or offenses charged;

(d) the defendant's remorse or contrition and his willingness to assume responsibility for his conduct;
(e) the desirability of prompt and certain disposition of the case;
(f) the likelihood of obtaining a conviction at trial;
(g) the probable effect on witnesses;
(h) the probable sentence or

other consequences if the defendant is convicted;
(i) the public interest in having the case tried rather than disposed of by a guilty plea;
(j) the expense of trial and appeal; and
(k) the need to avoid delay in the disposition of other pending cases.

U.S. Department of Justice, *Principles of Federal Prosecution* (Washington, D.C.: Government Printing Office, 1980), p. 23.

state lost twelve out of sixteen jury verdicts, the prosecutor quietly returned to the old policies (Carter: 109–111). Not all efforts at reform, however, are short-lived. Separate efforts in Detroit to use pretrial conferences (Nimmer and Krauthaus) and to abolish plea bargaining in cases involving the Michigan Felony Firearm Statute (Heumann and Loftin) were successfully implemented.

hydraulic process

Even when programs are successfully implemented, they may not have the impact intended. Discretion in the criminal justice system has been likened to a **hydraulic process.** Efforts to control discretion at one stage typically result in its displacement to another part of the process. Thus efforts to abolish or reform plea bargaining often result in the activity simply moving elsewhere. Such a hydraulic process occurred in California after the voters approved Proposition 8. One of the key provisions of this victim's bill of rights (see Chapter 9) prohibits plea bargaining for twenty-five of the most serious crimes. The ban applied only to the major trial court, however. One comprehensive study found that Proposition 8 did not abolish plea bargaining; rather its location shifted to the lower court where the proportion of bargained cases increased (McCoy). Alaska provides another clear example. In that state, the attorney general forbade assistant prosecutors from engaging in plea bargaining or from making sentencing recommendations to the judge.

> Judges complain now that, although their responsibilities have increased dramatically, they have very little opportunity to give sentencing thorough consideration, partly because of insufficient time to review the defendant's files, partly because of other calendar pressures which shorten the time available for sentencing hearings, and partly because the law itself offers so little guidance. (Rubenstein and White: 277)

An excellent in-depth study of a Michigan county revealed a similar pattern (Church, 1976). After a law-and-order antidrug campaign, the newly elected prosecuting attorney instituted a strict policy forbidding charge reduction plea bargaining in drug sale cases. One result was an increased demand for trials, although it was not as great as some judges feared. But at the same time, outright dismissals increased because of insufficient evidence. Moreover, a much greater percentage of defendants were sentenced as juveniles rather than adults, so that they would not have a felony record. Most important, plea bargaining involving defense attorney and judge continued in drug cases. Hence the assistant prosecutor's ability to control the disposition of the case weakened. Thus efforts to increase sentence severity by abolishing or constraining plea bargaining are not always successful. When the Coast Guard effectively eliminated plea bargains in special courts-martial, there was no increase in sentence severity (Call et al.). On the other hand, recent changes in California appear to have resulted in somewhat longer prison sentences (McCoy). Some contend that prosecutors push for more severe penalties in order to provide themselves greater leverage during plea negotiations. In short, attempts to abolish plea bargaining often produce a number of offsetting changes because overall policies fail to consider the reasons for negotiations.

Conclusion

Plea bargaining vividly illustrates the difference between the law on the books and the law in action. The rules of criminal procedure, appellate court decisions, and theories of the adversary system suggest that the trial is the principal activity of the criminal courts. Instead plea bargaining is the predominant activity. Bargaining is best understood not as a response to the press of cases but as an adaptation to some realities about the types of cases requiring court disposition. In most cases, there is little question about the defendant's legal guilt. A trial is a costly and sometimes risky method of establishing that guilt. A trial cannot wrestle with the most pressing issue of what sentence to impose on the guilty. Finally, through plea bargaining courthouse officials are able to individualize justice. In short, it is neither necessary nor desirable that every defendant have a trial.

It is important to bear in mind, however, that plea bargaining is not one single easily definable practice. All the complexities and differences of America's legal system are reflected in the wide variety of practices collectively referred to as plea bargaining. We defined bargaining as the process through which a defendant pleads guilty to a criminal charge with the expectation of receiving some consideration from the state. Some bargains are explicit; others are implicit. Some defendants plead guilty on the nose, others after a charge reduction, still others after count bargaining, and finally some after sentence negotiations. Equally varied are the processes through which such bargains are reached. Different persons with divergent concerns have observed roughly similar plea bargaining practices and procedures and reached very different conclusions about the justice dispensed and the improvements needed.

For Discussion

1. What form of plea bargaining—sentencing, charge reduction, or count pleading—predominates in your community? Why?
2. Observe the taking of a plea in a local court. Do you think the procedures follow the legal standards? What improvements might be made? What are your impressions of the dignity of justice? What are the most important characteristics of the cases where guilty pleas are entered?
3. Should a defendant be allowed to plead guilty without fully admitting guilt? Would you limit the *Alford* guidelines solely to situations in which the death penalty was involved? Why?
4. What do you consider the major disadvantages of plea bargaining? Why?
5. What would you recommend be done to standardize plea bargaining?
6. Discuss plea bargaining with criminal justice officials. Do they believe it is necessary? If so, why? Compare and contrast their views on the problems associated with negotiating justice.

References

ADAMS, KENNETH. "The Effect of Evidentiary Factors on Charge Reduction." *Journal of Criminal Justice* 11 (1983): 525.
ALSCHULER, ALBERT W. "Plea Bargaining and Its History." *Columbia Law Review* 79 (1979): 1.

——. "The Prosecutor's Role in Plea Bargaining." *University of Chicago Law Review* 36 (1968): 61.

——."The Defense Attorney's Role in Plea Bargaining." *Yale Law Journal* 84 (1975): 1179–1314.

BOLAND, BARBARA, AND BRIAN FORST. "Prosecutors Don't Always Aim to Pleas." *Federal Probation* 49 (1985): 10.

BRERETON, DAVID, AND JONATHAN CASPER. "Does It Pay to Plead Guilty? Differential Sentencing and the Functioning of Criminal Courts." *Law and Society Review* 16 (1981–1982): 45–70.

BUREAU OF JUSTICE STATISTICS. "The Prevalence of Guilty Pleas." *Bureau of Justice Statistics Special Report.* Washington, D.C.: U.S. Department of Justice, 1984.

CALL, JACK, DAVID ENGLAND, AND SUSETTE TALARICO. "Abolition of Plea Bargaining in the Coast Guard." *Journal of Criminal Justice* 11 (1983): 351.

CARTER, LIEF. *The Limits of Order.* Lexington, Mass.: D. C. Heath, 1974.

CASPER, JONATHAN D. *American Criminal Justice: The Defendant's Perspective.* Englewood Cliffs, N.J.: Prentice-Hall, 1972.

CHURCH, THOMAS W., JR. "Plea Bargains, Concessions and the Courts: Analysis of a Quasi-Experiment." *Law and Society Review* 10 (1976): 377.

——. "Examining Local Legal Culture." *American Bar Foundation Research Journal* 1985 (1985): 449.

DEGRUY, PIERRE V., AND JOHN ALAN SIMON. "Poll Official 'Forced' into Guilty Plea." *New Orleans Times-Picayune,* April 14, 1977.

EISENSTEIN, JAMES, AND HERBERT JACOB. *Felony Justice.* Boston: Little, Brown, 1977.

FEELEY, MALCOLM M. *The Process Is the Punishment: Handling Cases in a Lower Criminal Court.* New York: Russell Sage Foundation, 1979.

FRIEDMAN, LAWRENCE. "Plea Bargaining in Historical Perspective." *Law and Society Review* 13 (1979): 247.

HAGER, PHILIP. "Plea Bargaining—Is Justice Well Served?" *Los Angeles Times,* February 25, 1975.

HEUMANN, MILTON. *Plea Bargaining: The Experience of Prosecutors, Judges and Defense Attorneys.* Chicago: University of Chicago Press, 1978.

——, AND COLIN LOFTIN. "Mandatory Sentencing and the Abolition of Plea Bargaining: The Michigan Felony Firearm Statute." *Law and Society Review* 13 (1979): 393–430.

ILLINOIS ASSOCIATION FOR CRIMINAL JUSTICE. *The Illinois Crime Survey.* Chicago: Blakely, 1929.

KALVEN, HARRY, AND HANS ZEISEL. *The American Jury.* Chicago: University of Chicago Press, 1966.

LEVIN, MARTIN. *Urban Politics and the Criminal Courts.* Chicago: University of Chicago Press, 1977.

MATHER, LYNN M. *Plea Bargaining or Trial?* Lexington, Mass.: D. C. Heath, 1979.

——. "Some Determinants of the Method of Case Disposition: Decision-Making by Public Defenders in Los Angeles." *Law and Society Review* 8 (1974): 187–216.

MAYNARD, DOUGLAS. *Inside Plea Bargaining: The Language of Negotiation.* New York: Plenum Press, 1984.

MCCOY, CANDACE. "Determinate Sentencing, Plea Bargaining Bans, and Hydraulic Discretion in California." *Justice System Journal* 9 (1984): 256.

MILLER, HERBERT, WILLIAM MCDONALD, AND JAMES CRAMER. *Plea Bargaining in the United States.* Washington, D.C.: National Institute of Law Enforcement and Criminal Justice, 1978.

MOLEY, RAYMOND. "The Vanishing Jury." *Southern California Law Review* 2 (1928): 97.

NARDULLI, PETER. *The Courtroom Elite: An Organizational Perspective on Criminal Justice.* Cambridge, Mass.: Ballinger, 1978.

NARDULLI, PETER, ROY FLEMMING, AND JAMES EISENSTEIN. "Unraveling the Complexities of Decision Making in Face-to-Face Groups: A Contextual Analysis of Plea-Bargained Sentences." *American Political Science Review* 78 (1984): 912.

NATIONAL ADVISORY COMMISSION ON CRIMINAL JUSTICE STANDARDS AND GOALS. *Courts Report.* Washington, D.C.: Government Printing Office, 1973.

NEUBAUER, DAVID W. *Criminal Justice in Middle America.* Morristown, N.J.: General Learning Press, 1974.

NEWMAN, DONALD. *Conviction: The Determination of Guilt or Innocence Without Trial.* Boston: Little, Brown, 1966.

NIMMER, RAYMOND, AND PATRICIA ANN KRAUTHAUS. "Plea Bargaining Reform in Two Cities." *Justice System Journal* 3 (1977): 6–21.

PRESIDENT'S COMMISSION ON LAW ENFORCEMENT AND ADMINISTRATION OF JUSTICE. *Task Force Report: The Courts.* Washington, D.C.: Government Printing Office, 1967.

RHODES, WILLIAM. *Plea Bargaining: Who Gains? Who Loses?* Washington, D.C.: Institute for Law and Social Research, 1978.

ROSETT, ARTHUR, AND DONALD R. CRESSEY. *Justice by Consent.* Philadelphia: J. B. Lippincott, 1976.

RUBENSTEIN, MICHAEL, AND TERESA WHITE. "Plea Bargaining: Can Alaska Live Without It?" *Judicature* 62 (1979): 266.

RUBIN, ALVIN B. "How We Can Improve Judicial Treatment of Individual Cases Without Sacrificing Individual Rights: The Problems of the Criminal Law." *Federal Rules of Decisions* 70 (1976): 176.

RYAN, JOHN PAUL, AND JAMES ALFINI. "Trial Judges' Participation in Plea Bargaining: An Empirical Perspective." *Law and Society Review* 13 (1979): 479–507.

SANBORN, JOSEPH. "A Historical Sketch of Plea Bargaining." *Justice Quarterly* 3 (1986): 111.

SCHELLING, THOMAS. *The Strategy of Conflict.* Cambridge: Harvard University Press, 1960.

SPRINGER, J. FRED. "Burglary and Robbery Plea Bargaining in California: An Organizational Perspective." *The Justice System Journal* 8 (1983): 157.

UHLMAN, THOMAS, AND DARLENE WALKER. "He Takes Some of My Time: I Take Some of His': An Analysis of Judicial Sentencing Patterns in Jury Cases." *Law and Society Review* 14 (Winter 1980): 323–342.

VETRI, DOMINICK R. "Plea Bargaining: Compromises by Prosecutors to Secure Guilty Pleas." *University of Pennsylvania Law Review* 112 (1964): 901.

WINSBERG, JEROME. Telephone interview. July 1977.

For Further Reading

FEELEY, MALCOLM. *The Process Is the Punishment.* New York: Russell Sage Foundation, 1979.

HEUMANN, MILTON. *Plea Bargaining: The Experiences of Prosecutors, Judges and Defense Attorneys.* Chicago: University of Chicago Press, 1978.

KLEIN, JOHN. *Let's Make a Deal.* Lexington, Mass.: D. C. Heath, Lexington Books, 1976.

MATHER, LYNN M. *Plea Bargaining or Trial?* Lexington, Mass.: D. C. Heath, 1979.

MAYNARD, DOUGLAS. *Inside Plea Bargaining: The Language of Negotiation.* New York: Plenum Press, 1984.

MCDONALD, WILLIAM, AND JAMES CRAMER, eds. *Plea Bargaining.* Lexington, Mass.: Lexington Books, 1978.

NEWMAN, DONALD. *Conviction: The Determination of Guilt or Innocence Without Trial.* Boston: Little, Brown, 1966.

CHAPTER 14

Trial

Trials attract more attention than any other step of the criminal process. The national media provide detailed accounts of celebrity trials. The local media offer extensive coverage of trials involving local notables, brazen murderers, and the like. Books, movies, and television use courtroom encounters to entertain. Usually trials attract our attention because we want the answer to the age-old question: did he do it? At times, however, broader questions are raised. Like morality plays of an earlier era, some trials become the center of ritual dramas about good and evil.

The importance of trials extends far beyond the considerable public attention lavished on them. Under the common law, the trial serves as the ultimate forum for vindicating the innocence of the accused. For this reason, the right to be tried by a jury of one's peers is guaranteed in several places in the Bill of Rights.

Given the marked public interest in trials, as well as their centrality to American law, we would expect trials to be the prime ingredient in the criminal court process. They are not. Instead, trials are relatively rare events. As Chapter 13 established, roughly 90 percent of all felony convictions are the product of a guilty plea. In a very fundamental sense, then, a trial represents a deviant case. But at the same time, the few cases that are tried have a major impact on the operations of the entire criminal justice system. Trials are the balance wheel of the process, structuring how members of the courtroom work group bargain cases.

Trials generally proceed in the following steps: jury selection; opening statements; presentation of the state's case; presentation of the defense's case; rebuttal; closing arguments; judge's instructions to the jury; and finally a decision of the lay jurors. This chapter concentrates on the most important aspects of the trial. We will examine the history and function of trials, selection of juries, the prosecutor's approach to trial, the defense attorney's strategies during trial, and how jurors reach a decision. The end of the chapter discusses the important impact trials have on cases not brought to trial, as well as a persistent area of concern—prejudicial pretrial publicity.

History and Function

The primary purpose of the jury is to safeguard citizens against arbitrary law enforcement. Reinforcing this purpose is the jury's role of preventing oppression by the government and providing the accused a "safeguard against the corrupt or overzealous prosecutor and against the complaint, biased, or eccentric judge" (*Williams* v. *Florida,* 399 U.S. 780, 1970).

petit juries

Ideally, juries are made up of fair-minded citizens who represent a cross section of the local community. Once selected, they are the sole judges of the facts of the case. During trial the judge rules on questions of law, but the jury decides the weight of the evidence and the credibility to give to the testimony of witnesses. Trial juries are also called ***petit juries*** to differentiate them from grand juries. The use of juries represents a deep commitment to the role of laymen in the administration of justice. The views and actions of judges and lawyers are constrained by a group of average citizens who are amateurs in the ways of the law (Kalven and Zeisel).

trial by ordeal

The modern heritage of a trial by jury traces its roots deeply into Western history. Used in Athens five or six centuries before the birth of Christ, juries were later employed by the Romans. They reappeared in France during the ninth century and were transferred to England from there. These early bodies, however, served purposes vastly different from those of the modern institution. For example, in England prior to 1066 settling disputes by a trial took one of two forms. Trial by compurgation was based on a community approach. If the defendant could recruit thirty men to certify that he was an honorable person, then he was considered truthful. ***Trial by ordeal*** involved subjecting the accused to torture by fire or water. Those who survived were considered truthful because God had directed it. Trial by ordeal was used by the American Puritans who tested the truthfulness of witnesses by dunking them in a pond; those who did not float were lying.

The concept of the jury functioning as an impartial fact-finding body was first formalized in the Magna Carta of 1215 when English noblemen forced the king to recognize limits on the power of the Crown.

> No Freeman shall be taken or imprisoned, or be disseized of his Freehold, or Liberties, or free Customs, or be outlawed, or exiled or otherwise destroyed, nor will we pass upon him nor condemn him but by lawful Judgment of his peers or by Law of the Land. We will sell to no man, we will not deny or defer to any man, either Justice or right.

This protection applied only to noblemen (freemen). Its extension to the average citizen occurred several centuries later. As with much of English law, this early trial system was clearly oriented to protecting property rights.

In the centuries after the Magna Carta, the legal status of the jury continued to evolve. Early English juries did not determine guilt or innocence. They were composed of witnesses to a crime and served to compel testimony, thus functioning much like the modern-day grand jury. Only later did they become impartial bodies selected from citizens who knew nothing of the alleged event.

By the time the U.S. Constitution was written, jury trials in criminal cases had been in existence in England for several centuries. This legal principle was transferred to the American colonies and later written into the Constitution. The pivotal role that the right to trial by jury plays in American law is underscored by the number of times it is mentioned in the Constitution.

Article III, Section 2 provides that "the trial of all crimes, except cases of impeachment shall be by jury and such trial shall be held in the state where the said crimes shall have been committed." This section not only guarantees the right to a trial by jury to persons accused by the national government of a crime but also specifies that such trials shall be held near the place of the offense. This prevents the government from harassing defendants by trying them far from home.

The Sixth Amendment guarantees that "in all criminal prosecutions, the accused shall enjoy the right to a speedy and public trial, by an impartial jury." The requirement of a public trial prohibits secret trials, a device commonly used by dictators to silence their opponents. The Seventh Amendment provides: "In suits at common law . . . the right to trial by jury shall be preserved." This provision is a historical testament to the fact that the framers of the Constitution greatly distrusted the judges of the day.

Throughout most of our nation's history, these broad constitutional provisions had little applicability to trials in state courts. As part of the Warren Court revolution in criminal justice, however, the Supreme Court ruled that the jury provisions of the Sixth Amendment applied to state as well as federal courts (*Duncan* v. *Louisiana,* 391 U.S. 145, 1968). (Technically the Sixth Amendment was incorporated into the due process clause of the Fourteenth Amendment, which restricts state power.) Subsequent decisions grappled with the problem of defining the precise meaning of the right to trial by jury. The most important issues concerned the scope of the right to a jury trial, the size of the jury, and unanimous versus non-unanimous verdicts.

Scope of the Right to a Trial by Jury

Trial by jury is considered "fundamental to the American scheme of justice" (*Duncan* v. *Louisiana*). But not all persons accused of violating the criminal law are entitled to a jury trial. Youths who are prosecuted as juvenile offenders are typically denied the right to a jury trial. In addition, adult offenders *petty* charged with ***petty offenses*** enjoy no right to be tried by a jury of their peers. *offense* Thus the Sixth Amendment covers only adults charged with serious offenses. In this context, "no offense can be deemed 'petty' for the purposes of the right to trial by jury where imprisonment for more than six months is authorized" (*Baldwin* v. *New York,* 399 U.S. 66, 1970). Some states, such as California, guarantee a jury trial to anyone facing any criminal charge whatsoever, including traffic offenses.

Jury Size

Since the fourteenth century, the size of juries in England has been fixed at twelve jurors. Although some colonies experimented with smaller juries in less important trials, by the time of the American Revolution the number twelve was universally accepted. In *Williams* v. *Florida* (399 U.S. 102, 1970), however, the Supreme Court declared that the number twelve was a "historical accident, wholly without significance except to mystics," and therefore not required by the Constitution. The Court concluded that the six-person jury used in Florida in all but capital cases was large enough to promote group deliberations and to provide a fair possibility of obtaining a representative cross section of the community. Attempts to use juries with even fewer than six members was halted by *Ballew* v. *Georgia* (435 U.S. 223, 1978). The defendant's misdemeanor conviction by a five-member jury was reversed because "the purpose and functioning of the jury in a criminal trial is seriously impaired, and to a constitutional degree, by a reduction in size to below six members."

six-member   Use of ***six-member juries*** has been suggested as a way to relieve conges-
jury   tion of court calendars and reduce court costs for jurors (National Advisory Commission). Thirty-three states have specifically authorized juries of fewer than twelve (see Table 14-1), but most allow smaller juries only in misdemeanor cases. In federal courts defendants are entitled to a twelve-person jury unless the parties stipulate in writing to a small jury. Six-member juries in federal civil cases are quite common, however.

There has been a good deal of debate over whether or not small juries provide the defendant with a fair trial. Critics contend that six-member juries will be more likely to ignore conflicting points of view and will be too hasty in reaching a verdict. Social science evidence suggests there are few differences between six- and twelve-person juries. Both small and large juries, for example, spend about equal time deciding similar cases (Pabst). Research also indicates that small juries do not exclude important points of view in reaching a verdict (Roper, 1979). In terms of the types of verdicts reached, however, the evidence is mixed. A few studies suggest that case outcomes are about the same regardless of jury size. But other studies indicate that twelve-member juries were more likely to vote for the plaintiff in civil cases and were more

TABLE 14-1 State Provisions on Size of Criminal Juries

Twelve-member juries required
Alabama, Hawaii, Illinois, Maine, Maryland, New Jersey, North Carolina, North Dakota, Rhode Island, Vermont, West Virginia, Wisconsin

Juries of fewer than twelve specifically authorized
Alaska, Arizona, Colorado, Connecticut, Florida, Georgia, Idaho, Indiana, Iowa, Kansas, Kentucky, Louisiana, Massachusetts, Michigan, Minnesota, Mississippi, Missouri, Montana, Nebraska, New Hampshire, New Mexico, New York, Ohio, Oklahoma, Oregon, South Carolina, South Dakota, Tennessee, Texas, Utah, Virginia, Washington, Wyoming

Juries of fewer than twelve permitted by agreement
Arkansas, California, Delaware, Nevada, Pennsylvania

SOURCE: Based on data from National Center for State Courts, *Facets of the Jury System: A Survey* (Denver: 1976), pp. 41–44.

generous in their financial awards (Zeisel and Diamond; Beiser). Similarly, a study of 110 juries and a thousand jurors concluded that large juries are slightly more likely to be unable to reach a verdict than smaller ones. Providing a dissenter with an ally increases the ability of the dissenter to resist pressures to conform (Roper, 1980).

Unanimity

Like jury size, the requirement that a jury reach a unanimous decision became a firm rule in England during the fourteenth century. The colonies accepted this rule on the assumption that an agreement by all of the jurors served to legitimize the verdict, giving the community a sense that the conclusion must be correct. These assumptions were shaken, however, by a pair of 1972 decisions. While holding that verdicts in federal criminal trials must be unanimous, findings of guilty by votes of a 9 to 3 and 10 to 2 in state proceedings were upheld by the Supreme Court (*Johnson* v. *Louisiana,* 406 U.S. 356; *Apodaca* v. *Oregon,* 406 U.S. 404). Most state constitutions, however, specifically require unanimous verdicts in criminal trials. Thus only five states (Louisiana, Montana, Oregon, Oklahoma, and Texas) permit ***non-unanimous criminal verdicts.*** In any case, six-member juries must be unanimous (*Burch* v. *Louisiana,* 441 U.S. 130, 1979).

non-unanimous verdict

The purpose of allowing a non-unanimous verdict is as a hedge against a juror who does not agree with the finding of the others. Not only would it reduce the expensive and time-consuming process of conducting a second trial, but it is also likely to reduce deliberation time. Opponents of non-unanimous verdicts argue that the conservative majority on the Burger Court misread the history of the jury with the result that a basic constitutional right is being sacrificed. They point out that proof beyond a reasonable doubt has not been shown if only some of the jurors vote to convict. So far the Court has given no indication what size majority is constitutionally mandated.

Jury Selection

Before the first word of testimony, trials pass through the critical stage of jury selection. Many lawyers believe that trials are won or lost on the basis of which jurors are selected. Juries are chosen in a three-stage process that combines random selection with deliberate choice. The first step is the compilation of a master jury list. Next, the venire—the citizens available for jury duty on a particular date—is randomly drawn from the master jury list. Finally, some members of this jury pool are questioned (in what is called *voir dire*) about possible bias in a specific case. If juries are to function as a fair and impartial body that carefully weighs the facts of the case, it is important that fair and impartial jurors be initially selected. Whether the three stages of jury selection actually produce fair and impartial juries has been the subject of much concern.

Master Jury List

Juries are supposed to be made up of fair-minded laymen, representatives of the community in which the defendant allegedly committed the crime. Therefore the first step in jury selection is the development of procedures that will produce a representative ***cross section of the community*** (Simon and Marshall). These sentiments are well reflected in the Federal Jury Selection and Service Act of 1968, designed to ensure that juries are "selected at random from a fair cross section of the communities in the district or division wherein the court convenes [and that] no citizen shall be excluded from service as a grand or petit juror in the district courts of the United States on account of race, color, religion, sex, national origin, or economic status." This act was prompted by evidence that selection of federal juries was systematically biased. Similar concerns have been expressed about jury selection at the state level.

cross section of the community

The most frequent source for assembling the names for the ***master wheel*** or ***master jury list*** (sometimes called ***jury wheel***) are voter registration lists. These lists have major advantages: they are readily available, frequently updated, and collected in districts within judicial boundaries. Basing the master jury list on voter registration, however, tends to exclude the poor, the young, racial minorities, and the less educated. A recent study found that in one jurisdiction blacks constituted 30 percent of the population but only 17 percent of the jury list. In another jurisdiction, about 20 percent of the population were between the ages of twenty-one and forty-nine, but only 3 percent were on the jury list. In the same jurisdiction 53 percent of the population consisted of women, yet only 17 percent of the jury list did (Kairys et al.). In addition, blacks and Mexican-Americans have been prevented from registering to vote in the South, which meant that these minorities never served on juries.

master jury list (jury wheel)

Because of these limitations, many states as well as the federal government either require or allow the use of other sources—city or telephone directories, utility customer lists, or driver's license lists—in drawing up the master list. The use of multiple sources achieves a better representation of a cross section of the community on jury panels.

Jury panels can be challenged if they fail to include racial or other minorities. Appellate courts have ruled that the master jury list must reflect a representative and impartial cross section of the community. Blacks, Mexican-Americans, and women cannot be systematically excluded from petit juries solely on the basis of race or sex. This does not mean that every jury must include blacks (*Strauder* v. *West Virginia,* 100 U.S. 303, 1880), Mexican-Americans (*Castenada* v. *Partida,* 420 U.S. 482, 1977) or women (*Taylor* v. *Louisiana,* 419 U.S. 522, 1975) if they exist in the community. But such parties may not be denied the opportunity to be chosen for jury service equally with others in the community.

Venire

venire

The jury pool (or ***venire***) is a list or group of people from among whom a trial jury will be selected. Periodically the clerk of court, judge, or jury commissioner determines how many jurors are needed for a given time. A sufficient number of names is then randomly selected from the master jury list, and the sheriff issues a summons for these citizens to appear at the courthouse for jury duty.

Not all those summoned, however, will actually serve on the venire. Virtually all states have laws that require jurors to be citizens of the United States, residents of the locality, of a certain minimum age, and able to understand English. Most states disqualify convicted felons and insane persons. A majority also specify that jurors be of "good character" and/or be "well-informed." Persons who fail to meet these requirements are eliminated from the venire.

statutory exemptions

Others will be excused because of ***statutory exemptions.*** The identities of those exempted from jury duty by statute vary greatly but commonly include judicial and government officials, medical personnel, ministers, educators, and lawyers. Those not exempt by law may still be excused if they can convince the judge that jury duty would work an undue hardship.

Voir Dire

voir dire

Voir dire (Old French for "to speak the truth") refers to the preliminary examination of a prospective juror in order to determine his or her qualifications to serve as a juror. The veniremen are questioned by the attorneys and/or judge about their backgrounds, familiarity with the case, friendship or acquaintance with persons involved in the case (defendant, witness, lawyer), attitudes about certain facts that may arise during trial, and any other matters that may reflect on their willingness and ability to judge the case fairly and impartially.

challenge for cause

peremptory challenge

If during the interrogation it develops that a juror cannot fairly judge the case, the juror may be ***challenged for cause*** by either defense or prosecution. The presiding judge rules on the motion and, if sustained, the juror is excused. In practice, few challenges for cause are made, and even fewer are sustained (Simon and Marshall). ***Peremptory challenge*** is the second—and much more important—technique used by prosecution and defense in influencing who will sit on the jury. Each side has a limited number of peremptory challenges they can use to exclude a juror. Based on hunch, insight, whim, prejudice, or pseudoscience, a lawyer may peremptorily exclude a juror without giving a reason.

Attorneys have traditionally enjoyed carte blanche freedom in exercising peremptory challenges. For twenty-one years the Supreme Court tacitly protected the practice of some prosecutors who used peremptory challenges to keep blacks off the jury in any case involving a black defendant. But in

Batson v. *Kentucky* (54 LW 4425) the Court reversed its earlier decision. Now if there is an apparent pattern of purposeful discrimination, the prosecutor must explain his or her actions and may be ordered to change tactics.

In recent years attorneys have employed the assistance of social scientists to aid them in a more intelligent and systematic use of the *voir dire*. By determining the social characteristics and attitudes of the local population that would be beneficial to the accused, lawyers could reject some jurors while retaining others. These techniques were widely used in the trials of political radicals in the early 1970s. Now their use has broadened. Ford Motor Company, for example, hired jury scholar Hans Zeisel to advise them during the criminal prosecution resulting from the defective gasoline tanks in Pinto automobiles. Whether scientific jury selection is actually helpful has yet to be conclusively shown. In most trials where it has been used, though, the defendants were acquitted.

In practice, attorneys use the *voir dire* for more than just trying to choose a fair and impartial jury. The primary function is to educate the citizen into the role of juror. Attorneys and judges make frequent requests for the juror's assurance that he or she can set aside past experiences and biases to judge the case fairly and objectively. Some practicing attorneys interpret the answers given by the venire person as promises and restate them later in their summation. The questioning of jurors develops rapport between the attorneys and the jurors. In turn, the *voir dire* provides the lawyers the opportunity to attempt to influence jurors' attitudes and perhaps their later vote. Defense attorneys in particular view the *voir dire* as necessary for ensuring that potential jurors will presume that the defendant is innocent until proven guilty. Many lawyers view the *voir dire* as the final safeguard against unstated biases or prejudices by jurors, ensuring a fair and dispassionate jury.

In some areas the *voir dire* has become a time-consuming process. Some cases have consumed six weeks or more in the jury selection process. Usually, though, jury selection is accomplished in less than two hours. The delay caused by jury selection is a cause for concern; also some fear that through the selection process attorneys seek to select jurors prejudiced to their side. As the National Advisory Commission has stated, "A defendant is entitled to an unbiased jury; he is not entitled to a jury biased in his favor" (p. 99).

Jury Duty

jury duty   Every year thousands of Americans are called to serve as jurors. **Jury duty** is currently the only time that citizens are directly required to perform a service for their government. Unfortunately many jurors experience great frustration in the process. They are made to wait endless hours in barren courthouse rooms; minimal compensation often works a hardship because not all employers pay for the time lost from work; and some are apprehensive about criminals in general and criminal courthouses in particular.

In spite of these hardships, however, most citizens express an overall satisfaction with jury duty. Of three thousand jurors surveyed in one study, almost 90 percent stated that they were favorably impressed with jury duty (Pabst).

The report concluded that they "view their experience as a precious opportunity of citizenship rather than an onerous obligation" (p. 164). Just as important, there is every indication that jurors take their job seriously.

Considerable attention is being devoted to reducing the inconvenience of jury duty. Courts in all states use a juror call-in system. In these jurisdictions, jurors can dial a number to learn whether their attendance is needed on a particular day during their term of service. In addition, an increasing number of courts are reducing the number of days a person remains in the jury pool. Traditionally, jurors were asked to serve for a full thirty days. Although only a few were needed for a particular day, the entire pool had to be present in the courthouse each and every working day. A new approach is known as the ***One Day/One Trial jury system,*** which requires a juror to serve either for one day or for the duration of one trial. They are then exempt from jury duty for a year or more (Kasunic). One Day/One Trial jury systems are much more efficient than older practices because they spare many citizens the inconvenience of waiting in courthouses with no trials to hear.

*One Day/
One Trial
jury system*

The Prosecution Presents Its Case

Once the jury has been selected and sworn, the trial begins. (It is a common practice in many courts to select several ***alternate jurors*** who will serve if one of the regular jurors must withdraw during the trial.) Each side is allowed (but not required) to make a brief ***opening statement.*** It is not evidence but is intended to provide the jurors with a guide to the case. Both lawyers argue what they think the evidence will show and highlight areas they think are particularly important.

*alternate
jurors
opening
statement*

After the opening statement, the prosecution presents its main evidence. In preparing for trial, the prosecutor often must wrestle with difficult problems of how to prove each element of the offense. If the burden of proof is not met, the judge will grant the defense motion for an acquittal. How the prosecutor proceeds is affected by two important aspects of the law: the presumption of innocence and rules of evidence.

Q U O T A T I O N

What I don't want is some little old lady who has three locks on her door and who thinks that just because the defendant was arrested and is sitting in court means he is guilty.

Maurice Hattier, *New Orleans Times-Picayune,*
March 19, 1975.

Presumption of Innocence

One of the most fundamental protections recognized in the American criminal justice process is the right to be presumed innocent. The state has the burden of proving the defendant guilty of the alleged crime; the defendant is not required to prove himself or herself innocent. This difference is a fundamental one. A moment's reflection will give an idea of how hard it would be to prove that something did not happen or that a person did not do an alleged criminal

CLOSE-UP

The Jury: Two Hours of Duty

Some 200 of us are gathered in the Jury Assembly Room of the County Courthouse in Martinez on this hot summer day for that unique blend of civic responsibility, tedium and aggravation known as jury duty.

It is 9:30, and a bailiff is telling us that our names have been drawn from voter rolls and DMV registration lists. A few of us comment that the vote isn't really worth all this trouble but that, dammit, a person has to drive. Despite much talk about the money we're losing by being here (jurors get $5 a day plus 15 cents per mile, one-way; as one judge remarked, "I guess they only care if you get here"), most are stoic or even amused by it all.

We'll be here for anywhere from four days to the time it may take us to reach a verdict. Basically we're the markers in a game of judicial bingo, and few of us will even be called, let alone sworn in as jurors. But visions of complex homicides and parades of forensic and/or psychiatric experts dance in many heads—next to visions of shrinking bank accounts and impatient employers.

One graying gent in a brown jumpsuit sniffs irascibly, "If you don't show up they come and get you and throw you in jail, on $1000 bond. The damndest thing is, you can't be called if you've had a felony! Used to be you could get out by saying you were prejudiced, but they won't go for that anymore."

I mention that for a society concerned about both the victim and the accused, there's precious little consideration for the poor duty-bound slobs who decide what's what. Many in the room concur vehemently.

At 2:15 the first panel of 35 names is read, from which 12 good and true will be chosen. I'm on it. We follow a bailiff to a third-floor courtroom and sit in the spectator section. The principals enter: a young black male defendant, a black male DA (district attorney), a white male PD (public defender) and a white female judge, the latter three aged 30 to 40. The defendant is bearded, has short furrowed hair and black horn-rimmed glasses and looks equally like a scam artist or a black-history major at the University of California. He has alert and thoughtful eyes, not the studied indifference or opaque vacancy one usually associates with street criminals.

We jury panelists take an oath that boils down to a promise to be honest and do our best. Twelve names are selected from a tumbler: mine is number two. The judge tells us that as "the judges of the facts" our duty is to be fair and unbiased, and then defines "reasonable doubt" with gray phrases like "abiding conviction" and "moral certainty," whose ambiguity guarantees that we'll frame our own ideas of reasonableness and doubt.

The charge is felony intent to sell marijuana in North Richmond. Juror number seven, about 40, with receding hair, declares: "I feel I'd be helping enforce a bad law. If I have a choice, I'd rather not be here." Juror number four, some 15 years older, says he has an 18-year-old son in a rehab center and fears he'd "be at loggerheads" with juror number seven. Now we're having some fun.

The judge asks us if we have any friends or relations who've been arrested for marijuana use or sale. I reply that several friends of mine were popped for possession when I was in college, around 1968.

"And how many friends would you say?" she asks.

"Well," I shrug, "that was in Berkeley"—a big laugh sweeps the room—"and it was hard to keep track then. In fact, one of them is a lawyer

act, for it is very difficult to rule out all possibilities. Therefore a defendant is cloaked with the legal shield of innocence through the criminal justice system.

In meeting the obligation to prove the defendant guilty, the prosecution is required to prove the defendant guilty beyond a reasonable doubt. ***Reasonable doubt*** is a legal yardstick measuring the sufficiency of the evidence. This burden of proof does not require that the state establish absolute certainty by eliminating all doubt—just reasonable doubt.

reasonable doubt

---

today, practicing in this area."

Now we're on a laugh-roll, as the judge asks, "Well, how about between three and six?"

"Yes, I'd say so."

"And did any of these cases go to trial?"

"Yes. The guy who became a lawyer. Actually, I think that's why he became a lawyer."

Lots of mirth for everyone, including Her Honor now, with the exception of the DA, who isn't happy to have pot established here as a laughing matter. He eyes me dubiously. . . .

Most jurors are questioned at length. This is no cut-and-dried matter, like kidnapping or burning down an orphanage, but it involves a substance many find more benign than either the laws against it or the tax money spent to enforce them. Both attorneys are impressively smooth, erudite, ingratiating and able to reduce abstractions to a comprehensible distillate for a jury whose reading habits range from "computer journals" to "mostly TV Guide."

The DA questions me about any relevant attitudes I may have. The high point comes when he asks if I'm familiar with North Richmond, and I note, "Well, a former TV set of mine was once found there." This brings down the house. . . .

The next day the PD asks us our hobbies, our lifestyles, whether we'd defend ourselves if accused and whether we'd be prejudiced against a defendant who doesn't take the stand to testify. Things get intriguing—the DA has said no actual marijuana would be introduced in evidence; now it looks like a case of the police's word against . . . whose? Could we think of reasons an innocent man might have not to testify, he asks? Sure; but not as many as a guilty man would have.

The PD stresses the difference between *innocent* and *not guilty*: You may doubt a man's innocence, but if you also doubt his guilt, he goes free. Under the tight lexicon of jurisprudence, anything short of "definitely guilty" means not guilty. Indeed, all manner of trial laws state explicitly how we must vote, given various if-then considerations. The idea is to narrow the element of choice for us as much as possible, limiting the possibilities of "truth" to the minuscule dimensions of that which is entered as evidence—i.e. limited information presented for purely ulterior reasons by adversaries.

"Don't worry," the process seems to be assuring us. "Don't worry how you feel about pot, or blacks, or personal liberty, or even right or wrong. We've factored all that in and reduced it to your choice of two contradictory statements. Just pick the one you believe."

Fine. But then the process adds all the vagueness and subjectivity one can compact into two words: "reasonable doubt."

The PD asks us, lastly, "Do you believe you're the kind of person who belongs on this jury?" A vicious question for any honest soul, involving as it does the issue of "the kind of person" one truly is.

Finally come the peremptory challenges, of which each side has a specified number. The DA "thanks and excuses" juror number ten, then number seven, and then, at 1:47 of our second day, number two—me. "Surprise," he says, smiling, with cheery sarcasm. "We'll miss you," says the judge.

I don't know how the trial came out, though other panelists later told me nine prospective jurors were dismissed before 12 were seated. But the system worked at least in my respect: It got rid of me and my biases. I hope it worked as well for whichever side was in the right.

Mostly, I hope it works as well for me if I ever wind up facing the jury box, and not in it.

Robert S. Wieder, "The Jury: Two Hours of Duty," in "This World," *San Francisco Examiner and Chronicle,* September 2, 1984, pp. 16*ff.*

Rules of Evidence

evidence

real evidence

testimony

direct evidence

circumstantial evidence

The state tries to convince the jury to return a guilty verdict by presenting *evidence.* Evidence can be classified into real evidence, testimony, direct evidence, and circumstantial evidence. *Real evidence* includes objects of any kind—guns, maps, records and documents, for example. The bulk of the evidence during criminal trial consists of *testimony*—statements by competent witnesses. *Direct evidence* refers to eyewitness evidence. Testimony that a person was seen walking in the rain is direct evidence that a person walked in the rain. Indirect evidence is called *circumstantial evidence.* Circumstantial evidence can be used to prove the truth or falsity of a fact in issue. Testimony that the person was seen indoors with wet shoes is circumstantial evidence that the person had walked in the rain.

rules of evidence

The presentation of evidence during trial is governed by principles called *rules of evidence.* A trial is an adversary proceeding in which the rules of evidence resemble the rules of a game with the judge acting as an impartial umpire. These rules of evidence have developed primarily out of appellate court decisions rather than from legislative enactments. Although they may seem to be a fixed set of legal rules, they are not. Like all other legal principles, they are general propositions that courts must apply to specific instances. During such applications judges use a balancing test, carefully weighing whether the trial would be fairer with or without the piece of evidence in question (Rothstein).

privileged communication

The purpose of the adversary process is to get at the truth: the primary purpose of rules of evidence is to help achieve this end. For instance, a judge who feels that the jury would give certain evidence undue weight or would be greatly prejudiced would not allow that evidence to be presented. Some rules of evidence, however, have purposes other than truthfulness. Because the law seeks to protect the secrecy of communications (legally called *privileged communications*) between doctor and patient, lawyer and client, and husband and wife, such communications are not normally admissible in open court. Similarly, under the exclusionary rule illegally seized evidence is inadmissible (even if trustworthy) because the laws seek to discourage such activities. Most of the major rules of evidence, however, are directed at achieving the truth. These principles may be briefly summarized under the headings of trustworthiness and relevance.

trustworthiness

best evidence rule

Trustworthiness. The basic criterion for admissibility of evidence is *trustworthiness.* The object of the evidentiary system is to ensure that only the most reliable and credible facts, statements, or testimony are presented to the fact finder. The *best evidence rule* illustrates the point. Ordinarily only the original of a document or object is admissible because a copy or facsimile may have been altered. Similarly a judge may rule that a person of unsound mind or a very young child is not a competent witness because they may not understand what was seen or heard. The mere fact that evidence is legally ruled to be competent does not, of course, mean that the jury must believe it. A wife's alibi for her husband may be competent evidence, but the jury may choose not to believe her.

hearsay

Hearsay is secondhand evidence. It is testimony a witness provides that is not based on personal knowledge but is a repetition of what another said. An example is someone's testimony that "my brother Bob told me he saw Jones enter the store that evening." The general rule is that hearsay evidence is not admissible because it is impossible to test its truthfulness; there is no way to cross-examine as to the truth of the matter. There are exceptions, however. In some situations, dying declarations constitute a hearsay exception. In addition, hearsay evidence may be admissible if the defendant is charged with conspiracy. There are many such exceptions; the rules for whether or not hearsay may be used are among the more complex in the law.

relevance

immaterial
(irrelevant)
evidence

Relevance.   To be admissible, evidence must also be **relevant**; there must be a valid reason for introducing the statement, object, or testimony. Evidence not related to an issue at trial is termed **immaterial** or **irrelevant.** If, for example, a defendant is accused of murder, the issue is whether he killed the deceased. Evidence as to motive, intention to commit the offense, and ability to commit the offense are all relevant evidence. But information about the defendant's character—prior convictions or a reputation for dishonesty, for instance—would not normally be admissible because it is not material to the issue of whether the defendant committed this crime. If, however, the defendant testifies, such evidence would be admissible during **rebuttal** for the sole purpose of **impeaching** (casting doubt on) his credibility.

rebuttal
impeach

Traditionally common law allowed a defendant accused of rape to introduce evidence concerning the victim's past sexual activities. The past conduct of the defendant is not admissible, however. The women's movement views such a dual standard as sexist and argues that it works to discourage a rape victim from testifying at trial. California and Michigan, among other states, have adopted a new rule that past sexual activity is not generally relevant and therefore is inadmissible at trial. This example illustrates that rules of evidence touch on important social issues of interest to people other than lawyers.

Objections to the admission of evidence.   During trial, attorneys must be continuously alert, ready to make timely objections to the admission of evidence. After a question is asked but before the witness answers, attorneys may object if the evidence is irrelevant, immaterial, or hearsay. The court then rules on the objection and thus permits the evidence to be admitted or not. The judge may rule immediately or may request the lawyers to argue the legal point out of the hearing of the jury (termed a **side-bar conference**). If the objection is to a line of testimony, it may be necessary for the jury to retire to the jury room while the judge hears the testimony and makes a ruling. If the testimony may be admitted, it is then repeated before the jury.

side-bar
conference

Occasionally inadmissible evidence will inadvertently be heard by the jury. For example, in answering a valid question, a witness may overelaborate. When this occurs and the attorney objects, the judge will instruct the jury to **disregard the evidence.** But even with such a cautionary warning, jurors may still be influenced by that piece of evidence. If the erroneous evidence is deemed so prejudicial that a warning to disregard is not sufficient, the judge may declare a **mistrial.**

disregard
the evidence

mistrial

The Defense Presents Its Case

Although we generally expect a trial to be a battle between the prosecutor, who asserts that the defendant committed the crime, and the defendant, who maintains innocence, such a view greatly oversimplifies the tactical decisions involved. In deciding on the defense strategy at trial, attorneys must carefully consider the strengths and weaknesses of the state's case, the character of the defendant, how credible the defense witness may be, and how juries are likely to react. In weighing the various factors, defense attorneys invariably start from a position of weakness. They seldom are able to pick cases they wish to try. If the prosecutors consider the case to be weak, they may dismiss it rather than risk an acquittal or offer such a good deal that the defendant cannot turn it down. Defense attorneys are sometimes forced to trial even when they believe the client's story is implausible or dishonest. They must also consider whether *bench trial*   the trial should be before a jury or only the judge (a ***bench trial***). Most states allow defendants to waive their right to a jury trial and be tried by a judge. The other states require the prosecution to agree to a bench trial. Although studies indicate that a judge is more likely to find guilt than a jury, in some instances the defendant may wish to avoid a jury trial either because the crime is very inflammatory or because the defendant is using a technical legal defense that a jury is not likely to understand. Most trials, however, are jury trials. Within these constraints, the defense attorney can construct a case along one of three broad lines: reasonable doubt, a denial, or an affirmative defense.

Reasonable Doubt

Because the defendant is presumed innocent, the defense does not have to call any witnesses or introduce any evidence. Through cross-examination the attorney can try to undermine the state's case and create in the jury's mind a reasonable doubt as to whether the defendant committed the crime. The key to such a strategy is the skillful use of the right to confront witnesses, one of the criminal court procedures enumerated in the Sixth Amendment: "In all criminal prosecutions, the accused shall enjoy the right . . . to be confronted with witnesses against him." One meaning of this provision is that the defendant must be present during trial—that is, the state cannot try defendants who are absent. (Defendants who disrupt the trial may be removed, however.) *cross-* The right to be confronted with witnesses guarantees the right to ***cross-*** *examination* ***examination.*** As we have seen, a fundamental tenet of the adversary system is the need to test evidence for truthfulness, and the primary means of testing the truthfulness of witnesses is cross-examination. The following description of a trial illustrates how a defense attorney uses cross-examination to build a reasonable doubt case.

> Xinos [public defender] . . . on cross examination . . . picked skillfully at Parrish's [state's attorney's] case. Playing to his hard hat on the jury, he asked Castelli [victim] whether the stick-up man had one or two hands on the gun. "Only one, sir," said Castelli. "And was the trigger pulled in rapid succession— click-click-click?" Xinos pressed. "Yes, sir," said Castelli, and Xinos had his point: it takes two hands to keep pulling the slide and clicking the trigger.

Next came Patrolman Joe Higgins, who remembered, under Xinos's pointed cross-examination, that Castelli had described the gunman as weighing 185 pounds—30 more than Payne [defendant] carries on his spindly 6-foot-1 frame. Payne had nearly botched that point by wearing a billowy, cape-shaped jacket to court, but Xinos persuaded him to fold it up and sit on it so the jurors could see how bony he really was. The 30-pound misunderstanding undercut Castelli's identification of Payne—and suddenly the People and their lawyer, Walter Parrish, were in trouble. (Goldman and Holt: 33)

If a defendant has no valid defense but will not plead, the defense attorney's only choice is to force the state to prove its case and hope to create a reasonable doubt in the minds of the jury. But many experienced defense attorneys believe this is the weakest defense. They believe that to gain an acquittal the defense must give the jury something to "hang their hat on." Thus they must consider whether to let the defendant testify.

The Defendant as Witness

The most important part of defense strategy is the decision whether the defendant will testify. The Fifth Amendment—"No person . . . shall be compelled in any criminal case to be a witness against himself"—protects defendants from being compelled to take the witness stand. If the defendant chooses not to testify, no comment or inference can be drawn from this fact. The prosecutor cannot argue before the jury, "If he is innocent, why doesn't he take the stand and say so?" (*Griffin* v. *California,* 380 U.S. 609, 1965). But this legal protection aside, jurors are curious about the defendant's version of what happened. They expect the defendant to protest innocence and in the secrecy of the jury room can ponder aloud why the defendant refused to testify.

Defendants may, of course, waive the privilege against self-incrimination and take the stand in their own defense. In considering whether to call the defendant to the stand, a major concern of the defense attorney is whether the story is believable. If it is not, the jury will probably dismiss it, thus doing more harm to the defendant's case than if he had not testified at all.

A defendant who takes the stand is subject to cross-examination like any other witness. Because cross-examination is broader than direct examination, the defendant cannot tell a mere part of the story and conceal the rest. Once the defendant chooses to testify, the state can bring out all the facts surrounding the event testified to. Just as important, once the defendant has taken the stand, the state can impeach the defendant's credibility by introducing into evidence any prior felony convictions. The defense attorney must make the difficult decision whether to arouse juries' suspicion by not letting the accused testify or letting the defendant testify and be subjected to possibly damaging cross-examination.

alibi defense   **Alibi defense.**   In an *alibi defense,* defendants argue that at the time the crime was committed they were somewhere else. They may independently testify to this and/or call witnesses to testify that during the time in question, the defendant was drinking beer at Mary's or shopping downtown with some friends. Some states require that defendants provide a notice (warning) of alibi defense prior to trial along with a list of witnesses to be called to support this assertion. A notice of alibi defense allows the prosecution the opportunity to investigate the witness's story before trial. Prosecutors who suspect that witnesses have carefully rehearsed the alibi testimony can use clever cross-examination to ask questions out of sequence, hoping to catch each witness in a series of contradictions. Prosecutors can also call rebuttal witnesses to suggest that the witnesses were long-time friends of the defendant who are likely to lie.

Affirmative Defense

affirmative defense

An *affirmative defense* goes beyond denying the facts of the prosecutor's case; it sets out new facts and arguments that might win for the defendant. In essence affirmative defenses are legal excuses that should result in a finding of not guilty. They also require the defense to assume the burden of proving these defenses. Although the state has the ultimate duty of proving the defendant guilty beyond a reasonable doubt, under an affirmative defense, the defense has the duty called ''the burden of going forward with the evidence.''

Q U O T A T I O N

Now I submit that the jury is the worst possible enemy of this ideal of the "supremacy of law." For "jury-made law" is, par excellence, capricious and arbitrary, yielding the maximum in the way of lack of uniformity, of unknowability. . . . Yet little . . . is done to ensure that these . . . jurymen, "act upon principles and not according to arbitrary will," or to put effective restraints upon their worst prejudices. Indeed, through the general verdict, coupled with the refusal of the courts to inquire into the way the jurors have reached their decisions, everything is done to give the widest outlet to jurors' biases. If only a jury trial is properly conducted according to the procedural rules, the jurors' decision may be as arbitrary as they please in such circumstances, their discretion becomes wholly unregulated and unreviewable. . . .

If anywhere we have a "government of men," in the worst sense of the phrase, it is in the operations of the jury system.

Jerome Frank, *Courts on Trial: Myth and Reality in American Justice* (New York: Princeton University Press, 1973), p. 132 (Copyright 1949 by Jerome Frank; copyright renewed © 1976 by Princeton University Press). Reprinted by permission of Princeton University Press.

From the defendant's perspective an affirmative defense is tricky, for often it means that the defendant admits the prosecutor's case. Moreover, juries often view such defense strategies as an attempt by the defendant to wiggle out of a guilty verdict. The most common affirmative defenses are self-defense, insanity, duress, and entrapment (that is, someone induced the defendant to commit the crime).

Rebuttal

After the defense rests its case, the prosecution may call rebuttal witnesses, whose purpose is either to discredit the testimony of a previous witness or discredit the witness. The prosecutor may call a rebuttal witness to show that the previous witness could not have observed what she said she did because she was somewhere else at the time. Or the prosecutor may call witnesses or otherwise present evidence to show that the previous witnesses have dishonorable reputations. The rules of evidence regarding rebuttal witnesses are complex. In general, evidence may be presented in rebuttal that could not have been used during the prosecution's case in main. For example, the prosecution may legitimately inform the jury of the previous convictions of defendants who take the stand in an attempt to impeach their credibility.

The End of the Trial

closing argument

When all the evidence has been presented and both sides have rested (that is, completed the introduction of evidence), each side has the opportunity to make a *closing argument* to the jury. Closing arguments can be very important because they allow each side to sum up the facts in its favor and indicate why they believe a verdict of guilty or not guilty is in order. The prosecutor will carefully sum up the facts of the case, often tying together into a coherent pattern what appeared during the trial to be isolated or unimportant matters. They also typically call upon jurors to do their duty and punish the defendant who has committed the crime. The defense attorney will highlight the evidence favorable to the defendant, criticize the witnesses for the state, and show why they should not be believed. Finally the defense will call upon the jurors to do their sworn duty and return a not guilty verdict. Closing arguments to the jury call for lawyers to muster all the art and skill of their profession. They are often the most dramatic parts of the trial. There is a fine line, however, between persuasiveness and unnecessary emotionalism. Many jury verdicts have been reversed on appeal because the prosecutor interjected prejudicial statements into the closing argument.

Jury Instructions

jury instructions

The jury decides the facts of the case, but the judge determines the law. Therefore the court instructs the jury as to the meaning of the law applicable to the facts of the case. These *instructions to the jury* include discussions of general legal principles (innocent until proven guilty, proof beyond a reasonable doubt, and so forth), as well as specific instructions on the elements of the crime in the case and what specific actions the government must prove before there can be a conviction. If the defendant has raised a defense like insanity or duress, the judge instructs the jury as to the meaning of these defenses according to the law in that jurisdiction. In some states judges are also allowed to comment on the evidence. That is, they can express their own views on the credibility of the witnesses, the probabilities of certain acts occurring, and the truth of the matters testified to. Finally the judge instructs the jury on possible verdicts in the case and provides a written form for each verdict of "guilty" and "not guilty." Depending on the state or federal law involved, the jury may also have the option of choosing alternative forms of guilty verdicts called *lesser included offenses.* In a murder case, for example, the jury may find the defendant guilty of murder in the first degree, murder in the second degree, or manslaughter, or they may acquit on all charges.

charging
conference

Instructions to the jury are prepared by the judge and the attorneys during a special ***charging conference*** preceding jury deliberations. The prosecution and defense each draft the instructions they think the judge should give to the jury. The judge chooses the instruction that seems most applicable to the case. Each side therefore has an opportunity to enter on the record objections to the judge's instructions, thus preserving the issue for later appeal. Particularly in technical cases like embezzlement or fraud, the judge's instructions to the jury can greatly affect the final verdict. If the judge adopts a very narrow definition of the crime in question, the instructions to the jury virtually mandate an acquittal. The instructions are written out, signed by the judge, and then read to the jury. Some judges allow the jurors to take a copy of the instructions into the jury room as a guide.

C O N T R O V E R S Y

Judge's Charge to Jury May Seal Fate of Goetz

NEW YORK—Every morning for nearly six weeks, the judge in the trial of Bernhard Goetz has carried the same manila file folder under his arm as he strides to the bench in state Supreme Court in Manhattan.

The folder contains scrawled notes that the judge, Acting Justice Stephen Crane, has written to himself, typed drafts of specific legal language composed by his clerks and lengthy photocopied passages of the penal law. It is what the judge calls a "working draft" of the instructions, or charge, that he must give the jurors just before they retire to deliberate Goetz's fate. By all accounts, the fold-

er's contents loom larger and larger in importance as the trial nears its conclusion.

Both prosecution and defense attorneys say the wording of the charge, which is to be worked out in a hearing out of the jury's presence, is crucial. At stake are the signposts of the law—intent, justification and reasonableness—that the jurors will have to follow in reaching a verdict. It is a map that legal experts say is crucial in the Goetz case because so much of the jury's task deals with perceptions and interpretations, rather than simply deciding whether Goetz did what he is accused of doing.

Goetz, 39, is charged with attempted murder, assault, reckless endangerment and illegal weapons possession. He admits shooting four teenagers on a downtown subway in December 1984, and admits possessing the unlicensed weapon used in the shootings.

This leaves the jury, which is expected to get the case next week, to decide whether those actions were criminal or not, or whether, as Goetz asserts, the action was justified self-defense in the face of a robbery and the threat of physical violence.

These are among the key undecided issues of the judge's charge:

The court's instructions to the jury are a formal lecture on the law and are delivered in a formal manner. Because faulty jury instructions are a principal basis for appellate court reversal of the trial verdict, judges are careful in their wordings. Still, the net effect is that instructions to juries contain extensive amounts of legal jargon not readily understood by nonlawyers. There have been some efforts to increase jurors' understanding of these vital matters (Ellwork, Sales, and Alfini; Severance and Loftus). An experiment in Florida found that better instructions clarifying the meaning of the judge's charge to the jury did increase understanding. At the same time, juries still did not have an accurate knowledge of the law. For example, the Florida jury instructions stress that a defendant is presumed innocent until proven guilty by the evidence beyond any reasonable doubt. Yet after seeing and hearing the modern instruction on this matter, only 50 percent of the jurors understood that the defendant did not have to present any evidence of innocence; 10 percent were uncertain as to what the presumption of innocence was; and a small but still important 2 percent still believed that the burden of proof of innocence rested with the defendant (Strawn and Buchanan).

The Jury Decides

How juries decide has long fascinated lawyers and laymen alike. Jury deliberations are secret, and therefore there is great curiosity about what goes on behind the locked and guarded jury room door. What factors motivate a decision has always been an intriguing question. Until the deliberations begin, jurors have

---

• Whether a different legal standard of self-defense may be considered by the jurors if they find that a robbery was, in fact, in progress, as Goetz claims.

• Whether the jurors will be told by the judge that they must convict Goetz if they find sufficient evidence, or that they have an option of acquitting him on the basis of conscience even if his guilt is technically established by the prosecution.

• Whether the prosecutor's assertion that Goetz acted irrationally could undermine his own argument that Goetz consciously intended to murder and assault the four youths, one of whom remains paralyzed from the chest down.

"It really comes down to the intricacies," said one of Goetz's attorneys, Mark Baker, who was expected to argue for the defense at the hearing, called the charge conference.

Robbery Issue Is Key

One of the main issues at the conference concerns how the jurors are told to measure the actions of a person in the face of what he perceives to be a robbery. The prosecution, for example, argues that the defendant must be shown to be "reasonable" in his belief that a robbery was in progress, and also reasonable in believing that deadly force was necessary in the face of that robbery.

The defense position, by contrast, is that only the belief in the robbery itself must be valid, and that beyond that, the jurors should not be asked to judge how much force was excessive.

The issue of the jury's conscience, called the principle of "nullification," was raised by the defense, and is primarily aimed at what Goetz's attorneys said are the toughest aspect of the case for them—the illegal weapons charges.

Note: Bernhard Goetz was later acquitted of attempted murder but was found guilty of possessing an unlicensed revolver, a felony.

"Judge's Charge to Jury May Seal Fate of Goetz," *New Orleans Times-Picayune*, June 7, 1987, p. 6; copyright 1987 The New York Times Company. Reprinted by permission.

been passive observers. They are not allowed to ask witnesses direct questions. A juror may pass a question to the judge, who may raise it or ignore it. In most courtrooms jurors are also prohibited from taking notes during the trial. But after the charge to the jury, it is the lawyers', judge's, and defendant's turn to wait passively, often in tense anticipation, for the jury's decision. During

jury
deliberations

deliberations the jury may request further instructions or clarifications from the judge about the applicable law. Juries may also request to have portions of the testimony read in open court.

Because these deliberations are secret, research on this process is indirect. Much of what we know about how juries decide is based either by directly observing mock juries or by indirectly asking jurors to recall what occurred in the jury room. The major studies on jury deliberation were conducted by a team of researchers at the University of Chicago Law School. These studies found that rates of participation varied with social status. Men talked more than women. The better educated also participated more frequently. Persons with high-status occupations were more likely to be chosen as foremen (Strodtbeck et al.; Simon). Most of the jury discussions concerned trial procedures, opinions about the trial, and personal reminiscences. There was far less discussion of either the testimony or the judge's instructions to the jury (James).

hung jury

In the federal courts and forty-five of the states, the jury's decision must be unanimous. If the jury becomes deadlocked and cannot reach a verdict, the trial ends with a ***hung jury.*** The prosecutor then has the option of trying the defendant again. In most cases juries are able to agree on a verdict with little deliberation. After interviewing jurors in over two hundred criminal cases in Chicago and Brooklyn, the University of Chicago researchers found that almost all juries took a vote as soon as they retired to chambers. In 30 percent of these cases, only one vote was necessary to reach a unanimous verdict. In 90 percent of the rest of these cases, the majority on the first ballot eventually won out (Broeder). Most important, this research found that only very rarely did a lone juror produce a hung jury. The psychological pressures associated with small group discussions are so great that a single juror can buck predominant sentiment only if he or she can find at least one ally. Thus Kalven and Zeisel concluded that jury deliberations "do not so much decide the case as bring about a consensus" (p. 488).

The Verdict

verdict

After the jury informs the court that a decision has been reached, the judge, prosecutor, defense attorney, and defendant reassemble in the courtroom. Once the ***verdict*** has been publicly announced, either party can request that the jury be polled with each juror voicing his or her vote in open court.

How often do juries convict? Given that most of the easy cases have already been either dismissed or disposed of by a plea of guilty, we might expect that the defendant's chances at trial are roughly fifty-fifty; but in reality, juries convict two thirds of the time (Roper and Flango).

In evaluating the jury system, researchers have tried to discover whether judges view cases differently than juries do. Harry Kalven and Hans Zeisel attempted to answer this question by comparing, in more than 3,500 criminal trials, jury verdicts to the decisions judges would have made. Overall, judge and jury agreed three out of four times, which suggests that the evidence in the case is the primary factor shaping the jury's verdict. Judge and jury disagreed 22 percent of the time, however, with the jury voting acquittal when the judge would have convicted.

The finding by Kalven and Zeisel that judges convict at a higher rate than juries has been challenged by two recent studies. Roper and Flango examined data on juries for all fifty states and found that juries convicted felons at a much higher rate than did judges, whereas judges convicted non-felons at a much higher rate than juries. Another study, this time of federal courts, reached the same conclusion: juries convicted those accused of felonies more often than judges (Levine). Thus disagreements between judge and jury appear to vary according to the seriousness of the offense.

Post-Conviction Review

acquittal

A trial verdict of *acquittal* (not guilty) ends the case. The defendant can leave the courthouse a free person. Bond is immediately canceled and the person cannot be charged with the same offense again. A verdict of guilty, however, means that further proceedings will occur. The defendant must be sentenced (Chapters 15 and 16). In addition the guilty party can take further steps to contest the finding of guilt by filing post-verdict motions, appealing, and perhaps pursuing post-conviction remedies.

Post-Verdict Motions

post-verdict motions

If the jury returns a verdict of guilty, the defendant still has certain opportunities to be retried or to have the conviction dismissed. A guilty defendant may file *post-verdict motions,* which are heard prior to sentencing. These motions provide the defense attorney the opportunity to re-argue alleged mistakes made at trial. Thus the trial judge is given the opportunity to change his or her mind if she or he is convinced that any adverse decision made against the defendant was erroneous.

Post-verdict motions generally fall into two categories. One is a motion in arrest of judgment, which argues that errors in the actual trial require that the case be dismissed and the defendant discharged. In essence counsel is asking the court to reverse the jury decision. A common ground is the assertion that the evidence was insufficient for the jury to return a verdict of guilty. A second type of post-verdict motion is a motion for a new trial, which asserts that serious errors were made at trial by either the trial judge or the prosecutor and therefore the guilty verdict should be set aside and a new trial granted. The most common grounds are newly discovered evidence and errors committed during trial or pretrial hearings. Post-verdict motions are largely a formality; few are ever granted.

Appeal

appeal

An *appeal* asks a higher court to review the actions of a lower court in order to correct mistakes or injustices. The prosecutor cannot appeal a verdict of

double jeopardy

not guilty. The Fifth Amendment guarantees, "Nor shall any person be subject for the same offense to be twice put in jeopardy of life or limb." The purpose of this protection against **double jeopardy** is to prevent repeated harassment of an accused person and reduce the danger of convicting an innocent one. Once a not guilty verdict is returned, jeopardy is said to attach. Prior to a not guilty verdict, however, prosecutors may file an interlocutory (non-final) appeal on certain pretrial rulings that substantially hinder the state's ability to proceed with its case. For example, if the trial court suppressed a defendant's confession or excluded physical evidence because of an illegal search and seizure, the prosecution may file an interlocutory appeal arguing that the judge's ruling was in error.

appellate process

Unlike unsuccessful prosecutors, guilty defendants have the right to appeal. The major steps in the **appellate process** are as follows.

1. The appeal is initiated by filing a written notice of appeal within a specified number of days.
2. A transcript of the trial court proceedings is prepared and provided the appellate court.
3. Briefs are filed by the opposing parties.
4. If there are to be oral arguments, a hearing is scheduled and the arguments heard.
5. The court deliberates and announces its decision, which is often in writing, explaining the reasons for the conclusion reached.

right to one appeal

All appeals from U.S. District Courts and most appeals from state courts of general jurisdiction are heard by intermediate courts of appeals. In the less populous states, which do not have intermediate appellate bodies, the initial appeal is filed with the court of last resort (see Chapter 3). After the first reviewing body has reached a decision, the **right to one appeal** has been exhausted. Any further review is at the discretion of the next higher court. Defendants may request further review either to the state supreme court or the U.S. Supreme Court, but only a relative handful of these requests are granted. Most appeals go no farther than the first reviewing body.

appellant

On appeal, the **appellant** (the person bringing the appeal) commonly raises objections to trial procedures; defects in jury selection, improper admission of evidence during the trial, incompetent assistance of counsel, and mistaken interpretations of the law are some examples. The appellant may also claim constitutional violations, including illegal search and seizure, improper questioning of the defendant by the police, or the identification of the defendant through a defective police line-up (see Chapter 12). Finally, some defendants who have pled guilty may seek to set aside the plea of guilty on the basis of ineffective assistance of counsel or because the plea was not voluntary.

affirm

In the vast majority of appeals, the defendant's conviction is **affirmed.** After reviewing the lower court record, the reviewing body court determines that no legal errors occurred or that any error that did occur was harmless. If the appellate court finds that errors were made by the judge, the jury, the prosecutor, or the police, the conviction is **reversed and remanded;** that is, the verdict of guilty is set aside and the case is remanded (sent back) to the

reverse and remand

trial court. Often the defendant is tried a second time, but not always. On occasion the reviewing body will allow a retrial only with key prosecutorial evidence from the first trial not admissible. Thus, the state's case may be so weakened that the charges will be dismissed or a plea taken to a less serious offense. Although the public perceives that appellate courts free many defendants, in reality appellate courts only rarely reverse. During 1985 only 9 percent of federal criminal appeals were reversed compared to 16 percent for all appeals. Similarly, only 12 percent of appellants win in Louisiana (Neubauer).

Post-Conviction Remedies

post-conviction remedies

After the appellate process has ended, state as well as federal prisoners may challenge their convictions in federal courts on certain constitutional grounds. These post-conviction remedies are collateral attacks, meaning they are attempts to avoid the effects of a court decision by bringing a different court proceeding. *Post-conviction remedies* differ from appeals in several important ways. First, they may be filed only by those actually in prison. Second, they may raise only constitutional defects, not technical ones. Third, they may be somewhat broader than appeals. An appeal is limited to objections made by the defense during the trial. Post-conviction petitions, however, can bring up issues not raised during trial, assert constitutional protections that have developed since the original trial, and contest conditions of confinement. Finally, they are unlimited in number. A prisoner can file numerous petitions at all levels of the court system; this provides the procedural basis for lengthy challenges to capital punishment.

habeas corpus

Post-conviction remedies are collectively referred to as habeas corpus relief. *Habeas corpus* (Latin for "you have the body") is a term for a writ that is the instrument to bring an accused party immediately before a court or judge. Section 9 of Article I of the United States Constitution provides that "[t]he Privilege of the Writ of Habeas Corpus shall not be suspended unless when in Cases of Rebellion or Invasion the public Safety may require it." This provision traces its roots to seventeenth-century England, when the king's officers often detained Englishmen without ever filing charges. The writ of habeas corpus has been described as the great writ because it prevents the government from jailing citizens without ever filing charges. Many totalitarian regimes have no such protections; even some Western democracies allow the police or prosecutors to detain persons suspected of crimes for up to a year without formally accusing the person of any wrongdoing.

Originally, habeas corpus was thought of only as an extraordinary means to determine the legality of executive detention prior to trial. Virtually the only way one could get a state criminal conviction reviewed in the federal courts was to exhaust all remedies in the state courts and then seek review by the U.S. Supreme Court. But the great writ of liberty has undergone considerable transformation in the last decades. In three 1963 decisions, for example, the Warren Court greatly expanded the application of habeas corpus, making it much easier for state prisoners to seek judicial relief in federal courts (*Fay* v. *Noia,* 372 U.S. 391; *Towsend* v. *Sain,* 372 U.S. 391; and *Sanders* v. *United States,* 373 U.S. 1).

These decisions opened the floodgate for federal review. The number of habeas petitions jumped from about two thousand in 1960 to twenty-five thousand in the 1980s. Whether the actual workload of the federal courts increased as greatly as the number of petitions did is an open question. Most decisions are made on the basis of the papers. More time-consuming evidentiary hearings are relatively rare. How often prisoners actually win depends on the time period in question. In 1970 more than twelve thousand such petitions were granted—an indication that state courts were very slowly adopting the new procedural requirements of the Warren Court revolution in criminal justice. By the 1980s, however, prisoners were rarely successful; fewer than 2 percent gained release.

The right of convicted offenders to seek virtually unlimited review through habeas corpus proceedings has sparked a heated debate. The massive increase in federal habeas petitions has produced numerous calls to reduce or eliminate such review. Critics argue that post-conviction petitions contribute to the heavy caseload of the federal courts, are often frivolous, and undermine the value of a final determination of guilt. These strong arguments probably influenced the conservative Burger Court to restrict the grounds for prisoner petitions. In one major ruling, for example, the court held that if state courts had provided a fair hearing, federal courts could not consider Fourth Amendment search and seizure questions in habeas corpus proceedings (*Stone* v. *Powell*, 428 U.S. 465, 1976).

Trials as Balancing Wheels

Trials exert a major influence on the operation of the entire criminal court process. Although only a relative handful of cases go to trial, the possibility of trial operates as a balancing wheel on all other cases. The possibility of losing at trial is an important basis for the exercise of prosecutorial discretion during screening. The likelihood of conviction determines the bargaining position of lawyers during plea negotiations. The effects of jury trial must be measured not only by the impact on a specific case but also by the effect on similar cases at a later time.

One important way that trials affect the court process is by introducing popular standards of justice. The University of Chicago jury project found that by far the major reason for disagreement between judge and jury (29 percent) was "jury legislation." Jury legislation is defined as a jury's deliberate modification of the law to make it conform to community views of what the law ought to be (Kalven and Zeisel).

For example, federal jury conviction rates vary substantially according to the crime charged (Table 14-2). Whereas four out of five of those accused of violating food and drug laws were convicted, only about one third of the defendants in migratory bird and civil rights cases were found guilty. Rural juries appear to be more dubious about laws that restrict hunting privileges, and for many years southern juries (as well as some northern ones) have questioned federal laws proscribing racial discrimination. So federal defendants accused of these crimes have a good chance of finding friendly juries ready to come

TABLE 14-2 Federal Jury Conviction Rates for Selected Regulatory Crimes, 1961–1980

	Jury conviction rate	Number of jury trials
National defense	82.5%	143
Selective service	82.1	809
Immigration	80.4	1,084
Food and drug	79.8	376
Obscenity	72.1	258
Anti-trust	38.5	257
Civil rights	36.2	536
Migratory birds	35.8	358

SOURCE: James Levine, "Using Jury Verdict Forecasts in Criminal Defense Strategy," *Judicature* 66 (1983): 448. Reprinted by permission.

to their rescue (Levine). Similarly, state juries are less likely to convict if they perceive that the potential sentence is too severe (as when a defendant charged with drunken driving, who caused no damage or injury, stands to lose his driver's license for a long period of time). Jury verdicts thus establish boundaries on what actions the local community believes should (or should not) be punished.

By introducing uncertainty, trials affect the criminal court process in a second important way. During a trial the legal professionals are at the mercy of the witnesses, whose behavior on the witness stand is unpredictable. What witnesses say and how they say it often make the difference between conviction and acquittal (Eisenstein and Jacob). The presence of juries adds another layer of unpredictability. Part of the folklore of any courthouse are stories about the unpredictable jury. Here are two examples. During jury deliberations on a narcotics case, two women announced that "only God can judge" and by refusing to vote hung the jury. In another case, after a not guilty verdict, a juror put her arm around the defendant and said, "Bob, we were sure happy to find you not guilty, but don't do it again" (Neubauer: 228).

Judges and defense attorneys, as legal professionals, resent such intrusion into their otherwise ordered world and seek to reduce such uncertainties. They do so by developing the norms of cooperation we have talked about throughout this book. Viewed in this light, plea bargaining functions to buffer the system against a great deal of the uncertainty that results when lay citizens are involved in decisions on important legal matters.

Prejudicial Pretrial Publicity

For weeks the Cleveland press, through vivid headlines and front-page editorials, pressed for the arrest of Dr. Sam Sheppard. In July 1954, Dr. Sheppard's wife was bludgeoned to death in her bedroom. Sheppard claimed he was asleep on a couch, when his wife's screams awakened him. He went upstairs and grappled with the intruder, who struck him on the back of the head, causing him to lose consciousness. The local press was critical of the handling of the case and implied that Sheppard was guilty but that the police were not pressing hard enough because Sheppard was socially prominent. Later a public inquest was broadcast live with Sheppard being questioned for six hours without benefit of counsel. During the subsequent trial, a radio station broadcast from the room next to the jury room. The courthouse was so packed that newsmen sat right behind the defense table. Moreover, the local press carried detailed stories of the trial (including inadmissible evidence), which jurors were permitted to read. Dr. Sheppard was convicted. Years later the Supreme Court reversed (*Sheppard* v. *Maxwell,* 384 U.S. 333, 1966). It likened the trial to a Roman holiday and the atmosphere to that of a carnival. In holding that ***prejudicial pretrial publicity*** denied Sheppard the right to a fair and impartial trial, the Court set off a long and often heated battle over fair trial versus free press.

prejudicial pretrial publicity

The essential problem underlying the issue of prejudicial pretrial publicity is that two vital protections of the Bill of Rights are on a collision course. The Sixth Amendment guarantees defendants a trial before an impartial jury, a group of citizens who will decide guilt or innocence on the basis of what they hear during the trial—information tested according to accepted rules of evidence—not what they heard or read outside the courtroom. At the same time, the First Amendment protects the freedom of the press; what the reporters print, say on radio, or broadcast on television is not subject to prior censorship. Without the First Amendment, there would be no problem; courts could simply forbid the press from reporting anything but the bare essentials of a crime. This is the practice in England. The U.S. Supreme Court, however, has ruled that local courts cannot issue ***gag orders*** forbidding the press from publishing information about a criminal case. For example, when a trial judge in New Orleans issued a gag order forbidding the press from publishing testimony revealed in open court during a pretrial hearing, the Court held that this ruling infringed on freedom of the press (*Times-Picayune* v. *Schulingkamp,* 419 U.S. 301, 1975). Gag orders, though, pose another problem: a journalist who prints information in violation of a court order can be sentenced to jail for contempt of court, even if an appellate body later rules the trial judge's order was illegal.

gag order

The great majority of criminal trials do not involve problems of prejudicial pretrial publicity. News coverage usually extends to no more than police blotter coverage. But when there is extensive pretrial publicity, the normal *voir dire* process is greatly strained. Jury selection is geared to ferreting out ordinary instances of bias or prejudice, not correcting the possibility of a systematic pattern of bias. If, for example, one excuses all jurors who have heard something about the case at hand, one runs the risk of selecting a jury solely from the least attentive, least literate members of the general public. If, on the other hand, one accepts jurors on their assertion that they will judge the case solely on the basis of testimony in open court, one is still not certain that the juror—no matter how well-intentioned—can hear the case with a truly open mind.

Moreover, research has demonstrated that pretrial publicity does bias juries. A team of researchers from Columbia University provided one set of "jurors" with "prejudicial" news coverage of a case and a control group with nonprejudicial information. After listening to an identical trial involving a case where the guilt of the defendant was greatly in doubt, the study found that 78 percent of the ''prejudiced jurors'' voted to convict compared to only 55 percent of ''nonprejudiced jurors'' (Padawer-Singer and Barton: 131).

In trying to reconcile conflicting principles involved in the First and Sixth amendments, trial courts employ singly or in combination three techniques: limited gag orders, change of venue, and sequestered juries. Each of these methods is a partial one, however, and each suffers from admitted drawbacks.

Limited Gag Order

contempt of court

The First Amendment forbids the court from censoring what the press writes about a criminal case. It says nothing, however, about restricting the flow of information to the media. Thus in notorious cases in which it seems likely that selecting a jury may be difficult, judges now rather routinely issue an order forbidding those involved in the case—police, prosecutor, defense attorney, and defendant—from talking to the press. Violations are punishable as ***contempt of court*** (disobeying a judge's order). Since these are the people who know the most about the case (and often have the most to gain from pretrial publicity), the net effect is to dry up news leaks. The press, however, consistent with the First Amendment, is free to publish any information it discovers. The greatest difficulty is that sometimes one of the people involved in the case secretly provides information in violation of the judge's order. The judge can then subpoena the reporter and order a disclosure. Reporters believe that disclosing their sources will dry up their sources and therefore refuse to testify. They are cited for contempt and go to jail. The conclusion is obviously far from logical: the court—in the interest of respecting freedom of the press—takes an action the net effect of which is to send a reporter to jail.

Change of Venue

change of venue

Venue refers to the local area where a case may be tried. If the court is convinced that a case has received such extensive local publicity that picking an impartial jury is impossible, the trial may be shifted to another part of the state. Where a case has received statewide coverage, however, a change in venue is of limited use. Generally the prosecution opposes such a move because of a belief that the chance of conviction is greater in the local community and because it is quite expensive to move witnesses, documents, and staff to a distant city for a long trial. Defense attorneys face a difficult tactical decision. They must weigh the effects of prejudicial publicity against a trial in a more rural and conservative area, for example, where citizens are hostile to big city defendants, particularly if they are black.

Sequestering the Jury

sequestered jury

A prime defect during the trial of Dr. Sheppard was the failure to shield the jury from press coverage of the ongoing trial. To remedy the defect, it is common in trials involving extensive media coverage to ***sequester the jury.*** Jurors' activities are tightly regulated: they live in a hotel, take their meals together, and participate in weekend recreation together. Sheriff deputies censor newspapers and mail going to the jury and shut off television news. The possibility of being in virtual quarantine for six weeks or eight weeks, or in some cases even longer, makes many citizens reluctant to serve. When sequestering is probable, the jury selected runs the very obvious risk of representing only those citizens willing to be separated for long periods of time from friends, family, and relatives; who can afford to be off work; are unemployed; or look forward to a spartan existence.

Covering the Trial

The rise of the electronic media, radio and television, has added a new dimension to protecting the defendant's right to a fair trial. Because trials are open to the public, journalists can observe and report on the events of the trial. Other types of coverage, though, have been limited since the sensational Lindbergh trial of the thirties. German immigrant Bruno Hauptman was accused of kidnapping and murdering the son of the famous aviator Charles Lindbergh. The extensive daily press coverage of the trial was widely perceived as excessive. Since that time, court rules have generally forbidden the press or the public from bringing any cameras or recording devices into the courthouse. For this reason televison stations hire artists to provide sketches of courthouse scenes for the nightly news.

These restrictions are changing, however. The Supreme Court has held that the right to a fair trial is not violated by electronic media and still photographic coverage of public judicial proceedings (*Chandler et al.* v. *Florida,* 449 U.S. 560, 1981). However, only a handful of states and local courts allow such media coverage. Early experience indicated that after an initial burst of enthusiasm, television stations found trials too lengthy and tedious to attract viewer interest. The Claus von Bullow trial, though, was broadcast live on national television. Whether future trials of well-known celebrities will receive such treatment remains to be seen.

Conclusion

In many ways the trial is the high point of the criminal justice system. Indeed it stands as the symbol of justice. Many of our myths about the court and decisions of the U.S. Supreme Court emphasize the importance of the adversarial procedures at trial. Yet in examining the realities of trial, we are presented with two contradictory perspectives, for as we saw in the last chapter, full-fledged trials are relatively rare. At the same time, trials are a very important dimension of the court process. Every year two million jurors serve in some two hundred thousand civil and criminal cases. Long after trials have declined to minimal importance in other Western nations, the institution of a trial by jury remains a vital part of the American criminal process. Given the availability of counsel, any defendant, no matter how poor and no matter how inflamed the public is about the crime allegedly committed, can require the state to prove its case. Although only a relative smattering of cases are ever tried, the possibility of trial shapes the entire process.

For Discussion

1. Talk to some former jurors about their experiences. What did they like? What did they dislike? Do they have any suggestions about improvements in jury service?

2. Observe a *voir dire*. How many jurors are excused? Why do you think the lawyers excused the jurors they did? If possible, talk to the lawyers about the strategies they use in *voir dire*. Overall does *voir dire* take too long? What might speed up the process?

3. What do you think are the major benefits of a jury system? Disadvantages? Would justice be better or worse if America adopted the European model in which professional judges are used and juries have very limited powers?

4. What does the phrase "a jury of one's peers" mean in the context of contemporary society? Are inner-city residents provided equal protection of the laws if they are judged by middle-class, suburban jurors?

5. Follow the newspaper and television coverage of a major crime. Do you think that the defendant's right to an impartial jury is jeopardized? Why or why not?

References

BEISER, EDWARD. "Six-Member Juries in the Federal Courts." *Judicature* 58 (1975): 424.

BROEDER, D. W. "The University of Chicago Jury Project." *Nebraska Law Review* 38 (May 1959): 744–760.

EISENSTEIN, JAMES, AND HERBERT JACOB. *Felony Justice: An Organizational Analysis of Criminal Courts.* Boston: Little, Brown, 1977.

ELLWORK, AMIRAM, BRUCE SALES, AND JAMES ALFINI. *Making Jury Instructions Understandable.* Charlottesville, Va.: The Michie Co., 1982.

ETZIONI, AMITAI. "Scientific Jury-Stacking Puts Judicial System on Trial." *Boston Globe,* June 23, 1974.

GOLDMAN, PETER, AND DON HOLT. "How Justice Works: The People v. Donald Payne." *Newsweek,* March 8, 1971, pp. 20–37.

JAMES, RITA. "Status and Competence of Jurors." *American Journal of Sociology* 69 (May 1958): 563–570.

KAIRYS, DAVID, JOSEPH KADANE, AND JOHN LEHORSKY. "Jury Representativeness: A Mandate for Multiple Source Lists." *California Law Review* 65 (July 1977): 776–827.

KALVEN, HARRY, AND HANS ZEISEL. *The American Jury.* Boston: Little, Brown, 1966.

KASUNIC, DAVID. "One Day/One Trial: A Major Improvement in the Jury System." *Judicature* 67 (1983): 78.

LEVINE, JAMES. "Using Jury Verdict Forecasts in Criminal Defense Strategy." *Judicature* 66 (1983): 448.

NATIONAL ADVISORY COMMISSION ON CRIMINAL JUSTICE STANDARDS AND GOALS. *Courts.* Washington, D.C.: Government Printing Office, 1973.

NEUBAUER, DAVID. *Criminal Justice in Middle America.* Morristown, N.J.: General Learning Press, 1974.

NEUBAUER, DAVID. "Winners and Losers Before the Louisiana Supreme Court: The Case of Criminal Appeals." Paper presented at the Annual Meeting of the Law and Society Association, 1985.

NEW YORK TIMES, March 12, 1971.

PABST, WILLIAM. "What Do Six-Member Juries Really Save?" *Judicature* 57 (June–July 1973): 6.

PADAWER-SINGER, ALICE M., AND ALLEN H. BARTON. "The Impact of Pretrial Publicity on Jurors' Verdicts." In *The Jury System in America: A Critical Overview,* ed. Rita James Simon. Beverly Hills, Calif: Sage Publications, 1975.

ROPER, ROBERT. "Jury Size: Impact on Verdict's Correctness." *American Politics Quarterly* 7 (October 1979): 438–452.

———. "Jury Size and Verdict Consistency: 'A Line Has to Be Drawn Somewhere'?" *Law and Society Review* 14 (1980): 977.

ROPER, ROBERT, AND VICTOR FLANGO. "Trials Before Judges and Juries." *Justice System Journal* 8 (1983): 186.

ROTHSTEIN, PAUL. *Evidence in a Nutshell.* Minneapolis: West Publications, 1970.

SEVERANCE, LAWRENCE, AND ELIZABETH LOFTUS. "Improving the Ability of Jurors to Comprehend and Apply Criminal Jury Instructions." *Law and Society Review* 17 (1982): 153.

SIMON, RITA JAMES. *The Jury and the Defense of Insanity.* Boston: Little, Brown, 1967.

———, AND PRENTICE MARSHALL. "The Jury System." In *The Rights of the Accused in Law and Action,* ed. Stuart Nagel. Beverly Hills, Calif.: Sage Publications, 1972.

STRAWN, DAVID, AND RAYMOND BUCHANAN. "Jury Confusion: A Threat to Justice." *Judicature* 59 (May 1976): 478–483.

STRODTBECK, F. L., R. JAMES, AND C. HAWKINS. "Social Status in Jury Deliberations." *American Sociological Review* 22 (December 1957): 713–719.

ZEISEL, HANS, AND SHARI DIAMOND. "Convincing Empirical Evidence on the Six Member Jury." *University of Chicago Law Review* 41 (1974): 281–295.

For Further Reading

DIPERNA, PAULA. *Juries on Trial.* New York: Dembner Books, 1984.

HASTIE, REID, STEVEN PENROD, AND NANCY PENNINGTON. *Inside the Jury.* Cambridge, Mass.: Harvard University Press, 1983.

HANS, VALERIE, AND NEIL VIDMAR. *Judging the Jury.* New York: Plenum, 1986.

KALVEN, HARRY, AND HANS ZEISEL. *The American Jury.* Boston: Little, Brown, 1966.

KERR, NORBERT, AND ROBERT BRAY, eds. *The Psychology of the Courtroom.* New York: Academic Press, 1982.

NATIONAL CENTER FOR STATE COURTS. *Facets of the Jury System: A Survey.* Denver: 1976.

SAKS, MICHAEL. *Jury Verdicts: The Role of Group Size and Social Decision Rules.* Lexington, Mass.: Lexington Books, 1977.

SIMON, RITA, ed. *The Jury: Its Role in American Society.* Lexington, Mass.: Lexington Books, 1980.

———, ed. *The Jury System in America: A Critical Overview.* Beverly Hills, Calif.: Sage Publications, 1975.

VAN DYKE, JON. *Jury Selection Procedures: Our Uncertain Commitment to Representative Panels.* Cambridge, Mass.: Ballinger, 1977.

PART IV

SETTING
THE
PENALTY

Sentences are the currency of the realm. While reformers, law professors, and appellate courts spend most of their time debating and analyzing how courts determine guilt or innocence, judges, prosecutors, defense attorneys, and defendants focus much of their attention on sentencing. Whether the defendant will be granted probation and if not, how many years in prison are the main topics that fuel the dynamics of courthouse justice.

Chapter 15 considers the legal basis for the wide range of discretionary power over sentencing. In addition, the competing theories of sentencing are examined.

Chapter 16 examines how courtroom work groups choose between prison and probation. Of particular interest are competing criticisms of how these choices are made—whether they are too harsh or too lenient—and various proposals to correct perceived problems.

CHAPTER 15

Sentencing:
The Legal Basis
of Judicial Discretion

Sentencing encompasses both the beginning and the end of the criminal justice system. For society, sentencing is the starting point: the reasons for punishing law violators establish the very basis and purpose of the criminal justice system. For the defendant, sentencing is the last step in the process: whether he or she will be sentenced to prison or placed on probation will be decided. The courts stand in the middle: they must wrestle with a host of conflicting considerations, some of them with no easy answers. Dissatisfaction with how the courts perform these tasks is widespread.

The last two decades have witnessed an unprecedented questioning of all aspects of sentencing. The reasons for punishing wrongdoers have provoked intense debate. The previously dominant goal of rehabilitation has come under sharp attack, and in its place is a certain urge that punishment should be based on the principle of just desserts. Wide-ranging sentencing discretion has prompted calls for greater accountability in official decision making. Many question the broad sentencing discretion legislative bodies have traditionally granted judges and parole boards. The forms of punishment have, likewise, come under intense scrutiny. Increasing crime rates prompted citizens to demand longer prison terms. As a result, prison populations have soared. But at the same time substandard conditions of confinement have led federal courts to order revolutionary changes in prisons. Moreover, the death penalty was seemingly abolished but then restored under different conditions.

This questioning and debate has produced numerous and sweeping reforms in sentencing. After nearly forty years of stability, the indeterminate sentencing system has been abruptly rejected in state after state. Parole has been abolished in some jurisdictions. Administrative rules and guidelines now play a prominent role in almost every state.

Before we can understand the dissatisfaction with sentencing and the sentencing reforms that have resulted, we must examine the legal basis of sentencing. This chapter examines the why, the who, and the what of sentencing. Punishments for violators of the criminal law are shaped by philosophical and moral orientations. Asking *why* we sentence focuses attention on the competing and often partial justifications for sentencing. Probing *who* should make these choices reveals the complex and varied sentencing structure in the United States. Whereas the public associates the judge with sentencing, closer scrutiny indicates that other branches of government share sentencing responsibility as well. Finally, examining the *what* of sentencing shows that a variety of sentences may be imposed on the guilty, including probation, prison, fines, restitution, and—most controversial of all—the death penalty.

Why Do We Sentence?

- "An eye for an eye, a tooth for a tooth."
- "The punishment should fit the crime."
- "Lock 'em up and throw away the key."
- "This sentence will be a warning to others."
- "Sentencing should rehabilitate the offender."
- "The public demands a prison sentence."

These statements—variously drawn from the Bible, newspaper headlines, casual conversations, and statements by court officials—aptly demonstrate that there is no consensus on how the courts should punish the guilty. Retribution, incapacitation, deterrence, and rehabilitation are the four principal justifications offered. These sentencing philosophies differ in important ways. Some stress past behavior whereas others are future-oriented; some focus on the crime committed and others on the criminal. All, however, shape contemporary thinking about sentencing.

Retribution

retribution

"An eye for an eye, a tooth for a tooth." This Old Testament injunction expresses the oldest of sentencing philosophies. What is most distinctive about **retribution** is its focus on past behavior; the severity of the punishment is tied to the seriousness of the crime. This concept is based on strongly

moral principles

held ***moral principles***; individuals are held responsible for their own actions. Because they have disregarded the rights of others, or otherwise upset the social order, criminals are wicked people and therefore deserve to be punished. Punishing wrongdoers also reflects a basic human emotion, the desire for ***revenge***: the victim has suffered and the criminal should suffer as well. The concept of retribution, however, places important limits on sentencing. Because society as a whole is punishing the criminal, individuals are not justified in taking the law into their own hands. Moreover, in applying sanctions, the severity of the punishment is limited to the severity of the injury of the victim. This is how Leviticus 24:20 differs from other ancient notions about punishment. Finally, retribution also provides for reconciliation; through punishment the offender has paid a debt to society.

revenge

From biblical times through the eighteenth century, retribution provided the dominant justification for punishment. Its emphasis on punishing wrongful acts fit well with the dominant form of punishment: public and corporal. Horrible punishments were often inflicted even for trivial offenses. In England and Europe from the sixteenth through the eighteenth century, for example, punishments were particularly brutal: whipping, mutilation, and branding were used extensively, and in England death was the common sentence for a host of felonies. Beginning with the Enlightenment, however, retribution lost much of its influence. Criminal penalties based on revenge began to be viewed as barbaric. More utilitarian reasons for sentencing were preferred. Since the 1970s, however, retribution has attracted the interest of scholars and criminal justice reformers who use a more humane phrasing, ***deserved punishment***. One of the leading exponents, Andrew von Hirsch, writes, "Someone who infringes the rights of others . . . does wrong and deserves blame for his conduct. It is because he deserves blame that the sanctioning authority is entitled to choose a response that expresses moral disapproval; namely punishment." This punishment should be administered in accordance with the principle of ***just desserts***: the severity of the sanction should be proportionate to the gravity of the defendant's criminal conduct.

deserved punishment

just desserts

Q U O T A T I O N

When one man strikes another and kills him, he shall be put to death. Whoever strikes a beast and kills it shall make restitution, life for life. When one man injures and disfigures his fellow-countryman, it shall be done to him as he has done; fracture for fracture, eye for eye, tooth for tooth; the injury and disfigurement that he has inflicted upon another shall in turn be inflicted upon him.

Leviticus 24:17–22

As a sentencing philosophy, retribution suffers from several limitations. Its emphasis on vengeance does not easily square with the notions of individual rights fundamental to a representational democracy. Its focus on crimes of violence offers little apparent guidance for sentencing the far more numerous defendants who have committed property violations. Its moralistic stress on individual responsibility presents great difficulty in the context of twentieth-century explanations of human behavior based on social, physical, and psychological factors. Most important, though, its emphasis on the past behavior of the defendant exhibits no concern for future criminal activity. Some studies demonstrate that extended periods of custody may actually increase the likelihood that an inmate will commit future criminal acts. Thus, sentencing on the basis of retribution may even be contrary to the goal of crime reduction.

Incapacitation

*incapacita-
tion*

"Lock them up and throw away the key." Sentiments like this are often expressed by average citizens outraged by some recent and often shocking criminal act. The assumption of *incapacitation* is that crime can be prevented if criminals are physically restrained. The theory of isolating current or potential criminals differs from the theory of retribution in two important ways. First, it is future-oriented: the goal is to prevent future crimes, not punish past ones. Second, it focuses on the personal characteristics of the offender; the type of person committing the crime is more important than the crime committed. Unlike rehabilitation, however, incapacitation has no intention of reforming the offender.

From ancient times, societies have banished persons who have disobeyed the rules. England transported criminals to penal colonies, Georgia and Australia among them. Similar practices continue today. Russia exiles dissidents to cold, barren, and distant Siberia where they cannot threaten the government. In most nations, prisons are used to isolate guilty offenders, preventing them from committing additional crimes in the community. The death penalty is justified by some on the ground that it likewise prevents future crimes.

Incapacitation is probably the simplest and most straightforward justification offered for punishing wrongdoers. As a sentencing philosophy, however, it suffers from some important limitations. It cannot provide any standards about how long a sentence should be. Unlike retribution, it does not imply any limits on sentencing. Indeed the goal of crime prevention may be used to justify severe sanctions for both trivial and serious offenses. Moreover, isolation without efforts as rehabilitation may also produce more severe criminal behavior once the offender is released. Prisons "protect the community but that protection is only temporary. They relieve the community responsibility by removing the offender, but they make successful reintegration of the offender into the community unlikely" (National Advisory Commission, 1973a). Finally, of course, applying the incapacitation theory would require the building of many more expensive prisons.

The incapacitation theory of sentencing has never been well articulated. Its assumptions about crime and criminals are simplistic. In recent years, how-

selective in-capacitation

ever, a more focused variant, **selective incapacitation,** has received considerable attention. Research has shown that a relatively small number of criminals are responsible for a large number of crimes. Burglars, for example, commit many such offenses before they are caught. These findings have led to an active interest in targeting **dangerous offenders** (Moore et al.). Some studies estimate that sending serious offenders to prison for longer periods of time will result in a significant reduction in crime (Shinnar and Shinnar; Wilson). Not all researchers agree that selective incapacitation will greatly reduce crime (van Dine, Conrad, and Dinitz). Moreover, some argue that even though some offenders may be imprisoned, others on the verge of criminality are ready to take their place. But how would these offenders be singled out? Many believe that we do not have the knowledge or technology to make accurate predictions of future criminal activity by convicted defendants.

dangerous offenders

Deterrence

deterrence theory

"This sentence will be a warning to others." Phrases like this reflect one of the more modern and also most widely held justifications for punishment. According to **deterrence theory,** the purpose of punishment is the prevention of future crimes. Unlike retribution and incapacitation, this theory offers ideas about the causes of crime and how to alter those causes. However, it does not propose to change offenders—just deter them. Much like rehabilitation, special deterrence argues that the punishment should fit the criminal. Note that this is a different concern from retribution theory, that the punishment should fit the crime.

Deterrence theory was first articulated by Jeremy Bentham, a nineteenth-century British lawyer, reformer, and criminologist. To Bentham, punishment based on retribution was pointless and counterproductive. Instead, sanctions should be used to further society's goal of preventing crime. Punishment, therefore, is unjustifiable unless it can be shown that more "good" results when it is inflicted than when it is withheld. Bentham believed that human behavior is governed by individual calculation; people seek to maximize pleasure and minimize pain. Under this **utilitarian theory,** the basic objective of punishment is to discourage crime by making it painful. Because they seek to minimize pain, people will refrain from activities like crimes that produce sanctions.

utilitarian theory

general deterrence

special deterrence

Contemporary discussions of deterrence theories incorporate two subconcepts, often confused. **General deterrence** is the idea that the general populace will be discouraged from committing crimes by observing the public example of the punishment of wrongdoers. It has a strong education component, and public perceptions of punishment are very important. **Special deterrence** (which is sometimes called *specific* or *individual deterrence*) is concerned with producing changes in the behavior of the individual defendant. It seeks individualized punishment in the amount and kind necessary so that the criminal will not commit future crimes. A difficulty with deterrence theory is that the goals of general and special deterrence can be incompatible. The severity of the punishment needed to impress the general population about the price of committing a crime may be higher than that needed to deter the individual defendant from future crimes.

Notions of deterrence form the core of contemporary discussions about sentencing. In a general sense, many people refrain from committing illegal acts because they fear the consequences of being convicted. After a party, for example, an intoxicated guest may take a taxi home rather than run the risk of being arrested and disgraced by a drunken driving conviction. In this situation, one can easily argue that the threat of punishment does deter. When we move to more specific applications, however, the picture becomes much cloudier. The exact nature of the role that deterrence plays and the extent to which sentencing policies affect crime and criminals is unclear. An extensive literature examines deterrence but reaches no firm conclusions. Some studies find a deterrent effect and others do not (Nagin). Although discussions of deterrence are usually coupled with calls for increasing the severity of the sentence, some research suggests that ***certainty of punishment*** is more of a deterrent than the ***severity of punishment*** (Wilson). Moreover, deterrence rests on the assumption of rational, calculating behavior. Many crimes, particularly crimes of violence, are committed on the spur of the moment. For these reasons many question whether court sentences—particularly severe ones—do indeed deter.

certainty of punishment

severity of punishment

Rehabilitation

The most appealing modern justification for imposing punishment is to restore a convicted offender to a constructive place in society through vocational, educational, or therapeutic treatment. The idea of ***rehabilitation*** assumes that criminal behavior is the result of social, psychological, or physical imperfections, and that the treatment of such disorders should be the primary goal of corrections. Success means assessing the needs of the individual and providing a program to meet these needs. Ultimately, then, offenders are not being punished but ***treated,*** not only for their own good but for the benefit of society as well. Under rehabilitation, sentences should fit the offender rather than the offense. Rehabilitation shares a common orientation with deterrence—crime reduction. But they differ in a fundamental way: rehabilitation assumes that human behavior can be altered.

rehabilitation

treatment

The concept of rehabilitation has dominated thinking about sentencing through the twentieth century. It has provided the intellectual linchpin for such important developments as probation, parole, and indeterminate sentencing. It has been strongly favored by most court personnel and correction officials as well. It has also enjoyed widespread public support. Almost three out of four persons support the idea that the main emphasis in prisons should be to help the offender become a productive citizen.

During the last two decades, however, the rehabilitative ideal has been challenged on both empirical and normative grounds. There is growing evidence that rehabilitative programs do not substantially reduce the later criminality of their clients (Blumstein et al.). California, for example, where the rehabilitative model had been most completely incorporated, was also marked by high rates of recidivism. To some the key weakness is that one cannot coerce a person to change. This is reflected in the fact that some prisoners participate in prison rehabilitation programs, like counseling, education, job training, and religious services, out of a desire to gain an early release—not because they wish to change their behavior. Thus doubts have been expressed as to whether the causes of crime can be diagnosed and whether enough is yet known to engage in major behavior modification.

Apart from the empirical question whether rehabilitation programs have been successful, concern has also been voiced that sentencing structures based on the rehabilitative ideal grant too much discretion to judges and parole boards. As a result of this discretion, the humanitarian goal of rehabilitation can serve to mask punishment. In most prisons, rehabilitation programs are minimal or nonexistent. Yet, judges often sentence in the hope of rehabilitating the offender; this may produce lengthier prison sentences. To critics, sentencing an offender according to the rehabilitative ideal may be more punitive than sentencing for the sake of punishment alone.

Competing Sentencing Philosophies

Justifications for punishing wrongdoers are based on religious and moral understandings about right and wrong as well as empirical perceptions about human behavior. Of retribution, incapacitation, deterrence, and rehabilitation, however, none alone is adequate; the various goals must be balanced. Therefore elements of each of these four philosophies have been incorporated into society's efforts to control crime. In turn, sentencing decisions reflect ambivalent expectations about the causes of crime, the nature of criminals, and the role of the courts in reducing crime. Sentences also reflect ambivalent expectations about the likely results of following these philosophies.

During the last two decades the reasons for sentencing have been the subject of intense debate. After three quarters of a century the intellectual dominance of the rehabilitative ideal began to crumble and then collapse. Scholars and others began to explore alternative justifications for imposing punishment on wrongdoers. This questioning why we sentence resulted in widespread sentencing reforms, many of which focus on who should have the authority to impose sentence and what limits should be placed on that authority.

Sentencing Structures

sentencing structure

The power to punish is distributed among the three branches of government. The result is a varied and complex *sentencing structure.* Who is sentenced to prison and for how long can be understood only in terms of this blend of decision-making power.

Through most of this century, sentencing was exercised within broad limits set by legislative statute. The courts had primary control over who went to prison. Parole boards controlled the length of the prison term. This general model had many variations but was the predominant approach to setting prison terms. Since the mid-1970s, dramatic changes have been made in the laws under which offenders are sent to prison and in the mechanisms that control how long they stay there. Legislatures have increased their control over the sanctioning process. In some jurisdictions, the judiciary and the parole boards have taken steps to formalize their control over specific components of the sanctioning process. The result has been a significant narrowing of sentencing discretion in many jurisdictions.

Legislative Sentencing Responsibility

*legislative
sentencing
responsibility*

Legislatures are initially responsible for creating sentencing options. Recall from Chapter 4 that there can be no crime and no punishment without law. *Legislative sentencing responsibility* refers to the criminal codes enacted by legislative bodies. Legislatures have done a reasonably good job in providing precise and specific definitions of crime but have generally neglected doing the same for punishments. Instead they have enacted contradictory sentencing provisions and historically have given open-ended powers to judges.

Penal codes have evolved piecemeal, with the result that there are numerous sentencing distinctions. State laws may provide for fifteen or more different maximum penalties for first-conviction felons (Tappan). Moreover, as new crimes are defined or more severe punishments provided for existing ones, little effort is devoted to ensuring that a consistent set of penalties exist. The end result is a crazy quilt pattern of sentences. Less serious offenses may be punished more severely than more serious ones. To some, the number and variety of sentencing distinctions is "the main cause of the anarchy in sentencing that is so widely deplored" (Model Penal Code).

*sentencing
alternatives*

A broader concern is that legislators have given judges wide powers to impose sentences but have failed to provide guidance on how those powers should be used. Often *sentencing alternatives* range from granting a defendant probation to imposing various terms of imprisonment that may range up to life. Such wide-ranging power might be understandable if the legislatures at the same time provided some guidance as to how choices are to be made between these greatly diverging alternatives; generally, however, they have not. State law requires only that the judge consider the safety of the community or the possibility of the defendant's committing future crimes. Such general statements provide no effective guidance.

Legislators are elected officials who operate in a political world. A survey of four states undergoing sentencing reform—Minnesota, Indiana, Illinois, and Connecticut—found that legislators had difficulty differentiating among the four traditional justifications for punishment (Price). In their minds there were only two sets of goals: one encapsulating the values of retribution, deterrence, and incapacitation; the other, the values of rehabilitation. Most of the legislators were more interested in responding to public pressure for stiffer punishment than in developing a coherent set of sentencing laws. In a perceptive analysis of sentencing policy, Rosett and Cressey suggest that legislatures are influenced by a severity-softening-severity process. Severe criminal laws are passed on the assumption that the fear of pain will terrorize the citizenry into conformity. Court officials, however, soften these penalties because most of the offenders do not fit the criteria the legislatures initially had in mind. Finding that the severe sentences are not being handed out, the legislatures pass even more severe laws, and the process is repeated.

The past decade has witnessed a major rethinking of the purposes of punishment and the sentences created to carry out those purposes. As a result numerous legislative bodies have enacted major changes in sentencing laws, with the key objective to reduce the amount of discretion exercised by actors in the other branches of government. A number of states have restricted the carte blanche authority historically granted judges and have also limited and in some cases abolished the discretion of parole boards to release prisoners.

Judicial Sentencing Responsibility

Only judges have the authority to choose among the sentencing options provided by the legislature. Other members of the work group may recommend; only the judge can decide. Of course there are some minor exceptions to this general proposition. A few jurisdictions allow an appeal of the sentence. In death penalty cases only the jury can decide whether to impose the death penalty. In addition, a few states provide for jury-determined sentences for

---

QUOTATION

*U*nder current sentencing laws, state legislatures rarely decide what sentence a "typical" violator of a criminal statute should receive. Instead, they generally determine only what the minimum and maximum sentence for a given offense will be. As a consequence, attention has focused primarily on extremes. What is the most any armed robber should get? What is the *least* any armed robber should get? This tends to encourage unrealistic thinking about criminals. It forces the legislator to concentrate on the unusual cases, such as the mercy killer who "murders" a loved one suffering from a terminal illness, or, at the other extreme, the armed robber who forces his victims to the floor and systematically murders them. Since the imagination is virtually unlimited in coming up with extreme cases that warrant extremely different punishments, legislatures tend to set the minimum and maximum sentences at very great distances from each other.

The resulting legislation tells us what the legislature thinks the appropriate penalty should be for the statistically insignificant number of situations at the extremes of the statute. It does not tell us, however, what the legislature thinks the appropriate sentence should be for the fairly typical case.

The Twentieth Century Fund Task Force on Criminal Sentencing, *Fair and Certain Punishment* (New York: McGraw-Hill, 1976), pp. 11–12.

certain types of crimes. In Texas defendants may request jury sentencing. Reformers have recommended the abolition of jury sentencing on the grounds that it is unprofessional and likely to result in arbitrary and emotional sentences (National Advisory Commission, 1973b).

judicial sentencing responsibility individu- alized sen- tencing

These minor exceptions aside, American judges traditionally enjoyed virtu- ally unlimited ***judicial sentencing responsibility.*** Such wide judicial dis- cretion in sentencing reflected the rehabilitative model, which stressed that punishment should fit the criminal. No two crimes or criminals are exactly alike; sentences therefore should be ***individualized,*** with judges taking these differences into account. But there is no agreement on what factors should increase the penalty or should reduce it. To critics like former federal judge Marvin Frankel, judicial sentencing discretion is too vast.

> The sentencing powers of the judge are, in short, so far unconfined that, except for frequently monstrous maximum limits, they are effectively subject to no law at all. Everyone with the least training in law would be prompt to denounce a statute that merely said the penalty for crimes "shall be any term the judge sees fit to impose." A regime of such arbitrary fiat would be intolerable in a sup- posedly free society, to say nothing of being invalid under our due-process clause. But the fact is that we have accepted unthinkingly a criminal code creating in effect precisely that degree of unbridled power.

narrow judicial discretion

As a result of sentencing reform there are now major variations in judicial sentencing discretion. The states range from broad to narrow in the degree of judicial discretion over sentencing lengths they allow. Court discretion is defined as narrow if the range of sentencing options available to the judge is restricted by law to less than one third of the statutory maximum sentence length for each offense. For example, when a person is convicted of a crime carrying a twelve-year statutory maximum, judges with narrow discretion must select a sentence from within, at most, a four-year range (Bureau of Justice Statistics, 1983). Under this definition, ***narrow judicial discretion*** over sentencing is characteristic of twelve jurisdictions.

Executive Sentencing Responsibility

executive sentencing responsibility

Most sentences imposed by the judge are actually carried out by officials of the executive branch. Collecting fines is the responsibility of the judiciary, but sentences of probation or prison are generally part of ***executive sen- tencing responsibility.*** The decisions made by governors and parole boards play a major role in sentencing.

Few prisoners serve their maximum terms of imprisonment. Each year almost two hundred thousand inmates are released from prison. Only one out of six of these prisoners is released because his or her sentence has expired; the vast majority are released after serving only a part of the prison term imposed by the judge (Bureau of Justice Statistics, 1986). Typically these prisoners are re- leased conditionally; that is, they are subject to supervision. The criteria for early release are established and administered by correction officials. The most typical forms of early release are parole, good time, and to a lesser extent ex- ecutive clemency.

parole

Parole is the conditional release of an inmate from incarceration under supervision after a portion of the prison sentence has been served. Conditions of release are supervised by a parole officer and rule violations or new crimes may result in a return to prison for the balance of the unexpired term. **Parole**

parole boards

boards, which are usually appointed by the governor, vary greatly in their discretionary authority.

Decisions made by the executive branch affect how long an inmate must stay in prison in another way. In all but four states (Hawaii, Pennsylvania, Ten-

good time

nessee, and Utah) prisoners are awarded **good time**—days off their minimum or maximum terms for good behavior or participation in various vocational, educational, and treatment programs. The amount of good time that can be earned varies from five days a month to forty-five days a month in some states. Correctional officials find these sentence reduction provisions necessary for the maintenance of institutional order and as a mechanism to reduce overcrowding. Therefore, they typically have discretion in awarding good time.

State governors, as well as the president of the United States, have the power to pardon any prisoner in their jurisdiction, reduce the sentence, or make the

pardons

prisoner eligible for parole. **Pardons,** however, are not a major method of prisoner release. Only a small group of inmates are granted this executive clemency each year.

How long an offender will be imprisoned depends not only on the length of the sentence imposed by the judge but also on the criteria parole boards use in granting a conditional release and on how correctional officials compute good time. In a fragmented criminal justice system, such executive powers are clearly necessary. Based on experience with the offender and backed up with other information, parole and corrections officials may be in a better position than the sentencing judge to know when the inmate is ready for release. These powers also allow the executive to mute sentencing disparities.

The use of these powers is being questioned today. Prisoners and exprisoners are strong critics of extensive parole authority because they cannot predict when they will be released. A convict may be denied parole after only a brief hearing. Moreover, because release is tied to rehabilitation, prisoners can con parole and prison officials. Some may attend church on Sunday or enroll in rehabilitation programs not out of any desire to change but to gain an early release.

This questioning has produced significant changes in parole board authority in some jurisdictions in recent years. In the eleven states that have adopted determinate sentencing, there is no discretionary parole board release. Inmates are released from prison when they have served their original sentence less time off for good behavior or program participation. In the majority of jurisdictions, parole boards have discretionary authority to release prisoners after they have served a fraction of the sentence, often one third. Although nearly all states have legislative statutes defining general criteria for parole release, in fourteen states, the District of Columbia, and the federal system the discretion of the parole board to release prisoners is limited by explicit parole guidelines enacted by the legislature or voluntarily adopted by parole boards.

Forms of Punishment

Flogging, the stocks, exile, chopping off a hand, and branding are just a few examples of punishments historically inflicted on the guilty. Today such sanctions are viewed as violating the Constitution's prohibition against cruel and unusual punishment. In their place we use imprisonment, probation, fines, and restitution (see Table 15-1).

forms of punishment

Many states also make formal provisions for capital punishment, but the death penalty is rarely used. In essence these *forms of punishment* are tools created under the sentencing structure to advance society's theories of punishment. They are the options from which the sentencing judge must choose.

Imprisonment

imprisonment

Although employed from time to time throughout history, *imprisonment* became the dominant form of punishment only during the last two centuries. In the United States legislatures specify terms of imprisonment in two different ways. Consistent with the goal of rehabilitation, which dominated correctional thinking through most of this century, state legislatures adopted indeterminate (often called indefinite) sentences based on the idea that correctional personnel must have discretion to release an offender when that treatment has been

indeterminate sentences

successful. States with *indeterminate sentences* stipulate a minimum and maximum amount of time to be served in prison; one to five years, three to ten years, twenty years to life, and so on. At the time of sentencing the offender knows only the range of the sentence and that parole is a possibility after the minimum sentence, less good time, has been served. How long the person remains in prison is determined by the parole authority based on their assessment of the offender's progress toward rehabilitation.

determinate sentences

Growing disillusionment with the rehabilitative model and the ascendancy of the concept of deserved punishment has brought renewed efforts toward *determinate sentences.* Determinate sentences (sometimes called fixed sentences) consist of a specified number of years rather than a range of years. Thus the judge must sentence the defendant to five years—or ten years, or whatever—in prison.

The United States relies on imprisonment more than any other Western nation in the world except South Africa. Over five hundred thousand inmates are currently housed in state and federal prisons (see Table 15-2). The prison population grows yearly. From 1977 to 1985 the prison population increased by 68 percent. The length of sentences in the United States are also quite long compared to those imposed in Europe where it is rare for a defendant to be sentenced to more than five years.

prison conditions overcrowding

Prison conditions have often been described as substandard. Although a few prisons resemble college campuses, many are old and run-down. They have often been hot in the summer and cold in the winter. *Overcrowding* results in inadequate security for inmates, with assaults and homosexual rapes a constant part of prison life. These conditions affect how judges sentence. Prison overcrowding prompts some judges to seek alternatives to incarceration (Finn). Likewise, substandard conditions make some judges reluctant to

TABLE 15-1 What Types of Sentences Are Usually Given to Offenders?

Death penalty—In some states for certain crimes such as murder, the courts may sentence an offender to death by electrocution, exposure to lethal gas, hanging, lethal injection, or other method specified by state law.

- As of 1982, 36 states had death penalty provisions in law.
- Most death penalty sentences have been for murder.
- As of year-end 1982, six persons had been executed since 1977; and 1,050 inmates in 31 states were under a sentence of death.

Incarceration—The confinement of a convicted criminal in a federal or state prison or a local jail to serve a court-imposed sentence. Custody is usually within a jail, administered locally, or a prison, operated by the state or the federal government. In many states, offenders sentenced to less than 1 year are held in a jail; those sentenced to longer terms are committed to the state prison.

- More than 4,300 correctional facilities are maintained by federal, state, or local governments including 43 federal facilities, 791 state-operated adult confinement and community-based correctional facilities, and 3,500 local jails which are usually county-operated.
- On a given day in 1982, approximately 412,000 persons were confined in state and federal prisons and approximately 210,000 persons were confined in local jails.

Probation—The sentencing of an offender to community supervision by a probation agency, often as a result of suspending a sentence to confinement. Such supervision normally entails the provision of specific rules of conduct while in the community. If violated, a sentencing judge may impose a sentence to confinement. It is the most widely used correctional disposition in the United States.

- State or local governments operate more than 2,000 probation agencies. These agencies supervise nearly 1.6 million adults and juveniles on probation.

Split sentences and shock probation—A penalty that explicitly requires the convicted person to serve a period of confinement in a local, state, or federal facility (the ''shock'') followed by a period of probation. This penalty attempts to combine the use of community supervision with a short incarceration experience.

- 1977 and 1978 California data reveal that by far the most common disposition in felony cases was a combined sentence of jail and probation.

Restitution—The requirement that the offender provide financial remuneration for the losses incurred by the victim.

- By 1979, nearly all states had statutory provisions for the collection and disbursement of restitution funds. In late 1982, a restitution law was enacted at the federal level.

Community service—The requirement that the offender provide a specified number of hours of public service work, such as collecting trash in parks or other public facilities.

- By 1979, nearly a third of the states authorized community service work orders. Community service is often imposed as a specific condition of probation.

Fines—An economic penalty that requires the offender to pay a specific sum of money within the limit set by law. Fines are often imposed in addition to probation or as an alternative to incarceration.

- Many laws that govern the imposition of fines are undergoing revision. These revisions often provide for more flexible means of ensuring equality in the imposition of fines, flexible fine schedules, ''day fines'' geared to the offender's daily wage, installment payment of fines, and a restriction on confinement to situations that amount to intentional refusal to pay.

SOURCE: Bureau of Justice Statistics, U.S. Department of Justice, *Report to the Nation on Crime and Justice* (Washington, D.C.: Government Printing Office, 1983), p. 73.

TABLE 15-2 Prisoners Under the Jurisdiction of State and Federal Correctional Authorities, by Region and State, Year-end 1985 and 1986

Region and state	Total			Incarceration rate 1986
	Advance 1986	Final 1985	Percent change 1985–86	
U.S., total	546,659	503,271	8.6%	216
Federal	44,408	40,223	10.4	15
State	502,251	463,048	8.5	201
Northeast	82,388	75,706	8.8%	158
Connecticut	6,905	6,149	12.3	135
Maine	1,316	1,226	7.3	99
Massachusetts	5,678	5,390	5.3	97
New Hampshire	782	683	14.5	76
New Jersey	12,020	11,335	6.0	157
New York	38,449	34,712	10.8	216
Pennsylvania	15,201	14,227	6.8	128
Rhode Island	1,361	1,307	4.1	103
Vermont	676	677	-0.1	88
Midwest	103,101	95,704	7.7%	173
Illinois	19,456	18,634	4.4	168
Indiana	10,175	9,904	2.7	181
Iowa	2,777	2,832	-1.9	98
Kansas	5,425	4,732	14.6	220
Michigan	20,742	17,755	16.8	227
Minnesota	2,462	2,343	5.1	58
Missouri	10,485	9,915	5.7	206
Nebraska	1,953	1,814	7.7	116
North Dakota	421	422	-0.2	53
Ohio	22,463	20,864	7.7	209
South Dakota	1,045	1,047	-0.2	143
Wisconsin	5,697	5,442	4.7	119
South	215,713	202,926	6.3%	249
Alabama	11,710	11,015	6.3	283
Arkansas	4,701	4,611	2.0	198
Delaware	2,828	2,553	10.8	324
District of Columbia	6,746	6,404	5.3	753
Florida	32,228	28,600	12.7	272
Georgia	17,363	16,014	8.4	265
Kentucky	6,322	5,801	9.0	169
Louisiana	14,580	13,890	5.0	322
Maryland	13,326	13,005	2.5	280
Mississippi	6,747	6,392	5.6	249
North Carolina	17,762	17,344	2.4	258
Oklahoma	9,596	8,330	15.2	288
South Carolina	11,676	10,510	11.1	324
Tennessee	7,182	7,127	0.8	149
Texas	38,534	37,532	2.7	228
Virginia	12,930	12,073	7.1	215
West Virginia	1,482	1,725	-14.1	77
West	101,049	88,712	13.9%	198
Alaska	2,460	2,329	5.6	306
Arizona	9,434	8,531	10.6	268
California	59,484	50,111	18.7	212
Colorado	3,673	3,369	9.0	111
Hawaii	2,180	2,111	3.3	142
Idaho	1,451	1,294	12.1	144
Montana	1,111	1,129	-1.6	135
Nevada	4,505	3,771	19.5	462

TABLE 15-2   *(continued)*

Region and state	Total			Incarceration rate 1986
	Advance 1986	Final 1985	Percent change 1985–86	
New Mexico	2,701	2,313	16.8	170
Oregon	4,737	4,454	6.4	175
Utah	1,845	1,633	13.0	108
Washington	6,603	6,909	-4.4	147
Wyoming	865	758	14.1	170

SOURCE: Bureau of Justice Statistics, U.S. Department of Justice, *Prisoners in 1986* (Washington, D.C.: Government Printing Office, 1987).

send any but the worst offenders to prison. As a former prosecutor and defense attorney put it:

> Judges simply won't impose lengthy sentences to institutions that are over-crowded or that lack minimal standards. . . . [C]riminal trial judges . . . adjust their individual sentences in the light of their knowledge of the conditions in the institutions. Judges now rarely send an urban resident to state prison unless he has committed murder, or is over 25 and has committed rape, armed robbery, or atrocious assault. (Kwitny)

During the 1970s state and federal courts began to examine closely the operations of correctional institutions to ensure compliance with the Eighth Amendment's protection against cruel and unusual punishment. Federal courts have declared unconstitutional the entire prison systems of Alabama, Florida, Louisiana, Mississippi, Oklahoma, Rhode Island, Tennessee, and Texas. In at least twenty-one other states, one or more facilities are operating under a court order or a consent decree as a result of inmate overcrowding or conditions of confinement. Other states are in the midst of similar litigation. Thus, the majority of states are under some form of *federal court order* requiring upgradings in physical conditions, increased correctional supervisory personnel, better food, and so on.

federal court order

State officials allowed substandard prison conditions to exist because of a combination of political indifference and the high costs of remedying the situation. Conservative estimates of the costs of constructing a single cell for a prisoner range from $50,000 to $100,000. The costs of clothing, feeding, and guarding prisoners is also quite costly, running to roughly $15,000 per year per prisoner. In the face of swelling prison populations and federal court orders, state legislatures are being forced to spend considerably more on building new prisons and upgrading existing ones. Indeed in a growing number of states, prisons are targeted for the biggest percentage increase in governors' budgets. In an era of tight budgets, the requests are major. In Massachusetts the governor has requested over $200 million, in New York almost $100 million, and in Texas an extra $400 million (Peirce).

Probation

The principal alternative to imprisonment is probation. Indeed probation is granted to over 60 percent of the offenders sentenced in the United States.

probation
Over 1.7 million adults are on probation. Unlike incarceration, **probation** is designed as a means of maintaining control over offenders while permitting them to live in the community under supervision. The practice of probation initially evolved from efforts of judges to lessen the harshness of common law penalties by suspending sentences. Today the major justification is that prisons are inappropriate places for some defendants, and limited supervision is a better way to rehabilitate criminals. Youthful or first-time offenders may only be embittered if mixed in prison with hardened criminals, and may end up learning more sophisticated criminal techniques. Moreover, probation is significantly less expensive than imprisonment.

State and federal laws grant judges wide discretion in deciding whether to place a defendant on probation. Typically statutes allow probation when it appears that: (1) the defendant is not likely to commit another offense; (2) the public interest does not require that the defendant receive the penalty provided for the offense; and (3) the rehabilitation of the defendant does not require that he or she receive the penalty provided for the offense. Legislatures, however, often forbid the granting of probation for those convicted of serious offenses like murder, rape, and in some states armed robbery as well.

Often the sentencing judge imposes a prison sentence but then suspends its execution and places the offender on probation instead. A sentence of probation is often used in conjunction with some other form of non-incarcerative sanction, such as a fine, restitution, or the requirement of attendance at a drug or alcohol rehabilitation center. When probation is granted, restrictions are

conditions
of probation
placed on the defendant's activities. **Conditions of probation** typically include keeping a job, supporting the family, avoiding places where alcoholic beverages are sold, reporting periodically to the probation officer, and not violating any law. Because probation is a judicial act, the judge may revoke probation and send the defendant to prison if these conditions of probation are violated.

Fines

fines
The imposition of a *fine* is one of the oldest and most widely used punishments. Fines are used extensively for traffic offenses and minor ordinance violations. They generate well over $1 billion annually for local governments. The imposition of a fine, however, is not confined to the lower courts. Many trial courts of general jurisdiction depend quite heavily on fines, alone or as the principal component of a sentence in which the fine is combined with another sanction—probation, for example—in sentencing criminal defendants for a wide variety of offenses, including some generally considered serious (Hillsman, Sichel, and Mahoney).

In contrast to the great diversity of practices regarding fine use in America, some West European countries have adopted sentencing policies that explicitly make fines the sentence of choice for many offenses, including some crimes of violence that would result in jail sentences in many American criminal courts. In West Germany, for example, a major legislative goal is to minimize the imposition of jail terms of less than six months. Instead, courts make extensive use of ''day-fines,'' which enable judges to set fines at amounts reflecting the gravity of the offense but also taking account of the financial means of the offender. American judges, on the other hand, frequently cite the poverty of offenders as an obstacle to the broader use of fines as sanctions. Some courts, however, regularly impose fines on persons whose financial resources are extremely limited and are successful in collecting those fines (Hillsman, Sichel, and Mahoney).

Restitution

restitution

In its simplest form, **restitution** is repayment to a victim who has suffered some form of economic loss as a result of the offender's crime. Restitution has always been part of the American criminal justice system but has gone largely unpublicized. In recent years, however, it has received increased attention and has been endorsed by the National Advisory Commission on Criminal Justice Standards and Goals and the American Bar Association, among others. Some states have enacted laws encouraging restitutive sanctions, and programs have been started in other states to implement this approach.

community service

When used, restitution is usually made a condition of probation. In addition to financial payments to specific victims, restitution may also take the form of **community service**—for example, work in a social service agency for a specified period. As a criminal sanction it is largely restricted to property crimes. It has little relevance if violence figured in the commission of the offense. Although restitution has many supporters, some are concerned that if it is used as the sole sanction it may allow some offenders to purchase a relatively mild punishment. As a practical matter, however, the typical property offender lacks the financial resources to compensate the victim.

The Death Penalty

death penalty

Of all the forms of punishment, the **death penalty** is by far the most controversial. Although its use is highly debated, only a handful of offenders potentially face the ultimate sanction society can impose on the guilty.

capital punishment

Capital punishment was once almost the exclusive penalty applied to convicted felons. By the time of the American Revolution, the English courts had defined approximately 240 felony offenses, all of which were **capital offenses.** Many death penalties were not carried out, though; instead, offenders were pardoned or banished to penal colonies. Through time, courts and legislatures began to recognize other forms of punishment, such as imprisonment and later probation. By 1970 all but nine jurisdictions had provided for the death penalty, but it was limited to murder, treason, and (largely in the South) rape. Through the years the number of executions steadily fell. Since 1930, when statistics first began to be collected, executions declined from an annual average of 167 to only twenty-one per year between 1960 and 1967. From 1967 to 1972 an unofficial moratorium on executions existed. Table 15-3 shows executions between 1930 and 1967.

capital offenses

Abolition of the death penalty has been a hot political issue. Opponents contend that it is morally wrong for the state to take a life: it has no deterrent value and it is inherently discriminatory. These arguments have led all Western

TABLE 15-3   Profile of Capital Punishment Statutes

Jurisdictions authorizing capital punishment at some time during 1985	Revised or replaced by legislature	Automatic appeals required	Capital offenses
Federal			Aircraft piracy
Alabama		Yes	Murder
Arizona	Yes	Yes	First degree murder
Arkansas	Yes		Aggravated murder; treason
California		Yes	First degree murder with special circumstances
Colorado	Yes	Yes	First degree murder (includes felony murder); first degree kidnaping
Connecticut	Yes	Yes	Murder
Delaware		Yes	First degree murder with statutory aggravating circumstances
Florida			First degree murder
Georgia		Yes	Murder; treason; aircraft hijacking; kidnaping with bodily injury; armed robbery or rape in which victim dies
Idaho		Yes[a]	First degree murder, aggravated kidnaping (except where victim released unharmed)
Illinois		Yes	Murder
Indiana		Yes	Murder
Kentucky		Yes	Aggravated murder; kidnaping when victim is killed
Louisiana		Yes	First degree murder
Maryland		Yes[a]	First degree murder
Mississippi	Yes	Yes	Capital murder, capital rape
Missouri		Yes	First degree murder
Montana	Yes	Yes	Deliberate homicide, aggravated kidnaping (resulting in death)
Nebraska		Yes	First degree murder
Nevada	Yes	Yes	First degree murder
New Hampshire		Yes	Contract murder or murder of a law enforcement officer or kidnaping victim
New Jersey	Yes	Yes[b]	Kidnaping or purposeful murder or contract murder with aggravating circumstances
New Mexico		Yes[a]	First degree murder
North Carolina		Yes	First degree murder
Ohio			Aggravated murder
Oklahoma		Yes	Murder
Oregon		Yes	Aggravated murder
Pennsylvania		Yes	First degree murder
South Carolina	Yes	Yes	Murder with statutory aggravating circumstances
South Dakota		Yes	Murder, kidnaping (with gross permanent physical injury inflicted on victim)
Tennessee		Yes	First degree murder
Texas	Yes	Yes	Murder of public safety officer, fireman, or correctional employee; murder during specified felonies or escapes; contract murder; multiple murders

TABLE 15-3 *(continued)*

Jurisdictions authorizing capital punishment at some time during 1985	Revised or replaced by legislature	Automatic appeals required	Capital offenses
Utah		Yes	First degree murder; aggravated assault by prisoner sentenced for first degree felony where serious injury is caused
Vermont			Murder of police or corrections officer, kidnaping for ransom
Virginia	Yes	Yes	Capital murder
Washington		Yes	Aggravated, premeditated first degree murder
Wyoming		Yes	First degree murder

Note: Jurisdictions without capital punishment statutes are: Alaska, District of Columbia, Hawaii, Iowa, Kansas, Maine, Massachusetts, Michigan, Minnesota, New York, North Dakota, Rhode Island, West Virginia, and Wisconsin.
[a] Sentence review only.
[b] Automatic review after January 17, 1986.
SOURCE: Bureau of Justice Statistics, U.S. Department of Justice, *Capital Punishment, 1985* (Washington, D.C.: Government Printing Office, 1986).

democracies except racist South Africa to formally abolish the death penalty. Supporters counter that retribution justifies the taking of a life and that the death penalty does deter; they are generally unconcerned or unconvinced about allegations of discriminatory impact. For the last two decades the debate over the death penalty has largely focused on Supreme Court decisions.

Eighth Amendment Standards

cruel and unusual punishment

Is capital punishment consistent with the Eighth Amendment's prohibition against *cruel and unusual punishment*? The Supreme Court did not consider the constitutionality of capital punishment until 1972. The landmark decision of *Furman* v. *Georgia* (408 U.S. 238) invalidated all thirty-seven state death penalty statutes. The Court was deeply divided over the issue, however, with every justice penning a separate opinion. Only two justices, for example, believed that the death penalty itself was unconstitutional. Three other justices in the majority shared a common concern that the death penalty was arbitrarily and capriciously imposed. Similarly the four justices in the minority expressed widely divergent views as to why they believed that capital punishment was consistent with the Eighth Amendment.

Furman v. Georgia

mandatory death penalty guided discretion aggravating and mitigating circumstances

Furman raised more questions than it answered. Many legal scholars believed that state legislatures could write capital punishment laws consistent with the Eighth Amendment. By 1976 thirty-seven states had enacted new legislation designed to avoid the standardless and arbitrary application of capital punishment. These laws took two forms. Some states passed *mandatory death penalty* laws that removed all discretion from the process by requiring that anyone convicted of a capital offense be sentenced to death. Other states enacted *guided discretion* statutes, which required judges and juries to weigh various *aggravating and mitigating circumstances* in deciding whether or not a particular defendant should receive the death penalty.

Death Penalty Cases

These new laws were tested in a series of five companion cases collectively known as the ***Death Penalty Cases*** (*Gregg* v. *Georgia,* 428 U.S. 153, 1976). Again the Court was badly divided but a seven-justice majority agreed that the death penalty did not constitute cruel and unusual punishment under all circumstances. Thus, the Court considered under what circumstances the death penalty was unconstitutional. Mandatory death penalty laws were struck down because they failed to focus on the circumstances of the case. Thus the death penalty provisions in twenty-one states were invalidated, resulting in the modification to life imprisonment of death sentences imposed on hundreds of offenders in those states. Guided discretion death penalty laws on the other hand were upheld: "The concerns expressed in *Furman* that the penalty of death not be imposed in an arbitrary or capricious manner can be met by a carefully drafted statute that ensures that the sentencing authority is given adequate information and guidance." For a death penalty law to be constitutional,

bifurcated process

the high court ruled, it must provide for a ***bifurcated process.*** During the first or guilt phase of the trial, the jury considers only the issue of guilt or innocence. If the jury unanimously convicts for a crime carrying the death penalty, then the jury reconvenes. During the second or penalty phase of the trial, the jury considers aggravating and mitigating circumstances and then decides whether to impose the death penalty. If they decline, the defendant is typically sentenced to life imprisonment.

Many state legislatures, citing public opinion polls showing that a great majority of citizens favor the death penalty for murder, quickly revised their laws to conform with those upheld in the Death Penalty Cases. By 1985, thirty-seven states and the federal government had death penalty laws covering 78 percent of the population. (Only thirty-two states, though, held prisoners under sentence of death.) Thirteen states and the District of Columbia do not have capital punishment statutes. Table 15-3 indicates that there are some variations in these laws. All encompass murder, but there are some differences in specific types of homicide cases that are ***death-eligible.*** State death penalty

death-eligible

laws also differ in terms of a minimum age at which the death penalty may be imposed. Twenty-three states specify a minimum age, which most frequently is eighteen years but can be as low as ten years of age (Indiana and Vermont). Fourteen states and the federal system report no minimum age. It is important to realize that these and similar provisions are subject to change. During 1985, for example, legislatures in eleven states altered their death penalty laws. Moreover, courts have struck down laws in several states, including New York, Massachusetts, and Oregon.

Appeals and Evolving Standards

Like all defendants found guilty, those sentenced to death are entitled to appellate court review. In death penalty cases, though, special provisions govern appeal and special significance attaches to utilizing all potential avenues of post-conviction relief. The vast majority of states require appellate review of a death

automatic review

penalty case regardless of the defendant's wishes. Typically, this ***automatic review*** is heard directly by the state supreme court, bypassing any intermediate courts of appeals. Next, a writ of certiorari may be filed with the U.S. Supreme Court. Even though the chances of four justices voting to hear the case are not high, they are much higher than for ordinary criminal appeals. The Court "has become America's life-and-death tribunal. No other Supreme Court in history has been as preoccupied with—or bedeviled by—the questions of when life begins and when a state may snuff one out" (Press). Having exhausted these appellate remedies, defendants sentenced to death often file numerous writs of habeas corpus in various state and federal courts. As a result the review process is quite lengthy. For those executed since 1977, the average time between the imposition of a sentence of death and execution was six years. Some are quite critical of such delays. Then Justice, now Chief Justice, William Rehnquist criticized his colleagues for providing capital offenders "numerous procedural protections unheard of for other crimes," and "for allowing endlessly drawn out legal proceedings" (*New York Times*). Others counter that the death penalty is qualitatively different from other types of sanctions and therefore repeated scrutiny of the case is more than justified.

One reason for the lengthy appellate process is evolving standards concerning the application of the death penalty. Three issues illustrate some of the issues that have arisen in the aftermath of *Gregg*. For example, can the state impose the death penalty for crimes other than murder? The Court ruled that rape was not a grave enough offense to justify the imposition of the death penalty (*Coker* v. *Georgia,* 422 U.S. 584, 1977).

A longstanding issue has been the exclusion of persons opposed to the death penalty from juries in capital cases. In 1968 the Supreme Court rejected the classic "hanging jury." A state may not choose jurors to a jury organized to return a verdict of death just by excluding jurors simply because they voiced general objections to the death penalty or expressed religious scruples against its infliction (*Witherspoon* v. *Illinois,* 391 U.S. 510, 1968). This case was limited somewhat in *Wainwright* v. *Witt* (105 S.Ct. 844, 1985) when the high court held that, as a matter of principle, any juror can be excused if his views on capital punishment are deemed by the trial judge to "prevent or substantially impair the performance of his duties."

*proportion-
ality review*

There has also been considerable disagreement over whether *Gregg* required **proportionality review.** Proportionality is the concept that states should compare each death sentence with sentences imposed in comparable cases throughout the state to determine whether similar cases are being handled in a similar way. The Supreme Court upheld the death sentence in a California murder case, holding that a proportionality review by an appellate court was not a constitutional requirement (*Pulley* v. *Harris,* 104 S.Ct. 378, 1984). Many state laws, however, mandate such a review.

Death Row Inmates

As a result of post-*Gregg* statutes, 1,591 prisoners were under a sentence of death as of the end of 1985. Table 15-4 shows that the preponderance of those awaiting execution were in the South. Death-row inmates are predominantly male (a scant 1.1 percent are female), disproportionately black (42 percent),

TABLE 15-4   Prisoners Under Sentence of Death, by Region and State at Year-End 1984 and 1985

Region and state	Prisoners under sentence 1984	Changes during 1985			Prisoners under sentence 1985
		Received under sentence	Removed from death row (excluding executions)	Executed	
United States	1,420	273	84	18	1,591
Federal	0	0	0	0	0
State	1,420	273	84	18	1,591
Northeast	59	20	6	0	73
Connecticut	0	0	0	0	0
New Hampshire	0	0	0	0	0
New Jersey	10	7	0	0	17
Pennsylvania	49	13	6	0	56
Vermont	0	0	0	0	0
Midwest	174	54	6	1	221
Illinois	70	15	2	0	83
Indiana	26	10	1	1	34
Missouri	29	8	1	0	36
Nebraska	13	0	1	0	12
Ohio	36	21	1	0	56
South Dakota	0	0	0	0	0
South	900	167	50	16	1,001
Alabama	68	13	2	0	79
Arkansas	23	6	1	0	28
Delaware	6	0	2	0	4
Florida	215	27	13	3	226
Georgia	112	8	10	3	107
Kentucky	20	6	1	0	25
Louisiana	31	10	1	1	39
Maryland	19	0	2	0	17
Mississippi	39	5	3	0	41
North Carolina	37	20	1	0	56
Oklahoma	50	14	6	0	58
South Carolina	35	9	1	1	42
Tennessee	37	11	2	0	46
Texas	180	36	4	6	206
Virginia	28	2	1	2	27
West	287	32	22	1	296
Arizona	56	4	4	0	56
California	167	16	13	0	170
Colorado	1	0	0	0	1
Idaho	14	1	1	0	14
Montana	4	1	0	0	5
Nevada	28	7	3	1	31
New Mexico	5	0	0	0	5
Oregon	0	0	0	0	0
Utah	5	2	1	0	6
Washington	4	1	0	0	5
Wyoming	3	0	0	0	3

SOURCE: Bureau of Justice Statistics, U.S. Department of Justice, *Capital Punishment, 1985* (Washington, D.C.: Government Printing Office, 1986).

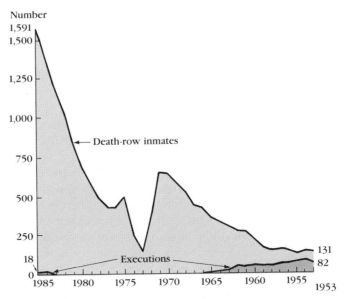

Figure 15-1 Persons under sentence of death and persons executed, 1953–85.   SOURCE: Bureau of Justice Statistics, U.S. Department of Justice, *Capital Punishment, 1985* (Washington, D.C.: Government Printing Office, 1986).

have never completed high school (58 percent), and have a prior felony conviction (two out of three). The median age is thirty-two years (the youngest was sixteen and the oldest seventy-four).

On January 16, 1977, convicted murderer Gary Gilmore's execution by a Utah firing squad attracted considerable national and international attention, not only because he was the first person executed in the United States since the unofficial moratorium began in 1967, but also because Gilmore had opposed all attempts to delay the execution. By the end of 1985 a total of fifty persons had been executed. The most common methods of execution are lethal injection (sixteen states), electrocution (fifteen), lethal gas (eight), hanging (four), and firing squad (two).

A sentence of death does not necessarily mean that the offender will be executed, however. From 1977, when the death penalty was upheld, through the end of 1985 a total of 2,110 prisoners were under a sentence of death. Fifty were executed. An additional 889 had their death sentences vacated on appeal or commuted by the governor or else died in prison. The others remain on death row pending the outcome of their appeals.

Conclusion

We usually identify sentencing with the judiciary. A closer examination, however, indicates that all three branches of government share sentencing responsibilities. The legislative branch establishes the forms of punishment.

Thus the judge must choose a sentence prescribed by law; in a typical felony case this means deciding between probation and imprisonment. For less serious offenses a fine, restitution, or both may also be considered. The executive branch largely determines the consequences of prison sentences. How long a person serves in prison is determined not only by the length of sentence initially imposed by the judge but also by state practices related to good time and parole release.

Over the last two decades considerable attention has been devoted to sentencing resulting in major alterations in the mix of sentencing responsibilities. The range of sentencing discretion granted the judge has been restricted in some states. Parole board authority over early release has also been restricted in some jurisdictions. These changes reflect widespread questioning of the purposes of criminal sanctions. Sentencing serves many frequently contradictory purposes. Asking why we sentence forces one to examine these contradictions. Pragmatic considerations of overcrowded and sometimes inhumane prisons, public concern over rising crime rates, the absence of rehabilitation programs, and high rates of unemployment are equally important in assessing whether retribution, incapacitation, deterrence, and rehabilitation are reachable goals.

For Discussion

1. Should the punishment fit the crime or the criminal? In what ways do the four justifications for punishment provide different answers to this question?
2. Which of the four justifications for sentencing comes closest to matching your own? How does this view influence your thinking about how the courts sentence?
3. What is the mix of legislative, judicial, and sentencing responsibility in your state?
4. What views of the purposes of sentencing are most often expressed in the local and national newspapers?
5. Interview a judge. What are his or her views of judicial discretion over sentencing? Too much, too little, or just right? Why?

References

BLUMSTEIN, ALFRED, JACQUELINE COHEN, SUSAN MARTIN, AND MICHAEL TONRY, eds. *Research on Sentencing: The Search for Reform.* Washington, D.C.: National Academy Press, 1983.

BUREAU OF JUSTICE STATISTICS, U.S. Department of Justice. *Setting Prison Times.* Washington, D.C.: Government Printing Office, 1983.

——. *Probation and Parole 1984.* Washington, D.C.: Government Printing Office, 1986.

FINN, PETER. "Judicial Responses to Prison Overcrowding." *Judicature* 67 (1984): 318.

FRANKEL, MARVIN. *Criminal Sentences: Law Without Order.* New York: Hill & Wang, 1972.

HILLSMAN, SALLY, JOYCE SICHEL, AND BARRY MAHONEY. *Fines in Sentencing: A Study of the Use of the Fine as a Criminal Sanction, Executive Summary.* Washington, D.C.: National Institute of Justice, U.S. Department of Justice, 1984.

KWITNY, MARTHA. "Our Overcrowded Prisons." *Wall Street Journal,* October 1, 1975. (Extract reprinted by permission of *The Wall Street Journal,* © Dow Jones & Company, Inc., 1975. All rights reserved.)

MODEL PENAL CODE, Comment 1. Tentative Draft No. 2. Philadelphia: American Law Institute, 1954.

MOORE, MARK, SUSAN ESTRICH, DANIEL McGILLIS, AND WILLIAM SPELMAN. *Dangerous Offenders: The Elusive Target of Justice.* Cambridge, Mass.: Harvard University Press, 1984.

NAGIN, DANIEL. "General Deterrence: A Review of the Empirical Evidence." In *Deterrence and Incapacitation: Estimating the Effects of Criminal Sanctions on Crime Rates,* ed. Alfred Blumstein, Jacqueline Cohen, and Daniel Nagin. Washington, D.C.: National Academy of Sciences, 1978.

NATIONAL ADVISORY COMMISSION ON CRIMINAL JUSTICE STANDARDS AND GOALS. *Corrections.* Washington, D.C.: Government Printing Office, 1973a.

———. *Courts.* Washington, D.C.: Government Printing Office, 1973b.

NEW YORK TIMES, June 14, 1981, p. 28.

PEIRCE, NEAL. "Large Chunks of State Budgets Targeted for Prisons," *New Orleans Times-Picayune,* February 9, 1987.

PRESS, ARIC, WITH DIANE CAMPER. "A Life-and-Death Tribunal." *Newsweek* 102 (July 18, 1983): 56.

PRICE, ALBERT. *The Politics of Definite Sentencing in Four American States.* Unpublished Ph.D. dissertation, University of Connecticut, 1980.

ROSETT, ARTHUR, AND DONALD CRESSEY. *Justice by Consent: Plea Bargains in the American Courthouse.* Philadelphia: J. B. Lippincott, 1976.

SHINNAR, SHLOMO, AND REUEL SHINNAR. "The Effects of the Criminal Justice System on the Control of Crime: A Quantitative Approach." *Law and Society Review* 9 (1975): 581.

TAPPAN, PAUL. *Crime, Justice and Correction.* New York: McGraw-Hill, 1960.

VAN DINE, STEPHEN, JOHN CONRAD, AND SIMON DINITZ. *Restraining the Wicked.* Lexington, Mass.: Lexington Books, 1979.

VON HIRSCH, ANDREW. *Doing Justice.* New York: Hill & Wang, 1976.

WILSON, JAMES Q. *Thinking About Crime.* New York: Basic Books, 1975.

For Further Reading

ALLEN, HARRY, CHRIS ESKRIDGE, EDWARD LATESSA, AND GENNARO VITO. *Probation and Parole in America.* New York: Free Press, 1985.

BLACK, CHARLES. *Capital Punishment: The Inevitability of Caprice and Mistake,* 2d ed. New York: W. W. Norton, 1981.

CLEAR, TODD, AND GEORGE COLE. *American Corrections.* Pacific Grove, Calif.: Brooks/Cole, 1986.

CULLEN, FRANCIS, AND KAREN GILBERT. *Reaffirming Rehabilitation.* Cincinnati, Ohio: Anderson, 1982.

JOHNSON, ROBERT. *Hard Time: Understanding and Reforming the Prison.* Pacific Grove, Calif.: Brooks/Cole, 1987.

PACKER, HERBERT. *The Limits of the Criminal Sanction.* Palo Alto, Calif.: Stanford University Press, 1968.

SELLIN, THORSTEN. *The Penalty of Death.* Beverly Hills, Calif.: Sage Publications, 1980.

VAN DEN HAAG, ERNEST, AND JOHN CONRAD. *The Death Penalty: A Debate.* New York: Plenum, 1983.

VON HIRSCH, ANDREW. *Doing Justice.* New York: Hill & Wang, 1976.

CHAPTER 16

Choosing Between Prison and Probation

There is no more powerful symbol of law than Lady Justice. Held high in her right hand are the scales of justice symbolizing fairness in the administration of justice. Draped across her eyes is a blindfold suggesting that all who come before her will receive impartial justice. Grasped low in her left hand is a sword standing for the power and might of law. Replicas of Lady Justice can be found adorning the exteriors of many American courthouses; but whether the sentencing process inside the courtrooms lives up to those high ideals is open to question.

The subject of this chapter is the sentencing process; it concerns who is and who is not sentenced to prison, granted probation, or executed. The scales of justice are the starting point. Before we can evaluate the criticisms leveled against the sentencing process, we need to know what factors judges and other members of the courtroom work group weigh in deciding between prison or probation. Normal penalties are the most important consideration in sentencing. Based on the seriousness of the offense and the defendant's prior record, courthouses have developed going rates. These normal penalties provide the parameters that members of the courtroom work group use as they fine tune a sentence for a given offender.

The blindfold is the next major topic. Sentences imposed on the guilty are expected to be fair and just. Many argue that they are not. Disparities and discrimination in sentencing are major topics of concern. Numerous studies probe the extent to which race, age, gender, and economic status improperly pierce the judicial blindfold when sentences are imposed.

The sword of justice also will be discussed. Whereas some worry that the scales of justice are tipped, others are concerned that the sword of justice is sheathed. Frustration over rising crime rates have produced charges that judges are too lenient. Demands that sentences be more certain as well as more severe have become a staple of American politics. Legislators have responded by increasing the severity of some punishments and altering sentencing structures in hopes of producing greater predictability in sentencing. The way these reforms actually work out in practice requires careful scrutiny.

Courtroom Work Groups and the Sentencing Process

Sentencing represents a joint decision-making process (Nardulli et al.). Although only judges possess the legal authority to impose sentence, other members of the courtroom work group are also influential. However, the extent of this influence varies from jurisdiction to jurisdiction and from judge to judge. Where sentence bargaining predominates, for example, the judge almost invariably imposes the sentence that the prosecutor and defense attorney have already agreed upon. Where count and charge bargaining is used, the actors reach agreements based on past sentencing patterns of the judge. The most significant actors in sentencing are probation officers, prosecutors, defense attorneys, and of course judges.

Probation Officer

Probation officers perform two major functions in the sentencing process. One is the supervision of offenders after a sentence of probation has been imposed. The other is investigation prior to sentencing. The primary purpose of a *pre-sentence investigation (PSI)* is to help the judge select an appropriate sentence by providing information about the crime and the criminal. Typically the PSI is ordered by the court following the defendant's conviction. A date is set for sentencing the offender, and in the interim the *probation officer* conducts the investigation. The report is based on police reports, prosecutor's records, an interview with the offender, and perhaps a talk with the defendant's family as well. A typical pre-sentence report contains a description of the offense, the defendant's version of the crime, prior criminal record, social history, and a psychological evaluation (if needed). Thus the pre-sentence report links the judge, who must select the appropriate sentence, to an appropriate data base. This is particularly important because in many cases, especially when the defendant has entered a plea of guilty, the judge knows

pre-sentence investigation (PSI) probation officer

little about the particulars of the crime or the background of the offender. For these reasons many groups have urged mandatory PSIs for all felony cases. Actual usage varies, however. Depending on state law and the workload of the probation department, a judge may request a pre-sentence investigation in all cases, for only certain categories of offenders, or only when probation is a likely sentence (Katkin).

Besides providing background information, many pre-sentence reports also include a recommendation of an appropriate sentence. Some judges, however, will not allow a recommendation, claiming that this is the prerogative solely of the court. Even if there is no explicit recommendation, most PSIs leave little room for doubt about what the probation officer thinks the sentence should be. If probation is recommended, the report typically includes a suggested level of supervision (ranging from intensive through regular to minimal), a listing of special conditions of probation, a plan for treatment, and an assessment of community resources available to facilitate rehabilitation.

Through sentencing recommendations, probation officers can play a significant role in the sentencing process. Although sentencing judges are not required to follow such recommendations, they usually do. Research has shown a consistently strong relationship between the recommendation of the probation officer and the final disposition made by the judge (Carter and Wilkins; Hagan, 1977). This correlation is subject to several different interpretations. One possibility is that judges seriously consider the recommendations and use them to guide their decisions. Alternatively, probation officers may anticipate what the judges' decisions will be and tailor their recommendations accordingly. In jurisdictions where sentence bargaining predominates, for example, prosecutors and defense attorneys may talk to the probation officer before the PSI is submitted to the court. The conversation indicates the information to be stressed to justify the sentence already agreed upon. The probation report then provides a rationale after the fact (Rosett and Cressey). One study concluded that the probation officer's role in sentencing is largely ceremonial (Hagan et al., 1979).

Prosecutor

Prosecutors can influence the sentencing decision in several important ways. By agreeing to a count or charge bargain, prosecutors limit the maximum penalties that the judge may impose. During the sentencing hearing, prosecutors can bring to the court's attention factors that are likely to increase the penalty—for example, that the victim was particularly vulnerable or that the defendant inflicted great harm on the victim. Alternatively, though, prosecutors can bring out factors that would lessen the penalty—for example, the defendant's cooperation with the police. Finally, prosecutors may make a specific sentencing recommendation. If, for example, there has been a sentence bargain, the prosecutor will indicate the penalty agreed on, with the usual result that the judge will adopt that recommendation as the sentence. When such prosecutorial recommendations are based on officewide policy, they can have the positive effect of muting sentencing disparities among the different judges.

In some courts, however, prosecutors are not allowed to make sentencing recommendations because sentencing is viewed solely as a judicial responsibility.

Defense Attorney

The defense attorney's role in sentencing begins early in the history of a case. The decision of whether to go to trial or enter a guilty plea is partially based on the attorney's realistic assessment of the likely sentence to be imposed. Based on the knowledge of what sentences have been handed out to other defendants accused of similar crimes and with similar backgrounds, the attorney must advise (and at times prepare) the client as to the probable sentence. At the same time, the defense attorney seeks to obtain the best sentence possible. One way to accomplish this goal is by trying to maneuver the case before a judge with a lenient sentencing record. Another way is to discuss the case with the prosecutor in hopes that he or she will agree to (or at least not oppose) a recommendation of probation in the pre-sentence investigation. Defense attorneys also try to show certain circumstances to make the defendant look better in the eyes of the judge, prosecutor, and probation officer. They may try to downplay the severity of the offense by stressing the defendant's minor role in the crime or the fact that the victim was not without blame, or they may have friends or employers testify about the defendant's general good character and regular employment.

Overall, though, defense attorneys are less influential than prosecutors in obtaining a less severe punishment than is typical. At times judges and prosecutors view defense attorneys' arguments for leniency as an effort to impress their clients that they tried as hard as they could.

The Judge

Courtroom work groups impose informal limits on how judges exercise their formal legal authority to impose sentences. Judges are well aware that the disposition of cases is tied to plea bargaining and that in turn plea bargaining depends on being able to anticipate the sentencing tendencies of judges.

> No matter how aloof a judge may think he is and no matter how eccentric others may think he is, he shares in a framework of understandings, expectations and agreements that are relied upon to dispose of most criminal cases. As does a prosecutor or a defense attorney, he can deviate from this consensus only slightly; otherwise he threatens the whole working structure of the courthouse. When he strays too far from expectations by imposing a sentence either substantially more lenient or more severe than the one agreed on by defendant, defense lawyer and prosecutor, it becomes more difficult for the prosecutor and defense counsel to negotiate future agreements. (Rosett and Cressey: 81)

In working within the limits established by the consensus of the courtroom work groups, judges are also constrained because the other members of the work group possess a more thorough knowledge of the details of the defendant and the nature of the crime. This does not mean that judges are without influence. Judges are the most experienced members of the courtroom team, and therefore their views carry more weight than the relatively inexperienced prosecutors' or defense attorneys'. Thus differing judicial attitudes on sentencing are reflected in the courtroom work groups' common understanding of what sentences are appropriate.

Factors in Sentencing

Sentencing is not an easy task. The vast majority of judges say it is the most difficult part of their job. Part of the reason is that sentencing requires weighing the possibility of rehabilitation, the need for protecting the public, popular demands for retribution, and any potential deterrent value in the sentence. But courtroom work groups do not consider these competing perspectives in the abstract. They must sentence real defendants. Each defendant and crime is somewhat different. Sentences are expected to be individualized—to fit the penalty to the crime and the defendant. The seriousness of the crime, prior criminal record, aggravating or mitigating circumstances of the crime, and the social stability of the defendant are just a few of the general factors that must be considered in seeking to individualize sentences. Recall also from the discussion in Chapter 13 that defendants who go to trial rather than plead guilty may also receive greater than normal sentences.

Normal Penalties

normal penalties

In seeking to produce individualized sentences, courtroom work groups employ what have been labeled ***normal penalties*** (Sudnow). Based on the usual manner in which crimes are committed and the typical backgrounds of the defendants who commit them, courtroom work groups develop typical sen-

---

Q U O T A T I O N

I have sentenced hundreds of criminal offenders and the difficult responsibilities that attach to sentencing haven't become any easier for me the longer I have done it. From my own experience, about ten percent of the time involves a case in which I can't readily determine what I want to do. I've got to think about it for a while, may confer with some of my colleagues. Figuratively speaking, it's a coin flip sometimes and that is rather drastic when you are talking about somebody's personal liberty.

Judge Critelli, Des Moines, Iowa, in Leslie Wilkins et al., *Sentencing Guidelines: Structuring Judicial Discretion* (Washington, D.C.: Government Printing Office, 1976), p. vii.

tences of what sentences are appropriate for given categories. It is within these normal penalties that individualization occurs. Upward and downward adjustments are made. Typical sentences are not used mechanically; rather, they guide sentencing.

CLOSE-UP

Labeling Defendants

POs [probation officers] did not so much process individuals as they *processed types of individuals who had been labeled in particular ways*. . . . [They] used a threefold typology of criminal defendants which was based on the defendant's risk of recidivism.

1. Low-risk defendants were usually in trouble with the criminal justice system for the first time, were between the ages of 18 and 25, and were either attending university or had a steady job. These defendants, therefore, had much to lose by possessing a criminal record and they took their current involvement with the courts seriously. As one PO put it, ''These people have made one screwy mistake and it's shaken them up so much we'll probably never see them again.'' For example, one defendant has been convicted of attempted theft after he had altered a sales receipt to obtain items he hadn't paid for. This defendant was unusually cooperative during the interview and expressed concern about the fact that business associates and local bankers would find out about the criminal record he now possessed. His PO told me, ''I don't think we'll see him come through here again. This was his first offense and I think it really made an impression on him.''

2. High-risk defendants usually had at least two prior arrests and convictions, little formal education, and were seen as unwilling or unable to hold a steady job. Often, they were perceived as not taking their involvement with the courts seriously. For these reasons, POs saw these defendants as likely to be in and out of trouble for much of their adult lives. For example, a defendant had been convicted of burglary and had several other theft-related convictions. In addition, he had never held a job for more than three months at a time. The PO who handled the case told me:

> This [defendant] is just too lazy to work. . . . He commits these burglaries because of that. I'll bet ya we see this guy again. He's definitely [high-risk] material.

3. The final category of defendants consisted of individuals whose risk of recidivism was neither definitely high or low, but was seen as problematic. Some of these defendants had been in trouble with the law before, generally involving minor offenses such as shoplifting. Other possessed characteristics of alcoholism or a ''bad attitude'' which POs considered likely to be related to future criminal behavior. While there was no specific set of characteristics which defined this category of defendants, POs pointed out that what they did share was the potential for ''heading for trouble.'' For example, a defendant had been convicted of theft and had two prior theft-related convictions. However, he also was working two jobs to pay off a student loan and return to the university. The PO described the defendant's risk of recidivism in the following way:

> It is hard to tell with him. He's got these [prior offenses], but he's got these things [two jobs, a car] going for him. If he was in a situation where he could steal, I don't know.

What was important for POs was that, whatever the problem, these defendants were ''workable.'' As one PO put it:

> I spend the most time with these [defendants]. I try to make them aware of alternatives . . . or refer them for heavy-duty counseling, or do some things myself so hopefully they won't get in trouble again.

Jack Spencer, ''Accounts, Attitudes, and Solutions: Probation Officer–Defendant Negotiations of Subjective Orientations.'' © 1983 by the Society for the Study of Social Problems. Reprinted from *Social Problems*, Vol. 30, No. 5, June 1983, pp. 570–581, by permission.

two-stage decision-making process

Sentencing involves a ***two-stage decision-making process.*** After conviction, a decision is made whether to incarcerate the defendant or grant probation. The second stage is determining how long the sentence should be. This process can be used to illustrate that different courtroom work groups employ varying concepts of normal penalties. From one courtroom to the next, there are important differences in the threshold for granting probation. And once it has been decided that a defendant should be imprisoned, there are important differences in the factors used to determine the length of that sentence. Stated another way, courtroom work groups tend to look at the same set of general factors in passing sentence. But there is no uniformity in the relative weights that are assigned these general or individual factors.

Seriousness of the Offense

seriousness of the offense

The most important factor in setting normal penalties is the ***seriousness of the offense.*** The more serious the offense, the less likely the defendant will be granted probation. And the more serious the offense, the longer the prison sentence. These conclusions are hardly surprising. Society expects that convicted murderers will be punished more severely than those found guilty of theft. What is important is how courtroom work groups go about the task of deciding what offenses are serious.

When weighing the seriousness of the offense, courtroom work groups examine the harm or loss suffered by the crime victim in what they perceive to be the "real offense" (what really happened, not the official charge). This information is provided either in the official version of the offense part of the pre-sentence report or by the police arrest report. By focusing on the "real offense" judges can counteract charge bargaining. For example, in some areas pre-sentence reports for simple robbery cases include the type of weapon used. Thus the defendant who has been found guilty only for unarmed robbery may often be sentenced on the basis that he really committed an armed robbery. The opposite also happens. By examining the prior relationship between the defendant and the victim, courtroom work groups often perceive that the underlying crime is a squabble among friends and therefore less serious than the official charge indicates (Vera Institute of Justice).

Court work groups vary in what offenses they view as serious and the severity of the penalties to be applied. Courts differ over the threshold of seriousness of the offense in granting probation. I found that in one downstate Illinois county, defendants convicted of aggravated assault with a weapon were never granted probation because this crime was viewed as very serious. But in Los Angeles, some defendants convicted of assault with a weapon would be considered for probation (Mather).

Sentencing on the basis of seriousness is one of the major ways courts attempt to arrive at consistent sentences. Most courts employ a rank ordering that incorporates the full range of offenses from the most serious crimes of armed robbery and rape, through middle-level crimes of domestic homicide to the lowest level of forgery, theft, and burglary. One reason that sentences appear to critics to be lenient is that most cases are distributed on the lowest level of this ranking. Many critics also fail to consider that judges do not wish to punish minor violators more harshly than serious ones. When a sentence is criticized for being too lenient, the usual response is that to give this defendant a longer prison term would necessitate an upward adjustment in all penalties.

Prior Record

prior record

After the seriousness of the offense, the next most important factor in sentencing is the defendant's ***prior record.*** As the prior record increases, so does the sentence (Welch and Spohn). In considering whether to grant the defendant probation or place him in prison, the courtroom work group carefully considers the defendant's previous criminal involvement. Often a single previous conviction is sufficient ground for denying probation (Neubauer; Welch and Spohn). But this is hardly an automatic policy. Several studies find that some courts will grant probation for a minor felony even if the defendant has previously been convicted (Dawson; Tiffany et al.). If the decision has been made to sentence the offender to prison, the prior record also plays a role in setting the length of incarceration. A study of seven cities found that a previous incarceration increased the length of sentence (Welch and Spohn).

How courts assess prior records varies. Some consider only previous convictions, whereas others look at arrests as well. In addition, courtroom work groups often consider the length of time between the current offense and the last one. If there has been a significant gap, the defendant will often receive a more lenient than normal sentence. If on the other hand the previous conviction is a recent one, this is often taken as an indication that the defendant is a bad actor and the severity of the punishment will increase. Finally, the prior record is assessed within the context of the severity of the crime itself. A study of federal defendants found that prior record had its greatest impact on less serious offenses. "When the crime is perceived as being less serious, individual factors such as prior record seem to be given relatively more weight than when the crime is more serious—there uniformly 'let the punishment fit the crime' seems to be more important" (Tiffany et al.: 379).

Aggravating or Mitigating Circumstances

In passing sentence judges and other members of the courtroom work group consider not only the formal charge but also how the crime was committed.

> We found that prosecutors and defense counsel engage in a very fine calculation of moral turpitude. Compared with the layperson's, the experienced criminal justice actor's analysis of moral turpitude is like the difference between measuring things in terms of pounds and ounces and measuring them in the finer units of grams, milligrams, and micrograms. There are subtle shades of differences and nuances which experienced attorneys appreciate but which are lost on the layperson.
>   For instance, in pretesting our hypothetical robbery with a knife case, prosecutors wanted to know such things as: Was the slashing completely unprovoked by the victim? Had the victim said anything at all or resisted in any way? Was the slashing necessary to accomplish the crime? Was it done out of nervousness? When the robber presented the knife, how did he present it? Was

there actual contact of the knife with the victim? . . . Prosecutors wanted to know not just whether there had been a slashing but how deep it was, whether there would be permanent injury or ugly scars in visible areas such as on the face. This kind of information was used by prosecutors to assess not only how serious the crime had been but also how "mean" or "bad" the defendant was. There was no question that a robbery with a slashing was a serious matter and had to be punished, but there was a question about the precise degree of punishment that this particular robbery deserved. (McDonald et al.: 157)

aggravating circum- stances

mitigating factors

Some of the ***aggravating circumstances*** that lead to higher penalty often include the use of a weapon and personal injury to the victim. For example, an offender who pistol whipped an elderly woman during a mugging would receive a higher penalty than one who merely threatened the victim with a weapon. ***Mitigating factors*** include youth of the defendant, lack of mental capacity, and role (principal or secondary actor) in the crime. There is no uniformity in what factors should be considered in weighing aggravating and mitigating circumstances, however.

Social Stability

social stability

The perceived ***social stability*** of the defendant is particularly important when probation is under consideration. Whether the defendant is married, the relationship with the family, length of employment, and prior alcohol or drug abuse represent some indicators of social stability. In an exhaustive study of factors in sentencing, Wilkins and his associates investigated over two hundred sentencing variables in the Denver and Vermont courts. They found that pre-sentence reports often contained significant missing data about social stability but concluded that judges have enough other data available to form a judgment. In both areas social stability turned out to be an important predictor of judges' sentencing.

Uncertainty and Public Opinion

uncertainty

Sentencing is more art than science. Judges, prosecutors, probation officers, and defense attorneys are well aware that in considering the seriousness of the offense, prior record of the defendant, aggravating or mitigating circumstances, and stability of the defendant, they will make mistakes. ***Uncertainty*** is deep-seated in the process. They may send someone to prison who should not be there or impose a prison sentence longer than necessary. Or they may err in the opposite direction. A defendant recently granted probation may commit a serious and well-publicized crime. Note, though, that only the second type of error will reach public attention. Mistakes of the first kind appear only later.

The uncertainties inherent in sentencing are particularly important at a time when public opinion is increasingly critical of the courts and sentencing. The majority of Americans feel that sentences are too lenient. In response, courts are sentencing a higher proportion of defendants to prison. Yet at the same time prisons are overcrowded, adding another complexity to the difficult task of arriving at a fair and appropriate sentence.

Discrimination in Sentencing?

Motivated by charges that sentencing is unfair, much sentencing research has investigated the extent of unwarranted variation in sentencing. These concerns include discrimination as well as disparity. Although widely used, terms like *discrimination* and *disparity* are rarely defined consistently. These concerns overlap somewhat, but they involve distinct behaviors. *Disparity* refers to inconsistencies in sentencing; the decision-making process is the principal topic of interest. *Discrimination,* on the other hand, refers to illegitimate influences in the sentencing process; defendant's attributes are the primary focus. Race is the clearest example of an illegitimate criterion in sentencing; it is a "suspect classification" from both a legal perspective and on moral grounds (Blumstein et al.). *Sentencing discrimination* exists when some illegitimate case attribute is associated with sentence outcomes after all other relevant variables are adequately controlled. These objectionable influences are referred to as *extralegal variables* (Hagan, 1974).

sentencing discrimination

extralegal variables

defendant's attributes

Numerous studies have probed the extent to which a *defendant's attributes,* such as race, age, gender, and economic status, pierce the judicial blindfold when sentences are imposed. The results are provocative not only because they raise important issues of equality before the law but also because they frequently appear to contradict one another (Blumstein et al.). To cite only one example, whereas Eisenstein and Jacob conclude from a study of sentencing in Baltimore, Chicago, and Detroit that "blacks are not treated worse than whites," Lizotte uses some of the same data from Chicago to calculate that "the 'cost' of being a black laborer is an additional 8.06 months of prison sentence." Thus some studies find patterns of discrimination, and many do not. These mixed results reflect at least four sets of issues that researchers debate: outcomes and controls, research sites, sentencing measures, and competing theories.

sentencing outcomes

Outcomes and controls.   Many laymen and even some academics equate any variation in sentencing with discrimination. It is quite clear that *sentencing outcomes* vary. Compared to the population as a whole, prisoners are much more likely to be young, minority males. To some this is sufficient evidence to prove that the sentencing process favors females, whites, and the rich (or at least the not-so-poor) and discriminates against young, minority males of lower socioeconomic status. Disparity in sentencing outcomes, however, is not necessarily indicative of discrimination (Wilbanks). As Chapter 9 indicated, criminal defendants are predominantly poor and uneducated. Thus any assessments of discrimination must examine not only outcomes but also consider the influence of legally relevant factors like seriousness of the offense and prior record. In statistical terms, the effects of these other variables must be controlled. Earlier studies often failed to do this. They considered only the single variables of race and sentencing, for example, and reported finding racial discrimination in the sentencing. Hagan (1974) found that the studies failed to include appropriate statistical controls for legally relevant variables like seriousness of the offense and prior criminal records. When these studies were reanalyzed he found that claims of racial discrimination were not supported by the data.

statistical controls

The necessity of using ***statistical controls*** becomes clear when we examine race and imprisonment (Hawkins). Blacks are incarcerated in state prisons at a rate eight times those of whites (Langan and Greenfeld). Does this indicate discrimination? Blumstein examined the degree to which the racial gap in prison populations could be attributed simply to racial differences in crime rates. He found he could attribute 80 percent of the racial gap to differences between races in their rates of arrest; blacks were more likely to be arrested for the most serious offenses of murder and robbery. Thus although some individual judges will behave in discriminatory ways and individual courts may display discrimination, the bulk of the racial disproportionality in the United States prisons can be attributed predominantly to nondiscriminatory responses to differences in involvement in crime.

Research sites. The American judiciary consists of numerous courts that differ in important ways. No one court is typical. It is difficult, therefore, to make general statements based on research in only one or a few places. Thus differing conclusions about the presence or absence of discrimination in sentencing may be the product of what court is studied and when. Hagan and Bumiller suggest that some "structural contexts" increase the likelihood of finding a race effect. These include the death penalty in the South, rural as opposed to urban courts, politically sensitive crimes like rape, and jurisdictions where probation officers make sentencing recommendations. In contrast, studies in the last decade that did not find discrimination focused on areas like large urban courts which are so constrained by courtroom work group norms that they lack the time and resources to allow discrimination by race.

Sentencing measures. As we indicated in Chapter 15, judges often must choose between a range of sentences that can range from very light punishment (fine, restitution, and/or probation) through a minimal period of incarceration (local jail or a year or two in state prison) to the very severe (many years to life in prison). In addition, a few murderers may be sentenced to death. No single statistical measure adequately summarizes this variation. Thus differing studies may reach different conclusions about discriminatory effects because they employ different measures of sentencing. Thus some studies examine the in/out decision (probation versus prison); others the sentencing length for those imprisoned; and others compare death penalties. Some studies use several complementary measures. One recent study illustrates how the conclusions reached depended on the measure used. The researchers found little evidence of racial discrimination in the decision to send an offender to prison, but they did find some evidence about sentence length (Welch et al.).

Competing theories. Divergent conclusions about discriminatory factors also reflect two different theoretical orientations. Functional or traditional theorists believe that the court process is basically impartial. Their studies find that apparent sentencing disparities result from valid legal factors, such as seriousness of the offense and prior record. When these factors are considered (actually controlled in a statistical sense) the sentences handed out do not discriminate against the poor or racial minorities. Stated another way, the reason that poor defendants (or minorities) receive longer sentences is that they have been convicted of more serious crimes, are more likely to have prior convictions, and employ more violence in committing these offenses.

Conflict theorists, on the other hand, view the court process as fundamentally discriminatory.

> Obviously judicial decisions are not made uniformly. Decisions are made according to a host of extra-legal factors, including the age of the offender, his race, and social class.
>   Perhaps the most obvious example of judicial discretion occurs in the handling of cases of persons from minority groups. Negroes, in comparison to whites, are convicted with lesser evidence and sentenced to more severe punishments. (Quinney: 142)

These views reflect a neo-Marxist perspective: because dominant interests in society manipulate the criminal law to keep the poor and the minorities politically powerless, the sentencing process is discriminatory. Social characteristics of the defendant play a major role in sentencing. Moreover, because the process is fundamentally discriminatory, conflict theorists are skeptical about viewing seriousness of the offense and prior record as unbiased factors.

The contrasting theories—functional and conflict—indicate that sentencing discrimination involves complex issues.

Economic Status

economic status

The courts are a sorting process. At several stages, it is obvious that *economic status* makes a difference. The poor receive differential or negative outcomes. We know, for example, that the poor are less likely to receive pretrial release and have little likelihood of hiring a private attorney. These differences are reflected in sentencing. Defendants not released on bail and/or represented by a court-appointed attorney are granted probation less often and are given longer prison sentences. Moreover it appears that only the poorest and least educated offenders are sentenced to death. Middle- or upper-income defendants are almost never executed. Do these patterns indicate that in sentencing, courts discriminate against the poor, or are they the product of other, legally permissible, factors? A number of studies yield conflicting answers but generally support the latter conclusion.

An analysis of California jury decisions in 238 first-degree murder cases between 1958 and 1966 showed that 42.1 percent of the blue collar defendants but only 4.8 percent of the white-collar defendants received the death sentence. The authors concluded that "the simplest hypothesis to explain this powerful association is that juries are lenient toward white-collar defendants on the basis of their occupational status alone" (Judson et al.: 1379). Hagan (1974) reviewed the Judson study as well as five others, several of which reported that poor defendants received harsher sentences. He argues that all except Judson's failed to consider legally relevant variables such as the seriousness of the offense and the prior record of the defendant, and also employed inadequate statistical techniques. Because of these weaknesses, he concluded that the evidence does not support a finding of economic discrimination in sentencing.

Several recent studies analyzing a large number of sentences employing commonly accepted statistical techniques point in the same direction. An examination of prison sentences of 10,488 inmates in three southeastern states found that socioeconomic status had no effect on sentencing (Chiricos and Waldo). Studies by conflict theorists, however, report that economic factors do influence sentencing (Jacobs; Lizotte). Most other recent studies find no empirical evidence for economic discrimination. In short, the conclusions drawn often reflect the theory favored by the authors.

Age

age

Another variable that might affect the sentence imposed is the ***age*** of the offender. Young defendants (variously defined as under twenty-one or under twenty-five depending on the study) are often viewed as more likely to be granted probation or, if sentenced to prison, receive a shorter term. This might indicate that court personnel adopt a more protective attitude toward young offenders because they are viewed as better candidates for rehabilitation. Prisons may also be viewed as inappropriate places for the young because prisons are dangerous.

A number of studies reject this interpretation, arguing that differential sentencing of the young results from other factors. Youthful offenders have fewer prior brushes with the law and commit less serious, less violent crimes than older defendants. When legally relevant factors like these are controlled, age has no independent effect on sentencing (Green; Burke and Turk; Clarke and Koch).

Race

Critics of the criminal justice system view the arrest and imprisonment rates for blacks and other minorities as evidence of racial discrimination. Although the law contains no racial bias, these critics claim that because criminal justice officials exercise discretion, discrimination can and often does enter in.

There are more studies of racial discrimination at the sentencing stage than at any other decision point in the criminal justice system. The reason does not appear to be that researchers view judges as those in the system who are most likely to discriminate; most would make that charge against the police. Rather, data are more readily available at this point for statistical analysis (Wilbanks). Over seventy studies of the possible impact of race on sentencing have been published. Some examine only capital punishment. Others analyze sentencing of adult felons. These studies are best reviewed separately.

Capital punishment studies. Capital punishment has figured prominently in studies of racial discrimination in sentencing. Marked racial differences in the use of the death penalty in the South provide the most obvious historical evidence of racial discrimination in sentencing. From 1930 to 1966, when the unofficial moratorium on executions occurred, 2,306 prisoners were executed in the South, 72 percent of whom were black. This proportion is dramatically higher than the ratio of blacks in the overall population or the ratio of blacks committing capital offenses. The racial gap was even more pronounced in rape cases. Only the South executed rapists, and of those executed for rape 90 percent were black. Those most likely to be executed were blacks who had raped white women (Wolfgang and Riedel; Hagan, 1974).

The executions in the South clearly show major racial differences, but as we indicated earlier variations in outcomes do not necessarily establish discrimination. Interestingly many studies found that the most obvious factor—race of the defendant—made little difference. Rather, what was important was the race of the offender in combination with the race of the victim. The *offender-victim dyad,* arranged according to perceived seriousness of the offense, is: (1) black offender, white victim; (2) white offender, white victim; (3) black offender, black victim; and (4) white offender, black victim. Blacks killing (or raping) whites were found to be most likely to be executed; conversely whites killing blacks were found least likely to receive the death penalty. These findings have been interpreted as indicating that severe punishments were motivated by a desire to protect the white social order. Some also argue that reverse discrimination was present and that black lives were not valued as much as white lives. A variety of studies indicate that the use of the death penalty in the South was racially discriminatory (Hindelang). A different conclusion emerges for the North. Studies of the death penalty in northern states find no evidence of racial discrimination (Kleck).

offender-victim dyad

Major racial differences in execution rates coupled with studies finding racial discrimination in the application of the death penalty figured prominently in the opinions of several justices when the Supreme Court struck down state death penalty laws in 1972 (*Furman* v. *Georgia,* 408 U.S. 238). The Court later upheld guided discretion statutes designed to reduce or eliminate the arbitrariness with which the death penalty is imposed. In the aftermath of *Gregg,* several studies have probed whether these new laws actually eliminated racial discrimination.

The prosecution of homicide cases involves several discretionary decisions that can affect the use of capital punishment. From the time the police classify a homicide until the case is presented in court, significant changes in the characterization of the homicide can occur. A study of more than a thousand homicide defendants in Florida compared original police classifications with the charges filed by the prosecutor. The results indicate that these decisions are related to race. Blacks accused of killing whites are the most likely to have the charges upgraded to a death-eligible charge and least likely to be downgraded (Radelet and Pierce). Similarly, in South Carolina the race of the victim is a significant factor structuring the district attorney's decision to request capital punishment. Black offenders who killed white victims were forty times more likely to have the prosecutor request the death penalty than black defendants accused of killing other blacks (Paternoster). A study by Baldus and others of the Georgia Supreme Court found that the application of capital punishment is related to the offender-victim dyad. Defendants convicted of killing a white victim are four times more likely to receive a sentence of death than those found guilty of slaying a black victim. These racial differences remained even after controls for relevant factors like prior record and type of homicide were introduced. The authors conclude that Georgia is operating a dual system of capital punishment based on the race of the victim (Baldus, Pulaski, and Woodworth).

These findings about racial discrimination in post-*Furman* death penalty laws have been challenged, however, by a recent study of all death-eligible cases appealed to the Louisiana Supreme Court from 1979 through 1984. The preliminary analysis revealed the impact of extralegal variables. The chance of receiving a death sentence steadily decreased as one moved down the offender-victim dyad. These findings clearly parallel earlier ones in other states. More sophisticated analysis, however, highlighted the importance of legal variables. Unlike previous researchers, Klemm also examined how the crime was committed. The prior relationship of the offender to the victim emerged as an important factor. Primary homicides are crimes of passion involving persons who knew one another. Non-primary homicides occur during the commission of another felony (most typically, armed robbery), and the victim is a total stranger. Those convicted of non-primary homicides were more likely to receive a sentence of death irrespective of the race of the offender or the race of the victim. Thus the chances of receiving a death sentence are greater if an offender kills a stranger. The details of the crime emerged as another key factor. Based on the state law, homicides were analyzed according to legally relevant aggravating circumstances present. The more aggravated the murder, the more likely the jury would recommend a sentence of death. An offender's prior record of conviction as well as the aggravation level of the homicide (based on the state's post-*Gregg* statute) provided a better explanation of differences in capital sentencing than extralegal variables. Overall, in Louisiana race of the victim had only an indirect effect.

The Court squarely addressed the issue of racial discrimination in capital punishment in a controversial 1987 decision (*McCleskey* v. *Kemp,* 55 LW 4537). By a 5 to 4 vote the majority rejected claims that statistical studies finding that murderers of white people in Georgia are eleven times more likely to be sentenced to die than those who murder blacks indicated that the state's death penalty law was wanton and freakish in application. To Justice Powell, "Disparities are an inevitable part of our criminal justice system." The opinion focused heavily on the Baldus study, arguing that the statistics do not prove that race enters into any capital sentencing decisions or that race was a factor in McCleskey's case. The net effect of the ruling was to move hundreds of death row inmates closer to execution.

Non-capital punishment studies. The first study of sentencing discrimination in the United States was conducted in the 1920s. Sellin asserted that judges in the Recorders Court in Detroit imposed more severe sentences on black than on white defendants. Over the next decades more than twenty similar studies were published. Most concluded that extralegal factors like race were responsible for differences in sanctions. These original findings, however, have not stood up to further analysis, because they failed to use appropriate statistical techniques. When Hagan (1974) computed measures of association for seventeen studies he found that race of the offender improved accuracy in predicting the sentence by a maximum of ony 8 percent. Moreover, when controls for relevant factors like type of offense and prior record were included, even this weak relationship between race and sentence was found to be not statistically significant.

Many recent studies using appropriate statistical techniques likewise fail to find a link between race and sentencing. Studies in Milwaukee (Pruitt and Wilson), Charlotte (Clarke and Koch), Indianapolis (Burke and Turk), three southeastern states (Chiricos and Waldo), and federal offenders (Tiffany et al.) all independently concluded that race had no effect on sentencing. Taken together, these studies seem to reflect a developing consensus that there is not as much racial discrimination in sentencing and other stages of the criminal process as had been assumed.

Yet a few studies report modest levels of racial discrimination (Spohn et al.; Lizotte). A study of six American cities found that in three southern cities (El Paso, Norfolk, and New Orleans) blacks were sentenced to prison more often than whites. No such differences were found in northern jurisdictions, however. Moreover in Norfolk, but not the other five cities, the defendant's race affected the length of sentence imposed (Welch et al.). Along similar lines, a study of Atlanta found that black defendants received the same sentences as whites after taking into account seriousness of the offense, prior record, and so on. In analyzing sentences handed down by individual judges, however, a more complex pattern emerged. Some judges were clearly anti-black, others pro-black, and some nondiscriminatory (Gibson, 1978).

Several major reviews of the literature have summarized and critiqued what we know about the impact of race on criminal sentencing (Hagan, 1974; Blumstein et al.). Kleck reviewed seventeen studies of the imposition of the death penalty and forty of noncapital sentencing. He summarizes his conclusions as follows.*

1. The death penalty has not generally been imposed for murder in a fashion discriminatory toward blacks, except in the South. Elsewhere, black homicide offenders have been less likely to receive a death sentence or be executed than whites.

2. For the 11 percent of executions that have been imposed for rape, discrimination against black defendants who had raped white victims was substantial. Such discrimination was limited to the South and has disappeared because death sentences are no longer imposed for rape.

3. Regarding non-capital sentencing, the evidence is largely contrary to a hypothesis of general or widespread overt discrimination against black defendants, although there is evidence of discrimination for a minority of specific jurisdictions, judges, crime types, and so on.

*From "Racial Discrimination in Criminal Sentencing: A Critical Evaluation of the Evidence with Additional Evidence on the Death Penalty," by G. Kleck, *American Sociological Review*, Vol. 46, 1981, p. 783. Reprinted by permission.

4. Although black offender—white victim crimes are generally punished more severely than crimes involving other racial combinations, the evidence indicates that this is due to legally relevant factors related to such offenses, not the racial combination itself.

5. There appears to be a general pattern of less severe punishment of crimes with black victims than those with white victims, especially in connection with imposition of the death penalty. In connection with non-capital sentencing, the evidence is too sparse to draw any firm conclusions.

These conclusions have not gone unchallenged. Austin maintains that Kleck's evidence "shows discrimination to be more widespread than he allows." According to Austin, some studies that Kleck claims showed no discrimination had been improperly interpreted. Kleck is sometimes misread as having concluded that there was *no* evidence of racial discrimination, when he actually concluded that the evidence was *largely* contrary to the discrimination theses and that discrimination was not general or widespread—not that discrimination did not exist (Wilbanks).

Sentencing Disparities

Fairness requires that equally blameworthy offenders receive substantially similar sanctions. To put it simply, we think justice demands similar punishments for similar offenders committing similar offenses. Numerous studies, however, have documented that this ideal is not being carried out in practice. One of the most detailed studies of sentencing disparities involved federal trial judges in New York, Connecticut, and Vermont, who were asked what sentences they would give twenty hypothetical defendants (drawn, however, from actual case files). As Table 16-1 shows, the judges varied in their responses

---

C O N T R O V E R S Y

The Myth of a Racist Criminal Justice System

I take the position that the perception of the criminal justice system as racist is a myth. . . . I believe that there is racial prejudice and discrimination *within* the criminal justice system, in that there are individuals, both white and black, who make decisions, at least in part, on the basis of race. I do not believe that the *system* is characterized by racial prejudice or discrimination against blacks; that is, prejudice and discrimination are not "systematic."

Individual cases appear to reflect racial prejudice and discrimination by the offender, the victim, the police, the prosecutor, the judge, or prison and parole officials. But conceding individual cases of bias is far different from conceding pervasive racial discrimination. . . . [T]he assertion that the criminal justice system is not racist does not deny that racial prejudice and discrimi-

nation have existed in or even been the dominant force in the design and operation of the criminal justice system in the past. There is evidence suggesting that racism did permeate the criminal justice system in earlier periods of American history, especially in the South. The evidence regarding northern cities, however, does not support the discrimination thesis.

William Wilbanks, *The Myth of a Racist Criminal Justice System* (Pacific Grove, Calif.: Brooks/Cole, 1987), pp. 5–6, 8.

TABLE 16-1 Sentences of Federal Trial Judges
for Defendants Convicted of Theft and Possession
of Stolen Goods

Imprisonment (in months)	Probation (in months)	Number of judges
90		1
72		1
60		6
48		10
36		18
24		6
12		1
6	30	1
	48	1
		45

SOURCE: Anthony Partridge and William Eldridge, "The
Second Circuit Sentencing Study: A Report to the Judges
of the Second Circuit," Federal Judicial Center (August
1974). Constructed from case 4, pp. A-12, A-13.

(Partridge and Eldridge). Even if the most extreme sentences are eliminated, the data clearly indicate that substantial disagreement exists among the judges about what constitutes a fair and appropriate sentence. These findings, based on comparing similar but hypothetical cases, parallel the results of other research that employs a different approach. These studies statistically analyze actual sentences imposed by judges in comparable (but not identical) groups of cases. Table 16-2 reports one such study. Major differences in sentences are again readily apparent. On average, narcotics violators in the Eighth Circuit received prison sentences almost twice as long as those in the Sixth Circuit. Numerous other studies reach roughly the same conclusion.

Describing actual disparities is a much simpler task than defining the term. Many commentators define a disparity as any variation in sentencing that they deem unwarranted. But such broad and subjective definitions of inappropriate sentences fail to address the key question adequately: when can we consider like cases to be alike? Sentencing represents the conflict between two important goals: equality and individualization (D'Esposito). The ideal of equal justice under the law means that all persons convicted of the same offense should receive identical sentences. But not all deviations from equality are unwarranted. The law also strives for individualized dispositions based on the character of the offender. Thus, some differences in sentences reflect varying degrees of seriousness of the offense, whereas others reflect varying characteristics of the offender. What may be disparity to one person may be justifiable variation to another. Combining these two conflicting goals can give us a useful definition. ***Sentencing disparity*** is the divergence in the lengths and types of sentences imposed for the same crime, or for crimes of comparable seriousness, without apparent justification. The most commonly cited types of sentencing disparity involve geography (variations across jurisdictions) and judicial backgrounds and attitudes (variations between judges within the same jurisdiction).

sentencing disparity

TABLE 16-2   Average Sentences, in Months, by Selected Offense and Judicial Circuit, of Federal Prisoners (Fiscal Year Ended June 30, 1972)

Judicial circuit	Narcotics laws	Forgery	Robbery	All offenses
1st (Me., Mass., N.H., R.I.,P.R.)	68.0	19.7	133.5	52.5
2d (Conn., N.Y., Vt.)	58.8	30.4	114.7	44.3
3d (Del., N.J., Penn., V.I.)	77.4	27.3	128.3	67.7
4th (Md., N.C., S.C., Va., W.Va.)	77.0	36.4	158.8	57.3
5th (Ala., Fla., Ga., La., Miss., Tex.)	74.8	36.7	144.0	41.3
6th (Kent., Mich., Ohio, Tenn.)	54.0	39.3	134.4	52.8
7th (Ill., Ind., Wisc.)	75.6	38.2	114.4	50.4
8th (Ark., Iowa, Minn., Mo., Neb., N.D., S.D.)	103.3	36.6	155.8	52.4
9th (Alaska, Ariz., Calif., Hawaii, Idaho, Mont., Nev., Ore., Wash., Guam)	70.8	42.9	131.1	40.5
10th (Colo., Kansas, N.M., Okla., Utah, Wyo.)	85.7	56.5	134.9	54.3
Totals	69.7	37.3	134.6	46.8

SOURCE: U.S. Department of Justice, Federal Bureau of Prisons, *Statistical Report, Fiscal Years 1971 and 1972* (Washington, D.C.: Government Printing Office, 1973), pp. 96–101.

The Geography of Justice

geography of justice

What counts against the defendant is not only what he does but also where he does it. Significant variations in the sentencing patterns of judges in different judicial districts within the same political jurisdiction is referred to as the **geography of justice.** The frequency of fines, probation, or prison varies from county to county. Turning back to Table 16-2, note that whereas the average sentence for forgery in the First Circuit Court of Appeals is 19.7 months, in the Tenth it is 56.5—a difference of almost three to one. There are similar differences among the states in prisoners imprisoned per hundred thousand people (Figure 16-1). Such differences are the product of a number of factors: the amount of crime, the effectiveness of the police in apprehending offenders, density of population, and types of screening employed by the court are examples. These differences also result from the fact that some courts deal with more serious offenses, as well as with a greater number of defendants with prior records. But even after controlling for factors like these, it is apparent that important geographical differences remain.

Overall it appears that the South imposes harsher sentences than other states. Executions, for example, are concentrated in this region. Urban courts are marked by a greater use of probation and shorter prison terms than are their rural counterparts. Such geographical patterns demonstrate that court officials, drawn as they are from the local communities, vary in their views of what offenses are the most serious as well as what penalty is appropriate.

Judicial Backgrounds and Attitudes

What counts against the defendant is not only what he does and where he does it, but also which judge will impose sentence. In any medium-sized to large community, it is an accepted fact that judges have different sentencing tendencies. One or two have reputations for handing out stiff sentences. "Maximum Max" or "Mean Geraldine" are examples of the colorful labels used by members of the courtroom work group to characterize these judges. One or two others

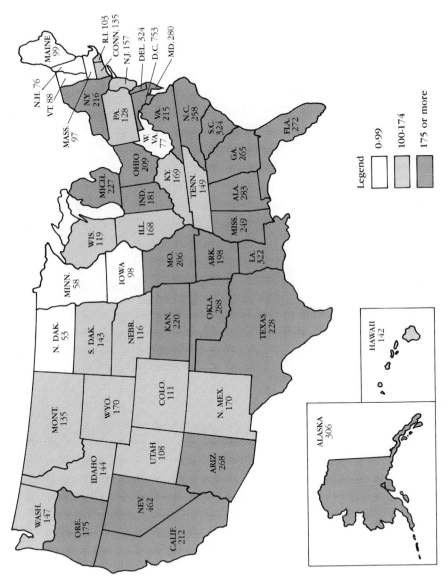

Figure 16-1 Number of prisoners in state institutions per 100,000 civilian population, December 31, 1980. SOURCE: U.S. Department of Justice, Bureau of Justice Statistics, *Prisoners in 1986* (Washington, D.C.: Government Printing Office, 1987).

are known for lenient sentences. "Cut 'em loose Bruce" is but one name given these judges by courthouse regulars. The sentences of most judges fall somewhere in between these extremes. Because they are less distinctive, the courtroom actors seldom get colorful nicknames.

Sentencing disparities based on attributes of judicial decision makers have fascinated social scientists for decades. A study of the women's court in Chicago is typical of this interest. Cameron found that the proportion of shoplifting defendants placed on probation ranged from a low of 10 percent for one judge to a high of 62 percent for another. Although sentencing disparities like this may be due to variations in the seriousness of the cases heard, differences in judges' backgrounds and attitudes are a more likely cause.

judges'
backgrounds
Judges come to the bench from a variety of ***backgrounds.*** We might reasonably expect that these differences will be related to varying patterns of judicial behavior. Studies of judicial decision making support this proposition. One comprehensive study of federal judges examined over ten thousand criminal cases decided between 1933 and 1977. The authors found that district court judges appointed by Democratic presidents were more likely to decide for the defendant than those appointed by Republican presidents. Similarly, judges from the North were more supportive of issues raised by defendants than those from the South (Carp and Rowland). Analyses of the voting patterns of appellate court judges point in the same direction. One key finding is that state supreme court justices who are Democratic and/or Catholic are more likely to vote for the defendant. By contrast former prosecutors are more prone to affirm the conviction (Nagel). Studies of federal appellate courts likewise have shown that background characteristics are related to judges' votes in criminal justice cases. Overall, though, the effect is only slight. Judges' backgrounds account for only about 10 percent of the differences in appellate court votes (Bowen; Goldman).

Martin Levin's study of the criminal trial courts of Pittsburgh and Minneapolis revealed a close link between judges' social backgrounds and the communities they serve. Pittsburgh judges came from humble backgrounds and showed greater sympathy toward defendants than did judges with upper-class backgrounds on the Minneapolis bench. Whereas the Pittsburgh judges tried to base their decisions on what they believed was best for the defendant, Minneapolis judges were more legally oriented, emphasizing society's need for protection from criminal behavior. The impact of these differing approaches is apparent in sentencing. Pittsburgh judges granted probation more often and also handed out shorter prison terms than their colleagues in Minneapolis. These sentencing disparities persist even when factors like prior record, plea, age, and type of offense were taken into account.

judicial
attitudes
Variations in judges' backgrounds indirectly indicate different perceptions of what crimes are serious as well as the relative weights to be assigned to conflicting sentencing goals. Several studies have directly examined ***judicial attitudes*** and sentences imposed (Gibson, 1980). Hogarth examined magistrates in Ontario, Canada, and found that those who stress deterrence are more likely to favor prison sentences over other forms of sentencing. Conversely, magistrates who are more treatment-oriented use suspended sentences,

fewer fines, and relatively few short jail sentences. In addition magistrates from working-class backgrounds tended to be more punitive than those from professional backgrounds, who were more committed to the rehabilitative ideal.

Hogarth concluded that there were marked inconsistencies in the principles of sentencing held by the magistrates. But most important, differences among magistrates were not random: although magistrates were inconsistent with each other, they were individually consistent themselves. A study of sentences imposed by the Philadelphia Court of Quarter Sessions also concluded that judges did not sentence by whim. Green found that the degree of disparity among judges was most pronounced in cases at the intermediate level of gravity, tapering off gradually as the cases approached the extremes of mildness or seriousness. For serious offenses, there was a high degree of consistency among the judges in the length of the prison sentence imposed.

The studies to date indicate that judges hold no single set of sentencing attitudes. Although the public views judges as either harsh or lenient sentencers, detailed studies indicate that the pattern is far more complex. A survey of federal judges in the Second Circuit found that the twenty-nine whose general sentences were in the middle range in most cases nonetheless varied in individual instances; each had a sentence ranked among the ten most severe in at least one case and sentence ranked among the ten least severe in another case (Partridge and Eldridge).

Reducing Sentencing Disparities

Sentencing disparity has concerned legal scholars, social scientists, criminal justice practitioners, and offenders themselves for most of this century. Not only do major differences in sentences for similar offenders violate deep-seated notions of equal justice under law, but such disparities also have very negative practical consequences. Correctional officials, for example, complain that disparate sentences work to defeat correctional objectives. When prisoners compare sentences, some discover that they have been treated leniently, reinforcing their views that they are smart or lucky and therefore do not need rehabilitation. Other prisoners, however, discover that for essentially the same offense they received a rather severe sentence. The resulting embitterment is directed toward the courts and prison programs rather than being channeled along more constructive lines.

Until recently, however, the evidence of sentencing disparities uncovered by researchers did not spur criminal justice policy makers to take corrective action. This can be partially explained by the methodological difficulties involved in proving the existence of disparities, discrimination, or both. More important, though, policy makers did not act because they adhered to an "individualized" sentencing model. Observed variations in sentences were justified by a commitment to take into account each offender's need for rehabilitation and potential for successful adjustment in society (Forst). Within the rehabilitative model, however, three types of reforms have been used or recommended for reducing sentencing disparities: sentencing institutes, sentencing councils, and appellate review of sentencing. We will discuss these proposals on the basis of how much constraint they place on judges' traditional sentencing discretion, starting with the least restrictive.

Sentencing Institutes

sentencing institutes

American trial judges work alone. Under indeterminate sentencing laws they have broad sentencing authority and are not required to account for their decisions. Partly to facilitate communications between judges, in 1958 Congress authorized **sentencing institutes** for the federal judiciary. Most states have followed this lead and conduct similar programs. Sentencing institutes are attended by judges as well as prosecutors, probation officers, parole officials, and sentencing experts. Some of the discussions are informal in nature, with recent sentencing developments and changes in the law addressed. In addition, the attendees engage in simulated sentencing exercises. The participants express their reactions to summaries of past cases and indicate the sentences they would impose. The exchange of views familiarizes judges with the perceptions and ideas of their colleagues. Newly appointed judges learn about the going rates used by more experienced colleagues. Veterans of the bench learn whether their own attitudes and opinions are consistent with general patterns.

> To nobody's surprise, the judges exhibit huge divergencies in their dispositions of the same case. Everyone tends to gasp a little upon the rehearing of this same old story. Sometimes, but not regularly, a judge seems to be persuaded toward some view different from his initial one (Frankel: 64).

Although sentencing institutes sensitize the participants to sentencing disparities and the complexities of determining when like cases deserve similar sentences, they provide no binding decisions.

QUOTATION

One of the most glaring flaws in our current system of criminal justice can be traced to the arbitrariness of criminal sentencing procedures. During the past decade study after study has demonstrated that unfettered sentencing discretion results in increasing unfairness and uncertainty. The impact of such unfairness is devastating. Sentencing disparity and uncertainty affect society, the victims and the offenders themselves. The inescapable conclusion remains—public respect for our criminal justice system requires a complete overhaul of the way we go about sentencing the offender.

Senator Edward Kennedy, "Foreword," in Jack Kress, *Prescription for Justice: The Theory and Practice of Sentencing Guidelines* (Cambridge, Mass.: Ballinger, 1980), p. xiv.

Sentencing Councils

sentencing councils

Sentencing councils were the first modern institutional innovation expressly aimed at reducing sentencing disparity (Blumstein et al.). They were initially used in several U.S. District Courts in 1960. ***Sentencing councils*** are composed of groups of judges who voluntarily meet on a regular basis to discuss sentences for pending cases. Before attending the council meeting, each participating judge reviews pre-sentence reports and prepares sentencing recommendations, which are then discussed during the meeting. The recommendations are purely advisory; the sentencing judge retains complete discretion in imposing sentence.

Sentencing councils reduce but do not eliminate sentencing disparities (Phillips). Several studies indicate that the initial recommendations of judges differ from their ultimate sentences in about one third of the cases. It is more likely for sentences to be reduced than increased (Diamond and Zeisel). Like sentencing institutes, sentencing councils work on the basis of peer pressure in trying to develop a general consensus. The overall effect is that participating judges are more likely to impose the average sentence of the group as a whole.

Appellate Review of Sentencing

In the vast majority of American jurisdictions, a convicted defendant can appeal only issues related to the finding of guilt. Because the sentencing decision is viewed as a matter for the sole discretion of the trial judge, the sentence cannot be appealed. As a result, U.S. appellate courts annually write volumes about the guilt adjudication process, but the most important decision in many criminal cases—the sentence—is unreviewable. This American doctrine of non-review of sentences stands in sharp contrast to practices elsewhere. In virtually all other Western nations, grossly excessive sentences are subject to routine appellate review. In England, West Germany, and the Scandinavian countries, for example, appellate review of sentencing has resulted over time in the accumulation of a body of case law that has developed and refined sentencing standards (Blumstein et al.).

appellate review of sentencing

Despite its limited use in the U.S., ***appellate review of sentencing*** remains a widely recommended sentencing reform. Several national commissions along with some commentators have called for its implementation. Proponents are concerned that unbridled judicial discretion results in excessive and/or disparate sentences. Judicial sentence review, as a regularized corrective mechanism, could alleviate this situation in two important ways. First, it could level the peaks of grossly excessive sentences; a sentence that is clearly out of line with prevailing norms could be set aside by the appellate court. Second, advocates contend that appellate review could be an important vehicle for developing legal principles of sentencing. Trial judges would be required to set forth reasons for the sentence imposed. Appellate court scrutiny of these reasons in written opinions would in the long run lead to sound sentencing principles.

The contention that sentencing is not regulated by rules of "law" subject to appellate review is an argument for, not against, a system of appeals. The "common law" is, after all, a body of rules evolved through the process of reasoned decision of concrete cases, mainly by appellate courts. English appellate courts and some of our states have been evolving general, legal "principles of sentencing" in the course of reviewing particular sentences claimed to be excessive. One way to begin to temper the capricious unruliness of sentencing is to institute the right of appeal, so that appellate courts may proceed in their accustomed fashion to make law for this grave subject (Frankel: 84).

Calls for appellate review of sentencing in the U.S. have met with limited success, however. The Louisiana Supreme Court is one of the few courts to adopt this practice (Neubauer). But several states that have enacted sentencing guidelines have also incorporated appellate review as an enforcement mechanism.

Increasing Predictability

In the mid-1970s a growing sense developed that existing sentencing practices resulted neither in fairness nor effective crime control. Opposition to existing sentencing practices produced an unusual consensus among liberals and conservatives. For very different reasons both opposed indeterminate sentencing and sought a greater degree of predictability in sentences.

Adherents of the due process model were concerned over the excess of discretion in decisions about individuals' liberty. They perceived that criminal justice officials, ranging from police officers to parole boards, were making decisions in a discriminatory manner, especially on the basis of race. They were also concerned that judges' sentencing discretion resulted in sentencing disparities. Thus the political left saw determinate sentences as providing the means to reduce individual discretion and thereby presumably to reduce disparity and discrimination.

Adherents of the crime control model were far more concerned with undue leniency and lack of certainty in sentencing than about disparity or discrimination. They viewed trial judges as all too ready to impose sentences well below statutory maximums. They perceived that parole boards were excessively ready to release prisoners early and were shocked that prisoners were back on the streets on parole well before the maximum sentence had expired. Thus, to conservatives the essential problem was that sentencing was not reducing crime. In an effort to make sentencing more effective, a "justice" model of sentencing came into increasing prominence. Wrongdoers should be punished on the principle of just desserts, which implies a certainty and uniformity of punishment.

For very different reasons, liberals and conservatives sought greater predictability in sentencing. This coalition focused their attention on sentencing guidelines and determinate sentencing.

Sentencing Guidelines

Most criminal laws permit a wide range of latitude in sentencing, leaving judges with little or no guidance on how to determine the proper sentence for each individual case. Sentencing institutes, sentencing councils, and appellate review

sentencing guidelines

of sentencing only partially fill this void. In recent years ***sentencing guidelines*** have been the most often mentioned procedure for providing certainty and consistency in sentencing. Guidelines direct the judge to specific actions should be taken. Besides providing guidance, guidelines are also designed to that constrain the sentencing discretion of the judge and thus reduce sentencing disparities.

Since their origin in the early 1970s, sentencing guidelines have evolved steadily. They were first proposed in the field of criminal justice by Don Gottfredson and Leslie Wilkins for use by parole boards when deciding whether to release offenders from prison. The U.S. Parole Commission has used various versions of the Gottfredson-Wilkins guidelines since 1977 (Gottfredson et al.). Later this approach was also applied to trial court sentencing (Wilkins et al.). Based on these early efforts, sentencing guidelines have been established on a statewide basis in three states (Minnesota, Pennsylvania, and Utah) and in selected courts in many other states, including Maryland, Massachusetts, Rhode Island, Vermont, Washington, and Wisconsin. In addition, Congress created the U.S. Sentencing Commission and charged it with developing guidelines for sentencing federal offenders. These standards automatically became law in November 1987 when both houses of Congress did not modify the recommendations or delay their implementation.

Most sentencing guidelines provide a sentencing range according to the seriousness of the crime and the criminal history of the offender. How they operate can be illustrated by the sentencing grid used in Minnesota (Table 16-3). The lefthand column ranks the seriousness of the offense according to ten categories. The upper rows provide a criminal history score. These seven categories are calculated by summing the points allocated to such factors as the number of previous convictions, the number of times incarcerated, whether the offender was on probation or parole; employment status or educational achievement, and the offender's history of drug and/or alcohol abuse. Having determined the offense severity ranking and the criminal history score, the judge determines the recommended sentence by finding the cell of the sentencing grid in the applicable row and column. The cells above the bold block line call for sentences other than state imprisonment; these numbers specify months of supervision. The cells below the bold line contain the guideline sentence expressed in months of imprisonment. The single number is the recommended sentence. The range varies by plus or minus 5 to 8 percent from the guideline sentence and can be used for upward or downward adjustments.

voluntary/ descriptive sentencing guidelines

Sentencing guidelines differ on two important dimensions, depending on their legal authority and how sentencing ranges were derived. Although there are four possible combinations of these dimensions, only two are actually found. ***Voluntary/descriptive sentencing guidelines*** were first developed by Wilkins and Gottfredson for the courts in Denver and Massachusetts. They are the most commonly employed type of sentencing guideline. Under this approach, recommended sentencing ranges are derived by empirically analyzing the types of sanctions judges in the jurisdiction have usually imposed in various types of cases in the past. Thus, descriptive guidelines articulate and codify past sentencing practices as standards for future cases. Once adopted,

TABLE 16-3   Minnesota Sentencing Grid: Sentencing by Severity of Offense and Criminal History

Severity levels of conviction offense		Criminal history score						
		0	1	2	3	4	5	6 or more
Unauthorized use of motor vehicle Possession of marijuana	I	12*	12*	12*	15	18	21	24
Theft-related crimes ($150–$2500) Sale of marijuana	II	12*	12*	14	17	20	23	27 25–29
Theft crimes ($150–$2500)	III	12*	13	16	19	22 21–23	27 25–29	32 30–34
Burglary—felony intent Receiving stolen goods ($150–$2500)	IV	12*	15	18	21	25 24–26	32 30–34	41 37–45
Simple robbery	V	18	23	27	30 29–31	38 36–40	46 43–49	54 50–58
Assault, 2d degree	VI	21	26	30	34 33–35	44 42–46	54 50–58	65 60–70
Aggravated robbery	VII	24 23–25	32 30–34	41 38–44	49 45–53	65 60–70	81 75–87	98 90–104
Assault, 1st degree Criminal sexual conduct, 1st degree	VIII	43 41–45	54 50–58	65 60–70	76 71–81	95 89–101	113 106–120	132 124–140
Murder, 3d degree	IX	97 94–100	119 116–122	127 124–130	149 143–155	176 168–184	205 195–215	230 218–242
Murder, 2d degree	X	116 111–121	140 133–147	162 153–171	203 192–214	243 231–255	284 270–298	324 309–339

Note: 1st degree murder is excluded from the guidelines by law and continues to have a mandatory life sentence.
* One year and one day.
SOURCE: Minnesota Sentencing Guidelines Commission (1981: 23).

these guidelines may be used by judges voluntarily, but they are advisory only. Voluntary/descriptive sentencing guidelines do not have the force of law and noncompliance by a judge creates no right to sentencing appeal.

presumptive/ prescriptive sentencing guidelines

Presumptive/prescriptive sentencing guidelines are found in Minnesota, Pennsylvania, and Washington, and are the basis of the work of the U.S. Sentencing Commission. Under this approach, the legislature delegates to a sentencing commission the authority for developing detailed sentencing criteria. The resulting guidelines are prescriptive because they express what sentence should be imposed irrespective of existing practices. Once adopted, these guidelines are presumptive; they must be followed by the sentencing judges. If a sentence is imposed outside of the guidelines, the judge must provide reasons for such deviations. Both defendants and prosecutors have the right to have the sufficiency of that explanation reviewed by an appellate court. Thus prescriptive/presumptive guidelines have substantial legal authority.

The sentencing guideline approach is seriously questioned by some. To critics, much of the empirical work involved in developing guidelines has serious methodological flaws resulting in inaccurate and misleading statistical descriptions of previous sentencing practices (Sparks; Rich et al.). These findings illustrate law professor Norval Morris's concern that sentencing guidelines give "a false precision of that which by its nature can never be precise." The experience of the U.S. Sentencing Commission bears this out. In developing rankings of offense seriousness the initial draft specified a 360-point scale that was widely criticized as too complex and too drastic a curtailment of judges' discretion. The second draft incorporated forty-three offense levels, which led some to charge that the proposed guidelines merely retained existing judicial discretion.

Evaluation. Researchers have evaluated the actual impact of guidelines on sentencing practices. Two studies illustrate that differing types of guidelines have varying impacts. Florida and Maryland adopted voluntary/descriptive sentencing guidelines. As one would expect, not all judges employed the guidelines. In 15 percent of the cases in one state and 43 percent in the other, the judges did not consider the guidelines when imposing sentence. Moreover, the judges also fell significantly short of full compliance with the requirements to provide reasons for sentences outside the guidelines. As a result, the goal of reducing sentencing disparity met with mixed results. In Florida the guidelines did not reduce sentencing disparity. In Maryland the findings were somewhat more ambiguous. Although there were modest decreases in disparity in at least some of the four test sites, decreases were also observed in the comparison sites as well. According to Carrow, the limited success of sentencing guidelines in Florida and Maryland was not primarily due to the guidelines themselves, but rather to the effort by judges to voluntarily address the problem of sentencing disparities.

Minnesota's presumptive/prescriptive guideline law, on the other hand, appears to have achieved its goals of more predictable, more uniform, and more socioeconomically neutral sentencing. During the first year of operation the law achieved significant increases in both uniformity and neutrality. But not all judicial discretion was eliminated. The law allowed judges some leeway. An analysis of these sentencing departures revealed a pattern suggesting that exceptions to the presumptive sentence may be used as a means of adjusting sentencing outcomes to fit judges' individual sense of justice. Moreover, some sentencing decisions—for example, granting probation—were not covered under the law. These decisions continued to be influenced by sentencing philosophies very different from those endorsed by the Minnesota State Guidelines Commission. The exceptions aside, the Minnesota sentencing guideline law has been more successful than other sentencing reforms. The chief reason for this success, at least in the areas of conduct governed by the guidelines, is that the state's sentencing guidelines were backed by the weight of law (Moore and Miethe).

Determinate Sentencing Laws

In response to criticisms of the rehabilitation model, with its emphasis on indeterminate sentences and discretionary parole release, a number of states have adopted determinate or fixed sentencing laws (see Chapter 15). Emerging from the just desserts model of sentencing, these new sentencing laws are based on the assumption that judges should give offenders a specific amount of time to serve rather than a minimum and a maximum. The movement to determinate sentencing was usually accompanied by a move to abolish release on parole as well. Under determinate sentencing the prisoner is automatically released to community supervision at the end of the term, less credit for good time.

determinate sentencing laws

Maine was the first to adopt this approach in 1976. Since then a number of other states have enacted ***determinate sentencing laws***; among them are Alaska, Arizona, California, Colorado, Connecticut, Indiana, Illinois, Minnesota, New Mexico, and North Carolina. The statutory systems in these states vary widely, however. At one extreme, judges in Maine retain broad discretion to determine time served in prison. Because of the abolition of parole, however, prisoners can predict at sentencing when they will be released. California's Uniform Determinate Sentencing Law, at the other extreme, abolished parole release for most prisoners and enacted detailed statutory sentencing standards. The law provides that when sentencing offenders to prison judges choose one of three specified sentences as the ''base term'' for persons convicted of a particular offense (for example, two, three, or five years for robbery). The middle term must be chosen in the absence of either mitigating or aggravating factors, the latter of which must be charged and proven in court. The other determinate sentencing laws range between those of Maine and California. They provide more guidance to judges than the former but less than the latter.

Determinate sentencing laws were passed as a result of a temporary coalition of liberals and conservatives. Whether these laws have proved successful depends somewhat on one's political vantage point. While some hoped that these laws would increase the certainty of punishment (or in some cases the severity as well), others feared that prison populations would swell. A number of studies have investigated the impact of determinate sentencing laws but reach no clear conclusions. There is some evidence from California (Brewer et al.; McCoy) and North Carolina (Clarke) that the offender's chances of receiving probation declined. Yet, in Colorado (Covey and Mande) there was no change in the rate of commitments to prison. Analysis of sentence length yields a slightly different pattern. In Indiana (Clear, Hewitt, and Regoli) there was a projected 50 percent increase in actual length of sentence of first offenders (an effect likely to be counteracted by actions of the courtroom work group). In California (McCoy) the length of prison sentences has not increased, while in North Carolina (Clarke) sentence length was less severe and varied less. Finally, one can examine overall prison population. In California (Casper, Brereton, and Neal) as in other states (Carroll and Cornell) there have been significant increases in prison population following the passage of determinate sentencing legislation. Evaluations of long-term trends, however, show that the growth in prison population was much more a continuation of the previous trends than a change attributable to alterations in sentencing laws (Blumstein).

The lack of clear findings is not surprising. The American legal system consists of numerous independent units. In addition, the laws in question vary in important ways. For these reasons the research findings from one area may not be applicable in another. Moreover, early trends may not be indicative of long-term impacts. A comprehensive evaluation requires an appropriate time frame because it may take a substantial amount of time for an innovation to work its way through the implementation process and for an observer to be sure that it had an effect, was modified, or made no difference (Casper and Brereton).

Increasing the Severity of the Penalty

The majority of the American public believes that prison sentences are too lenient. Elected officials often share these views. When confronted with a crime problem, legislators thus often believe that the answer is to get tough with criminals by increasing the severity of the penalty. Such actions reflect the notion that harsher sentences will deter criminals and reduce crime. These ideas are more often justified by moral claims than supported by valid scientific evidence. Researchers are skeptical that this type of deterrent effect actually exists. A number of studies conclude that increasing the severity of the penalty does not result in lower crime rates (Zimring and Hawkins). For instance, separate studies of increased penalties for rape (Schwartz), marijuana possession, and assaults on police officers (California State Assembly) all report that there were no changes in crime rates.

Increasing the severity of the penalty, though, does have a major impact on courtroom work groups. In particular, harsher sentencing laws are associated with the exercise of increased discretion and negative side effects. After considering these impacts we will examine mandatory minimum sentencing laws as a specific illustration.

Nullification by Discretion

Sharp increases in formal penalties tend to be sidestepped by those who apply the law. As James Q. Wilson writes, "No one should assume that any judicial outcome can be made truly 'mandatory'—discretion removed from one place in the criminal justice system tends to reappear elsewhere in it" (1975: 187). At a variety of points in the application of legal sanctions—police arrest, prosecutorial discretion, judge and jury convictions, and sentencing—discretion may be exercised to offset the severity of the penalty (McCoy).

When the severity of the penalty is increased, the police may stabilize or reduce the number of arrests for violations subjected to those penalties. A study of Connecticut's crackdown on speeders reported that police arrests for speeding decreased after the severe penalties were announced (Campbell and Ross).

Prosecutors often responded by reducing the number of charges for that category. In 1973, the New York legislature enacted the toughest drug law in the nation. It provided for stiff mandatory sentences (up to life) and sought to prevent plea bargaining. The Association of the Bar of the City of New York Drug Abuse Council evaluated this law and reported that although indictments for drug violations in New York State remained constant through the first year of the law's implementation, the number of indictments fell by 14 percent the next year. Because they anticipate that judges and juries will be reluctant to convict, prosecutors may also choose to file charges for an offense that does not carry the most severe penalties.

A number of studies indicate that convictions decrease when the penalties are severe. The most commonly cited example is capital punishment in late eighteenth- and early nineteenth-century England, when most felonies were punishable by death. Judges strained to avoid convicting defendants, often inventing legal technicalities to acquit the defendant (Hall). In New York State, after the tough drug law was passed, the number of convictions dropped.

Finally, after conviction, judges are reluctant to actually apply the severe penalty. Thus when Chicago traffic court judges sought to crack down on drunk drivers by voluntarily agreeing to impose the seven-day jail term, a study found that the penalty was rarely applied (Robertson et al., 1973).

There is thus a relationship between punishment policy and the system that administers it. Through the discretionary actions of police, prosecutor, judges, juries, and executive, harsh penalties are nullified. The more severe the penalty, the less likely it will be imposed when its severity exceeds the limits of punishment viewed as appropriate. The final result is that more produces less. Stepping up the severity of the punishment does not increase the threat of punishment; it reduces it.

Negative Side Effects

One reason that legislators find raising penalties so attractive is that they appear to be fighting crime but do not have to increase appropriations. It is a policy apparently without costs. But a number of studies suggest that increasing the severity of the punishment produces "hidden costs" and "side effects." Harsher laws have effects, but often not the ones intended. One of these hidden costs is the greater time, effort, and money courts must expend.

Faced with severe sanctions, defendants demand more trials, which consumes more court time. This clearly happened in New York State. Before the drug law, 6.5 percent of the drug cases went to trial; after it, 13.5 percent (Association of the Bar). As a result, a backlog of cases develops, delay increases, and the certainty and speed of conviction drops. Moreover, the courts were forced to spend $55 million to comply with the law.

A second unintended consequence is that increasing the severity of penalties increases the pressure to plea bargain. To ensure convictions, avoid expensive and cost-consuming trials, and give expression to their views of benevolence, prosecutors and judges will try to get a guilty plea in return for a lesser sentence (Wilson, 1975). To cite but one example, Illinois prosecutors allowed first offender drunk-driving offenders to plead to reckless driving, which did not carry a mandatory one-year suspension of the driver's license (Neubauer, 1974).

A final unintended consequence of raising the severity of penalties is that sentencing disparities increase. Even though convictions decrease overall and there is a tendency not to apply the law to the fullest, some defendants are still caught in the net. The *New York Times* surveyed convictions in March 1976 under the New York drug law and found that only thirty-one persons drew the maximum penalty. They found that "suspects sentenced to the severest imprisonment appeared to be low-level dealers—not major traffickers in heroin or cocaine." In short, when severe penalties are applied, they are often applied randomly (*New York Times*).

Mandatory Minimum Sentences

mandatory minimum sentencing

In response to allegations that lenient judges allow many serious and/or violent offenders to go free, all but two states have passed ***mandatory minimum sentencing.*** They are most often legislated for violent crimes, habitual offenders, drug violations, and crimes involving the use or possession of a firearm. The best known examples include: the Massachusetts Bartley-Fox law, providing that all persons convicted of unlawfully carrying a firearm be imprisoned for at least one year; New York's Rockefeller drug law (since repealed), mandating a ten-year minimum prison sentence for all defendants convicted of selling drugs; and the Michigan Felony Firearm Statute, mandating an additional two-year prison sentence for those who possess firearms while committing felonies.

Mandatory minimum sentencing laws take many forms but have as their common characteristic a legislative directive that offenders convicted of certain offenses must be sentenced to a prison term of not less than a specified period of years. Many laws expressly preclude granting probation or other non-prison sentences and mandate a term of imprisonment regardless of the circumstances of the offense or the background of the individual. Under some other mandatory sentencing laws judges retain the option to impose probation or other non-incarcerative sentence, but if a prison sentence is imposed it must be at least the given minimum.

Mandatory minimum sentencing laws have proven popular for several reasons. First, they promise certainty of punishment. "If Every Criminal *Knew* He Would Be Punished If Caught . . ." is the title of an article by James Q. Wilson, professor of government at Harvard. He argues that the way to improve the deterrent effect of the law is to concentrate on increasing the certainty—but not necessarily the severity—of punishment. Second, the public supports more severe sanctions. Groups like Mothers Against Drunk Driving (MADD), for example, have effectively lobbied many statehouses for mandatory prison sentences for those convicted of drunk driving. Thus to elected officials, passing mandatory minimum sentencing laws is one way to demonstrate a "get tough on crime" attitude to the voters. Finally, mandatory minimum sentencing laws represent an attempt to assert legislative dominance over sentencing, thus replacing traditional judicial discretion with legislative mandates.

As mechanisms for controlling judicial discretion and reducing sentencing disparities, mandatory minimum laws have limited scope. Because they deal with a narrow range of offenders committing limited sets of offenses, the overwhelming percentage of convicted offenders is completely unaffected. In addition, these laws provide little guidance on the actual length of the prison term (Kress). Critics are also concerned that mandatory minimum sentencing legislation results in a rigid, mechanical, and inflexible overreaction to problems of judicial discretion. As the Twentieth Century Fund Task Force on Sentencing noted, flat-time sentencing and mandatory minimum sentences go too far in eliminating all flexibility.

> By requiring every single defendant convicted under the same statute to serve the identical sentence, it threatens to create a system so automatic that it may operate in practice like a poorly programmed robot. This is especially true if statutory definitions of crime remain as broad and inclusive as they are today. (p. 17)

CLOSE-UP

Judicial System Review Urged by Police Group

The Brotherhood, a Denver police organization, Friday called for a review of the entire judicial system, including methods of sentencing criminals and the possibility of mandatory sentencing of violent criminals.

A spokesman, Detective James Lux, pointed to a number of recent court actions and sentences which he called "appalling and should be frightening to the general public."

Lux directed his remarks toward a number of recent judicial actions which he said were improper and violated the safety of the public. . . .

"We're called upon time after time to re-arrest these dangerous criminals that the courts are always seeing fit to let loose into society without any rehabilitation," Lux said.

Lux said even when a dangerous criminal is convicted of a major crime, the judges too often give him such a lenient sentence he's "right back out on the street."

The example cited was the case of James A. Lang, one of two men involved in a robbery attempt in which Denver Patrolman Ed Smith was shot to death in January.

"Lang, who had fired shots and menaced innocent people during the robbery attempt, pleaded guilty to aggravated robbery and first-degree murder charges," Lux said.

"The opinion of the district attorneys presenting the case before Salida Dist. Judge Howard Purdy was that due to the seriousness of the crime, Lang be sentenced to the state penitentiary for life, the maximum sentence," Lux said.

"However, the action taken by Judge Purdy was sentencing the defendant to the Colorado State Reformatory at Buena Vista. After a period of nine months, the defendant may be eligible for parole."

Lux said it is the contention of the Brotherhood that criminals can't be rehabilitated in a short time.

"It has been proven in the past that the vast majority of ex-convicts return to society to become repeat offenders," Lux said.

"It is the board of trustees of the Brotherhood concern that the general public is being endangered through the premature release of dangerous criminals."

"The Brotherhood feels it is time for local government agencies to review the judicial sentencing systems and are asking that this review be immediately undertaken together with an investigation of the possibilities of mandatory sentencing for crimes of violence."

Denver Rocky Mountain News, September 6, 1975.

To the courtroom work group, mandatory provisions are infeasible. Members of the work group encounter defendants who would suffer an undue hardship by going to prison or whose crime is too minor to justify such a sentence. Thus there is considerable evidence that courtroom work groups seek ways to avoid the application of mandatory sentencing laws that they believe are unduly harsh (Blumstein et al.).

Two complementary articles analyzing the Michigan Felony Firearms Statute illustrate some of the issues involved in assessing the actual effectiveness of mandatory minimum sentencing laws. The law was widely advertised as introducing greater equity in sentencing, ensuring certainty of punishment, and decreasing violent crimes in the state. These goals were not met. Discretion was not eliminated but rather shifted. The law did decrease judicial sentencing discretion, but at the same time it stimulated prosecutorial discretion (Heumann and Loftin). There was a decrease in the probability of conviction for felonious assaults and perhaps armed robberies. The law did not result in adding an additional two years to the sentence. Finally there was no reduction in gun crimes (Loftin, Heumann, and McDowall). Experience in other states likewise indicates that mandatory minimum sentencing laws have little effect.

Conclusion

Sentencing is the most difficult task faced by the trial judge. In deciding whether to send an offender to prison or grant probation, the courtroom work group weighs the normal penalty for the offense, the seriousness of the crime, the defendant's prior record, and his or her social stability. The results of these decisions have become the focus of heated public dialogue. To some, sentences are too harsh; to others, too lenient. Some find sentences discriminatory and unpredictable; others say that they fail to protect the public from crime. These concerns have prompted numerous changes since the mid-1970s. Determinate sentencing laws, mandatory minimum sentencing provisions, and sentencing guidelines are the most prominent changes undertaken.

Sentencing is likely to remain on the nation's political agenda, because all too often members of the public, as well as elected officials, have ignored an important reality: prison populations are swelling. America sends more people to prison than any other Western nation, and the rate of incarceration is growing steadily. The result is severe prison overcrowding, compounded by federal court orders requiring major improvements in prison conditions. Limitations on the number and quality of available prison beds create a political dilemma. Even though citizens and public officials want to send even more offenders to prison, they are unwilling to spend large sums of tax dollars to build the needed facilities. Sentencing is thus likely to remain an important public policy issue for the foreseeable future.

For Discussion

1. Discuss with a judge and a prosecutor local practices concerning presentence investigations. What type of information is collected? How influential are these reports in setting the penalty?

2. Discuss the effects of courtroom work groups on the sentencing process.
3. Interview a judge, prosecutor, and defense attorney about the most important factors in sentencing in your community.
4. What are the arguments opposed to increasing the severity of sentences? What are the arguments in favor?
5. How do the general goals of equality and individualization lead to sentencing disparities? What do you think are the most relevant factors leading to sentencing disparities?
6. What do the studies of sentencing discrimination indicate? Is there evidence of systematic bias based on age, race, sex, or economic status?
7. What types of press coverage do sentences receive in the local press? (Remember to examine letters to the editor.) What impact do you think such coverage has on judges, prosecutors, defense attorneys, and probation officers?
8. Which reform—sentencing institutes, sentencing councils, sentencing guidelines, or appellate review—do you think would be most effective in reducing sentencing disparities? Why? Which do you think has the greatest chance for adoption? Why?

References

ASSOCIATION OF THE BAR OF THE CITY OF NEW YORK DRUG ABUSE COUNCIL. *The Effects of the 1973 Drug Laws on the New York State Courts.* New York: 1976.

AUSTIN, ROY. "Unconvincing Rejection of the Hypothesis of Racial Discrimination in Sentencing: A Commentary on Kleck." Unpublished manuscript, Pennsylvania State University, 1981.

BALDUS, DAVID, CHARLES PULASKI, AND GEORGE WOODWORTH. "Comparative Review of Death Sentences: An Empirical Study of the Georgia Experience." *Journal of Criminal Law and Criminology* 74 (1983): 661.

BLUMSTEIN, ALFRED. "Research on Sentencing." *Justice System Journal* 7 (1982): 307.

BLUMSTEIN, ALFRED, JACQUELINE COHEN, SUSAN MARTIN, AND MICHAEL TONRY, eds. *Research on Sentencing: The Search for Reform,* vol. 1. Washington, D.C.: National Academy Press, 1983.

BOWEN, DONALD. *The Explanation of Judicial Voting Behavior from Sociological Characteristics of Judges.* New Haven, Conn.: Yale University Press, 1965.

BREWER, DAVID, GERALD BECKETT, AND NORMAN HOLT. "Determinate Sentencing in California: The First Year's Experience." *Journal of Research in Crime and Delinquency* 18 (1981): 200–231.

BURKE, PETER, AND AUSTIN TURK. "Factors Affecting Postarrest Dispositions: A Model for Analysis." *Social Problems* 22 (1975): 313.

CALIFORNIA STATE ASSEMBLY, Office of Research. *Crime and Penalties in California.* Sacramento, Calif.: California State Assembly, 1968.

CAMERON, MARY. *The Booster and the Snitch.* Glencoe, Ill.: Free Press, 1964.

CAMPBELL, DONALD, AND H. LAURENCE ROSS. "The Connecticut Crackdown on Speeding: Times-Series Data in Quasi-Experimental Analysis." *Law and Society Review* 3 (1968): 33.

CARP, ROBERT, AND C. K. ROWLAND. *Policymaking and Politics in the Federal District Courts.* Knoxville: University of Tennessee Press, 1983.

CARROLL, LEO, AND CLAIRE CORNELL. "Racial Composition, Sentencing Reforms, and Rates of Incarceration, 1970–1980." *Justice Quarterly* 2 (1985): 473.

CARROW, DEBORAH. "Judicial Sentencing Guidelines: Hazards of the Middle Ground." *Judicature* 68 (1984): 161.

CARTER, ROBERT, AND LESLIE WILKINS. "Some Factors in Sentencing Policy." *Journal of Criminal Law, Criminology and Police Science* 58 (December 1967): 503–514.

CASPER, JONATHAN, AND DAVID BRERETON. "Evaluating Criminal Justice Reforms," *Law and Society Review* 18 (1984): 121.

CASPER, JONATHAN, DAVID BRERETON, AND DAVID NEAL. *The Implementation of the California Determinate Sentencing Law.* Washington, D.C.: U.S. Department of Justice, 1982.

CHIRICOS, THEODORE, AND GORDON WALDO. "Socioeconomic Status and Criminal Sentencing: An Empirical Assessment of a Conflict Proposition." *American Sociological Review* 40 (1975): 753.

CLARKE, STEVENS. "North Carolina's Determinate Sentencing Legislation," *Judicature* 68 (1984): 140.

CLARKE, STEVENS, AND GARY G. KOCH. "The Influence of Income and Other Factors on Whether Criminal Defendants Go to Prison." *Law and Society Review* 11 (1976): 57–92.

CLEAR, TODD, JOHN HEWITT, AND ROBERT REGOLI. "Discretion and the Determinate Sentence: Its Distribution, Control and Effect on Time Served." *Crime and Delinquency* 24 (1979): 444.

COVEY, HERBERT, AND MARY MANDE. "Determinate Sentencing in Colorado." *Justice Quarterly* 2 (1985): 259.

DAWSON, ROBERT O. *Sentencing: The Decision as to Type, Length, and Conditions of Sentence.* Boston: Little, Brown, 1969.

D'ESPOSITO, JULIAN C. "Sentencing Disparity: Causes and Cures." *Journal of Criminal Law, Criminology and Police Science* 60 (1969): 182–194.

DIAMOND, SHARI SHEIDMAN, AND HANS ZEISEL. "Sentencing Councils: A Study of Sentencing Disparity and Its Reduction." *University of Chicago Law Review* 43 (Fall 1975): 109–149.

EISENSTEIN, JAMES, AND HERBERT JACOB. *Felony Justice: An Organizational Analysis of Criminal Courts.* Boston: Little, Brown, 1977.

FORST, MARTIN. "Sentencing Disparity: An Overview of Research and Issues." In *Sentencing Reform: Experiments in Reducing Disparity,* ed. Martin Forst. Beverly Hills: Sage Publications, 1982.

FRANKEL, MARVIN. *Criminal Sentences: Law Without Order.* New York: Hill & Wang, 1972.

GIBSON, JAMES. "Environmental Restraints on the Behavior of Judges: A Representational Model of Judicial Decision Making," *Law and Society Review* 14 (1980): 343.

——. "Race as a Determinant of Criminal Sentences: A Methodological Critique and a Case Study." *Law and Society Review* 12 (1978): 455–478.

GOLDMAN, SHELDON. "Voting Behavior on the U.S. Court of Appeals Revisited." *American Political Science Review* 69 (June 1975): 491.

GOTTFREDSON, DON, LESLIE WILKINS, AND PETER HOFFMAN. *Guidelines for Parole and Sentencing: A Policy Control Method.* Lexington, Mass.: Lexington Books, 1978.

GREEN, EDWARD. *Judicial Attitudes in Sentencing.* New York: St. Martin's Press, 1961.

HAGAN, JOHN. "Criminal Justice in Rural and Urban Communities: A Study of the Bureaucratization of Justice." *Social Forces* 55 (1977): 597.

——. "Extra-Legal Attributes and Criminal Sentencing: An Assessment of a Sociological Viewpoint." *Law and Society Review* 8 (1974): 357–381.

HAGAN, JOHN, AND KRISTIN BUMILLER. "Making Sense of Sentencing: A Review and Critique of Sentencing Research." In *Research on Sentencing: The Search for Reform,* vol. 2, ed. Alfred Blumstein, Jacqueline Cohen, Susan Martin, and Michael Tonry. Washington, D.C.: National Academy Press, 1983, pp. 1–54.

HAGAN, JOHN, JOHN HEWITT, AND DUANE ALWIN. "Ceremonial Justice: Crime and Punishment in a Loosely Coupled System." *Social Forces* 58 (1979): 506.

HALL, JEROME. *Theft, Law and Society.* Indianapolis: Bobbs-Merrill, 1952.

HAWKINS, DARNELL. "Race, Crime Type and Imprisonment." *Justice Quarterly* 3 (1986): 251.

HEUMANN, MILTON, AND COLIN LOFTIN. "Mandatory Sentencing and the Abolition of Plea Bargaining: The Michigan Felony Firearm Statute." *Law and Society Review* 13 (Winter 1979): 393–430.

HINDELANG, MICHAEL. "Equality Under the Law." In *Race, Crime and Justice,* ed. Charles Reasons and Jack Kuykendall. Pacific Palisades, Calif.: Goodyear Publishing, 1972, pp. 312–323.

HOGARTH, JOHN. *Sentencing as a Human Process.* Toronto: University of Toronto Press, 1971.

JACOBS, DAVID. "Inequality and the Legal Order: An Ecological Test of the Conflict Model." *Social Problems* 25 (1978): 515–525.

JUDSON, CHARLES, JAMES PANDELL, JACK OWENS, JAMES McINTOSH, AND DALE MATSCHULLAT. "A Study of the California Penalty Jury in First Degree Murder Cases." *Stanford Law Review* 21 (1969): 1297.

KATKIN, DANIEL. "Presentence Reports: An Analysis of Uses, Limitations and Civil Liberties Issues." *Minnesota Law Review* 55 (November 1970): 15–31.

KLECK, GARY. "Racial Discrimination in Criminal Sentencing: A Critical Evaluation of the Evidence with Additional Data on the Death Penalty." *American Sociological Review* 46 (1981): 783.

KLEMM, MARGARET. *The Determinants of Capital Sentencing in Louisiana, 1979–1984.* Unpublished Ph.D. dissertation, University of New Orleans, 1986.

KRESS, JACK. *Prescription for Justice: The Theory and Practice of Sentencing Guidelines.* Cambridge, Mass.: Ballinger, 1980.

LANGAN, PATRICK, AND LAWRENCE GREENFELD. "The Prevalence of Imprisonment." Washington, D.C.: Bureau of Justice Statistics, U.S. Department of Justice, 1985.

LEVIN, MARTIN. *Urban Politics and the Criminal Courts.* Chicago: University of Chicago Press, 1977.

LIZOTTE, ALAN. "Extra-Legal Factors in Chicago's Criminal Courts: Testing the Conflict Model of Criminal Justice." *Social Problems* 25 (June 1978): 564–580.

LOFTIN, COLIN, MILTON HEUMANN, AND DAVID McDOWALL. "Mandatory Sentencing and Firearms Violence: Evaluating an Alternative to Gun Control." *Law and Society Review* 17 (1983): 287.

McCOY, CANDACE. "Determinate Sentencing, Plea Bargaining Bans, and Hydraulic Discretion in California." *Justice System Journal* 9 (1984): 256.

McDONALD, WILLIAM, HENRY ROSSMAN, AND JAMES CRAMER. "The Prosecutorial Function and Its Relation to Determinate Sentencing Structures." In *The Prosecutor,* ed. William McDonald. Beverly Hills, Calif.: Sage Publications, 1979.

MATHER, LYNN. "Some Determinants of the Method of Case Disposition: Decision-Making by Public Defenders in Los Angeles." *Law and Society Review* 8 (Winter 1974): 187.

MOORE, CHARLES, AND TERANCE MIETHE. "Regulated and Unregulated Sentencing Decisions: An Analysis of First-Year Practices under Minnesota's Felony Sentencing Guidelines." *Law and Society Review* 20 (1986): 253.

MORRIS, NORVAL. "The Sentencing Disease: The Judge's Changing Role in the Criminal Justice Process." *The Judges' Journal* 18 (Summer 1979): 8–13, 50.

NAGEL, STUART S. *The Legal Process from a Behavioral Perspective.* Chicago: Dorsey Press, 1969.

NARDULLI, PETER, ROY FLEMMING, AND JAMES EISENSTEIN. "Unraveling the Complexities of Decision Making in Face-to-Face Groups: A Contextual Analysis of Plea-Bargained Sentences." *American Political Science Review* 78 (1984): 912.

NEUBAUER, DAVID. "Appellate Review of Sentencing: The Louisiana Experience." Paper presented at the 1984 annual meeting of the Southern Political Science Association, Baton Rouge, La.

——. *Criminal Justice in Middle America.* Morristown, N.J.: General Learning Press, 1974.

NEW YORK TIMES, September 5, 1976.

NEWMAN, DONALD. *Conviction: The Determination of Guilt or Innocence Without Trial.* Boston: Little, Brown, 1966.

PARTRIDGE, ANTHONY, AND WILLIAM ELDRIDGE. *The Second Circuit Sentencing Study: A Report to the Judges of the Second Circuit.* Washington, D.C.: Federal Judicial Center, August 1974.

PATERNOSTER, RAYMOND. "Prosecutorial Discretion in Requesting the Death Penalty: A Case of Victim-Based Racial Discrimination." *Law and Society Review* 18 (1984): 437.

PHILLIPS, CHARLES. *Sentencing Councils in the Federal Courts.* Lexington, Mass.: Lexington Books, 1980.

PRUITT, CHARLES, AND JAMES Q. WILSON. "A Longitudinal Study of the Effect of Race on Sentencing." *Law and Society Review* 17 (1983): 613.

QUINNEY, RICHARD. *The Social Reality of Crime.* Boston: Little, Brown, 1970.

RADELET, MICHAEL, AND GLENN PIERCE. "Race and Prosecutorial Discretion in Homicide Cases." *Law and Society Review* 19 (1985): 587.

RICH, WILLIAM, L. PAUL SUTTON, TODD CLEAR, AND MICHAEL SAKS. *Sentencing by Mathematics: An Evaluation of the Early Attempts to Develop and Implement Sentencing Guidelines.* Williamsburg, Va.: National Center for State Courts, 1982.

ROBERTSON, LEON S., ROBERT F. RICH, AND H. LAURENCE ROSS. "Jail Sentences for Driving While Intoxicated in Chicago: A Judicial Action That Failed." *Law and Society Review* 8 (1973): 55.

ROSETT, ARTHUR, AND DONALD R. CRESSEY. *Justice by Consent.* Philadelphia: J. B. Lippincott, 1976.

SCHWARTZ, BARRY. "The Effect in Philadelphia of Pennsylvania's Increased Penalties for Rape and Attempted Rape." *Journal of Criminal Law, Criminology, and Police Science* 59 (1968): 509–515.

SELLIN, THORSTEN. "Race Prejudice in the Administration of Justice." *American Journal of Sociology* 41 (1935): 212.

SPARKS, RICHARD. "The Construction of Sentencing Guidelines: A Methodological Critique." In *Research on Sentencing: The Search for Reform,* ed. Alfred Blumstein, Jacqueline Cohen, Susan Martin, and Michael Tonry. Washington, D.C.: National Academy Press, 1983, pp. 194–264.

SPOHN, CASSIA, JOHN GRUHL, AND SUSAN WELCH. "The Effect of Race on Sentencing: A Re-Examination of an Unsettled Question." *Law and Society Review* 16 (1981–1982): 71–88.

SUDNOW, DAVID. "Normal Crimes: Sociological Features of the Penal Codes in a Public Defender Office." *Social Problems* 12 (1965): 254.

TIFFANY, LAWRENCE P., YAKOV AVICHAI, AND GEOFFREY W. PETERS. "A Statistical Analysis of Sentencing in Federal Courts: Defendants Convicted After Trial, 1967–1968." *Journal of Legal Studies* 10 (1975): 369.

TWENTIETH CENTURY FUND TASK FORCE ON SENTENCING. *Fair and Certain Punishment.* New York: McGraw-Hill, 1976.

VERA INSTITUTE OF JUSTICE. *Felony Arrests: Their Prosecution and Disposition in New York City's Courts.* New York: Vera Institute of Justice, 1977.

WELCH, SUSAN, AND CASSIA SPOHN. "Evaluating the Impact of Prior Record on Judges' Sentencing Decisions: A Seven-City Comparison." *Justice Quarterly* 3 (1986): 389.

WELCH, SUSAN, CASSIA SPOHN, AND JOHN GRUHL. "Convicting and Sentencing Differences Among Black, Hispanic and White Males in Six Localities." *Justice Quarterly* 2 (1985): 67.

WILBANKS, WILLIAM. *The Myth of a Racist Criminal Justice System.* Pacific Grove, Calif.: Brooks/Cole, 1987.

WILKINS, LESLIE, JACK KRESS, DON GOTTFREDSON, JOSEPH CALPIN, AND ARTHUR GELMAN. *Sentencing Guidelines: Structuring Judicial Discretion, Final Report of the Feasibility Study.* Washington, D.C.: Government Printing Office, 1976.

WILSON, JAMES Q. "If Every Criminal *Knew* He Would Be Punished If Caught . . ." *New York Times Magazine,* January 28, 1973.

———. *Thinking About Crime.* New York: Basic Books, 1975.

WOLFGANG, MARVIN, AND MARC RIEDEL. "Race, Judicial Discretion, and the Death Penalty." *Annals of the American Academy of Political and Social Science* 407 (1973): 119.

ZIMRING, FRANK, AND GORDON HAWKINS. *Deterrence: The Legal Threat in Crime Control.* Chicago: University of Chicago Press, 1973.

For Further Reading

BLUMSTEIN, ALFRED, JACQUELINE COHEN, SUSAN MARTIN, AND MICHAEL TONRY, eds. *Research on Sentencing: The Search for Reform,* vol. 1. Washington, D.C.: National Academy Press, 1983.

FORST, MARTIN. *Sentencing Reform: Experiments in Reducing Disparity.* Beverly Hills: Sage Publications, 1982.

HEWITT, JOHN, AND TODD CLEAR. *The Impact of Sentencing Reform: From Indeterminate to Determinate Sentencing.* Lanham, Md.: University Press of America, 1983.

JOHNSON, ROBERT. *Hard Time: Understanding and Reforming the Prison.* Pacific Grove, Calif.: Brooks/Cole, 1987.

KRESS, JACK. *Prescription for Justice: The Theory and Practice of Sentencing Guidelines.* Cambridge, Mass.: Ballinger, 1980.

WILBANKS, WILLIAM. *The Myth of a Racist Criminal Justice System.* Pacific Grove, Calif.: Brooks/Cole, 1987.

PART V

WHAT IS WRONG HERE?

P *arts II, III, and IV have examined numerous reform proposals. This last part examines some additional reform proposals and provides a general overview of the topic.*

The nation's lower courts operate very differently from the major trial courts. Chapter 17 considers some of the major criticisms of "conveyor belt justice" and various proposals to improve the quality of justice.

Whether the courts are too slow—and if so, why—is the focus of Chapter 18, which considers the important issues involved in judicial administration.

CHAPTER **17**

The Lower Courts:
Rapid, Rough Justice

Ninety percent of the nation's criminal cases are heard in the less prestigious lower courts. These are the courts that process the millions of Americans accused each year of disturbing the peace, shoplifting, being drunk, and driving too fast. Although individually these cases may appear to be minor—almost petty—collectively the work of the lower courts is quite important.

For decades reformers have pointed out the problems of the lower courts. Only a fraction of the adversary model of criminal justice can be found in these courts. Many defendants are not represented by an attorney. Trials are rare. Jail sentences are imposed, sometimes with lightning speed. Informality, rather than the rules of courtroom procedure, predominates. In short, practices that would be condemned if they occurred in higher courts are commonplace in the lower courts. Is this justice, we might ask? The President's Commission on Law Enforcement and Administration of Justice asked the same question and expressed shock over the conclusions it reached: "No findings of this

Commission are more disquieting than those relating to the conditions of the lower criminal courts'' (1967b: 29).

There is little doubt that lower courts do not always administer justice as well as they might, but placing this shortcoming in perspective is difficult. The literature on the lower courts has been impressionistic rather than systematic. As a result, our knowledge of the operational realities of misdemeanor courts is less advanced than for the felony trial courts (Alfini and Passuth). Some recent studies have suggested that we need to take a more objective and realistic approach in evaluating the lower courts. These studies maintain that there are two major factors to bear in mind when assessing the work of the lower courts. First, the lower courts are not just felony courts with a higher volume of less serious cases. Fundamental differences exist between how the lower courts and the major trial courts operate. Lower courts demonstrate greater flexibility because the judges and prosecutors more directly focus on trying to produce substantive justice (rather than just adhering to procedures). Second, lower courts exhibit immense variation. The big city drunk court operations are very different from the rural justice of the peace court. Moreover, even lower courts in big cities differ vastly according to the particular city.

This chapter discusses the rapid, rough justice dispensed by the lower courts. Some specific topics include the conditions of the nation's lower courts, their impact on citizens, their effects on the criminal justice system, their problems, and what might be done to improve them.

Problems of the Lower Courts

The lower courts are important because they interact with so many citizens. It is in the trial courts of limited jurisdiction that the bulk of cases are heard. Filings and dispositions outnumber those in the more prestigious trial courts of general jurisdiction by a ratio of six or seven to one. To be sure, most of these cases stem from the staggering number of traffic violations that occur each year (estimates range from fifty to seventy-nine million). But these courts also decide from eight to fourteen million criminal cases each year (Lieberman).

nonjudicial atmosphere   The most lasting impression is of the ***nonjudicial atmosphere*** of the proceedings. One of the most widely quoted passages of the President's Commission aptly summarizes these conditions:

> The commission has been shocked by what it has seen in some lower courts. It has seen cramped and noisy courtrooms, undignified and perfunctory procedures, and badly trained personnel. It has seen dedicated people who are frustrated by huge case loads, by the lack of opportunity to examine cases carefully, and by the impossibility of devising constructive solutions to the problems of offenders. It has seen assembly-line justice. (1967a: 128)

There is little in the process that instills in defendants, witnesses, observers, or court officials respect for the criminal justice system. Because these courts occupy the lowest rung on the judicial ladder, they have been treated as a judicial stepchild. The municipal courts in large metropolitan areas, as well as the justice of the peace courts in small towns, suffer from long-term neglect. By general consensus, the lower courts are the principal weakness in the state court system (Ashman).

To identify the most pressing problems of the trial courts of limited jurisdiction, the American Judicature Society surveyed six states: Colorado, Illinois, Louisiana, New Hampshire, New Jersey, and Texas. They found the problems confronting the lower courts as varied as the courts themselves, but four are particularly important: inadequate financing, lax procedures, inadequate facilities, and imbalanced caseloads.

Inadequate Financing

Generally lower courts are funded locally. As a result, sparsely populated counties and small municipalities often lack funds to staff and equip their courts adequately. Even when local funds are available to local governments, there is no guarantee that these funds will be spent on the lower courts. The suspicion is that in many cities these courts are expected to produce revenue for local governments. Even though they may generate a fairly large amount of income from assessing fines and imposing court costs, the local courts have no control over how these funds are spent. A survey found that 150 Texas municipal courts have revenues five times greater than their operating expenses. Yet over half of these courts lacked adequate courtrooms, supplies, office space, and the like (Ashman). The remainder of the funds went to pay for city services. In short, such local funding has meant *inadequate financing* for the nation's lowest tribunals.

inadequate financing

Court Procedures and Administration

lax court procedures

Critics of lower courts often cite *lax court procedures* and lack of uniformity in the day-to-day administration of these courts. There is a wide divergence in the way in which cases are handled in the trial courts of limited jurisdiction. Many do not have written rules for the conduct of cases. Conventional bookkeeping methods are often ignored. If records are kept, they are usually of use only to the individual judge. How much fine money was collected and how it was spent is often impossible to determine. The lack of uniformity and absence of records frustrate any attempts to assess the effectiveness of these courts.

Inadequate Facilities

Courtrooms that are dirty, crowded, or noisy and makeshift courtrooms hastily created in a store or garage convey a justifiably bad impression. The lack of dignity that such *inadequate facilities* and conditions convey is detrimental to the attributes of the defendant, prosecutor, judge, and all others involved in the justice process (Ashman). As an example of outdated and rundown facilities, the American Judicature Society singled out Atlantic County Juvenile and Domestic Relations Court (New Jersey). The old stone structure, which once was used as a roller skating rink, is now in a deteriorated condition, with high ceilings, soiled walls, and a wooden floor.

inadequate facilities

Imbalanced Caseloads

imbalanced caseloads

Many lower courts are characterized by moderate to heavy caseloads. But others appear to have little to do. Thus there are often wide differences in caseload from court to court. The ***imbalanced caseloads*** result in some courts being flooded with huge backlogs for which they are unequipped. But because these courts are locally controlled, there is no way to equalize the work load.

Any general statement about the problems of the lower courts must, however, be immediately coupled with a cautionary note, for the nation's lowest tribunals have been the least studied. Moreover they are tremendously varied. From state to state, between one county and its neighboring county, and even within a city, there are wide discrepancies in the quantity and quality of justice rendered. These wide-ranging variations illuminate the fact that these courts are locally controlled and are not generally part of the state judiciary. In short, there is no easy way to determine what is wrong (or even what is right) about these courts (Ashman). Given this wide-ranging disparity, it is best to examine the rurally based justice of the peace courts separately from the urban municipal courts. Although they share many problems, they are also sufficiently different to warrant separate treatment.

Justice of the Peace Courts

justice of the peace (JP)

In rural areas, the lower courts are collectively called ***justice of the peace courts.*** The officeholder is usually referred to simply as a ***JP.*** This system of local justice traces its origins to fourteenth-century England when towns were small and isolated. The JP system developed as a way to dispense simple and speedy justice for minor civil and criminal cases. The emphasis was decidedly on the ability of local landowners (squires), who served as part-time JPs to decide disputes on the basis of their knowledge of the local community.

The small-town flavor of the JP system persists today. By and large present-day JPs are part-time nonlawyers who conduct court at their regular place of business—the back of the undertaker's parlor, the front counter of the general store, or next to the grease rack in the garage. Most of the nation's fifteen to twenty thousand JPs are locally elected officials who serve short terms. Some, however, serve ex officio—that is, many small town mayors also serve as judges in city court. Although a few are able to earn a comfortable income from the job, overall the salaries are low. Moreover support personnel is often limited. In the smaller courts, the JP's spouse may serve as clerk. But many courts have no clerks at all. JPs in Texas, for example, seldom have any clerical help for record keeping.

Critics argue that the JP system has outlived its purpose. It may have met the needs of small, isolated, and rural towns of a century ago, but it is out of step with the modern era. A Maryland trial judge criticized his own state's JPs in the following terms:

> "[They have] treated some good, decent citizens like common criminals."
> "The justice of the peace system is completely outmoded. . . . If things keep going like they've been going, some of these people are going to get us into serious trouble. . . ."

Many of the JP's are just plain nasty to people.

"There have been all sorts of instances where they've been rude to people and when the person complains they tell him to 'go to see your congressman.'

"These people aren't controlled by us. They deny they have any connection with the police department. They tell the police to jump—and they tell us the same thing.

"It's time these people were put under us—or the circuit court—or somebody." (President's Commission, 1967b: 35)

Examples like these abound to show that the justice a defendant receives in JP court reflects the personality of the judge. Or that out-of-town motorists are treated very differently (high fines to keep the city treasury full) from local speeders. While some lower courts administer fair and even-handed justice, all too many do not. Critics doubt whether the current diversified and fragmented JP system can ever deliver fair, impartial, and even-handed justice. Efforts at improving the quality of justice dispensed by the rurally based lower courts focus on three topics: abolition of the JP courts, elimination of the fee system, and upgrading the quality of the personnel.

Abolition of the JP

abolition of JP

The ultimate goal of the judicial reformers is to **abolish the JP.** A major defect of the JP system is that these courts are not part of the state judiciary; instead they are controlled only by the local governmental bodies that create them and fund them. Only recently have judicial conduct commissions (see Chapter 8) been granted the authority to discipline or remove local judges who abuse their office.

courts of record

Nor are the activities of the lower courts subject to appellate scrutiny. Rarely are trial courts of limited jurisdiction **courts of record**; no stenographic record is kept of the witnesses' testimony or the judges' rulings. Thus when a defendant appeals, the appeal is heard by a trial court of general jurisdiction, which must conduct an entirely new trial, taking the testimony of the same witnesses and hearing the identical arguments of the attorneys as the

trial de novo

lower court did. This is called a **trial de novo.** The *trial de novo* system often unnecessarily increases the already heavy caseload of the state trial courts. But by far the major weakness of the *trial de novo* system is that it insulates the lower courtroom from scrutiny. No opportunity exists for higher courts to discover or correct errors in court procedure, the taking of evidence, the denial of defendant's constitutional rights, or the court's interpretation of the criminal law. The absence of appellate court review also hides patterns and practices that although not illegal are nonetheless problems—ineffective management of the courtroom or disparaging remarks by the judge, for example (Bing and Rosenfeld).

Unifying state courts into a three-tier system of a single trial court, an intermediate appellate court, and a supreme court (see Chapter 3) would abolish the justice of the peace, require all judges to be lawyers, and eliminate the *trial de novo* system.

Reformers have had only limited success in their efforts to abolish the JP system. One major obstacle is the powerful influence of nonlawyer judges, who do not want their jobs abolished. Another significant obstacle is the belief that JPs are easily accessible, whereas more formal courts are miles away. For example, they are readily available to sign arrest warrants for the police or to try a motorist accused of driving too fast. Supporters contend that a knowledge of the local community better prepares JPs to solve minor disputes than does a law degree, mainly because few minor disputes involve any complex legal issues. Thus JP courts are often viewed as people's courts. As one Florida supporter phrased it, "These are the last bastions of the people without much money. It's a place they can go to resolve their problems" without the necessity of having a lawyer (MacFeely: 10A).

Elimination of the Fee System

fee system

Historically rurally based, part-time justices of the peace were paid for their services from the fees assessed against a convicted defendant. To many, the *fee system* meant that JP stood for "justice for the plaintiff"; since the judge was paid only if the defendant was found guilty, few were acquitted. In 1927 the Supreme Court seemingly abolished the direct fee system by ruling that it denied defendants the right to trial before an impartial judge (*Tumey* v. *Ohio,* 273 U.S. 510). Yet as late as 1965, three states still used the direct fee system (President's Commission, 1967b). Many others used an indirect fee system for compensating lower court judges. Indeed, the President's Commission reported that in thirty-two of the thirty-five states where JPs had criminal case jurisdiction, pay was still tied to the fees; the state covered court costs if the defendant was acquitted. But even with this refinement, "justice for the plaintiff" continued. Since states were slow in forwarding funds, the JP tended to convict in order to avoid a lengthy wait for the county to pay. Then too, the fee system exerted pressure on each justice to get more business. Police officers— the major source of the JP's business—naturally patronized JPs sympathetic to the police and prone to convict (President's Commission, 1967b).

Since the President's Commission report, which singled out the fee system as one of the worst features of the JP courts, major changes have occurred. As states have reexamined their lower courts, the first thing to be abolished has been the fee system. In less than a decade the fee system has gone from the primary way of paying local judges to virtual extinction; only a small handful of states now use it. It has been replaced by paying lower court judges a salary irrespective of how many cases they handle or whether they find the defendant guilty. The major issue involved now is whether the local government or the state will pay the JP's salary. Typically local governments wish to retain the revenues they receive from JP courts but want the state government to bear the operating costs. A major consequence of the abolition of the fee system has been a marked decrease in the number of JPs.

Upgrading the Quality of the Personnel

The low pay and equally low status of the JP have not attracted highly qualified personnel. One survey found that only 5 percent of the JPs in Virginia were college graduates. Another, conducted in California, showed that between a third and a half of that state's lower court judges were not even high school graduates. Perhaps most shocking of all, the assistant attorney of Mississippi, in his brief in a state court case, estimated that "33 percent of the justices of the peace are limited in educational background to the extent that they are not capable of learning the necessary elements of law" (Justice Brennan, dissent, *North* v. *Russell,* 1976).

The average JP's unfamiliarity with basic legal concepts is shown in the following testimony of a South Carolina magistrate:

Q. Do you presently have an understanding of what your duties as a magistrate are?

A. Well, not really, no.

Q. Tell me what your understanding of the Code of Laws is. What is contained in the Code of Laws, as you understand?

A. Well, I never have done any reading in it.

Q. You never have had occasion to refer to it?

A. No, sir. [Neither had he read any case of an appellate court.]

Q. What would you do if someone were to request a trial by jury?

A. I would come to Mr. George Stuckey [the county attorney] and find out what I had to do.

Q. What is the purpose of bail?

A. It is for violation and a good reminder not to do it again.

Q. Are you familiar with the concept of probable cause, in connection with preliminary hearings?

A. No, sir.

Q. Or in connection with the issuance of search warrants, or arrest warrants?

A. No, sir.

Q. Have you ever refused to issue an arrest or search warrant?

A. No, sir.

Q. Are you familiar with the rules of evidence which govern the admissibility of evidence at trials?

A. No, sir. (Ashman and Chapin: 418)

High on the judicial reformers' list of priorities, therefore, is upgrading the quality of lower court judges. Some states have instituted training programs for lay judges, but only a few of the judges have yet received any training in basic legal concepts or the duties and responsibilities of the office.

Nonlawyer Judges

nonlawyer judges

A longstanding issue confronting the American judiciary is whether lower court judges should be attorneys. Whereas judges in the trial courts of general jurisdiction and appellate tribunals must be lawyers, forty-three states do not require lower court judges to have graduated from law school. ***Nonlawyer judges*** are more numerous than usually realized. All together there are over eleven thousand judges who are not legally trained in the United States, which adds up to almost half (46 percent) of all state judges (Bronstein). A disproportionate number of these part-time, nonlawyer judges are located in the states of New York and Texas (Alfini and Passuth). Judicial reformers argue that only lawyers should be allowed to judge defendants innocent or guilty and to sentence them to a year (or sometimes more) in jail. On the other hand, defenders of the status quo argue that these courts led by nonlawyer judges are people's courts where common sense is as good a guide as lawbooks in settling disputes. The U.S. Supreme Court considered this issue in *North* v. *Russell,* a case that features a number of problems in the lower courts.

The Lynch City Police Court meets every Thursday night, Judge C. B. Russell presiding. Like most others born and raised in Lynch, a small town in Kentucky's coal mining region, Russell dropped out of high school and worked in the coal mines. A few years ago he was elected judge. He is not a lawyer nor has he received any training in the duties of a city judge. On July 8, 1974, Judge Russell found Lonnie North guilty of drunk driving and sentenced him to thirty days in jail. But Kentucky law allows only a fine for Lonnie North's charge. The judge, it seems, exceeded his legal power. Nor was this the only legal irregularity in the proceedings that day. Judge Russell refused the defendant's request for a jury trial, did not inform him of his right to a court-appointed lawyer, and failed to advise the defendant of his right to an appeal.

CLOSE-UP

Rural Justice

More than 55 million Americans get their justice off the main road. For them, the law is meted out in rural courthouses often presided over by part-time judges, argued by inadequately trained lawyers, and administered by overworked and underpaid court clerks.

Consequently, the process is sometimes more convenient than constitutional, more community-oriented than concerned with individual rights, and particularly stacked against women, minorities, the poor—and "outsiders."

These are the conclusions of a little-publicized but highly respected series of studies being conducted by the New Hampshire–based Rural Justice Center (RJC). The results coincide with other assessments made by judicial scholars, social activists, and legal experts.

"There's a lack of an independent judiciary and a weak adversary process in many parts of rural America," says social activist Kathryn

Fahnestock, one of the cofounders of RJC. "Community knowledge is substituted for the Constitution," she says.

"Nobody Holds the System Accountable"

The . . . team so far has conducted its research in off-the-beaten-path court systems in Vermont, Indiana, North Carolina, Kansas, Ohio, and Michigan.

Among their findings:

- Seventy-nine percent of the 3,082 courts of general jurisdiction in the United States are in rural areas. Yet these country courtrooms have been virtually ignored by the judicial reform movement of the past two decades.
- With publicly funded legal services to the poor drastically reduced in recent years, rural areas have been hardest hit—with the result being ever greater injustice for non-urban residents.

- In many places, lack of funds, lack of expertise, inadequate knowledge about proper procedures, and even unfamiliarity with constitutional mandates have often resulted in an uneven, unequal, unresponsive judicial process.

Mr. Geiger says that the "isolation of rural judges and court clerks also tends to undermine the system." He also says that "nobody holds the system accountable from the outside."

"Justice is administered by those who grew up in the community," says Miss Fahnestock. "And what they want to do is preserve the peace and traditional community values."

Geiger and Fahnestock stress that they are not probing public corruption. They say their criticism of rural court procedures is meant to be "loving" and constructive. Admittedly, their assessments

Moreover, during the trial, Judge Russell listened only to the arresting officer's story and did not allow the defendant to tell his version (*North* v. *Russell,* 96 S.Ct. 2709, 1976).

Chief Justice Warren Burger's majority opinion argued that nonlawyer judges do not violate the due process clause of the Fourteenth Amendment. He described the JP system as courts of convenience for citizens in small towns and spoke favorably of the fact that ''the inferior courts are simple and speedy.'' Burger argued that any defects in the proceedings (which were numerous in this case) could be corrected by the availability of defense attorneys, the right to a jury trial, and a *trial de novo.* Significantly, though, these were the specific things that Judge Russell failed to inform the defendant about.

In a dissenting opinion, Justice Brennan stated the case for requiring judges to be lawyers. He found it constitutionally intolerable that a nonlawyer judge could send a defendant to jail or to prison. Brennan further noted that a

---

are candid, and sometimes harsh.

An RJC study in a North Carolina county reported, among other things, that the court tended to rubber stamp police and prosecutorial decisions; citizens were arrested capriciously; unduly high bail was set; and defendants were often pressured into pleading guilty.

Laying Groundwork for Reform

Geiger and Fahnestock allow that this kind of justice system will not change overnight. But they insist that RJC has laid the groundwork for significant reforms that community leaders have pledged to implement.

Predictably, reformers and social activists tend to embrace the judicial reform team. Others in local court systems challenge the validity of study findings.

Nancy Habig, a school-board member and citizen activist in Dubois County, Ind., says judges and court personnel in her area balked at first at an RJC probe. ''They didn't want urban solutions to rural problems,'' she explains.

One aspect of what RJC investigations found in Dubois is common in smaller communities in the U.S. Geiger and Fahnestock call it ''comity.'' Generally, it speaks to courtesy and polite conduct. But in this context, explains Mrs. Habig, it means: ''You scratch my back, and I'll scratch yours.''

''It's not always a conscious thing. The judge and the prosecutor are friends. Sometimes they're related. People back off when they know people too well. . . . And the local paper only covers major cases in the courts,'' Habig says.

Dubois courts—prodded by citizen oversight—are slowly changing procedures and wiping out abuses, reports Habig. ''There are still things to work out,'' she admits. ''But we now know what can happen.''

RJC's approach is generally hailed by those who advocate court reform. But many warn that progress will be slow.

For instance, Albert Barney, long-time chief justice of Vermont's Supreme Court, says that local mores and loyalty tend to work against an effective justice system in small towns.

Judge Barney, who recently stepped down from the bench after 31 years of service, likens rural attitudes toward justice to whites support of apartheid in South Africa. ''It's all in the name of protecting the community,'' he says.

But the Vermont jurist says that RJC is helping to neutralize this local bias by developing invaluable data for rural jurisdictions that are willing to adapt it to their own situations.

A basic premise of RJC is that the courts set the tone for how people generally behave. ''If people see that the courts are lawless,'' Fahnestock says, ''it is easier for them to be lawless themselves.''

Curtis Sitomer, ''Rural Justice Affects Many, But May Serve Few,'' *Christian Science Monitor,* May 28, 1985, p. 23. Reprinted by permission from *The Christian Science Monitor.* © 1985 The Christian Science Publishing Society. All rights reserved.

defendant's right to a lawyer in the lower court is eroded if the judge is not capable of understanding a lawyer's argument on the law.

To many, the JP's unfamiliarity with the law erodes the court's traditional role of independence. Nonlawyer judges may be too easily swayed by a lawyer's argument, often place undue reliance on the opinions of the district attorney, and may give unjustifiable weight to police testimony (Ashman and Chapin). A study in the state of New York, for example, determined that lay judges were slightly more favorable toward police officers and prosecutors than were legally trained officials (Ryan and Guterman).

States are beginning to eliminate nonlawyer judges. The California supreme court has ruled that the nonlawyer magistrate violates that state's contitution. Moreover, when states adopt court reorganization they invariably abolish the nonlawyer JP (although typically incumbents are retained). The movement to eliminate the nonlawyer JP is a slow one, however. One reason is that such proposals can appear to be full employment manipulations for the advantage of the legal profession. In an era when there is an oversupply of lawyers, the requirements that all lower court judges be lawyers may be partially motivated by a desire to keep the profession working.

Studies have shown that the shift to legally trained judges may alter the decisions reached. Green and associates found that Iowa's new state constitution requiring legally trained lower court judges resulted in more formal proceedings that frightened away the individual civil plaintiffs of the courts. Moreover, decisions in small civil cases increasingly benefited the merchants. A handful of other studies, however, have found few, if any, differences between behavior of lay versus lawyer judges (Provine, 1981). A comprehensive survey concluded that, despite the opposition of the legal profession to nonlawyer judges, they are as competent as lawyer judges in carrying out judicial duties in courts of limited jurisdiction (Provine, 1986).

Municipal Courts

municipal courts

Municipal courts are the urban counterparts of the justice of the peace courts. Decades ago the increasing volume of cases coupled with the anonymous conditions of the big cities overwhelmed the ability of the rurally conceived JP system to dispense justice. The forerunner of the municipal court was the police magistrate, who was closely tied to another major nineteenth-century innovation—organized police forces in the big cities. In actuality, police magistrates were combination law enforcement officials and judicial officers. Located in the precinct houses, the police magistrate served as a legal adviser to the police and conducted criminal investigations. At times these police functions obviously conflicted with judicial duties of setting bond, conducting preliminary hearings, and the like. Increasingly, therefore, *police magistrates* evolved into purely judicial officers. Today most municipal courts hold court in a central location rather than a police station house, which reduces the ties to local police stations.

police magistrates

Municipal courts have also been shaped by another important aspect of the urban political landscape: the political machine. Urban political machines viewed the lower courts as opportunities for patronage. Party bosses controlled the election or appointment of judges. Similarly, the positions of bailiff and clerks were reserved for the party faithful. Not surprisingly, therefore, municipal courts were often tainted by corruption. Charges would be dropped or files mysteriously disappear in return for political favors or cash. The judicial reformers of the 1920s and 1930s sought to clean up the courts by removing them from politics.

The Assembly Line

"Sausage Factories" headlined a *Time* article on municipal courts (November 25, 1974). "Hurricanes of Humanity" wrote the American Judicature Society in the first national survey of the lower courts. Both analogies draw our attention to the overriding reality of municipal courts in the nation's big cities: the press of cases (Ashman). All too often the major concern is moving cases. "Obstacles" to speedy disposition—warning of constitutional rights, presence of counsel, trials—are neutralized. In a process some have labeled an *assembly line,* shortcuts are routinely taken to keep the cases moving. Thus the municipal courts more closely resemble a bureaucracy geared to mass processing of cases (and not necessarily defendants) than an adjudicative body providing consideration for each case.

assembly line

Arraignment.   The handling of cases begins when the defendant is arraigned. Instead of advising defendants individually—a time-consuming process—municipal court judges often open court by generally addressing everyone in court roughly as follows:

> All of you who have charges against you, listen. You have a right to remain silent if you wish. If you speak, what you say can and probably will be held against you. You have a right to an attorney and to have time to get one. You also may have a right, in some cases—if you have no money—to apply for a court-appointed attorney, and under certain conditions one will be assigned to you. And if your offense is bondable you have a right to bond.

Later the judge may individually or in groups advise defendants more specifically. But some defendants are never advised of their rights at all. One study in a large eastern city found that in one fourth of all cases, the judge did not inform the defendants of their rights (Table 17-1). Few efforts are made to determine whether defendants understand what is said or even whether, in the noise and confusion of the crowded courtroom, the defendant heard at all. Appraisal of rights is treated by the court as a clerical detail to be dispensed with before the taking of guilty pleas can begin.

Absence of counsel.   Other potential obstacles to the speedy disposition of cases are defense attorneys. Defendants have a constitutional right to be represented by an attorney. In practice, however, the presence of an attorney in the lower courts is rare. A study in one eastern city found that only 12 percent of the misdemeanor defendants were represented by a lawyer (Mileski). This absence of defense attorneys is partially the product of the minor nature of most municipal court cases; some defendants believe the charge is too

TABLE 17-1 Appraising of Rights

| | Offense charged | | |
Appraising of rights	Misdemeanor minor	Serious	All cases
None	35%	6%	26%
In courtroom audience	22	11	18
Groups before bench	20	23	23
Groups before bench with individual follow-up	6	28	11
Individual before bench	18	31	22
Total	101	99	100
(N)	(220)	(35)	(292)

SOURCE: Maureen Mileski, "Courtroom Encounters: An Observation Study of a Lower Criminal Court," *Law and Society Review 5* (May 1971): 485.

minor to justify the expense of hiring a lawyer. The more serious the alleged offense, however, the more likely a defendant will have an attorney. Thus in Boston, "two out of three defendants charged with 'real crimes' are represented by a lawyer" (Bing and Rosenfeld: 264). The absence of attorneys is also a product of the economics of the legal profession. Since fees are low, few attorneys will take a case in one of these courts. The general absence of defense attorneys reinforces the informality of the lower courts and does nothing to deter the lack of attention to legal rules and procedures (Bing and Rosenfeld).

But what of those too poor to hire a lawyer? In *Argersinger* v. *Hamlin* (407 U.S. 25, 1972) the Supreme Court ruled that "absent a knowing and intelligent waiver, no person may be imprisoned for any offense, whether classified as petty, misdemeanor, or felony unless he was represented by counsel." Thus an indigent defendant may be fined without having a lawyer, but if the judge is considering imposing a jail term, he or she must give the impoverished defendant the opportunity to have a court-appointed counsel at state expense. Although legal experts viewed *Argersinger* as a landmark decision potentially commanding wholesale changes in the lower courts, actual changes have been far less dramatic. After a comprehensive survey, the Boston University Center for Criminal Justice concluded: "Compliance has generally been token in nature," reform "has been chaotic and uneven at best," and the legal right to counsel remains "an empty right for many defendants" (Krantz et al.).

Dispositions. In municipal courts the defendant's initial appearance is usually the final one. Most persons charged with a traffic violation or a minor misdemeanor plead guilty immediately. In one of the few truly systematic studies of the lower courts, Mileski found that 85 percent of the defendants plead guilty at the first appearance. The rate of guilty pleas varied with the severity of the offense, however. For minor offenses (like public drunkenness) the rate was 98 percent; for more serious cases it was 68 percent. The quick plea represents a fatalistic view of most defendants: "I've done it—let's get it over with." Realistically, a defendant charged with crimes like public drunkenness or disorderly conduct cannot raise a valid legal defense.

What has struck all observers of the lower courts is the speed with which the pleas are processed. Typical are the following rough calculations:

> The Court generally disposes of between 50 and 100 cases per day, but on any Monday there are 200 to 250 and on Monday mornings after holiday weekends the Court may handle as many as 350 cases. I would estimate that, on the average, cases take between 45 seconds and one minute to dispose of. (Wiseman: 235)

More systematically, Mileski calculated the median time to accept a defendant's plea and impose sentence at less than a minute. More serious cases were given more time, but the average time was still only two minutes.

Absence of trials.   Few trials are held in the lower courts. A defendant has a right to a jury trial only if the offense can be punished by imprisonment for more than six months (*Baldwin* v. *New York,* 399 U.S. 66, 1970). The general absence of attorneys and the minor nature of the offenses combine to make requests for jury trials rare. If there is a trial it is a bench trial. The informality of the lower court dominates trials (and almost everything else): rules of evidence are not necessarily followed, no trial record is kept, and trials last only a few minutes.

The Courtroom Work Group

It is no accident that the vast majority of defendants waive their rights to counsel, trial, and so on, thus enabling the court to dispose of its day's business rapidly. The courtroom work group tries to encourage such behavior by controlling the flow of defendants, making quick pleas part of the routine. Some courts manipulate bail to pressure defendants into waiving their right to a lawyer. During the arraignment, each defendant is informed of the right to a full hearing with a court-appointed attorney. But the hearing cannot be held for two or three weeks, which the defendant will have to spend in jail (Wice). Not surprisingly the vast majority of defendants choose to waive their right to counsel in favor of a speedy disposition. Quick pleas represent a defendant's unwillingness to take a chance; they surrender the possibility of an acquittal because they fear a harsher penalty if they try but are unsuccessful (Mileski).

The routines of the lower courts also may be threatened by uncooperative defendants. Defendants who unreasonably take up too much of the court's time can expect sanctions. Judges and prosecutors dislike defendants who "talk too much." Mileski provides an example of a young middle-class white man who made a detailed inquiry into his rights and then gave a relatively lengthy account (roughly two minutes) of his alleged offense of vagrancy. Although the defendant was polite, the judge interrupted him with "That will be all Mr. Jones" and ordered him to jail. Other defendants who "talked too much" received longer than normal sentences.

Sentencing

Municipal courts, in a sense, are not really trial courts because few defendants contest their guilt; in actuality they are a sentencing institution. The courtroom encounter is geared to making rapid decisions about which sentence to impose. Lower court judges, unlike felony judges, typically have a wide range of alternative sanctions from which to choose. These alternatives may include jail, probation, fines, community service work, victim restitution, alcohol treatment programs, and driver clinics, among others. Despite the diversity of potential sanctions, fines play a predominant role. Table 17-2 reports sentencing practices in four cities. Note that few defendants were sentenced to jail. Instead approximately two thirds of all defendants pay a fine of some amount (Ragona and Ryan, 1983). A longstanding practice of lower courts was the **option sentence** of five days or $25. To poor defendants this was not an effective option, and jail was the only alternative. The Supreme Court has ruled that convicted defendants cannot be jailed because of the inability to pay a fine (*Tate* v. *Short,* 401 U.S. 395, 1971). The continued widespread reliance on fines or other forms of economic sanctions, such as court costs, is by no means accidental or coincidental. Fines paid by guilty defendants can be a significant source of revenue for local governments. In some communities, pressures are placed on judges to generate more revenue through fines (Ragona and Ryan, 1984).

option sentence

The sentencing process in the lower courts involves elements of both routinization and individualization of justice. Readily identifiable characteristics of the defendants are used in sorting defendants into typical or modal categories. Through time virtually every court has evolved a set of penalties deemed appropriate for given types of offenders in combination with the crimes they have committed. Thus, in the lower courts sentencing involves a process of quickly determining group averages. The result is a high degree of uniformity; by and large a defendant gets the same sentence as all others in the same category. To the casual observer the process appears to be an assembly line. Yet a closer probing indicates that sentences can also be fitted to the specific defendant. During plea negotiations there is some individual attention to cases. Despite sentencing consistencies, exceptions are made (Ragona and Ryan, 1983). The most important factors in both the routinization and individualization of sentencing in the lower courts are the type of crime and prior record.

Nature of the event.   Offenses can be categorized along two dimensions: the official charge and what actually occurred (substance). Although the charge is never more serious than the substance, at times the substance is more serious than the charge. For example, a defendant may be charged with breach of the peace when he had engaged in a more serious violation—threatening his wife with a knife. When the substance is more serious than the charge, judges usually sentence on the basis of the ***nature of the event.*** Even when the charges have been reduced (after plea bargaining, for example), the defendant receives the penalty typical for the more serious charge.

nature of the event

The opposite may also be true. What is perceived by the police officer as trouble serious enough to warrant an arrest may not be viewed equally as seriously by the prosecutor or the judge. On the whole, the court has a higher tolerance for trouble than the police (Feeley). An arrestee who is loud and threatening during booking may appear quiet and nonthreatening the next day in court. As a result court officials may treat some cases as minor. Indeed,

TABLE 17-2   Frequency of Type of Sentence in Four Lower Courts

	Austin, Texas	Columbus, Ohio	Mankato, Minnesota	Tacoma, Washington
Probation	15.0%	NA	5.6%	3.0%
Jail	6.7	5.1	10.7	4.2
Fine	6.7	57.2	62.7	54.4
Fine and probation	49.0	NA	4.4	4.8
Fine and jail	22.2	29.6	2.0	3.2
Other combinations	.4	—	4.8	2.1
None of above	—	8.1[a]	9.8[b]	28.3[c]
(N)	(1,216)	(1,281)	(803)	(565)

[a] Includes fines and jail terms suspended in their entirety; possibly also probation sentences, for which data are unavailable.
[b] Includes fines and jail terms suspended in their entirety, as well as community work and counseling/treatment programs.
[c] Includes court costs imposed in lieu of fines, as well as community work.
SOURCE: Anthony Ragona and John Paul Ryan, "Misdemeanor Courts and the Choice of Sanctions: A Comparative View," *Justice System Journal* 8 (1983): 203.

some arrests are regarded as so trivial that prosecutors and judges resent the police for bringing such cases to court. Feeley has argued that situations like the one just mentioned represent situational justice. Criminal charges are abstractions. Courts respond to the actual events from a perspective of hindsight and cooler temperaments. He concluded that prosecutors and judges look beyond the specific charges to assess the real damage in establishing an appropriate sentence.

Defendants are pigeonholed according to offense. The four-city study found that drunk driving and traffic cases nearly always resulted in a fine, possibly along with jail or probation. By contrast, theft and other miscellaneous criminal offenses much less often resulted in a fine; more commonly these defendants were sentenced to jail or placed on probation. The decision not to fine in minor criminal cases may stem from a philosophy that such crimes are "too serious" to be treated merely with a fine and that such offenders are in need of ongoing counseling or supervision, the practical realization that many defendants cannot afford to pay a fine, or some combination of the two (Ragona and Ryan, 1983).

criminal record

Criminal record.   A key factor in sentencing is the defendant's prior ***criminal record*** (unless the offense was very serious). First offenders rarely receive a jail term. Indeed, given the pettiness of the offenses, first offenders may be released without any penalty whatsoever. Repeaters are treated to more severe sanctions. The jailing of defendants for public intoxication increases strikingly as the length and recency of prior arrests increase, for example. The importance of a record in sentencing partially explains an otherwise unaccountable pattern. One study found that serious misdemeanants were fined while minor misdemeanants were jailed. The explanation is that few of the serious misdemeanor defendants had prior records, while more of the minor misdemeanor defendants did (Mileski).

The Process Is the Punishment?

Several recent studies have begun to question the image of the lower courts as assembly line operations. Susan Silbey, for example, argues that the standard picture of lower courts as wholesale, mechanical processors of a high volume of cases is only partially correct. In the first place, the operations of the misdemeanor courts are not as chaotic, disordered, or unreasonable as they may first appear. A second consideration is that the lower courts do try to provide justice. They do so, however, by responding to problems rather than crimes, concentrating their efforts on producing substantive justice rather than focusing on purely formal (due process) justice. Separate studies in New Haven, Connecticut (Feeley), and Columbus, Ohio (Ryan) have assessed the disparate functions served by the lower courts.

Malcolm Feeley spent several years studying the lower court in New Haven firsthand. He concluded that the major punishment of defendants occurs during the processing of cases and not after a finding of guilt. He contends that the pretrial process imposes a series of punishments ("price tags") on the accused. These price tags often include staying in jail (briefly), paying a bail bondsman, hiring a private attorney, and losing time and perhaps wages due to repeated court appearances. These costs far outweigh any punishment imposed after the defendant pleads guilty. Moreover, these price tags affect the roughly

---

$Q\ U\ O\ T\ A\ T\ I\ O\ N$

By and large, the judge's function is to ratify the decisions of the prosecutors and defense attorneys.

But even in those cases in which judges have "freedom" to sentence, they are left feeling frustrated. "What do you do," one judge asked, "in these petty cases? They're not serious enough to put a person in jail; yet you want to do something to show society's disapproval. Normally a fine would be appropriate, but so many of these people don't have any money. So we end up giving meaningless conditional discharges or probation, and it becomes something of a joke. It's frustrating; there's little we can do."

In the main the courtroom judge is not even manager of his own domain; the activity is too diffuse and the pace too quick. It is perhaps more accurate to say that the judge endures rather than presides over his courtroom.

Malcolm Feeley, *The Process Is the Punishment: Handling Cases in a Lower Criminal Court* (New York: Russell Sage Foundation, 1979), p. 69.

40 percent of the defendants eventually found not guilty. In short, the pretrial process itself is the primary punishment, according to Feeley.

Another study, this time of Columbus, Ohio, reaches a different conclusion. Analyzing statistical data on court sentences, John Paul Ryan concludes that the outcome is the punishment. Unlike those in New Haven, lower court judges in Columbus routinely impose fines on convicted defendants. Often these fines are substantial, averaging over $100. Further, 35 percent of the guilty in Columbus are sentenced to jail, six times as many as in New Haven. Finally, in traffic cases defendants often have their driver's licenses suspended and/or are ordered to attend drunk-driver schools. In short, Columbus defendants are more likely to be fined, to pay heavier fines, to go to jail, and to be required to participate in some sort of treatment program than their counterparts in New Haven.

These sharp contrasts between New Haven and Columbus accentuate the point made earlier in the chapter—misdemeanor courts are very diverse in their operations and procedures. A principal reason for such diversity relates to important differences in the political and legal culture. Recall from Chapter 8 Levin's comparison of Pittsburgh and Minneapolis. We find similar differences in the cities studied by Feeley and Ryan. New Haven is a very ethnic, Democratic, and political town. In contrast Columbus is middle-class, Republican, and "good government" in orientation.

Another reason for such diversity stems from variations in court procedures. In New Haven the prosecutor controls case processing, whereas in Columbus the police are the dominant influence. In short, any assessment of the activities of the lower courts requires an awareness of their diversity.

Reducing the Caseload

The overriding problem of the urban courts is the high volume of cases. To judicial reformers, these excessive caseloads are the crux of the problem, for they cause the routine, summary, and often perfunctory disposition process. Reduction of the caseload is viewed as an essential first step if the nation's lower tribunals are ever going to employ a true adversary process. One way to accomplish this is to expand the number of judges and support personnel. But more fundamentally, many believe that the key to making lower court caseloads more manageable is by removing certain types of cases from the courthouse. Diverting public drunkenness cases, creating nonjudicial, private-dispute-settling institutions, and shifting traffic violations to an administrative body are three programs that reflect current thinking on how to shrink lower-court caseloads. Although programs like these are usually presented as methods for reducing administrative burdens, the issues actually are much more fundamental and deep-seated. The root issues are whether minor criminal cases should be handled through formalistic court procedures and whether some of these offenses should be criminal.

Diverting Public Drunks

Yearly the police arrest two million people for public intoxication. After a brief encounter with the lower courts, they are fined or sent to jail for a few days or a few months. Drunk court is simply a revolving door; many of those arrested for public intoxication have been arrested before and will be arrested again. Jail sentences certainly do not seem to deter. There is general agreement that this process of jailing public drunks is ineffective, inefficient, and all too often inhumane as well. Moreover, the revolving door process greatly strains the criminal justice process.

> [T]he present handling of public drunkenness offenders is often demoralizing to the police, judicial, and jail personnel. It is an immense economic drain—in terms of men, time and space—on these agencies. Furthermore, it seriously undermines the professional character of the work of policemen, judges, district attorneys, and others, and often makes a mockery of the American judicial system. In most courts the average time spent by the judge in the "trial" and sentencing of each public drunkenness offender probably is less than three minutes. This system of handling defendants undoubtedly violates the traditional American conception of the "due process of law." (Plaut: 110–111)

diverting
public drunks
In searching for alternatives to the traditional handling of public drunkenness, emphasis has been placed on ***diverting public drunks*** to programs that provide better social services while at the same time reducing strains on the criminal justice system. The current thinking has been summarized in a model program the Law Enforcement Assistance Administration has found workable. First, because alcoholism is largely a public health problem, better medical assistance should be available. Second, many persons arrested for public

CLOSE-UP

Turnstile Justice

The breakdown of New York City's Criminal Court begins with facilities that are often filthy and dilapidated. It ends with a pattern of case disposition that most participants agree is unpredictable and unfair.

In eight key areas, according to the judges, prosecutors and defense lawyers who work there, Criminal Court has become a mockery of what was intended when it was created 21 years ago to judge lesser crimes and begin the legal process in the most serious ones. The areas of failure are these:

• Courtrooms are so crowded, dirty and noisy that some judges have taken

to warning juries not to let their surroundings discourage them from treating cases seriously.
• The court's clerks, typists and court officers are too few and often too poorly trained. Courtroom decorum and legal research both suffer, judges say.
• The volume of cases has grown unmanageable to everyone from the judges and lawyers to the clerical staff.
• The number of judges assigned to the court is not adequate, participants agree. Every day, judges must deal with a calendar of as many as 100 cases.
• The issuing of summonses has far outstripped the

ability of the court to handle them. Seventy percent of those who get summonses ignore them with impunity.
• Trials have become an expensive rarity, and defendants know it. Fewer than 1 in 200 of last year's cases ever went to trial.
• Plea bargaining has become the rule, leading to sentences that often bear little resemblance to the seriousness of crimes committed, some judges and prosecutors say.
• Dismissals are often handed out as much from judges' frustration as from the merits of the case, some lawyers and judges say.

drunkenness actually suffer from being homeless. A shelter would not only get the drunks off the street (the public's major demand) but would also provide facilities for medical treatment. Third, intermediate care should be provided for those who may want to break the skid-row cycle. Fourth, after detoxification many alcoholics are not ready to return to autonomous community living. Therefore, a halfway house facility should be available. Finally, aftercare services should be provided (Weis).

Alternative Dispute Resolution

The steady diet of the police and the lower courts is private disagreements between friends, neighbors, spouses, or landlord and tenant. Two factory workers argue over Saturday's football game and a fight develops. After work the loser goes to the police station to file an assault and battery charge. An older neighbor, upset over dogs in his front yard, threatens to shoot the next dog in his yard. The irate dog owner calls the police and wants his neighbor arrested. These actual examples from Columbus, Ohio, are typical of the types of situations confronting the courts and the police (Palmer).

private dispute
    The role the courts and the legal system can play in resolving such *private disputes* is not clear. In such cases a trial would only obscure the source of the problem because it is either irrelevant or immaterial to the legal issues. Further, in such interpersonal disputes the person who files a complaint is often as guilty as the defendant. Such disputes are essentially civil matters that the

---

Criminal Court began its life in September 1962, after the State Legislature decided to replace two tribunals that were thought to have outlived their usefulness—the Magistrate's Court and the Court of Special Sessions.

"The Criminal Court is a stepchild of the system," said the Brooklyn District Attorney, Elizabeth Holtzman. "Once you understand that, you see how everything flows from that. The cases are not thought to be as important. The facilities are atrocious, which does not breed respect. The judges are paid less and are given no staff. The truth is, the bulk of the crimes in the city are treated in the Criminal Court."

Robert M. Morgenthau, the Manhattan District Attorney, said: "The impact is seen in a tremendous backlog and not enough trial parts. It makes it very difficult to dispose of cases on an equitable basis."

With a branch in each of the five boroughs, the court touches the lives of hundreds of thousands of New Yorkers each year—as accused, as families and friends or as victims. Its problems are citywide, but they are worst in Manhattan and Brooklyn, the boroughs with the most crime and the biggest caseloads.

The Criminal Court is where several hundred thousand lesser crimes and violations are processed every year, from arraignment through disposition. Included are 75 percent of all the Police Department's arrests for serious crimes, felonies, which are ultimately reduced to misdemeanors.

It is also where anyone accused of a felony is arraigned and where some preliminary hearings are held.

"There is no feeling of justice there," said Richard Emery, a staff lawyer for the New York Civil Liberties Union. "A lot of stuff is done off the record. It looks like everyone is dealing, which they probably are. It doesn't give the look and feel of justice to the hundreds of thousands of people whose only glimpse of justice is that court."

E. R. Shipp, "The Failure of Criminal Court: 8 Crucial Areas," *New York Times,* June 30, 1983, pp. 1 and 16. © 1983 by the New York Times Company. Reprinted by permission.

agencies of the criminal law are forced to cool off lest a more serious crime—murder, shooting, or what have you—occurs. It is worth noting that other societies place much greater reliance on informal procedures for resolving these essentially private conflicts. Socialist nations, for example, employ neighborhood tribunals that emphasize conciliatory, nonadversarial techniques (Robertson).

alternative dispute resolution

Issues like these have prompted considerable interest in ***alternative dispute resolution*** (Alfini, 1986). Over 160 ***neighborhood justice centers*** in about forty states have been established. These programs handle disputes between non-strangers, generally on a referral from police, prosecutor, court clerk, or the court itself (Marks et al.). In addition there are also many different kinds of specialized mediation programs involving divorce, consumer, landlord–tenant, and juvenile delinquency disputes (Edelman). These programs are founded with the belief that less formal, nonjudicial types of dispute resolution will promote the dual goals of efficiency and effectiveness. The overworked criminal justice system will be aided by removing cases between parties who know each other and that involve essentially a minor civil dispute. In addition, through the process of mediation and compromise, a more lasting solution to the underlying causes of such a dispute can be obtained. Evaluations indicate that system-centered goals of efficiency tend to dominate the client-centered goals. Much like pretrial diversion programs, neighborhood justice centers can be a mechanism for control over behaviors and activities of those not formally processed (Tomasic and Feeley).

neighborhood justice centers

Traffic Court

Few citizens make it through life without driving too fast and being caught. Yet in many localities a simple traffic violation is treated the same way as a minor criminal violation: the traffic ticket (actually a court summons) requires attendance at ***traffic court.*** And after a long wait the motorist is allowed to pay the fine. Not only do such traffic cases unnecessarily clog up many lower courts, but they also give the average citizen a negative view of justice. The National Advisory Commission on Criminal Justice Standards and Goals has urged that traffic cases no longer be treated as criminal violations (except serious traffic violations like drunk driving or negligent homicide).

traffic court

Administrative disposition of minor traffic cases would work as follows. All minor traffic violators would be allowed to enter a plea by mail, except where the violator is a repeater or where the infraction resulted in a traffic accident. No jury trials would be available. If the alleged violator desires a hearing, one would be provided by a legally trained referee. During the hearing the government would be required to prove the case by clear and convincing evidence (a standard less rigorous than the criminal prosecutor's burden in a criminal case of beyond a reasonable doubt). Appeal would be permitted to an appellate division of the administrative agency. The only grounds for appeal to a court would be abuse of discretion by the administrative agency (National Advisory Commission).

Conclusion

The lower courts come into contact with more citizens every year than virtually any other governmental institution. All too often, however, the average citizen comes away from such encounters with the impression of a nonjudicial atmosphere. The overriding concern appears to be a hasty disposition before sending the citizen to the cash register to pay the fine.

Several factors have led to this state of affairs. First, most cases are relatively minor. Perhaps citizens' expectations are too high concerning the quality of courts society uses for processing the large volume of cases where there are essentially no disputes over the facts. Second, the lower courts have historically been neglected by citizens, lawyers, and judges alike. In most states the lower courts operate separately from the other trial courts, which handle more serious offenses. Finally, the courts are extremely diverse. The problems faced by a rurally based JP differ entirely from those of a municipal court judge in a large city. All of these factors raise obstacles to efforts to improve the quality of justice. But as noted throughout this chapter, numerous and varied reforms are being recommended and some implemented.

For Discussion

1. Discuss with your friends, parents, and neighbors any experiences they have had with the nation's lower courts. What do these experiences suggest about the nonjudicial atmosphere of these courts?
2. Has your state incorporated the lower courts into the state judicial system? If so, what factors do you think led to abolition of the JP? If not, what are the principal obstacles to abolition?
3. Do you think that all judges should be required to be lawyers? Discuss the pros and cons.
4. Observe a local lower court. Are defendants advised of their rights? How many defendants are represented by counsel? How quickly are cases disposed of? Are there any trials? Does the judge typically impose the sentence recommended by the prosecutor? In many communities there is more than one lower court (one for the city, another for the county). Compare these courts on the above measures. In which court would you prefer to have your case heard? Why?
5. Lower courts have been described as sentencing institutions. Discuss how the courtroom work group influences sentencing.
6. Interview a lower court judge and/or a prosecutor. What frustrations do they express about their job? What problems do they perceive? What reforms do they propose?
7. What proposals do you favor for reducing the caseload of municipal courts? What factors inhibit the adoption of such proposals?

References

ALFINI, JAMES J. "Introductory Essay: The Misdemeanor Courts," *Justice System Journal* 6 (Spring 1981): 5–12.

——, ed. *Misdemeanor Courts: Policy Concerns and Research Perspectives.* Washington, D.C.: National Institute of Justice, 1980.

——. "Alternative Dispute Resolution and the Courts: An Introduction." *Judicature* 69 (1986): 252.

——, AND PATRICIA M. PASSUTH, "Case Processing in State Misdemeanor Courts: The Effect of Defense Attorney Presence." *Justice System Journal* 6 (Spring 1981): 100–116.

ASHMAN, ALLAN. *Courts of Limited Jurisdiction: A National Survey.* Chicago: American Judicature Society, 1975.

——, AND PAT CHAPIN. "Is the Bell Tolling for Nonlawyer Judges?" *Judicature* 59 (1976): 417–421.

BING, STEPHEN, AND S. STEPHEN ROSENFELD. "The Quality of Justice in the Lower Criminal Courts of Metropolitan Boston." In *Rough Justice: Perspectives on Lower Criminal Courts,* ed. John Robertson, pp. 259–285. Boston: Little, Brown, 1974.

BRONSTEIN, JULIE. *Survey of State Mandatory Judicial Education Requirements.* Washington, D.C.: The American University, 1981.

EDELMAN, PETER. "Institutionalizing Dispute Resolution Alternatives." *Justice System Journal* 9 (1984): 134.

FEELEY, MALCOLM M. *The Process Is the Punishment: Handling Cases in a Lower Criminal Court.* New York: Russell Sage Foundation, 1979.

GREEN, JUSTIN, ROSS RUSSELL, AND JOHN SCHMIDHAUSER. "Iowa's Magistrate System: The Aftermath of Reform." *Judicature* 58 (1975): 380–389.

KRANTZ, SHELDON, CHARLES SMITH, DAVID ROSSMAN, PAUL FROYD, AND JANIS J. HOFFMAN. *Right to Counsel in Criminal Cases: The Mandate of Argersinger v. Hamlin.* Cambridge, Mass.: Ballinger, 1976.

LIEBERMAN, JETHRO. *The Role of Courts in American Society: The Final Report of the Council on the Role of Courts.* St. Paul, Minnesota: West Publishing, 1984.

MACFEELY, F. T. "J. P. Courts Last Hope for Little People." *Gainesville Sun,* October 9, 1971.

MARKS, JONATHAN, EARL JOHNSON, AND PETER SZANTON. *Dispute Resolution in America: Processes in Evolution.* Washington, D.C.: National Institute for Dispute Resolution.

MILESKI, MAUREEN. "Courtroom Encounters: An Observation Study of a Lower Criminal Court." *Law and Society Review* 5 (May 1971): 473–538.

NATIONAL ADVISORY COMMISSION ON CRIMINAL JUSTICE STANDARDS AND GOALS. *Courts.* Washington, D.C.: Government Printing Office, 1973.

PALMER, JOHN. "The Night Prosecutor: Columbus Finds Extrajudicial Solutions to Interpersonal Disputes." *Judicature* 59 (1975): 23–27.

PLAUT, THOMAS, ed. *Alcohol Problems: A Report to the Nation.* New York: Oxford University Press, 1967.

PRESIDENT'S COMMISSION ON LAW ENFORCEMENT AND ADMINISTRATION OF JUSTICE. *Challenge of Crime in a Free Society.* Washington, D.C.: Government Printing Office, 1967a.

——. *Task Force Report: The Courts.* Washington, D.C.: Government Printing Office, 1967b.

PROVINE, DORIS MARIE. "Persistent Anomaly: The Lay Judge in the American Legal System." *Justice System Journal* 6 (Spring 1981): 28–43.

——. *Judging Credentials: Nonlawyer Judges and the Politics of Professionalism.* Chicago: University of Chicago Press, 1986.

RAGONA, ANTHONY, AND JOHN PAUL RYAN. "Misdemeanor Courts and the Choice of Sanctions: A Comparative View." *Justice System Journal* 8 (1983): 199.

——. *Beyond the Courtroom: A Comparative Analysis of Misdemeanor Sentencing.* Washington, D.C.: National Institute of Justice, U.S. Department of Justice, 1984.

ROBERTSON, JOHN, ed. *Rough Justice: Perspectives on Lower Criminal Courts.* Boston: Little, Brown, 1974.

RYAN, JOHN PAUL. "Adjudication and Sentencing in a Misdemeanor Court: The Outcome Is the Punishment." *Law and Society Review* 15 (1980–1981): 79–108.

——, AND JAMES H. GUTERMAN. "Lawyers versus Non-Lawyer Town Justices." *Judicature* 60 (1977): 272–280.

"THE SAUSAGE FACTORIES." *Time,* November 25, 1974, p. 91.

SILBERMAN, LINDA J. *Non-Attorney Justice in the United States: An Empirical Study.* New York: Institute of Judicial Administration, 1979.

SILBEY, SUSAN S. "Making Sense of the Lower Courts." *Justice System Journal* 6 (Spring 1981): 13–27.

TOMASIC, ROMAN, AND MALCOLM FEELEY, eds. *Neighborhood Justice: Assessment of an Emerging Idea.* New York: Longman, 1982.

WEIS, CHARLES. *Diversion of the Public Inebriate from the Criminal Justice System.* Washington, D.C.: Government Printing Office, 1973.

WICE, PAUL. *Freedom for Sale.* Lexington, Mass.: D. C. Heath, Lexington Books, 1974.

WISEMAN, JACQUELINE. "Drunk Court: The Adult Parallel to Juvenile Court." In *The Criminal Justice Process: A Reader,* eds. William Sanders and Howard Dandistel, pp. 233–252. New York: Praeger Publishers, 1976.

For Further Reading

ASHMAN, ALLAN. *Courts of Limited Jurisdiction: A National Survey.* Chicago: American Judicature Society, 1975.

FEELEY, MALCOLM M. *The Process Is the Punishment: Handling Cases in a Lower Criminal Court.* New York: Russell Sage Foundation, 1979.

NATIONAL CENTER FOR STATE COURTS. *Rural Courts: The Effects of Space and Distance on the Administration of Justice.* Denver: National Center for State Courts, 1977.

PROVINE, DORIS. *Judging Credentials: Nonlawyer Judges and the Politics of Professionalism.* Chicago: University of Chicago Press, 1986.

TOMASIC, ROMAN, AND MALCOLM FEELEY, eds. *Neighborhood Justice; Assessment of an Emerging Idea.* New York: Longman, 1982.

CHAPTER 18

Administering the Courts

Delay in processing cases is one of the most visible problems facing American courts. Newspapers highlight cases that languish in courts for years. Public commissions decry the effects of delay on the delivery of justice. The general public voices similar concerns. Over half of those surveyed by the Yankelovich, Skelly and White polling organization rate the inefficiency of courts as a "serious" or "very serious" social problem. Two specific findings from this poll press home the public's dissatisfaction. First, persons with direct court experience were more likely to rate the inefficiency of courts as a problem than were those with no experience. Second, the general public was more likely to perceive delay as a major problem than were judges and lawyers. Court officials, however, are becoming increasingly alarmed that the effectiveness of the criminal justice system is jeopardized by mismanaged and inefficient courts. Others worry about assembly line justice that rushes cases through without careful consideration.

Concern that "justice delayed is justice denied" is as old as the common law itself. In the thirteenth century the nobles forced King John to sign the Magna Carta and promise not to "deny or delay right or justice." In the nineteenth century the novelist Charles Dickens condemned the tortuous process of litigation in English courts. In America in the late 1960s systematic attention finally began to be directed toward court management. And in the last few years, a new field of interest has arisen: judicial administration. The concept embodies a central concern: justice is affected not simply by how the courts decide the legal merits but also by how the courts process cases (Wheeler and Whitcomb).

This chapter examines some of the major topics included under the general heading of judicial administration: the problem of court delay and its causes, case scheduling, paperwork, court managers, and speedy trial acts.

The Problem of Delay

Case backlog and trial delay are problems that affect many of the nation's courts. The magnitude of the backlog and the length of the delay vary greatly, however, depending on the court involved. This was the conclusion of a comprehensive survey of how long it takes for cases to proceed from arrest to disposition (Table 18-1). The National Center for State Courts found that the typical criminal case in Detroit, Portland, and Phoenix reached disposition rather rapidly—within about two months. But in other courts the duration was much more extensive. In Newark the median disposition time was over eight months. These variations caution us that in some areas the delay problem may be less pressing than commonly assumed.

delay

It is best to view delay not as a problem, but as a symptom of a problem (Neubauer et al., 1981). In a general sense, the term *delay* suggests abnormal or unacceptable time lapses in the processing of cases. Yet, some time is needed to prepare the case. The inherent subjectivity of the term *delay* becomes apparent when we try to define *unnecessary delay*. The total time that a case is on the court's docket may consist of acceptable (normal) time as well as unacceptable (abnormal) time. Many empirical measures of delay are actually measures of the total time taken to case disposition. It is better, therefore, to employ a neutral term, like *case-processing time* (Neubauer, 1983).

case-processing time

The difficulties in defining what delay is help explain why there is no consensus about how long is too long. Past commissions have provided yardsticks ranging from six months to two years (American Bar Association, 1968; President's Commission, 1967; National Advisory Commission, 1973). Most recently, a special committee of the Conference of State Court Administrators (COSCA) proposed a maximum of 180 days from arrest to trial in felony cases and ninety days in misdemeanors (Moran). Efforts to specify time standards are initially useful because they provide criteria for assessing current court practices; but a closer probing reveals that proposed time standards are too abstract. In focusing on "typical" cases, commission standards fail to recognize the importance of diversity in case processing.

TABLE 18-1 Median Criminal Disposition Time for Selected Cities, 1983

	Median total court disposition time (in days)
Oakland, CA (Alameda County Superior Court)	81
Detroit, MI (Detroit Recorders Court)	69
San Diego, CA (San Diego County Superior Court)	89
Phoenix, AZ (Maricopa County Superior Court)	64
New Orleans, LA (Orleans Parish Criminal District Court)	73
Wayne County, MI (3rd Judicial Circuit Court)	96
Portland, OR (Multnomah County Circuit Court)	62
Dayton, OH (Montgomery County Court of Common Pleas)	88
Minneapolis, MN (4th Judicial District Court)	84
Cleveland, OH (Cuyahoga County Court of Common Pleas)	123
Pittsburgh, PA (Allegheny County Court of Common Pleas)	135
Miami, FL (11th Judicial Circuit Court)	108
Wichita, KS (18th Judicial District Court)	116
Jersey City, NJ (Hudson County Superior Court)	213
Newark, NJ (Essex County Superior Court)	253
Providence, RI (Superior Court for Providence and Bristol Counties)	197
Bronx, NY (Bronx County Supreme Court)	218

SOURCE: Barry Mahoney, Larry L. Sipes, and Jeanne A. Ito, *Implementing Delay Reduction and Delay Prevention Programs in Urban Trial Courts* (Williamsburg, Va.: National Center for State Courts, 1985) p. 11.

An important question is which time periods to measure. The evaluation of the Law Enforcement Assistance Administration's court delay reduction program divided total case processing time into three segments: lower court time, upper court time, and sentencing time. This subdivision highlighted important variations in elapsed time in the courts of Providence, Dayton, Detroit, and Las Vegas (Neubauer, 1983). Courts do not control all case processing time. For example, time spent by probation departments in preparing pre-sentence investigations is seldom controllable by the court. Similarly, if the lower courts are slow in processing cases, trial courts can do little to speed up these dispositions.

A second question is how to measure case processing time. Simple summary measures are suspect. Statistical averages (means), though commonly used, are often inappropriate because a handful of unusual cases skew estimates. A better summary statistic is the median: half the cases took more time and half took less than the median score. Medians, though, provide only a limited picture of what is often a complicated reality (Neubauer, 1983).

Consequences of Delay

Concern with court delay flows from a set of common assertions about its costs. Cases that take too long to reach disposition are more than a minor inconvenience. Concern with delay in the courts is warranted, not because of slowness or inconvenience, but because the values and guarantees associated with the legal system may be jeopardized. A number of different costs of delay are commonly cited. We can conveniently group these perceived costs under four headings: defendant, society, citizen, and system resources.

Defendant's rights.   In the past, court delay was defined as a problem because it jeopardized the defendant's right to a speedy trial. The Sixth Amendment provides that "in all criminal prosecutions, the accused shall enjoy the right to a speedy and public trial. . . ." Defendants may languish in jail for a number of months before guilt or innocence is determined. Some suggest that lengthy pretrial incarceration pressures defendants into pleading guilty (Casper). A number of states have enacted speedy trial laws premised on the need to protect the defendant's rights.

Societal protection.   More recently, delay has been viewed as hampering society's need for a speedy conviction. This view stresses harm done to the prosecution's case. As the case becomes older and memories of the witnesses diminish, the defendant's chance for an acquittal rises. Delay also strengthens a defendant's bargaining position. Prosecutors are quicker to accept a plea of guilty when dockets are crowded and cases are growing older. Also, when delay occurs for defendants out on bond, the potential for additional criminal activity weighs heavily in the public's mind. In short, the state is also viewed as possessing the right to a speedy trial.

Citizen confidence and convenience.   Despite costs or benefits to either the defense or prosecution, a third perspective emphasizes that delay erodes public confidence in the judicial process. Citizens lose confidence in the swiftness or certainty of punishment. Additionally, victims and witnesses make repeated and, for them, wasted trips to the courthouse. Appearances can cost citizens a day's pay and lost time, and ultimately discourage them from prosecution.

Strain on resources.   Delay in disposing of cases strains criminal justice system resources. Pretrial detainees clog jail facilities. Police officers must appear in court on numerous occasions, at public expense. Attorneys are forced to expend unproductive time because of repeated court appearances on the same case, costs ultimately passed to defendants. Moreover, efforts to reduce delay on the criminal docket may exacerbate delay in disposing of civil cases.

Assessing the Costs of Delay

Assertions about the alleged costs of delay require careful scrutiny. A general consensus has emerged that delay is a problem facing the courts, but there is no agreement about the particulars. The four perspectives just described stress varying and at times contradictory reasons that delay is a problem. Some perceive that lengthy pretrial incarceration forces the defendant to enter into a less than advantageous plea bargain. Others, however, portray caseload pressures as forcing the prosecutor into offering unduly lenient negotiated bargains. The four perspectives, of course, are not necessarily mutually exclusive. Concerns about system resources as well as citizen confidence and convenience may be jointly held. The critical point is that assessment of the costs of delay are inherently subjective.

Not only is agreement absent on the specific costs of delay, but documentation of the evils that flow from it is lacking. The National Center for State Courts noted that "few of the foregoing assertions [about the social costs of delay] have been subjected to empirical examination" (Church et al., 1978b: 15). They find some evidence to indicate that jail overcrowding, failure-to-appear rates, and citizen respect for the judiciary are tied to case delay. But they find no support for the assertions that deterioration of cases, diminished deterrence, decreased possibilities of rehabilitation, or plea bargaining are the products of case delay.

Conventional Wisdom about Court Delay

conventional
wisdom

Different people have identified many causes for court delay. The literature on the subject contains varying and sometimes conflicting diagnoses. Typically, discussions of the causes of delay are linked to proposed remedies. The central difficulty in understanding the causes of delay is that most analyses have not been grounded in an understanding of the dynamics of the judicial process (Church et al., 1978b). Let us proceed by first discussing some of the *conventional wisdom* about court delay and then examining more recent research. Factors commonly asserted to cause delay can be grouped under two headings: (1) resources and work loads, and (2) administrative and procedural factors.

CONTROVERSY

23½ Hours in Court: 1,636 Cases Later

With arrests and indictments up significantly this year, the day is long and arduous at the complex on Centre Street in lower Manhattan.

Last Thursday, one of the busier days of the week for the courts, the machinery came to life at 1:30 A.M. with a marijuana sales case—15 days in jail on a guilty plea. It ended, 23½ hours later, when a Brooklyn man received 90 days at Rikers Island for picking pockets.

Between those points, in courtrooms and complaint rooms, in the offices of assistant district attorneys, probation officers and the police, it was a fairly typical Thursday in the state's busiest court jurisdiction.

Together, in State Supreme Court—which handles felonies—and the city's Criminal Court—which hears misdemeanors 24 hours a day—1,636 cases were on the calendar.

There were 483 defendants arraigned. About 350 guilty pleas were entered and about the same number of defendants were sentenced. Thirty-three jury trials and six non-jury trials were under way, and four State Supreme Court juries came back with verdicts: three convictions, one acquittal. Twenty-four defendants who were out on bail did not show up in court. Warrants were issued for their arrests.

Solving a Space Shortage
A shortage of space to hold prisoners awaiting court appearances in Manhattan has changed the way the cases are assigned to judges, administrators say.

New cases assigned to the 30 Supreme Court justices who sit at 111 Centre—the building with the worst space problem—are now predominantly those in which the defendant remains free on bail. The justices at 100 Centre—which has courtrooms of both Criminal and Supreme Court—will receive

resources vs. caseloads

It is an article of faith among many commentators that the problem of delay results from an imbalance between available **resources** and mounting **caseloads** (Church et al., 1978b). A common response is to supplement resources—add judges, prosecutors, clerks, and so on. Others urge reducing the number of cases going to court.

administrative and procedural factors

Traditional understandings of delay have also identified **administrative and procedural factors,** which stress the legal and managerial aspects of criminal court processing. Various stages of criminal court processing have been mentioned as sources of delay—initial appearance, preliminary hearing, grand jury indictment, and pretrial motions, for example. The recommended solutions involve "streamlining" the courts by eliminating these procedural roadblocks (Church et al., 1978b).

A major difficulty with the conventional wisdom about court delay is that it rests on a meager and inadequate knowledge base (Gallas). Our understanding of the causes and remedies of court delay has progressed little beyond Roscoe Pound's (an early judicial reformer) much-quoted comments on delay in 1908 (Church et al., 1978b: 45). Many studies of delay, particularly those purporting to show that delay has been reduced in a particular jurisdiction, are methodologically weak (Luskin).

Some recent studies call the conventional wisdom into question (Church, 1982). In *Justice Delayed,* the National Center for State Courts reports on

---

cases where defendants are jailed while awaiting trial.

Further changes will be introduced this week to ease the problem for the cases the 111 Centre Street judges already have on their calendars. Vans will begin taking prisoners back and forth between the comparatively large pens at 100 Centre and those at 111. Meanwhile, additional pens are being built at 111 Centre.

Justice Peter J. McQuillan, the Administrative Judge of State Supreme Court, said that on three occasions in the last two months, the holding pens at 111 Centre Street became so crowded that he had to tell the justices there to adjourn the rest of their cases.

Thursday's noon report at 138 prisoners—in a system with a capacity of 120—was well below the 175 level that causes a shutdown.

From Station to Station

The sluggish pace of the court system in Manhattan is resulting in many prisoners—especially on the peak arraignment days of Thursday, Friday and Saturday—being shuttled between police stations before their arraignment, law enforcement officials say.

Take Michael Cole and Benjamin Davis for example. By the time Mr. Cole, 26 years old, and Mr. Davis, 22—both of Manhattan—came before a judge for arraignment Thursday at noon, they had been held for nearly 40 hours and been transferred four times.

Arrested at 8:45 P.M. on

Tuesday and charged with the slaying of a New Jersey man in a dispute over drugs, the defendants were taken to the 25th Precinct in Manhattan.

From there, they were taken downtown to central booking at Police Headquarters, where their records were searched and they were fingerprinted. Because booking was completed before the courts were ready to take the defendants, however, they were sent back uptown to 51st Street to the 17th Precinct to wait. Thursday morning they came back downtown for the second time to 100 Centre.

They both left for Rikers Island later that afternoon after pleading not guilty.

Kirk Johnson, "23½ Hours in Court: 1,636 Cases Later," *New York Times,* November 25, 1986, p. B1. © by The New York Times Company. Reprinted by permission.

twenty-one metropolitan courts. The study focused on the linkage between formal aspects of court operations and case-processing time (see Table 18-1). These formal aspects constitute the traditional model of court delay and are the factors most often cited by practitioners as the reasons for delay. The study found that the relationships were weak (Church et al., 1978a). The size of court was unrelated to delay. Court caseload and trial utilization (as opposed to plea bargaining) also bore little relationship to case-processing time. The type of charging system was the only external variable related to delay; grand jury systems consumed more time.

These findings suggest considerable need to revise conventional wisdom about court delay. The rationale for reassessment is set forth by the National Center for State Courts.

> Consideration of the "state of the art" in pretrial delay research had led us to several broad conclusions regarding this literature. There are few accepted truths in this field. Commentators seldom support theories or perceptions with data. Research often is inadequately designed or executed, and leads to inconclusive results. Moreover, research frequently is concentrated on courts solely as they exist on organization charts. More study should be devoted to the less formal aspects of courts, especially the network of relationships, motivations, and perceptions among court participants. (Church et al., 1978b: x)

Delay and the Dynamics of Courtroom Work Groups

The essential problem of the conventional wisdom is that it ignores the dynamics of courthouse justice. All too often the problems of case backlogs and trial delays are discussed in legalistic and mechanistic terms. The impression conveyed is that case flow management is somehow removed from other issues and problems in the criminal court process, with the result that the question is falsely viewed in apolitical, administrative terms. In short, the formal, the legal, and the structural have been stressed to the neglect of the informal pattern of discretionary relationships that exists.

Case backlogs, trial delay, and case management are intimately intertwined with the dynamics of courthouse justice. Typically proposals for reducing delay are based on a simple and straightforward analysis: cases produce delay; therefore better management of caseloads will reduce delay. But this equation is not as inherently logical as common sense may indicate. The evidence from an increasingly large number of studies shows that delay results from the voluntary actions of court participants (Oaks and Lehman; Banfield and Anderson; Levin). According to Levin, discussions of the causes and remedies of delay tend to take on an unreal and irrelevant air. Reformers approach the subject as if most defendants and most victims were middle-income persons, as if court officials considered their entire caseload to be composed of serious cases and thought many of the defendants innocent, and as if most of the accused spent the delay in jail (Levin). Such conditions simply do not exist in the real world.

Delay is tied not so much to caseload pressure as to the goals of the participants in the decisional process. Defense attorneys seek continuances to avoid harsh judges, to maximize their own goals (for example, fee collection and limiting court time), and to satisfy clients. Prosecutors use delay to increase the stakes of plea bargaining, or to postpone weak cases that they are likely to lose. Judges acquiesce in continuances to pursue their own goals of organization maintenance and enhancement. Viewed in this framework, delay is not simply a question of managing the court docket more efficiently and providing more resources.

local legal culture

Lawyers and judges are generally content with the existing pace of litigation in their courts. Case-processing time is influenced by shared courthouse norms regarding how fast cases *ought* to move. These practitioners' attitudes reflect **local legal culture** (Church et al., 1978a). A recent study asked practitioners to provide appropriate case-processing times for twelve hypothetical cases slightly modified from actual cases. Within the four courts studied—the Bronx, Detroit, Miami, and Pittsburgh—there was little systematic disagreement between judges, defense counsel, and prosecutors on the appropriate pace of case dispositions. Between the courts, however, major differences are apparent. Sampling from case files shows that the courts differed in case-processing time, with variations in disposition times closely paralleling intercourt differences on attitude measures. Church (1985: 464) concludes that the study ''provides strong support for the existence of a distinctive practitioner attitude regarding proper case-disposition times in each of the four courts.''

Case Scheduling

Waiting is one activity that people in the courthouse inevitably engage in: waiting for a defense attorney or prosecutor who is in another courtroom on another case, waiting for a vital witness to show up, waiting for the court reporter.

From an administrative perspective, the courts are extremely complex institutions. A hearing on a pretrial motion, accepting a guilty plea, or conducting a trial requires that numerous people come together at the same time and place. The disposition of a case often requires the presence of the following diverse people: judge, clerk, court reporter, bailiff, defendant, prosecutor, defense attorney, police officer, victim, and witness. Depending on the procedural stage, the appearance of jurors, a probation officer, a pretrial release representative, and an interpreter may also be necessary.

Many of these people have several different courts to appear in during a single day. Defense attorneys, prosecutors, the probation officer, and the translator may have several cases set for the same time. There can be administrative problems too. Heavy traffic can delay a juror or witness. Because of slow mail delivery, notices of court appearances may arrive the day after the scheduled hearing. An illegible address means the defendant never receives a notice. Or the jailer may inadvertently forget to include the needed defendant on the day's list. If just one person is late, the others must wait. And if one person never shows up at all, the hearing must be rescheduled.

To complicate further the administrative complexity of the courts, judges have only limited authority to control the other agencies. The court is actually a collection of separate and independent organizations: judge, police department(s), prosecutor, sheriff, clerk, probation officer, and court reporter. Most of these organizations in state court are headed by elected officials or, like the police, report to elected officials. They have their own base of power and their own separate legal mandates. Judges, then, have only limited administrative control (although they are often held responsible when something goes wrong). When a group of Minnesota district judges was asked to state the major organizational and administrative problem facing the trial courts, 36 percent chose "inadequate" control by the courts of the services or functions required to support court operations (Beerhalter and Gainey).

In turn, each of these separate organizations has scheduling problems. Typically each tries to establish a schedule of court appearances that is best for them. But such schedules often inconvenience other agencies. The sheriff, for example, may decide to bring prisoners to court only once a day. If a defendant is inadvertently left off the day's list, the case must be set for another day.

A major study of the federal courts concluded that most of the best-run district courts held regular meetings of top officials of the various organizations to iron out administrative problems. In the other, less well-run courts, each agency head was critical of operating procedures of the others for causing delay and inconvenience. But they never met to work out a coordinated plan (Flanders). A report on the success of four state trial courts in reducing delay pointed to improved communications between the principal agencies as a chief factor. Meeting periodically, the heads of the court agencies were able to share information and work out common problems (Ryan et al.).

Trial Schedules

*case
scheduling*

Case scheduling is a juggling act. A profusion of cases involving numerous different people must constantly be rearranged in order to accommodate conflicts in schedules. For example, at the last minute a prosecutor cannot make a scheduled trial because a trial in another court has taken longer than expected.

A key ingredient in effective court management is the ability to set a certain date for trial. The District Courts Studies Project (Flanders) reported that courts with low backlogs and little delay were ones that set a date for trial early in the history of a case. Lawyers knew they must be prepared by that date. The key is that the date must be certain. Often dates are set, but lawyers, knowing the case will not be reached by then, do not prepare.

continuance

Judges vary both in their authority and willingness to enforce the certainty of trial settings. In some jurisdictions only the judge can grant a request for *continuance.* In others, however, the judge has no legal power to deny a request from both parties for a continuance. Even when judges have this authority, though, they are often reluctant to use it. Many do not wish to antagonize the local lawyers. Judges are understandably reluctant to force a case to trial when one party states they are not prepared. To complicate matters further, in some areas prosecutors—not judges—determine trial settings. There are two principal methods courts use in scheduling cases: individual and master calendars.

individual
calendar

Individual calendar. The simplest procedure is the **individual calendar.** A case is assigned to one judge for all matters—arraignment, pretrial motions, and trial. A central advantage is continuity. All parties know that a single judge is responsible. Judge shopping is minimal. Administrative responsibility is fixed. One can easily compare judges' dockets to determine who is moving the cases and who is not.

Where the individual calendar system is used, there are often major differences in the dockets, though. Some judges are speedy, others slow. The speed of disposition is tied to the luck of the draw. For example, if a judge

---

C O N T R O V E R S Y

Typing Error Helps Would-Be Rambo Slip Away

A Cook County Circuit Court clerk who typed ''reckless driving'' when she should have typed ''reckless conduct'' has inadvertently helped a transient arrested for allegedly setting up a deadly Rambo-style camp near southwest suburban Oak Forest evade recapture by Cook County sheriff's police.

John E. Cotey, 25, whose last known local address was in northwest suburban East Dundee, was arrested May 14 in the Mascoutin Woods Forest Preserve after he was found in the camp.

Cook County forest preserve police and Oak Forest police found fishing line strung around the camp at neck level. They also found trip lines and two camouflaged pits with sharpened wooden spears pointing up from their floors.

Oak Forest Officer Gary Tyssen, who had been sent to investigate complaints of after hours camping in the woods, stepped into one of the pits but narrowly missed the spears. Inside the tent where Cotey was arrested, police also

found blow guns, martial arts ''throwing stars,'' a knife and an ax, Tyssen said.

Cotey was charged with reckless conduct, violating the forest preserve curfew and damaging county property. Last Monday, when he failed to appear in Cook County the charges, Associate Judge John T. O'Donnel issued a warrant for his arrest.

But in processing the warrant, a court clerk incorrectly typed Cotey's charge as reckless driving. While reckless driving and reckless conduct are both misdemeanors and carry similar punishments, the mistake made a big difference to sheriff's police. By policy, the fugitive warrants division of the sheriff's police does not actively hunt for fugitives charged with traffic violations.

The division assigned investigators to search for Cotey only late Friday after learning of the mistake. Lt. Philip Dalen of the warrants division said:

''Someone slipped up. We now have changed that and have a team out looking for him.''

Ray Murphy, chief clerk in the Chicago Ridge branch said of the error, ''It's a serious mistake.'' But he said, ''It's a rare one. In the 1 ½ years I've been here, it's the first one that's been brought in to me like this.''

Dalen said the warrants division adopted the policy of not actively pursuing fugitives charged with traffic violations because of a shortage of officers.

''There are some 76,000 active warrants in Cook County,'' Dalen said. ''With traffic violators, we just hope they are picked up on another stop somewhere.''

Dalen said that despite the mistake, Cotey eventually would have been arrested.

''There was still a warrant for him in the computer,'' Dalen said. ''Eventually he would have been grabbed.''

Rob Karwath, ''Typing Error Helps Would-be Rambo Slip Away,'' *Chicago Tribune,* August 23, 1986, p. B5. © Copyrighted 1986, Chicago Tribune Company, all rights reserved, used with permission.

is assigned a difficult and complex case that takes a long time to try, all the other cases are delayed.

The main difficulty in setting certain trial dates is that there are potentially more cases to try than dates available. Thus cases must be stacked—more than one case set on a given day. Because most cases will plead out, such stacking can work. But there are dual dangers. Some judges set too many. As a result, when two cases do not plead out, only one can be tried; the other must be rescheduled. If this happens too often, the certainty of the trial date is eroded. The opposite can also happen. Fearful of not being able to try a case that is ready, the judge stacks too few cases. When they all settle, a trial date is vacant. This often leads to a situation in which judges with large backlogs have little to do on a given day.

master calendar

Master calendar.   The ***master calendar*** is a more recent development. Judges specialize (typically on a rotating basis) on given stages of a case—arraignment, motions, bargaining, and trial. The central advantage is that judges who are good in one aspect of litigation (settling cases, for example) but feel less comfortable in other areas (jury trials, for instance) can be assigned what they do best. The disadvantage is that it is hard to locate responsibility for delay. Cases move to the top of the list in each section of court and when they are finally reached, the case goes on the next list. Judges have less incentive to try to keep their docket current because when they dispose of one case, another appears. Say three judges handle pretrial motions. If two work hard but the third does not, the hard-working judges are penalized because they end up with more cases.

Under a master calendar system a case is set on the trial docket and when it reaches the top of the list, it is supposed to be tried. Flexibility is a clear advantage. If there is a single long case, one judge is available to handle it. However, the master calendar is less able to establish firm trial dates. Cases that reach the top of the list may not be able to be tried on that date; a lawyer may be busy on another case in another court, or the case may require witnesses who are not available.

An Evaluation

There is a running debate over which calendaring system is best. Which system is "best" depends partly on the nature of the court. Small courts, such as U.S. district courts, use the individual calendar system successfully. Because of the complexity of their dockets, big city and state courts almost uniformly use master calendars. Although both the individual and master calendars have advantages as well as drawbacks, research indicates that courts using the master calendar experience the greatest difficulty. Typical are problems identified in Detroit and Las Vegas: (1) some judges refused to take their fair share of cases; (2) the administrative burden on the chief judge was too great; (3) as a result a significant backlog of cases developed. In these courts when the master calendar was scrapped in favor of the individual calendar, major reductions in delay were achieved (Neubauer et al., 1981).

Paperwork

Courts are paperwork bureaucracies. Even the simplest case requires stacks of papers: charging document, bail papers, pretrial motions and responses, appearance of counsel, and so on. Courts have been slow to adopt modern management techniques or equipment to process this ***paperwork.*** Papers are processed by hand, which is both cumbersome and time-consuming. Papers get lost, thus delaying the case. Moreover, there is no ability to generate the type of statistical data vital for managing the courts. Former Chief Justice Burger put it this way:

> In terms of methods, machinery, and equipment, the flow of papers—and we know [that] the business of courts depends on the flow of papers—most courts have changed very little fundamentally in a hundred years or more. . . .
>
> As litigation has grown and multiple-judge courts have steadily enlarged, the continued use of the old equipment and old methods has brought about a virtual breakdown in many places and a slowdown everywhere in the efficiency and functioning of courts.

Beginning in the 1960s, records management in the courts has been undergoing important changes (Saari). The computer offers major advantages. It can organize, index, and docket information so that it is useful to all the parties—judge, prosecutor, clerk, defense, probation, sheriff—who need to know about what is currently happening in a specific case. It can help schedule cases and aid in avoiding conflicts in court appearances. It can account for the large sums of money handled by courts and related agencies. By centralizing information it can generate data on the extent of case backlog and bottlenecks in the system. Finally, it can provide the documentation needed to evaluate the effectiveness of court operations.

For a number of reasons, courts have been slower than virtually all other major organizations in America to adopt such techniques. One factor is cost. Courts are short of funds to finance new equipment and hire the skilled personnel to utilize them. But more fundamentally, many court officials are not prone to innovate. Some judges falsely fear that a computer will replace them altogether. At times the benefits of the computer have been greatly oversold. Some courts have attempted to computerize many of their operations, but after several years—and substantial expenditures—the computer was able to produce only limited information. Such failures are partially the product of the fact that many court docket systems are so primitive. The old methods used are not systematic enough to be incorporated into a modern management system.

In short, courts require better statistical information than most currently possess if they are to successfully tackle their administrative and management problems. But the specifics of the technology, the computer in this case, must be viewed not as an end in itself but as a means to an end—the more effective management of the courts.

Managing the Courts

A constant complaint is that the courts are mismanaged. The attorney general of Massachusetts characterized the court system in his state as "ineffective, inaccessible, chaotic, archaic, ponderously slow, and beginning to fall almost by its own weight" ("Bellotti"). In most states there are three distinct sets of court managers: court clerks, chief judges, and court administrators.

Clerks of Court

clerks of court

The **clerks of court,** variously referred to as prothonotaries, registers of probate, and clerks, are pivotal in the administration of local judiciaries. They are responsible for docketing cases, collecting fees and costs, overseeing jury selection, and maintaining court records. Although these local officials often have enormous power, they have been overlooked by academics and reformers alike (Gertz). They have traditionally competed with judges for control over judicial administration. Given that they are elected officials in all but six states, they can operate semiautonomously from the judge. Typically clerks have not been associated with effective management. The reasons are summarized thus:

> Generally they are conservative in nature and reflect the attitudes and culture of the community. Their parochial backgrounds coupled with their conservative orientation, in part accounts for this resistance to change. This resistance often compels judicial systems to retain archaic procedures and managerial techniques. (Berkson: 164)

Although there are notable exceptions, most clerks are not trained to manage the local courts.

Chief Judges

Although judges are responsible for court administration, they have historically been ineffective managers. This fact is primarily the result of the unique environment in which the courts operate. For example, judges may be held responsible, but they seldom have the necessary authority. Moreover they are not trained in management. The skills of the lawyer center on treating each case individually, and most practicing attorneys handle only a few cases at any one time. The end result is that the lawyers who become judges are not accustomed to analyzing patterns of case dispositions or to managing large dockets. Yet those are the essential skills a manager needs.

chief judge

These problems are reflected in the position of **chief judge.** Although the chief judge has general administrative responsibilities, the position is really one of first among equals with the other judges. Particularly when the chief judge assumes the position by seniority, as many do, there is no guarantee that the person will be interested in management or will be effective at it. Election by the other judges sometimes does result in selecting a powerful and effective manager. But election can also produce a candidate who will not rock the boat.

Court Administrators

One of the most innovative approaches to the solution of court problems has been the creation of a professional group of trained administrators to assist judges in their administrative duties. The guiding theory is that well-trained managers can infuse the courts with managerial talent they often have lacked.

> "Management—like law—is a profession" today. Few judges or lawyers with severe chest pains would attempt to treat themselves. There would be slight hesitation about consulting the medical profession. Congested dockets and long delays are symptoms that court systems need the help of professionals. Those professionals are managers. If court administration is to be effective, judicial recognition that managerial skill and knowledge are necessary to efficient performance is vital. (Meyer: 234)

Underlying this theory is the assumption that the managers can perform administrative tasks (case management, budgeting, personnel) without interfering with the judges' primary task of adjudicating (deciding specific cases).

court admin-istrator

The development of the professional position of **court administrator** has been sporadic. In 1937 Connecticut established the first centralized office of court administrator. It was not until after World War II, however, that many other states followed; by the 1980s, every state had established a statewide court administrator. The primary duties of these officials are preparing annual reports summarizing caseload data, preparing budgets, and trouble-shooting. Typically they report to the state supreme court or the chief justice of the state supreme court. Increasingly trial courts are also employing court administrators. Few, if any, major metropolitan areas are without professional judicial employees.

Because the position is so new, several aspects of the court administrator's role are still being debated. Arguments among advocates of professional court executives center around two topics: qualifications and administrative relations with other agencies.

Qualifications.   In the past, it was common for the court administrator to be merely another patronage position. Moreover, there was no agreed-upon body of knowledge or set of skills court administrators needed. To counter these factors reformers have sought to professionalize the position. The creation of the Institute for Court Management in 1970 was a landmark. By creating the mechanism for training court administrators, it legitimized their standing within the legal establishment. But there is still no agreement as to the skills and qualifications the court administrator should possess. Many reformers believed that managerial expertise was needed and a law degree was unnecessary. On the other hand, many judges contend that a law degree is essential. For example, some complain that some court administrators hired for their background in business techniques have been ineffective because they know too little about courts and the common law.

Administrative relationships.   A second area of concern is the proper relationship between the court administrator and other agencies of the judiciary. For example, what supervisory powers should the court administrator have over the clerk's office? Often clerks view the position as a threat and resent any intrusion. Yet to be an effective executive, the court administrator requires the type of data on cases that only the clerk can provide. This means many

potential conflicts are associated with creating the new position of court executive. Court clerks have assumed a central role in resisting the creation of court
executive. If the position is created, they can greatly reduce the administrator's
effectiveness by not cooperating.

Tension between judges and the court administrator may arise too. Some
judges are reluctant to delegate responsibility over important aspects of the
court's work—case scheduling, for example. In practice, the distinction between administration and adjudication is not clear-cut. A court administrator's
proposal to streamline court procedures may be viewed by the judges as an
intrusion on how they decide cases. For example, deciding whether the power
to transfer the judge from one assignment to another is a judicial or nonjudicial
responsibility is not an easy task.

An Evaluation

Despite their potential ability to improve the efficiency of the court, court administrators have encountered opposition from both clerks and judges. Most
have not been given full responsibility over most aspects of the court's nonjudicial duties. A survey in Florida, for instance, found that most court administrators handle only relatively minor tasks (Berkson). In other areas, however,
judicial administrators have been able to fulfill the reformers' expectations that
they would be able to innovate. As is typical of emerging positions, substantial confusion still exists over the role of the court administrator (Stott).

Speedy Trial Acts

Although the Sixth Amendment guarantees the right to a speedy trial, the
Supreme Court has refused to give this rather vague concept any precise time
frame (*Barker* v. *Wingo,* 407 U.S. 514, 1972). Likewise, thirty-five state constitutions have speedy trial guarantees, but these provisions apply only when
the delay has been "extensive." In the last few years, though, there has been
considerable interest in putting some teeth into the guarantee of a speedy trial.
The best known and most comprehensive such effort is the *Speedy Trial Act*
of 1974, amended in 1979, which specifies time standards for the two primary
stages in the Federal court process. Thirty days are allowed from arrest to indictment, and seventy days from indictment to trial. Certain time periods, such
as those associated with hearings on pretrial motions, and mental competency
hearings are considered excludable time.

Speedy trial statutes exist in all fifty states (Misner). These laws, however,
have a different orientation from that of their federal counterpart. Most state
laws are defendant-centered; that is, they are designed to protect defendants
from suffering extensive delay, particularly if they are incarcerated prior to
trial. By contrast, the federal law is designed to protect the interests of society; that is, a speedy trial is viewed as an important objective irrespective of
whether the defendant's interests are in jeopardy. These laws differ in many
respects, such as what kinds of events count as excludable time, and they vary
widely in the amount of time they allow for bringing a case to trial. Among
the most restrictive states is California, which specifies fifteen days in felony

cases from arrest to indictment and sixty days from indictment to trial. Other states, on the other hand, stipulate only that cases be processed with "no unnecessary or unreasonable delay."

Most striking about efforts to mandate speedy trials is their generality. These laws are not based on an analysis of why delay occurs; they incorporate none of the conflicting explanations of why courts are too slow. Moreover they do not provide for any additional resources (more judges, court reporters, and so on) to aid the courts in complying. This can produce some unforeseen consequences. A number of federal courts have had great difficulty in complying.

CONTROVERSY

Judge Dismisses Wall Street Case

Judge Louis Stanton, an ex-Marine who hates unfinished business, is probably the last person a lawyer would want to make excuses before.

"He never had any sympathy for someone who says 'I haven't had time to do this,' " recalls Robert McTammaney, managing partner at Carter, Ledyard & Milburn, the law firm here where Judge Stanton was a partner from 1967 to 1985, before President Reagan appointed him to the federal bench in July 1985.

So, in retrospect, it wasn't surprising when the 59-year-old U.S. District Court judge in Manhattan decided this week not to give government prosecutors the extra time they said they needed to prepare their major inside-trading case against three top Wall Street abritragers. Judge Stanton's ruling forced the government to make its stunning, and embarrassing, decision Wednesday to move to dismiss the current charges against the three rather than proceed with the trial scheduled for next week.

Judge's Rationale
In denying the prosecution's

request to delay the start of the trial until July 20, Judge Stanton cited the constitutional guarantee of a speedy trial.

"It was somewhat surprising that the judge didn't give the government more time," says Edward Brodsky, a former government prosecutor who is now a defense lawyer, expressing a view common among courthouse lawyers here. But, adds Charles L. Brieant, chief judge of the court: "So long as the speedy trial act is on the books, courts should enforce it, as he apparently has done."

'You Have Assistants'
At the law firm for which he worked, Judge Stanton was known for quickly and efficiently moving a case along—sometimes by dictating long briefs off the top of his head while scouring his notes and reference books. In the pretrial hearings preceding Wednesday's decision, the judge's impatience with the prosecutors' pleas that they needed more time to digest their

mountains of evidence was clearly building.

"You have assistants," he said at one point, cutting off prosecutor Neil S. Cartusiello, who was trying to explain that he needed to postpone a hearing. "Here you have people who are suffering by reason of public arrests initiated by the government and they're being told they will be advised of the ingredients of the case against them in due course. I cannot stand (for) that."

In refusing to allow the government two extra months to get its case together, the judge expressed a far greater sympathy for the defendants' rights to a speedy trial than for the government's pleas that the high-stakes case is too complex to rush to court. "The government arrested these people and charged them publicly. It must have known what its plans were," he told the prosecutors.

Judge Stanton said yesterday that he wouldn't comment on any cases pending before him.

William Power, "Judge Who Derailed Wall Street Case Is an Ex-Marine Who Hates to Dawdle," *Wall Street Journal*, May 15, 1987, p. 33.

Often compliance has come at the price of delaying civil cases. Speedy trial acts, because they reduce flexibility in scheduling, can also result in courts' expending greater effort per case.

Potential difficulties also arise because not all cases easily fit into the mandated time frames. A major case or a complex drug conspiracy case take longer to prepare than an ordinary burglary case. State laws generally allow trial judges wide discretion in deciding that in the interest of justice the time frames can be waived. These laws also specify general periods that can be excluded.

Finally, enforcement is a problem. Ten states provide that the case must be dismissed. This can result in a guilty defendant's going free because of an administrative problem. It can also allow the prosecutor not to proceed deliberately because there is no case and then later blame the judge when the case

reprosecution   is dismissed. Other states permit dismissal but allow ***reprosecution.*** This latter approach can undermine the effectiveness of speedy trial provisions by subjecting defendants to a series of reprosecutions. Dismissal with or without

CLOSE-UP

Drug Crackdown Puts Judicial System in Crisis Situation

Campaigns by Los Angeles County law enforcement agencies to arrest more drug dealers have further clogged an already jammed criminal justice system, bringing closer the specter of judicial "gridlock," according to numerous authorities.

The trend has implications not only for the criminal courts but for the everyday civil litigant, such as the man who sues his insurance company for refusing to pay a claim.

Today, it takes nearly 3½ years for such civil cases to come to trial because of a backlog of more than 30,000 lawsuits. By the end of 1987, that wait may be closer to five years because an increasing number of civil courts are being borrowed for the growing number of criminal trials, said Frank S. Zolin, executive officer of the county's Superior Court system.

"It's really a crisis situation," he said.

Felony narcotics cases filed by the district attorney's Central District have been running as much as 36% ahead of the 1985 pace, and the total number of felony cases filed countywide rose 24% during the fiscal year that ended in June.

Prosecutors and judges insist that the quality of prosecution has not been eroded by the increased workload, but warn that without an infusion of additional personnel the system will run out of flexibility.

"We all think we're approaching that limit," said Michael E. Tranbarger, a special assistant to Dist. Atty. Ira Reiner for branch operations.

The central problem, authorities say, is the shortage of Superior Court judges, who try felony cases. The county has 224, only 18 more than it had five years ago.

With increasing frequency, the daily calendar of new felony trials exceeds the number of criminal court judges available to hear them.

Suburban criminal courts that were once used to take the pressure off judges in the downtown Criminal Courts Building are now equally jammed, and often need to transfer their overflow downtown.

The overflow is aggravated by speedy-trial laws that limit postponements. A criminal suspect is entitled to have his trial begin within 60 days of the time the charges were filed.

When the county runs out of available criminal courts, the remaining "last day" trials (those in which the delay has reached 60 days) are transferred to civil courtrooms.

This shifting, in turn, forces postponements or interruptions of lawsuits that have

the right for reprosecution at the discretion of the judge is provided for in other state provisions and in the federal act as well.

Overall, speedy trial laws have had only a limited impact in speeding up the flow of cases through the criminal court process (Nimmer). The primary reason is that most state laws fail to provide the court with adequate and effective enforcement mechanisms. As a result, time limits specified by speedy trial laws are seldom a guide to actual practice.

Conclusion

By general consensus, delay constitutes a major problem confronting the American judiciary. Once we begin to discuss specifics, however, this consensus breaks down. There is, for example, no agreement on how to define *delay*. Not all case-processing time involves delay. Time needed for case preparation must be distinguished from unnecessary delay. Similarly, there is no agreement

---

already waited an average of 40 months to come to trial because of the county's civil court backlog.

Such techniques have been used for years in Los Angeles County. They are an informal alternative to more severe steps, such as those taken two months ago in New York City, when 20 civil court judges were transferred to criminal assignments because of New York's large backlog of narcotics cases related to the sale and use of "crack," a cheap, highly addictive derivative of cocaine.

However, there are now some fears that Los Angeles' system may not be sufficient.

For example, in the past it has been common for court officials to find their criminal courtrooms filled with ongoing cases and seven or eight new criminal trials scheduled to begin. But on a recent day, said Assistant Presiding Superior Court Judge Jack E. Goertzen, "there were 40 'last-day' criminal cases that had to be gotten to trial" immediately somewhere in the system.

Officials were able to delay

a number of these trials when the suspects either entered guilty pleas or agreed to waive their right to a speedy trial.

However, it is impossible to predict what percentage of suspects will forgo or postpone the start of their trials. Hence county officials are for the first time confronting the possibility that several consecutive days of massive overflow will paralyze civil aggregation by filling all the county's civil courts with criminal cases.

"That has not happened, but it's not inconceivable," Goertzen said. "When you get a little worried about what the future might hold."

If such a scenario did occur, the county would have to ask the Judicial Council for judges from other counties to break the logjam.

The prosecutors who feel increased pressure from the heightened number of cases are those who do not have the luxury of doing any one of the district attorney's specialized

units. These lower-level deputies juggle a variety of rape, robbery, murder and drug cases or are assigned to more tedious jobs, such as supervising the flow of defendants through Municipal Court preliminary hearings, where judges determine whether there is sufficient evidence to justify holding a trial.

"We've almost doubled (the caseload) with the same number of deputy district attorneys," said Andrew W. Diamond, the prosecutor in charge of Van Nuys Municipal Court.

Among the deputy district attorneys responsible for guiding two dozen cases a day through preliminary hearings, "Twelve-hour days are not unusual," Diamond said. "A lunch hour is something that you spend out of court over your files nine out of 10 times. Legal research is something you do in your spare time. It's been increasing like that on a direct surge in the last year."

Bob Baker, "Judicial System Put in 'Crisis Situation' by Drug Crackdown," *Los Angeles Times,* October 26, 1986, p. II–1. Copyright 1986, Los Angeles Times. Reprinted by permission.

on why delay is a problem. Historically speedy trial requirements were designed to protect the rights of the accused. More recently *speedy trial* is defined in terms of protecting the rights of society.

Our understandings of the causes and consequences of delay have been shaped by a conventional wisdom that is at best partial and at worst misdirected. The essential problem of the conventional wisdom is that it ignores the dynamics of courthouse justice. How long cases take to reach disposition reflect the voluntary activities of members of the courtroom work group. Thus, local legal culture is more important than internal court procedures or external forces in understanding why delay occurs and developing solutions to the problem.

Eliminating delay is one of the central themes of court reformers who have variously recommended speedy trial rules, abolition of the grand jury, priority case scheduling, limitations on *voir dire* and so on. These proposals typically view delay as the primary problem, overshadowing and unrelated to other court problems. The premise is false. There is little doubt that courts can better manage their diverse activities. Improved record keeping, targeted docketing of cases, and better trained personnel will help reduce needless delays and provide data to monitor other inequities in the system. But reformers greatly overestimate the improvements likely to result from speedier and more efficient court dispositions. Well-run courts, staffed by capable persons and using modern management techniques, will continue to be confronted with the same conditions that currently plague some courts—large case volume, sentencing disparities, and overcrowded jails (Neubauer and Cole).

For Discussion

1. What advantages would result from greater centralized administration of state courts? What disadvantages?
2. Examine docket sheets, analyze news accounts of criminal cases, and talk to court officials. Try to develop an estimate of how long it takes to dispose of criminal cases in your community. Is the time too long or too short? Why? Using the same sources develop an estimate of the case backlog.
3. Why do you think delay is a problem? Which of the four perspectives comes closest to your own? Why?
4. What procedural steps do you think contribute to unnecessary delay? What might be done?
5. In Chapter 1 we argued that the criminal justice system is fragmented. How does this fragmentation contribute to delay? What can be done to overcome the problem?
6. Examine the court files in several cases. Do they seem to be complete? Are notations made in pen, typewritten, or by computer? Are the courts able to provide accurate data on the number of cases pending, what stages the cases are at, and the average length of delay? Interview a professor from your department of business. Ask about the types of modern paperwork management techniques that might be successfully used in the courts.

7. What advantages do you see to the Speedy Trial Act? What disadvantages? To be effective the law must have enforcement provisions, but typically these involve dismissing the case. Do you favor case dismissal? What other enforcement mechanisms might be considered?

8. Interview a judge, prosecutor, defense attorney, and court clerk about delay. Do they think the local court has a problem? Do they agree or disagree on what might be done to speed up case dispositions?

9. In designing and implementing programs to reduce case backlog and delay, why is it important to consider the dynamics of courtroom work groups?

References

AMERICAN BAR ASSOCIATION COMMISSION ON MINIMUM STANDARDS FOR CRIMINAL JUSTICE. *Standards Relating to Speedy Trial.* Chicago: American Bar Association, 1968.

BANFIELD, L., AND C. DAVID ANDERSON. "Continuances in the Cook County Courts." *University of Chicago Law Review* 35 (Winter 1968): 259–316.

BEERHALTER, SUSAN, AND JAMES GAINEY. *Minnesota District Court Survey.* Denver: National Center for State Courts, 1974.

"Bellotti Calls Judicial System Inaccessible, Archaic, Chaotic." *Boston Globe,* February 1, 1976, C1.

BERKSON, LARRY. "Delay and Congestion in State Court Systems: An Overview." In *Managing the State Courts: Text and Readings,* ed. Larry Berkson, Steven Hays, and Susan Carbon. St. Paul, Minn.: West Publishing, 1977.

CASPER, JONATHAN. *American Criminal Justice: The Defendant's Perspective.* Englewood Cliffs, N.J.: Prentice-Hall, 1972.

CHURCH, THOMAS. "The 'Old' and the 'New' Conventional Wisdom of Court Delay." *Justice System Journal* 7 (1982): 395.

———. "Examining Local Legal Culture," *American Bar Foundation Research Journal* 1985 (1985): 449.

———, ALAN CARLSON, JO-LYNNE LEE, AND TERESA TAN. *Justice Delayed: The Pace of Litigation in Urban Trial Courts.* Williamsburg, Va.: National Center for State Courts, 1978a.

———, AND VIRGINIA McCONNELL. *Pretrial Delay: A Review and Bibliography.* Williamsburg, Va.: National Center for State Courts, 1978b.

FLANDERS, STEVEN. *Case Management and Court Management in United States District Courts.* Washington, D.C.: Federal Judicial Center, 1977.

GALLAS, GEOFF. "The Conventional Wisdom of State Court Administration: A Critical Assessment and an Alternative Approach." *Justice System Journal* 2 (1976): 35.

GERTZ, MARC. "Influence in Court Systems: The Clerk as Interface," *Justice System Journal* (1977): 30–37.

LEVIN, MARTIN. "Delay in 'Five Criminal Courts.'" *Journal of Legal Studies* 4 (1972): 83.

LUSKIN, MARY. "Building a Theory of Case Processing Time." *Judicature* 62 (1978): 114–127.

MEYER, BERNADINE. "Court Administration: The Newest Profession." *Duquesne Law Review* 10 (Winter 1971): 220–235.

MISNER, ROBERT. *Speedy Trial: Federal and State Practice.* Charlottesville, Va.: The Michie Company.

MORAN, J. DENIS. "Stating the Case for Timely Standards." *State Court Journal* 8 (1984): 23–25.

NATIONAL ADVISORY COMMISSION ON CRIMINAL JUSTICE STANDARDS AND GOALS. *Courts.* Washington, D.C.: Government Printing Office, 1973.

NEUBAUER, DAVID W. "Improving the Analysis and Presentation of Data on Case Processing Time." *Journal of Criminal Law and Criminology* 74 (1983): 1589.

——. "Are We Approaching Judicial Gridlock? A Critical Review of the Literature." *Justice System Journal* 11 (1986): 363.

——, AND GEORGE F. COLE. "A Political Critique of the Court Recommendations of the National Advisory Commission on Criminal Justice Standards and Goals." *Emory Law Journal* 24 (Fall 1975).

NEUBAUER, DAVID W., MARCIA LIPETZ, MARY LUSKIN, AND JOHN PAUL RYAN. *Managing the Pace of Justice: An Evaluation of LEAA's Court Delay Reduction Programs.* Washington, D.C.: Government Printing Office, 1981.

NIMMER, RAYMOND. *The Nature of System Change: Reform Impact in the Criminal Courts.* Chicago: American Bar Foundation, 1978.

OAKS, D., AND W. LEHMAN. *A Criminal Justice System and the Indigent.* Chicago: University of Chicago Press, 1968.

PRESIDENT'S COMMISSION ON LAW ENFORCEMENT AND ADMINISTRATION OF JUSTICE. *Task Force Report: The Courts.* Washington, D.C.: Government Printing Office, 1967.

RYAN, JOHN PAUL, MARCIA LIPETZ, MARY LUSKIN, AND DAVID NEUBAUER. "Analyzing Court Delay-Reduction Programs: Why Do Some Succeed?" *Judicature* 65 (1981): 58–75.

SAARI, DAVID. *American Court Management: Theories and Practice.* Westport, Connecticut: Quorum Books, 1982.

STOTT, E. KEITH. "The Judicial Executive: Toward Greater Congruence in an Emerging Profession." *Justice System Journal* 7 (1982): 152–179.

WHEELER, RUSSELL, AND HOWARD R. WHITCOMB. *Judicial Administration: Text and Reading.* Englewood Cliffs, N.J.: Prentice-Hall, 1977.

EPILOGUE

The Troubled Courthouse

Clearly, the criminal courts face serious problems. Rising crime rates swell the court dockets. Arrestees often languish in overcrowded jails. Cases may take months or years to wind through the process. Plea bargaining practices are questioned. Witnesses meet with indifference. Victims often feel mistreated. Prisons are filled to overflowing.

The problems of the courthouse are real. But acknowledging these problems does not mean that the courts are on the brink of collapse. Exaggerated assertions about the crisis facing the courts detract from realistic assessments about what the problems are and what can be done to solve them. The primary problems of the courts are not the result of external calamities, such as increased crime rates and expanded caseloads. Rather they are due to increased attention and raised standards (Feeley, 1983).

Historical Perspective

Exaggerated statements about the problems of the courts stem from the lack of a historical perspective. What many label as new problems have actually

443

been around for a long time. The last few years are not the only time Americans have discovered the problem of crime; it only seems that way. In an often-cited speech given in 1906, ''The Causes of Popular Dissatisfaction with the Administration of Justice,'' legal scholar Roscoe Pound warned that a legal system created within the framework of a rural, agrarian America could not meet the needs of an urban, industrialized society. Pound's warnings went largely unheeded until the turmoil of Prohibition and the rise of modern gangsters like Al Capone focused attention on the state of the courts. In 1931 the *Wickersham Reports* labeled the court system inefficient and called for major overhauls. But the nation's interest in the sorry state of the criminal courts was soon replaced by more pressing matters—the Great Depression and, later, World War II. It was not until the 1960s that national attention again returned to criminal justice. To study the crime problem, President Lyndon Johnson created the *President's Commission on Law Enforcement and Administration of Justice,* which probed the entire spectrum of the criminal justice process, identified problems, and made general suggestions for improvements.

In 1971, President Nixon created the *National Advisory Commission on Criminal Justice Standards and Goals* with a mandate to ''formulate for the first time national criminal justice standards and goals for crime reduction and prevention.'' By and large these standards and goals express the agreement within the legal community about the direction of reform. In 1981 President Ronald Reagan created a task force on violent crime (President's Task Force on Victims of Crime). The work of these prestigious national commissions has been supplemented by the activities of a diverse array of citizen groups, business associations, ex-offenders, and court officials themselves.

The result has been a period of unprecedented activity aimed at improving the criminal justice system. Whereas most early concern focused on the police and corrections, the problems of the courts have also come to occupy a place of importance.

Increased Expectations

This increased attention to the troubled courthouse has contributed to an exaggeration of the problems in a second important way—expectations have increased. This tide of rising expectations is clearly legitimate. Confronted with cases that take years to be processed or misdemeanor courts that provide only rough justice, society can reasonably expect more. What is of concern, though, is that some of these increased expectations are unrealistic. Unrealistic expectations create frustration when lofty goals are not met. We need to ask hard-headed questions. How much delay is too much? How much due process can the lower courts reasonably be expected to provide?

The troubled history of the Law Enforcement Assistance Administration (LEAA) provides a case in point. Initially created by President Johnson, showcased by President Nixon, and later abolished by Presidents Carter and Reagan, LEAA was plagued with difficulty. Crime rates did not fall. Hopes for far-reaching changes in police, courts, and prisons did not materialize. Why? The typical criticisms of LEAA centered on a rigid bureaucracy, the lack of firm leadership, too much partisan politics, and at times just plain ineptitude. In their thoughtful review, however, Malcolm Feeley and Austin Sarat point to more fundamental problems. The Congressional Act itself was flawed. Congress had no clear idea about what needed to be done, only a general sense that change was necessary. Instead of providing policy direction, the act created a planning process. But this left unclear what was to be planned. Overall the stated goals were overly ambitious. LEAA did foster important changes and some much-needed improvements. But unrealistic expectations distracted attention from these achievements and contributed to a sense of frustration about reform.

Sorting out where the courts have been and where they are going is obviously a difficult task. The purpose of this epilogue is to offer a realistic assessment of the troubled courthouse. The attempt is to walk the line between two extremes: the rhetoric of crisis and the endorsement of the status quo. The core concerns of this epilogue are several. The nature of the problems facing the criminal courts are not always self-evident. Expectations of reformers have been set unrealistically high. The nation must learn to live with inevitable tensions in the court process. We must acknowledge that fundamental social changes are outside the capacity of the courts. Much reform activity places too much emphasis on legalistic and mechanistic matters and gives too little attention to the dynamics of the courthouse justice.

QUOTATION

My thesis is that, because our understanding of the courts is flawed and our expectations about what the courts can do are unrealistic, many innovations fail. Some fail because we try to impose bureaucratic structures on a protean if imperfect adversary process. Some fail because we mistake discretion for arbitrariness. Some are misdirected because we focus on isolated horror stories. Others respond to the symbols of legal formalism and ignore actual practices. Some strive to extend the courts beyond their capacities.

Conversely, many concerned observers have unrealistic expectations about what courts can do, while others fail to appreciate that some of their concern stems from increased standards and expectations; as a result, they underestimate the significance of changes that have taken place.

Malcolm Feeley, *Court Reform on Trial: Why Simple Solutions Fail* (New York: Basic Books, 1983), p. xiv.

Disagreement over Goals

The starting point in constructing realistic expectations is the realization that there is a lack of agreement on the fundamental goals of the courts. Like beauty, statements of the problems of the courthouse often lie in the eye of the beholder. What one person applauds as progress, another denounces as a step backward. Are pretrial release practices too limited or not restrictive enough? Are sentences too lenient or unduly harsh? Reasonable persons disagree over issues like these. The disagreements need to be recognized. The essential difficulty is that reform efforts mask these areas of disagreement.

Consider, for example, the National Advisory Commission on Criminal Justice Standards and Goals recommendations on the courts. The primacy given to procedural improvements comes at the expense of substantive policy issues. Examination of different governmental reform movements suggests that while they purport to be neutral ways of doing the same thing better, they actually disguise policy alternatives. Thus, it is necessary to separate the reformers' rhetoric from their underlying and sometimes unarticulated concerns.

For example, at several points the report indicates displeasure with such fundamental policies of prosecutors as non-filing or certain cases because they are low on the DA's list of priorities and charge reductions during plea bargaining to avoid harsh sentences. In each instance the Commission discusses changing these procedures when it is really quarreling with the policies themselves. Not only does the emphasis on procedure mask substantive policy issues, it diverts attention from questions about the fairness of the system and protection of defendants' rights (Cole and Neubauer). We thus need to consider efforts to improve court efficiency in substantive terms.

Efficiency

Clearly the criminal court process needs better management. Reformers are certainly correct in stressing the need for improved efficiency. All too often poor management prevents actors in the system from focusing on priorities, at times resulting in truly dangerous criminals somehow falling between the cracks. But a realistic appraisal of the court process indicates that increased efficiency will not solve many of the basic difficulties. Well-run courts staffed by capable persons using modern management techniques will face the same conditions—large volume of cases, sentencing disparities, and over-crowded jails—as the courts do now (Cole and Neubauer).

We may also ask, efficiency for whose benefit? The failure to confront directly conflicts over goals of the court process can blind us to the fact that some reforms may make the process harsher. This was the conclusion of a study that probed the effects of the no plea bargaining policy in Alaska. The study found that the strongest negative impact was on middle-class defendants charged with property crimes (Rubinstein and White). We must always be mindful that reforms based on the goal of efficiency may involve hidden political agendas (Ryan). A stress on improving efficiency that does not take into account important substantive concerns serves to promote unrealistic expectations. Justice must be considered as well.

Evenhandedness

In considering what the courts can do better, one must keep in mind the overriding criterion: justice must be served. The process by which justice is administered, as well as the results achieved, must be perceived to be fair and impartial. Alas, the public rhetoric concerning the criminal courts all too often neglects to consider evenhandedness.

There are clear areas where evenhandedness is a major concern. Disparities in treatment based on race or poverty do not conform to the ideals of equal justice under the law. Likewise harsher penalties for those who go to trial rather than plead guilty raise questions. Perceptions that the rich receive undue leniency in white-collar crimes prompt attention.

Recent studies indicate that these factors operate in a more indirect fashion than was often thought. Rather than being direct and blatant, research indicates that the influences are actually subtle. To apply the old cliché, issues of disparity emerge as shades of gray rather than stark contrasts of black and white.

At the same time studies indicate that courthouse officials do wrestle with important issues of doing justice. Judges, prosecutors, and defense attorneys are not preprogrammed computers who merely examine a few immediately obvious factors and crank out a decision. Rather they consider various nuances: the true nature of the crime and the individual nature of the defendant. Court actors attempt to produce substantive justice rather than procedural justice—merely following the book (Feeley, 1979).

But where justice ends and expediency begins is difficult to decipher. Courthouse officials are expected to both do justice and move cases. As Rosett and Cressey write, "When Steve Ohler the [hypothetical] public defender exercises his discretionary power to settle a case, no one is able to tell whether the settlement is made in the interests of justice rather than in the interests of bureaucratic efficiency. Even Steve himself is not certain" (p. 131).

Settling cases in the interest of justice reflects a group sense of justice. Each courthouse has a "going rate"—a typical penalty applied to a crime category, based on the defendant's background. Properly assessing how substantive justice is meted out in the courthouse requires an understanding of the courtroom work group.

The Dynamics of Courthouse Justice

A flawed understanding of the court process contributes to unrealistic expectations (Feeley, 1983). Reformers focus on individual problems in isolation from the broader process. They stress the formal dimensions of the process to the neglect of the informal ways that discretionary power is controlled and channeled.

The courts are a community of actors. Throughout this book we have stressed the central role of the courtroom work group. Judges, prosecutors, defense attorneys, juries, and in some cases the police are tied together by more than a shared workplace. Because these actors appear daily on the same judicial stage, their interactions combine to create what is best described as a social organization.

Unfortunately the reform efforts as typified by the National Advisory Commission on Criminal Justice Standards and Goals do not recognize the dynamics of the process. Much the same criticism was made about the 1967 report: "The President's Commission reports deal with the formal, the legal, the structural—and virtually ignore the reality of the criminal court as a social system, as a

---

QUOTATION

A reform is an external variable, and the systemic reaction to it is determined in large part by the preexisting relationships and personal interests of the participants in the judicial process. If it is to produce system impact, a reform must disrupt the prior balance and accommodation of interests sufficiently to induce the participants to engage in a new pattern of behavior. . . .

A basic fallacy of most current reform planning is that it ignores these factors. Reformers plan the enterprise as if the sole relevant activity were to enable practitioners to act more correctly from the reform perspective. . . .

The idea that participants in the judicial process desire change is, at best, naive. In part, it is perpetuated by the absence of systematic attention to the process of reform. However, there is also a seeming desire to displace attention from the behavior of judicial professionals to alleged artificial barriers and constraints. This amounts to an implicit unwillingness to recognize the true nature of most judicial problems. These problems are typically not the product of artificial barriers or constraints but of conscious behavioral choices made both individually and as a group by professionals within the system. These choices may be related in complex ways to various environmental influences. However, it is to these conscious choices and the resulting behavior that a reform must be directed and not merely to removing a seemingly undesirable influence in the environment, such as caseload pressure. Environmental reforms can succeed only to the extent that they supply incentives to participants to change their behavior. To the extent that they do not, other measures designed to induce change and to manipulate behavior are necessary.

Raymond Nimmer, *The Nature of System Change: Reform Impact in the Criminal Courts* (Chicago: American Bar Foundation, 1978), pp. 175–176.

community of human beings who are engaged in doing certain things with, to, and for each other'' (Blumberg: viii–ix).

The inattention paid by the *Report on Courts* to the existence of a social control network necessarily limits its analysis of discretion. The recommendations to formalize the standards that guide discretion are substantially off target, for they fail to grapple with the real source of limitations: the courtroom work group.

Limited and partial knowledge about the dynamics of courthouse justice explains why numerous reform efforts have not been successful. Efforts to limit or control discretion at one point in the process typically result in increased discretion elsewhere. Our discussions of efforts to abolish plea bargaining (Chapter 13), alter sentencing (Chapter 16), and reduce delay (Chapter 18) are cases in point.

Once we recognize that the courtroom work groups set standards that structure discretion, we can proceed to the central task of examining and analyzing these standards. Typically the screening criteria employed by one young assistant prosecutor differ from that of another. The same variation occurs between sections of courts on sentencing. We need to confront these differences in order to achieve more consistency. But at the same time, we must recognize that the uniformity that is the product of the lowest common denominator must also be avoided.

Crime Reduction

A realistic assessment indicates that the courts cannot be expected to solve the problems of crime. This perspective stands in sharp contrast to political rhetoric that lashes out at the criminal courts for their failure to protect the community.

Americans remained troubled by high crime rates. Despite recent decreases in crime rates, they still perceive that crime is on the increase. Compared to other industrialized nations of the world, the American crime rate is indeed high in both absolute and relative terms. Just as disturbing are the indications that violent crime is on the increase (Radzinowicz and King). The American public remains very fearful of crime, and demands that something be done. What can be done, of course, is unclear to politicians and court officials alike.

Despite these public concerns, however, it is unrealistic to expect that the courts can have much impact upon the crime rate. Consider for example the facts discussed in Chapter 10 on case attrition. Putting these numbers together indicates that roughly only about 5 percent of crimes ever make it as far as sentencing. It is not realistic to expect that how the courts sentence this small percentage of wrongdoers will have much impact on the overall crime problem (Feeley, 1983; Miller, 1981). Proper sentencing will have at best a marginal impact.

Conclusion

Throughout this book we have discussed a number of major reform efforts. We have suggested that some of these reform efforts require a healthy dose of skepticism. But at the same time one needs to note that in a number of important ways the court process is fairer and more focused than in earlier times. Future efforts require the establishment of realistic expectations about the nature of the court process, how change occurs, and what can be done to make courts better.

It is appropriate to conclude that reform efforts must avoid the trap of perceiving that nothing works. As part of the increased attention to the court process a number of works have suggested the futility of reform. Evaluations of sentencing reforms, pretrial release programs, and diversion efforts have shown that the reformers' claims of success have been greatly overinflated. These evaluations indicate that programs have been poorly implemented or not implemented at all; expectations for success were unduly optimistic; and measures of actual success are hard to come by (Feeley, 1983). Concluding that nothing works, though, is unduly pessimistic. Part of the difficulty is that these evaluations have themselves suffered from important limitations (Casper and Brereton).

The last decade has been a period marked by a great deal of experimentation. While some of the programs have not necessarily shown a direct impact, they have often had important indirect effects. Pretrial release practices have been liberalized. Alternatives to incarceration have gained legitimacy (Feeley, 1983). Court delay has been reduced in some, but certainly not all, jurisdictions (Neubauer et al.). The message to be drawn from reform efforts is a better sense of how changes actually occur in complex organizational entities like the criminal courts.

Patterns of behavior, once established and routinized, become hard to change because the participants often see no need to act any differently. Moreover, some reform efforts resemble thunderbolts from a far-off Mount Olympus. Outsiders proclaim that a problem exists and reform is needed to correct the problem. But those on the working level either fail to see the problem or if they perceive the problem find that the proposed solution bears little resemblance to how the court system actually operates. When the reform fails because it was poorly tailored to local conditions, the sense that nothing works gains greater momentum. In short, reform efforts need to refocus by taking into account the legitimate practices reflected in the courtroom work group.

The recommendations of the presidential commissions exemplify the lawyer's approach to reform: reform procedure. If decisions are being made poorly or badly, the lawyer's solution is to create a better procedural structure. But the fundamental problems of justice cannot be solved by imposing more adversarial due process, for such efforts ignore the fact that the exercise of discretion is a response to the need for flexibility. The inevitability of trying to regularize discretion in this way is that it simply reappears elsewhere. To be successful, reforms must recognize the fundamental role of the courtroom work group. Of course, there are important disagreements over the direction of these reforms. Some argue that the central task is to improve the ability of courts to reduce crime. Others doubt that the courts can ever play a role in crime reduction; they stress instead the need to improve the fairness of justice that defendants receive or to upgrade the public's confidence in the courts by working more effectively with jurors, witnesses, and so on. In short, the public dialogue surrounding the courts continues.

References

BLUMBERG, ABRAHAM. *Criminal Justice*. Chicago: Quadrangle Books, 1967.

CASPER, JONATHAN, AND DAVID BRERETON. "Evaluating Criminal Justice Reforms." *Law and Society Review* 18 (1984): 121.

COLE, GEORGE, AND DAVID NEUBAUER. "The Living Courtroom: A Critique of the National Advisory Commission Recommendations." *Judicature* 59 (1979): 293–299.

FEELEY, MALCOLM. *The Process Is the Punishment: Handling Cases in Lower Criminal Court*. New York: Russell Sage Foundation, 1979.

———. *Court Reform on Trial: Why Simple Solutions Fail*. New York: Basic Books, 1983.

FEELEY, MALCOLM, AND AUSTIN SARAT. *The Policy Dilemma: Federal Crime Policy and the Law Enforcement Assistance Administration, 1968–1978*. Minneapolis: University of Minnesota Press, 1980.

GALLAS, GEOFF. "Court Reform: Has It Been Built on an Adequate Foundation?" *Judicature* 63 (1979): 28–38.

MILLER, J. L., MARILYN ROBERTS, AND CHARLOTTE CARTER. *Sentencing Reform: A Review and Annotated Bibliography*. Williamsburg, Va.: National Center for State Courts, 1981.

NATIONAL ADVISORY COMMISSION ON CRIMINAL JUSTICE STANDARDS AND GOALS. *Report on Courts*. Washington, D.C.: Government Printing Office, 1973.

NEUBAUER, DAVID, ET AL. *Managing the Pace of Justice: An Evaluation of LEAA's Court Delay-Reduction Programs*. Washington, D.C.: Government Printing Office, 1981.

NIMMER, RAYMOND. *The Nature of System Change: Reform Impact in the Criminal Courts*. Chicago: American Bar Foundation, 1978.

POUND, ROSCOE. "The Causes of Popular Dissatisfaction with the Administration of Justice." *American Bar Association Reports* 29 (1906): 395.

PRESIDENT'S COMMISSION ON LAW ENFORCEMENT AND ADMINISTRATION OF JUSTICE. *Task Force Report: The Courts*. Washington, D.C.: Government Printing Office, 1967.

PRESIDENT'S TASK FORCE ON VICTIMS OF CRIME. FINAL REPORT. Washington, D.C.: Government Printing Office, 1982.

RADZINOWICZ, SIR LEON, AND JOAN KING. *The Growth of Crime: An International Experience*. New York: Basic Books, 1977.

ROSETT, ARTHUR, AND DONALD CRESSEY. *Justice by Consent: Plea Bargains in the American Courthouse*. Philadelphia: J. B. Lippincott, 1976.

RUBINSTEIN, MICHAEL, AND TERESA WHITE. "Plea Bargaining: Can Alaska Live Without It?" *Judicature* 62 (1979): 270.

RYAN, JOHN PAUL. "Management Science in the Real World of Courts." *Judicature* 62 (1978): 144–146.

For Further Reading

DUBOIS, PHILIP. *The Analysis of Judicial Reform*. Lexington, Mass.: Lexington Books, 1982.

———. *The Politics of Judicial Reform*. Lexington, Mass.: Lexington Books, 1982.

FEELEY, MALCOLM. *Court Reform on Trial: Why Simple Solutions Fail*. New York: Basic Books, 1983.

JACOB, HERBERT. *The Frustration of Policy: Responses to Crime by American Cities*. Boston: Little, Brown, 1984.

NEELEY, RICHARD. *Why Courts Don't Work*. New York: McGraw-Hill, 1982.

INDEX